CREATIVE LIVING

Basic Concepts in Home Economics

Fourth Edition

Reviewers

Joyce Armstrong, C.H.E.
Home Economics Teacher
W. W. Samuell High School
Dallas, Texas

Marie S. Bell, C.H.E.
Consumer and Homemaking Teacher
Columbia High School
Columbia, South Carolina

Mary G. Blevins
Home Economics Instructor
Mifflin High School
Columbus, Ohio

Linda L. Dannison, Ph.D., C.H.E.
Teacher Educator
Western Michigan University
Kalamazoo, Michigan

Doris H. DeSarro, C.H.E.
Home Economics Teacher
Plaza Junior High School
Virginia Beach, VA

Ruth Felty
Vocational Supervisor
Northside Independent School District
San Antonio, TX

Joan M. Fredeen, C.H.E.
Living Skills Teacher
Armstrong Senior High School
Plymouth, Minnesota

Eva Mae Lloyd
Home Economics Department Chairperson
Ballard High School
Louisville, Kentucky

Vicki A. Risinger, C.H.E.
National Future Homemakers of America Consultant
James Rumsey Vocational Technical Center
Martinsburg, West Virginia

Linda G. Smock, C.H.E.
Supervisor of Home Economics
Pinellas County Schools
Largo, Florida

Judy G. Theriot, Ph.D., C.H.E.
Teacher Educator
Nicholls State University
Thibodaux, Louisiana

Areatha Wells, C.H.E.
Coordinator, Family and Consumer Education
Racine Unified School District
Racine, Wisconsin

Fourth Edition

CREATIVE LIVING

Basic Concepts in Home Economics

Consulting Authors

Josephine A. Foster, Ph.D.
Assistant Superintendent
Alexander County Schools
Taylorsville, North Carolina

M. Janice Hogan, Ph.D.
Head, Family Social Science Department
University of Minnesota
St. Paul, Minnesota

Bettie M. Herring, Ph.D.
Director of Vocational and Adult Education
Fort Worth Independent School District
Fort Worth, Texas

Audrey G. Gieseking-Williams, Ph.D.
Former Chair, Department of Home
Economics
California State University, Los Angeles

GLENCOE

Macmillan/McGraw-Hill

New York, New York
Columbus, Ohio
Mission Hills, California
Peoria, Illinois

Send all inquiries to:
GLENCOE DIVISION
Macmillan/McGraw-Hill
3008 W. Willow Knolls Drive
Peoria, IL 61614-1083

ISBN 0-02-675980-2 (Student Text)
ISBN 0-02-675990-X (Teacher's Wraparound Edition)

Printed in the United States of America.

6 7 8 9 10   VHJ   99 98 97 96 95 94 93 92

Co-developed by
Glencoe/McGraw-Hill Educational Division and
Visual Education Corporation,
Princeton, New Jersey

Design Office, Bruce Kortebein: Text Design
FPG International, Orion Press: Cover

Contents

UNIT 4: MANAGEMENT 238

FOCUS ON YOU

You as an Individual

OBJECTIVES

This chapter will help you to:

- Explain how different characteristics combine to make each person unique.
- Describe the influence of emotions and attitudes on personality.
- Define self-concept and discuss the importance of developing a realistic self-concept.

WORDS TO REMEMBER

attitude
characteristic
environment
heredity
personality
self-concept

William and Daniel are identical twins. Most people cannot tell them apart at first. Both boys are tall and slim, with brown eyes and dark curly hair. In personality, however, they are quite different, and their friends have no difficulty telling the twins apart. William is quiet and shy. He has a few close friends, but spends a lot of time alone in his room listening to music. Daniel, on the other hand, is rarely alone. He is outgoing and energetic and spends a lot of time participating in after-school activities.

You might expect that identical twins would have similar personalities as well as similar looks. After all, they have usually been brought up in the same home by the same parents. However, even twins are like the rest of us in one important respect: each is a unique individual with a personality unlike that of any other individual.

Unless you are an identical twin, there is no one in the world who looks exactly like you. More importantly, whether you are a twin, an only child, or part of a large family, there is no one who feels, thinks, and acts exactly as you do.

"Her admirers knew her by what she did rather than by her appearance. She was average looking—medium height, medium weight, medium brown hair. What her friends admired her for were her actions, which were always kindnesses done without a hint of seeking any type of repayment."

When authors want to describe people for us, they write about **characteristics.** These are the special features or traits that distinguish one individual from another. Characteristics may relate to a person's appearance or actions. Looking at your characteristics will help you form a picture of yourself and help you see yourself as others see you.

Your Characteristics

No single word could be used to describe you—or any human being. Each person is a complex combination of characteristics. These characteristics—physical, emotional, mental, and social—combine to make you the unique person you are.

You Are Unique

"He had dark, brooding eyes, and when he was with people he held himself apart from them, as if afraid to be drawn in by their friendliness."

Look at any group of people and you will discover that each individual is unique, with his or her own personality.

People experience a wide range of emotions. What emotions do you think this girl is expressing in each situation?

- **Your body.** People notice your physical characteristics first. You might be tall or short, straight-haired or curly-haired, dark or fair. Perhaps you wear glasses or have a turned-up nose. Your physical features affect the way people see you. Most likely, you are pleased with some but may want to change others.

- **Your emotions.** Your emotional characteristics also affect the way people see you. Perhaps you are very even-tempered, or maybe you are easily upset. You may find that your emotions swing from feeling very happy one day to feeling quite low the next.

- **Your mind.** Your mental characteristics involve your abilities, attitudes, and interests. Perhaps you are good at thinking through math problems. Do you like watching baseball, or would you rather curl up with a good book? Almost everything you say or do tells people something about your mind.

- **Your relationships.** Your social characteristics include how you get along with other people. Are you quiet and shy or talkative and outgoing? Do you like to be with large groups of people or just one or two friends?

Your Actions

Your behavior with others also helps add to the picture of who you are. Are you a good listener? Do you prefer spending time with a group of people or with only one special friend? Do you like sharing with others? Are you the leader of a group? These are social characteristics that people notice; they, too, add to the picture of who you are.

People see the world from different viewpoints, so the people who know you will probably notice different characteristics in you. Your parents may notice your kindness to a younger sister or your willingness to help with household chores. Your teachers will know that you are good in some subjects and have trouble with others. Your friends may know that you like to tell jokes or that you are good at organizing activities.

Nobody's picture of you is complete. Your friends at school might not know that you enjoy singing, while your friends at choir are not aware that you hate sports. Everyone sees a different side of you. To fully appreciate yourself, you must realize that you are all of the people that others see, and more.

Your Personality

Your **personality** is the combination of characteristics and actions that makes you different from every other person. Nobody has the same personality as you. The great variety in human personalities results from the interactions of heredity and environment.

Your **heredity** involves the characteristics that you inherit from your parents and ancestors. It is your heredity that determines many of your physical characteristics, such as the color of your skin, hair, and eyes, and whether you are tall or short. Your heredity also determines many of your personality traits. The way you express emotions such as happiness or anger, for example, may be strongly influenced by your heredity.

The other major influence on personality is environment. Your **environment** is everything that surrounds you. It includes your family, friends, teachers, and the neighborhood and society in which you live. Ever since you were born, your environment has helped shape your emotions, attitudes and interests.

The members of this family have inherited similar physical characteristics.

Emotions

Every living person experiences the same basic emotions, yet each person feels and expresses emotions in different ways. For example, to show happiness you might yell and jump up and down. Your friend, however, might simply smile and look pleased when she feels happy. A movie that brings tears to your eyes may seem to have little effect on your friend.

The emotions you experience are part of the one-of-a-kind you. Learning to recognize, accept, and express your emotions in socially responsible ways is an important part of growing up.

Attitudes

Closely linked to your emotions are your attitudes. Your **attitudes** reflect the thoughts and judgments you have about the world around you. It is this part of your personality that makes you approve of some people or issues, but disapprove of others.

Most people's attitudes begin to form when they are children. Perhaps, as a child, you learned from your family to place a high value on helping other people. Perhaps you were taught to be honest and polite at all times.

As you grow older, some of your attitudes may change. Others are likely to remain a basic part of your personality.

Your Self-Concept

When people react to you as a person, they are responding to the set of characteristics that makes up your personality. They do not see all of those characteristics: everyone sees different things about you.

Even you don't have a complete picture of yourself. True, you know things about yourself that nobody else knows. You know what makes you sad, the kinds of people you admire, your dreams for your future. Still, it's quite likely that other people see things about you that you've never noticed.

Many factors help shape your self-concept. Your family, friends, neighborhood, school, beliefs, past experiences, skills, and talents all influence your view of yourself.

The particular view that you have of yourself is your **self-concept.** Your self-concept includes your views about what you like and what you think you're good at. You may see yourself as an athlete, or a computer expert, or a good cook. Your self-concept also includes what you see as your weaknesses. Perhaps you are shy about expressing your opinions, or perhaps you lose your temper easily.

Your self-concept is important to you for a number of reasons. It has an enormous influence on the way you feel about yourself. It also affects the way others see you. For example, if you think of yourself as a cheerful person and if you greet people in a cheerful, friendly manner, others will also think of you as cheerful.

are and how you want to act. You'll be able to focus on your good points and to find the confidence to improve the things you don't like about yourself.

Many teens find it hard to bring their view of themselves into focus. You might find, for example, that you feel different when you're with different people. You might behave a certain way when you're with your parents, yet you might feel that you're a completely different person when you're around your friends.

Uncertainties such as these are normal, but you need to resolve them. It's important that you build a realistic self-concept over the next few years. Being realistic about yourself will help you make the decisions about your life that are right for you.

How Self-Concept Develops

You start forming your self-concept when you are very young. Perhaps your grandfather often commented on your warm smile or happy laugh. Maybe your mother praised you for running fast or for helping out around the home. Your sister may have teased you about your red hair and freckles. All of these comments helped build your self-concept.

As a teen, you know that some of your childhood characteristics are changing and that you are developing many new qualities. As a result, your self-concept is changing. The way you see yourself now is different from the way you viewed yourself a few years ago. There is still much to discover about yourself.

The Importance of Self-Concept

Your self-concept—your view of yourself—is your key to becoming the person you want to be. If you are realistic about yourself, you'll know who you

A strong, positive self-concept will help you understand who you are and why you are important. It will help you make choices and decisions that affect your life.

Your Self-Concept

It's one thing to know that you're unique, but quite another to figure out just who you are. Developing an objective picture of yourself—a realistic self-concept—takes some time and effort. Many teens feel confused about their identity. That confusion is natural when you consider all the changes you're going through and adjusting to. Such confusion can sometimes cause teens to focus on negative aspects of themselves. You may become overly conscious of your apparent failures and, in so doing, you may overlook some of your strong points.

Study the questions below. They may help you see some of your pluses, and help to put your picture of yourself in perspective.

- **Are you reliable?** Do you show up for team practices? When you tell a friend you'll visit, do you arrive on time? Can your parents rely on you to do chores?
- **Are you a good listener?** Even if you don't think you're good at making conversation, showing that you can listen, and that you care about what others have to say, is an asset that people will appreciate.
- **Are you polite?** Good manners help you get along with people of all ages and are a sign that you respect other people.
- **Are you cooperative?** Are you willing to lend a hand in activities such as the school play, local fund-raising efforts, or community events?

- **Do you show other people that you care?** Just as you need to know that other people care for you, the people in your life—especially your family and friends—appreciate your efforts to show interest in and concern for them.

Think It Through

1. Do you think it is possible for a teen to have a realistic self-concept? Why or why not?
2. Why do you think it's important for people to be realistic about themselves?

CHAPTER

1 REVIEW

Reviewing the Facts

1. What are characteristics?
2. What four types of characteristics does every person have?
3. What are the two main influences that shape a person's personality?
4. What is environment?
5. Explain what attitudes are.
6. How do people develop a self-concept?
7. Why is it important to have a realistic self-concept?

Sharing Your Ideas

1. What are some ways in which young people can be taught to express their emotions in socially responsible ways?
2. How might you be able to help a friend develop a realistic self-concept?

Applying Your Skills

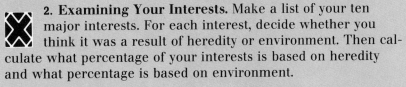

1. Making a List of Characteristics. List three of your positive characteristics in each of the following categories: your body, your emotions, your mind. Then choose two of the characteristics you have listed and write one way that you could use each to help someone else.

2. Examining Your Interests. Make a list of your ten major interests. For each interest, decide whether you think it was a result of heredity or environment. Then calculate what percentage of your interests is based on heredity and what percentage is based on environment.

3. Analyzing Descriptions. Read a weekly magazine that describes people and their lives. Keep track of the adjectives used to describe the personalities of the people featured. Are there some characteristics that appear more frequently than others? How important would you say these characteristics are in your own life? Are there characteristics that are important to you that are not included in the article?

The Teen Years

OBJECTIVES

This chapter will help you to:

- Describe the physical, emotional, mental, and social changes that take place during the teen years.
- Explain how to build self-esteem.
- Explain why you need to develop management skills.

WORDS TO REMEMBER

adolescence
hormones
management
peer group
self-esteem

The teen years are often described as the best time of life. Whether or not you agree may depend on the day you are asked. Some days seem terrific; others you would like to forget.

On the plus side, you have much more knowledge and experience now than you did when you were a child. You have acquired a storehouse of information and skills. You can solve difficult problems. You've learned how to get along with many different types of people.

Still, there are times when life seems to be a real struggle. You may do graceful dives, but then sometimes stumble over your own feet (always when someone is watching). Your skin breaks out the day your class pictures are to be taken. Your emotions sometimes seem to get out of control. When you finally understand algebra, it's time to take geometry.

This is the period of life called **adolescence,** when you grow from being a child to being an adult. It is a period marked by unfamiliar feelings and new experiences. It can be a confusing time, but all these changes and feelings are signs that you're growing up.

A Time of Growth

As the most important growth stage before adulthood itself, adolescence affects your physical, emotional, mental, and social characteristics.

Physical Changes

The first changes most teens are aware of are physical. You probably noticed that some of your classmates seemed to grow taller overnight. You're probably aware, too, that certain classmates have developed far more rapidly than others. The natural differences in rates of development can be difficult to cope with. No one wants to be the first or the last person to develop an adult figure. Some of the temporary "side effects" of adolescence can also be embarrassing. Acne or a squeaky voice may seem unbearable, but it helps to keep in mind that they will pass.

The physical changes that take place during adolescence are triggered by the release of substances in your body called **hormones.** Certain hormones enable you to reach adult height and to develop adult characteristics. Sometimes, swift changes in size cause you to feel awkward until you get used to your new body. As you grow taller, the proportion of fat and muscle in your body changes. Other changes are listed in the chart below.

Changes in Adolescence

- Girls' growth spurt begins between ages 10 and 13. (At ages 11 and 12, the average girl is taller than the average boy.)
- Boys' growth spurt begins between ages 12 and 15. (In adulthood, the average man is taller than the average woman.)
- You develop more muscles and curves.
- Your legs and arms grow longer.
- Your hands and feet grow bigger.
- Your hair darkens.
- Your voice lowers.
- Your nose and chin become more sharply defined.
- Your skin becomes oilier and you perspire more.
- Your lungs and stomach can hold more air and food.
- You develop sexual maturity.

Physical

Emotional

Mental

Adolescence is a time of growth and development as you change from a child to an adult.

Social

Emotional Changes

The hormones released by your body also produce emotional changes. You may feel emotions such as happiness or sadness more intensely than ever before. You may discover new emotions as well. Perhaps you feel embarrassed if someone teases you, or confused by your attraction toward someone you barely know.

Chances are that your emotions now change more abruptly than they once did. One day you may feel lonely and want to be with friends. The next day, for no obvious reason, you find you want to be by yourself.

Emotional swings such as this usually stop once the levels of hormones in your body come into balance. Fortunately, the new richness of your emotions will last into your adult years.

Mental Changes

Your teen years are characterized by mental development, too. You begin to reason and to think in more abstract terms. You may begin to ask questions such as "Why is this true?" or "Why not do it this way?" You are ready to test new ideas and to think things through for yourself.

Your new mental abilities make it possible for you to make realistic plans. You're able to imagine the consequences of actions you may take, and to think about alternatives to those actions. Equally important, you are developing the ability to reflect on the results of your decisions and to learn from your mistakes.

Adolescence is a time of self-discovery, as you assume more responsibility for your decisions and actions.

Social Changes

When you compare a fourth grader with a ninth grader, it's easy to see that the two interact with others in very different ways. Adolescence marks a significant change in how individuals deal with their family and friends.

Some social changes are internal—they come from within the individual. By early adolescence you probably found yourself drawn to your **peer group**—people your own age. You wanted to spend more time with your friends. You might also have found that you felt awkward around teens of the other sex.

Some social changes are caused by other people. Your parents expect more of you because you are becoming an adult. They probably expect you to take more responsibility around the house. Your teachers also have higher expectations—they expect you to take more responsibility for your own learning. Sometimes these responsibilities may conflict with what you would like to do. Learning to manage and balance your obligations is an important part of growing up.

Changes in Thinking

Keith's parents are confused. Every time they turn around, Keith seems to view the world differently. Last month he was signing petitions to stop the spread of nuclear power. Now he favors nuclear energy as an alternative to the fossil fuels that he feels are polluting the environment. Why, his parents wonder, does Keith keep changing his mind?

Changes such as Keith is experiencing are not unusual in a teen. Around the beginning of adolescence, teens become capable of **abstract thinking**. Things are not as black and white as they once were. It's common for teens to change their opinions whenever they get new information.

Whenever you think in terms of what might be possible, you are using your developing thought processes. Whether you're speculating about justice or politics, or fantasizing about life on distant planets, you're exploring the possibilities of different subjects.

Changes also take place in the reasoning that teens use concerning moral issues. They begin to make decisions based on a concern for others. They can experience a sense of guilt if their actions cause harm to others. They begin to understand that rules and laws are designed to help people interact in a society, not just to punish them.

Young people also begin to recognize situations and problems involving justice. For example, when Chris was young, he believed that all people who steal should be punished for breaking the law. Now he believes that their intentions also matter. He wonders if a mother who steals food to feed her children should be treated differently from a person who steals a car to go joy riding or to make some easy money.

Issues such as these become the subject for many discussions and debates among teens. You might find that by exchanging ideas you see a whole new side to an issue. Learning to understand and respect other people's points of view is important for your future growth.

Think It Through

1. What do you think are the advantages of being able to think in abstract terms?
2. Why do you think it is important to respect other people's points of view?

A Time of Change

Each person reacts to the changes that adolescence brings in different ways. Many teens move smoothly through this period in their lives. They enjoy using their new mental abilities to solve problems. They feel stimulated by the greater demands that are placed on them. They are excited by their closer relationships with their friends.

However, many teens find the adolescent years troublesome. Their changing physical appearance makes them feel self-conscious, and the emotional ups and downs may leave them feeling confused, even depressed.

Some of the self-consciousness that teens feel is actually a result of their mental growth. As your mind matures, you become capable of imagining what other people think. You may worry, unnecessarily, that other people are being critical of you. You may believe, for example, that other people find you unattractive, think that your clothes are old-fashioned, or that you laugh too loudly. You are often mistaken—maybe those people aren't thinking of you at all, or perhaps their thoughts are positive. This will become clearer to you as you become more experienced at "reading" other people.

Your increasing intellectual abilities can help you expand your relationships with your parents, teachers, and other adults. You'll notice, in your discussions with grown-ups, that they're beginning to treat you more as an equal and to respect your point of view. However, such discussions may also create tension or lead to misunderstandings. You may find yourself questioning your parents' ideas and causing conflict within your family.

It may help you to remember that you're not the only one who is experiencing change. Just as you must adjust to the changing you, so must those around you. It's not always easy for parents to decide how much freedom and responsibility to give their teen children during the years between childhood and adulthood.

Your Self-Esteem

When you look in the mirror, are you happy about the person you see there, or do you spend a lot of time wishing you could change some of your characteristics?

The way you feel about yourself is called your **self-esteem.** You can have high self-esteem, meaning that you have a favorable opinion of yourself, even though you are aware of some faults. You can also have low self-esteem, meaning that you don't like yourself very much. Self-esteem does not just concern your physical appearance, although the way you look certainly affects the way you feel about yourself. Rather, it concerns the whole you—your feelings about your body, your mind, your emotions, and your interactions with others.

Your self-esteem is closely linked to your self-concept—the view that you have of yourself. In Chapter 1, you learned that your self-concept might be realistic: you see yourself clearly and are aware of your strengths and weaknesses. It could also be unrealistic: you focus too heavily on your faults and overlook some of your good points. People suffering from low self-esteem often have an unrealistic self-concept.

People who have high self-esteem usually relate well to others.

Low self-esteem is a problem for many teens. They may feel concerned about their looks. They may be upset about conflicts with the people around them. They may be confused about new kinds of friendships and new emotions. All of these problems can cause them to think less of themselves.

If you suffer from low self-esteem, you are not alone. However, it is a problem that you should begin working on immediately. If you learn to feel good about yourself, you will be more confident that you can handle the things you want to do. You will be more able to see the positive feelings that people have toward you. You will also be less likely to be influenced by others to do things you would rather not do. For example, teens who use drugs are often suffering from low self-esteem. For these reasons, developing high self-esteem is an important task for the teenage years.

Building Your Self-Esteem

There are many things you can do to develop a more positive view of yourself. Here are some of them:

- **Learn to accept praise.** When someone compliments you, don't belittle yourself or your accomplishment. People praise you because they feel you really deserve it.
- **Focus on your strengths.** Everyone has talents. You might sew well, or play the piano, or be good at gymnastics. You might be a sensitive listener or a good organizer. Write down these strengths to remind yourself of the good things others have said about you.

■ **Accept yourself as you are.** Accept the fact that you are not perfect and that you have some faults. After all, you accept your friends as they are. Why should you be any harder on yourself? If you spent less time criticizing yourself, you could spend more time trying to adjust characteristics that you think need improvement.

■ **Learn from what you do.** Recognize and keep developing your strengths, and try to view your mistakes as learning experiences. When you make a mistake, don't label yourself a failure. Use the opportunity to figure out how you can avoid a similar mistake in the future.

■ **Use your strengths to help others.** Becoming involved in activities that help others lets you know that you can accomplish something really important. It can also reinforce your strengths.

■ **Take responsibility for your own life.** Learn how to deal with the different demands that are made of you. Managing your own life successfully will make you feel very competent and good about yourself.

You can raise your self-esteem by focusing on your successes. What experiences have you had that bolstered your self-esteem?

Managing Your Life

Just what is management, and why is it so important that you develop management skills? **Management** involves making decisions about the things you want to do and then accomplishing the goals you have set for yourself. By developing management skills, you begin to take responsibility for your life. That is especially important now because you will soon be making some very crucial decisions about your future.

Managing your life involves, among other things, taking charge of your health. Every day you make decisions—about food, exercise, sleep, work, and relaxation—that can have long-term effects on your health. In Chapter 3 you will learn why health is important and how to establish healthy habits.

Managing your life also involves setting goals for yourself. Having goals—about making a team, going to camp, or graduating from high school, for example—helps you make decisions now that will help you in the future.

Chapter 4 focuses on goal setting and helps you figure out how to achieve the goals that you set for yourself.

Finally, managing your life means making the decisions that are right for you. When you were a child, your parents and other adults made most of the decisions about your life. Now you are beginning to make more of these decisions yourself, and eventually you will take full responsibility for your own life. Chapter 5 walks you through a decision-making process that you can apply to all your important decisions.

The teen years are not easy for anyone. Adapting to change is a challenge at any stage in life, and no other stage involves so many changes so quickly. This book is designed to help you understand the changes that occur between childhood and adulthood, and to help you develop the skills for dealing with this period in your life.

Managing your life involves making decisions about a wide variety of things—from daily tasks, such as grooming, to long-range plans for your future.

CHAPTER
2 REVIEW

Reviewing the Facts

1. Give two reasons why the teen years might be described as the best time of life.
2. What causes the physical and emotional changes experienced by adolescents? Name two physical and two emotional changes.
3. What are three examples of mental abilities that are developed during the teen years?
4. List six ways to build self-esteem.
5. What is management and why is it important?
6. Name three aspects of your life for which you need management skills.

Sharing Your Ideas

1. How might you help a friend who is having a particularly difficult time adjusting to the changes of adolescence?
2. How might feeling good about yourself—having high self-esteem—affect the ways you relate to other people? Give several specific examples.

Applying Your Skills

1. Evaluating Personalities. Select two characters from books or television shows, one with high self-esteem and one with low self-esteem. Write a few paragraphs on how each character's level of self-esteem affected his or her actions and what it did to the lives of others around them.

2. Generating Solutions. Read the advice columns in at least three teen magazines, noting the kinds of problems that are covered. Select a letter and be prepared to discuss the advice that you would have given in the same situation.

3. Describing Biological Aspects of Development. Read the section of a life science, health, or biology textbook that describes changes in hormones during adolescence. Write two or three paragraphs in your own words to explain what occurs.

Your Health and Wellness

Marcie started jogging three months ago and now she's enjoying the results of her efforts. All her friends tell her how terrific she looks. Most important to Marcie, though, is the fact that she feels so much better. She has more energy, her skin is clearer, and she feels more confident about herself. She's determined to keep to her new regimen.

Perhaps, like Marcie, you need to take greater control of your health. In the last chapter you learned about the physical changes that take place during the teen years. You also learned that this is the time when you develop your decision-making skills. A decision to practice good health habits could be one of the smartest moves you ever make.

Why Health Is Important

Many people believe that if they're not sick, they're healthy. In fact, being healthy means a lot more than not having a disease. People who are truly healthy are physically fit, emotionally and mentally sound, and have a satisfying social life.

To emphasize the difference between a moderate and a high level of health, many people now use the word *wellness.* **Wellness** is a state of good health that you achieve by making a conscious effort to look after yourself.

Here are some of the benefits of maintaining a wellness program:

- You will look and feel better.
- You will have more energy to do the things you want to do.
- You will have a better outlook on life.
- You will enjoy being around people.
- You will enjoy being alone.
- You will be able to handle your emotions better.
- You will feel more confident.

Wellness involves four main aspects of health: physical, mental, emotional, and social. To achieve wellness, you need to pay attention to all four.

Regular exercise is beneficial for your physical health, as well as your mental and emotional health. You can make exercise a part of your social life, too.

Physical Health

As you mature, you can begin to take responsibility for your own physical health. That means making decisions about what you eat, how much you sleep, and how much exercise you get. Physical wellness also involves safety, grooming, and making judgments about harmful substances such as tobacco, alcohol, and drugs. In addition, you need to develop a basic awareness of your physical condition. For example, you can no longer expect your parents to notice if you have a sore throat or a rash. It's up to you to pay attention to any signs that you may be sick and to get advice from an adult.

Nutrition

Your body needs a balanced diet to stay well. When you eat a variety of foods you have a better chance of resisting infection and disease. You also have a higher level of energy for both studying and playing.

Although achieving a balanced diet takes some thought and planning, the basic rule is quite simple. You should eat a variety of nutritious foods such as whole-grain breads, fruits, vegetables, poultry, fish, and dairy products.

Sleep

Regular sleep contributes greatly to your health. It affects your appearance, the amount of energy you have, and your mental and emotional state. Basically, you look better and feel better if you get a good night's sleep.

Your body needs sleep to refresh itself. Going to bed late occasionally will probably not hurt you, but most teens require about eight hours of sleep each night.

Exercise

The human body is designed for movement and it needs exercise. Yet many people spend their days at a desk and their evenings in front of the television. You need to make a conscious effort to include exercise in your daily routine so that it becomes a habit.

The benefits of regular exercise are numerous:

- It gives you strength and endurance.
- It gives you greater agility.
- It helps release tension.
- It helps you maintain your weight.
- It makes you feel and look better.

When you are planning an exercise program, try to choose activities that you think you'll enjoy. Some people prefer to exercise alone, so they might decide to start jogging, or swimming, or biking regularly. Others prefer team sports, such as soccer or softball, that allow them to be with other people. Working out with a group can help motivate you to continue an exercise program.

One key to fitness is to make sure you exercise regularly. It doesn't always have to be an organized sporting activity. If you occasionally choose to walk instead of going by car, or if you rake leaves instead of watching television, you will be doing your body a favor.

Safety

Accidents are the leading cause of death among teens, yet most accidents could have been prevented.

Make sure you take preventive measures to protect yourself from accidents. For example, always wear a safety belt when you're riding in a car. And follow traffic rules and safety regulations when biking or driving.

Wear protective gear such as helmets, pads, and goggles to prevent sports injuries. Before diving, make sure the water is deep enough. Never swim alone. Accidents often occur when people take unnecessary risks.

Grooming

Good grooming is particularly important for teens. The physical changes that occur at adolescence can lead to such temporary conditions as oily skin and hair, acne, and increased perspiration.

Good grooming involves regular showers or baths, the use of a deodorant or antiperspirant, and greater attention to hair care and skin care. Daily brushing and flossing of your teeth is important—both for your appearance and for your health. You should also make sure you keep your hands and nails clean. Good grooming contributes to your overall appearance and helps you feel better about yourself.

Substance Abuse

Choosing wellness means deciding against harmful substances such as tobacco, alcohol, and drugs. All of these substances are bad for your health and most are **addictive**—people who start using them find it difficult, and sometimes impossible, to stop.

All forms of tobacco—whether smoked or chewed—can cause serious health problems. The use of tobacco has been directly linked to cancer, strokes, and heart disease. Even occasional smokers find that tobacco stains their teeth and fingers, dulls the taste buds, and causes "cigarette breath." Smoking is offensive and harmful to nonsmokers, too.

A clean, neat personal appearance communicates to others that you care about yourself.

Learn about substance abuse and its physical, mental, emotional, and social effects on individuals and families. Such knowledge can help you say "no" to using tobacco, alcohol, or drugs.

Alcohol affects the body by slowing down the nervous system. Your muscle coordination and mental judgment are affected. Alcohol abuse can cause vomiting, unconsciousness, and even death. Alcohol is also involved in one-half of all automobile accidents. Unfortunately, many teens and adults become problem drinkers or alcoholics. They come to depend on the regular use of alcohol.

The word *drugs* is used to mean many different kinds of substances, from medicine to illegal crack and heroin. Drug abuse can affect a person physically, mentally, and emotionally. It can cause severe health problems, bizarre behavior, and even death. Prescription drugs should be used only under the care of a doctor. Buying or selling illegal drugs, from marijuana to cocaine, can result in arrest, fines, and jail sentences.

Why do teens use tobacco, alcohol, or drugs when these substances are so harmful to their health? Reasons vary from a desire to act older and pressure from others to low self-esteem and personal problems. School programs, support groups, and counselors help people deal with drug problems. The best way to avoid substance abuse is never to start using tobacco, alcohol, or drugs.

Mental, Emotional, and Social Health

Physical fitness is an important component of wellness. However, to be truly healthy you need to give attention to your mental, emotional, and social health, too. The four components are interrelated.

Mental Health

Just as there are different levels of physical fitness, there are different levels of mental health. In general, people who are very healthy mentally feel good about themselves, are comfortable with other people, and are able to cope with the demands of life.

The level of your mental health is closely related to your self-concept and your self-esteem. It is not unusual for teens to be confused about their self-concept. After all, you're in a stage of transition from child to adult, and you're not sure who you are or what you want. That, in turn, affects your self-esteem. At times you feel confident and positive. You *know* you can do well in school. You feel good about your friendships. Then at other times you feel unsure about yourself. You feel clumsy and awkward. You want to try out for the soccer team but you're afraid of being rejected.

It may help if you realize that your self-concept is based on years of "input." The positive and negative experiences you've had since childhood have all affected the way you see yourself today. You can't change that perception of yourself overnight. However, as you read in Chapter 2, you can take measures to improve your self-esteem.

Emotional Health

Just as you have certain physical needs, you also have basic emotional needs. You need to give and receive love, you need to have a sense of belonging, and you need to feel worthwhile.

You can satisfy your need to love and be loved by building close relationships with your family and friends. These relationships also give you a feeling of being a valued member of a group. The approval and recognition of others help you think of yourself as a worthwhile person.

Learning to express your emotions is another important part of growing up. When you were a child, you didn't think twice about crying or throwing a tantrum. You reacted the only way you knew. Since then you have learned that there may be more appropriate ways of expressing your feelings. Sometimes, you might feel like talking things over with someone else. Other times, you might prefer to let off steam by doing strenuous exercise. Everyone has different ways of expressing emotions. Just remember that it's important that you don't bottle up your emotions.

Social Health

Your involvement in the society in which you live has an effect on your health. There are two main aspects of social health. One concerns the people with whom you have direct contact—your family, friends, neighbors, and so on. If you enjoy good, supportive relationships with the people you know, you are likely to be healthier than someone who does not.

The other aspect of social health concerns your role within society as a whole. For a society to function well, its members need to work together. There are many things you can do to contribute to the overall health of your community. You can volunteer your time to help people in need. You can take a first aid course given by your local Red Cross. You can support the local recycling effort. You can help keep your environment clean.

Stress Can Be Good for You

Most people think of stress as always bad—something to avoid. Some stress, however, can be good for you. In fact, a certain amount of stress is helpful.

One of the body's responses to stress is to prepare for action: the heart and breathing speed up, for example. If you are in danger—or even if you are preparing to run a race—these changes will benefit you. Many people find that stress gives them the boost of energy or courage needed to do a difficult task well.

Certain studies have even shown that a degree of stress can help people cope with a difficult situation. Researchers have found that people who were moderately concerned about surgery recovered better than both those who were extremely fearful and those who seemed not to be concerned at all. The slight worry apparently helped patients to construct inner defenses.

Recognizing that stress can be helpful will allow you to use it to your advantage. If you feel nervous about beginning a new job, realize that the stress may be helping you in many ways. Perhaps it will cause you to take extra care with what you do, or it may help you pay attention and remember a new procedure. Being too comfortable too soon might cause you to become careless.

Everyone encounters stressful situations in daily life. If you can see moderate stress as a helpful aid, you will find that you are taking control of situations instead of letting them control you.

Think It Through

1. Why do you think the individuals who were not at all concerned about surgery did not do as well as those who were moderately concerned?
2. Choose a type of stress that you encounter in everyday life. List ways that the stress might help you perform better.

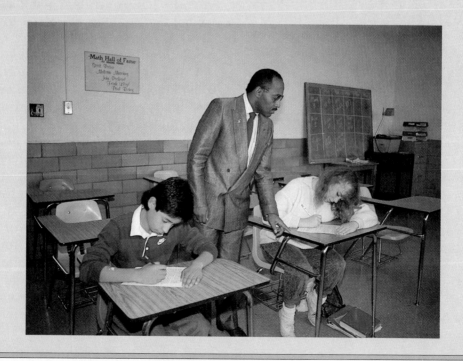

Stress

Even the healthiest person feels tense and nervous on occasion. For example, you might become nervous before a team tryout, or performing in a school play, or dating someone for the first time. Serious events, such as a death, a divorce, or a major illness in the family, can leave you feeling emotionally drained.

The physical and emotional tension that is caused by important happenings or changes in your life is called **stress.** It might cause you to lose your appetite for a while, or you might suffer from headaches or sleeplessness. Usually, such effects are temporary and cause no harm. Your body is equipped to handle a certain amount of stress. In fact, stress can actually be good for you at times.

Dealing with Stress

There are many things you can do to deal positively with stress. The important thing is to recognize signs of stress early and to take action quickly.

- **Try to relax.** Sometimes just getting away from everything and spending time by yourself can help you relax. Make a point of taking time out each week to read a book, listen to music, work on a hobby, or just daydream.
- **Get some exercise.** When you are starting to feel overwhelmed, go out and run, shoot some baskets, or do some other physical activity that will help you unwind.
- **Plan ahead.** If you're nervous about an upcoming event such as a speech, take time to prepare yourself and rehearse so you feel more confident.

- **Think about the situation.** Perhaps your imagination is making it seem worse that it really is. Ask yourself, "What's the worst thing that could happen? How can I prevent that from happening?"
- **Learn from the experience.** If you're miserable because you failed an important test, think about what you can do to pass the test next time.

If the feeling of stress continues, you may need to get outside help. Although everyone feels unhappy from time to time, a prolonged feeling of stress can develop into **depression.** This can cause people to feel hopeless, to lose enjoyment of life, or to even consider suicide. If you suffer from depression, talk about your problems to someone you trust—a close friend, your parents, a teacher, or a counselor.

Remember that stress is perfectly normal, and everyone experiences it. If you take care of your health—physical, mental, emotional, and social—you'll be better equipped to deal with stress.

If you can relax during stressful times, you will feel more in control. You can also use the time to think of solutions to the problems.

Reviewing the Facts

1. What is wellness?
2. Name three benefits of maintaining a wellness program.
3. Why does your body need a balanced diet?
4. Name three benefits of regular exercise.
5. What substances should you avoid when you're concerned with wellness?
6. How does a person with a high level of mental health feel?
7. What are your basic emotional needs?
8. What are the two main aspects of social health?
9. List five ways to cope with stress.

Sharing Your Ideas

1. What could your school do to help promote wellness among students?
2. Why do you think stress has become such a major health problem in American society?

Applying Your Skills

1. Describing a Method. Choose one of the following stressful situations: waiting in traffic; entering a new school; having an argument with your parents; beginning a new job; having a close friend move away. List five words that would describe your physical and emotional reactions. Then write a short essay describing how you might reduce the stress that the situation created.

2. Analyzing Your Behavior. Make a chart to check your physical wellness habits for a week. Set up columns for wellness habits such as eating breakfast, exercising, getting eight hours of sleep, cleaning teeth, etc. Every day, make a check mark in each column if you took that step. At the end of the week, total the check marks. Then determine your wellness index by computing your total marks as a percent of the number of check marks you could have made.

3. Observing Accurately. With a partner, select ten emotions to express. Then play a variation of charades, with one person attempting to convey each of these emotions using only facial expressions. Are some emotions harder to express than others?

CHAPTER

4

Examining Your Goals

OBJECTIVES

This chapter will help you to:

- Explain how to examine needs, wants, and values in order to determine what's important.
- Discuss different types of goals.
- Describe the resources used to accomplish goals.
- Explain how to choose between conflicting goals.

WORDS TO REMEMBER

fixed goal
flexible goal
goal
long-term goal

prioritize
resource
short-term goal
values

Every day you have to make many decisions. Some of them are fairly easy—like what you'll wear to school or what you'll eat for lunch. Others are more difficult. Should you buy that cassette you want or should you save your money for a new bike? Should you go swimming with your friends or should you stay home and help around the house?

As you get older, you'll find that you have to make more and more decisions, and some will require careful thought. For example, how will you decide what courses to take in school? How can you earn extra money on the weekends?

The way to make the decisions that are right for you is to examine your goals. A **goal** is a target you set for yourself to accomplish. If you think carefully about what you're trying to achieve, you'll find it easier to make decisions. Equally important, the decisions you make will help you achieve your goals.

What's Important To You?

You have a problem: you have tickets for a concert Saturday night, but now you've been invited to a friend's party on the same night and you really want to go. What should you do? One way of settling problems like this one is to sort out what's most important to you. You can do this more easily if you examine your needs, wants, and values.

Your Needs

Everyone needs certain basic things in order to survive. You need food, water, clothing, and a place to live. Needs are things that are essential—things you can't get along without.

However, you must have more than these basics for your life to be satisfying. You need the love and companionship of your family and friends. You need to know that there are people you can turn to when you have a problem. You need to do things that make you feel good about yourself and help build your self-esteem.

Right now, you probably don't have to worry about satisfying your basic needs for food, shelter, and so on. Your parents take care of that. At some time in the future, though, you will have to figure out how you are going to earn enough money to meet those needs.

The needs that you are most concerned with at present are those that help you feel good about yourself. You might feel that you need to make the soccer team, or get an A on the next math test, or be chosen for the school play.

Your Wants

Wants are things you would like to have in order to make your life more enjoyable. They have to do with preferences and desires. You might want, for example, a new leather jacket, or a CD player, or a dirt bike, or a gold chain.

Some wants are also needs. Everyone has the need to eat, for example, but when you choose pizza and your friend chooses salad, you are both satisfying your need in different ways because you have different wants. You might also argue that your desire for a leather jacket (a want) is also a need because wearing it will make you feel good about yourself. Chances are, though, that you could find some other, less expensive way to feel good about yourself if a leather jacket was beyond your means. In general, wants are not essential to your life, but you think they would make you happier.

How might needs, wants, and values influence this teenager's goal of owning a car?

Wants also include much larger desires. You may dream about becoming a movie star, or a sport commentator, or an Olympic athlete. There's nothing wrong with such wants. Dreams such as this have inspired many dedicated people to achieve their desires.

Your Values

Some of your actions are based not on your needs and wants, but on your values. **Values** are guidelines that you have for living with yourself and others. Values are based on what you believe to be right or wrong, important or unimportant.

Your values are shaped by people you like and respect, such as your parents and friends, by what you learn in school, and by your religion. They are also influenced by people you admire, such as heroes from history, or politicians, celebrities, or athletes of today.

Perhaps you value physical fitness. It's important to you that you be strong and healthy. If so, you will be sure to exercise regularly and eat the right foods. If education is what you value, you will study hard and work toward your graduation.

TECHNOLOGY

Acquiring Computer Literacy

If you are like most teens, you are still finding out about the world and you're not yet ready to settle on a particular career. How, then, can you set short-term goals to prepare for your future?

Experts predict that no matter what you decide to do in the years to come, computers will be a part of your life. Technology has changed the way most people do their jobs. Office workers who once used typewriters and adding machines now use word-processing computers and high-speed electronic calculators. Computers help travel agents, lawyers, and police officers to work more efficiently. Increasing numbers of factory workers are using computers to operate the machines on assembly lines. You may even be able to see technology at work at your local supermarket, which may have electronic scanners to read price codes.

How can you prepare to take your place amid this technological revolution? Here are a few suggestions:

- Become familiar with computers. Your school probably offers computer courses; if you haven't signed up for one, try to do so soon.

- Look for locations where computers are in use. If you can, ask what the computers are used for and what type of training is required to operate the computer.

- Read about computers in newspapers and magazines. Many articles describe new uses for computers, advances in computer technology, or predictions about how computers will continue to change the way we live.

- Keep an open mind. Be ready to accept change in technology and in other areas. Some people who lose their jobs because of technological advances are those who are unwilling to adapt to the new technology.

You are just beginning to plan for your future. As you set goals, keep in mind all the ways that technology has changed your life and will continue to do so in the future.

Think It Through

1. What are some ways in which your own life has been affected by the computer?

2. What are some home uses of the computer now and what new uses can you suggest for the future?

Setting Goals

Analyzing your needs, wants, and values will help you set goals for yourself. At the same time, setting goals will help you satisfy your needs, wants, and values. Where do you begin? First, you must think about the different types of goals that you have.

Types of Goals

Suppose your goal is to buy a new pair of athletic shoes. This may be a need because you have worn out your current shoes, or it may be a want—you'd love to have a pair of high-tops just like your friends are wearing. A need is usually a more important reason for setting a goal than a want is.

Many goals meet a combination of needs, wants, and values. At lunch, you plan to have an apple for dessert. This would help meet your *need* for food. However, many foods could satisfy this need—one of your friends prefers a brownie. Your exact choice depends on what you *want,* but what you want may also depend on your values. If you *value* good health, you'll choose an apple over a brownie because you know it's better for you.

Short-Term or Long-Term

The way you go about reaching your goals also depends on whether they are short-term or long-term. When you have more time to do something, you usually have more options.

A **short-term goal** is something you can accomplish soon. Your short-term goals might include the following:

- Read a novel.
- Go on a hike.
- Fix your bike.
- Buy a birthday gift.
- Lose five pounds.
- Write to your grandmother.

Your goals can be short-term or long-term. This student spent several years developing his artistic skill before winning an award.

A **long-term goal** is something you plan to accomplish sometime in the future, perhaps in six months, or a year, or after you finish high school. Examples of long-term goals are:

- Make the basketball team.
- Go to computer camp.
- Buy a used car after you get your driver's license.
- Graduate from high school.

You can establish short-term goals as steps toward reaching your long-term goals. Suppose, for example, that your long-term goal is to buy a computer. You can build toward that goal by setting several short-term goals. One short-term goal will be to put aside a certain amount of money each week. Another will be to start reading magazines about computers so that you will know which computer is best for you when the time comes. Another may be to spend more time in the computer lab at school so that you'll know more about computers when you get yours. Dividing a long-term goal into several short-term goals often helps make the goal seem more attainable.

Resources

When you're deciding about your goals, you also should consider your resources. A **resource** is something that you need to accomplish a goal. There are many different types of resources:

- Your own knowledge, skills, energy, and imagination.
- Money, tools, equipment, and other possessions.
- Time.
- Other people, such as your family, friends, teachers.
- Community facilities, such as the Y, the library, and courses offered by local schools or colleges.

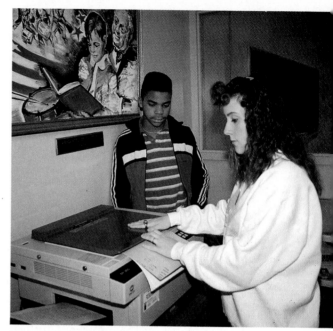

Resources include knowledge, skill, energy, time, money, equipment, other people, and community facilities. What resources might these students be using?

When you establish your goals, then, you must consider if you have the resources to reach them. If you don't, you have two options: you can establish different goals, or you can figure out how you can obtain the resources.

Suppose, for example, that your goal is to buy a new bike. One resource you will need is money. You have about half the money you need for the bike, but it will take you a long time to save the rest. Next, you consider some of your other resources—like your possessions. Perhaps you could raise some of the money by selling the albums that you never listen to any more, or by selling your old bike. Maybe you could offer to mow lawns during the summer to earn the extra cash.

Often, there are different ways of meeting the same goal. Examining your resources helps you consider the alternatives available to you.

Fixed or Flexible

Sometimes you'll find that your goals conflict. Perhaps you'd planned to clean up your room this afternoon, but now your father has asked you to mow the lawn. Deciding between conflicting goals is easier if you consider which ones are fixed and which are flexible.

A **fixed goal** is one that can only be met at a certain time. The lawn-mowing may be a fixed goal if the grass is so high that it can't wait another day. Fixed goals are often tied to specific dates. For example, if your goal is to sign up for a community athletics program, you must set time aside to attend the registration on the specified date.

A **flexible goal,** on the other hand, is one that has no definite time limit. Cleaning your room is a flexible goal— you can do it any time. Reading a novel for pleasure is another example of a flexible goal. If you have to read that same novel in time for a class, though, then it's a fixed goal.

Usually, goals that involve you alone are more flexible than those that involve others. Changing a plan that involves three or four people can be difficult. You will also find that long-term goals are usually more flexible than short-term goals.

Sometimes, a goal starts out being flexible but becomes fixed. If you want to work on a mid-semester assignment, it is a flexible goal for the first few weeks. As the deadline approaches, however, it becomes a fixed goal—you can't put it off any longer.

Many times you have to set priorities. Some tasks have to be done at a specific time, while others are very flexible.

Goals and Choices

Learning to prioritize your goals is a key to taking responsibility for your own life. When you **prioritize** your goals, you rank them in order of importance. This helps you to make choices between goals when they conflict. Which goals should you go for? Which should you postpone or forget about? These are the kinds of decisions that you have to make throughout your life.

Whenever you're confused about which goals you should pursue, take time to ask yourself these questions:

- Does this goal satisfy my needs or wants?
- Is it in line with my values?
- Do I have the resources I need?
- Is it a fixed or a flexible goal?

Examining your goals carefully will help you decide which ones you should concentrate on. It will also help you figure out alternative ways of meeting conflicting goals.

Reviewing the Facts

1. How can you sort out what is most important to you?
2. What are values?
3. What is the difference between a short-term goal and a long-term goal?
4. List the five resources you might use to accomplish a goal.
5. Define and give an example of a fixed goal; define and give an example of a flexible goal.
6. How can you choose between conflicting goals?
7. What four questions should you ask yourself when prioritizing goals?

Sharing Your Ideas

1. Do you think the basic needs of people have changed since your grandparents were children? How about wants and values? Explain your answers.
2. What do you think is the most important resource for accomplishing a goal?

Applying Your Skills

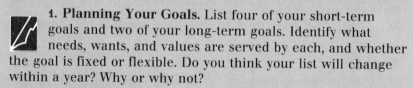 **1. Planning Your Goals.** List four of your short-term goals and two of your long-term goals. Identify what needs, wants, and values are served by each, and whether the goal is fixed or flexible. Do you think your list will change within a year? Why or why not?

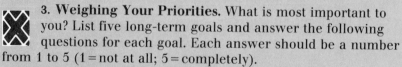 **2. Researching a Valued Person.** Study back copies of your local newspaper to find information about someone in your community whose strong values influenced people or events. Describe the values that person displayed.

3. Weighing Your Priorities. What is most important to you? List five long-term goals and answer the following questions for each goal. Each answer should be a number from 1 to 5 (1 = not at all; 5 = completely).
  1. How much does this goal satisfy my needs?
  2. How much does this goal satisfy my wants?
  3. How important is it that I achieve this goal?
For each goal, add your three answers. The goal with the highest total is most important to you—you have prioritized your goals. How do your goals rate? Does the rating surprise you?

CHAPTER

5

Making
Decisions

OBJECTIVES

This chapter will help you to:

- List different types of decisions and explain how decisions can affect people.
- Explain the five-step decision-making process.
- Discuss the importance of taking responsibility for decisions.

WORDS TO REMEMBER

alternative
decision
evaluate

One of the differences between childhood and adolescence has to do with the number of decisions you make. When you were a child, your parents decided a lot of things for you—what you would wear, what you would eat, what movies you might watch, how you could spend your money, and so on. Now you're beginning to make these and many other kinds of decisions for yourself.

A **decision** is the choice you make between different possibilities. Decisions are directly related to your goals. As you learned in Chapter 4, goals are the targets you set for yourself to accomplish.

Part of the process of decision making involves examining your goals so that you can figure out which ones are most important.

Some of the decisions you make are easy and you probably don't give them much thought. Others need careful consideration. After all, every decision you make, large or small, affects you and other people in your life. In this chapter you'll study a step-by-step process you can apply to your decision making, and you'll learn why it's important that you accept responsibility for your decisions.

Decisions and You

Are you the kind of person who makes decisions on impulse? Do you walk past a store window, see an item you really like, and rush in and buy it without thinking carefully about your purchase? Instead, you may be a creature of habit. Perhaps you chose to have breakfast before you got dressed this morning because you do that every morning.

The decisions you make affect not only yourself but other people around you, such as your family, friends, or classmates.

Different people have different ways of making decisions. When the decisions are small ones, making a choice based on impulse or habit probably won't do you any harm. Bigger decisions, however, require a better, more organized, method of choosing.

Types of Decisions

Decisions can be of major or minor importance. They can be easy or difficult to make. They can be made by you alone, by you after you have consulted others, or by a group. Even *not* making a decision is a decision.

Decisions are part of every area of your life. You make decisions about family matters, such as how to divide telephone time or household responsibilities. You make decisions about friends too. For example, you might spend more time with one friend than another.

Other decisions concern how you spend your time and money as well as what you eat and wear. You need to organize your evenings so that you can get everything done—homework, cleaning your room, and watching a particular television program, for example. You also have to budget your money so that you save enough for special purchases like birthday presents. Food choices involve looking at nutrition, and clothing decisions are made when you purchase as well as wear garments.

The Effects of Your Decisions

Decisions vary in the ways they affect you. The small decisions you make each day may not seem important, yet the effects of some of these can build up. For example, if you choose high-calorie snacks every day, you risk gaining weight and threatening your health.

Sometimes your decisions affect others, not just you. Your family is affected when you decide to skip household duties. Your friends are affected by the way you spend your time after school and on weekends. Even the feelings of others may be influenced by your decisions. If you help with the dishes, someone in your family will probably be appreciative. When you choose a special birthday gift for someone, you show that person how much he or she means to you.

Not all decisions are small ones, however. Some can affect you for years to come. Your decisions about the use of tobacco, alcohol, and other drugs will have both immediate and long-term effects. Entire families experience deep stress when someone is involved in substance abuse. When you decide not to smoke, drink, or use other drugs, you show that you care about your own health as well as the feelings of people around you.

Other important decisions you make affect your life's work. The classes you choose to take in high school may influence what you do after graduation, whether it be a job, training, or college. Since you are likely to spend 30 or more years of your life working, choosing a satisfying career is very important. To make the right decision, you will need to examine all aspects of a potential job. Jobs with rigid hours, seasonal work, or unsteady income are not right for everyone. Those who value time spent with families or time for personal activities will need to consider how a certain career could affect these plans. Many jobs are stressful by nature, and most have stress to some degree. When people are not happy on the job, stress increases and affects their personal and family lives. As you can see, making a careful career choice can have a tremendous influence on your life for many years to come.

Thought-provoking games and activities help develop critical thinking and decision-making skills. They also help you learn about people and how you react in situations.

Decisions that are important to your future are also felt by other people. For example, a young person's decision to go to college can have a major effect on his or her parents' finances. The personal decisions you make about friendships and dating can make their mark on the lives of others, too. Your choices may lead to close relationships and commitments that are just as important to other people as they are to you.

The Decision-Making Process

Many of the decisions that you make each day don't require much thought. When you're trying to decide between a blue or a yellow T-shirt, or between two television shows, you don't spend much time thinking about your options. However, when it comes to major decisions careful thought makes sense.

Here is the basic five-step procedure for making decisions:

1. Define the problem.
2. Identify alternatives.
3. Compare possible outcomes.
4. Make the decision.
5. Evaluate the results.

For small, quick decisions, you might follow these steps in seconds, without even being aware of them. For more important decisions, you'll probably want to go through each step carefully.

How the Method Works

Here's a real-life situation that will help you understand how the decision-making process works. Stephanie and Jessica are two friends who decided to make extra money by working in neighborhood yards after school and on weekends. One month after they started working together, Stephanie was offered a chance to work at a local kennel. She very much wanted to do it—Stephanie loves animals and she would like to own her own pet shop one day. However, if she took the job at the kennel, Stephanie would have to stop working with Jessica. Since Jessica could not handle the gardening job alone, she would have to give it up, too. Stephanie needed to work through the decision-making model in order to figure out what to do.

- **Define the problem.** Stephanie's problem was that she wanted to take the job at the kennel but she didn't want to let Jessica down. Still, she knew she could only be in one place at a time.

  You might have a similar problem. Perhaps two of your friends have invited you to spend time with them next weekend and you only have time to see one. Perhaps you want to get to know someone who just moved into your neighborhood but you can't decide how to go about doing it.

- **Identify alternatives.** At first, Stephanie thought she had only two **alternatives,** or choices. She could take the new job and risk upsetting Jessica, or she could keep working with Jessica and forfeit her opportunity to work in the kennel. As Stephanie thought about it more, though, she realized there was a third alternative. Maybe she could find somebody else to work with Jessica.

  Often, you will find that exploring your options will help you see that you have more choices than you first thought. Sometimes, at this point, it helps to discuss your problem with somebody else. Other people may be able to suggest alternatives that you hadn't thought of.

- **Compare possible outcomes.** Stephanie then considered her three possible solutions, in light of her goals. One of her goals was to keep Jessica as a friend. They had been best friends for a long time and Stephanie valued that. If she turned down the job at the kennel she would not be endangering her friendship. Another of Stephanie's goals was to own her own pet shop one day. She knew that the experience at the local kennel would be helpful. It would help her decide if she did, indeed, want to work with animals. It would also give her valuable experience. Stephanie then thought about her third option. It would enable her to meet her goal to work in the kennel, but the risk she took was that the person who replaced her on the gardening job might also replace her as Jessica's best friend.

- **Make the decision.** In order to make her decision, Stephanie had to prioritize her goals. She decided to give top priority to her plans for a pet shop. Although she hoped to keep Jessica as her best friend, she was prepared to risk having another person take her place. She decided to accept the job at the kennel after explaining everything to Jessica.

- **Evaluate the results.** A few weeks later, Stephanie and Jessica got together for pizza one evening. They wanted to talk about Stephanie's decision and determine whether she had done the right thing. It's always useful to **evaluate,** or judge, a decision in this way—it helps with future decision making. Stephanie and Jessica spend a lot less time together now, but they are still best friends and enjoy talking about their different job experiences. Most important, Stephanie believes that she made the right choice and she expects to take a full-time job at the kennel once she finishes school.

Whenever you make a major decision, or even a fairly unimportant one, it's a good idea to evaluate the decision's effects and to compare them with what you expected would happen. Evaluations such as this help you see your strengths and weaknesses and help you with your decision making in the future.

Taking Responsibility for Your Decisions

Sometimes it's tempting to let other people make decisions for you. That way, if something goes wrong you have someone to blame. You may also be tempted to put off making a decision. You prefer to "wait and see."

At times such as these, you may need to remind yourself that you're in charge of your own life. If you let others decide things for you, you're letting them take charge.

Imagine, for example, that Stephanie had chosen to talk over her dilemma with Jessica, and then let Jessica decide what was best. Jessica would have seen the problem from a different point of view. Her goal was to keep the gardening business going. She might have persuaded Stephanie to turn down the job at the kennel. If that had happened, Stephanie would have missed out on an important opportunity because she let someone else make a decision for her.

You know yourself better than anyone, and you know what's important to you. Making your own decisions, and accepting responsibility for them, is part of the process of growing up. As with anything else, responsible decision making takes practice. The more practice you get now, the better equipped you'll be when you need to make major decisions about your future.

When making major decisions, seek information and advice from parents, teachers, counselors, and other resources.

Everyday Decision Making

How did you decide what to wear today? What to eat for lunch? What to do after school? Chances are you didn't follow the five-step decision-making process when reaching those decisions. If you had, you might not have found time to do much else. You probably took one of the following shortcuts:

- **Default.** You're at home studying when a friend drops by to talk. If you keep talking until it's too late to study, you've decided by default to talk rather than to study. This means that you have backed into a decision by not deciding.

- **Imitation.** You might make decisions by following the examples of others. Imitating others can lead to good decisions—you might see a new movie because a friend recommends it. Sometimes, however, imitation limits you and may even be dangerous. Imitation plays a role when teens feel they have to wear the same clothes as their friends. It also influences people to use drugs, alcohol, and tobacco.

- **Habit.** Many people make decisions purely by habit. They wake up at the same time every day or take the same route to school. Sometimes, though, habit can keep you from trying new things. If you always order a hamburger when you go out to dinner, try another food for a change.

- **Impulse.** When you decide on impulse, you don't give yourself any time to think about your decision. If you are in line at the cafeteria to buy milk and you grab some candy instead, you're acting on impulse, which means that you're doing what you feel like at that moment.

When a decision is minor, these shortcuts are harmless. However, sometimes people make a decision according to habit or by default without realizing how important the decision is and how much impact it might have on their life.

Think It Through

1. Who are some of the people whose example might lead you to imitate decisions?
2. What kind of decisions should not be left to impulse or default?

Reviewing the Facts

1. What is a decision?
2. What is affected by the decisions you make?
3. List the five steps in the decision-making process.
4. Why is it important to think through all your options?
5. How do you prioritize goals?
6. What is the point of evaluating decisions?
7. Why should each person take responsibility for his or her decisions?

Sharing Your Ideas

1. What are the advantages of beginning now to think about your career decisions? What might happen if you don't think about your options?
2. Do you think it's possible to improve your decision-making skills? Why or why not?

Applying Your Skills

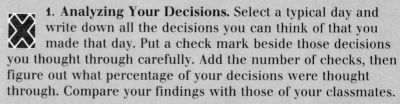 **1. Analyzing Your Decisions.** Select a typical day and write down all the decisions you can think of that you made that day. Put a check mark beside those decisions you thought through carefully. Add the number of checks, then figure out what percentage of your decisions were thought through. Compare your findings with those of your classmates.

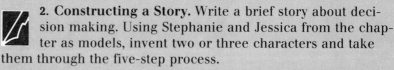 **2. Constructing a Story.** Write a brief story about decision making. Using Stephanie and Jessica from the chapter as models, invent two or three characters and take them through the five-step process.

3. Evaluating a Decision. Use an encyclopedia to learn about a court decision on a specific topic, such as prayer in school, women's rights, or a libel issue. Pretend you were the judge making the decision. Describe how you would apply the five-step process. How is this example similar to a personal decision? How is it different? What would have been the result had the judge decided differently?

CHAPTER

6

Managing Your Life

OBJECTIVES

This chapter will help you to:

- Discuss reasons for developing good management skills.
- Describe the four-step management process.
- Explain why it is important to take responsibility for managing your life.

WORDS TO REMEMBER

back-up plan
flexible
implement
improvise

"You mean this coming weekend?" Brian was talking to his mother on the phone. It was Thursday and she had just told him that his grandparents were planning to attend a funeral and would be staying with them for the weekend.

Brian was happy at the thought of seeing his grandparents again. Now that they lived so far away he didn't get to see them very often. He wondered, though, how he was going to be able to rearrange his weekend around their visit.

Already, he had too much to do. He had promised to sell raffle tickets for a class fund raiser on Saturday morning. Then he had soccer practice in the afternoon and had been invited to a party on Saturday evening. He had also promised his neighbor that he would mow the lawn some time over the weekend, and he had to put in at least three hours on his science project. His mother's birthday was on Tuesday, meaning that he had to shop for a present. He'd also promised his mother that he would help with the barbecue that she had planned for a few friends on Sunday afternoon.

Now Brian had to figure out how he could squeeze still more into the weekend. After all, he wanted to spend time with his grandparents. He'd also have to clean up his room before they came—they always wanted to see his various collections. Brian had too much to do.

Managing a Busy Life

You've probably had days that were too full, and no doubt you muddled through as best you could. "Muddling through" isn't the best way to handle difficult situations, though. If you develop sound management skills, you'll be better equipped to deal with conflicting demands on your time and energy.

The need for good management skills increases as you grow older and as your various roles become more numerous and more complex. Your family roles change as your parents expect you to assume more responsibility around the home. Perhaps your brothers and sisters also need more of your time and energy than they once did.

Many teens lead very busy lives. Management skills can help you make better use of your time and energy, and help you accomplish more.

In addition, your role as a student places more demands on your time and energy than it did when you were in elementary school. Moreover, your friendships, with your own sex and the other sex, have become more complex. You're a neighbor and a member of a community—these roles carry responsibilities. Furthermore, you may be a part-time worker, a babysitter, an athlete, a scout, a member of a club.

Think, for a moment, about Brian, whom you read about at the beginning of this chapter. During one weekend he would be juggling a number of roles: son, grandson, friend, teammate, neighbor, student. Each role was making certain demands on him.

When you think about the number of roles you have and realize how much more complex your life has become, you may see why management skills are so important. Those skills will become even more important when you take on additional, and more responsible, roles in the future.

The Management Process

Whether you are sorting out a conflicting schedule, planning a party, or preparing a meal, the same management process can be applied. Management involves four steps:

- Planning.
- Organizing.
- Implementing.
- Evaluating.

This management process, just like the decision-making process that you learned about in Chapter 5, can be applied to many different aspects of your life, including your school work, social activities, and spare time.

Planning

After Brian got the phone call from his mother, he started to make a list of all the things he had to do that weekend. This is a good way to see clearly the decisions that you face. He also tried to include all the details associated with each activity: for example, helping his mother get the spare room prepared for his grandparents, checking that there was enough charcoal for the barbecue, washing his soccer uniform.

The first step of any project is planning. Planning involves assessing the situation, figuring out what resources you have, and deciding on your priorities. Writing a list is often a good way to assess the situation—it helps you see all the things you have to consider. Before you begin preparing a meal, for instance, you might find it useful to list all the steps you need to take. A food-shopping trip will be more productive if you prepare a list of needed supplies.

Another part of planning is thinking about your resources. Your resources are the things you need to accomplish your goals. They include equipment, skills, knowledge, time, energy, money, and other people.

Brian thought about the resources he would need for the different tasks on his list. His biggest problem seemed to be time: most of his time was already accounted for before he heard about his grandparents' visit. His mother had told him they would be arriving late Saturday morning. Brian decided that he needed to spend Saturday morning helping his mother get the spare room ready and cleaning up his own room. He'd promised to sell raffle tickets, though. Then Brian thought of another resource: his friends. He'd ask his friend Alan to sell raffle tickets for him. He could return the favor another time by doing something to help Alan.

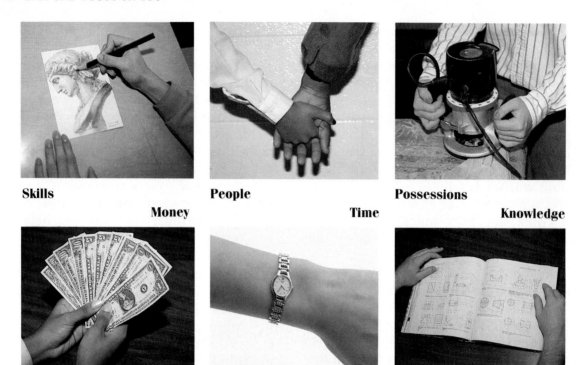

Skills People Possessions

Money Time Knowledge

Identifying available resources is an important part of the planning step. Which of these resources will Brian need to use during the weekend?

Thinking about resources is an important part of the management process because careful thinking can prevent things from going wrong later. You should start by imagining each step of the project that you're preparing, and picturing, in your mind's eye, what equipment or people you will need and how long each step will take. If you're preparing a meal, for example, thinking it through will help ensure that you don't discover at the last minute that you're missing a needed ingredient or utensil.

Once you've assessed the situation and figured out what resources you have, you need to set priorities. This is phase three of the planning stage.

Brian decided that his top priorities were to get his own room and the spare room ready, to spend some time with his grandparents, to attend team practice, to mow his neighbors' lawn, and to help with the Sunday afternoon barbecue. He wanted to go to the party, but it wouldn't be the end of the world if he missed it. He could put off his science project until the following weekend, though he preferred not to. If necessary, he could go shopping for his mother's present on Monday evening.

To sort out your priorities, you should follow the decision-making process described in Chapter 5. Priorities are determined by your goals, which are in turn determined by your needs, wants, and values. Brian placed a high value on helping his mother and on spending time with his grandparents, so those two items were high on his list.

Organizing

The organization stage of the management process involves developing a schedule, getting your resources together, and preparing to act. First Brian drew up a schedule. That helped him realize that he'd be able to spend Saturday lunchtime and Saturday evening with his grandparents, if he didn't go to the party. He also realized that he had no plans for Friday night—he could work on his science project then. He could mow the lawn before the barbecue. Maybe his grandmother would like to go shopping for his mother's birthday present with him. That would allow them to spend some more time together.

Then Brian called Alan and arranged for him to sell raffle tickets Saturday morning. After that, he checked to make sure there was enough charcoal, washed his soccer clothes, and wrote down some of his ideas for presents for his mother. He'd show the list to his grandmother before they set out for the stores.

Good organization is necessary for any project to go smoothly. When you have a schedule that tells you what needs to be done when, things are less likely to go wrong. If your project involves other people, it's important that they, too, know what their duties are.

It's also a good idea to have some **back-up plans**—alternative ways of doing something if the original plan does not work out. For example, what if it rained on Sunday? Brian would gain time because he wouldn't have to mow the lawn, but he would also have to help his mother prepare food that could be served indoors.

Implementing

After you've planned and organized your project, you're ready to **implement** it, to put it into action and monitor it. During the implementing stage you make sure that everything gets done.

In an ideal world, a well-planned and well-organized project would go smoothly. Very often, though, things don't turn out exactly as you expected. Problems arise along the way, and you may have to improvise as the project progresses. **Improvising** means coming up with new ideas when some of your plans don't work.

To make the car wash a successful fund-raiser, the group spent time planning and organizing the event.

For example, after Brian had mowed the lawn and had gone shopping with his grandmother on Sunday, clouds began to gather and rain started before the friends arrived for the barbecue. Brian and his mother had to put their back-up plan into action: they baked potatoes and chicken in the oven instead of on the grill, and served the food in the dining room.

Flexibility is one of the keys to good management. People who are **flexible** are able to adapt to different plans if the original plans don't work out.

Evaluating

As with decision making, it's important to evaluate your project once it is over. You learn from your successes and failures.

Overall, Brian's plans worked out well. He had managed to do all that he had wanted to do, except go to the party, and he had been able to spend several hours with his grandparents. He realized that the weekend would have been less hectic if he had been better prepared beforehand. For example, he rec-

ognized that he should have bought his mother's present earlier so that he wouldn't be forced to do it at the last minute.

After his grandparents left, Brian and his mother talked about their weekend. They had enjoyed the visit, and even though the barbecue plans had had to be changed, everyone had enjoyed their time together.

Responsible Management

In this chapter, you read about how Brian managed one weekend. In real life, of course, you have to manage every day of your life and deal with many different situations.

Over the next few years you will take more and more responsibility for managing your own life. In your home life, you will take on added responsibilities related to keeping the home clean, buying supplies, and choosing meals. That will give you experience you will need when you move into an apartment or home of your own. At school, you will find that your teachers will give you increasing responsibility for managing your time and getting your work done. In your relationships with your family and friends, you'll find that you'll be making more and more decisions for yourself.

Taking responsibility for managing your own life is an exciting prospect. During the next few years you'll have many opportunities to use your management skills. Practice applying the management process to different projects that you undertake. Practice now will help you for years to come.

Management skills can help you with added responsibilities—both now and in the future.

MANAGING RESOURCES

You Can Be Your Own Best Resource

Becky knows that when she has to accomplish a goal, she needs certain resources. She also knows that she cannot always count on having enough money, equipment, and help from other people. There is one thing, however, that she is sure she can always count on: herself.

Even when you do have everything you need at your disposal, you are still your most important resource because you have to manage all the others. Money must be spent with care. Equipment needs to be taken care of. People have to be given guidance and consideration. The following rules of resource management should help you make the most of your most important resource—you.

■ **Look after yourself.** Learn to look after yourself by promoting your own wellness. Eat a balanced diet, get regular exercise, and follow the other health-related suggestions in Chapter 3. This way you will have enough energy for the projects you undertake—and energy is a valuable resource to bring to any undertaking.

■ **Develop skills.** Whenever you get the opportunity, develop skills that you think will be useful and make you more able to look after yourself. Home economics and technology courses will help you become more self-sufficient. You should also practice working on projects, both alone and with your friends. Don't forget skills that will help you to get and hold a job, especially general ones like communication, math and computer skills.

■ **Expand your knowledge.** Take advantage of all chances to expand your knowledge of the world by taking a wide variety of courses at school and by reading newspapers, books, and magazines. Become an expert at finding things out: know how to use the library, where to call to get information, and who to contact for help when you need it.

■ **Cultivate your relationships.** People can be a resource to you, not only by helping you with a particular project, but also by providing you with encouragement, support, and affection. You will find that you are more prepared to tackle a project when others are rooting for you, or when you have taken time to recharge by enjoying the company of people you like.

Think It Through

1. Do you think that it is better to develop yourself in areas where you are strong already, or to work on what you view as your weaknesses? Why?
2. Which area do you think you need to work on the most? How would you go about it?

Reviewing the Facts

1. Why should teens develop good management skills?
2. List the four steps in the management process.
3. What three steps are involved in planning?
4. List the three steps in the organization stage.
5. What does improvising mean?
6. Why should you be flexible?
7. Why is it important to take responsibility for managing your life now?

Sharing Your Ideas

1. Why would having good management skills help you to feel more relaxed?
2. How has your role as a student changed in the past two years? In what ways do these changes require greater management skills?

Applying Your Skills

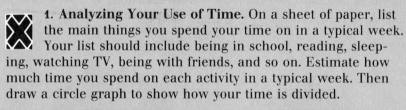

1. Analyzing Your Use of Time. On a sheet of paper, list the main things you spend your time on in a typical week. Your list should include being in school, reading, sleeping, watching TV, being with friends, and so on. Estimate how much time you spend on each activity in a typical week. Then draw a circle graph to show how your time is divided.

2. Evaluating Management's Benefits. Make a list of the three people who are most strongly affected by the way you manage your life. For each person, list a specific example of a way that good management has or might possibly benefit that person. How can you improve your life management further to benefit these three people?

3. Analyzing Management Skills. Use an encyclopedia or biography and read about Lee Iacocca, Jesse Jackson, Ronald Reagan, or Margaret Thatcher to discover the role that management plays in that person's life. Describe how the person managed to get where he or she is today and how he or she relies on management skills still. Does this leader seem to apply the four-step process efficiently? Do you admire him or her?

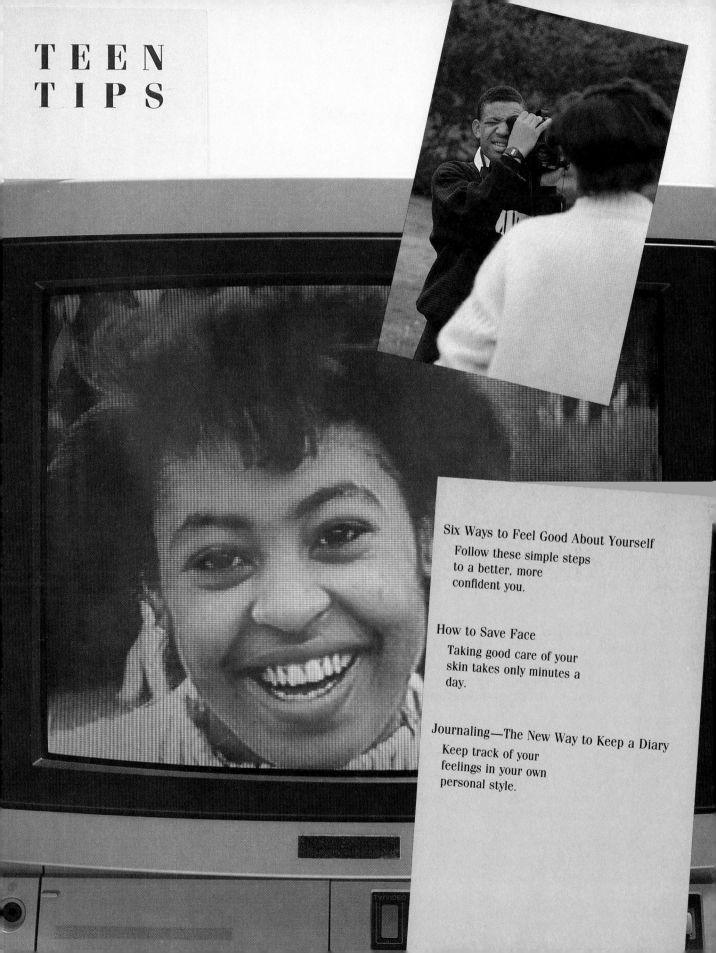

TEEN TIPS

Six Ways to Feel Good About Yourself
Follow these simple steps
to a better, more
confident you.

How to Save Face
Taking good care of your
skin takes only minutes a
day.

Journaling—The New Way to Keep a Diary
Keep track of your
feelings in your own
personal style.

Six Ways to Feel Good About Yourself

Sometimes you feel great—on top of the world. Other times it seems that life is just the pits. Don't worry, that's normal. On those days that you're feeling down, you have to work harder than usual at feeling good about yourself. Here are six ways that are guaranteed to lift your spirits and tell the world you're feeling great:

Look your best to feel your best. Take a little extra time and extra care in dressing, whether for school or a special event. Walk confidently so everyone will know you feel great about yourself.

Learn to relax. If you feel mentally tired after studying, a good physical workout may be what you need to unwind. On the other hand, if you've just finished mowing the lawn or working on your car, a hot bath and some music might make you feel great.

Send positive messages to yourself. If you say to yourself "I'm not popular" or "I'm not smart," you give yourself an excuse to feel bad. Instead, make a list of your strengths or the things you like best about yourself. Then give yourself a pat on the back for all your good qualities.

T
E
E
N

T
I
P
S

☺ **Enjoy life.** Being interested in life is what is attractive to other people. If you enjoy yourself and your interests, you will be fun to be with—and it will be easier to make good friends.

☺ **Cope with problems.** Accept the things that you can't change, but be able to make decisions about those things that are within your control. If you avoid making decisions, others may make them for you. Take responsibility for your own life.

☺ **Focus on what's happening right now.** If you're dwelling on mistakes you made in the past, you're not helping your self-esteem. Evaluate how you handled the situations, and forgive yourself for your mistakes. Then start focusing on the present—and the future.

68

How to Save Face

Did you know that the average adult has about 17 square feet of skin? Your skin serves as a waterproof covering for your body, acts as a barrier to germs, and regulates your body temperature.

How you take care of your skin affects your overall appearance—both now and when you are older.

Skin and Sun

Too much sun can result in a severe sunburn, as well as premature aging of the skin and skin cancer. How can you protect your skin and still be active outdoors?

The sun's ultraviolet rays are most damaging to skin. These rays are most intense during the middle of the day, and up to 80% of the rays can penetrate haze and light clouds. That's why you can get sunburned even on hazy or cloudy days. Also, snow and water reflect ultraviolet rays upward.

To protect your skin, avoid overexposure to the sun's ultraviolet rays. *Suntan lotions* offer little or no protection against ultraviolet light unless they contain a sunscreen. *Sunscreens* can

TEEN TIPS

absorb some of the rays, and are rated according to their sun protection factor (SPF). The higher the SPF number, the more protection provided—the number 2 offers only minimal protection, while the number 15 provides a lot of protection. *Sun-blocking agents* deflect the harmful rays and offer maximum protection—and are good for areas that burn easily, such as lips, ears, and nose. When choosing suntan products, read the labels carefully.

Skin and Acne

What causes some people's skin to break out, while others have flawless skin through their teen years? There are several factors. For starters, heredity is involved. Just as you inherited your father's build or your mother's eye color, you also inherited your skin type and any tendency toward blemishes.

Hormones are another factor. During the teen years, rapidly rising hormone levels cause the oil glands to enlarge and produce more oil. These oil-producing glands can cause your pores to clog. When oils or bacteria get trapped in your pores, the result can be whiteheads, blackheads, or pimples.

Stress may also contribute to skin problems. That's why your face seems to break out during test week or the day before a big party.

Here are some suggestions for controlling acne:

- Wash your face morning and night with warm water and a mild soap or cleanser.

- If you wear makeup, be sure to remove all traces before you go to bed.

T E E N T I P S

- Eat a well-balanced diet and get plenty of rest and exercise.

- Select cleansers and astringents, which help to clean clogged pores, carefully. Read the labels and ask the pharmacist for advice.

- If necessary, use a cream or gel containing benzoyl peroxide to help clear up pimples. Do not use too frequently, because it can dry out the skin.

- Avoid picking or squeezing any affected area as this can worsen the problem or even cause scarring.

- For a severe case of acne, contact a dermatologist, a doctor specializing in skin disorders.

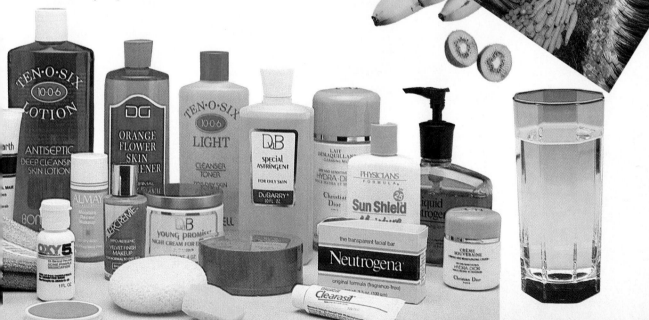

Journaling  The New Way to Keep a Diary

Have you ever kept a diary of the events that happened in your life? Perhaps you went on a trip and kept a record of the things you saw and did along the way. You might have shared this diary with your friends or relatives when you came back.

Journaling is different from keeping a standard diary. Your journal is a private place where you write your thoughts and feelings. It mirrors what is going on inside your head and heart at the time.

A journal can be used to help you through difficult times, make it easier to understand yourself better, or give you a way to deal with someone who is a source of trouble to you. Because you are writing for yourself, you can use any style or form that you want to use. If you want to share your journal with anyone else, that is your personal choice.

Professionals who encourage journal writing suggest four different themes for journal entries:

Memory. Do you remember something that happened to you in the past that seems to be affecting your life now? It may be a pleasant memory of a day with your family that all of a sudden makes you feel very happy. If you write about something you remember as being uncomfortable, you may be able to deal with the memory in a more positive way.

Imagination. Do your teachers or parents ever tell you that you spend too much time daydreaming when there seems to be something more practical to do? You may be dreaming about the future or something you want that will make you feel more confident. Perhaps you dream about a special relationship in your life. Keep track of these dreams in your journal. It may help you focus on your ideas and goals.

Dialogue. Have you ever had a conversation in your mind with someone who you have a hard time communicating with in real life? It may be a parent, a brother or sister, a teacher, a friend, or a classmate. You may think that if you could only tell that person how you feel, he or she would understand you better. Try writing the conversation in the form of a dialogue. By writing the other person's side of the conversation, you may begin to understand the other person better.

Spirituality. What gives meaning to your life? Sometimes it's difficult to talk to your peers about your beliefs. Your private journal is for your eyes alone, so it is a place where you can express things that you may not feel comfortable talking about to others.

A journal may surprise you. You may discover that you are able to handle things better than you thought you could. By writing down your feelings, you will become more aware of yourself as the special person that you are.

Unit Two

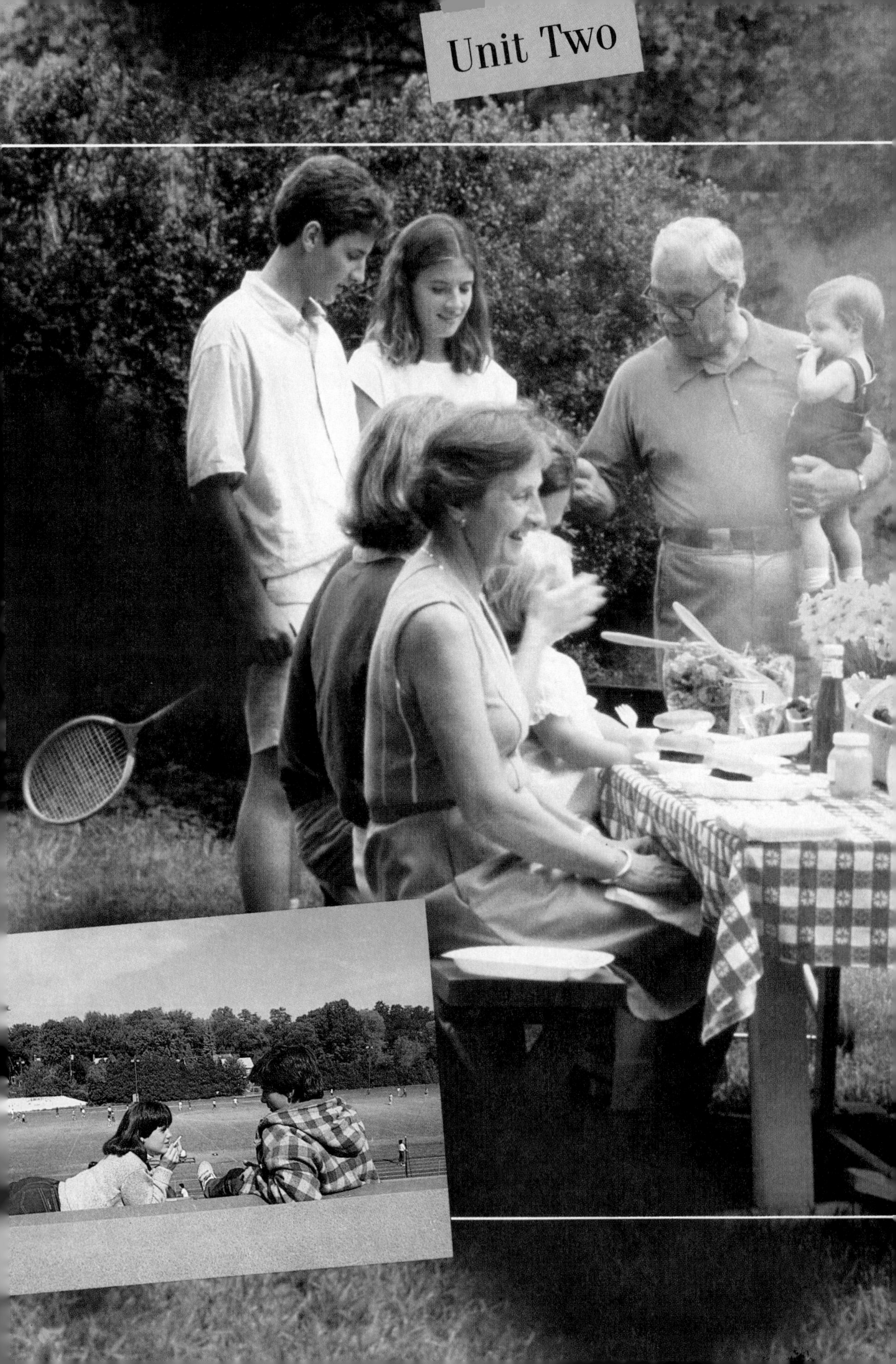

YOUR FAMILY
AND FRIENDS

Relationships and You

OBJECTIVES

This chapter will help you to:

- Describe different types of relationships.
- Explain why relationships are important.
- Describe how successful relationships involve both giving and receiving.
- Identify skills that help to build strong relationships.

WORDS TO REMEMBER

acquaintance   relationship
compromise   respect

A large part of your life is shaped by your relationships. **Relationships** are your connections with other people. Understanding how you interact with others is an important step in knowing who you are.

People who have good relationships are not just lucky. They learn to think before they speak and not say things that might hurt other people's feelings. They learn to see situations through other people's eyes. They learn that everyone has something to offer, whether the person is a young child, a great grandparent, a neighbor, or a best friend. People who like themselves usually treat others fairly and are liked in return.

Types of Relationships

Your relationships are not all the same. Your relationships with family members are different than those with friends. You probably get along better with some classmates than with others.

Your relationships can be divided into three groups: family, friends, and acquaintances.

- **Family.** Have you ever thought what you would be like if you had been born into a different family? Without your parents, brothers and sisters, and other relatives, you would not be the person that you are today.

  Your family helps to shape your personality: you learn how to think and act mainly from your parents. Your family teaches you values and what is important in life. It provides you with food, clothing, and shelter. More important, your family gives you love and emotional support.

- **Friends.** As soon as you were able to talk, you began to form friendships outside your family. You enjoyed running, playing, and trying new games and toys. Your playmates were your friends.

  When you started school, some of your classmates became friends. Perhaps you singled out one person as a "best friend," or you and your friends formed groups. Friends become even more important as you enter your teens.

- **Acquaintances.** You also form relationships with people you don't know very well. A schoolmate, co-worker, or neighbor can be an **acquaintance**: someone you know, but not as well as you would a good friend. An acquaintance can be someone you just met or someone you see occasionally. Sometimes these relationships develop into friendships.

  Throughout this unit you will learn to strengthen your relationships with these three groups.

The love you receive as a child helps you to form satisfying relationships as an adult.

Older Family Members

Teens and grandparents have much to offer one another. Still, like every relationship, the one between young and old sometimes requires extra effort.

Many teens may think of their grandparents simply as close relatives they see often, or only once in a while. That view is limited; it leaves out the fact that grandparents are individuals, too, with a wide range of abilities and experiences.

How can you find out about your own grandparents' unique characteristics and experiences? There is one simple way—you can ask them.

Duane's American history class was compiling an oral history of the local community.

Duane's assignment was to tape-record an interview with his grandparents, who were known as longtime residents.

That assignment started Duane thinking about his grandparents. He loved them, but he realized he didn't know much about their lives. He decided to make a list of questions to ask them: What were they like as teenagers? How did they meet? How did they decide to settle down in this community? What made them keep on working when many others their age had retired?

Duane was delighted with the answers he received. He felt he knew his grandparents much better. His grandparents were pleased that he cared about the stories they had to tell.

Following are some hints for strengthening the ties with your grandparents. (They also apply for other older family members.)

- Ask your grandparents to recall what your parents were like as children.
- Find out if they can teach you a special skill or share a hobby.
- At family gatherings, tell them about your school and social activities.

Think It Through

1. What are some activities that teens and grandparents could do together?
2. Why is it sometimes easier for teens to discuss problems with grandparents than with parents?

The Importance of Relationships

You will continue to form relationships throughout your life. Each relationship can enrich your life and teach you something about yourself. Relationships are important because they help meet your needs, provide you with companionship, develop your self-concept, and broaden your horizons.

Meeting Needs

Corey enjoys going camping with his family. He likes the way he and his brother joke about the dinners they cook. At night in the woods, he feels secure knowing that the members of his family are all around him. Corey's relationships with the members of his family satisfy his important emotional needs.

Your relationships with your family and friends help fulfill your need for affection, love, and a sense of belonging. You also look to your family, friends, teachers, coaches, and counselors for acceptance and approval. A hug, a pat on the back, and a word of praise help you feel appreciated and loved. Spending time together with family and friends helps you feel that you are part of a group that cares about you. Think about some of your own relationships. What emotional needs do they fulfill?

Providing Companionship

One of the reasons why relationships are so important is that they allow people to share ideas, feelings, and experiences with another person. Every relationship you have involves some level of companionship and sharing, but the level is different for each relationship. For example, Sasha may enjoy going to football games with one friend. If she wants to go to a concert, she may ask another friend. When her father became seriously ill, however, she felt most comfortable talking about it with another family member.

Friendships can enrich your life. What do you receive from your relationships with your friends?

Developing Self-Concept

One way that people form their self-concepts is through relationships. How people see themselves largely comes from the way other people see them. When Tony's friend Ellen told him that she really liked his new haircut, he felt pleased. Later, however, when Kevin laughed at the shoes that Tony bought, he felt embarrassed. Tony felt intelligent when his teacher told him that his book report was good, but not so smart when his older brother yelled at him for leaving the front door unlocked.

The way people respond to you in certain situations can help to strengthen your self-concept. Suppose the children you babysit for tell you they think you are the best babysitter they ever had, or your mother thanks you for folding the laundry without being asked. In both cases, the compliments will make you feel good about yourself.

Obviously, your self-concept also affects your relationships. The way you look at yourself helps determine how you get along with others. When you feel good about yourself, getting along with others is much easier.

Broadening Horizons

Relationships do more than form the way people see themselves. Since Risa introduced Sue to Mexican food, Sue has been ordering tacos and enchiladas instead of burgers when she goes out. In this way, relationships can also introduce you to new experiences.

What is more, the comfort you feel in certain relationships—perhaps with your family or with your best friend—can give you the confidence to try new things and discover parts of yourself you might not otherwise have known about.

Getting involved in school or community activities can help you develop friendships with people who have similar interests.

Shawn didn't want to try out for the school play all by himself, but when his friend Joel agreed to try out, too, it gave him the confidence he needed. Now he is a member of the drama club and appears in club productions regularly.

Good relationships also offer opportunities for growth. Family and friends can help you learn about consideration and compromising. (See the explanation of "compromise" on page 80). They can also help you explore different ways of solving a problem. Strong relationships teach you how to listen to other people and accept their differences. In fact, many of the relationships you have now are helping you discover what makes for lasting adult relationships.

Getting Along with Others

Learning how to get along with others can benefit you and those around you. By developing certain attitudes and skills, you can improve the relationships you have and form strong ones in the future.

Giving and Receiving

In every relationship there are two actions—giving and receiving. At least one person gets something from another person. Students learn from teachers. Friends receive companionship from other friends.

We all have to give a little to get something in return. We must be aware of other people's problems, so that we can be helpful and supportive to them. In this way, they will usually be responsive to our problems when we need a shoulder to lean on.

In order to get along well with others, you should treat them the way you want to be treated.

Few relationships require one person to do all the giving and the other to do all the receiving. In fact, people usually will not stay in a relationship for long unless they get something in return for their efforts. Satisfying relationships involve giving and receiving on both sides.

Building Positive Relationships

You can learn how to get along better with others. The following characteristics are important ones to develop:

- **Patience.** Nobody is perfect. Being patient with another person's habits and faults will minimize conflicts and the disagreement they can cause.
- **Understanding.** Try to see things through the other person's eyes. It is easy to get caught up in your own view of things and forget there is another perspective.
- **Trust and honesty.** Trust grows as a relationship grows. Naturally, you don't trust everyone in the same way or to the same extent, but trust is an important part of every relationship. Honesty is related to trust. If you want others to trust you, you must be honest with them.
- **Respect.** You can show **respect** by being polite and considerate to others. Respect is something all people need. Try to respect other people's opinions. They may be different from yours, but they are just as important to others as yours are to you.

- **Willingness to compromise.** When two people **compromise,** each gives up a little of what he or she wants in order to come to an agreement. Suppose that you want to spend the afternoon shooting baskets, but your friend wants to go to the mall to play video games. If the mall is not too far away, you might be able to get in some time at the video arcade and then go shoot baskets. Another solution would be to do what your friend wants this time, but agree that you will choose the activity the next time you get together.
- **Willingness to communicate.** Communication lets the other person know what you need and want as well as what you are feeling. It can clear the air and prevent future problems.
- **A sense of humor.** A sense of humor, especially about yourself, can get people to laugh and often can lighten an embarrassing or tense situation.
- **Acceptance.** People who get along well with others accept others as they are, with their differences and their faults.

You can practice relationship skills, such as patience, understanding, honesty, and respect, when you are with family members.

CHAPTER
7 REVIEW

Reviewing the Facts

1. What are three basic types of relationships?
2. Name two needs that relationships can satisfy.
3. How do relationships provide companionship?
4. In what ways can relationships influence self-concept?
5. Describe how a relationship could provide enrichment in your life.
6. Name five qualities that are important for creating positive relationships.
7. What does it mean to compromise?

Sharing Your Ideas

1. How do you think family relationships differ from relationships with friends? Why do you think people need different kinds of relationships?
2. Which two qualities that contribute to positive relationships do you think are the most important? Which one do you think you need the most improvement in?

Applying Your Skills

1. Writing a Description. Write a 100-200 word essay that describes the way your relationships have enriched your life.

2. Writing a Scenario. Create a fictitious situation in which two people must compromise. Write a short story or script describing how the problem is resolved.

3. Analyzing Relationships. Read a short story and study the relationship between the main character and another character. Are these two characters relatives, friends, or acquaintances? What needs and wants does this relationship satisfy? Is it a positive or negative relationship? Explain your answer.

Communication Skills

OBJECTIVES

This chapter will help you to:

- Define verbal and nonverbal communication.
- Describe how your words and actions, your body language, and your appearance send messages to others.
- Explain how to improve listening skills.

WORDS TO REMEMBER

body language
communicating
eye contact
first impression

manners
nonverbal
verbal

as your best friend ever asked you "What's wrong?" before you said a word? How could your friend know something was wrong? He or she could probably sense that something was different about you. Perhaps you were walking more slowly than usual. Perhaps you were looking at the ground. Maybe it was just that you didn't say "Hi."

Communicating means sending messages from one person to another. These messages don't travel just one way—from you to others. You receive messages as well as send them. Understanding the messages you get from others requires you to listen, not just to hear. This chapter will discuss ways to improve the quality of the messages you send and receive.

The Messages You Send

When people first meet you, they receive many different messages. Communication is not always **verbal**, or using words. If you have ever seen a mime artist, you know that someone's body or facial expression can speak very clearly. The way you stand or sit, the clothes you wear, how you move, and the tone of your voice all send messages about you to others. These are types of **nonverbal** communication: communication without words.

People put together all they see and hear to create a picture of you. The images people have of someone they have just met are their **first impressions.** They use those impressions to form an opinion about the person. After meeting someone, have you ever thought "I'd like to get to know her better"? Sometimes first impressions are wrong.

Someone who seems unfriendly may simply be shy. Keep this in mind, and get to know people before you decide what they are like. At the same time, remember that many people make judgments based on first impressions. After just meeting you, what judgment would people make about you?

Your Words and Actions

You also send messages with your words and the tone of your voice. Your little brother excitedly says, "Look at the picture I drew!" You answer, "That's terrific." It's *how* you say those words that is the key to your message.

Both your words and tone of voice convey messages to your listeners.

If your voice shows enthusiasm, your brother will be pleased that you like the drawing. If, however, you speak in a flat tone of voice and don't look up from your magazine, your brother will think that you don't really care, and he may feel hurt. Thinking before you speak can keep you from sending the wrong messages.

The way you act is another form of communicating. Your **manners** are the way you behave on the whole toward other people. They interpret your behavior as nonverbal messages you are sending. For example, if you are polite and friendly on the telephone, people will enjoy speaking with you. If you are rude, people assume that you are thoughtless.

How you react to events can also tell people about you. If you are able to solve a problem calmly, for example, people will see you as mature. If you get flustered very easily, they may think of you as childish.

People can express many feelings without saying a word. What message is this boy communicating?

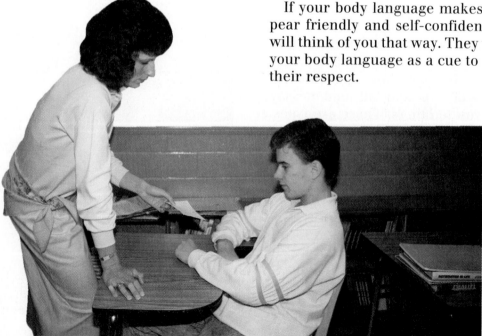

If you are concerned about how you seem to others, your family and friends can help. Ask someone you trust about the impression you make. Does your voice sound harsh or friendly? Are you usually polite to others? A good friend can give you honest answers.

Your Body Language

Body language refers to your posture and the way you move, walk, or sit. It also affects how others see you. Earl stands up straight and walks with his shoulders held high. This shows that he respects himself. Justin slouches and gives the impression that he thinks very little of himself.

An important form of body language is **eye contact:** direct visual contact with another person's eyes. Lee doesn't like to look directly at people who speak to her. She may be shy or nervous, but by avoiding eye contact, she sends the message that others should not approach her. Sheila looks directly at a new acquaintance. The message she sends is that she is interested, confident, and glad to be approached.

If your body language makes you appear friendly and self-confident, others will think of you that way. They will take your body language as a cue to give you their respect.

Your Appearance

Grooming is another part of the message you send about yourself. Good grooming shows that you are trying to look your best. It includes things like brushing your hair and putting on a clean shirt. A clean, healthy appearance communicates to others that you care about yourself.

Keep in mind that appearance is more important in some circumstances than in others. For example, the type of clothes you wear matters more at an interview for a part-time job than on an outing with friends.

The Messages You Receive

"I heard you, I heard you," Anita grumbled to her friend Tanya.

"Yes, I know you heard me, but did you really *listen*?" Tanya asked in exasperation.

What is the difference? Isn't hearing the same as listening? Not at all. Hearing is merely receiving sound waves in your ears. Listening, on the other hand, involves concentrating on, understanding, and remembering what was said.

Why Listen Well?

Why should you try to become a good listener? Because being a skillful listener helps you in your daily life—at home, in school, and on your job, if you have one.

Listening can help relationships to grow. You have to listen closely to what people are saying to get to know them better.

In addition, listening well helps you to know more. You can learn about a variety of subjects in an enjoyable manner while talking to someone else. Listening is also a natural way to build your vocabulary. All these benefits can help you make a better impression on others.

Good listening skills are important, not only in school, but in all types of relationships.

To improve your listening skills, start by actively listening to what the other person is saying.

How to Listen Better

Now that you know *why* you should gain listening skills, you need to know how to do it. Here are some techniques for becoming a better listener:

- **Concentrate on what is being said.** This is the single most important part of becoming a good listener. Sometimes you can aid concentration by eliminating distractions—turning off the radio or TV while someone is speaking, or moving to a quieter area.

- **Listen with a purpose.** Most people do a job better if they know why they should do it. This is certainly true with listening. It helps to decide beforehand why you need to listen. In class, you probably want to listen well to improve your grades. You might want to listen to your friends' problems to help them find solutions. Having a purpose helps you to concentrate.

- **Be positive about listening.** Assume a positive attitude before a person starts talking so you will get something out of what you hear. Then you will be motivated to listen and remember.

- **Control your emotions.** Sometimes what the speaker is saying affects you emotionally. This can act as a barrier to listening. Suppose, for example, your mother is talking to you about when you should be in at night, and you begin to feel impatient. Your impatience may cause you to tune her out. It is better to keep your emotions in check, listen to what she has to say, and try to see things from her perspective. Then present your point of view. She will be much more likely to listen to you, and even compromise, if she knows that you have really been listening to what she has been saying.

A Positive Message

Very often, you will have only one opportunity to make an impression. That means it is important to be sure that your image, which is made up of what you say, how you act, and the clothes you wear, creates the kind of impression you want to make.

Take a close look at the image others see. Are you communicating your real self, or are you pretending to be someone else? When you talk, act, or even dress in ways that are not natural to you, you may send mixed and even conflicting messages to others.

You also need to send the right messages to yourself. If you are sad, you may walk with your head down. It is also true that if you walk with your head down, you may begin to feel sad. On the other hand, smiling can sometimes make you feel better on a gloomy day. One way to send the right messages to yourself, then, is simply to act positively.

Of course, smiling all day is not a substitute for solving a problem that bothers you. Even so, a positive image of yourself will help you get over the smaller problems in life as well as give you strength to handle the bigger ones.

People enjoy being around others who are cheerful and happy, rather than those who are grouchy or sad.

Communication for People with Disabilities

Every day we communicate in ways that we take for granted: we talk, we write, we wave hello or good-bye. For many people with disabilities, these methods of communication are difficult or impossible. With the help of technology, however, many of these people are experiencing the rewards of communicating with others. Below are just a few of the ways that technology is helping.

■ Most hearing-impaired people communicate through lip reading or sign language, in which hand gestures are used to represent specific words or letters. There is also a relatively new invention that helps hearing-impaired people to communicate by telephone. A machine called the TDD, or Telecommunications Device for the Deaf, is a typewriter connected to a telephone that signals incoming calls with a blinking light. The hearing-impaired person types in a response when the light blinks, and the person making the call uses the same kind of machine on the other end to talk. The conversation is printed out as it is being typed.

■ For those who are visually impaired, engineers have designed a special computer that can aid communication. The sender types out a message on a computer keyboard. The computer then translates the message into signals that control an electromechanical hand, which transfers the message to the sender's hand. Another way to send messages to visually impaired people is to use a Braille writer, a machine that writes in braille. Braille is a system of raised dots, with each letter of the alphabet having a different combination of dots.

■ ERICA (the acronym for "Eyegaze Response Interface Computer Aid") responds to the gaze of a paralyzed user rather than to touch. On the screen are a variety of choices for the user, such as displaying a book on the computer screen or requesting a cup of coffee. The user merely looks at the appropriate part of the screen, a camera records which part is being gazed at, and the message is transmitted.

These are only a few examples of the technology being used today in this area. Scientists hope that future inventions will help many people communicate easily and in more ways.

Think It Through

1. Some people feel that computers are dehumanizing; they believe they take the human touch out of life. Would this report change their opinion? Why?
2. How might the new technology change people's perceptions of people with disabilities?

CHAPTER

8 REVIEW

Reviewing the Facts

1. Describe the difference between verbal and nonverbal communication, using examples.
2. Why might it be unfair to make a judgment about another person from a first impression?
3. What message is communicated through good manners?
4. How does your body language affect the way people see you?
5. What are the differences between hearing and listening?
6. List three advantages of being a good listener.
7. How can you become a better listener?
8. Why should you control your emotions when you listen?

Sharing Your Ideas

1. When a person's words say one thing but the person's body language says another, which do you believe? Why?
2. What can you do to show people that you are listening to them?

Applying Your Skills

1. Selecting Criteria. Write five to ten "Good First Impression Guidelines" for teens. They should be appropriate for your lifestyle but also show respect for others. Illustrate the guidelines using pictures from magazines.

2. Writing a Description. Think about a movie or television character you have seen or a speaker that you have heard recently. Describe all the ways in which the person communicated. What methods did he or she use most effectively?

3. Performing an Experiment. Why can you say something to another person who acknowledges what you said—but then the person seems to forget about the conversation? This is because people often hear and respond without really listening. Perform an experiment in which the entire class sits in a circle. Think of a detailed sentence and pass it on to the next person, and so on, until the statement makes it around the circle. Did the statement change? What do you think the experiment has demonstrated?

Improving Relationship Skills

OBJECTIVES

This chapter will help you to:

- Describe how roles and expectations affect relationships.
- Give examples of strategies for resolving conflicts in your relationships.
- Discuss how prejudice and stereotypes hurt relationships.

WORDS TO REMEMBER

conflict	role
expectation	stereotype
prejudice	tolerance

sk yourself the following questions about relationships:

- Do I understand why my friends make the choices they do?
- Do I appreciate the ways in which my family is special?
- Can I accept that decisions that are right for me may not be right for everyone?

The answers to these questions bring out an important point: there are skills involved in getting along with others. You can work to improve these skills so your interactions with others are a source of joy, satisfaction, and personal rewards. This chapter will show you how to improve your relationship skills through understanding others, resolving conflicts, and improving attitudes.

Understanding Others

In order for a relationship to be satisfying, each person involved must work at understanding what the other one wants or needs. Relationships work best if you understand your different roles and expectations.

Roles

Roles are the parts you play when you interact with others. Remember, you have many roles. You are your parents' child, your teacher's student, your friends' friend. You might also be a team member, a musician in the band, an employee, or a neighbor.

You may have many different roles, depending on who you are with. What different roles might this girl have?

Expectations

Different roles produce different **expectations,** what each person wants in a relationship. As roles change, expectations change, too. When you were a child, for example, you expected your parents to provide everything—food when you were hungry or a blanket when you were cold. As you mature, you may expect to be treated more as an adult. In turn, your parents will expect you to assume more responsibility for your own life.

Erica has been elected captain of the basketball team. She expects each team member to be interested in the game, to follow directions, and to work together with teammates. Her team members expect the captain to give directions, to treat all members fairly, and to support and encourage them.

Sometimes, the expectations of two people in a relationship differ. Beth and Amber are good friends who enjoy talking and studying together, but Beth likes to spend time with other people, too. For example, she would like to ask Carmen to come along sometimes, but Amber likes it better when she and Beth are alone.

How can Beth and Amber solve this difference in their relationship? One way is to talk about the expectations each has of the other. Once each person understands what the other wants, they can decide what to do. Beth may decide to do certain things with Amber and to see Carmen at other times.

Resolving Conflicts

At one time or another, you can expect to have **conflicts,** or problems in your relationships. Often, these conflicts occur because each person expects something different.

Eric has always looked up to his father and has spent a lot of time with him. He has always discussed his feelings and problems with his father. Lately, however, Eric has been keeping more things to himself. Even though he sometimes

When expectations differ in a relationship, problems may develop. It helps to talk about the expectations that each person has of the other.

asks for advice, he often resents his father's giving it. Eric's father has noticed that their relationship is changing. Yesterday he said to Eric, "What's wrong with you these days? You're very moody." Eric was hurt and angry.

Changing roles and differing expectations make many demands on people in relationships. Handling these demands calls for relationship skills. Close relationships are worth preserving, even if that means compromising more than you would like. Here are a few guidelines to help you in controlling your feelings, communicating honestly, and accepting others.

Controlling Your Feelings

When people disagree with friends or family members, they should not speak in anger. If they do, they might say something that would hurt the other person. Eric was so angry at his father's remark that he almost shouted back. Instead, he turned and walked away.

In such a situation, give yourself time to cool off. Anger can be released in different ways. You might talk about the problem with another adult or with a friend. Then you could try to work the problem out with the person who made you angry when you are calm enough to control your feelings.

Communicating Honestly

Whether your relationship is with your mother, your stepfather, your best friend, your teammate, or anyone else, communicating is important. You learn what the other person expects from you, and you get a chance to tell the other person what you expect as well.

Eric's father, who had spoken out of his own hurt and anger, was not thinking about how his statement would af-

Discussing an emotional topic in a calm manner is far more productive than getting angry or shouting.

fect Eric. When Eric approached him to talk things over, his father apologized. Eric also apologized for walking away angrily. As Eric explained the way he was feeling, he and his father came to understand that Eric was just trying to become more independent. Eric's father agreed to work with Eric toward that goal. They both promised to keep their communication open and honest.

Some people find it difficult to talk about their angry feelings. If that is how you feel, let the other person know it. You might feel more relaxed if you admit your feelings. If you say something like "This is hard for me to say . . .," it might actually become easier to say. In addition, expressing your feelings will show the other person that you care.

Honest communication can win you the respect of others. For example, John asked Cathy to meet him at the football game on Friday night. She really wanted to, but she had already made plans with Matt for the same evening. This left her with a decision to make.

Cathy's first impulse was to accept John's invitation. After all, this was what she wanted to do the most. "I'll just go to the game," she thought, "and tell Matt that I've been grounded so I can't go with him." Something inside her, however, made her think some more.

Lying to Matt would be dishonest. If he found out about the lie, which was likely, he would no longer trust or respect her. He would also be hurt. If John found out, he might wonder if she would do the same thing to him. The result could be the loss of two friends.

Instead, Cathy decided to honor her commitment to Matt. She turned John down because she already had plans, but she let him know that she hoped they might go another time. Although Cathy was a little disappointed, she felt right about her decision.

Accepting Others

Tolerance is the ability to accept people as they are. It is sometimes difficult to accept the fact that your friends and family don't behave exactly as you want them to. To preserve your relationships, you have to allow for people's individual traits.

Tolerance is especially important when there are problems in a relationship. If your best friend has different ideas about something that is important to you, you must learn to accept these ideas as something your friend believes in, if your relationship is to continue. Rarely does one disagreement destroy a strong relationship. Tolerance, though, will help to avoid conflicts.

Relationships and Attitudes

People's likes and dislikes are reflections of their attitudes. An attitude is a way of looking at people, events, and things. Like values, attitudes are usually learned from family and friends.

Attitudes can have a strong effect on you and your relationships. People with positive attitudes feel good about themselves and treat others with fairness. They don't label or reject people, but instead try to give everyone equal treatment. On the other hand, people with negative attitudes are often insecure, afraid, or ignorant. They let these feelings interfere with their relationships, and they often judge people unfairly.

Prejudice

Whenever groups or individuals have fixed mental pictures of what people are like, they are guilty of **prejudice,** an opinion or feeling that is not based on fact. Prejudice is a form of rejection in which you decide about people before really knowing them. Whether you are prejudiced in favor of or against someone, it means that the person is not being judged fairly.

Prejudice is at work when you play favorites. The baseball coach is prejudiced if he leaves Kyle on the bench and puts Ron in every game, not because Ron is a better player but just because he is his nephew. It is a form of prejudice whenever a person is treated better on the basis of something other than ability or experience. It also almost always hurts those other people who are denied the same treatment.

When there is prejudice against an entire group of people, the society as a whole is hurt. If talented people are refused jobs or training because of their age, race, color, religion, or sex, everybody suffers. Society loses the work of people it needs, and many individuals in society lose the chance to meet people who might make their lives richer.

Stereotypes

One form of prejudice is stereotyped thinking. A **stereotype** is an unfair label that is automatically given to strangers. For example, someone may think that members of a certain group who share the same skin color or a particular way of speaking are also exactly alike in other ways.

One of the problems with stereotypes is that they sometimes cause you to act differently toward an individual than you would if you were not influenced by that image. For example, if you believe that a person confined to a wheelchair leads a boring life, you probably will stop yourself from getting to know someone you might like.

Stereotypes abound in our society and serve to limit people's experiences and possibilities. Perhaps you have heard stereotypes about races, professions, different ages or disabled people. See "Labels that Limit" on page 96.

Treating people as stereotypes rather than individuals can keep valuable relationships from beginning.

Prejudice is harmful because it limits and restricts people's opportunities. Learn to judge people as individuals, not as members of any stereotyped group.

Labels That Limit

Many general statements about people are stereotypes. Can you recognize stereotypes when you hear or read them? Here are ten general statements about people. See if you can determine why each one is a stereotype.

1. Teens are bad drivers.
2. People who wear glasses are bookworms.
3. Old people are absentminded.
4. All athletes are dumb.
5. Rural people are ignorant.
6. All doctors are rich.
7. Teenage girls only think about clothes.
8. Teenage boys only think about cars.
9. Women are too emotional to run a business.
10. Men never cry.

You don't have to let your ideas about people be governed by stereotypes. You can fight stereotypes. Here are three suggestions:

- **Avoid thinking or speaking in stereotypes.** Try to make your thoughts reflect reality.
- **Refuse to accept stereotypes.** Point out to others that their statements involving stereotypes are untrue. Mention the exceptions you know about personally.
- **Try to influence your friends.** Help them to be more flexible in their thinking. If you encourage them, they are likely to think for themselves and reject stereotypes.

Think It Through

1. Choose two of the stereotypes listed above. Explain why they are false.
2. Do you think that first impressions are made up of stereotypes? Why or why not?

CHAPTER
9 REVIEW

Reviewing the Facts

1. What is a role?
2. What is a common source of conflict in relationships?
3. Why should you avoid speaking in anger?
4. How can communication help prevent conflicts that arise over differing expectations?
5. What does it mean to be tolerant?
6. What is the difference between prejudice and stereotypes?

Sharing Your Ideas

1. What role changes have you experienced in your life so far? As a result of these changes, how have your expectations and those of other people changed?
2. Discuss with the class an experience you had at one time when you stereotyped someone before knowing the person. What happened?

Applying Your Skills

1. Analyzing Criteria. Prepare an advertising campaign for an organization that fights stereotyping and prejudice. Examples include the American Civil Liberties Union, the National Organization for Women, or Amnesty International. Design a public service message for television and a print advertisement.

2. Expressing Your Feelings. Suppose that your friend Larry agreed to purchase tickets to a concert for several of his friends, including you. When Larry returns, he says that he forgot to buy a ticket for you and that the concert is sold out. Write a skit of the conversation or conversations you would have with Larry. Be sure to use the tips on how to resolve conflicts as a guide.

3. Designing an Experiment. Act out a scene with another classmate in which one represents a parent and the other represents a teenage son or daughter. The parent wants the teen to get home from a party earlier than the teen thinks is fair. Try to incorporate the concerns that parents have and communicate these feelings effectively. What does this show you about the roles that parents play?

Understanding Families

OBJECTIVES

This chapter will help you to:

- Define family.
- Explain how a family provides for, nurtures, and guides family members.
- Identify different types of family structures.
- Give examples of how you can develop a better understanding of parents and siblings.

WORDS TO REMEMBER

adopted
blended family
extended family
foster child
nuclear family

nurture
sibling
single-parent family
stepparent

Can you remember your first steps, or who held your hand? Perhaps not, but chances are that someone in your family was there to help you along. Back then, you learned how to talk and that it hurt to touch a hot range.

Many of your ideas, opinions, and tastes also came from your family. Do you like card games? You probably learned to play them at home. Do you love spicy food? Your family probably cooks it that way.

In addition, as you grew, your family taught you to value what is important in life. You not only developed a feeling about who you are, but also about what your place is in the world. Even after you no longer needed a hand to hold, you felt secure, a part of something. You belonged.

What Is a Family?

If you asked 12 people what a family is, you would probably get 12 different answers. A person's definition of the word *family* comes from experience, which can vary a lot. One person might say a family is a father, mother, and two sons. Another person might say that it is a mother and a daughter. A third would say that a family is a husband and wife. Even though all these definitions of family are different, they are still all correct.

A family is often defined as a group of individuals who share common values, goals, and resources. Each family member is responsible for certain decisions, and they all share emotional bonds.

No two families are the same, yet most families perform certain functions that set them apart from other groups. These functions are providing, nurturing, and guiding.

Providing

A newborn baby needs a lot of care, so it is easy to see how necessary a family is at the beginning of a child's life. The family, though, must satisfy the basic needs of all its members, young and old alike. The job of providing the physical things we need—food, clothing, and shelter—is a difficult one, and one that never ends.

Although families may have different structures, they are responsible for providing basic needs, and nurturing and guiding family members.

However, a family provides much more than physical needs. Many emotional needs are provided for as well: the need to belong, to laugh, to share with others, to feel loved and cared for.

Some families do a better job of providing for family needs than others. Usually it is not a matter of money, but rather of time, energy, and experience.

Nurturing

A family also **nurtures** its members, or helps them develop. Your family helps you grow as a person. Growing up is not just a matter of getting taller. Your mind grows just as your body does; you have to grow emotionally and socially, too. None of this happens all at once. It is gradual, and much of it happens in your family.

Your family teaches you about feelings and how to express them. At home, you can express your pride at making the track team or your disappointment at losing the school election.

You learn your first social skills from your family. Even before you could talk, you were introduced to playmates and asked to share toys. You saw how older family members got along with their friends, and people showed you how to take on new responsibilities.

Guiding

In addition, a family gives guidance to its members. Children are taught to distinguish between right and wrong. Family values help determine what kind of behavior is accceptable and what kind is not. Guidance also involves encouragement to set goals, make decisions, and take responsibility for your actions. Your family helps you learn how to live in society.

Types of Families

You have just looked at some of the ways in which families are similar. Families can also differ. One of the main ways in which they differ is in their structure.

Family Structures

All of the following groups of people are families:

- Rudolph and Yvonne Johnson have been married five years. Although they have no children, they are a family.
- The Vasquez family is an example of a **nuclear family**: two parents and one or more children sharing a household. Mr. and Mrs. Vasquez have three children: Maria, Anna, and Roberto.
- Mr. Webster heads another kind of family. He is divorced and cares for his son, Cody, and his daughter, Sherry. They are an example of a **single-parent family**: children living with one parent. Single-parent families are more common today than in the past.
- The Rosens are a **blended family**: a family that joins two separate families through marriage. Their new family consists of Mr. and Mrs. Rosen, plus Amy, Mrs. Rosen's daughter from her previous marriage, and Richard and Mindy, the children from Mr. Rosen's first marriage.

When a child gains a parent by marriage, the parent is called a **stepparent**. Mr. Rosen is Amy's stepfather and Mrs. Rosen is Richard and Mindy's stepmother. Similar terms are used for the relationships between children. Mindy is Amy's stepsister, and Richard is Amy's stepbrother.

Different generations enrich each other's lives.

■ Another type of family is the **extended family**, which is a family that may include grandparents, uncles, aunts, and cousins, as well as parents and children. The DeLauras are an extended family. There is Mr. and Mrs. DeLaura; their two children, Donald and Rebecca; Mrs. DeLaura's mother, Audrey Swenson; and Joe DeLaura, Mr. DeLaura's father.

These are five of the most common family structures, but many others exist as well. It is not unusual in our society for family structure to change many times. For example, single adults, or adults who are not married, are also part of a family—the family they grew up in. They may not live with their family, yet they are still part of them.

Also, when people do not live close to other family members, they may look upon close friends as almost a family group. Thus family structures are very flexible and have different variations. Every family has special characteristics that can be appreciated and enjoyed by its members.

Appreciating Your Family

Have you ever wished that your family was different? Does your dad embarrass you by telling jokes to your friends? Does your younger sister tag along wherever you go, or your older brother act like he knows everything?

Perhaps you envy a friend who is an only child and doesn't have to share or compete with her brothers and sisters. She may even seem to have a perfect relationship with her parents.

Did you ever stop to think that your friend might envy you? To her, a larger family looks like fun—there are more people to do things with and share experiences with. She may wish that she could talk to her parents the way you can talk to yours.

Family Styles

People may see family styles that are different from their own as being better or worse, but they are simply different. The fact is that all families are different—in size, in the way members interact, and in how responsibilities are divided. No one style is right. Each family finds a system that works well for its members.

Why are families different? Each family is unique because its members have special abilities and characteristics. For example, your grandfather makes hand-crafted items, your sister plays the flute, and your father sings in the church choir. All this variety makes family life more interesting. It would not make sense for all these different people to try to follow the same pattern.

The culture, customs, and religious background of a family also make it one of a kind. Does your family always celebrate birthdays with a cake? When you go to family weddings, do you dance traditional dances that are a part of your cultural heritage, such as the Polish polka, Irish jig, or Italian tarantella?

A family's cultural pride and heritage play a very important part in family life. They influence the food you eat and the holidays you celebrate. Your cultural background also influences the role you have in your family, how decisions are made, and how responsibilities are divided. Your family style is different from the way of life of other families. Appreciating the differences helps you enjoy the ways your family is special.

Understanding Your Parents

Understanding your family means thinking about your parents' roles, too. When you were younger, you may have thought that your parents knew everything and could do anything. Now, as you grow older, you may be seeking more understanding and acceptance from your parents as you begin to make more of your own decisions.

Special celebrations, such as weddings, may reflect the culture, customs, and religious background of families.

As you become ready for more responsibilities, it is important to remember that parents need understanding and acceptance, too. Teens sometimes forget that parents are people with interests, thoughts, desires, and their own dreams. They are individuals with strengths and weaknesses. They, too, have good and bad days.

As you learned in Chapter 9, honest communication will help you see your parents' point of view. Getting to know your parents may help you see things differently. You will better understand why they care about where you are going, who you will be with, what you will be doing, and when you will be home.

Remember that parents' love helps you build a strong self-concept. Their caring makes you feel safe. Their guidance helps you decide what is right. Their listening proves how important you are to them. Their sharing teaches you to give.

This family consists of biological children, adopted children, stepchildren, and foster children. The parents love them all!

Understanding Your Siblings

Many families include one or more children. These children may be born into the family, adopted, or stepchildren. An **adopted** child is one who has been legally made a permanent member of a new family. Some children from troubled homes are taken into families for shorter periods. They are called **foster children**.

If you have brothers or sisters, or **siblings**, it is important to understand their feelings. If you are an older child, try to include your younger siblings in your activities sometimes. If you are a younger child, you need to understand your older siblings' need for privacy.

Whether you are the oldest or youngest child, or in the middle, when you feel pleased with a brother or sister, say so. Your affection and admiration probably mean more than you realize.

Everyone who has a brother or sister feels jealous sometimes. It is important to remember that parents love all their children. In treating each child as a unique person, they may not treat them all alike.

Oldest, Middle, Youngest, or Only?

Whether you were born first, last, in the middle, or are the only child in the family affects both how you feel about yourself and how your family treats you. What effect does the order of your birth have?

- **Oldest.** Oldest children are "only children" until the next child is born. The undivided attention of your parents gives you a good start in life. You may be given more responsibility because your parents depend on you. Because you are used to helping out, you may be more confident about your abilities than younger family members.

  Sometimes, however, as an oldest child you may feel that your parents expect a lot from you or that they want you to act more grown-up than you are. You may feel you had to abide by stricter rules than your younger siblings did at a particular age. Having a younger sister or brother admire you can make you feel good about yourself, though.

- **Middle.** Being in the middle has its ups and downs, too. By the time they have you, your parents have had experience in caring for children. They probably feel more relaxed about bringing you up. You may feel less pressure to be perfect than an oldest child. Because you are used to playing with older and younger siblings, you may be more sociable.

  On the other hand, you may feel left out. You don't have the privileges of the oldest child or the same degree of attention paid to the younger ones.

- **Youngest.** Youngest children often join older siblings in doing new and exciting things. You may be given privileges earlier than older children, and you have the advantage of having the most experienced parents.

Of course, following older sisters or brothers through childhood can be difficult. If they had some special talent or ability, then you may feel you have to have it, too. You also probably get tired of being treated like the baby in the family. Still, your position as the youngest can make you feel especially accepted or secure.

- **Only.** As an only child, you receive a great deal of your parents' attention and often are given a lot of responsibility. You don't have to share your possessions or get along with other children in the family.

  Being an only child can be lonely, though. Also, if your parents have very high hopes for you, you can feel pressured to please them. On the other hand, your closeness with your parents provides you with a very special relationship and a great deal of support. As for the companionship that other children get from brothers and sisters, you can get it from your relationships with friends.

Think It Through

1. What can parents do to make middle children feel special?
2. Do you think the descriptions above apply to your own family? Why or why not?

CHAPTER
10 REVIEW

Reviewing the Facts

1. Explain what a family is.
2. What are the three functions of a family? Give an example of how a family performs each of those functions.
3. List three specific ways a family provides guidance for its members.
4. What is the difference between a nuclear family and an extended family?
5. What is a blended family?
6. Why is it important to develop an appreciation of your family rather than comparing your family to other families?
7. What can you do to understand your parents?
8. What can you do to understand your siblings?

Sharing Your Ideas

1. What are some unique characteristics and talents of your family members that make a special contribution to your family?
2. Identify a family tradition or custom of your family. How did it develop? Is it one that you would want to continue with your future family? Why or why not?

Applying Your Skills

1. Giving Some Examples. Write a brief description of the ways you provide family members with support. How do you provide for, nurture, and guide the other members of your family?

2. Writing a Comparison. Think about a family television show that you watch regularly. In several paragraphs, explain the ways that this family is the same or different from real families that you know.

3. Forming a Model. Create a family tree that is as complete as you can make it without having to ask an older family member. Who does your version of the family tree include? How close of a relationship do you have with these people? Explain how these people contributed to your development.

Strengthening Families

OBJECTIVES

This chapter will help you to:

- Identify qualities that make families strong.
- Explain ways to communicate about family problems.
- Describe how brainstorming and compromising help to solve problems.
- List sources that will help with family conflicts.

WORDS TO REMEMBER

brainstorming
confidentiality
counseling

In many ways, a family is a team, and it functions just like any other team. For a baseball team to win, each player must do what he or she is best at, but they must still work together as a group. Members of winning teams communicate their plans and share responsibilities. They build confidence by appreciating one another's strengths and weaknesses and showing one another respect and trust. In fact, the players of a baseball team could not accomplish as individuals what they can accomplish as a team. A family is like that—they need to work together to be successful.

What Makes Families Strong?

Families that are vital and strong have certain qualities that help bind the family together and strengthen individual members. Here are some ways that family members provide support for one another:

- **Building self-esteem.** Families can build high self-esteem by praising each other's accomplishments. Family members need to know that they are accepted and loved as they are, with all their strengths and weaknesses. This helps them accept others.

- **Communicating effectively.** Families can aim to communicate in ways that are clear and honest. It is easy to fall into the trap of assuming that everyone else in the family knows what you are thinking. You might, for example, be upset with a friend and mope around the house, assuming that your family knows why. However, unless you tell them, they won't know, and they may become annoyed at your behavior.

- **Sharing responsibilities.** Family members can share responsibility for certain tasks such as preparing food, cleaning, and doing the laundry. Even young children can participate by setting the table, making beds, or folding clothes. Many families have rules that govern household chores along with the use of money, methods of communication, and even what happens when someone breaks the rules. Rules should be clear so everyone knows what they are. When circumstances change, family rules may need to change. For example, your curfew may get later as you get older.

- **Showing respect and trust.** Family members need to respect one another's opinions and show one another attention and concern. They can earn respect and trust by being truthful and dependable.

- **Spending time together.** The time that a family spends together is much more important than what it is they do together. They might rake the lawn, go on a hike, wash the car, make cookies, play with a board game, go biking or canoeing, or plan a vacation.

- **Establishing traditions.** Families usually have some traditions that have been handed down and are based on their ethnic or cultural background. They might also establish new traditions such as reading a favorite story or poem on a particular holiday, celebrating special occasions at a favorite restaurant, or cooking specific foods at a certain time of year.

- **Reaching beyond the family to the larger society.** Families can have a good relationship with people outside the family. They do this by maintaining an attitude of friendliness and openness toward others. Often, families become involved in some project in their neighborhood or community.

This family enjoys going on weekend trips together. What activities does your family enjoy?

These seven qualities work together. The high self-esteem that a family provides, for example, allows its members to go out into the world as people who are more likely to respect themselves and to help others. Communication skills learned in the family help family members to take an active part in the larger society. In addition, sharing responsibilities helps family members to develop respect and trust for other people. Spending time together and establishing traditions contribute to the special enjoyment of family life.

No family, however, is perfect. Families are made of people, and people have weaknesses and faults as well as strengths and virtues. That means that sometimes problems arise in families.

Handling Family Problems

Problems are bound to occur in family life. Families include individuals, each with his or her own likes and dislikes, desires, and plans. There are, however, ways to deal with family problems or conflicts that can help a family grow stronger.

What's the Problem?

The first step in dealing with family conflict is identifying the source of the problem. Suppose you and your brother, Carlos, are responsible for washing the dinner dishes. You and Carlos alternate cleaning nights. You also divide the vacuuming on weekends. Carlos, however, has just joined the volleyball team at school, and this week he has been getting home late because of practice. Your father asks you to clean up on Carlos's nights, too. You feel this is unfair, but you don't know what to do about the situation.

Talking It Over

Resolving family problems, like any other problems, requires communication skills. Here are a few guidelines for getting your point across.

- **Choose the proper setting.** Wait for a relaxing moment in a quiet place. Instead of stopping your father when he is getting ready for work in the morning, ask him if you can talk to him that evening when he gets home.

If you want to be taken seriously, you need to present your position clearly and calmly.

- **Keep to the point.** Think through what you want to say before you begin. Be direct. Your family will not get your point if you can't state it clearly. Offer a reasonable solution if you have one.
- **Keep calm.** If you are upset or angry, you will not be able to get your point across. Crying or slamming doors will not change people's minds.
- **Listen.** Listening well is just as important as speaking well. Don't think about your side of the argument when someone else is talking. Listen and try to understand the other person's point of view.
- **Avoid accusation, sarcasm, and threats.** Showing respect for another person's ideas will earn respect for your own. Saying "You're wrong!" or "That is ridiculous!" can end communication fast. Some communication experts suggest avoiding "you" statements entirely and speaking in "I" statements. Rather than saying, "You don't make Carlos wash the dishes!" you might say, "I feel like I am doing more than my share of the work."

■ **Avoid generalizations.** When you use words such as "never" and "always," you confuse the issue and can't talk about the specific conflict you have. Saying "I always have to wash the dishes" does not explain the problem. Instead, you might say, "I am upset because I am doing my share of the washing and Carlos's, too."

Family Discussions

Some problems can best be solved by the whole family, but finding a solution that everyone accepts is not always easy. Resolving conflicts will be easier if everyone communicates openly and honestly, respects each person's opinion, listens, and allows give-and-take.

Family discussions can help solve conflicts by allowing members to share their opinions.

One way to find solutions is by listing as many ideas as you can think of, or **brainstorming.** This free-for-all approach to problem solving is an excellent way to get ideas flowing and to promote discussion. All it takes to brainstorm is a pen, a piece of paper, and several open minds.

Suppose your family decides to brainstorm about your conflict with Carlos. For a designated period of time, family members write down any idea they think of, without considering whether the idea is good or bad. The goal at the beginning is simply to list ideas.

Here are just a few of the solutions that might emerge:

■ Carlos could do the dishes after volleyball, even though it is late and he is tired.

■ Carlos could clean up after all the meals on the weekends.

■ Carlos could do the dishes every evening that he doesn't have volleyball and do all the vacuuming on the weekends.

- Carlos could be given a different job entirely, one that would not interfere with volleyball. Perhaps you could do the dishes every night, but he could vacuum the whole house on the weekends.

Once family members have listed all their ideas, each person gets a chance to defend the solution he or she thinks will work best. Try to give good reasons for feeling the way you do, and listen to your family's objections without getting upset. Remember to use "I" rather than "you" statements.

Compromising

An important part of handling problems in a mature way is being able to compromise. As you learned in Chapter 7, compromising means that each person gives up a little of what he or she wants in order to find a solution that satisfies everyone. In other words, you give a little to get a little.

Suppose that as a result of your brainstorming session you and your family decide you will do the dishes every night, and Carlos will vacuum the whole house on weekends. He will not have to rush home after volleyball, and you will not have any additional chores on weekends. Usually, if each family member is willing to compromise, a workable solution can be found.

Seeking Outside Help

Sometimes, when a family has a very serious problem, even talking openly and honestly may not help. Not every family problem can be solved at home. When you have tried everything and you are no closer to solving a problem, it is time to reach out beyond the family.

Professional counseling can help families solve serious problems.

Lisa, for example, knows that her family needs help. Lisa's home has become a battleground. Her parents fight constantly. After a fight, her father often storms out, and her mother ends up drinking too much. Lisa's older sister, Alicia, has completely withdrawn from her parents and refuses to speak to them at all. What can Lisa do?

Community Counseling

Lisa can go many places to receive **counseling**, the advice and guidance given by experts, religious leaders, or support groups. She can consult:

- **Teachers and guidance counselors.** The adults you see in school every day are a good source of help. They may come up with solutions to the problem or give you the name of a community agency that offers help.
- **Religious leaders.** Many ministers, priests, rabbis, and mullahs know a great deal about counseling. They sometimes set up workshops to deal with family problems.
- **Youth leaders.** Adults who volunteer to work with young people are usually willing to help out in any way they can. If you are a scout or belong to the YWCA, YMCA, the 4-H, the Future Homemakers of America, or other organizations like these, ask your leader for help and guidance.
- **Social workers.** These people are trained to listen and to help people overcome their problems.
- **Community agencies and organizations.** Many agencies and organizations help families deal with specific problems such as drug abuse or family violence. Al-Anon, for example, has helped millions of family members who live with alcoholics. To find these groups in your neighborhood, ask at your local library or check the white and yellow pages of your local telephone directory.
- **Crisis centers.** Crisis centers have volunteers who are eager to help people with problems. Some of the centers operate telephone hot lines for people who need help immediately, such as teens running away from home or considering suicide.

Making a Choice

Lisa, like many other people, feels uncomfortable and embarrassed about telling her problem to a stranger. Sharing personal problems with someone you don't know well is not easy to do. Professionals, however, know that you are discussing important feelings and will try to make you feel as comfortable as possible.

Lisa does not need to worry about her counselor telling someone else what she has said. Any professional counselor will maintain your **confidentiality**, or privacy. He or she will not reveal your problems to anyone else.

In the end, Lisa decided to talk with her minister. He suggested that she, her sister, and her parents come to a workshop being held at the church. After he talked with the whole family, Lisa's parents and sister finally agreed to attend. Together, as a family, the members were taking an important first step toward working out their problems.

MANAGING RESOURCES

Balancing Work and Family

The struggle to balance work and family life is a reality that many families are facing today. A family may be headed by a single parent who works full time, or both parents may work outside the home. These situations require strong management skills to ensure that family members get all the attention they need.

When there are young children in the family, thought must be given to protecting and caring for them. Questions such as these may come up: Who will take care of the children when the parents are working? What will happen if a single parent has to work late? Who will take a sick child to the doctor?

Families juggle the demands of work and family by making different kinds of long-range plans. Here are some possible options:

- **Postponing work.** A parent may choose not to work outside the home while the children are young. When the children are older, the parent returns to work.
- **Flexible schedules.** Two parents schedule different working hours. Then one parent can be at home while the other parent is working.
- **Part-time work.** A parent may work part-time, perhaps during the hours when the children are in school. As the children grow older, that job may become full-time.

- **Working at home.** In some jobs, a parent can use the home as a workplace. This can be an advantage when children are young.

Trying to meet work and family obligations often leads to stress in a family. Careful planning of time can reduce the stress, but emergencies such as illness or the need for a single parent to work late may still arise. Here are two strategies that many families rely on to get necessary things done:

- **Delegating responsibilities.** When necessary, tasks usually done by one member of the family can be given to other family members who have more time. Shopping, cleaning, cooking, and laundry are tasks that can be delegated, or assigned to others.

- **Building a support system.** A support system is especially important for working parents. It includes people who would respond in emergencies: relatives, friends, neighbors, and community groups. A support group makes it possible to share the difficult job of balancing work and family.

Think It Through

1. What could you do to provide a neighbor who is a single parent with a few hours of help?
2. What can young school-age children do to make it easier for the parents to balance work and family responsibilities?

Reviewing the Facts

1. List the seven qualities that help strengthen family ties.
2. What are some of the household responsibilities that family members can share?
3. Name three ways that families can spend time together.
4. What is the first step in dealing with family problems?
5. What are some guidelines for handling family problems?
6. Explain what brainstorming is.
7. When should you seek outside help for a family problem?
8. List six sources of help for families in need of counseling.

Sharing Your Ideas

1. What family traditions and rituals does your family share? Explain how these help to strengthen your family.
2. Do you think conflict is natural in a family? Why or why not?

Applying Your Skills

1. Choosing Appropriate Examples. Reread the seven qualities that make families strong on page 107. For each quality, write a short paragraph that gives a concrete example of how this quality might be exhibited by a real family. Do not repeat examples given in the text.

2. Evaluating Ideas and Suggestions. Imagine that you and your brother often argue about who should answer the telephone. Brainstorm possible solutions to this conflict. Be sure to write down everything that comes to mind, without trying to decide whether it is a good or bad idea. Then choose the idea that you think is fair to both of you, and explain why you think it is the best solution.

3. Designing a Survey. Create a survey of at least ten questions that would measure how strong a family is. Include questions about how well the family members support each other and how well they handle family problems.

CHAPTER

12

Adjusting to Family Changes

Do you remember when a younger brother or sister was born or when your family moved to a new town? There are many reasons that changes like these happen in families. Some changes may occur suddenly, while others may happen slowly. Some changes occur because time passes—members of a family grow up and take on different roles. This chapter will discuss the most common family changes.

The Family Life Cycle

Just as a human being develops from a dependent baby to a toddler, an adolescent, then finally an adult, so every family goes through different stages, from birth to maturity. This growth is part of the **family life cycle**, the stages of life that the average family goes through.

Learning about the family life cycle will help you understand the changes that families go through. The chart on page 118 pictures families in the various stages of the life cycle. Of course, families vary greatly. Many families are headed by a single parent. Some couples have no children. Partners may divorce, remarry other people, and begin new families. At each stage of the life cycle, families have some common characteristics even though their experiences are different.

Factors Causing Family Changes

Some changes in a family are set in motion by factors outside the home. A parent may get a job transfer, for example, or may be the victim of an accident.

Other factors come from within the family and may happen more slowly. A new baby may be born or parents may divorce. All these events require adjustments by family members.

Job Changes

A change in employment affects both the individual making the change and the rest of the family. A parent may have less time to spend at home if a new job requires additional hours or more commuting time. In some cases, a parent's new job may require a move.

Sometimes parents will change their job status. If a parent gives up an outside job to become a homemaker, the family may have to live on a smaller income. If, on the other hand, a homemaker decides to take a job outside the home, other family members may have to take on more responsibilities. Karla, for example, had to babysit a few afternoons a week for her younger sister when her mother took a job in an insurance office.

When parents lose jobs, everyone is affected. If the job provided the main or only income, the family may go through very difficult times. In addition, feelings of rejection and depression are commonly experienced by people who lose jobs.

If a parent is unemployed, everyone can help. Children might begin by showing their support. They might put off requests for new clothes or spending money until the crisis passes. Occasionally teens are able to obtain part-time jobs to help their families financially.

Moving Away

Your family may decide to move to another community. Maybe a parent's job requires it, or perhaps you are moving

Part-time jobs can provide additional money or an opportunity to meet people and learn about a new community.

- Find out as much as possible about the new community and school. What courses are offered? What clubs or sports seem interesting?
- Remember that it takes time to make new friends. If possible, find other new people at school who are experiencing many of the same feelings as you. Join a club or activity, such as a newspaper, chorus, drama club, or pep club where you can meet other students with interests like yours.
- Join community groups such as youth groups at a church, temple, or YMCA.

It takes an effort to make new friends. The classmates and neighborhood kids you will be meeting already have friends, so you will have to take the initial steps. Especially in the beginning, it helps to stay in touch with old friends through letters and visits.

closer to the rest of the family. Moving is a big change. Family members must get used to a new home, new friends, and new schools.

When Jamie's father told the family that he was being transferred from Ohio to South Carolina near the coast, Jamie was not excited. He felt nervous about going to a new school. He was afraid that he would not make any new friends and that he would miss his old ones. However, the family talked about how they could make the adjustment easier for Jamie and his younger sister. Here are some of the suggestions they offered:

Divorce

Many families experience **divorce**, the legal termination of a marriage. Divorce affects not only the two people involved in the marriage, but others in the family as well. If parents announce that they are going to divorce, their child may be surprised and shocked, even if family life has been unhappy for some time. Both young children and teens may feel angry or resentful toward one or both parents for divorcing. They may be afraid that they will no longer be loved or protected.

The Family Life Cycle

Beginning Stage
A couple marries and establishes a home.

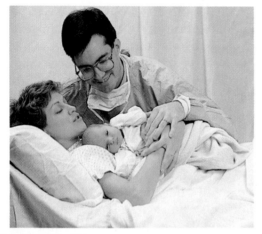

Childbearing Stage
The couple prepares for and adjusts to parenthood.

Child-Rearing Stage
As children grow, the parents work to meet their children's needs and to help them develop independence.

Launching Stage
Children gradually leave home to support themselves. Parents help children adjust to their new way of life.

Empty-Nest Stage
After the last child has left home, the couple renews the marriage relationship and adjusts to the change in their parenting role.

Retirement Stage
The couple adjusts to the aging process. They may develop new interests or renew old ones.

Children may worry about who will care for them. This brings up the issue of **custody**, the right of caring for children granted by a court. Issues of custody often present the most painful problems in divorce.

When custody is settled, children may wish they were living with the other parent. They may hope and dream that their parents will remarry.

Children and teens whose parents are divorcing may act differently toward those around them. They may withdraw, lose interest in schoolwork, or pick fights with classmates. They may even feel guilty, as if *they* caused the divorce.

It must be explained for them, however, that their parents are divorcing because of their own problems, and that the children are in no way the cause of divorce.

In some cases, children feel a sense of relief when their parents separate. This may be true especially when there has been much turmoil in the home. Divorce may also provide relief for family members who have been abused.

No matter how family members feel about the divorce, time helps everyone to adjust. Children should be urged to share their feelings with their family. They may also want to talk with other teens who have gone through the experience of divorce. This will help them adjust more easily to their situation. Community groups may also provide adults and teens with a place to share their feelings and find ways to cope with divorce.

When parents are divorcing, children need to be reassured that they are not the cause of the divorce.

New Family Members

The coming of a baby is usually a happy event. A new baby can be a lot of fun—fun to hug and hold and play with. Still, babies are a 24-hour job. Their care takes lots of time, and this requires adjustments from every member of the family.

A new baby in your home will mean that other family members need to take on more responsibility. Older children can help feed, bathe, dress, or play with the baby. Parents, up nights with a fussy infant, may be more irritable and less patient than usual. Try to be especially understanding during this time.

New family members sometimes come through adoption or foster care. For these children also, there is a period of adjustment. If the adopted or foster child is not an infant and has become accustomed to life in a different environment, love and patience on the part of family members are very important.

If a parent remarries, adjustments in family life need to be made. Household routines are likely to change to accommodate additional people. Rivalries may occur between stepbrothers and stepsisters. Teens especially may feel resentful or jealous of the new stepparent—they may believe the stepparent is destroying the relationship they have with their own parent. Good communication is important during this trying period, and gradually many blended families can unite in a few years.

Perhaps an older relative, such as a grandparent, comes into the home. These extended family arrangements can enrich family life. Older family members contribute to the family in many ways. They are a source of support for parents, offering advice and understanding. They often share in household responsibilities such as cooking, cleaning, or child care.

Coming to live with your family may not be easy for an aging relative, however. A person who has lived in one area for many years will miss old friends and familiar sights. Accustomed to being independent, an older adult may not like feeling dependent on his or her children.

Illnesses and Accidents

When someone becomes very ill or experiences a serious accident, family life can be disrupted. The individual may be in a lot of discomfort; watching someone you love in pain can make you feel helpless and frustrated.

Illnesses and accidents are more than emotionally trying. They may also put a strain on family finances. Long-term illnesses or disabling accidents can create large medical bills. Fortunately, medicine today enables doctors to do much to heal physical and mental illness and to speed recovery from accidents.

During a time of illness, families often find strength in each other or in religious faith. You may discover qualities and strengths in others, or in yourself, that you never knew you had. Sharing their feelings and responsibilities will help families through difficult times.

Death

When Salim's Uncle Jerome died, Salim had trouble coping with his feelings. At first, Salim tried not to think about Uncle Jerome at all. Then he felt guilty about the times when he had argued with his uncle. He wished those moments had been happier ones. He felt angry, too, at his uncle for leaving him.

Salim's feelings frightened him. He felt that there was something wrong with him. All these emotions, however,

Change can be frightening to both young children and teens when a parent has an accident, becomes critically ill, or dies.

together with loneliness and sadness, are natural after a death. If someone close to you dies, allow yourself to grieve. Don't be ashamed to cry. If you ignore your feelings, you may suffer from more serious problems later on.

A death is **traumatic**: it causes family members severe emotional shock that may take some time to heal. When someone dies, everyone in the family needs care and consolation, even very small children. Sharing sad feelings is one way to deal with them. Sometimes family members need to take turns putting their own sorrow aside to comfort one another. If family members help a grieving parent or sibling, they may feel better, too.

Adjusting to Change

Changes that take place in your family may be exciting and challenging, or they may be painful and confusing. No matter what kind of situation is involved, there are ways you can adjust to them.

- **Plan ahead.** When you know that a change is unavoidable, prepare for it in advance, even if you wish it were not going to happen. If you are moving, you can learn as much as possible about the new community and school ahead of time. Perhaps you can even arrange a visit. Often, difficult changes are not as bad as you thought they would be because you prepared for them.

- **Discover something positive about the change.** This is not always easy to do. For example, what can be positive about Tom's older brother moving back home? Well, although Tom will have to once again share his room with his brother, he will enjoy using his brother's bike when he returns.

- **Share, support, and communicate.** While you are going through changes in your life, members of your family are changing, too. It helps to talk about your feelings within the family. Just having someone listen can ease your pain and confusion. Support others in your family as they try to adjust, too. When Joanne's mother was struggling to manage a job and finish her college degree, Joanne started to get up early and make breakfast for her. It was Joanne's way of showing how much she cared for and admired her mother.

- **Accept your feelings.** Changes may bring anger, sadness, or fear as well as joy or pride. You may even have conflicting feelings. When Bob's father had a serious operation, Bob was scared and angry about his father's illness, but he was also thankful that his father would eventually recover. It is important in such a situation as this that you accept the way you feel and find ways to express yourself that will not hurt you or others.

- **Stay active.** Getting involved in activities will keep you from brooding about your situation. When Suzanne's parents were getting divorced, she stayed active in the swimming team and chorus at school. Her teammates and friends helped her to cope.

- **Seek help if necessary.** Sometimes family changes may be very difficult to deal with or resolve. As you learned in Chapter 11, there are many places where individuals and families can get counseling to help them adjust more easily and successfully.

To help you adjust to family changes, get involved in school or community activities. Share your feelings with your family, your friends, or a counselor.

HEALTH WATCH

Family Violence

Most people don't think of the home as a violent place, but family violence is a serious problem that accounts for many physical and emotional injuries. Experts who study families have collected a great deal of information about the problem. Here are some questions that are often asked about family violence and the answers that most experts support:

Q: Who are the most common victims of family violence?

A: Women and children are usually the ones abused, but some men have been victims. Elderly people are also the victims of abuse.

Q: What kinds of family violence take place?

A: Physical abuse can range from pushing and slapping to hitting and beating. Victims may suffer black eyes and broken bones. Verbal abuse is another kind of violence. Victims may be repeatedly criticized or berated by being told that they are stupid, bad, worthless, unwanted, or even hated. Such humiliation and shame results in low self-concept and self-esteem. Another form of abuse is neglect. Children may be malnourished or poorly clothed, for example. Another type of violence is sexual abuse.

Q: Is family violence a problem of a particular group of people?

A: No. The problem exists among all income levels, ethnic backgrounds, and occupational groups.

Q: What causes family violence?

A: Anger during an argument may lead to violence. Often economic problems play a part. When a parent is unemployed, family violence tends to increase. Other reasons include alcoholism, drug abuse, and mental illness.

Q: Why do some parents and stepparents abuse their children?

A: Stress within the family is sometimes the cause. When parents can't handle a stressful situation, they may take out their frustrations on their children by hurting or humiliating them. Parents who were abused when they were children often abuse their own children. You can learn more about child abuse on p. 206.

Q: Why don't women just leave home when they are victims of violence?

A: Many women worry that they will be without financial support if they leave their spouses. Others are ashamed and lack self-esteem. Many women do leave once the violence spills over and hurts their children.

Q: What kind of help is available for abused family members?

A: Counseling at community health centers is available to help families in trouble. Shelters for abused women and children have opened in many communities. Special hot lines also offer advice and support.

Q: What should teens do when they suspect violence in a family?

A: They should report any cases of suspected abuse to parents, teachers, or guidance counselors, who can then assist in getting help from experts.

Think It Through

1. Although there is no evidence that family violence has increased, there is more discussion about the problem than ever before. What do you think is the reason?
2. What are some techniques you might suggest for people to try when they are angry and might be in danger of hurting someone in the family?

Reviewing the Facts

1. What is the family life cycle?
2. How can teens help if a parent becomes unemployed?
3. What can you do to make the adjustment easier when moving to a new community?
4. List three feelings or set reactions that are common in children when their parents divorce.
5. If a parent remarries, what adjustments might the family have to make?
6. What purpose does grieving serve?
7. List six strategies for adjusting to change.

Sharing Your Ideas

1. Families in today's society are moving more than ever before. What do you think accounts for this? What are the positive and negative consequences?
2. What could you do to help your parents prepare for a new family member?

Applying Your Skills

1. Indicating Appropriate Methods. Reread the material on adjusting to change on pages 121-122. Choose one type of family change discussed earlier in the chapter and rank the methods of adjusting as they apply to that type of change. Which would be the most helpful, and which the least helpful? Are there any methods of adjustment that do not apply to that type of change?

2. Describing Adjustments. Write a short story about a teen who must move from a small town to a major city. Describe the changes the teen experiences and the adjustments that were needed to adapt to this move.

3. Investigating a Cause-and-Effect Relationship. Take a poll of your classmates. Find out how many of them have experienced a major change in their family life. Describe the changes, their cause, their immediate effect, their long-term effect, and how these changes were handled.

CHAPTER
13

Friendships

OBJECTIVES

This chapter will help you to:

- List the five qualities of strong friendships.
- Explain how to make new friends.
- Describe the characteristics of friendships in the teen years.
- Explain how to communicate effectively with friends.

WORDS TO REMEMBER

caring
clique
empathy
loyalty
reliability
self-confident

There is an old saying that the only way to have a friend is to be one. What do you suppose the saying means?

How do you make friends? Usually, the first friends you make are those who live near you or attend your school. Often these early friendships last for years, long after school days are over.

Although you may spend time thinking about your friends, you may have given little thought to friendship itself. Have you ever wondered what makes friendships last? Friendships grow differently and at different paces. They may come easily or they may take work to develop. All friendships have some of the same qualities. You can develop satisfying and memorable friendships; some of them may even last all your life.

Qualities of Friendship

In order to answer the questions—how do you make friends and what makes friendship last—you need to know what makes a good friendship. A strong and lasting friendship is built on five qualities.

- **Sharing.** Friendships are often based on common interests. You and a friend may both work on the school newspaper, or perhaps you like to go shopping together. You can learn from your friends. You might show a friend how to change a flat tire on a bicycle, and your friend might help you find an error in your computer program. Experiences are more enjoyable if you share them. A funny movie is funnier if you can laugh at it with a friend.

- **Reliability.** If you always arrive on time to meet friends, you will be known as a reliable person. **Reliability** means being a person others can count on. If you have ever gotten homework assignments for a friend who was home with the flu, you showed your reliability.

- **Loyalty.** Suppose a friend who means a lot to you is the target of gossip. Speaking up for your friend is a sign of loyalty. **Loyalty** is being faithful to others, especially when they need it.

- **Empathy.** Just as friends can increase happiness, they can make sadness easier to bear. **Empathy** is being able to understand what someone else is experiencing. Everybody has unhappy times. Friends can encourage you if you are feeling upset about a low test grade at school. They can also help you deal with family problems. When you are feeling down, friends can help you see your situation clearly, and they can help you explore some ways to feel better.

A good friendship is based on personal qualities that are demonstrated by both persons. What qualities do you admire in your friends?

- **Caring.** The basic quality of friendship is caring, the one from which all the others seem to grow. People are real friends when they truly care about each other. **Caring** is the emotional bond that one person feels for another. A friend who cares remembers birthdays or helps a friend rehearse for the school play. Caring means valuing your friends' feelings as much as your own. It means making the effort to be kind, trusting, and honest.

Making New Friends

You might want to make new friends for any number of reasons: because you have moved to a new area, because old friends have moved away, or even because of changes within yourself. Some people seem to have a gift for making friends easily, but there is nothing magical about it. Developing friendships is a skill, and, like most skills, it improves with practice.

How to Meet People

You can make new friends if you take the initiative, treat people with kindness, and are yourself. You should also be aware of the situations that promote friendship. Friendships generally occur between people who have something in common: the area where they live, special interests, attitudes, or activities. One way to approach making new friends, then, is to look closely at yourself. What do you enjoy doing? What is important to you? Choosing people who share your basic interests or values provides a basis for lasting friendships. Here are some ideas on how to get started.

- **Join a club or group.** Talking with someone who shares a common interest is a natural way to start a friendship. There are plenty of groups to satisfy every type of interest, whether it is drama, photography, or modern dance.

- **Join someone in an activity.** You could study with a classmate for a science test or join a neighbor in collecting canned goods for a community food bank. Working together can be an effective way to start a friendship.

- **Start a conversation.** For example, you could compliment a neighbor on something you admire or ask a classmate about the class assignment.

Shared activities, such as cleaning up a local park or playground, bring people together and lead to new friendships.

INTERPERSONAL SKILLS

Peer Pressure

Many teens are strongly influenced by their friends or other teens. That influence is known as peer pressure.

Peer pressure can be a good thing when it influences you to do something that is right for you. Here are three examples of situations in which peer pressure is a positive influence:

- Aaron decides to join the FHA/HERO group because his friends are members.
- Alexandra warmly welcomes a new student because Sonya and Wes give the girl a friendly greeting.
- Kara decides to bring cans of food to a community food bank when several of her friends praise the project.

Sometimes, however, peer pressure can work against your best interests. Here are three examples of situations in which peer pressure could be a negative influence:

- Stacy is wondering whether to cut her hair after her friend Elysha comes to school with a short haircut.
- Two of Kurt's friends have been experimenting with drugs on the weekends, and Kurt is afraid of feeling left out.
- Jennifer notices a student being bullied and wants to defend him, but her friends pull her away.

Even the most determined teens may not find it easy to handle peer pressure. Everyone wants to have friends and be part of a group. If you are afraid of losing your friends or being laughed at, you might be tempted to do things that are wrong for you.

What can you do to resist peer pressure? Here are three suggestions:

- Take time to review the things you value most. If you value your health, for example, you will resist any pressure to use drugs.
- Tell those who want to pressure you your reasons for refusing to go along. Stand your ground against arguments.

- Decide what actions you will take to pursue the things you believe in, such as choosing certain groups to join or speaking out on issues of importance to you.

Think It Through

1. Do you think peer pressure is good or bad? Discuss examples from your own experiences.
2. Suppose your friends try to persuade you to stay out later than you want to. What reasons can you give to resist them?

How to Develop New Friendships

Once you have established a bond with someone, how can you build a new relationship? Suppose you meet someone that you enjoy talking with. After the conversation, one of you will have to make a second move if you want to develop a friendship. If you don't hear from new acquaintances, don't assume they are not interested in you. They may be waiting for you to call, or they may simply be busy. If you make the move yourself, you could follow up with a telephone call or an invitation to do something together.

Keep in mind that friendships don't happen in an instant. It takes time to get to know and be comfortable with another person.

Each time you meet or talk to your new friends, you are likely to find new interests in common. You share your experiences and problems, and, just as important, you listen to your friends' experiences and problems. These things cement new friendships together and make them last.

How to Be Self-Confident

What is so hard about meeting new people? Why do so many people get butterflies in the stomach when faced with the prospect? Meeting strangers means facing the unknown, and it is human nature to feel a bit uncomfortable about the unknown.

Most of our fears about dealing with new people come from doubts about ourselves. We imagine that other people are judging us—finding us too tall or too short, too quiet or too talkative. Remember that people meeting you probably have similar fears. If you accept yourself as you are and concentrate on putting other people at ease, everyone will feel more comfortable.

Try to act **self-confident**, or sure of yourself, even if you don't feel that way.

It takes both time and effort to develop lasting friendships.

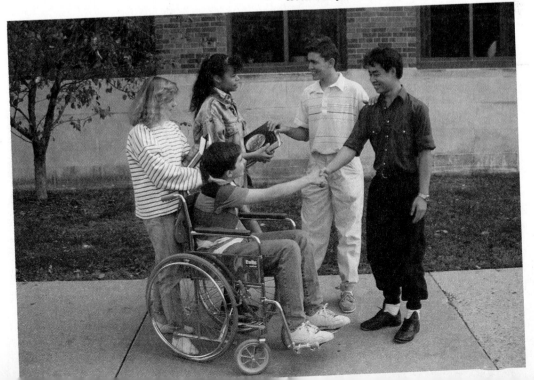

When you enter a room full of strangers, walk tall and straight, look directly at other people, and smile. If you see someone you would like to speak to, say something. Don't wait for the other person to start a conversation.

Meeting new people and getting to know them may or may not lead to new friendships. Not all hoped-for friendships work out. Learning how to handle these situations is an important part of the skill of making friends.

Friendships in the Teen Years

During the teen years, the nature of friendship changes. In childhood, friendships came from sharing activities. Now personal qualities often become the focus of attention. Intense friendships that are based on sharing thoughts and feelings often develop during these years.

Peer Groups

Peer groups, groups of people of the same or similar age, are very important during the teen years. If you manage your peer relationships well, you can benefit from them in many ways.

Your peer group can help meet your need for closeness and give you a sense of belonging. You can relax among others like yourself as you talk about and think through what you value. Your peer group also provides you with support as you begin to establish your own identity. It offers opportunities to learn and to practice how to act in new situations.

There are times, however, when peer groups can have a negative influence. Peers may expect you to behave in a certain way and even reject you if you don't. This pressure is especially difficult for teens, who are often concerned with being accepted.

Sometimes friendships change and a person may feel excluded from a particular peer group or clique.

Cliques

Within a peer group, there may be many **cliques**, or small, exclusive groups of people. People may form cliques without even realizing it, because they belong to the same club or sports team. Sometimes cliques are based on similar appearance or similar social or economic status.

Cliques often exclude people they think don't fit in. This can be devastating for teens who feel they need to be accepted by certain "in" groups. In fact, some teens make every effort to try to fit into groups that they want to be a part of. What the members of cliques don't realize is that by isolating themselves, they are losing opportunities to make new friends and develop new interests.

Communicating with Friends

When Ashley and Sarah started high school, they were best friends. They went virtually everywhere together, and they told each other everything.

During freshman year Sarah joined the basketball team. Ashley realized that their relationship would probably change a little during basketball season, but she didn't realize that Sarah would make new friends that she would enjoy seeing. Even though Sarah and Ashley still get together occasionally, Ashley feels left out. She wants to tell Sarah how she feels but is afraid of her reaction. She also wonders why things ever had to change.

Changing Friendships

What Sarah and Ashley are going through is common during the teen years. Changes in tastes and interests or in attitudes and beliefs can cause friends to grow apart. Sometimes those changes mean that friends just spend less time together. At other times, those changes may cause friendships to end.

Keeping Friends

Most people don't consciously work to keep their friends. In fact, many even take their friends for granted. Neither Sarah nor Ashley realized that friendship requires honest communication of thoughts and feelings.

It is important for friends to spend time together so their relationship can grow. They can benefit from sharing in each other's lives, talking about what is important to them, making new discoveries, and having fun.

Keeping friends also involves being considerate. If Sarah has to cancel plans because of basketball practice, then she should be considerate enough to tell Ashley right away and explain the situation. When friends respect each other's feelings, they are showing how much they care.

Best Friends

During the teen years, best friends take on more significance than before. You may consider just one person a best friend, or you may have several best friends. A best friend helps fulfill the need for affection and emotional closeness and helps you discover many of your own qualities. When a friend values you, it adds to your good feelings.

Sometimes teens face problems with close friendships. They can feel torn between an old friend and a new group. At times like these, it is helpful to talk the problem over with an adult.

Reviewing the Facts

1. List the five qualities that help make a friendship strong.
2. Explain what empathy is.
3. Why should caring be considered the basic quality of friendship?
4. Name three ways to meet new people.
5. How can you cement new friendships?
6. What positive and negative influences can peer groups have?
7. What is a clique?
8. Why do some friends grow apart during the teen years?
9. What two elements are essential to keeping friends?

Sharing Your Ideas

1. What would you do or say to help a very shy person make friends?
2. Describe the qualities your best friend has that are most important to you.

Applying Your Skills

1. **Writing a Dialogue.** With a classmate, write a dialogue between two people who are interested in initiating a conversation in order to build a friendship. Act out the dialogue in class.

2. **Ranking Ideas.** Reread the qualities of friendship on pages 126-127 and rank them in your own order of importance. Be prepared to discuss your choice for the most important quality and the ranking of the others.

3. **Forming Hypotheses.** You probably have at least one very close friend, if not a whole circle of friends. Why do you think you became friends with these people? Describe the cricumstances. Why do you suppose you remain friends?

CHAPTER

14

Special Relationships

OBJECTIVES

This chapter will help you to:

- Describe ways that teens become interested in and attracted to the other sex.
- Identify what teens can gain from dating.
- List and describe common problem areas in relationships.

WORDS TO REMEMBER

infatuation
platonic
unrequited love

Imagine a group of teens your age. Bruce thinks about girls a lot, but his shyness keeps him from asking a girl out or even approaching one for friendship. Leann is interested in boys, but her parents don't let her date yet. Brett has no great interest in the other sex; he enjoys spending time with his male friends. Zack would love to have a girlfriend. So far, however, no one he has been interested in has shown any interest in him.

Every one of these teens is different, and all are normal. There is no timetable, no set of steps to follow, that dictates when and how teens should take interest in and interact with the other sex. No one but you can say when you are ready for romantic relationships.

New Interests and Attractions

At some point during their teen years, most people become attracted to the other sex, even if they decide to do nothing about it right away. They feel strong emotions as well as sexual attraction. Such feelings may start to be expressed in friendships.

Just Friends

When Trea was in grade school, all her closest friends were girls. Now she has formed a close friendship with Nathan, a boy she knows from the debating team. Neither of them is interested in getting romantically involved yet, but they really enjoy being together. Trea says that Nathan helps her understand boys better. Nathan finds that he can relax with Trea because their relationship doesn't have the demands or the pressures of a romantic relationship.

Sometimes friendships like the one between Trea and Nathan *do* turn into romantic relationships. More often they are just **platonic** relationships—close friendships that are not romantic.

One-Sided Relationships

Whether you call them crushes, puppy love, or **infatuations**, most people experience intense, but usually short-term, feelings of love for someone who may not even know the yearnings exist. Usually the crush is on someone who is unattainable, such as a friend's older sibling, a teacher, or a rock star. The

Many teens experience crushes or infatuations. Such experiences help you begin to understand what love is all about.

person experiencing the crush daydreams about the object of the crush and often becomes fascinated with the details of his or her life.

Such one-sided relationships are part of learning to love. Respect and admiration are important elements in a love relationship. Also, an infatuation allows you to explore relationships in a safe way, since the other person is not required to respond.

If you get a crush on someone, you may be told that a crush is not real love. That is not exactly true. Unlike mature love, a crush *is* limited and one-sided, yet it is a kind of love. In any case, the feelings of excitement, yearning, sadness, and despair are very real to you.

First Steps

Children's first steps are wobbly and unsteady, and often they fall, but it is only through this experimentation that they learn to walk. The beginning steps that you take in relationships with the other sex are a little like that. It is normal to feel awkward about telephoning someone to talk or to get together, or even approaching someone you like at school for a conversation. Tess can talk to most boys with ease. When she speaks to Dave (whom she would like for a boyfriend), however, she feels tongue-tied.

Because of such fears and shyness, the first interactions between teens often occur in groups. In Camille's high school, a popular meeting place is the mall. Separate groups of boys and girls spend Saturdays there, talking, laughing, and having fun. Sometimes one group tries to attract the attention of another group, often through teasing and flirting. They may spend time talking in small groups.

As you begin to reach out, remember that any shyness you might feel is normal. You are learning how to talk and act with the other sex. Other people are probably not judging your every move; more likely, they are concerned about how they appear to you.

Many teens feel shy or awkward when they first talk to someone they like. It takes time for relationships to grow.

Dating

In time, these first contacts give way to dating relationships. Though the point at which you begin dating is not important, dating itself is a valuable activity. Through dating you:

- Learn to evaluate others.
- Learn what kinds of characteristics you like in another person.
- Learn how to determine the characteristics that are best for you and those you want in a mate.
- Learn how to share your interests, opinions, and feelings.

Dating helps you learn about the other sex as well as about yourself. There is one more purpose of dating that should not be forgotten: having fun!

Going Out in Groups

Sometimes dating starts with a group of friends who have fun together. Teens might meet for bowling, skating, parties, or movies. In a group date, people can relax and have fun with both males and females.

In fact, that is one of the advantages of a group date: you will feel less self-conscious with your friends around. It is easier to talk in a group. Each person has less responsibility for keeping the conversation going. In addition, some parents will not allow young teens to go out on an individual date, but they may allow them to go on a group date.

Dating as a Couple

Nadia was always surprised at how nervous she felt on a first date with someone new. Making conversation seemed especially difficult.

Perhaps the most popular thing to do on a first date is to see a movie, because you can relax while you are watching the film instead of worrying about making conversation. In addition, the movie gives you something to talk about later. Your separate opinions can tell you a lot about each other.

Group dating provides fun opportunities to get to know other people better.

Remember that the object of the date is to learn about the other person and to have fun. Don't worry about doing everything right. If you concentrate on making the other person comfortable, you will find you have a better time.

Some teens prefer to date different people. This gives them the advantage of gaining lots of experience in getting to know and understand many types of people. Sometimes a couple decides to date each other exclusively. This is sometimes referred to as going steady. It has some advantages. You get to know another person well, you derive a feeling of security, and your self-esteem is boosted. Yet going steady can also rob you of the chance to meet and date many people and to learn what you really like in a person. It may also have a negative effect on your same-sex friendships.

Problems with Relationships

It seems odd that love, which is something that is supposed to make people feel happy, can also bring sadness or hurt. Yet it is because loving and being loved mean so much that having something go wrong causes unhappiness. Knowing how to handle problems with relationships can help you cope with them and make better decisions.

When Love Is Not Returned

Rock stars sing about it, movies show it, soap operas thrive on it: **unrequited love**, or love that is not returned. Loving someone who does not love you in return is painful. Your friends and family may tell you to forget about the person, but you end up thinking about him or her all the time.

Ryan thought Lily was the only girl for him. After a few dates, however, she told him that she didn't think they should go out anymore because she didn't feel as strongly about him as he did about her. For a while, he tried to win her over. He knew her schedule, and he would turn up after her classes and at her table at lunch. After some time, however, he began to feel resentful and angry at her. He began to see faults that he had not seen before.

What happened to Ryan is normal. As a defense against the pain of unrequited love, Ryan experienced feelings of anger and resentment, which helped him to stop pursuing Lily. Eventually he could focus his attention on another girl, who cared for him in return.

Poor Communication

When Gina said to Tory, "I really like being with you," she only meant that she felt comfortable with him. When Tory heard those words, though, he thought Gina was saying she wanted an exclusive relationship with him. He was hurt when she explained that was not it at all.

Misunderstandings like these often happen when people are just starting out in a romantic relationship. They even happen to people who have been in a relationship for some time. Unfortunately, people don't always say what they mean. People don't always hear what others say, either; instead, they may hear what they *want* others to say.

It is important to be as honest and clear in your communication as possible. If there is a problem, discuss it. When the other person is speaking, listen. If you aren't sure what the message is, ask. Open communication is the best way to keep a relationship going strong.

Disagreements and Quarrels

Disagreements in relationships can begin for many reasons. Sometimes two people have different values or ideas about what is important. You will learn more about relationship problems in Chapter 15.

Sometimes a power struggle is the underlying problem. Power struggles come from the desire of the two people in a relationship to be in control. Sometimes one person will give in for a time. Soon, however, he or she tires of putting up with this and begins to fight back, perhaps in subtle ways. Jon, for example, really enjoys playing basketball, both on the school team and in more informal games with friends. He expects Robin to come and watch him. In fact, that is how most of their dates are spent. Robin didn't mind at first. When she did get upset, however, she didn't tell him directly. Instead, she started coming to the games and bringing her homework with her. Sometimes she would disappear for long stretches during the game.

Power struggles occur in some relationships. To solve them, people need to sit down and talk about what they want and how they are willing to work together. Unless Jon is willing to be less domineering, or Robin is willing to give in gladly, their relationship will probably end.

In another kind of disagreement, the two parties will fight about almost everything. Luke and Penny's friends joke about their quarrels. One day one friend said to another, "They seem to create situations just so they can break up. Do they really like fighting?"

"I think what they really like," said the other friend, "is making up after the fight." For some people the attention and feelings that go with making up make the quarrel worthwhile. Others, not confident in their partner's love, provoke fights as a kind of test. Games like these may be fun for a while, and they are one way to experiment with relationships. In the long run, however, they are a waste of time. Most people outgrow relationships built on games like these.

Frequent disagreements or quarrels may mean that the relationship is not based on mutual interests or values.

Outgrown Love

"I don't really understand what happened. I thought I loved Libby," said Doug. "But the relationship just doesn't seem to be working anymore. What's wrong with me?"

There really is not anything wrong with Doug, or Libby either. During your teen years you are growing and changing very quickly. Two teens in a relationship may change in different ways. When this happens, one person usually becomes dissatisfied with the relationship before the other. The often painful process of breaking up must then take place.

From every relationship—no matter how long it lasts—you can learn about yourself and the qualities that you seek in your future mate.

Breaking Up

Breaking up is not easy. Sometimes a relationship ends by mutual agreement, but more often one person wants to end it before the other. In such cases, one person usually feels hurt and may be angry while the other feels guilty. There are ways, though, you can make breaking up easier on you and the other person. (See "Ending a Relationship" on page 140.)

With every relationship you experience in your teen and young adult years, you will probably ask, "Is this love?" No one can really explain to anyone else what love is. Some say that when you are in love, you care about the whole person, not merely his or her looks or talent. You want to give as well as take. Whatever real love is, it should endure the test of time. It should not be here today, gone tomorrow. Maturity will help you define love and determine what role it will play in your future.

INTERPERSONAL SKILLS

Ending a Relationship

During the teen and early adult years, people often have several close relationships with the other sex. That means that some of them will end. There are ways to make the experience of breaking up less painful.

If you are the one ending the relationship, do it with honesty and sensitivity. Express your feelings, but try not to make the other person feel unlovable. Try to use "I" statements rather than "you" statements. Instead of saying, "You're too possessive," say, "I don't want to tie myself down to one person just yet." Avoid blaming and insulting the other person. Be kind, but firm.

If you are on the other side of the relationship, avoid pressure, sarcasm, or threats. Trying to keep a relationship from ending by clinging to the other person is bound to make him or her resentful. It will also make you feel worse about yourself.

After a breakup, give yourself time to recover from the hurt and disappointment. You will eventually regain your self-confidence and feel happy again. Don't expect, however, to remain friends with the person you broke up with. Although this is sometimes possible, more often it creates jealousy. Also, it may keep you hoping for a reconciliation when none is possible.

Though breaking up is hard, don't be afraid to try having a relationship again. Breaking up does not mean that your love was a waste. The experience of loving and being loved is part of you now. You have even learned from breaking up that you can bear the pain, and that it passes.

Think It Through

1. What do you think are some ways to get over the hurt of breaking up?
2. If you broke up with someone, would you want to remain friends? Why or why not?

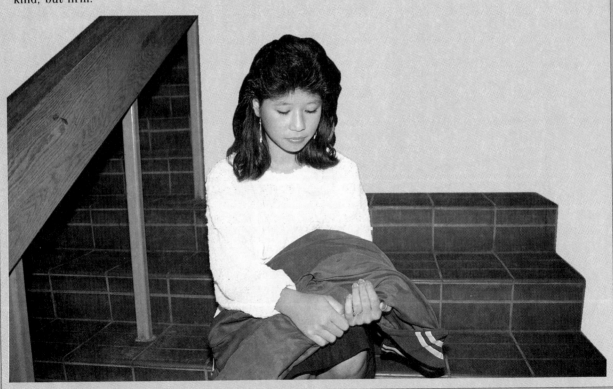

CHAPTER
14 REVIEW

Reviewing the Facts

1. What is an infatuation?
2. Why do early interactions between teens often happen in groups?
3. List three reasons why dating is important.
4. Name one advantage and one disadvantage of going steady.
5. Explain why good communication is important in a relationship.
6. What are two reasons why disagreements occur in relationships?
7. Why do teens sometimes outgrow their partners in a love relationship?

Sharing Your Ideas

1. Do you think there are pressures on teens today to begin romantic relationships early? Explain your answer.
2. How might the following aspects of an early dating relationship lead to poor communication: shyness, nervousness, and lack of knowledge of each other?

Applying Your Skills

1. Analyzing a Problem. Think of a book you have read or a movie or television show you have seen that has portrayed some troublesome aspect of relationships between teens of different sexes. Write a paragraph in which you describe ways that poor communication played a part in the problem, and give several suggestions for how communication might have been improved.

2. Writing a Dialogue. Derek and April have been going out for about a year. During a six-week vacation in California, April realizes that she wants to go out with boys other than Derek. She still likes Derek but does not want to tie herself down to one boy just yet. Write a dialogue in which April breaks this news to Derek in a sensitive manner.

3. Making Inferences. Usually Natalie asks Jake to come to her track meets. Jake used to go all the time. All of a sudden Jake is busy on some of the days of the track meets. Should Natalie infer something from this behavior? Explain your answer. What should Natalie and Jake do?

Decisions in Relationships

OBJECTIVES

This chapter will help you to:

- Identify ways of dealing with inner conflicts and peer pressure.
- Explain how to decide what is right for you.
- Discuss how to handle emotions, such as anger, jealousy, and possessiveness, in relationships.

WORDS TO REMEMBER

conscience
jealous
self-control

Andy and Vince were walking home from school when Vince asked Andy if he wanted to go to a party that night and drink a few beers. Vince had moved to town a few months ago. Andy had immediately liked him and thought that he and Vince could become good friends. Now Andy was surprised and couldn't stop thinking about the offer. After a few minutes he told himself, "If Vince does it, then it must be OK." He decided to ask Vince about it.

"I didn't know you drank," Andy said.

"Yeah, and it's great," Vince exclaimed. "Why don't you come try it?"

Suddenly Andy remembered what the football coach had said: "If I ever catch any of you guys drinking alcohol or doing drugs, you're off the team for good."

"No, I don't think so, Vince," Andy finally replied. "Coach said that if he ever caught any of us doing any of that stuff, we would be off the team for good."

"Oh, come on," Vince said. "Nobody will ever find out."

"Nope," Andy said. "It's not worth taking the chance."

Relationships and Values

Andy turned down the drinks because of his values. To him, being on the football team meant more than drinking beer. He and his parents had discussed teenage drinking, and he knew they were opposed to it. He also knew that drinking under the age of 21 was illegal in his state. Andy's values have an effect on his relationships. Although he may not develop a close relationship with Vince, he has strengthened the trust of his parents and coach.

Throughout the teen years, relationships change. Values change, too, as people make more decisions for themselves and figure out what is really important to them.

Inner Conflict

It is common for teens to feel torn between their relationships and their values. Many of them have not decided what is most important to them. They may experience conflicting feelings when faced with a decision, and, after making one, they may be overcome with doubts.

Andy was undecided at first, until he remembered the coach's warning. Even though Andy's feelings may have been in favor of going along with Vince, his mind told him that he didn't want to risk being kicked off the football team or having his parents or the police find out about the drinking.

Your values can help you sort out conflicting feelings when you make decisions.

At times you may, like Andy, feel as if there are two or even three people inside you. Your feelings may tell you to do one thing, your mind another.

Everyone has a **conscience**, the "little voice" that tells you whether, according to your values, what you are doing is right or wrong. When Cassie's friend tried to convince her that cheating on a test was OK, Cassie's conscience told her that it was wrong but she did it anyway. Afterward, Cassie felt very guilty.

A conscience isn't any help if it merely produces guilt. Your conscience should be helping you to develop **self-control**: an inner control over your own behavior. With self-control, you don't depend on someone else to look out for you. You become responsible for yourself, and you begin to feel better about who you are and what you can do.

Peer Pressure

Many teens find that their decisions are strongly influenced by their friends. Andy almost gave in to Vince's pressure because he wanted to be better friends with him.

A good friend will respect your values and not pressure you into making decisions that might be wrong for you.

In order to deal with peer pressure you need to know what your values are. Then you can make the decisions that are right for you.

Because Andy valued being on the football team and maintaining his parents' trust, he resisted the pressure to drink alcohol. Some teens might resist drinking because they value their health or because they don't want to be arrested. The important thing to remember is to act according to your values or what *you* think is right.

Deciding What Is Right

When you know what your values are, you can decide what is right for you. However, when you feel pulled in two different directions, those decisions may seem more difficult than ever. What can you do so that the tough decisions are easier to make? The following suggestions can help:

■ **Think about the possible outcomes.** For example, shoplifting or using an illegal drug even once may result in your getting arrested.

■ **Think about the physical consequences.** Smoking cigarettes, marijuana, or crack has serious physical effects. People have died from using cocaine just once.

■ **Think about the emotional consequences.** What if you have lied to a friend? How will you feel when that friend discovers you haven't told the truth?

Once you have made a choice, how do you communicate your decision so that others respect it? Andy said no and then explained why. Explaining your reasons can be an effective way to say no. See "Refusal Skills" on page 147 for more information on this subject.

Relationships and Emotions

Emotions are a part of all relationships. At times, you may feel love, joy, or enthusiasm. There might also be times that you will feel annoyed, impatient, or depressed. Emotions can have many different shadings as well. You might feel one kind of love for your parents, another kind for your best friend, and even a third kind for someone special.

It is even possible to experience several different emotions at the same time. Have you ever been excited and scared at the same time? What is most important is how you express the emotions you have.

Anger

Everyone experiences angry feelings occasionally. In relationships, it is important to learn how to express that anger responsibly.

When you have a disagreement with a friend, the thing you should *not* do is speak in anger. You will only be tempted to say something that will hurt the other person. You may even say something you don't really mean, which will drive you and your friend further apart.

When you are angry with anyone, avoid name-calling and threats. You should also learn how to express your anger in a nonviolent way.

Give yourself time to cool off. This does not mean that you should not express your anger. You might talk about the problem with your parents or with another friend. Try to work the problem out with your friend when you are calm enough to be able to control your feelings.

During the teen years, you may feel deep emotions about someone special. How might such emotions influence your decisions?

Although anger is a common emotion, it is important to learn how to express your anger in nonviolent ways.

Jealousy and Possessiveness

Relationship problems can also occur because of other strong emotions like jealousy and possessiveness. You are **jealous** when you feel hurt or resentful if a boyfriend or girlfriend spends time with or pays attention to someone else. You may also get these feelings when he or she does something that does not include you.

When making decisions about relationships, always maintain respect for yourself and for the other person.

These emotions are normal parts of relationships, and everyone has them. That does not mean they should be ignored or exaggerated. If they build up, they can threaten a relationship.

Special Considerations

There are also other important emotions and actions that can affect relationships. For example, dating brings new responsibilities as well as new experiences. In the teen years, the same hormones that bring physical maturity may also cause strong sexual feelings. Lack of understanding of or control over sexual feelings can lead to problems such as pressure by one person on another to get sexually involved, sexually transmitted diseases, and teen pregnancy.

It is important to base decisions about these subjects on both a personal sense of responsibility and a respect for others. Emotional or physical pressure on another person to become more physically involved than he or she wants is unfair and selfish.

Feelings can be very strong in the teen years, but part of growing up is learning how to control your own feelings and express them in ways that are good for everyone.

Respect for Yourself and Others

Teens are faced with so many conflicting emotions they have never felt before that it may be especially difficult for them to make decisions sometimes. Those emotions can be both exciting and frightening at the same time. It is important to keep in mind that emotions are changeable, and that what you do with them shows how much respect you have for yourself and for others.

Refusal Skills

If friends try to talk you into doing something you don't really want to do, you need to be prepared. You have to make sure that other people really understand and accept your refusal. If you are in a situation where you need to say no, you can use these four steps to refuse firmly.

■ **Step 1: Plan ahead.** You need to decide in advance what you will do in case certain situations arise. Doing this allows you to make up your mind without pressure from other people. You can also be ready to stand up for your own beliefs and values. For example, if your parents are going to be away on Saturday night and your friends ask if they can come over and have a party, you will be prepared to say no because you have made an agreement with your parents not to do this. You can also plan ahead by asking yourself some specific questions such as: Is it safe? Is it legal? Can it hurt me or anyone else?

■ **Step 2: Say no.** It is important to say no and to mean it. Look straight at the other person. Don't smile, because your smile will communicate yes. Keep your voice steady, and watch your body language. Don't send confusing messages or the other people involved will doubt your statement.

■ **Step 3: If necessary, repeat your refusal and give reasons why.** There may be times when saying no is not enough. You should be prepared for a put-down, but don't get into an argument. Give your reasons calmly but firmly. For instance: "It's against school rules," "I wouldn't feel right doing it," "I might get hurt," "It's illegal," or "I've promised my parents that I will not do that."

■ **Step 4: Suggest an alternative.** Put on your own pressure by suggesting another activity, one that is fun, healthy, safe, and legal. If that does not work, you should get away from the pressure as soon as you can. You might even say that you have already made plans to do something else.

If you use the four steps, you will let your friends and acquaintances know that you are not rejecting them or their friendship. You are just making your own decisions. More often than not, your friends will respect you for making your decisions.

Think It Through

1. Suppose a friend dares you to join a group that plans to pocket several items at a department store just for fun and then return the items afterward. Use the four steps to tell your friend why you don't want to take part.

2. What could you do if a friend threatened to end the friendship with you after you refused to do something you didn't want to do?

Reviewing the Facts

1. Explain what your conscience is.
2. Describe self-control and how it helps you handle inner conflicts.
3. What do you need to know in order to deal with peer pressure?
4. What three things should you think about when you are deciding what is right for you?
5. What should you do when you are angry?
6. Define jealousy.
7. When making decisions about dating, what should you base your decisions on?

Sharing Your Ideas

1. What do you think is the relationship between self-esteem and self-control?
2. Do you think anger and jealousy should be expressed? Why or why not?

Applying Your Skills

1. Analyzing a Sequence of Events. Write a paragraph describing a time when you felt pressured by your peers. Try to analyze what you did on the basis of whether you thought about the three suggestions on page 144.

2. Dissecting Behavior. Write a paragraph about a television show you have seen or a book you have read in which one or more characters took responsibility for their emotions. Discuss specifically what the characters did that showed responsibility.

3. Discovering Cause-and-Effect Relationships. Have you ever been asked to do something that you didn't want to do? Describe the situation. How did it arise? How did it make you feel? What was the outcome?

CHAPTER
16

Your Future Relationships

OBJECTIVES

This chapter will help you to:

- Explain the benefits of new friendships at school and at work.
- Describe the elements of a successful love relationship.
- Discuss how family relationships can change.
- Define the roles of a leader and a good citizen.

WORDS TO REMEMBER

citizen
parliamentary procedure
role model

Your teen years are a time of preparation. In getting ready to be an adult, you learn how to be a friend and how to be a member of a family. The success of your future relationships might depend on what you learn now.

Of course, no one knows what your future relationships will be like. Everyone takes a different path. You may stay in your town and remain friends with the people you know now. You may go to college in a new city and decide to stay there. Perhaps you will go away for a period—in the armed services, for example—and then return to your hometown to work at another job.

Whatever you do, wherever you go, there will always be people with whom you can form satisfying relationships.

Friendships

As you get older, you and your friends may grow apart. Sometimes, a friend moves away and it is harder to keep the closeness over a long distance. Sometimes, you grow apart because of a change in interests. Changes in your life don't mean that you *must* lose your current friends, though. You can talk about your new experiences whenever you are together. At the same time, you may develop new friendships with people at school or at work.

New Relationships at School

When you think of your relationships at school now, you probably think of your friendships. However, your relationships with teachers, counselors, coaches, librarians, and other adults are also opportunities for growth.

Your relationships with these adults help you to learn how to get along with those in positions of authority. You also learn, through these contacts, skills in listening, understanding, and following directions that are crucial in all parts of your life. These people are your **role models**, people you admire and whose behavior you use as an example.

After high school, perhaps you will go to college away from home and live in a dormitory with a roommate. Both you and your roommate will need to adjust to living with someone who has different habits. Getting along will be easier if you speak honestly, listen patiently, and are considerate. A sense of humor helps, too.

Finding new friends at college—especially at a big school—may seem impossible. Actually, though, it is like making friends in school now. As you read earlier, you can meet people in classes, at the cafeteria, in special clubs, or on teams.

In seeking these friendships, remember to be yourself. You have built a self-concept and identified your interests. Now act on what you have learned.

New Relationships at Work

People spend so much time at the place where they are employed that they often make friends of the people they meet there. Of course, being friendly at work does not mean chatting all day, but it does mean being pleasant, cooperative, and considerate of others.

The people you work with have different opinions and personalities, but you will have to get along with all of them, not just the ones you like. A positive aspect of getting along with co-workers is that you may develop friendships with people who are different from you.

You will also have to learn to follow suggestions and to accept criticism of your work. If you remember that your boss is discussing your *work*, not judging your character, you will find criticism easier to accept. It is natural to make a few mistakes, and your boss wants to help you learn from those mistakes. Just be sure that you aren't making the mistakes because you are afraid to ask questions.

Finally, you may often find yourself working in a group or team. Team workers share ideas and responsibility, and this means sharing responsibility for both success *and* failure.

Love

Sometimes a friendship will undergo a change and turn into a love relationship. Love is based on the give-and-take of two people so that the deepest needs of both people are met.

The Four C's

For love to grow and develop, it helps to follow the four C's. These are caring, commitment, communication, and compromise.

- **Caring.** The most satisfying part of a love relationship may be the caring. Knowing that someone else cares makes you feel more secure and worthy. You can show how much you care, too, by helping when your partner is feeling low or has a problem.
- **Commitment.** A strong relationship also depends on both people's making a commitment. Each partner must want to make the relationship work. Love relationships don't just happen; they require teamwork.
- **Communication.** Commitment requires communication. Talking honestly can help solve the problems that arise. Just talking is not enough; you must listen, too.
- **Compromise.** To settle differences, both partners must be willing to compromise. They must be willing to give a little so that they can reach a solution that satisfies them both. The result is a stronger relationship.

An enduring, lasting love is based not just on physical attraction, but on qualities such as trust, understanding, and respect.

Marriage

Deciding to marry someone is a major decision. It means being willing to practice the four C's every day. It usually also requires a lot of adjustment by each person, especially during the first year. If both partners work hard, however, they can get over the rough spots. The joy that may result can make it all worthwhile.

Of course, not everyone chooses to marry. You may prefer to dedicate your life to a career. Single people can still have satisfying relationships with other people: old friends, new friends, and family members.

Family

Your family relationships also will change in the future. You may start to care for younger siblings or perhaps help take care of your grandparents. When you move away from home, however, you begin a whole new stage in your life. Your family will not play exactly the same role as it did before.

Independence and Moving Out

In many other countries, grown children live with their parents until they are married, and sometimes even after. In our society, though, young adults often leave their homes and become independent. They live on their own or with roommates and begin setting up their own household.

It can be an exciting time, doing what you want on your own schedule. This new freedom carries its responsibilities, however. You will have to manage your money to meet your expenses for food, clothing, shelter, and leisure activities, for example.

As you meet the new challenges, you gain more confidence in yourself. You prepare yourself to take on even more new experiences. Still, it can be comforting to have family members who are willing to lend a helping hand.

New Family and Old

If you marry, you will probably acquire more than just a spouse. New relatives are likely to be involved. Your spouse's family may be very different from your own, and your family may seem strange to your spouse. In fact, accepting one another may be difficult for everyone at first.

Remember that your spouse draws strength and love from his or her family, just as you do from yours. A good relationship with your new relatives is important to you and to your marriage.

Neighborhood, Community, and Nation

Beyond your family, school, and workplace, you are a part of your neighborhood, your community, and your nation. Your relationships in these larger groups will also help determine your future.

Groups consist of leaders and followers, and all groups need both. There are times you may assume the role of leader, such as when you serve as a student council officer or get your group involved in an after-school project. At other times you may be a follower, as when you help with a car wash or participate in a community walkathon.

Different skills are required of each position, and each is needed to get the job done. Whether you are a leader or a follower, you relate to the group in different ways.

Being a Leader

A good leader uses the best talents of a group to achieve the group's goals. These might range from running a bake sale to cleaning up a park. Whatever the project, an effective leader enables group members to work together efficiently to reach the goal.

What characteristics make a leader effective? The following five skills are very important.

- **Management.** A leader must know and follow the management process: planning, organizing, implementing, and evaluating. Good leaders don't do it all themselves; they use the special talents of everyone in the group to get things done.

- **Motivation.** To use the resources of the group fully, a leader must be aware of the talents and abilities of each member, as well as sensitive to the ways that each person can best be motivated. Some people, for example, work well with little direction. Others require more help in getting started. An effective leader understands people's talents and abilities and tailors management to each person's needs.

- **Problem solving.** A good leader solves the problems that naturally arise when people work together. Creative thinking, conflict resolution, and decision-making skills are all necessary for good leadership.

- **Communication.** A good leader communicates effectively. He or she must be able to explain to the group what needs to be done and how each person can help do it. A leader needs to listen to suggestions, problems, and complaints, and to communicate praise and encouragement to group members.

- **Conducting meetings.** A good leader gives group members at a meeting an opportunity to voice their opinions following rules developed first by the English Parliament. This democratic method, known as **parliamentary procedure,** permits the reaching of a majority decision. Knowing parliamentary rules can help you become a leader at school and at work.

Leadership skills, just like other skills, can be learned and developed.

Being a Good Citizen

A **citizen** is a member of a group such as a school, a community, or a nation. Your role as a citizen is the role of follower and group member. You already know what it means to be a good citizen within your family, and you have discovered how working together helps everyone.

What makes a good citizen? Several qualities stand out:

- **Respect.** A citizen respects other people, their individuality, their needs, and their property. Some property is shared by all people in a group. The earth, for example, belongs to all of us. By trying to live in ways that minimize pollution, you act as a good citizen of the world who respects this common heritage. Being respectful also means acting honestly and obeying the rules or laws of the group.

- **Cooperation.** No group can achieve its goals if the members do not cooperate with each other and share ideas and resources. Part of good citizenship is working together with others to achieve a common goal, such as running the student government smoothly and effectively.

- **Responsibility.** Being a good citizen means thinking before you act—you need to consider how your action will affect others. It also means taking responsibility in your daily life. For example, your walking your dog on a leash will be appreciated by others in your neighborhood.

- **Participation.** Part of being a good citizen means pitching in with the group for everyone's good. As a citizen of the United States, for example, you participate by staying informed and by voting when you come of age. At some point in your life, you may decide to open up your own business, buy a home, or invest in the stock market. All of these actions contribute to the nation's economy.

Being an effective leader or citizen benefits everyone. Doing your job well will make you feel good about yourself, and it will make others feel good about you. You will know that you can make a difference in the world of the future by controlling your own life and affecting the lives of others for the good of all.

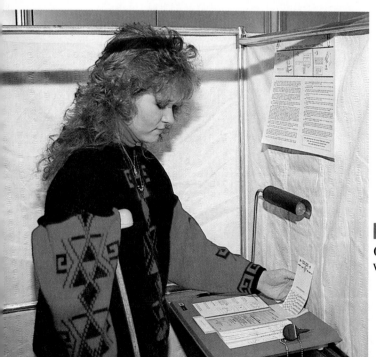

One of the responsibilities of citizenship is voting in every election.

TECHNOLOGY

Keeping Memories Alive

Long ago . . . it must be. . . .
I have a photograph.
Preserve your memories;
They're all that's left you.
—Paul Simon, *Bookends Theme*

Families have always passed memories from generation to generation, to be kept and treasured. While the human need to preserve these memories has not changed, methods for recording memories have. Here are some of the popular ways of holding on to memories.

- **Storytelling.** Stories have preserved memories for thousands of years. Even today most families treasure and retell favorite anecdotes. When old friends get together, they say, "Do you remember when . . ." Stories are word-snapshots of important times in our lives.

- **Photographs.** Photographs are another way of preserving memories. They capture visually a moment in time. Many families enjoy reviewing old photographs or slides and remembering the special times together.

- **Home movies.** Home movies, especially popular a few decades ago, provide another way of preserving memories. A baby's first step, a toddler's gift of wildflowers, a sweltering sixth-grade graduation, and the senior prom are all examples of events that can be preserved—in sometimes embarrassing detail—for future viewing.

- **Video technology.** Today's technological advancement is the home video camera. Used with videocassette players, video cameras can record events to be watched immediately or to be viewed months or years later.

Technology has strongly affected the ways memories have been passed along. Even so, people today use a variety of old and new technology: stories are still told, photos taken, and video cameras roll. Perhaps our personal and family histories are too important for us to discard *any* method of preserving them.

Think It Through

1. Which of these methods of preserving memories is most vivid for you? Why?
2. The memory-preserving methods mentioned here use our senses of sight or hearing. Other senses, especially the sense of smell, also trigger memory. Give at least one specific example of a scent that brings back a memory for you.

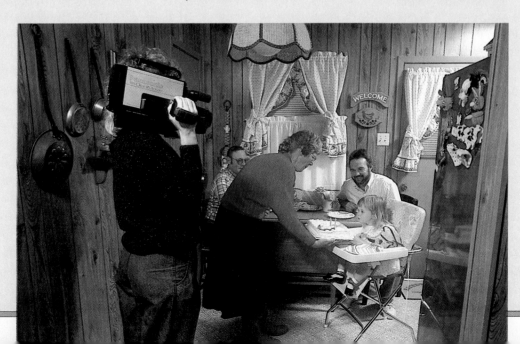

Reviewing the Facts

1. How can your relationships with teachers help you in the future?
2. Why do friendships often start in the workplace?
3. What are the four C's of a strong love relationship?
4. What are two ways in which your family relationships can change as you grow older?
5. Why are leaders and followers needed to get a job done?
6. What five qualities are important for good leadership?
7. Define the term citizen.
8. Why is cooperation within a group important to good citizenship?

Sharing Your Ideas

1. List two things that you learn in your relationships at school that you expect will also help you at work.
2. How can you be a good citizen of your family? At school? In your neighborhood? Give two examples for each.

Applying Your Skills

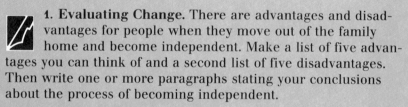

1. Evaluating Change. There are advantages and disadvantages for people when they move out of the family home and become independent. Make a list of five advantages you can think of and a second list of five disadvantages. Then write one or more paragraphs stating your conclusions about the process of becoming independent.

2. Applying Characteristics. Reread the section on being a leader. Think of a goal your school or community wants to achieve, such as cleaning up the local playground. How could you use the five qualities that effective leaders possess to accomplish that goal?

3. Supporting Theories. Think about a couple you know who has been married for several years. How do the four C's fit into this relationship? Then think about some of the couples in your school. How do the four C's fit into those relationships? Compare your answers for the couples still in school. Explain your answer.

CHAPTER

17

Careers in Working with People

OBJECTIVES

This chapter will help you to:

- Identify the interests and skills required for a career in working with people.
- List personal goals and achievements.
- Give examples of jobs that involve helping people.
- Distinguish between entry-level jobs and jobs that require training.

WORDS TO REMEMBER

aide	entry-level job
clergy	objective
client	personal inventory

Very often people need help in improving their relationships with others. Consider the following situations:

- Looking for new friends, you join a youth group at a community center, where a young adult plans activities for teens with common interests.
- Your best friend's family begins weekly meetings with a family therapist to help settle some conflicts peacefully.
- Your elderly neighbor has suddenly become a widow and hires a companion to avoid loneliness.

These are only a few of the situations that may require the help of workers with certain skills. Helping people improve their relationships with others can be the basis of a rewarding career.

Helping People: Which Qualities Are Needed?

Ask yourself some questions to find out whether you have the personal qualities that could lead to a career in helping people improve relationships. Many of the jobs focus on helping a **client**, a person who is given help and information by a professional. Most of your working hours would be spent listening to people with problems. Do you have many of the following qualities?

Interests and Skills

- **Do you relate well to people?** You need to understand people's fears and hopes, how they learn, and why they act as they do. Some of this knowledge comes from studying, but much is learned on the job.
- **Are you a good listener?** You need to learn about the particular client who wants help. You must be able to let the clients tell their story, while you keep an open mind.

This teenager enjoys tutoring other classmates. What qualities would she need for a job that focuses on helping others?

■ **Can you allow the client to make independent decisions?** You must be careful to let the client choose what to do. If you force a client to take a certain action, it is very likely to fail.

■ **Are you assertive?** If you are positive and confident, a client will be more inclined to trust your ability to help with problems.

■ **Can you negotiate well?** With individuals, and especially with families, you may need to help clients see all the sides of a conflict. It is important for you to help them discuss their problems and reach a compromise.

■ **Are you interested in people?** Listening to people with problems is often very demanding. Although you must be prepared to put a lot of energy into this type of work, the results can be very rewarding. One reward is the satisfaction of helping a client deal with a problem.

■ **Do you have empathy?** You must have empathy, the ability to understand what the client is experiencing. You may feel that your client's problems are minor, but the client is likely to disagree. Being able to see a problem from the client's point of view is essential.

■ **Can you be objective?** To help a client, you must be **objective**, or able to listen without becoming emotionally involved. Balancing empathy and objectivity is a great challenge.

■ **Can you handle conflict?** By being calm, you can put a client who is very upset at ease. Often, this helps the client see solutions to the problem.

■ **Are you trustworthy?** Since clients may reveal deep and important secrets, they need to feel confident that you will keep those secrets.

A Personal Inventory

Even if you are not ready to choose a specific career, it is a good idea to examine your goals and achievements. Then you will be more prepared in the future to decide which careers you might be suited for.

Making notes about what you discover about yourself will help you develop a **personal inventory**, or a review of your interests and skills. The chart below shows a method of organizing details about your interests, skills, and your future goals.

Finding Out About Yourself

What I like to do: _____

What I am good at: _____

Activities I enjoy: _____

Work I have done: _____

My goals for the future: _____

Jobs I think I would enjoy: _____

Fully Qualified

Nina Johnson and her mother are sitting in the living room of their home.

"Mom, Tim just told me that his mother is getting her master's degree in business administration. Isn't that great?" Nina says.

"Yes, it's wonderful. She certainly deserves it after working so hard," Mrs. Johnson replies.

"Why don't you go back to school, Mom? You're just as smart as Tim's mother. You should have a career, too," Nina says.

"I already have one. I'm a homemaker," Mrs. Johnson says.

"That's not a real career, like being a lawyer or a big executive. You know what I mean," Nina says. She stands up and gets her trombone. "So long, Mom," she says, waving. "I have band rehearsal at school."

After Nina leaves, Mrs. Johnson thinks for a minute, takes a notepad from the table, and begins to write. When she has finished, she folds the paper, puts it in an envelope with Nina's name on it, and leaves it in Nina's bedroom.

When Nina returns from school, she finds the envelope on her dresser. She tears it open and begins to read.

Memo to Nina from Mom:

Do you know anyone who could fill this job I heard about? There is a position available for a mature individual with at least fifteen years of experience in the following areas:

- **Instructor.** Giving direction to others.
- **Consultant.** Serving as a major source of information on a wide variety of subjects.
- **Scheduler.** Planning and organizing tasks to achieve specific goals.
- **Financial Planner.** Making budgets, distributing income, and paying expenses.
- **Manager of Human Resources.** Having chief responsibility for the health and safety of other human beings.

After reading the note, Nina looks for her mother. She finds her in the dining room. "Mom, what is this?" She holds up the note. "Are you really applying for this job?"

"No, I don't have to. I've had that job for fifteen years."

Nina looks at the note again and says, "Oh, I get it. You really do all those things as a homemaker, don't you?"

"I like to think so," Mrs. Johnson replies. "And I would like to hold on to my career as a homemaker. I think it suits me."

"You're right. I guess I just didn't think of it that way."

Think It Through

1. **Why is it hard for some people to accept the idea that homemaking is a career?**
2. **How would you go about paying homemakers for the work they do?**

Jobs Working with People

You may have already decided that you want a job helping people deal with relationships. To prepare for such a job, you need to know how much training is required at each job level.

Some people are hired for **entry-level jobs,** or those jobs for which little or no experience is needed. Jobs at the next level require some training. That training could be education in a community college or technical school, work in an apprenticeship program, or on-the-job training.

The third group of jobs requires at least a degree from a four-year college. Some jobs call for higher degrees as well, such as master's, doctorate, or medical degrees.

Entry-Level Jobs

A companion may help a person who is elderly, disabled, or recovering from illness. If you work as a companion, you might keep house, prepare meals, and even entertain the client. Companions can work full-time or part-time. They may live in the home of the person they care for, in which case they might get room and board along with a wage. Experience working in a hospital can be helpful for this job.

Government agencies hire social worker aides. **Aides** are workers who assist higher-level workers with their jobs. Some ask clients questions to learn whether they are eligible for income or jobs programs. Others explain programs to clients and provide information. Social worker aides also can work part-time or full-time. Typing skills can be valuable for this job.

Many support groups have hot lines, telephone numbers that people can call for emergency help. Some hot lines help people who are thinking about committing suicide. Others assist people with drug problems. Since they offer important care to people who need it right away, hot-line workers need to be calm and understanding. Most programs train their workers, but college courses in counseling will help.

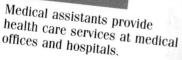

Medical assistants provide health care services at medical offices and hospitals.

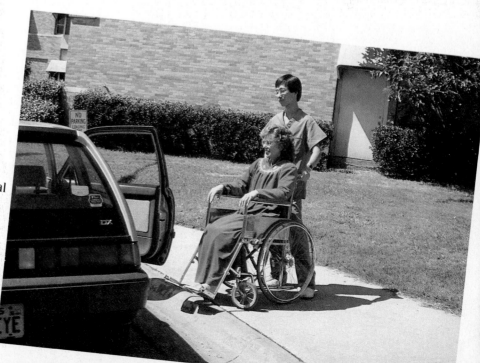

A medical assistant works with doctors and nurses in providing health care: you might handle office records, do lab work, or do simple physical tests on patients. Most medical assistants work in doctors' offices, though some are employed by hospitals. Usually, they are trained on the job, but some junior colleges offer courses.

Jobs That Require Training

Among their many duties, police officers sometimes handle emergency family problems. In such instances, it is very important for them to act calmly, since situations involving family violence can be dangerous. To become a police officer, you must first pass a test. Then you will be trained in a police academy. The number of jobs in police work is expected to grow in the future, so there will be many openings for applicants.

Child care workers care for preschool children whose parents work. These workers help the children grow emotionally, socially, and mentally. Because many families are now headed by a single parent who works, or by two parents who both work, the demand for child care workers is growing. Training can be obtained on the job, although some employers require a degree from a two-year or four-year college.

Physical therapist assistants help people who are recovering from illness or an injury. Physical therapist assistants use equipment, exercise, and massage to help patients overcome their physical problems or pain. They might also instruct patients in using wheelchairs or braces. Training is given in two-year colleges.

Jobs That Require an Advanced Degree

Some jobs require a college degree or additional study. Sometimes a master's degree is needed and sometimes even a doctorate.

Families that are having conflicts often turn to family therapists. These highly trained people work with the whole family rather than with one or two individuals. They can work for clinics and hospitals, or in private practice. Family therapists must have a college degree and usually a master's degree.

Many police officers are called upon to handle emergency family problems.

Social workers help individuals and families deal with problems, such as obtaining help from various agencies. They can provide advice and counseling, as well as hold classes for clients. Social workers may be based in schools, hospitals, or government agencies. Most have a college degree and a master's degree as well.

Many people turn to a religious worker or a member of the **clergy** such as priests, ministers, rabbis, and mullahs when they need help. These people can be important sources of comfort and advice. Training for religious workers varies from one religion to another, but a college degree and study at a religious school are the usual requirements.

Psychologists study how the mind works. They offer counseling to clients who want therapy. Psychologists may work in a hospital or have their own practice. These professionals have a college degree and usually an advanced degree. They also get extra training by talking with patients and helping them resolve difficulties.

Following Up

The more you plan and prepare ahead in pursuing your career goals, the better off you are. Here are three suggestions to follow if you think you might be interested in a career helping people:

- Talk to school guidance counselors. They can help you determine whether you would be happy in a career that involves dealing with people's problems. They might also suggest ways for you to gain a little experience to help you decide.

- Ask students who have spent time caring for small children or for people with disabilities to share their experiences with you. You will then have a better idea of what it means to meet the needs of people who may not be independent.

- Volunteer for several hours a week at a child care center, hot-line service, or other facility in your community that provides aid to people. Having direct contact with social service centers can help you decide whether a career helping people is a good choice for you.

Religious leaders can provide counseling for both individuals and families.

Reviewing the Facts

1. How would most of your time be spent in a career that helps people with their relationships?
2. What are three qualities needed for a career of helping people?
3. Define entry-level jobs and give an example of one.
4. Why is the number of child care workers growing?
5. What kind of training does a physical therapist assistant need?
6. What are two suggestions for finding out more about careers helping people?

Sharing Your Ideas

1. Why do you think a social worker's job is difficult?
2. A friend is painfully shy and wants you to suggest who could help. What questions would you ask to determine who could best help?

Applying Your Skills

1. Evaluating a Controversial Issue. Child care is an issue about which people have many views. Find two articles that present different points of view. Compare them and explain the differences to the class.

2. Requesting Information. Choose one of the professions in the chapter. Write a letter with questions that would help you determine whether you would be interested in that type of job. Ask a librarian to help you find the name and address of a national organization to send the letter to.

3. Proposing Theories. Consider the interests and skills presented in this chapter. Then choose one of the professions mentioned in the chapter. How would the interests and skills described be helpful in that profession? Describe a situation or two in which those qualities are called into play.

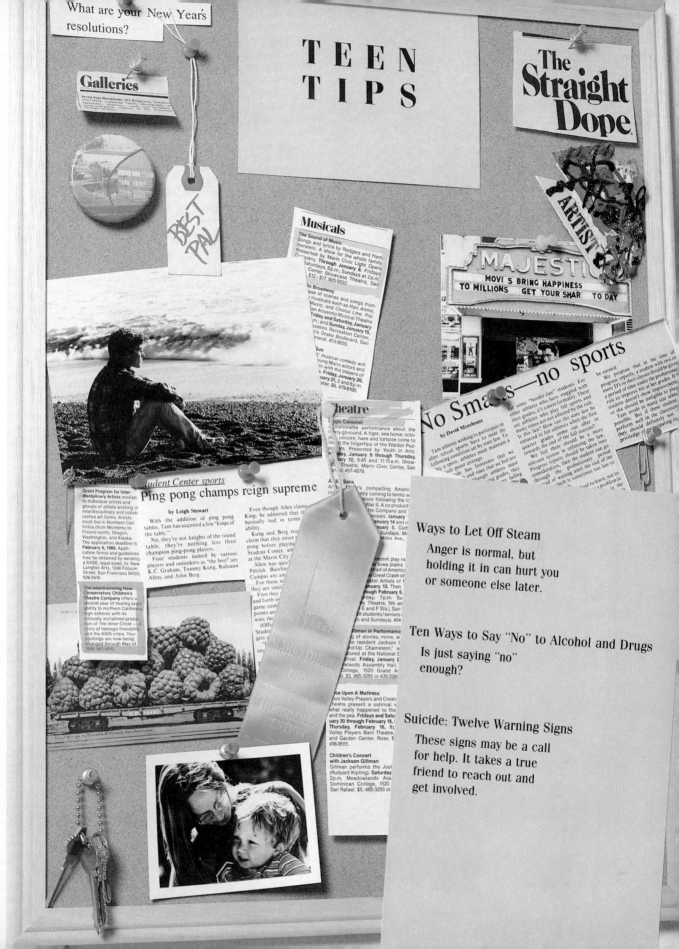

Ways to Let Off Steam

Anger is perfectly normal, and "blowing off steam" can be a healthy way to clear the air. When you are angry and don't express it, tension builds. Anger held inside too long can cause headaches, backaches, and stomach troubles. Unexpressed anger can even cause depression.

If you put off dealing with anger, you may end up hurting others or getting into trouble. Often, bottled-up anger results in a big explosion when it comes. An angry outburst usually makes it harder to solve the problem that caused your anger.

Here are ten helpful ways to let off steam:

1   Count to 10. Better yet, count to 20. Or say the alphabet out loud.

2   Breathe deeply, concentrating on your breathing, until you feel calmer.

3   Call a time-out. Go into another room or outside until you cool off.

TEEN TIPS

4 Get a pencil and notebook and write down what you're feeling. What caused the anger?

 5 Put on your favorite tape or turn on the radio and play some quiet music.

 6 Phone a friend. If you can't reach a friend, phone for the weather.

 7 Do some sit-ups, go for a run, or ride a bike.

 8 Splash some cold water on your face or take a hot bubble bath.

 9 Hug a pillow.

 10 Lie down on the floor and concentrate on a spot on the ceiling.

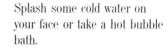

Ten Ways to Say "No" to Alcohol and  Drugs

Imagine this: You've been hanging around with a group of friends and having a great time. You really like these people because you seem to have a lot in common. Then you discover that the group wants you to drink alcohol or take drugs. How can you say "no" to your friends?

Here are ten ways to resist peer pressure:

1 **Just say "No."** Keep your response short and your voice firm. Let your facial expression tell your friends exactly how you feel about their pressure. Shake your head and say:
"I'll pass."
"I'm not interested."
"Forget it."

2 **Leave the situation.** You don't have to explain your reasons for saying no. When you walk away, your actions speak louder than words.

3 **Ignore the offer.** Pretend to read a book. Be distracted by someone else. Just don't listen.

T E E N T I P S

4 **Make an excuse.** Think of something you could or should be doing instead.
"I've got other plans."
"I have to practice _____ ." (the piano, football, dancing, etc.)
"I promised I'd be home by _____ o'clock."

5 **Change the subject.** Pick a topic that will get their interest or take them by surprise.

6 **Make a joke.** Use humor and say:
"Are you kidding? If I did that, my reputation might improve."
"Sorry, I'd like to but I need to spend more time with my plants."
"No thanks. I'm not into body pollution."

7 **Act shocked.** Show that you can't believe what your friends have asked you to do. Roll your eyes, let your mouth drop open, and say:
"I can't believe what I just heard."
"I know you didn't mean that. How did I pick such crazy friends?"

8 **Try flattery.** Say something kind and thoughtful to one of your friends.
"You're too smart to really mean that."
"You're too good a friend. I don't want to see you do anything crazy and get hurt."

THIS SCHOOL SAYS "NO" TO DRUG ABUSE

Just say no

"a symbol of commitment for young people everywhere"

9 **Suggest a better idea.** Suggest something else to do—say it with excitement and enthusiasm.
"Hey, I've got a good idea. Let's go get pizza or burgers."
"Why don't we _____ ?" (go biking, practice shooting baskets, play a video game, etc.)

10 **Return the challenge.** If someone calls you a "chicken" because you won't join them, throw the challenge right back with a comment such as:
"Scared to do it by yourself?"
"Yeah, I'm a chicken. Anybody smart would be."
"I'd rather by a chicken than a jailbird."

HUGS NOT DRUGS
TWIN LAKES HOSPITAL

Suicide WARNING Twelve Warning Signs

Each year, more than 8,000 teenagers commit suicide. Suicide is now the third leading cause of death for 15- to 24-year-olds. Many teens who commit suicide feel unable to handle the pressures in their lives—at home, at school, or with their friends.

For many teens, attempting to commit suicide is a way of asking for help or of getting attention. Many teens who tried suicide later admitted that they hoped they would be found before it was too late. Fortunately, they were—others were not so lucky.

Professional counselors feel that many suicides can be prevented if help is obtained when warning signs appear. How can you know if someone is feeling suicidal? Here are some warning signals:

- A sudden change in behavior characterized by withdrawal, rebellion, irritability, or taking extreme risks.

- A dramatic change in eating or sleep patterns—eating or sleeping too much or too little.

- Social withdrawal—dropping out of activities, quitting a job, or spending less time with friends.

- Sudden drop in grades or performance; lateness or absence from school or work.

TEEN TIPS

◆ A depressed mood—crying for no apparent reason, trouble concentrating, apathy.

◆ Loss of interest in personal grooming.

◆ Increased use or abuse of alcohol or drugs.

◆ Suicide threats or statements revealing a desire to die: "I can't take it anymore" or "I won't be around much longer."

◆ Giving or throwing away personal possessions; paying off old debts.

◆ Preoccupation with songs, poems, or movies dealing with death, dying, or suicide.

◆ Buying a means of suicide, such as pills, rope, or a weapon.

◆ A sense of failure or feelings of shame or guilt.

The best way to help a person who is suicidal is to let him or her know that you are aware of a change in behavior—and are concerned. Try to get this person to seek professional help. Talk to your parent, a teacher, a counselor, or a suicide prevention hot line for advice.

CHILD CARE AND DEVELOPMENT

Children
and You

OBJECTIVES

This chapter will help you to:

- Explain the rewards of caregiving.
- Identify the needs of children that are met by parenting.
- Explain the difference between parenting and parenthood.
- Explain the roles of nurturing and guidance in a child's development.
- Describe the resources used in parenting.

WORDS TO REMEMBER

caregiver   nurture
guidance   parenting

Monica is feeling good; she is happy about the money she has earned babysitting and pleased that her day has gone so well. She is proud of the way she has handled the Vega children. Mrs. Vega even complimented her on her work and told her that she recommended her to a neighbor who needed a babysitter two days a week.

Monica thinks of herself as a babysitter, but she can also be called a caregiver. A **caregiver** is someone who takes care of children or who cares for people who are sick or elderly. Because Monica works only occasionally, she is called a part-time caregiver. The people who take the main responsibility for rearing children, usually the parents, are called main caregivers.

Rewards of Caregiving

Many young people enjoy working as part-time caregivers. They often begin to learn the skills they need to take care of children by caring for younger brothers and sisters. Then, when they feel comfortable enough to manage other people's children, they seek jobs as babysitters, camp counselors, and similar occupations. The skills they develop and the trust adults place in them help to build their self-esteem.

Through her babysitting job, Monica is earning extra money, learning skills for the future, and showing that she is a dependable and responsible employee. Monica's goals in this job are to take good care of the children, to please her employer, and to earn money.

If she has children of her own someday, she will find that her child-care goal is somewhat different. She will still want to do a good job, but for different reasons. Her goal then will be long-term: to rear happy, healthy children who will grow into responsible, well-adjusted adults.

Many people, including grandparents, older brothers and sisters, and babysitters, can be caregivers. Have you had any experience being a caregiver?

If you are either a part-time or full-time caregiver, you have to make many decisions. The decision-making skills that you learned in Chapter 5 can help you.

When Monica sat for the Vega children, she had to decide:

- What can I do to stop the baby's crying?
- How will I give her a bottle and fix lunch for the older child at the same time?
- What activities are fun for a two-year-old?

By making decisions such as these, Monica is developing her management skills.

As a part-time babysitter, Monica was responsible for the Vega children for only a few hours. If she were the children's parent, she would be responsible for them for years, and she would have to make dozens of decisions daily that would affect them throughout their lives.

What Is Parenting?

Parenting involves taking care of children in all the ways that children require. It means meeting children's physical, emotional, mental, and social needs.

Parenting is not the same as *parenthood*, which means to be a father or mother of a child. Many people use parenting skills, including parents and babysitters. In some families, parenting is shared by the parents, grandparents, older brothers and sisters, and child caregivers. Parenting involves three basic skills: providing physical care, nurturing, and giving guidance.

Physical Care

- **Food.** Caregivers are responsible for providing nutritious meals and snacks to help children grow and develop. They should offer a wide variety of foods to ensure giving children a balanced diet with all of the vitamins, minerals, and nutrients that growing bodies need.

  Infants begin by drinking either milk from their mother or formula. During the first year, they begin eating strained foods and, later, food cut in small pieces. As they get older, children can eat the same meals as adults.

  Caregivers should avoid giving children rich, spicy, or fried foods, which can upset a child's digestion, or foods that are high in sugar, salt, or fat. They should also avoid giving very young children foods like nuts and popcorn, which can get stuck in a child's throat.

- **Clothing.** Caregivers must provide proper clothing for children so that they are kept warm and dry. Infants need fresh diapers—often! Other good clothes for infants include T-shirts and one-piece outfits such as footed sleepers.

  Once children are able to dress and undress themselves, they need clothes that they can put on and take off easily. Whatever their age, children need clothing that is appropriate for the weather. For example, in cold weather a child needs to wear a coat, hat, boots, and mittens. In addition, caregivers are responsible for making sure that the children's clothing is kept clean and in good repair.

- **Rest.** Children need more sleep than adults. They need naps during the day and many hours of sleep at night. It is up to the caregiver to keep the children on the same routine each day and night so they can get the rest they need.

Newborns can sleep in cradles or carriers. Once they are larger, they should sleep in cribs. Since they can hurt themselves by hitting the crib sides, the crib should have padded bumpers. Washable sheets and a waterproof pad covering the mattress are also necessary.

■ **Hygiene.** Children need to be bathed and washed when they are infants. Once they are older, they should be taught to wash themselves and brush their teeth, but even after they learn these things, they will still need supervision. When they are ready, young children also need toilet training so they can learn to go to the bathroom by themselves.

■ **Safe environment.** Children are not aware of the dangers of stairs, electric outlets, or poisons. Adults must protect them from accidents that their exploring can cause. Chapter 21 explains how to make the home safe for children.

Nurturing

Caregivers are also responsible for nurturing children. To **nurture** means to help children learn, and it involves providing love, support, attention, and encouragement.

Children are constantly learning because the whole world is new to them. To help them learn, they need stimulation: chances to see, hear, touch, taste, and smell. Infants learn by exploring with their senses. Older children build on this base as they experience even more. They learn a variety of skills, from walking and talking to reading and climbing. They also must learn how to get along with others. Children first learn how to relate to family members, then how to relate to friends. Chapter 20 offers some ideas on how to help children learn.

Children need a safe, stimulating environment where they can play and explore their surroundings.

Caregivers also provide children with love, affection, and a sense of security. Children need someone to comfort them when they are hurt or upset. They need to know that the people who are responsible for them really care about them. Showing affection can be as simple as saying a few kind words when a child scrapes a knee or praising a drawing when a child proudly displays it.

Guidance

Finally, caregivers need to provide **guidance** to children. In other words, they need to help children understand what type of behavior is acceptable and what type is not. For example, kicking a younger brother or sister is not acceptable. Young children do not yet know right from wrong. If given complete freedom, they may be confused about what to do and may be frightened.

Caregivers help children by setting limits: they tell them when to go to bed, what to eat for a snack, which programs to watch on TV. Of course, children may *test* limits and purposely do the wrong thing. They are not trying to be bad; they only want to make sure that the caregiver meant it.

Setting these limits is the responsibility of the parents. Part-time caregivers simply remind children what the limits are, and they get the children to stick to them. Of course, it's the responsibility of the part-time caregivers to find out from the parents what the limits are.

Nurturing involves comforting children when they are unhappy, hurt, or scared.

Resources for Parenting

When you parent a child, you are, in effect, a manager. You are responsible for the child's needs, activities, and behavior. Parenting is demanding work. It requires knowledge, skills, and personal qualities such as understanding, patience, love, and respect. Some of these things can be learned in classes and by reading. Others must be learned through experience.

Knowledge

Effective parenting requires knowing about children. You wouldn't expect a one-year-old to speak in complete sentences. Similarly, you wouldn't expect a five-year-old to write a book report. A caregiver (whether it is the parent or babysitter) must understand the stages of development that children reach at various ages. Then, he or she will know what to expect from the child and how to respond.

Skills

If you become a caregiver, you must learn more than just how to take care of children physically. Along with bathing an infant and dressing a two-year-old, you may need to know how to stop an argument between two children, how to deal with a child's fears, and how to help with a child's homework. You will also need to be able to plan appropriate activities, communicate positively, and act wisely and quickly in an emergency.

Personal Qualities

As a caregiver you need certain personal qualities in order to deal effectively with children. Basically, you need to have an understanding of the needs and abilities of children so that you know what to expect from them. You also need patience so you can remain calm even in the most difficult circumstances, such as when a child repeatedly throws food on the floor. In addition, you need to love and respect children.

Are you concerned about what you are teaching children by the example you set? That is a sign that you respect them. There is a good chance that the children who are shown respect will, in turn, learn to show respect to others.

A realistic understanding of yourself is the key to deciding whether you would make a good caregiver. That means knowing your strengths and weaknesses. For example, if a child became frustrated or angry because she couldn't tie her shoes, how would you react? Would you be patient and sympathetic?

Approaches to Parenting

In the past, most people believed that everyone automatically knew how to be a good parent. Now society recognizes that parenting involves skills and abilities that are usually learned through practice.

This does not mean that there is only one correct approach to parenting. Different parents have different values and philosophies that affect the way they rear their children. What works for one family may not work for another, but there are some characteristics that are common to every successful approach.

Whatever the approach, for it to succeed, parents must provide for their children's physical, mental, social, and emotional needs. They must also give children care, guidance, and a loving and supportive atmosphere.

Parenting Skills: A Learning Process

Knowledge is the most important resource that you can use as a caregiver. The more you know about how children develop and behave, and the more parenting skills you learn, the better you will be at meeting the needs of the children you care for. Here are some ways that you can acquire the knowledge you need to be a good caregiver:

- **Ask your own parents or other knowledgeable adults.** Your parents are experienced caregivers who can provide you with a lot of useful information and help. Don't be embarrassed to ask them for help if you find yourself in a situation you can't handle. It is much better to get help from experienced adults than to make a mistake that might harm or endanger the children you are caring for.

- **Read about caregiving.** Your library and local bookstores have dozens of books and magazines on child care that offer sound advice and very specific information about how to care for children of all ages. Some books tell you about games you can play with young children, others tell you how to make nutritious snacks, and still others advise you about how to handle illnesses and emergencies.

- **Take a course.** Check around your community to see who offers child care courses. The Red Cross holds babysitting classes, and the Girl Scouts offer child care merit badges. Some school districts, hospitals, and community service organizations also offer child-care courses.

- **Learn by doing.** Volunteer at a child care center, nursing home, or hospital where you can learn caregiving skills under the supervision of trained professionals. Volunteering is also an excellent way to find out whether you are interested in a caregiving career.

Think It Through

1. List five topics related to children that you would like to know more about. Where would you go to find this information?
2. If you were considering a child care career, what would you begin doing?

CHAPTER

18 REVIEW

Reviewing the Facts

1. How do the responsibilities of a main caregiver and a part-time caregiver differ? How are they similar?
2. What are some of the rewards of caregiving?
3. What is the difference between parenting and parenthood?
4. What are the three basic parenting skills?
5. What physical needs do children have?
6. Name two ways to nurture a child.
7. What is guidance? Why do children need it?
8. List three personal qualities that you need to be a good caregiver.

Sharing Your Ideas

1. What resources do you possess that would help you be an effective caregiver? What additional resources do you need?
2. If you were interviewing people for the job of caregiver, what two questions would you ask first? Why?

Applying Your Skills

1. Recalling a Decision. Identify a person in your life who has provided a parenting role in your development. How did the person prepare for the role of a caregiver? What was the most serious decision the caregiver faced in your presence, and how did he or she handle it? Write a brief report.

2. Planning for a Babysitting Job. Assume that you have been hired to babysit for a two-year-old child. Read the section of a child development textbook, a parenting book, or an encyclopedia that describes the developmental stage of toddlers. What limits would you need to set for the child? How could you provide a nurturing environment?

3. Selecting Important Qualities. Imagine that you are a parent and that you are looking for someone to take care of your child two afternoons a week. Write a want ad for your local newspaper listing the personal qualities of a caregiver that you think are most important.

Ages and Stages

OBJECTIVES

This chapter will help you to:

- Explain how development occurs in stages.
- List the four stages of development.
- Describe the physical, mental, and social characteristics of each stage.
- Explain how children with special needs can learn to develop to their full potential.

WORDS TO REMEMBER

developmental tasks
fine-motor skills

gross-motor skills
hand-eye coordination
parallel play
reflex
stages

Most nine-month-old babies can crawl, and by the time they are a year old, most are able to walk. Two-year-olds can speak a few words, and by the time they are three and a half, they can talk in sentences. Walking, talking, drawing, eating with a knife and fork, and learning colors and letters are all examples of **developmental tasks**: the skills and abilities that children acquire as they grow.

Nearly all children master these tasks in the same order. They crawl before they walk and speak in single words before they talk in sentences. Children build on what they've already learned. Walking becomes running and scribbling becomes drawing.

A major function of caregivers is to encourage and help children master these developmental tasks. If adults do not help children in such tasks as learning to talk, the children will not grow and develop properly.

Stages of Development

Researchers have found that children, after birth, go through four developmental stages:

- Infant (birth to one year).
- Toddler (one to three years).
- Preschooler (three to five years).
- School-age (five to ten years).

These **stages** are periods during which the child can perform certain tasks. The chart on page 184 shows what some of the developmental tasks are for the first three stages of development. It is important to remember that the ages given are just averages. Some children develop more rapidly and some more slowly. One child may walk at nine months and another may not walk until fourteen months. However, both are developing normally.

Remember, too, that the stages are not rigid categories. An infant does not suddenly become a toddler the day after his first birthday. The change is very gradual. Still, you can refer to this table as you read the chapters in this unit to learn what things a young child has probably learned.

Infant

For the first year of a baby's life, growth and development are very rapid. Most of the changes are fairly predictable and occur in the same sequence.

Physical Development

Although she is only a few days old, Gloria is already quite a complex individual. She has strong **reflexes**, or automatic, involuntary responses. If you stroke her cheek, she turns her head toward your hand and sucks. If you place your finger in her palm, she will curl her tiny fingers and grasp it tightly. Gloria cries to signal unhappiness. She can see, hear, taste, smell, and touch.

As she gets older, Gloria will learn about shapes and textures by putting objects in her mouth. Bringing objects to her mouth will help her develop **hand-eye coordination**, the ability to get her eyes and her muscles working together so that she can make complex movements. Batting a baseball or eating with a fork are examples of movements that require good hand-eye coordination.

Stages, Ages, and Tasks

Stage (approximate age)	Physical Tasks	Mental Tasks	Social Tasks
Infant (birth to 1 year)	Lifts head (1–2 months) Grasps rattle (3 months) Rolls over (3–5 months) Puts objects in mouth (4–5 months) Sits (5–9 months) Crawls (5–9 months) Begins teething (6 months) Eats finger foods (9 months) Stands (9–12 months)	Cries to communicate (birth) Follows object with eyes (1 month) Babbles (3 months) Forms sense of self (6 months) Explores by touch and taste (7 months)	Develops trust of caregivers (1–6 months) Smiles (3–5 months) Recognizes own name (4–12 months) Is afraid of strangers (6–8 months)
Toddler (1–3 years)	Walks (12–15 months) Climbs out of crib (12–15 months) Picks up small objects (12–15 months) Runs (15–18 months) Climbs stairs (15–22 months) Eats with spoon (15–22 months) Can undress self (18–30 months) Begins toilet training (1½–3 years)	Imitates words (12 months) Follows simple instructions (12 months) Points to objects when named (12–18 months) Makes single-word sentences (12–18 months) Makes 2-word sentences (18–24 months)	Learns meaning of "no" (12–15 months) Waves "bye-bye" (18–24 months) Has temper tantrums (2–2½ years) Can play in groups (2–3 years)
Preschooler (3–5 years)	Runs, jumps, hops, skips (3 years) Rides a tricycle (3 years) Feeds and dresses self (3 years) Climbs jungle gym (4 years) Draws recognizable pictures (4 years) Walks straight line (5 years) Skips rope (5 years) Pours liquids (5 years) Uses knife and fork (5 years)	Attention span lengthens (throughout) Identifies objects in pictures (3 years) Speaks 5- to 6-word sentences (3½ years) Learns counting and colors (4–5 years) Repeats rhymes, songs (4 years)	Develops sense of self (throughout) Begins using simple manners and grooming (3½ years) Begins cooperative group play (4 years) Learns fair play (5 years)

Gloria's first year will be full of tremendous change and growth. During this period, she will develop her **gross-motor skills.** These skills enable her to control the large muscles of her body, such as her arms and legs. As her muscle control develops, she will roll over, sit up, and finally stand.

Mental Development

At the age of one month, Gloria is awake for only short periods of the day, but she is beginning to take notice of the world. She will follow a toy with her eyes when it is moved in front of her face.

As her vision develops, Gloria will become more aware of the mobile hanging in her crib, and she will recognize familiar faces. With a rattle, she will begin to learn about cause and effect: if she shakes the rattle, it makes a sound.

At first, Gloria's only way of communicating is by crying. Around her third month, she will begin to use sound to communicate pleasure. She will gurgle and coo at familiar people and toys.

When Gloria reaches the age of eight to twelve months, she will learn that people or toys exist even after they are gone from sight. This concept is called object permanence.

Social Development

From the time babies are born, they begin to develop a sense of trust. They learn very quickly how to respond to others so that their needs are met.

Gloria will smile for the first time when she is about three months old. At six to eight months, she may become afraid of new people. This is probably because she is learning to tell familiar and unfamiliar faces apart.

Infants begin to develop a sense of themselves very early. Caregivers often provide babies with unbreakable mirrors so that they can see what they look like. Within a few months of birth, they begin to understand that they are separate from their parents.

During the first year, babies develop very rapidly—physically, mentally, and socially. Their self-concept is already forming.

Reading aloud helps a child learn to talk. The child can listen to the sounds of the words and imitate them.

Toddler

Physical growth usually slows a bit as an infant becomes a toddler. During this stage, however, children master an amazing number of physical, mental, and social skills.

Physical Development

Manuel's first steps were a thrill for him and his family. Once Manuel felt steady, he wanted to walk everywhere, including up every flight of stairs. After he became more sure of himself (he was then one and a half to two years old), he often wanted to run everywhere as fast as he could. His gross-motor skills were improving every day.

Manuel was also beginning to gain more control over his smaller muscles, such as those in his hands. He was developing the **fine-motor skills** he will need to be able to feed and dress himself and, later, to draw and write. Of course, Manuel's parents encouraged these efforts—even though they had to pay special attention to some skills, such as Manuel's being able to climb out of his crib and high chair.

Mental Development

Much mental growth occurs during the toddler years. Manuel will go from speaking single words to saying short phrases and finally whole sentences. He will build on his knowledge of cause and effect by noticing that if he lets something go, it falls.

As a toddler, Manuel will learn a lot about size and space and about how objects relate to one another. He will learn which object is larger and which is smaller and which objects go on top of or inside other objects. During this stage, children may spend a lot of time putting blocks and toys together and taking them apart, or playing with groups of objects, such as pots and pans. Manuel will also learn what tasks objects are meant to do. He will learn, for example, that spoons help you eat and sweaters keep you warm.

Social Development

Sometimes parents are concerned because their toddlers aren't interested in playing with other children. However, this is natural for children this age. Toddlers tend to play alongside each other, rather than together. This is called **parallel play.**

Around the age of two, children get caught in a struggle between their dependency on others and their desire for independence. The struggle usually shows up in fits of frustration. Often, Manuel wants to do everything for himself and realizes that he can't. At the same time, he resents his parents' efforts to help. When he isn't able to feed himself, climb into his high chair, or put together a puzzle, he may have a temper tantrum because he is frustrated. Adults can help by providing children with objects to assist them: low tables, step stools, and clothes they can put on by themselves. Adults should also be patient and allow children enough time to do things by themselves.

Little by little, Manuel is beginning to acquire the ideas that will form his self-concept: the knowledge that he is unique, that he has his own feelings, that others have certain feelings about him. Many of Manuel's early attitudes about himself will come from people who care for him. Caregivers must help children to feel good about themselves and must promote their self-esteem.

The Preschooler and the School-Age Child

Preschoolers and school-age children practice and refine their physical abilities. They also ask lots of questions and develop their communications skills. In addition, they develop friendships and become more independent.

Physical Development

From the age of four until the teen years, the changes that occur in children's bodies are not as dramatic as those that took place in infancy. During the preschool years and middle childhood, children continue to get bigger and stronger and to have more control over their bodies and emotions.

Children at these stages eat the same food as adults. By the time they start school, they can handle such personal tasks as bathing and dressing. They also learn to be aware of their own feelings of wellness and illness.

Mental Development

The exploring and testing that began during infancy will continue as a child grows. This is a time for exploring, asking questions, and thinking about things.

The preschool stage is when children refine their thinking processes. They learn to count and name colors, and many children also learn to identify the letters of the alphabet. By three or four, preschoolers have mastered the ability to speak in sentences, and many of them can print their own names.

School-age children build on these skills to master more complex tasks. They learn arithmetic and reading, and they refine their fine-motor skills so they can draw and write.

Children in these stages are able to sit still doing one thing for a longer time than toddlers can. These are also the years when children's imagination plays an important role, when children may brag or have scary dreams.

Social Development

During the preschool years, a child begins to learn what it means to enjoy the company of others. Around age four or five, a child is likely to single out another child as a best friend.

In day care, nursery school, and kindergarten, children learn social behavior: how to get along in a group, how to share, how to play together. Children at this stage also learn how to argue and how to compete. Winning contests becomes very important to them.

Belonging to a group is important for school-age children, but during this time they continue to need close family relationships. It is important that they have acceptance from family members, and encouragement and reassurance from caregivers.

Children with Special Needs

Some children need special attention. They may be mentally, physically, or emotionally disabled. In some cases, the disabilities are present at birth; in others, they occur as a result of an accident or illness. Other children may have certain learning difficulties or may be unusually bright. All these children are children with special needs.

Physical Development

It's important to remember that children with physical disabilities are children *first*. They have the same basic needs as other children—to be loved, to be cared for, and to be stimulated. Like any child, Paul, who uses a wheelchair, needs to develop self-confidence. Colette, who wears leg braces, is just as concerned about what she wears as any other child. Emil's hearing loss affects some parts of his life, but not his involvement in sports.

Children with physical disabilities may need special exercise or equipment, but they still need to be given the chance to help themselves as soon as possible. Help them learn to wash and dress themselves. Give them chores that they are capable of doing so that they will feel better about themselves.

Mental Development

The mental development of children with special needs varies greatly. Some children are mentally retarded. Their mental capabilities may develop very slowly, and development may stop at a low level. Other children have learning disabilities. Still others are mentally gifted. All of these children need special attention.

Children who are mentally retarded must be given every chance to develop their skills, abilities, and interests. They may be slower in completing a developmental task, but eventually many are able to do it. Encouraging these children, as well as rewarding them for what they do learn, can lead to further learning. Whenever possible, emphasize what children *can* do.

Children with learning disabilities are of normal intelligence, and some may even be very bright. They just have diffi-

Children with disabilities have the same needs and go through the same stages of development as other children.

culty mastering certain mental skills. Some children find reading or mathematics difficult, for example, because letters or numbers appear inverted or backward to them. These children require extra help in school so they can keep up with their classmates.

Children who are unusually intelligent need special attention, too. Many schools offer extra projects or special classes to stimulate and interest gifted children. This enables the children to do challenging work and still take part in regular school activities.

Social Development

Children with special needs have the same social and emotional needs that all children do. They need to make friends and to learn how to get along with others. As with all children, the way they feel about themselves will influence their relationships with others.

Sometimes a child's social behavior can indicate an emotional disturbance. For example, children who are very withdrawn, or constantly afraid, or very aggressive may be emotionally disturbed. Such children might need professional counseling.

All children, regardless of their abilities, share a common need. They all need to feel loved and accepted by their family and friends.

INTERPERSONAL SKILLS

Tempering a Tantrum

Have you ever seen a child throw a temper tantrum? Tantrums often occur when children become frustrated because they cannot do something they want to do, such as unbutton a coat. Tantrums may also happen when children are denied something they want, such as a toy or an ice-cream cone. They may fall on the floor and cry and kick for several minutes. Some also bang their heads against the floor or pull their hair.

If you are caring for a child who throws a tantrum, here are some ways to handle it:

- **Try to distract the child.** If children have a tantrum because they want something, try to offer another object. Turn the children's attention to something else to help them forget what they wanted.

- **Remain calm.** Remember that occasional temper tantrums are normal behavior for children in the toddler stage. Stay calm and talk soothingly. Losing your own temper and yelling at the child will not stop the tantrum; it will only make things worse.

- **Ignore the tantrum.** Many experts believe the best way to deal with a tantrum is to ignore it. If you walk out of the room, the child has no audience and gets no reward for the tantrum. Usually it will soon stop.

- **Physically restrain the child.** When children bang their heads against the floor or act violently during a tantrum, they may harm themselves physically. These children need to be held or hugged tightly until the tantrum subsides.

- **Remove the child from the situation.** Many children throw tantrums in the middle of a shopping mall or supermarket. The best thing to do is pick the child up and leave. If you take children home whenever they have a tantrum in a public place, they soon learn that one of the costs of tantrums is losing the pleasure of an outing.

Think It Through

1. If you were caring for a young child, what are three things you would do to help avoid a temper tantrum?

2. Why do you think that temper tantrums are most likely to occur in children between the ages of two and four? How can tantrums be redirected into more socially acceptable behavior?

CHAPTER

19 REVIEW

Reviewing the Facts

1. What are the four stages of children's development?
2. Define *reflexes* and give two examples of reflexes that infants possess.
3. What is hand-eye coordination? Give an example.
4. What can an infant learn by shaking a rattle?
5. What is object permanence? At what age does a child learn about it?
6. What is the difference between gross-motor skills and fine-motor skills? Give an example of each.
7. At what stage does parallel play become common?
8. Describe the mental development that occurs during the pre-school stage.
9. What is the main thing to remember about children with special needs?

Sharing Your Ideas

1. Why is it important for caregivers to know what changes they can expect to see in a child at each stage of development?
2. Why is the age of a child not always a determining factor in what a child can do?

Applying Your Skills

1. Classifying Activities. Make a list of ten activities that you remember from your early childhood. Then beside each activity on your list, state if it was a physical, mental, or social task. Identify those activities that helped build fine-motor skills and those that helped build gross-motor skills.

2. Listing Services. Use the local telephone directory to find out what programs are available in your community to help meet the needs of gifted and disabled children. Prepare a list of all the places that offer such services.

3. Sequencing Events. With two other students, make a time line showing the physical, mental, and social changes that take place in a child between the ages of one and three. Each student should be responsible for recording one type of development.

The Importance of Play

Playing comes so naturally to children that you may never have given it much thought. If you sometimes take care of a younger brother or sister or your neighbors' children, you've probably noticed how children enjoy playing.

When children play there is more going on than just amusement. Playing teaches children about their environment and how to interact with others. It also influences how they grow. Only recently have experts realized the great importance of play in children's learning.

Play and Development

Playing helps children develop in many different ways. It helps them develop physically by giving them the opportunity to exercise their muscles and improve their fine- and gross-motor skills. Play also helps children to grow mentally. When they put puzzles together, stack blocks, and play with nesting toys, they are also learning about sizes and shapes, colors, and counting. Board games and books help them learn numbers and letters. Play also helps children develop socially because it gives them practice in sharing and taking turns.

Children change as they grow and develop, and so does their play. An infant develops his fine-motor skills by grasping toys and bringing them to his mouth. A preschooler improves her fine-motor ability by making drawings.

When you know about the stages of development, you can provide children with opportunities to play that match their skill levels. Remember, though, that children develop at different rates and have different interests. One child can be ready for one kind of play before another child of the same age. To get the best results, adapt your play suggestions to children's actual skills.

How Infants Play

Infants play by exploring the world through their senses. Adults can help them to do this by spending time with them, by playing games with them, and by providing them with safe, interesting objects that they can enjoy and learn from.

Young children learn through their senses. They need toys they can see, touch, suck, and hear.

Here are some suggestions on how to play with infants:

■ Stimulate their senses by holding and cuddling them, by singing and playing music for them.

■ Talk and read to them so they become familiar with words.

■ Surround them with **sensory toys**: objects to touch that have different textures and shapes, rattles and squeak toys they can listen to, brightly colored objects and mobiles they can look at and watch, and teething rings they can put in their mouth.

■ Once they can sit up (at about five months), prop them up in a comfortable, safe chair, or in a playpen, or on the floor, so they can enjoy different sights and sounds.

■ Play games with them like peekaboo, funny faces, and hide-and-seek.

■ Give them new toys occasionally so they can make new discoveries.

How Toddlers Play

Toddlers are busy developing their gross-motor skills, so they need lots of space to walk and run. At this age, children love large dolls, wooden or soft plastic vehicles, balls, books, play telephones, and housekeeping toys, such as shopping baskets, vacuum cleaners, and brooms.

Here are some hints for playing with toddlers:

■ Set aside time for active play so they can exercise their muscles and use up their store of energy.

■ Be prepared to change games or activities when toddlers become bored or restless.

■ Help toddlers develop language skills by talking and reading to them. Using simple terms, describe what you are doing or what you see on a walk.

■ Children at this age have not yet learned to share or take turns, so don't be disturbed if they try to take toys away from other children or hit them. Be patient and correct their behavior in a gentle way.

Young children like to imitate adults. Can you explain how going shopping might influence this child's physical, mental, and social development?

Choosing Toys and Equipment

If you have ever gone shopping for a birthday present for a child, you will know that there are literally thousands of toys to choose from. Your first concerns were probably to find something that the child would enjoy, and that was suitable for the child's age. There is another important factor that you need to consider when buying a toy for a child: is it safe?

Here are some important safety points that you need to consider when choosing toys:

- Does the toy have any small parts that a young child could swallow or that could get stuck in the child's ears or nostrils? (Young children *do* put things in unlikely places!)

- Are the decorations, such as the eyes on stuffed animals and dolls, firmly attached so that the child can't pull them off?

- Are there any sharp edges or points that could cause cuts?

- Is the toy strongly constructed, so it won't break? Broken toys might have sharp and dangerous edges.

- If the toy is made of fabric, is it washable? If not, it could become unhygienic.

- If the toy is for a crib, is it designed for safety? You should avoid anything that has strings that could get wrapped around a baby's neck.

Choosing equipment for children demands a similar attention to safety. When buying cribs, playpens, swings, and jungle gyms, caregivers need to pay attention to what *might* happen, and to make their purchase cautiously.

For example, when choosing cribs, buyers should make sure that the bars or slats are no more than 2 1/2 inches apart. With wider spacing, the infant could get his or her head lodged between the bars. Buyers should also ensure that the mechanism that allows the side of the crib to be dropped cannot be accidentally released.

Swings and jungle gyms should be strongly constructed. There should be no rough edges or exposed bolts, and no parts that could pinch or trap a young child.

Ensuring safety is an important responsibility of caregivers. Remember, when you are buying toys, or taking care of children, those children don't know what can harm them. It's up to you to protect them, by choosing safe toys and equipment.

Think It Through

1. In what ways can product labels help you determine if a toy is safe?
2. What safety measures would you take if you were babysitting for children who had a jungle gym?

How Preschoolers Play

Preschoolers are proud of themselves and their abilities. Their muscles are developing rapidly, and their favorite words are "Watch me!" as they run, jump, and climb.

Preschoolers are also mastering many fine-motor skills. Good toys for this age group include blunt-edged scissors, coloring books and crayons, finger and poster paints, modeling clay, plastic and wooden construction sets, dolls with changeable clothes, small cars and trucks, tricycles, and swings and jungle gyms.

Children at this age tire quickly. Some still take a daily nap, and all need a change of pace at the end of an hour of active play. That is the time for gluing a collage or looking at a book.

Because preschoolers' abilities are increasing quickly, they want and need many opportunities for learning. Here are some suggestions:

- Taking them on walks through the neighborhood or to the local store. Talk about whatever you see along the way.

Preschoolers like to dress up in old clothes and pretend to be other people. This role playing helps them develop emotionally and socially.

- Encouraging questions and safe exploration.
- Helping them resolve their disputes and learn to take turns with their favorite toys when they are playing in groups.

Can you remember dressing up in your mom's or dad's old clothing and playing house? Maybe you had clothes or props for playing cowboys or pirates. Preschoolers are very interested in using their imagination. They enjoy **role playing**, pretending to be someone else. Role playing helps them express their feelings and practice the behaviors they are learning. Providing children with old clothes and props will amuse them for a long time.

Passive Activities

Passive activities are those that you watch or listen to, but do not join in. Watching a baseball game is passive, as is watching television or listening to a story.

Although passive activities don't get children into the action, they still affect them. Children learn how to do things by imitating people they watch, and their ideas and attitudes are affected by what they see and hear.

Reading Books

Young children love to be read to. They especially like it when you vary the pitch of your voice and use facial expressions and body movements to act out the characters in a book. Try to get them to join in whenever possible. They can cheer for heroes, boo the bad guys, and repeat simple rhymes as you read.

If the children are old enough to read simple books, let them read to you or to younger children. Help them with words they don't know and praise them for the parts they do well. Don't be too quick to help, though. They may just need a little more time to figure out a word.

Here are some tips on reading:

- Choose books and stories that are appropriate for the child's age. Most children have favorite books they love to have read to them again and again.
- Let the children look at the pictures in the book you are reading for as long as they like.
- Ask questions about the pictures or the story in order to involve the child. Let the child turn the page.
- Act out the stories when you're done.

Watching Television

Some caregivers use television to keep children busy. They might let children watch television so they can do other things without any interruption. It's important to keep in mind that television programs can have a great impact on children. They may contain violence or scary situations that children do not understand.

Watching television can be a good change of pace for children, but, like anything, too much of it can be harmful. Children should not be watching television because they can't think of anything else to do. Challenge yourself to find interesting activities for children instead of relying on television.

If the children do watch television, you should get into the habit of sitting and watching it with them. Be ready to discuss what is going on and to explain situations that may confuse them. Turn off the set or turn to another channel if the program is not suitable for children.

Children learn through actual experiences. What might these children learn by seeing live snakes rather than photographs?

Watching Real Things

Children are fascinated by watching people do things. You can use that fascination as part of playing and learning. If you are looking for a change of pace, let the children help you make brownies or watch the neighbor work in his garden. You might take a walk and look at colorful flowers or watch a building being constructed. You could even just sit on the front porch or stoop together and watch people go by.

Playing in Groups

If you are taking care of more than one child, it is sometimes difficult to make sure that everyone is fully included in the activities you plan. It is important, though, that no child feels that he or she is being left out. To prevent this, plan activities in which everyone has to work together toward a common goal, such as putting together a puzzle or collecting rocks.

Each child has different abilities. It is easy for children to feel like failures if they are playing something in which they are not as good as the others around them. If you see that happening to some of the children in the group, suggest a different game, or help them master the game they are not good at by giving them practice.

Competitive Sports

If the children are playing competitive sports, be sure that some are not left out from the start. A horrible feeling for a child is to be chosen last for teams all the time. Avoid the problem by finding an inventive way to choose teams. You might put all the children who like chocolate ice cream on one side and all those who prefer strawberry on the other.

Finally, in any team game, try to play down the importance of winning. Make it clear that the main goal is to have fun.

CHAPTER

20 REVIEW

Reviewing the Facts

1. How does play help children develop?
2. What should you do when a toddler you are caring for grabs a toy from another child?
3. How do preschoolers benefit from role playing?
4. Give three examples of passive play activities.
5. How can a caregiver turn reading into an active learning experience?
6. How can television be harmful to children?
7. How can a caregiver help a child who is not as good at a game as the others in the group?

Sharing Your Ideas

1. Some experts claim that the only toys a child needs are a book, a ball, and a doll. Do you agree? Why or why not? If not, what other toys do you think a child needs?
2. Why do you think children enjoy role playing so much? What do you think they gain from it? In what ways could it be harmful?

Applying Your Skills

 1. Using Imagination. Make a list of five of your favorite childhood toys. Use your imagination to suggest a substitute for each toy, using recycled items from your home. For extra credit, make the homemade toy and bring it to class.

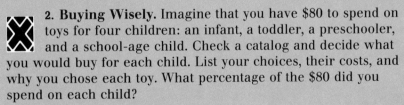 **2. Buying Wisely.** Imagine that you have $80 to spend on toys for four children: an infant, a toddler, a preschooler, and a school-age child. Check a catalog and decide what you would buy for each child. List your choices, their costs, and why you chose each toy. What percentage of the $80 did you spend on each child?

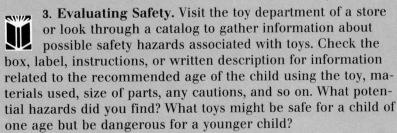 **3. Evaluating Safety.** Visit the toy department of a store or look through a catalog to gather information about possible safety hazards associated with toys. Check the box, label, instructions, or written description for information related to the recommended age of the child using the toy, materials used, size of parts, any cautions, and so on. What potential hazards did you find? What toys might be safe for a child of one age but be dangerous for a younger child?

Care and Safety

OBJECTIVES

This chapter will help you to:

- List and describe ways to meet children's physical, mental, emotional, and social needs.
- Discuss the importance of setting limits and communicating positively.
- Describe the basics of accident prevention and first aid for children.

WORDS TO REMEMBER

child abuse
childproof
distract
first aid
Heimlich maneuver

When you care for children, you have to be able to meet all of their needs. Children need someone to feed and dress them, to teach them about their world and the people in it, and to comfort them when they are hurt or upset.

As a parent or caregiver, you help guide children's behavior by setting limits and sticking to them. In doing this, you will make the children feel comfortable and loved, and give them opportunities to play and learn.

You are also responsible for keeping the children in your care safe. This means not only protecting them from obvious dangers such as electrical outlets and sharp objects, but also protecting them from people who might want to hurt them. If you do your job well in all these areas, you will help the children you care for to grow, to learn, and to become confident and self-reliant.

Caring for Children

In Chapter 18 you learned that parenting means taking care of children and meeting all their needs. Whether you are a babysitter, a camp counselor, or a nanny, for some period of time you will be doing the parenting for the children in your care. The children will look to you to provide them with many of the things their parents provide, from a glass of milk to a bedtime story. You must meet their physical, mental, emotional, and social needs.

Meeting Physical Needs

Think back to the ways you have been cared for in your life. When you were a small child, you were helped at special times in your day: mealtime, bedtime, bathtime, and playtime. With this help, you could have your physical needs for sleep, food, cleanliness, and exercise satisfied.

Here are some tips for helping you meet the physical needs of the children in your care:

- **Bedtime.** Getting children to bed is often the caregiver's most difficult task. Younger children may be fussy and tearful at bedtime, and older children may try to persuade you to let them stay up later. It helps to follow the children's usual bedtime routine. A warm bath, a bedtime snack that includes milk, and a bedtime story often help children to relax and go to sleep. Once they are asleep, check on them often.

- **Mealtime.** If you are going to make a simple meal for the children, find out from their parents what foods to serve and how to prepare those foods. If you are expected to use a microwave oven or other appliances, make sure you

When caring for children, you must meet all their needs. Bedtime might involve nurturing and guidance, as well as physical care.

know how to operate them or ask the parents to show you. You should follow the children's normal mealtime routine. Have them eat in the same place and at the same time as they usually do.

- **Bathtime.** When you are bathing toddlers or infants, never, ever leave them alone in a bathtub, not even for an instant. In addition, before you place a child in bathwater, check the temperature of the water to make certain it is warm, but not hot. Drowning and scalding are two very common childhood accidents.

- **Playtime.** When you play games with children or read to them, you provide companionship and you help them learn about their world. If children are playing together, you need to monitor their play and intervene if they start squabbling, name-calling, or hitting each other. Use such incidents as opportunities to teach children how to share and take turns.

Whatever activity you are engaged in as a caregiver, you need to keep the children safe. As much as possible, a child's environment should be made **childproof**, or safe for children. Childproofing should be done by parents, but a babysitter who knows what to look for can help make sure a child is safe.

Here are some things that should be done to childproof a home:

- Dangerous objects, such as glass knickknacks, scissors, and matches should be placed out of reach.

- Plastic caps should be placed over any unused electrical outlets.

- Gates should be installed at the top and bottom of stairs until children can climb the stairs safely.

- Any cabinets or closets that contain medicines or dangerous substances should be kept locked.

Meeting Mental Needs

Caregivers can help children learn about the world and develop their mental skills in these ways:

- By playing games that are appropriate to a child's skill.

- By changing to a new game when a child tires of what he or she is doing.

- By talking to the child to help him or her learn and develop language.

You can review some of the play ideas in this unit to help you meet children's mental needs.

Meeting Social and Emotional Needs

Children look to caregivers for emotional support and guidance. Be ready to praise a drawing or a project that a child has done. Encourage a child who becomes tired or frustrated with a game or toy.

You can help children socially and emotionally in other ways:

- Give them love and pay attention to them; this helps them feel loved and secure.

- Respond quickly when they are hurt or upset.

- Teach them to get along with others—by sharing toys, for instance.

- Help them learn to communicate.

Young children may cry when their parents leave. Be understanding. Often, you can quiet them by interesting them in a toy or a song. They usually get over their unhappiness quickly.

Children who wake up frightened need to be reassured that they are safe. Never make fun of their fears. Comfort them by talking or singing to them, or by holding or rocking them.

These caregivers are helping the children develop their mental skills as they learn about animals. What rules or limits might the caregivers have set?

Rules and Limits

Children need to have limits placed on what they can do and where they can go. Setting these limits is the parents' responsibility, but other caregivers must uphold them. It is always important to ask parents what limits they have set.

Setting Limits

Some limits are set to protect the children's safety. You should refuse to take children in, or near, dangerous areas that cannot be childproofed.

If the children are going to be outdoors near water, make sure that you review their parents' rules for water play. If they are going to use bicycles or other wheel toys, show them exactly where they can ride and review bicycle safety rules with them. Such boundaries and rules prevent accidents.

Limits also apply to behavior. For example, children learn what time to go to bed or how they should play together.

Communicating Positively

Children like to try out forbidden activities when someone new is in charge of them, but they need to know that the limits hold true at all times. Be firm about what is and is not permitted.

One way to handle this problem is to focus on what children may do, rather than on what they may not do. "You can run all the way to . . ." is a more positive way of suggesting limits than starting every sentence with *Don't*. See the chart on page 204 for examples of how to give children positive directions.

Of course, sometimes you can't enforce a limit by gentle reasoning. When a child chases a ball into the street, you don't have time to reason with him. You must take immediate and complete control. Either call out a sharp command or grab him, or do both.

Positive Communication

Children respond better to positive statements than to negative ones. They will also be happier if they are told what they can, rather than what they can't do.

What to Say	What Not to Say
"Let's read a story."	"Stop running around!"
"You can play here in the living room."	"Get out of the kitchen!"
"You can phone George to say hello."	"Don't go out!"
"You can play on the swings."	"Stay off the jungle gym!"
"Let's play with the toy truck."	"Put down your brother's toys!"
"Pet the dog gently."	"Don't hit the dog!"
"You can stay up until 8:00."	"You have to go to bed soon."

Providing Distractions

A good way to prevent arguments over limits is to provide distractions. Children who are busy with safe, interesting play are far less likely to become restless and get into trouble. You can **distract** children, or lead them away from something they shouldn't do, by interesting them in another activity.

Planning interesting activities is important. If it is raining and you are stuck indoors, try an art project. You can organize a finger-painting session, which preschoolers enjoy, with a minimum of effort and supplies. You can help children build something with their blocks.

If you take the children outside, organize races and games or take them for a walk, perhaps to a nearby park. Have a picnic lunch or play on the swings and jungle gym. When you can keep children busy in these ways, you prevent the arguments and fights that result from boredom.

Keeping Children Safe

Keeping children safe is your most important job. When children miss a meal or go to bed later than usual, little harm is done. When they are not protected from danger, however, serious and even fatal accidents can occur.

Fingerpainting is a good activity to amuse preschoolers on a rainy day.

Preventing Accidents

Children don't understand the dangers that surround them, and in their eagerness to learn and explore, they will try anything. Babies put things in their mouths; toddlers poke things into electrical outlets or wander into busy streets; preschoolers may be fascinated by water or fire; and older children may wander off in stores or crowds.

To prevent possible accidents, follow these guidelines:

- Don't give babies small toys or objects that they could accidentally swallow. Toys should not have any breakable or sharp parts. Give babies playthings that are large and soft.
- When changing diapers, never leave an infant alone on a table. He or she may turn over and fall off.
- Keep plastic bags away from children to prevent suffocation.
- Restrict crawling babies and toddlers to places they can explore safely. Don't let them play on stairs, with electrical outlets or wires, or with any breakable or dangerous objects.
- Take toddlers off any piece of furniture that isn't sturdy. Also take them off if they are reaching too far and might lose their balance.
- In the kitchen, keep children away from the top of the range and oven so they can't burn themselves.
- Keep knives and breakable dishes away from children.
- Outside, always watch toddlers to prevent their running out into the street or riding their wheeled toys into the paths of automobiles.
- At a playground, make sure children use the equipment safely. It is very easy for a child to slip or fall off a piece of playground equipment.
- At a public pool, keep your eye on the children at all times and call the lifeguard immediately if any child is in trouble in the water. If you are watching children at a home with a pool, be especially alert. Small children can slip away from you and drown in a pool in a matter of moments.
- In a car, a child should always ride in a child car seat, no matter how short the trip. The safest spot for a child is in the middle of the backseat.

Gates can restrict babies and toddlers from exploring areas where they might get hurt.

HEALTH WATCH

Facts on Child Abuse

Sometimes children are physically or emotionally mistreated. That mistreatment is called **child abuse,** and it involves more than just an occasional scolding or spanking. Child abuse has long-lasting effects on the physical, emotional, mental, and social health of its victims.

Child abuse occurs in all levels of society: among rich and poor, and among all races and ethnic groups. Parents who are under extreme stress are more likely to abuse their children than are other parents. Financial problems, family problems, and drug and alcohol abuse are sometimes causes of abusive behavior.

Child abuse can be divided into the following categories:

- **Neglect.** A parent or guardian fails to give a child basic love and care. The parent may not feed or clothe the child or provide medical care. The child may be left unattended for long periods of time.
- **Physical abuse.** The abuser physically injures a child in some way. Beating, scalding, scratching, or burning are some types of physical abuse.
- **Sexual abuse.** An adult forces or persuades a child to have sexual contact with him or her. Usually the abuser is a person the child knows well, such as a family member or neighbor.
- **Emotional abuse.** Emotionally abused children may be constantly yelled at, intimidated, ridiculed, or humiliated. They may be continually made to feel bad about themselves and may suffer from a loss of self-esteem. They may even be told, "You're stupid. I hate you."

Abuse tends to be repeated and to increase in frequency and severity unless help is obtained. Child abuse can be treated and the cause prevented. Help must be given to both the abused child and the abuser to stop the pattern and to prevent it from recurring.

A child who is being abused may bear visible signs of neglect or physical abuse. Signs of sexual and emotional abuse are usually harder to identify, but the children may give unconscious signals. Abused children may not want to go home. Some abused children are withdrawn, while others act like bullies. Some may even give hints, such as saying that a "friend" is being hurt.

If you suspect that a child is being abused, seek guidance from your parents or from an adult you can confide in, such as a teacher, a counselor, or a member of the clergy. Most communities have resources to help deal with child abuse. Every state and county has an agency to protect children. Various hot lines are available, on the city and national level, for calling and reporting the abuse or for getting advice about what to do.

Think It Through

1. What do you think could be done to help cut down on the number of cases of child abuse?
2. Why do you think some people are afraid to report suspected incidents of child abuse?

Giving First Aid

Children dash around with abandon, unaware of the many dangers that surround them. As a result, they tend to hurt themselves fairly often, though usually in very minor ways. As a caregiver, you should know the basics of **first aid**: emergency care or treatment given to an ill or injured person.

In case of very serious illness or injury, or if you feel uncomfortable administering first aid, call an adult for help Call an ambulance immediately if a child has difficulty breathing, is unconscious, is badly burned, has a broken bone, or is bleeding severely.

First Aid

Always contact the parents if there is a serious injury or illness.

Scrapes and bruises Clean scrapes with soap and water; apply antiseptic and bandage. For bruises, apply a clean washcloth wrung out in cold water.

Nosebleed Keep child seated and leaning forward. If head is tilted back, child may choke. Apply direct pressure by pressing on bleeding nostril. Apply a cold towel to nose and face.

Earache Pain can be relieved by covering the ear with a warm towel or heating pad set on low. Call doctor.

Cuts Apply direct pressure to stop bleeding. Wash and apply antiseptic and a bandage. If cut is deep, call doctor.

Bites (insect) For minor bites, wash the area and apply antiseptic or calamine lotion. For bee, hornet, or wasp stings, scrape against the stinger with a flat object, like a piece of cardboard, until you pull out the venom sac. Wash area thoroughly with soap and water. **Caution:** Some people are highly allergic to stings. If child is short of breath or faint or has stomach pain, call doctor immediately.

Bites (animal or human) Wash the wound with water; clean with soap and water, and cover with gauze. Call doctor.

Burns For minor burns, immediately run cold water on the burn for about five minutes and apply a clean, dry dressing. For major burns, rush to hospital immediately. Do not try to remove burned clothing.

Sprains Don't allow child to walk. Elevate foot and apply a cold pack. Call doctor.

Choking First, look into the throat to see if something is caught there. Next, try to get the child to cough up the object. If these methods don't work, you can use the **Heimlich maneuver**. This procedure works by your using pressure to force the object that is interfering with breathing from the throat. For older children and adults, stand behind victim and place your fists just below her rib cage. Have her lean forward while you give one quick, upward push against her abdomen. This forces the air in her lungs to expel the object. Repeat if necessary. If the object doesn't come out, seek help immediately.

For infants and toddlers, turn child face down over your arm. Using the heel of your other hand, give four quick blows between the child's shoulder blades. Turn child over, supporting his head, neck, and back. Position your two fingers below the rib cage and above the navel, and give four quick thrusts. Repeat if needed.

Poisoning If a child swallows a poisonous or irritating substance, call the nearest poison control center immediately. Report the name and quantity of the substance and follow the center's instructions. Take the container with you if you go to the doctor or hospital.

Electric shock Don't touch the child until his or her contact with electricity is broken, or you will get a shock, too. Turn off electricity if you can, or pull or push child away from source of shock with a stick, cloth, or rope, but never with anything metal. If child is not breathing, apply mouth-to-mouth respiration if you know how. Call ambulance immediately.

Reviewing the Facts

1. List four daily activities that give caregivers opportunities to help children meet their physical needs.
2. What are three things parents can do to childproof their home?
3. Describe four ways that a caregiver can meet the emotional and social needs of a child.
4. Why is it a good idea to provide children with distractions?
5. What are four safety guidelines to follow to prevent possible accidents?
6. When should you call an adult for help with first aid?
7. What is the Heimlich maneuver?

Sharing Your Ideas

1. Imagine that a niece (a toddler) is coming to stay at your house. What would you need to do to make the house childproof?
2. What kinds of accidents are most likely to happen to the children in your neighborhood? What could be done to prevent such accidents?

Applying Your Skills

 1. Planning a Meal. Look through cookbooks and get ideas for nutritious meals that could be served to young children. Plan a lunch or dinner and explain how it would be attractively served.

 2. Preparing a Brochure. Put together a brochure about childproofing that could be distributed to prospective parents. Explain the importance of childproofing a home, then provide a list of step-by-step procedures that parents could follow.

 3. Developing Questions. When you care for somebody else's child, you need to know what rules and limits the parents have set. Make a list of the questions you should ask parents so that you can enforce their rules while they are absent.

CHAPTER

22

Babysitting: Earning and Learning

OBJECTIVES

This chapter will help you to:

- Explain how to run a babysitting business.
- List the information you need to be a responsible babysitter.
- Describe ways to handle the problems babysitters may have.

WORDS TO REMEMBER

day-care center
family day care
licensed
reference

One thing has become very clear to fourteen-year-old Caitlin in the last several months: she loves children. Because of this interest, Caitlin has thought about different caregiver roles. Caregivers can be parents, foster parents, family members, child care workers, and babysitters. All of these people need skills as they care for children, either on a short- or long-term basis. Caitlin hopes to have several caregiving roles in her future.

For now Caitlin is satisfied to be with the children she babysits. While parents are away for short periods of time, Caitlin takes on the responsibility for their children's safety, welfare, and happiness. When a child is sick or unhappy, she meets the child's needs and feels good about her success.

Babysitting offers Caitlin several rewards. Not only is she earning money, but she is also preparing herself for her future roles. She especially wants to be a child care worker, someone who has a regular job caring for children. Caitlin realizes that much of what she does now as a babysitter will help prepare her for this career.

Running a Babysitting Business

Babysitting gives you practice in caring for children, making decisions, and dealing with new people and new situations. It can help you decide if you would like a career working with children, and it can also be fun. One other benefit that you can gain from your jobs is that you may develop close relationships with the children you care for.

Babysitting is a business. You will earn money and gain experience in managing your own time and resources. If you are organized and if you understand what the job requires, you should be very successful.

If you want your child care jobs to multiply, you will have to be businesslike in your dealings with each of your employers. Your rates, hours, and responsibilities should be clear to both you and your employer before you start work. Then both parties should stick to the agreement.

Making and Keeping Appointments

One of the biggest mistakes you can make as a babysitter is to forget an appointment. Almost as bad in parents' eyes is a last-minute cancellation.

To prevent these mistakes, keep an appointment calendar next to the telephone at home. Write everything you are scheduled to do in it: club meetings, a friend's birthday party, swim team practices, and all your child care jobs. Then when someone calls to offer you a job, you will be able to check your calendar and tell at a glance whether you are free that day at that time.

If you have to cancel, let your employers know as early as possible. If you find someone capable to take your place, they will appreciate it and will remember that you are a responsible person.

Agreeing on Rates and Hours

When parents call, clearly state what you charge for your services. You won't seem very businesslike if you tell your employers to pay you what they think is fair. Also, it is possible that you will end up being underpaid.

Find out what others in your area charge and set the same rate. You may want to charge extra for difficult jobs, such as those that involve large families, infants, or late hours.

When caring for children, always get needed information from parents before they leave. Be sure you know where they can be reached in emergencies.

You should also establish the length of the job. Find out what time to arrive and what time the parents expect to return home. Make arrangements for transportation. Will the parents be picking you up? How will you get home? By being clear about these details from the start, you will prevent confusion later on.

Getting the Information You Need

When parents hire you to care for their children, you become their employee. Like any employee, you have a responsibility to carry out your duties competently. To do this, you need to obtain certain information.

Before the parents leave, make sure you find out the following:

- What is the schedule for mealtime and bedtime?
- What foods are the children allowed to have for meals and snacks?
- Do they take any medicines?
- Do they have any allergies or fears?
- What are the rules for watching television?
- Where are the children's rooms and bathrooms?
- Where are the light switches?
- How do you work the appliances you will need to use?

- Where are flashlights and first-aid supplies kept?
- Where are the fire escapes?

You should also find out what rules and limits the parents want you to follow with their children. You need to know, for example, if it is acceptable to take away privileges when a child misbehaves. Sometimes, it helps to go over rules with the parents while the children are there. Then the children know that you are aware of the limits.

It is also essential that you get the phone numbers of the following:

- Place where you can reach a parent.
- Fire department.
- Police department.
- Child's doctor.
- Local poison control center.
- Nearest hospital emergency room.
- Local ambulance service.
- Nearby family member or friend.

The chart on page 212 shows what this "emergency card" would look like.

Emergency Information Card

Parent's names _____

Phone number where parents can be reached _____

Fire department _____

Police department _____

Poison control center _____

Child's doctor _____

Ambulance _____

Hospital emergency room _____

Nearby relative or friend _____

    name _____

    number _____

Acting Responsibly

Your employers may tell you to make yourself at home, but that does not mean that you can behave exactly as you would in your own home. Here are some do's and don'ts:

- Check with the parents about snacks and about using the phone, the television, and the stereo.
- If you do use the phone, keep your calls short. You would not want to tie up the line, because the parents might be trying to reach you.
- Don't entertain friends on the job. Your job is to watch the children, and friends would be a distraction.
- While the parents are out, you are responsible for their house. You should leave it as neat as you found it. If you prepare a meal or a snack for the children, you should clean up the dishes. Help them put away any toys or games they have played with.
- Take a few precautions. Keep all doors and windows locked. Never open the door to strangers. Don't give information over the phone. Don't tell the caller who you are, where the par-

ents are, or when they will be back. Ask to take a message and get the caller's name and number. If the message is very important, you can call the parents and tell them.

Doing Work, Not Favors

While employed, your job is to care for the children, not to clean the house or do the laundry. Some chores, like cleaning up the children's dishes after a snack, should be done. If your employers expect extra favors, however, like taking out the garbage or cleaning the living room, explain politely that your rate does not include housework. Also point out that the extra work takes you away from the children.

You have a right to expect certain things from your employers. If they find themselves out later than planned, they should call to let you know. If they don't, tell them in a friendly way that you would appreciate a call next time. They should also provide you with the information and instructions you need to do your job.

Dealing with Problems

When you care for children, you are responsible for their safety and welfare. Part of that responsibility includes being prepared to handle unexpected situations, such as crying, illness and accidents, fire, and other problems.

Crying

Young children may cry when their parents leave. Be understanding and try to get them interested in something else, such as a toy or a song. They usually get over their unhappiness very soon.

At other times, children may cry because they are tired, hungry, hurt, or upset. If this happens, you should respond quickly. Ask them what is wrong, and try to solve the problem if possible. Children need someone to comfort them and to reassure them.

Illness and Accidents

Sometimes, you may be asked to care for a sick child. You should get detailed instructions from the parents about how to manage the child's illness while they are away. Be sure you know when to administer medication and how much to give the child, and follow the instructions on any medicine bottle or pill vial very carefully.

If you are caring for a sick child, you will need to find some quiet play activities to amuse him or her. Play board games with the child, provide coloring books and crayons, or give the child blunt scissors, old magazines, and paste with which to make collages. Older children can build models, work on jigsaw puzzles, or do craft projects. When children are sick, their attention span is shorter, so you may have to change activities more frequently.

As you learned in Chapter 21, accidents sometimes happen, and you have to be prepared to handle them. One general rule to remember for any problem or emergency is *stay calm.* You may feel upset, but acting excited or panicky will only frighten the child and make things worse.

Review the first-aid tips on page 207, and always keep the list of emergency telephone numbers near the phone. Then, if an accident occurs, you can easily find the right number to call.

After feeding children, be sure to leave the kitchen as clean as you found it.

Fire

In case of fire, don't take the time to call the fire department or try to put out the blaze yourself. Be sure that you know where *all* the children are. Get them and then walk, don't run, to the nearest exit. Once you are all safely out, call the fire department from a neighbor's home.

If the home is filled with smoke, cover your face with a damp cloth and stay close to the floor. Feel each closed door that you come to. If the door is hot, don't open it. Find another way out.

Other Problems

Caring for children also means taking responsibility for them—as well as for yourself—during emergencies such as severe weather or break-ins. Each situation will be different, but follow these general rules:

- Stay calm.
- Use the telephone to call the police, fire department, or ambulance for help.
- If the emergency is threatening weather, such as a tornado or hurricane, listen to bulletins on the radio or television.

A Job Well Done

By being clear about things like rates, hours, and responsibilities, good caregivers help themselves and their employers. By acting responsibly and giving children their undivided attention, they live up to the trust their employers have placed in them.

Babysitting is a good way to find out if you want a job working with children. You may want to become a teacher, a children's nurse, or a worker in a **day-care center** (also called a child care center), a place where infants and preschool children are cared for while their parents work. You may even want to run your own center someday.

The skills you learn as a babysitter will be useful in other jobs. These include being punctual, following directions, making decisions, and acting responsibly.

The Business of Caring for Children

Vanessa was interested in starting a babysitting business, but she realized that she needed to learn more about children. When she asked her older brother for suggestions, he told her to get some child care books out of the library and to practice by sitting for their younger brother. She could take a child care and first-aid course offered by the Red Cross, or by a church, hospital, or school in the area.

Vanessa took her brother's advice, and now, after a few months of learning and practical experience, she has started her own business. The first few families she sat for were very pleased with the way she handled the children. The parents even supplied her with **references;** that is, they agreed to give Vanessa's new customers a good report about her performance. Parents who don't know Vanessa are likely to ask for references so they can learn about her before they entrust their children to her care.

When Vanessa is older, she hopes to make a full-time job of babysitting by offering child care in her home. Caring for children at home is usually called **family day care** (or family child care), and it requires many more resources than Vanessa's part-time business does. To run a family day-care center, Vanessa must have a home and she must be able to provide equipment, toys, food, and supplies. She will also have to establish regular business hours.

Vanessa may have to consider whether or not she wants her business to be licensed. A **licensed** business is one that receives permission from the state government to operate. In exchange, the business must meet certain standards for safety and cleanliness.

If Vanessa wants her home to be licensed, she will have to childproof it and have smoke detectors and fire-escape routes. She will also need to have adequate space for playing and napping, and a clean, sanitary kitchen for preparing and serving meals and snacks to the children. There will also be limits on the number of children she can care for.

If Vanessa does not want to become licensed, then it will be her responsibility to make sure that her home is safe and sanitary. Chances are that parents would expect her to meet the same high standards as family child care workers with licensed homes.

Think It Through
1. Why do you think that some states require family child care businesses to be licensed? What are the advantages of licensing? What are the disadvantages?
2. What do you think would be the advantages and disadvantages of caring for children in your own home?

Reviewing the Facts

1. Name four benefits that you gain from babysitting.
2. What three topics should you discuss with parents when they call to hire you to care for children?
3. Give three examples of information you need to obtain from parents when babysitting for their children.
4. List five telephone numbers you should keep by the telephone when you care for children.
5. What should you do if you are babysitting and a stranger calls?
6. What can you do to amuse a sick child?
7. What is the most important rule for handling accidents when you are caring for children?
8. What should you do if a fire breaks out while you are babysitting?

Sharing Your Ideas

1. What management skills do you think you acquire by running a babysitting business?
2. How would you go about convincing new customers that you are competent to care for their children?

Applying Your Skills

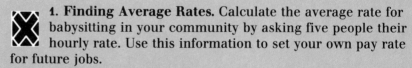

1. Finding Average Rates. Calculate the average rate for babysitting in your community by asking five people their hourly rate. Use this information to set your own pay rate for future jobs.

2. Writing an Ad. Write an ad or flyer to publicize your services. Include information about your age, experience, and the hours you are available. What other information would you include?

3. Compiling Emergency Information. Consult your local telephone directory for the numbers of the police and fire departments, poison control center, and hospital. Make a checklist of emergency telephone numbers to take with you each time you care for children.

CHAPTER

23

Ready for Parenthood?

OBJECTIVES

This chapter will help you to:

- Describe some of the challenges of being a parent.
- Discuss the financial and personal costs of parenthood.
- Describe the rewards of parenthood.

WORDS TO REMEMBER

emotional maturity
fetus
financial stability
premature birth
prenatal

Parents have a 24-hour job. They have complete responsibility for their child's health, safety, and development every day over the course of many years.

Parents have to invest a lot of time, energy, and money in their children, and they often have to postpone some of their plans and dreams. However, parenthood has many rewards. Seeing their children's accomplishments and helping them develop into happy, productive adults brings great joy to parents.

The Challenge of Parenthood

Donna and Mario had fallen in love. They knew they were young for marriage, but they wanted to get married anyway. Their parents asked them to wait. Donna's parents knew she wanted to go to college and become a teacher, and Mario's parents knew he planned to go to a local community college to study accounting.

Despite their parents' concerns, however, Donna and Mario got married right after they graduated from high school. They rented a small apartment, and Donna went to work in a department store. Mario took a part-time job at a garage and enrolled in classes at the community college.

Dreams and Realities

Two months later, Donna became pregnant. Neither of them had planned it that way or had even thought much about having a baby. Donna quit her job before the baby was born and postponed plans for college. Mario quit school and got a second job driving a truck.

In spite of these changes in plans, they were both excited. They were in love with each other, and they looked forward to having a child to care for and share their happiness. They wanted to help this new person grow and learn. They were a little scared, but they had each other and a lot of hope.

The Baby

Once Jan arrived, Donna's and Mario's lives changed completely. They still had their love, of course, and some fun, too, but they had many more responsibilities as well. It was hard for them to believe that anything as small as an infant could require so much work.

A lot of time and energy goes into being a parent. Changing diapers is only one of the many daily tasks that parents must do for a baby.

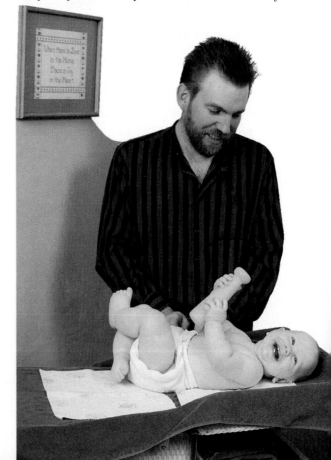

There was washing and diapering and feeding around the clock. The list of needs seemed to go on and on. Donna and Mario found they had to rearrange their lives around Jan's needs. Still, they were lucky. They cared for each other and for their baby. They were able to get help and advice from their parents, and they were smart enough to use that advice to help them over the rough spots.

The Responsibilities of Parenthood

Having a child affects a parent's life in many ways. When a new baby arrives, both parents must consider their child in everything they do. They must also adapt to their new financial and personal responsibilities.

Financial Responsibilities

Parenthood involves financial responsibilities for the present and the future. There are doctor's bills to pay and baby food to buy. Babies require a lot of special baby furniture and equipment, such as cribs and car seats. They outgrow their clothing very quickly.

While two may live in a small apartment happily, three people need more space; this may mean moving to a larger and more expensive apartment. In addition, if both of the baby's parents want or need to go back to work after the child is born, they have to pay for child care.

For this reason, it is important for parents to have **financial stability**. They need to be able to meet all their expected, everyday living costs, which increase significantly when a couple has children.

Personal Responsibilities

Because caring for an infant is a full-time job, there may be little time left over for outside activities. Mario and Donna found that they had less time to spend with their friends. A child needs constant care and attention; you can't punch a time clock at five o'clock and quit working for the day.

Basic supplies for a baby include clothing and diapers, as well as equipment for eating, sleeping, bathing, and traveling. Some items can be borrowed to reduce costs.

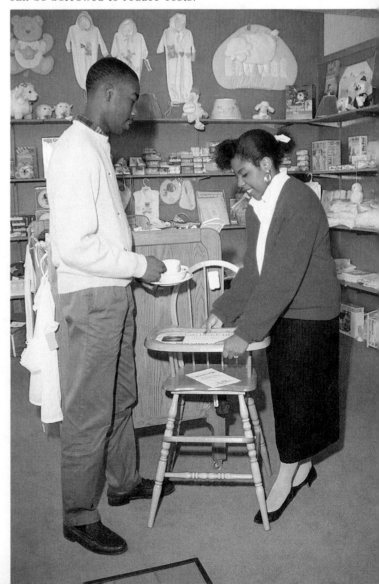

Caring for a baby also takes a lot of energy. Parents of young infants often find that they are too tired for other activities or interests.

One of the biggest adjustments that new parents face is the change in their personal lifestyle. Because parents are responsible for providing for all of a baby's needs, they have to deal with limits on their personal freedom. Young adults who are just beginning to get to know themselves and to find out what they want out of life may be affected even more by this adjustment. For example, Donna and Mario want to continue their education, but they have decided to postpone their plans until their baby is older.

For many people, having a baby may mean having to postpone or change a rewarding and fulfilling career. Fortunately, babies grow to be toddlers, then preschoolers. Once children are older, parents can spend more time on their own interests, and parents and children can always enjoy doing things together.

Parenthood may require many emotional adjustments, too. One parent may feel left out if the baby occupies most of the partner's time. Those feelings may be difficult to deal with if a young couple has not spent much time together before becoming parents.

Also, loving an infant may seem like a one-way street. The baby can't talk about love or other feelings, but a smile or a hug helps keep you going.

To meet these emotional demands, parents need something more important than money—they need **emotional maturity**. They must be secure enough in their own self-image to be able to meet the emotional demands and responsibilities they face.

This maturity includes being able to give love without expecting it back right away. It also means being grown up enough so that they don't think of their own needs all the time.

Sometimes one parent feels left out after the arrival of a new baby. What could parents do to solve this problem?

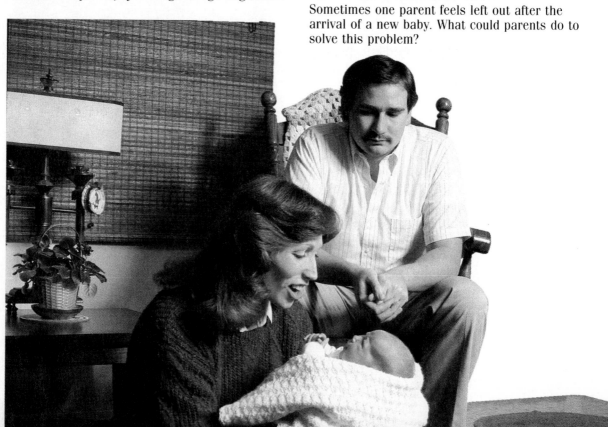

The Rewards of Parenthood

There is more to parenthood than the costs. Some moments make up for everything. Listen to the way parents speak of their children. Watch the light in their eyes when they say, "Do you know what my little Christopher did yesterday?"

Children are long-term investments. The bond formed by love and shared experience, by two lives helping each other develop, is emotionally very rewarding for parents.

Children also change the way you think about yourself and your world. Before you became a parent, you needed to think only about yourself and, if you are married, about your partner. When you become a parent, you think more about the future. What kind of a world will it be when your children are grown? Is that the kind of world you want for them? If not, what can you do to change it?

Helping children learn brings special satisfaction. Parents thrill to see their children master new skills. From the infant who begins to walk to the student graduating from high school, children give joy to their parents.

Parents enjoy watching a child grow, and they find it fascinating to observe all the changes. Seeing a child develop his or her self-concept leads parents to think about themselves, and, in fact, parents learn and grow along with their children.

Becoming a parent may be the most rewarding step to take in life. Parenthood involves a lot and requires even more than you expect, but for those who are ready for it, parenthood makes their lives richer and more satisfying.

Parents gain joy and satisfaction in helping their children learn about the world, master new skills, and develop positive self-concepts.

Caring for the Unborn

The responsibilities of being a parent don't begin when a baby is born. They start long before that. From the moment a child is conceived, the mother must begin caring for herself to ensure that her child gets the best possible start in life. This helps to prevent a **premature birth,** a birth that occurs before development is complete.

Here are some ways that an expectant mother can care for herself and her unborn child:

■ Every pregnant woman should begin receiving regular **prenatal** (pree-NAY-tul), or before birth, medical care as soon as she realizes she is pregnant. If the first prenatal visit has not taken place before pregnancy, it should come during the early weeks. The mother should then return monthly until the seventh month, when more frequent examinations are recommended. Pregnant women can develop several physical problems or conditions, which can be life-threatening to the **fetus** (FEE-tuss), or the unborn child, if they are not treated. These include high blood pressure and German measles.

■ The most important factor in prenatal care is good nutrition. If a pregnant mother wants to help her baby develop properly, she must eat a balanced diet consisting of food from the basic food groups.

■ Expectant mothers should also get plenty of rest and moderate exercise. They should avoid becoming overtired and relax whenever necessary.

■ Pregnant women should not take any medication without consulting their doctors. During pregnancy, both prescription and over-the-counter drugs such as aspirin can affect the growth of the fetus or cause a malformation as the fetus is developing.

■ Alcohol, tobacco, and illegal drugs should be avoided. The use of these substances can result in serious problems such as low birth weight and birth defects.

■ A pregnant woman should avoid having sexual contact with people who have sexually transmitted diseases such as syphilis, gonorrhea, genital herpes, or AIDS. She could pass it on to her unborn child, who could become seriously ill, deformed, or even die.

■ If a woman is pregnant, she should tell medical personnel, dentists, and orthodontists, so that special precautions can be taken when X rays are needed. The radiation from X rays and other sources can be dangerous to an unborn child.

Think It Through

1. How can the father participate in the care of the unborn child?
2. Many doctors recommend that women quit smoking and drinking alcohol and eat healthy foods *before* they become pregnant. Why do you think they make this recommendation?

CHAPTER
23 REVIEW

Reviewing the Facts

1. Why is parenthood more demanding than a nine-to-five job?
2. How does parenthood affect a couple's material resources?
3. Why is financial stability an important factor in starting a family?
4. What are two ways that parenthood affects a couple's social life?
5. Give two examples of the emotional adjustments new parents may have to make.
6. What is emotional maturity?
7. Describe two of the rewards of parenthood.

Sharing Your Ideas

1. Why is emotional maturity especially important for parents? What could happen when people who are not emotionally mature become parents?
2. Discuss some of the ways that young adults find out what is important to them and develop a sense of self. How can becoming parents hinder that process?

Applying Your Skills

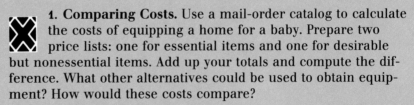

1. Comparing Costs. Use a mail-order catalog to calculate the costs of equipping a home for a baby. Prepare two price lists: one for essential items and one for desirable but nonessential items. Add up your totals and compute the difference. What other alternatives could be used to obtain equipment? How would these costs compare?

2. Exploring Effects. Imagine that your long-term goal is to be a computer programmer; then imagine that while you are still in vocational school, you are about to become a parent. Write a short essay describing how you think parenthood would affect your goals.

3. Developing a Survey. Think about the questions you could ask parents in order to discover more about the pleasures that children bring. List your questions in a logical sequence. Use your list to conduct a survey of four or five parents.

Careers Helping Children

OBJECTIVES

This chapter will help you to:

■ Identify the personal qualities a person needs to work well with children.

■ Describe some jobs that involve working directly with children.

■ Discuss some kinds of jobs in which people work for children.

WORDS TO REMEMBER

creativity
dietitian
pediatrician

hildren make a lot of noise and have a lot of energy, and they constantly demand attention. Working with children can be exhausting, but when they smile at you or at something they have learned, the work seems worthwhile. People who enjoy working with children often have such characteristics as an interest in children, creativity, sensitivity, and a sense of humor.

Being a parent means working with children. Parents have the full-time responsibility for their children's health, safety, learning, and happiness, but parents can't do everything themselves. They need teachers, doctors, coaches, child care workers, writers, and many other kinds of people who work with young children and teens. Perhaps you will want to perform one of these jobs when you become an adult.

Characteristics for Careers Working with Children

Before exploring some actual jobs and careers that involve working with young children or teens, let's find out what characteristics are needed. Some of these personal traits are mental and some are emotional.

Interests and Skills

- **Are you interested in children and how they learn and grow?**
- **Can you treat each child as an individual, with his or her own unique qualities?**
- **Do you have creativity? Creativity** is the ability to use your imagination to do things in new ways. This characteristic can help you think of new and interesting activities for children.
- **Do you respect children as people?** You must show children that you respect their feelings and that you take their needs seriously.

This teacher is using her creativity and enthusiasm to interest the young children in a story. She enjoys helping them learn new concepts and skills.

- **Are you patient, tolerant, and calm?** These qualities can help you play repetitive games and settle arguments.
- **Do you have a sense of humor?** If you do, you can help children learn to laugh at themselves and see the funny side of their mistakes.
- **Are you enthusiastic and willing to join with children in their play?** Playing with them shows them that you think they are important.
- **Are you adaptable?** Child care workers need to switch activities when children tire of what they are doing.
- **Are you sympathetic?** Can you put yourself in the children's place? Are you able to imagine what the world looks like from their perspective? If so, you will be able to calm their fears and respond to their needs more effectively.
- **Are you willing to learn about children?** To understand a child's behavior and needs, you must know what to expect at each stage of development.

If you have these qualities, you may be interested in some of the careers described below. Although this is just a sampling of the many jobs available, it should give you a basic idea of the variety of work you can do.

Jobs Working with Children

Many people work directly with young children or teens. Some provide day care or health care. Others help children learn or play.

Other people work in jobs related to children or teens. Some may create or sell products for children, such as clothes or toys. Others may work behind the scenes in schools, hospitals, or camps.

Entry-Level Jobs

A nanny cares for the children of a working parent or parents. This work is usually done in the child's home. (A child care worker, whom you read about in Chapter 17, does similar work in a child care center.) A nanny usually lives with the family, cares for the child in the evenings as well as the day, and receives free room and board as well as a salary. Babysitting experience and home economics courses are helpful for this job.

Camp counselors work with children at summer camps. They teach the children new skills, such as swimming, boating, and crafts, and they care for children who often are experiencing their first time away from home. Camp counselors are usually high school or college students. They may also work in day camps, where the campers go home every night. Scouting and babysitting experience is useful training for being a camp counselor.

Cafeteria workers prepare food and serve it to children in the school lunchroom. These workers should enjoy cooking and being with children. Patience and friendliness are a big help, too. Many mothers find this a convenient job, because it allows them to work when their children are at school and to be home after school is out.

Jobs That Require Training

A teacher's aide helps a teacher either with paperwork or with actual instruction in the classroom. The training needed for this job varies from one school system to another. Many two-year colleges offer a course of study leading to a degree for teacher's aides. With more course work, the aide can eventually become a teacher.

Cafeteria workers are responsible for preparing nutritious meals for students.

A team coach works with children who enjoy athletics. Many coaches are hired by school systems, but some work for the community parks department. Coaches have a very important role. They instruct children not only in the basic skills of a particular sport, but also in good sportsmanship. The training for this job includes experience in sports and, usually, a certain number of college credits. Coaches who are also teachers need college degrees.

Children's book authors write books for children. They may write picture books for toddlers or novels for teenagers. There is no single way of becoming a writer, though most writers have college degrees. However, the most important requirements are the desire to write and the creativity to capture children's interests.

Coaches are employed by schools and recreational departments. If you like sports and working with people, a coaching job may be for you.

Jobs That Require an Advanced Degree

How heavy is the earth? How many breeds of dogs are there? These are the kinds of questions asked of children's librarians. Whether they work in a school or a public library, librarians help children find books and information and teach them how to use reference materials. Children's librarians also purchase books and magazines for libraries. A children's librarian needs to have a college degree and often a master's degree as well.

The doctors who care for children are called **pediatricians**. Like all doctors, they have extensive training in both college and medical school, as well as in an internship at a hospital. They may have their own practice or work in a hospital or clinic. Some nurses also specialize in caring for children. These pediatric nurses may work for a doctor, advising parents about how to cope with childhood illnesses and other problems, or they may work on a hospital ward caring for gravely ill youngsters.

Children spend more time with their teachers than with any other adults except their parents. Teachers are responsible for helping children learn mental concepts and skills that they will need to succeed later in life. Even though teaching often means spending long hours at home planning lessons and grading papers, teachers receive a great deal of satisfaction from their careers. Teachers need a college degree and usually a teacher's certificate. Many also go on to get a master's degree.

A school dietitian plans and directs the purchase and preparation of the food in the school cafeteria. A **dietitian** is a person who has studied food and nutrition and their relationship to health and fitness. The aim of the school dietitian is to provide food that appeals to children, satisfies their nutritional needs, and meets the school's budget. Dietitians usually have a college degree in nutrition or food service, and most have a master's degree in food service. Management training is also a helpful background to have in this profession.

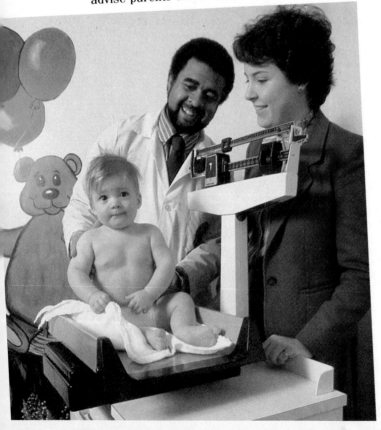

Pediatricians examine and treat children and advise parents about child care.

Getting a Job

If you think you might like a career working with young children or teens, you can start preparing now. While you are still in high school, you can get some basic experience by babysitting, scouting, or working as a camp counselor. Any experience you can gain will probably help you get the job you want.

Volunteer to Learn

One of the best ways to find out whether you would want a career working with or for children is to do volunteer work that involves being with youngsters. Volunteer work gives you the opportunity to develop the skills you need to work with children, but it does not impose more responsibilities on you than you can handle.

If you can't figure out how to get two children to stop fighting or what to do for a child who is sick, you can always call on the other people around you for help. By watching the other workers, you learn how to care for children, how to remain calm in the face of emergencies, and how to control your own anger and frustration when things are going badly. Here are some ways you can volunteer:

■ Become a candy striper or volunteer worker at a children's hospital or in the children's ward of your local hospital. Sick children demand a lot of extra attention, and they will sharpen your skills at providing them with amusement and comfort.

■ Volunteer at a day-care center, Sunday school, or a children's group at a church or synagogue. You could also work in a summer recreation program for children. You will learn how to manage groups of children as you lead them in games and activities. You will probably also learn how to treat minor injuries, such as scrapes and insect bites, which commonly occur when children play outdoors. Working with groups of children will also help you develop the skills you need to handle the fighting, bickering, and name-calling that sometimes erupt among children.

■ Volunteer to help the parent of an infant for an afternoon a week. You will learn how to bathe, feed, and handle a small baby, and you will see how much time and attention even the smallest child needs and demands.

Think It Through

1. If you were to choose one type of volunteer work discussed above, what would it be and why?
2. In addition to learning child-care skills, what else can you learn by volunteering to work with young children?

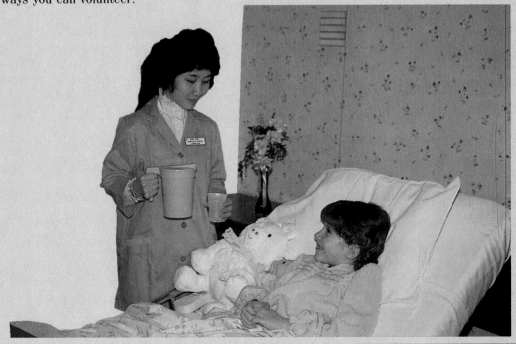

Reviewing the Facts

1. Name three personal qualities that are useful for working with children.
2. Name two entry-level jobs that involve working with children.
3. What is the difference between a nanny and a day-care worker?
4. What does a teacher's aide do?
5. Why is creativity important for writers of children's books?
6. What jobs do pediatricians and pediatric nurses do?
7. How do school dietitians help children?
8. What experience could you get now to help you know if you would like a career working with children?

Sharing Your Ideas

1. Discuss your own experiences in working with children. What were the most rewarding and the most difficult parts of the job?
2. Think of some of the people you know who work well with children. What words would you use to describe them? What special qualities do they have that make them good at their job?

Applying Your Knowledge

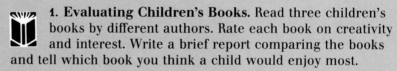 **1. Evaluating Children's Books.** Read three children's books by different authors. Rate each book on creativity and interest. Write a brief report comparing the books and tell which book you think a child would enjoy most.

 2. Creating an Advertisement. Suppose that you work for an advertising agency. Write a toy advertisement that would appeal to parents of young children. Illustrate your ad with drawings or photographs.

3. Identifying Special Qualities. Write a description of your favorite teacher. Explain why you think this person does a good job. What special qualities does she or he have?

TEEN TIPS

Baby Basics
   A handy set of hints for
   feeding, diapering, and
   bathing infants and
   toddlers.

Tidbits Toddlers Love to Eat
   Here are some tasty
   temptations that make
   mealtime fun for
   everyone.

The Quiet Times
   Calming activities for
   rainy days or for getting
   children ready for naps or
   bedtime.

Baby  Basics

How to Feed Babies

Here are some hints on how to feed a bottle to a baby:

- Warm the milk by setting the bottle in warm water for one or two minutes.

- Always check the temperature of the milk by shaking the bottle upside down so that a few drops fall on your wrist.

- Make sure that the neck of the bottle is full of liquid so the baby takes in less air.

- Midway through the feeding, burp the baby to release any air in the stomach. Cover your shoulder with a towel in case some milk comes up. Hold the baby against your shoulder and pat firmly but gently on the baby's back. The baby can also sit on your lap as you pat gently on the back.

wipe from front to back. Apply powder, oil, or ointment if parents use it to prevent diaper rash.

- Lift baby's legs by holding both ankles with one hand, and slide clean diaper underneath. Fasten a cloth diaper with pins; a disposable diaper with the attached tapes.

- Place wet or soiled diaper in a diaper pail, if cloth, or in the garbage, if it is disposable.

How to Diaper Babies

Parents may use either cloth or disposable diapers. Here are some diapering tips:

- Use a clean, flat surface such as a changing table, crib, or towel on the floor. Have all supplies nearby before you begin.

- Never leave the baby alone on a table—she may turn over quickly and fall off.

- Remove wet or soiled diaper and clean the baby using warm water or diaper towels. Be sure to

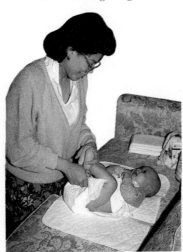

How to Bathe Babies

Bath time can be fun, but safety is very important. Here are some bathing tips:

- For an infant, use a small tub or sink lined with a towel. Fill with water up to the level of the baby's navel when placed in the bath.

- Test the temperature of the water by using your elbow—it should be warm and not hot.

- Hold the baby securely, keeping the head out of the water and away from the sink fixtures.

- Wash the head and face first, using a face towel and a mild baby soap. Rinse and dry the head. Then wash and rinse the rest of the body, remove the baby from the water, and wrap in a towel to dry.

- Older babies and toddlers can sit up in the bathroom tub in a small amount of warm water. To wash hair, use a baby shampoo and rinse by pouring water on the head but away from the face.

- Never leave a baby alone in water—not even for a second!

Tidbits Toddlers Love to Eat

Mealtime should be a happy time for toddlers and preschoolers—and for the people who care for them. Sometimes a new name or a new presentation makes food more fun to eat. Here are ten examples:

Bunny Food

Combine grated carrots with raisins. Mix with some mayonnaise, or a little honey and lemon juice.

Baked Banana Boat

Peel firm bananas and place in a greased baking dish. Brush with a little butter or margarine, and bake at 350°F for 12-15 minutes. When done, make a groove the length of the banana and fill with honey. Let cool before serving.

Devilish Eggs

Add a face to deviled eggs—using strips of green pepper or carrot for eyes, nose and mouth.

Yummy Apples

Peel and core a whole apple. Mix peanut butter with raisins or granola. Stuff the peanut butter mixture into the hole of the apple and slice into eighths to serve.

Personalized Pancakes

Using a teaspoon of pancake batter, draw a letter or number *backwards* on a hot pan or griddle. When the letter is browned, pour more batter over the letter so the pancake completely surrounds it. Bake until bubbles appear, then turn and brown the second side. The letter or number will be darker on the finished pancake.

Oatmeal Faces

On the top of a bowl of hot cereal, such as oatmeal or farina, make a face with chocolate chips or raisins for eyes, peach slices for mouth and ears, a dot of jelly for a nose.

Finger Food Buffet

Place finger foods such as fresh strawberries, cheese cubes, and hard-cooked egg wedges in an empty ice cube tray—for a fun-to-eat snack or meal.

Meat Loafies

Bake meat loaf mixture in muffin tins. Freeze individual meat loaves and reheat in a toaster oven or microwave oven.

Rainbow Pastas

Serve multicolored pasta (tomato, spinach, egg) in a sauce with multicolored vegetables.

Bean Dip

Combine chick peas, lemon juice, oil, garlic powder, and water in a blender or food processor. Blend or process until smooth. To serve, spread dip on crackers, breadsticks, or celery pieces.

The Quiet Times

Children need a balance of active and quiet play for healthy growth. Quiet play is especially important if you're caring for a child who doesn't want to settle down for a nap or bedtime. Try some of these calming activities for quiet times:

- Read a story aloud.

- Make up stories—and include the child as one of the characters in the story.

- Draw pictures to illustrate the stories.

- Identify shapes.

- Identify animals in pictures. (If the children decide to make animal noises, this activity may not be so quiet!)

- Finger paint with aerosol whipping cream on a cookie sheet.

- Play card games—Go Fish, Concentration, Old Maid, Crazy Eights.

- Do a jigsaw puzzle.

- Make a collage—cut out pictures from magazines and paste them on colored paper.

- Cut out shapes and make abstract designs.

- Make shapes with clay or Playdough.

- Make paper airplanes, hats, and boats.

- Place paper over a coin and rub with a pencil until the picture can be seen.

- Play guessing games such as "I'm thinking of an animal" or 'I'm thinking of a place."

- Listen to music—even two-year-olds love "Peter and the Wolf."

- Cut a potato, carrot, or turnip in half and carve out a design. (You do the cutting with the knife.) Brush with poster paint or use an ink pad, and stamp the design on note paper or wrapping paper.

- Make flashcards with objects to identify.

- Play with a book or toy that teaches how to manage clothing fasteners, such as zippers, snaps, buttons, and shoelaces.

- Count or recite the alphabet.

MANAGEMENT

Managing Resources

OBJECTIVES

This chapter will help you to:

- Identify human resources and describe their benefits.
- Give examples of material, community, and natural resources.
- Determine how to manage your resources to achieve your goals.

WORDS TO REMEMBER

barter
community resource
conserve
human resource

material resource
natural resource
pollution

Sharon never seems to have enough time and money to do the things that interest her. On the weekends she is tired from her hectic week and doesn't feel like cleaning her room or making plans for the upcoming week. She usually has little of her allowance left to spend.

Sharon's friend Charlie doesn't seem to have the same problems. He always seems to have the money and time to do the things he wants. Sharon saw Charlie taking photos at school with an expensive-looking camera. She watched him playing an electric guitar in the school's talent show. Charlie also finds time to help coach a Little League baseball team.

One day, Sharon asked Charlie jokingly how he was able to do so many things. Charlie explained that he had no secrets but that his older brother taught him one important thing—how to manage the resources he has.

Charlie had borrowed the camera from his older sister in exchange for babysitting services, Sharon learned. He had rented the guitar from the music store and was taking guitar lessons in return for cleaning up the store. Charlie's healthful diet and adequate rest give him the energy to do many things during his spare time, such as coaching the team.

You might decide that you, like Charlie, could benefit by learning how better to manage your resources. Resources are the things you use to help you meet your goals. By managing your resources more effectively, you will find you can better achieve your goals and feel more in control of your life.

This boy is using several resources to help him accomplish his goal of becoming an artist. Can you name at least three of the resources?

Your Resources

You have many resources that you can use to accomplish your goals. You might have a special talent, such as a pleasant singing voice or the ability to fix a machine that breaks down. You may have an outgoing personality or a great sense of humor. Your friend may be good with numbers and have a good memory for people's names and famous dates. Time, money, possessions, family and friends, and even your community are other available resources.

Individuals and families have differing amounts of resources available to them, but one resource can often be substituted or traded for another. This flexibility can help you and your family make the best use of your resources.

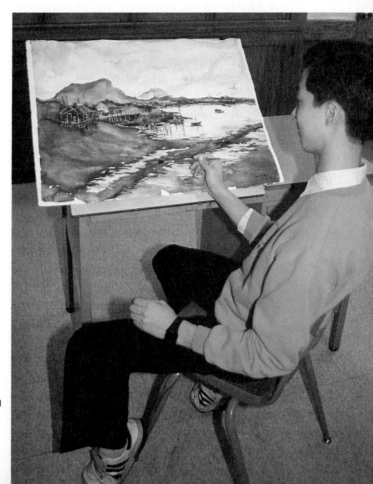

Human Resources

Human resources may be the easiest to draw upon because they are easily available and everybody possesses some. Human resources include knowledge, skills, imagination, energy, time, family, and friends.

- **Knowledge.** Knowledge, the information you acquire from your experience, includes the things you know about and the things you know how to do. Can you diaper a baby? Do you know how to use a computer? Have you learned the capital cities of the fifty states? These are different kinds of knowledge. You acquire your knowledge from your family, from school, from watching television, and from observing the world around you. You use your knowledge every day in hundreds of ways, but it never gets used up.

- **Skills.** Skills are your abilities to perform specific actions or techniques. Skills can be mental or physical. Walking on a balance beam is a physical skill, whereas working out mathematics problems in your head is a mental skill. The more you practice your skills, the better you will perform them.

- **Imagination.** Imagination is another valuable human resource. Have you ever tried to work out a problem in your mind, such as how to retrieve a box from a high shelf or how to redecorate your room on a tight budget? Those tasks require imagination. Your imagination helps you solve problems and make decisions by letting you think the situation through before you have to use any other resources. Artists and writers use imagination to envision the stories and pictures they will create.

- **Energy.** Energy is the power that allows you to get things done. You always use some mental or physical energy to accomplish a task. You can replenish your supply of energy by following four steps: get plenty of rest, eat nutritious foods, exercise, and avoid harmful substances. Following these steps will help prevent you from feeling tired; you will be better able to utilize your other resources.

- **Time.** Time is a resource that affects everything you do—working, resting, and playing. You would probably agree that time is often used up much too quickly. You probably know people who accomplish a lot. How do they do so much? In the next chapter you can learn some specific techniques for managing your time more effectively.

- **Family and friends.** Family and friends are irreplaceable resources. Your family helps you meet your basic needs for food, clothing, and shelter. Family members also have skills and knowledge that you can draw on. Your family is a resource that provides love, companionship, and support.

  Friends provide companionship and support. It's nice to have friends you can rely on when you need someone to talk to and laugh with. They often have skills that you don't have, and you can sometimes trade your skills for theirs. For example, if you help a friend with her homework, she may help you redecorate your room.

Material Resources

Material resources are objects that you can use to provide or make other things. They include possessions and money.

Other people are valuable resources. They can help you in many ways, from teaching you a new skill to providing support and friendship.

■ **Possessions.** Possessions are the things you have or own. Some possessions, like the furniture in your room, can be used for years before they have to be replaced. Others, such as looseleaf paper, ballpoint pens, or the film for your camera, need to be replaced often. Taking good care of your possessions can make them last longer.

Some possessions can help you use other of your resources more efficiently. A bicycle speeds travel and conserves time. Other possessions, such as a sewing machine or lawn mower, help you increase certain resources. By sewing, you can have more clothes. By using your lawn mower to mow other people's lawns, you can increase the amount of money you have.

■ **Money.** Money, another material resource, is known as a "medium of exchange" because it can be traded for almost anything. Your skateboard would not be accepted by the owner of a pizza shop in exchange for a pizza. The shop owner would rather have money, which he can then use to buy supplies.

Money is a resource that you can earn by working or performing a service. Some teens receive money as a weekly or monthly allowance from their parents. Learning to manage money by saving and spending wisely will help you to better meet your goals. Although money is useful, it cannot buy everything. Money can't buy the fun you have with your friends or the love of your family.

MANAGING RESOURCES

There's Only One World

Do you like to spend time in the sun, or visit beaches or woods? Can you imagine a world where you can't do those things? That kind of world may be in our future. Why? Because people are misusing our natural resources.

Pollution, or waste that is not properly disposed of, can harm beaches and forests. Solid wastes are showing up on the nation's beaches and they are causing people to become ill. Forests are being cleared and burned. Pollutants in the air are making rain more acidic, damaging forests and lakes.

Natural resources used as fuel, such as coal, wood, and oil, are causing wastes that threaten the world. For example, cars emit carbon dioxide, a gas that thickens the layer of atmospheric gases surrounding the earth. This so called "greenhouse effect" keeps the earth warm and, in the future, might cause the polar ice caps to melt.

Another type of pollution is caused by the production of chemical compounds such as those found in Styrofoam fast-food containers and in the Freon used in air conditioners. Those compounds break down the shield that protects the earth from the sun's harmful ultraviolet radiation. Not only could this adversely affect plant growth, but it could also cause people to become more susceptible to skin cancer.

Here are things that you can do to use our natural resources more efficiently:

- Walk, bicycle, or take public transportation instead of a car whenever possible. One bus or train generates less pollution than the 50 or 60 cars that would be needed to move an equal number of people.
- Conserve energy and fuel at home. Take shorter, cooler showers, and lower the thermostat in cool weather and turn it up in hot weather. Don't keep the refrigerator door open, and do shut off the lights when you leave a room. Conserving electricity reduces the amount of coal, oil, and gas used to generate more electrical energy.
- Don't throw away magazines, and empty soda bottles or cans. If you recycle glass, paper, and aluminum, fewer natural resources will be required to create new products.

Think It Through

1. What else could you do to make better use of natural resources or to help curb pollution? Give at least one original example.
2. If certain fuels are so harmful, why do you think they have been used in our society for so long?

Community Resources

Community resources are people and facilities in your community that help you enjoy your life, improve your skills, and achieve your goals. For example, schools are staffed with many people who serve as resources. Teachers, coaches, and counselors help you to increase your knowledge and improve your skills. Schools offer you opportunities to explore a wide variety of interests—such as art, foreign languages, child care, and computers—and also provide facilities such as libraries and gymnasiums that you can use.

People go to church, synagogue, and other places of worship for spiritual support and a sense of belonging. Individual religious leaders and other members provide guidance and friendship. Teen groups and functions provide opportunities to have fun and meet people.

People and places in your city or town provide many other resources. You can use the services of doctors, dentists, police officers, social service workers, child caregivers, and volunteer agencies. You can explore the varied offerings of museums, zoos, parks, movie theaters, libraries, restaurants, and stores. All these places enrich your life by enabling you to experience things you couldn't provide on your own, such as Bengal tigers, French paintings, and Vietnamese food.

Natural Resources

Air, water, soil, trees, minerals, and petroleum products are all **natural resources** that we use every day. We use water and soil to grow our food, trees to make paper and lumber for our houses, and gas and oil to heat our homes and fuel our cars. It is important to save, or **conserve**, our natural resources so that we don't use them up faster than we can replace them. Natural resources are important to us in other ways as well. They often provide a sense of beauty that improves our quality of life.

Community resources include members of your school staff, such as guidance counselors. What other people and places in your school can serve as valuable resources for you?

Managing Resources

Once you have identified the resources that are available to you, you can begin to plan the best way to use them to accomplish your goals. One important reason to think about managing resources is that your resources are limited. For example, you only have so much available money or time or energy. You need to make many decisions every day about how to use these resources most efficiently.

Choosing and Substituting Resources

You often have a choice of resources you can use to reach a goal. Before you decide which resource you will use, you need to determine what your choices are. For example, suppose that one of your household jobs is to wash the family car every week. To do that job, you can choose among several different resources:

- You can use your own time and energy to wash the car yourself.
- You can spend your money to have the car washed at a car wash.
- You can use your imagination to convince your brother or sister that washing the car is so much fun he or she will help you do it.
- You can **barter**, or directly exchange one resource for another. For example, you can trade homework help for help in washing the car.

Your choice of what resource to use will depend on several things: your supply of time, energy, and money, and the availability of a little brother or sister. You can try to substitute one resource for another when you are faced with a job to do. It's up to you to choose which resource you will use.

Using Resources Wisely

All of your resources are limited. Once you use them they are gone, so it is important to use resources wisely. Some resources, such as knowledge and skills, can be increased through education, experience, and training. Other resources, such as clean water and fuel, must be conserved for future use.

You have to decide which resources to use and how to use them efficiently. Decision-making and management skills can help you to better manage your resources—to satisfy your needs now and throughout your lifetime.

Here are some guidelines to help you increase your resources and to use them wisely:

- **Knowledge.** By reading, talking to people, and asking questions, you can increase your knowledge.
- **Skills.** Practicing is the best way to master skills. Reading and getting advice from skilled people also help.
- **Time.** If you plan what to do in the time available to you, you will be able to get more done.
- **Energy.** You can maximize your source of energy by following healthy living habits. Then you can use your energy for more activities.
- **Possessions.** You can take care of the things you own to make them last longer. You may be able to make or trade some possessions.
- **Money.** By careful planning and savings, you can get the most out of your money. You can work part-time to earn money in order to increase your savings or acquire what you need or want.
- **Imagination.** Use your imagination to think out problems and find creative ways to solve them. Use brainstorming to develop new ideas.

25 REVIEW

Reviewing the Facts

1. What is a resource? Identify four groups of resources.
2. What human resources do all people possess?
3. How can family and friends be a resource?
4. How is money different from other resources?
5. Name three community resources.
6. What are some strategies you can use in managing your resources?

Sharing Your Ideas

1. How do the following human resources—your knowledge, your energy, and your imagination—help you reach your goals? Why?
2. What types of resources do you have in your community that can help you achieve your goals? How can they help?

Applying Your Skills

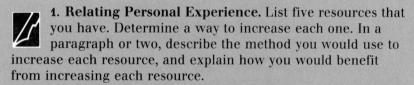

1. Relating Personal Experience. List five resources that you have. Determine a way to increase each one. In a paragraph or two, describe the method you would use to increase each resource, and explain how you would benefit from increasing each resource.

2. Using Library Resources. Look at a local telephone directory and list five community resources. Read the title of the organization carefully and come up with the purpose of each. Summarize the information for your class.

3. Evaluating a Decision. Each individual must decide how to use natural resources. Write a brief summary explaining how you use particular natural resources. Evaluate those decisions on the basis of what you've learned. Then write about measures you can take to conserve those same natural resources.

CHAPTER

26

Managing Time

OBJECTIVES

This chapter will help you to:

- List five benefits of time management.
- Explain how to use calendars, schedules, and lists.
- Describe the advantage of keeping a time schedule flexible.
- List techniques for using time effectively.

WORDS TO REMEMBER

calendar
deadline
procrastinate
schedule

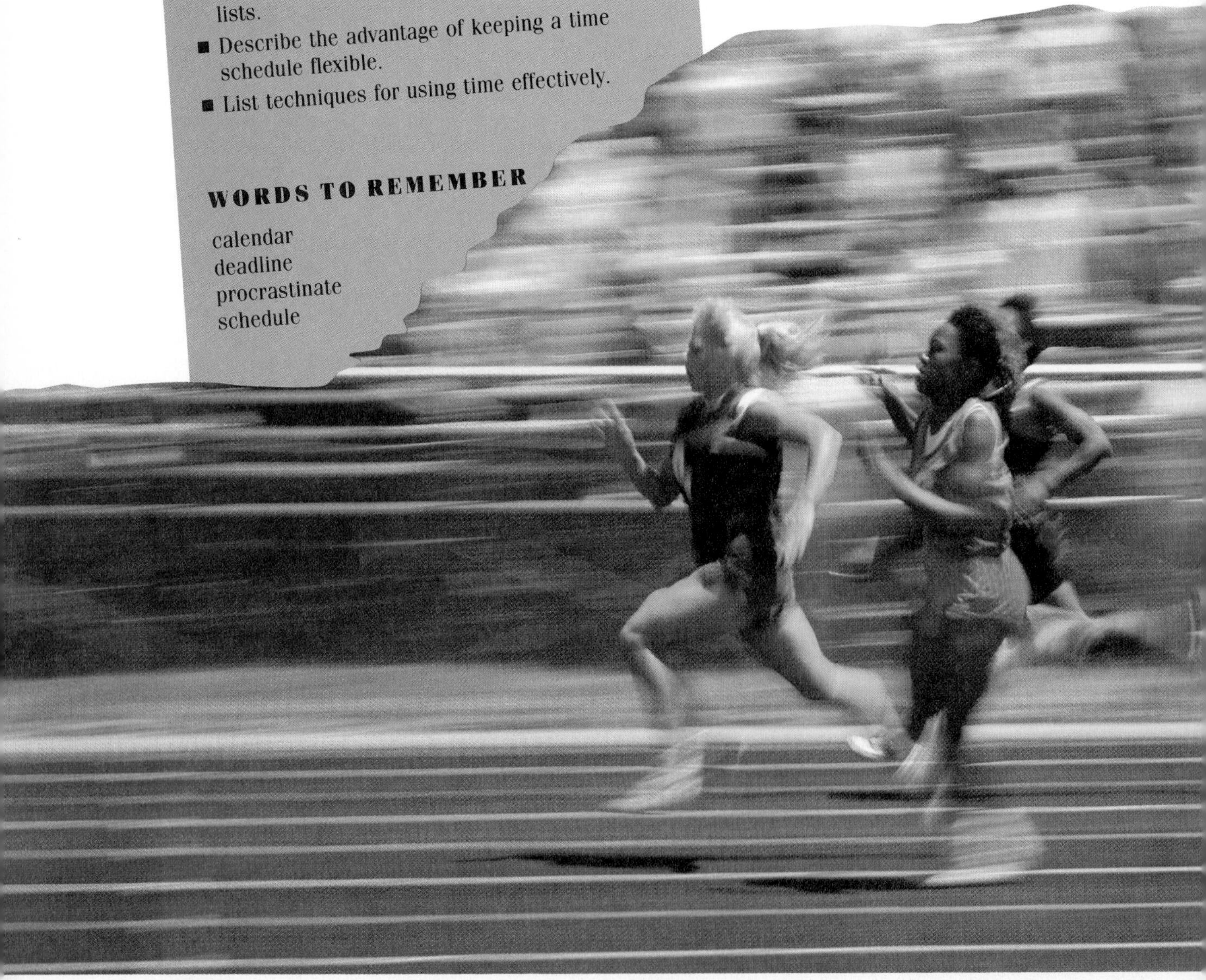

Colin mentioned to his mother that he didn't think he was doing too well in his Spanish class. "I don't always finish my assignments and then I have to struggle to catch up." Colin and his mother talked about what he could do and agreed he could concentrate better on his homework if he spent less time talking on the telephone in the evenings. Fifteen minutes later when his mother went upstairs, Colin was on the telephone again.

Colin is fighting himself. He hasn't really thought about his needs and his resources, so he has trouble setting goals. He could benefit from examining how he uses—and wastes—his time.

Time is a resource, like money and knowledge. You can plan how to spend time, and you can learn to manage what you do in the time available to you. Then you will have more time to spend on the people and things you value the most.

Planning Your Time

When you wake up in the morning, do you think about the day ahead? How much time do you have to get ready for school? Remember that you promised to eat lunch with Sara and Josh today. Basketball tryouts begin right after school. Tonight, besides studying for a math test, you're babysitting for your four-year-old brother, Bobby. When you plan ahead, you consider how your time will be used throughout the day. Planning your time has several benefits.

- You'll be better able to achieve your goals.
- You'll be able to get more done by fitting in more activities that are important to you.
- You'll be less likely to leave important tasks undone.

When you learn to plan your time, you will have more time to relax and do the things you enjoy.

- You'll be able to do all that's expected of you—at the time when it's expected. Others will be able to rely on you, and they will appreciate that you are considerate of their time.
- You'll gain extra time to do the things you enjoy or just to relax.

Setting Your Goals

Before you can start planning your time, you need to set goals for all the things you hope to accomplish. Setting goals will help you think about the time you will need to achieve each thing you want to accomplish.

If you need to write a thank-you note for a gift you have received, you may decide to set aside ten minutes today. If you plan to try out for a part in a school play, you may decide to spend a half hour each day this week reading aloud several parts in different plays. It's important to think about the kind of activities or tasks you are planning, so that you will allow realistic amounts of time to complete them.

Setting Priorities

Once you've identified your goals and the things you need to accomplish, you can set your priorities. That is, decide which tasks are most urgent and should be done first and which ones can wait. If your priority is to make the basketball team, you may want to practice basketball every day to improve your jump shot. You may need to decide which task is more important to you—the basketball team, your homework, your chores, or spending time with your friends.

Making Time Work for You

You are probably already doing some things to manage your time. When you look at all your tasks, you might group some of them together so that you can accomplish them more efficiently. For example, if you want to buy a jacket and a birthday card, you can save time by buying both on the same shopping trip.

This kind of planning also helps you break large tasks into smaller units. Instead of studying for a big test for two

Setting priorities helps you identify which tasks are most important and need to be done first.

hours the night before, you can plan to study 20 minutes each night for a week. Managing your work in this manner helps you make time work for you. Another way of managing your activities is to rely on three useful tools—a calendar, a schedule, and a list.

Using a Calendar

A common tool for managing your activities is a **calendar**—a weekly, monthly, or yearly record of your appointments, important events, holidays, birthdays, and so forth. Most people keep a calendar for a month or two ahead at a time.

To use a calendar, begin by writing down all of the events and obligations you have scheduled for the month on a wall or desk calendar. If you have soccer practice every Tuesday and Thursday evening, put that down. Include your work schedule, club meetings, dental appointments, babysitting jobs, sports events, and anything else that you need to set aside time for during the month. As other activities come up, include those on the calendar as well.

Whenever you want to go somewhere or do something with friends on a specific day and time, you can look at your calendar and see if you are free then. Another advantage of keeping a calendar is that you don't have to memorize dates and times or take the risk of forgetting an activity or appointment.

Making a Schedule

A **schedule** can be another important tool for managing your activities. This is a daily or weekly plan showing the time and length of each of your activities. You are already familiar with class schedules that show when and where each of

your classes meet each day of the week. Making a daily schedule, with a space for every hour in the day, will enable you to keep track of the starting time for every activity.

Organizing a List

An excellent way to organize the activities you want to accomplish is to plan your schedule in the form of a "To-Do List." A "To-Do List" allows you to set your priorities because it helps you to list your tasks in order of importance.

To make a "To-Do List," write down the things you must do each day. Include all your after-school activities and all the tasks that must be done at home. Then divide each day's tasks and activities into three groups—A, B, and C.

Tuesday – To Do:
1) Turn in math homework (A)
2) Complete outline for history report (A)
3) Clean room (A)
4) Cut grass (B)
5) Call Frank about party (C)
6) Read two chapters of Lincoln for next week (C)

- The A items on your list are your "must-do" items. These tasks are the ones with **deadlines**—dates by which these tasks must be completed.
- The B items are important, but they don't have to be done that day.
- The C items are those you would like to get done, but they can be put aside with little loss.

If you are honest with yourself when you set up these categories and if you concentrate on getting the A items done, you will be less likely to **procrastinate**. Procrastinating means putting things off. Most people tend to procrastinate when faced with tasks they dislike, even the important ones.

You won't need to make a list every day because on some days your schedule will be routine. You will already have a sense of what you want to do and how you can fit it all in. On other days, when you have many tasks, a list can help you to do them all.

By following these simple steps, you will manage your time better.

1. Choose a time to make your "To-Do List"—either the first thing in the morning or in the evening for the next day. Keep in mind that your priorities may change during the day.
2. Assign each task to a category—A, B, or C.
3. Cross out each item as you complete it. You'll feel good when you see how much you are accomplishing.

Planning for the Unexpected

One advantage of planning beforehand is that you can change your plans if something unexpected comes up. Even when your day is going just as you had planned, things may arise that you hadn't foreseen. Managing your time well means not only handling all the expected tasks you face each day but also dealing with the unexpected.

Let's look at a "To-Do List" for a typical day you might have planned:

- Walk and feed dog (A).
- Finish science report (A).
- Empty the wastebaskets (A).
- Do exercises (B).
- Attend meeting at teen center (B).
- Watch favorite TV show (C).

When you get home from school, you're ready to start on your tasks, but you're faced with a sudden change of plans. Your mother has left you a note saying that she's gone to pick up your aunt at the airport and will be back with her around 9:00 p.m. You'll have to heat up the stew for your dinner and get the spare room ready for Aunt Carol.

You need to change your list to reflect the new situation. Your A list must now include getting the room ready and fixing dinner. To fit those tasks in, you have to make some other changes. Your revised list might look like this:

- Get Aunt Carol's room ready (A).
- Walk and feed the dog (A).
- Prepare and eat dinner (A).
- Finish science report (A).
- Empty the wastebaskets (B).
- Attend teen center meeting (B).
- Do exercises (C).
- Watch TV show (C).

Now work through as much of the list as you can. If you get through all of the A items and all or most of the B items, you can feel a sense of accomplishment. If you can't get to the C items, you can always make exercising a high priority on tomorrow's list, and watch the next episode of your favorite TV series.

Take Time for "Time-Out"

John's been working hard all day—going to school, mowing the lawn, helping with dinner, and doing his homework. Now he is taking a half-hour break to read a magazine. Is he just wasting time he could be using to study? No, not at all.

Everyone needs to take time-outs. Far from being a waste of time, they relieve physical and mental stress, relax the body, and replenish energy so that time can be used more efficiently. That's why people have weekends off from school and work and why they take vacations and have hobbies.

Here are a few ways you can take a time-out:

- Athletics and exercise help relax tense, tight muscles, making you feel more energetic and fit. Physical activity is a great way to escape from the mental stress you've built up sitting in a classroom. You could go for a jog, walk the dog, ride a bike, or work out.

- Switching channels mentally is another good way to relax. If you find you can no longer concentrate on your homework or studying, take a 15-minute break. Read a magazine, listen to music, work on a crossword puzzle, eat a snack, or work on a hobby.

Remember when you take time for a time-out, you're not wasting time. You're "recharging your mental and physical batteries" so you can use your time and energy to its fullest.

Think It Through

1. Do you think exercise is a good form of time-out? Why? What kind of exercise do you enjoy for time-out?
2. If you wanted to "recharge your batteries" while studying for a test, what would you do? Why?

Hints for Good Time Management

The following strategies will help you use your time more effectively.

- **Group activities together to save time.** Suppose you have two errands during the school day—getting a form from your counselor and turning in a permission slip to the principal. Since both stops are in the same part of the building, do both on the same trip.
- **Alternate chores with more enjoyable tasks.** Having something pleasant to look forward to will help you finish a chore more quickly.
- **Do unpleasant tasks first.** They seem easier if you get them out of the way.
- **Don't overload.** If you try to do too much, you may do something wrong. Then you'll spend time fixing it.
- **Allow enough time to do things.** You can bet that a problem will occur if your schedule is too tight. If you planned on spending only one hour to write a paper that actually takes two hours, your schedule will be off.
- **Be prepared.** Even the best time-saving plan can fail if you don't organize each task. Before you begin a task, think it through and decide what you will need to accomplish it. If you're cleaning your room, bring both the vacuum cleaner and the dust cloth. If you have to go back to get supplies, you're wasting time.
- **Learn from your mistakes.** If you find it hard to get all your A items done, don't be discouraged. Step back and think. Try to find out what went wrong. Are you putting too many items on your A list? Are you allowing too little time for each item? Learn to limit your commitments and to leave a little extra time in the schedule—just in case.

You should reward yourself for good time management. This will encourage you to keep up the routine. If you have accomplished your tasks all week, reward yourself by going out to a movie or having a special lunch. If you get your homework done early, enjoy phoning a friend, reading a magazine, or relaxing.

Time is the one resource that you cannot increase. You only get 24 hours in each day. You can't save an hour from one day and add it to the next, and you can't get back the hours and days that have already gone by. You can, however, learn to use your time more effectively so that you have more time to do the things you like.

What time management strategies could this girl follow when training or grooming her dog?

CHAPTER 26 REVIEW

Reviewing the Facts

1. Name four benefits you can expect when you plan your time well.
2. Why must you first set goals in order to plan your time more effectively?
3. Explain the difference between a personal calendar and a schedule.
4. Why is it helpful to divide tasks into groups on a "To-Do List"?
5. What does procrastination mean?
6. What should you do if the unexpected happens and you cannot get through all the A, B, and C tasks on your list?
7. List three strategies for using time effectively.

Sharing Your Ideas

1. What problems do you have when it comes to managing time? How could you solve these problems? Do these problems affect other people? How?
2. Give some examples of situations where flexibility in a schedule is important.

Applying Your Skills

1. **Solving Scheduling Problems.** Plan a daily schedule that includes your usual activities, such as studying for a test, doing homework, and attending after-school activities. Make a note of the time each activity takes. Are there any activities that conflict with one another? How could you solve the problem?

2. **Specifying Criteria.** Make a "To-Do List" for today. Set your priorities for the day by assigning each task an A, B, or C rating. Cross off each task as you complete it. At the end of the day evaluate your list and write a paragraph about how this time-management tool worked for you.

3. **Planning a Workload.** Assume that you need to accomplish these things on Saturday: doing your homework, washing the car, spending time with friends, and cleaning your room. What steps would you take to handle these tasks? Write a brief summary.

Managing Money

OBJECTIVES

This chapter will help you to:

- Explain the goals of money management.
- Identify sources of income.
- Make and use a budget to manage money.
- Define and explain the difference between fixed and flexible expenses.

WORDS TO REMEMBER

budget
electronic funds transfer (EFT)
expense
income

What does money mean to you? Some people feel that money is for spending. They like to spend their money going to the movies, or buying clothes, or eating out, or selecting nice gifts for their family and friends. People with this attitude think that money's primary purpose is to provide fun—today.

Money can mean other things. To some it means security. Such people feel a great need to save money for their future needs, although most people save some money for a particular purpose. You may already be saving money to buy new stereo equipment, or a used car, or to pay for college.

Money can also mean a sense of power. Some people, for example, feel that money makes them look more successful. It can also determine a family's style of living—its choice of neighborhood, type of home, schools, and entertainment.

Remember that it's not how much money you have that's important, but how well you manage the money you do have. In order to manage your money well, you will need to do two things: carefully consider your values and goals, and learn some money-management skills.

Your Goals and Money Management

Although you can buy some of the things you want, it's almost impossible to have enough money to buy all of them, because wants are limitless. If you learn to manage your money well—planning ahead and saving—you can have more money to buy the things you want most.

Money for Things You Need

Your first responsibility is to use your money to meet your needs. Right now, your family probably provides your most basic needs for shelter and food. Even so, you may have to set aside some of your own money for other needs, such as lunches, school supplies, and perhaps clothes. Good money management is the key to providing for these needs.

Learning to manage your money involves choices and decisions about how you spend your money.

Money for Things You Want

Most people enjoy being able to buy some of the things they want. Putting on a new outfit or playing a new tape for the first time can be a lot of fun.

Some people make the mistake of putting their wants before their needs. Do you have friends who spend more than they can afford on extras? When they run short of money, they may borrow from others or skip lunches. That method of money management may work for these people for a while, but it causes them to constantly worry as to whether they will have enough money. Most people have to spend a large portion of their money on their needs, and only when their needs are met can they spend money on the things they want.

Money management includes planning for unexpected expenses, such as buying a present for a friend.

Money for Unplanned Expenses

It's also important to manage your money so that there is some left in case of an unexpected expense. Suppose someone invites you to a birthday party and you need to buy a present. Perhaps your tape player breaks and must be repaired. By putting some of your money aside, you'll have the savings to take care of unexpected expenses like these.

Making a Budget

One of the best ways to manage your money is to make a budget. A **budget** is a plan for using your money. A budget doesn't give you any more money, but it will help you decide how to best use the money you have.

Before you start a budget, make a list of your needs and wants. Set priorities. What are your specific needs? Which of your wants are most important?

Step 1. Determine Your Income

Before you start to plan the use of your money, you have to figure out how much income you have. **Income** is the money you take in and have available to spend.

What are your sources of income? As with adults, many teens depend on work to earn money. Jobs vary from baby-sitting and walking dogs to shelving books in a library or working in a fast-food restaurant. If you work for your spending money, you may find yourself more careful about spending it.

One of your main sources of income may be an allowance. If you receive one, you may be permitted to spend it as you please or you may be expected to pay for your school supplies and lunches. To avoid problems, it's a good idea to discuss how your family expects you to spend your allowance.

Do you sometimes receive money from your family for birthdays or holidays? If so, consider setting this money aside for special purchases. That way, when you find something you really want but cannot afford, you can use your gift money.

To figure out your income, decide on a period of time—maybe a week or a month—then add together all the money you expect to receive over that period of time. The total is the amount you have to spend in your budget.

Step 2. Keep a Record of Your Spending

Your **expenses** are the things that you spend your money on. A record of your expenses will be helpful in determining which items to include in your budget and how much money to allow for each item. There are two types of expenses.

- **Fixed expenses.** These are the important expenses that you need to pay—costs that you are committed to. You might have a piano lesson each week that you have to put aside money to pay for, or you might need money to buy lunch each day at school.
- **Flexible expenses.** These are expenses that don't stay the same, which you can make new decisions about in each budget. You go to the movies some weeks but not others, and you don't buy clothes or school supplies every week.

Making a Budget

Weekly Income		Weekly Expenses	
Allowance	$10.00	Savings	
Babysitting and odd jobs	20.00	Emergencies	$ 3.00
		For bicycle repairs	4.00
		Fixed expenses	
		Piano lesson	6.00
		Flexible expenses	
		Entertainment	6.00
		Clothes	9.00
		School supplies	2.00
Total	$30.00	**Total**	$30.00

Sometimes it can be hard to estimate your expenses. If you have a lot of trouble doing so, keep track of each amount you actually spend for two or three weeks. Write everything down. Then, take an average. For instance, if you spent $5.89 for school supplies over three weeks, you spent an average of $1.96 each week. Now you know that if you budget $2.00 per week for school supplies, you'll probably stay within that amount and still meet your needs for supplies. Compute the average amount for each item you want to budget.

Step 3. Define the Goals for Your Plan

When making a budget, it's important to keep your goals in mind. Short-term goals might include paying for lunches or buying a birthday present for your best friend. Long-term goals could be saving for summer camp or for new school clothes.

Set aside money for these goals before you allow money for extras. If you want to buy more clothes, set aside money for that before spending it on a movie.

One of your goals should include saving some money. Financial experts recommend trying to save something each time you receive money. The habit of saving is an important one. It will give you money for emergencies and for purchasing expensive items.

Some people first figure out everything they need or want to spend money on. Then they plan to save any money that may be left over. The problem with that method is that there often isn't anything left over.

Make saving a priority. Put aside a small amount, for example, $1.50 a week for a year. You'll be surprised at how quickly your small amount of savings will grow.

If your goal is to buy an expensive guitar, you can set aside a little money each week until you have saved enough to pay for it.

TECHNOLOGY

Electronic Money

What do you think of when you hear the word *banking?* Filling out forms, waiting in lines, and speaking with a teller? Well, now there is a new meaning to the word. It's now possible to bank and pay bills automatically with the use of computers. The method is called **electronic funds transfer (EFT).** EFT cards can be used to handle many transactions with just the push of a button:

Here are some EFT services.

- **Automatic teller machines.** You can skip the long lines at the bank by using these machines. The bank gives you a plastic EFT card and a secret identification number. You put your card into a machine and punch in your secret number on a keyboard. You can then make deposits or withdrawals, check your account balance, or move money from one account to another.

- **Point of sale terminals.** These machines are located in some stores. Instead of paying cash or using a check, you put your EFT card into one of the machines. It instantly transfers the money from your account to the account of the store.

- **Home computer transactions.** Some banks offer customers with home computers the option of paying bills and transferring funds from one account to another by means of computer. Customers can also use their computers to check their bank balances.

- **Telephone transfers.** Some banks allow people who don't have computers to call on the telephone to pay bills or transfer money between accounts.

If you use any of these EFT services, be sure to keep your personal identification number a secret. If you think there's an error in your statement, notify the bank immediately.

Think It Through

1. Can you think of possible disadvantages in using EFT services? Explain.
2. Some writers have imagined that bills and coins will no longer be used in the twenty-first century, and that all money transactions will be done with plastic cards and computers. Do you agree? Explain your answer.

Step 4. Revise the Plan If Necessary

If you aren't coming close to your budget, it's not right for you yet. Are you getting caught short of lunch money at the end of the week? You might want to adjust your budget to allow more money for lunch and less for entertainment or clothes.

Changes in income also mean that you will need to adjust your budget. You might find a part-time job or ask for a raise in your allowance. You should adjust your budget to include changes in income as well as changes in expenses.

Step 5. Stick to the Plan

Making and using your budget is a learning experience. You haven't failed if it doesn't work out exactly right the first time. Change things and try again until you are getting what you want from your money.

Using Your Budget

Keep the following points in mind as you practice managing your money:

- If you rely on your budget regularly, you will find it a useful tool. It won't help you at all if you don't use it.
- If you are on target in estimating your income and your spending, your budget should be accurate—especially if you revise it several times to reflect any changes.
- If your budget is not helping you manage your money, consider the possibility that your estimates of income and spending are unrealistic. You may want to make an extra effort to control any spending beyond your limits.
- Remind yourself that the person in charge of managing your money is you. Your budget can be a valuable tool for wise money management, but all decisions on planning, spending, and saving are in your hands.

A budget can help you decide how best to spend and save the money that you have.

CHAPTER

27 REVIEW

1. What are the three goals of money management?
2. What is a budget? What is the main purpose of a budget?
3. What is income?
4. What is the difference between fixed and flexible expenses?
5. What is one technique you can use to help you figure out your estimated monthly or weekly expenses?
6. What is one example of a short-term goal in using money and one example of a long-term goal?
7. What two kinds of changes might require you to revise your budget?
8. Name three transactions that you can perform on an automatic teller machine.

Sharing Your Ideas

1. What are some fixed and flexible expenses that you have? What types of adjustments can you make to your flexible expenses?
2. Why do you think it is important to include savings in your money management plans?

Applying Your Skills

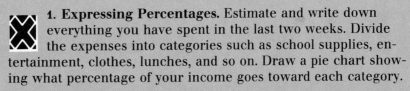

1. Expressing Percentages. Estimate and write down everything you have spent in the last two weeks. Divide the expenses into categories such as school supplies, entertainment, clothes, lunches, and so on. Draw a pie chart showing what percentage of your income goes toward each category.

2. Budgeting Expenses. Use your estimates of the amount of money you spend every two weeks to devise a weekly budget for yourself. First estimate your income. Then write down your fixed expenses, including the amount you expect to save. Take an average of your flexible expenses over the two-week period. Your income should equal your savings and expenses. See page 259 for a sample budget.

3. Writing a Summary. Write a short report describing any difficulties you anticipate in staying within your budget. Discuss how you expect to handle these difficulties, and describe the changes you would propose in your budget plan to make it fit your income and expenses more accurately.

Saving and Borrowing

There may be times when you want something very much but can't afford it. What can you do about this problem? You may find quite a few solutions. There may be a less expensive substitute. You could start a special savings effort to accumulate the money needed. (You might, for example, find a job to help you earn extra money.) You might borrow the money you need.

It's also important to take a second look at what you want to purchase. Will it still look as important to you next month? Because money is a limited resource, you know that you can't buy everything you want. To avoid disappointments, you will want to choose carefully the ways you save, borrow, and spend your money.

Another important reason for having a plan for savings and borrowing is that it can be quite difficult to tell in advance what you'll need next month or next year. If you plan for ways to meet unexpected expenses, you will be giving yourself some freedom.

Why do people save money? There seem to be three basic reasons.

- **For unexpected expenses.** Although a budget should cover usual expenses, if your bike is stolen or your tape deck has to be repaired, extra money will be needed.
- **To make large purchases.** For you, that might mean saving for a new sweater or stereo for your room. Your family might be saving for a new car or television. If everyone spends a little less, the extra money can be put aside for something everyone will enjoy.
- **For the future.** Are you saving to go to camp, college, or vocational school? Then you are saving for the future. Adults often start saving for their retirement after they begin work. Saving for the future helps to give you a sense of security.

Despite the benefits of saving, people sometimes find that saving does not quite give them enough. They might need a large sum of money right away. At such times, people might consider borrowing money.

Saving and borrowing are different kinds of money transactions, but they have at least one thing in common. Both require an understanding of how to act wisely to protect your best interests. You will find useful information about both saving and borrowing in this chapter.

Establishing Bank Accounts

There are several ways to save the money you have earned. No doubt you want your money to increase in value and to be available when you need it. Commercial banks, savings and loan associations, and credit unions offer savings and checking accounts. Let's take a look at these to determine the differences between them.

Savings Accounts

A **savings account** is an account that holds the savings you deposit. Some institutions give you a passbook when you open an account. You must present this book to the teller who will record your deposits and withdrawals in it. Other institutions have statement savings accounts. With this type of account you are given deposit and withdrawal slips. Every month you receive a statement of the account's transactions to check against your records.

Because savings accounts differ, it is important to compare how much interest your money will earn in an account. **Interest** is a fee paid for the use of money. When you put money into a savings account, the institution pays you interest in exchange for the right to use your money for investments and loans. Generally, the higher the interest rate the more you will earn.

How does the institution know how much interest to pay you? That's determined by four factors:

■ The **principal,** or amount of money you have in your account.

■ The interest rate, or percentage of the principal that is paid as interest.

■ How long the money will earn interest.

■ How often the interest is paid.

Suppose that you have $100 in your savings account at the interest rate of 5 percent per year. At the end of the year, your $100 will have earned 5 percent of that $100, or $5.00. The institution adds that to your savings account, giving you a total of $105.

Once the interest is added on, it becomes part of your principal. Since your principal is now $105, you will earn even more interest the next year. If the interest is paid quarterly (every three months), your total will increase faster.

Before you open a savings account, you should find out if you have to leave a certain amount of money in your account in order to earn interest. Ask whether you lose interest if you withdraw money often.

Checking Accounts

A **checking account** is an account on which you can write checks directing the bank to pay money as instructed. It provides an easy way to pay for things and helps you to keep track of both your spending and your savings. To open a checking account, you deposit your money in the bank. You then receive checks and a booklet for recording each by number, date, amount, and the person or business receiving the check.

Before opening a savings account, you should find out how much interest your money will earn. How does the rate compare with other types of savings accounts?

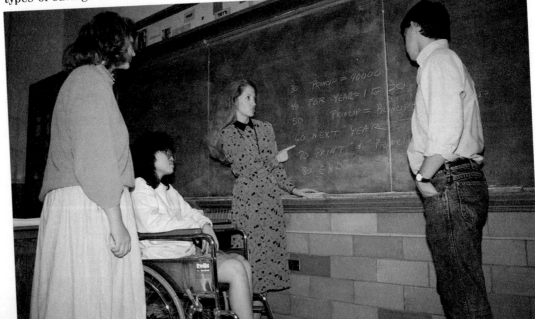

There are different types of checking accounts. Some require that you maintain a minimum balance. Others charge a specific amount for each check that you write. Until recently, most checking accounts did not pay interest on their balance. However, because of changes in banking laws and competition, most banks now offer checking accounts that pay interest. If you are thinking about opening a checking account, consider these questions:

- Do you need it? If you expect to write only one or two checks a month, you might be better off paying for your purchases with cash or a money order. A **money order** can be used like a check and is sold in banks and post offices.
- What will it cost? There are often fees for writing checks or monthly service charges.
- Will you be tempted to overspend by carrying a checkbook?
- Would writing checks be convenient?

If you open a checking account, you need to know how to write your checks correctly so that the person or business to whom the check is written is able to collect the money. To keep track of your transactions, subtract the amount of each check from your balance. If you forget to do this, your balance will show a figure higher than the amount of money that is actually in your account. Then you might write checks amounting to more money than is in your account, known as an overdraft or "bouncing" a check. Also remember to record any deposits.

Be sure to record each check you write. Also add any deposits and subtract any fees the bank charges.

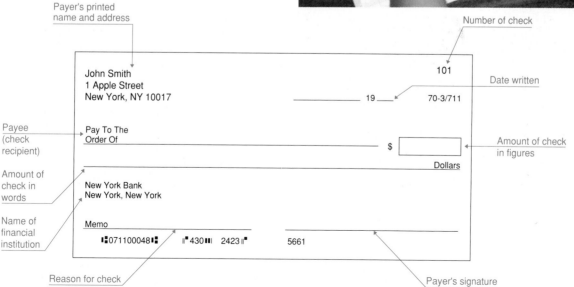

Payer's printed name and address

Number of check

John Smith
1 Apple Street
New York, NY 10017

101

19 ____ 70-3/711

Date written

Payee (check recipient)

Pay To The
Order Of

$ ____

Amount of check in figures

Dollars

Amount of check in words

New York Bank
New York, New York

Name of financial institution

Memo

⑆071100048⑈ ⑆430⑈ 2423⑈ 5661

Reason for check

Payer's signature

Making Money Grow

When Curtis received a savings bond for his birthday, he was disappointed. He wondered why his grandmother hadn't given him money, like she had every other year. What Curtis doesn't realize is that a savings bond is money with a value that increases the longer he holds it.

At some point in your life, you might consider investing your savings so that you earn a higher interest than you would in a traditional savings account.

Some investments are riskier than others. You need to consider the amount of risk involved versus the return on your money to decide what investment is best for you.

- **Savings bonds.** Savings bonds are certificates that represent money that you lend to the government. The bonds pay you interest as long as you own them. They are insured, and you can cash them in any time you want. They are sold in smaller amounts than most other types of investments.

- **Savings clubs.** Many banks offer a Christmas Club or a Vacation Club to help customers save. Club members put a certain amount of money into the account every week until the account is used to pay for presents or a trip.

- **Certificates of deposit.** A certificate of deposit, (CD) is a form of savings account in which a certain amount of money is deposited for a specific amount of time at a guaranteed interest rate.

- **Stocks.** Companies need money to operate. They get it by selling shares of stock. When you buy stock, you buy a share in the business.

- **Bonds.** In addition to the government, some businesses also sell bonds. The people who buy them are lending the company money. In return, they are paid interest.

- **Mutual funds.** Mutual funds are a method of saving and investing for people who don't want to buy stocks and bonds on their own. Mutual fund companies pool the money of many people to buy stocks, bonds, and other investments. Then they divide any money that the investments earn.

Think It Through

1. Which investment option would you choose if you had $1,000? Why?
2. Do you think investments are a resource?

Borrowing Money

People borrow money for all sorts of reasons. **Credit** is an arrangement for receiving money, merchandise, or a service now and paying for it later. For example, a family on vacation pays for a motel room with a credit card so they won't have to carry large amounts of money. A new car buyer takes out a loan to repay in monthly installments because she doesn't have the total amount needed to buy the car now.

Trust is an important part of using credit. Every day millions of people use some form of credit. This is possible because the lenders trust that the money will be repaid. Borrowing money involves a serious obligation to pay it back according to the terms agreed on.

Credit is available in many forms, such as credit cards, installment loans, and layaway.

- **Credit card.** A credit card is a form of identification that allows a person to purchase items on credit and pay for them over a period of time, usually with monthly payments.
- **Installment loan.** With an installment loan, the money that is lent is to be repaid in regular payments over a specified period of time. Installment loans are often used to pay for cars and major appliances.
- **Layaway.** Layaway is an agreement with a store to hold an item for you as long as you make regular payments. You receive the item after you have completed paying for it. Layaway is used for clothing purchases.

People can apply for loans at banks, savings and loan associations, credit unions, and certain stores or dealers. They must prove that they will be able to repay the loan.

Getting Credit

Companies that offer credit look for certain qualities in the people they lend to. They want borrowers to be of a certain age, usually at least 18 years old. They want them to have some steady source of income, such as a job. They also want the borrower to have shown that he or she was responsible about paying off past debts.

Young people just starting out haven't yet had a chance to build a credit record so they may have trouble getting loans. There are a few things that young people can do to establish credit. The first is to open a savings account.

One of the quickest ways to begin building a good credit history once you turn 18 is to obtain a department store or oil company credit card. Open a checking account to show you can pay bills and handle money, and when you begin to use your credit cards, always make sure you make payments on the bills promptly each month. This will ensure that you have a good credit rating if you ever need to take out a bank loan.

If you need to borrow money before you can establish a credit record, you may have to ask a parent or guardian to co-sign a loan with you. He or she must agree to be responsible for the loan payments if you can't meet them yourself.

Shopping for Credit

One important factor you should bear in mind when considering using credit is that there is a charge for borrowing money. The **finance charge** is the money you pay to the lender for allowing you credit. It includes interest, service charges, and, possibly, additional fees as well. A service charge is a fee the lender charges you to pay for the cost of processing the loan. The finance charge can add a great deal to the amount that you borrow.

For example, if you borrow $100 you might pay $18 in interest. In addition, there might be a service charge of $1. That would make the total finance charge $19 for the year.

A good way to compare finance charges is by using the **annual percentage rate (APR)**. It is the percentage cost of credit on a yearly basis. The APR in the previous example is 19 percent; you would pay $19 in one year for a $100 loan. Most often, the lower the APR, the

better it is for you. Banks, car dealers, and other lenders are required by law to tell you how much their APR rates and finance charges are. Be sure to get these figures in writing; then choose the lowest APR.

Making the Most of Savings and Credit

If you use savings and credit wisely, you can greatly expand your resources. It is a good idea to save because money in a savings account grows and gives you more to spend. It gives you financial security. Sometimes it makes good sense to use a credit card or take out a loan for things you cannot afford to pay for all at once.

There are no hard-and-fast rules for when to borrow money, but a few guidelines may be helpful:

- Use credit to meet emergencies when savings are not available.
- Use credit to pay for goods and services that you need, such as new automobile tires, rather than for wants.
- Use credit for expensive purchases, such as a refrigerator, that will give you benefits after payments are completed.
- Remember to consider the finance charges as part of the total price.

When you think about savings and borrowing, remember to start simply. Open a savings account. Build your credit record carefully. Once you feel comfortable, you can move to more complex financial strategies when you need them. The credit history you establish for yourself is another important resource for financial management.

CHAPTER
28 REVIEW

Reviewing the Facts

1. When comparing savings accounts, what is most important?
2. What is the principal in a savings account? How is the interest related to the principal?
3. What are the two main advantages of a checking account?
4. What is layaway?
5. Why is borrowing money more expensive than it seems?
6. What is the APR? Why is it important to know the APR when applying for credit?

Sharing Your Ideas

1. If you had some extra money for starting an account, which kind would you start and why?
2. Why is it necessary to shop around for credit? What questions should you ask?

Applying Your Skills

1. Analyzing Financial Information. Compare credit card applications either from two banks or two department stores. Read the applications carefully and search for information telling you how much it would cost you to use each credit card. Are there annual or monthly fees? What is the APR for each card? How much time would you have to pay each bill before each credit card company starts charging interest? After you compare the two credit card applications, write a brief report explaining which company you would choose and why.

2. Comparing Loans. Sharon wants to borrow $3000 to buy a used car. Bank A will loan her the money for one year at an APR of 12 percent. Bank B will make the same loan at an APR of 10 percent. How much is the finance charge on each loan? How much will Sharon save by getting the loan from Bank B?

3. Predicting Outcomes. You and a partner should act out the role of a banker and a person applying for credit. In one scene, the person applying for credit should be a student like yourself; in the next scene, the person should be older and have a full-time job. What questions might the banker ask? How should the person respond? Predict whether each person would get the loan.

CHAPTER

29

Advertising

OBJECTIVES

This chapter will help you to:

- List the advantages of advertising.
- Identify two types of advertisements.
- Describe several kinds of advertising techniques.
- Identify sources of reliable information about products.
- Discuss several strategies to evaluate advertisements.

WORDS TO REMEMBER

bait and switch
direct mail ad
image ad
information ad
media

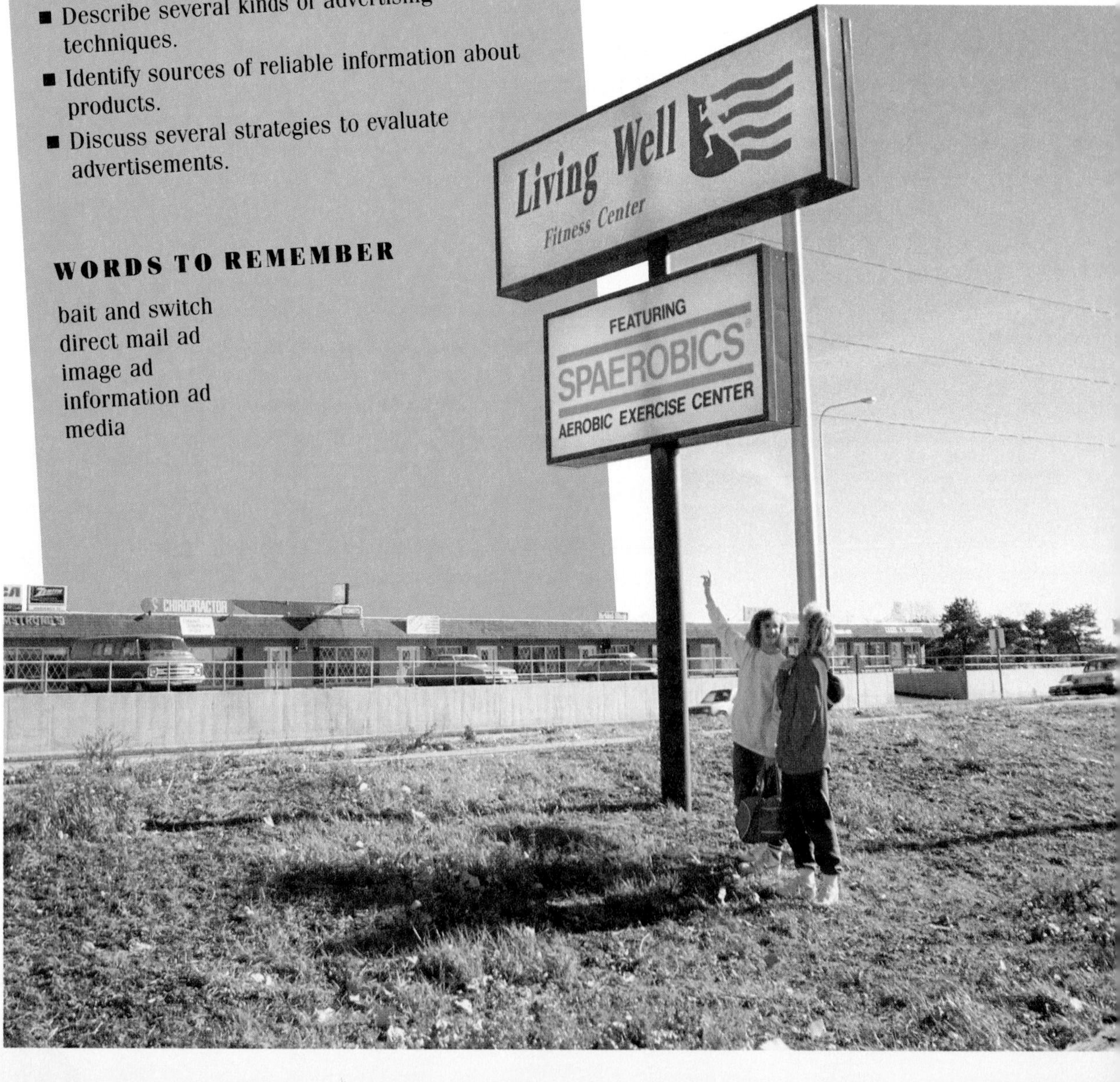

The ad in Sunday's newspaper for Whitney's Sporting Goods Store caught Brian's eye. The tennis racket he had been wanting was on sale for almost half the regular price.

After school on Monday, Brian and his friend Randy went to the store to look at the tennis racket. As Brian paid for it, he remarked to Randy, "I'm sure glad I saw that ad. I thought it would take me another three months to save enough money to buy this."

Advertisements can be very helpful to shoppers because they provide a wealth of information about products. However, some advertisements can also be very misleading. To shop wisely, you need to learn how to separate the facts from the fiction in the advertisements you see and hear every day.

The Pros and Cons of Advertising

The ability to make decisions about where and when to spend their money gives people great power in the marketplace. If too few people buy a product, that product will be taken off the market and its manufacturer may go out of business. All manufacturers and stores want you to spend your money on their products, so they compete for your dollars by offering attractive packaging and by advertising.

Advertisements are everywhere, in newspapers and magazines, on radio and television, on buses and roadside signs, sometimes even on the clothes you wear. They are all designed to make you want to buy the product or service they display.

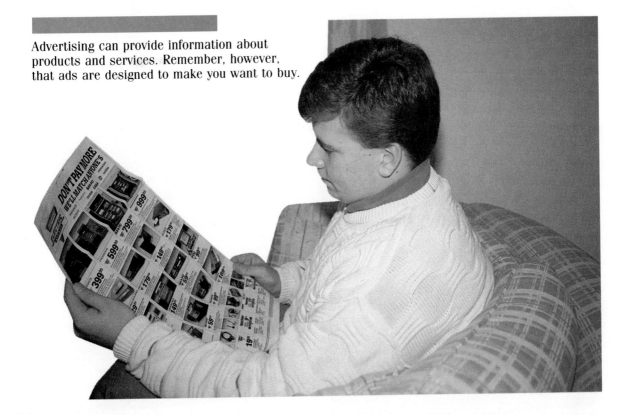

Advertising can provide information about products and services. Remember, however, that ads are designed to make you want to buy.

The Purposes of Advertising

When you buy a soft drink, do you ask for a certain brand? Do you look for a particular restaurant chain when you go out to eat? You probably learned about both through advertising. Another major purpose of advertising is to make people familiar with products, services, or ideas—to provide us with information.

Companies that make or sell products advertise. People running for political offices and special interest groups supporting various causes do, too. The American Cancer Society has used advertising very effectively in recent years to get out the message that smoking is harmful to your health.

Advertising also shapes our tastes, habits, and attitudes. For instance, a television advertisement for a new movie not only lets you know that the movie has arrived at local theaters but it also attempts to make you want to see that movie by showing a few funny or dramatic scenes from the movie.

Types of Advertisements

All advertisements aren't the same. They fall into two basic types—information ads and image ads:

- **Information ads.** An **information ad** provides specific information about a product such as its size, color, price, and features. Stores usually use this kind of ad in their catalogs or in newspapers when they want to promote special products or sales.
- **Image ads.** These are the kinds of ads that feature rock stars selling sun glasses or beautiful women driving sports cars. **Image ads** attempt to associate the product with a popular image so that you'll want to try it. Image ads also try to appeal to you to buy the product by making you think that if you do, you will be more popular, better looking, or smarter. Many magazine and television ads are image ads.

Which ads are information ads and which are image ads?

A NEW BREED

Sweaters to Create a New Relaxed Attitude...
...Striking a Balance Between Traditional and Contemporary Styling.

Advertising Media

Advertising **media** are the means by which ads are broadcast or displayed. The three most common advertising media are print (newspapers and magazines), electronic (radio and television), and direct mail. To advertise in a newspaper or magazine, the advertiser must purchase space in the publication in which the ad will appear. Newspapers are useful to local advertisers, like supermarkets and department stores who want to reach nearby residents.

Magazines, on the other hand, can reach millions of readers nationwide. The ads they carry are called national ads. Advertisers who want to reach a specific group of people, such as cooks or stamp collectors, can advertise in magazines devoted to these specialties.

When advertisers want to buy an ad on radio or television, they buy time instead of space. For example, they can buy 15 or 30 seconds of time in the middle of, or between, programs in which to air their ads. The national ads that appear on television can reach 30 or 40 million viewers at one time.

Direct mail ads are the kind of ads that are delivered by the postal service. These include catalogs from mail-order houses, advertising circulars for local supermarkets and stores, and any other advertising you get through the mail.

Other kinds of advertising include store window displays, roadside billboards and neon signs, point-of-sale displays, and bus and taxi signs. Clothes that carry the designer's name or symbol are a form of advertising also.

Many point-of-sale displays include attention-getting signs. What advertising information would be most helpful to this consumer?

Evaluating Advertisements

Will a new pair of designer jeans really make you more popular, as the ad suggests? Probably not, but the "popularity ploy" is just one of many methods that advertisers use to persuade you to buy things you may not really need or want. Here are some other common advertising techniques:

■ **Attention-getting headlines.** "Buy!", "Save!", "Lose 25 pounds in one week!" These kinds of headlines lure you into reading the rest of the ad and often promise you some benefit.

- **Testimonials.** Your favorite athletes, actors, or rock stars tell you how great a product is.
- **Product characters.** Cartoons or fictional characters are frequently associated with a product. For example, cartoon characters are often used to advertise breakfast cereal to appeal to children.
- **Emotional appeals.** These ads tell you that you'll be happier, healthier, more beautiful, or more popular if you use a certain product.
- **Slogans.** Ads use a slogan over and over again until it (and the product) sticks in people's minds.

Advertisers can use any and all of these methods, but the consumer should be aware that they are creative techniques and don't necessarily represent the nature or quality of the products they advertise.

Before truth-in-advertising laws, ads made claims for miracle cures. Today advertisers must be able to prove what they say in their ads.

CELEBRATED SKIN LOTION

Retail price . . . . $ .50
Our price, each . . . . . . $ .29
Our price, per dozen . . $2.70

Superior to every other skin lotion in the market.
This skin lotion is guaranteed to cure all eruptive and skin diseases.
You could obtain no remedy that is better or can equal it in healing qualities.
Those that have tried it will accept no other lotion under any circumstances.

Truth in Advertising

A hundred years ago, advertisers could make the most outlandish claims for their products and buyers had no way of knowing whether those claims were true or not. Today, advertisers can be challenged legally for making false or grossly misleading claims about their products. Advertising is regulated by several U.S. government agencies, including the Federal Trade Commission (FTC), and, if the ads are aired on radio or television, the Federal Communications Commission (FCC). These agencies can force advertisers to prove their claims or to pay fines if they violate federal laws. The FCC can even make an advertiser run a new ad to correct false claims made in earlier ads.

Sources of Information

Despite federal regulations, advertisers often exaggerate in an attempt to persuade you to buy their products. However, you don't have to rely solely on ads to gather information about products. One way to get information about products is to ask your friends questions about the products they use, such as "What do you like or dislike about a product?" "How much did it cost?" and "Would you recommend this product to others?"

You can also look for information in consumer magazines, such as *Consumer Reports* and *Consumer Research*, which test and rate many different products to see how well they perform and how closely they meet advertising claims. The *Consumer Index*, available in most libraries, lists which products and services have been reviewed in the consumer magazines.

HEALTH WATCH

Read That Label!

After weeks of allergy testing, the doctor gave Allison a list of foods and fibers that she was allergic to. Allison wondered how she could avoid buying products that contained the items on the list. She discovered that product labels provide important information about both the contents and safety of a product.

- **Food.** The Federal Food and Drug Administration (FDA) requires that food manufacturers list the weight, ingredients, additives, and added nutrients contained in their products on their packages and cans. Ingredients must be listed by weight in descending order, so if the first item on a list of ingredients is flour, the product contains more flour than any other ingredient.

- **Clothing.** Clothing sold in the United States must have a label showing what fibers were used in making the item and a care label that must include information on how the garment should be cleaned and whether it can be bleached or pressed.

- **Furniture.** Furniture that is stuffed or covered with fabric must have a label showing what materials were used and whether the material is flame-resistant.

- **Household cleaners.** Some household cleaners, painting supplies, and lawn-care products are poisonous, irritating, flammable, or explosive near heat. The labels on these products usually give safety and storage information.

Think It Through

1. Rachel was trying to choose between two breakfast cereals. The first four ingredients listed on one cereal box were whole wheat, sugar, rice flour, and soybean oil. The first four ingredients listed on the other box were whole wheat, wheat bran, raisins, and sugar. Which cereal do you think Rachel should choose? Why?

2. Do you think that product labels give enough information? Do they give too much information? Explain your answer.

Strategies for Evaluating Advertisements

Here are some strategies to use to help you evaluate what advertisements are telling you:

- Read and listen carefully to separate the facts from the opinions in an ad. The ingredients in a pizza are facts. The idea that eating a pizza will make you and your friends feel terrific is simply the restaurant's opinion.

- Remember that the famous people who appear in commercials are well-paid for telling you how wonderful a product is. Actors and rock stars may sincerely like the products they are advertising, but they do not necessarily know about the nutritional content or effectiveness of one product over another.

- Remember that advertisements only talk about the best features of a product. If a product tends to break down under certain conditions, the advertiser isn't going to tell you that.

- Watch out for **bait and switch** advertisements. These are ads that offer a model of a product at a very low price. When you get to the store, however, you discover that it has run out of the item or that the item is of very poor quality. Then the salesperson steers you toward a more expensive model.

When you read, watch, or listen to advertisements, remember that the advertisers are doing everything possible to persuade you to buy their products. It is up to you to separate the facts from the techniques used to impress you. Don't be easily convinced that products are good, just because an advertisement says so. To be a wise shopper, you have to take the responsibility for finding out what you need to know. The information is out there, but you have to analyze it before you purchase a product.

When gathering information about products or services, evaluate ads carefully to separate facts from advertising techniques.

CHAPTER 29 REVIEW

Reviewing the Facts

1. What are two main purposes of advertising?
2. Name two kinds of advertisements.
3. What is the difference between an information ad and an image ad?
4. What do the words "advertising media" mean?
5. What is direct mail advertising?
6. What is a testimonial?
7. What do magazines such as *Consumer Reports* do?
8. What does "bait and switch" advertising mean?

Sharing Your Ideas

1. What ads do you pay the most attention to? What advertising techniques are being used? Do they influence your buying decisions? Why or why not?
2. Luis saw an ad for a local discount store that advertised a bicycle for $59, but when he went to the store, the department manager claimed that that model was sold out. Instead, Luis was urged to buy another model that cost $79. What would you do if you were Luis?

Applying Your Skills

1. Writing an Analysis. Choose a product, such as a television, compact disc player, lawn mower, automobile, or microwave oven, and look up a recent article on that product in *Consumer Reports* or *Consumers' Research*. Using the information in the magazine, write a report explaining which brand or model you would buy and why.

2. Comparing Advertising Techniques. Cut out or photocopy three or four advertisements from a national magazine. Analyze each ad for factual information and for persuasive messages. Make two lists. List the facts contained in each ad on the first list and the opinions or persuasive messages contained in each ad on the second list. Which list is longer?

3. Composing an Advertisement. Choose a familiar product, such as a brand of soft drink or a favorite snack food. Create a 15- to 30-second radio ad or a full-page magazine ad. Use one or more of the advertising techniques described in the chapter.

Consumer
Skills

OBJECTIVES

This chapter will help you to:

- Describe how planning your purchases can make the best use of your resources.
- List the advantages and disadvantages of different types of stores.
- Evaluate sales and sales ads.

WORDS TO REMEMBER

clearance sale
consumer
department store
discount store

factory outlet
impulse buying
mail order
specialty store

Angela was shopping in a local department store when she noticed a denim jacket she really liked. The jacket was very expensive, however, and Angela decided to wait and see if she could find a similar jacket for less money somewhere else.

A week later, Angela was in a nearby clothing store when she saw another denim jacket for sale. She read the labels and learned that this jacket was very similar in quality and workmanship to the one she had seen in the other store but it was a good deal cheaper. This time, Angela decided to buy the jacket. She felt good about the purchase because she was sure she had made the right decision by waiting.

Planning Your Purchases

Without even being aware of it, Angela had planned her purchase of the jacket. She made a better decision than she would have if she had bought the first jacket she saw.

When you plan your purchases, you use the same strategies you learned about in Chapter 25. You set a goal by deciding what you want to purchase, and you decide how to use your resources to achieve the goal.

As a **consumer**, or a person who buys and uses things, your major resources are money, time, and knowledge. If you do not have enough money to buy the product you want, you can earn, save, use credit, or shop around for a less expensive model. If you don't have the time to shop around, you may end up spending more money for an item.

As Angela demonstrated, planning your purchases means using knowledge as well as time and money. You have to know when and where to shop and how to compare goods. You will find that knowledge can save you time and money. For example, you may want to buy a particular model bicycle because you researched bicycles in consumer magazines and found the model that suits you best. If a local store offers that model in a special sale, then you can buy it at a good price without having to spend a lot of time in stores.

Knowing Your Stores

Different kinds of stores serve different purposes. People can save time and money by shopping at the most appropriate store.

- A **specialty store** sells only a certain kind of merchandise, such as tapes and records, sporting goods, or shoes, and therefore offers a wider selection of those items.

Speciality stores usually offer a wider selection of choices than stores that carry a variety of merchandise.

- A **department store** offers shoppers a wide variety of goods, often in different price ranges, under one roof. Department stores issue their own credit cards and offer many services such as gift-wrapping and home delivery.

- A **discount store** carries nationally advertised brands at reduced prices. They usually also carry lines of clothing and shoes that are cheaper and of lesser quality than found in department stores.

- A **factory outlet** is a store in which the manufacturer of a product sells goods directly to shoppers. Prices are low,but the goods may be slightly imperfect or out of style.

Other Ways to Shop

Stores aren't the only places where you can shop. You can also buy from mail-order companies and shopping clubs. You can shop by telephone, by direct sales in your home, and even by television. (See "Remote Control Shopping" on page 283.)

Mail-order companies are businesses that send catalogs to people who can order various products from them. Some mail-order companies sell all kinds of merchandise, whereas others specialize in certain types of goods, such as sporting equipment, clothing, cooking utensils, or garden seeds.

Several major department store chains issue mail-order catalogs that enable people to use the telephone or mail to purchase many of the same goods that are sold in their stores. Many magazines also include advertising sections in which people can shop by mail. Mail-order shopping is a convenient way for teens to shop when they have no transportation to get to stores.

Shopping by mail is very convenient, although you may have to wait several days or weeks to receive your order. Read product information carefully and fill out the order form accurately.

TECHNOLOGY

Remote Control Shopping

Did you know you can go shopping without leaving your living room? All you have to do is turn on the television set and tune into the shopping channel on the cable network.

Television shopping programs are like electronic catalogs. You watch the items being presented, then call a special telephone number to order. In most cases, you have to charge the purchase on a credit card.

Here are some advantages and disadvantages of shopping by television that you should know:

■ You can shop without leaving your home, charge your purchases, and have them delivered to your door.

■ You can sometimes find real bargains, but to do that you have to be familiar with the brand names, features, and retail prices of items.

■ Most television shopping programs have liberal return policies. However, if you receive a damaged item or a product that you don't want, you still have to pack it up, ship it back, and wait for a refund.

■ Most home shopping programs only let you order an item while it is on the screen. This means that you may have to sit through several hours of the program before something comes on the screen that you want.

It is unlikely that shopping by television will ever replace shopping at your local shopping mall, but it may become more common in the future. When you venture into television shopping, you need to follow the same basic rules you would follow in a store—shop for the best quality at the lowest price, and learn as much as you can about the product beforehand.

Think It Through

1. What effect do you think shopping by television will have on shopping malls?
2. You purchased several Christmas presents from a home shopping program, but the presents didn't arrive before Christmas. You had to buy more presents at the last minute. What would you do when the gifts finally arrive? What might you learn from this experience?

A shopping club is a kind of mail-order shopping service that usually sells one kind of merchandise, such as books or records. When you join a shopping club, you may be offered a low-cost introductory bargain, such as four books for one dollar. In return, you agree to make a minimum number of additional purchases at regular prices within a specified time period, usually one year. See "Clubs Are More Than You Bargain For" on page 291.

In direct, or door-to-door sales, the salesperson brings products such as vacuum cleaners, encyclopedias, cosmetics, and magazine subscriptions to your home. Direct sales are a convenient way to shop, but you need to be cautious. Sales representatives may try to pressure you to buy on the spot without giving you time to compare the prices and quality of their products to similar ones.

Other ways to shop include cooperative (co-op) organizations that buy in bulk at wholesale prices and pass the savings on to their members. Food co-ops are the most common of these kinds of organizations.

You can also shop at thrift shops, garage sales, and flea markets, which are places that sell used and new merchandise at low prices. In addition, people sell cars, household furnishings, and a variety of other items through the classified advertisements in newspapers.

You can sometimes discover great bargains at flea markets and garage sales or in the classified ads, and occasionally you can find a true treasure such as an antique, an old record, or an out-of-print book. Shop carefully at these places. Examine anything you plan to buy very thoroughly because you cannot return defective goods. In some cases, you may not be able to find the seller again, and you may end up spending money on a worthless product.

Knowing When to Buy

You probably wouldn't like it if you bought a shirt at a store for $20 only to learn that the same shirt was marked down to $15 for a special sale the following week. That's why knowing when to buy is as important as knowing where to shop. This means knowing what time of year stores customarily hold sales on various kinds of products. For example, you can purchase bath and bed linens on sale during the annual January white sales. You can often get good buys on winter and summer clothing when you buy them at the end of that season.

Knowing when to buy also means that you know when *not* to buy. When you go into a grocery store or discount store, you may have the urge to engage in **impulse buying**, purchasing things that you hadn't intended to. Store managers deliberately display goods to tempt you to buy on impulse. For example, you will find gum, candy, magazines, and inexpensive items such as batteries and key chains right at the checkout counter on the chance that you'll decide to buy them while you wait.

To help avoid impulse buying, make a shopping list and stick to it. If you're not sure whether to buy a particular item, such as a sweater, wait. A store may be willing to hold an item aside for you for several hours. This allows you time to check other stores.

When you are shopping, you should be aware that sale items are sometimes out of fashion or out of season. Sometimes clothing is discounted when a particular color, style, or length is no longer fashionable. In the case of food, sale items may have passed their peak of freshness and may not be worth buying. Many food items have only a limited shelf life left (that is, time during which they can be legally sold). If a food item is dated, don't buy it after that date.

Counter displays encourage impulse purchases.

Understanding Sales

Stores use sales for two purposes—to attract new and regular customers, and to clear out merchandise that may be selling poorly or slowly. Stores also hope that you will buy regular-price items as well as the sale merchandise.

When Stores Hold Sales

You'll often see sales at certain times of the year. Summer clothes, for example, go on sale in July. Many sales traditionally are held on or around holidays such as Easter and Labor Day. Stores that are closing have going-out-of-business sales to get rid of their remaining stock.

Stores also hold **clearance sales** when they are seeking to get rid of old stock to make room for new items. Car dealerships, for example, have sales on last year's models when the new models come out. Some stores schedule sales when they know more people will be out shopping—back-to-school and Christmas sales—to try to lure these shoppers to their stores. And stores also hold sales at the end of a season to move leftover seasonal or dated merchandise.

Is It a Bargain?

When reading ads for sales, be sure to question these phrases.

- **List price.** The list price, the manufacturer's suggested selling price, is seldom the retailer's actual selling price.

- **Below manufacturer's cost.**This phrase suggests that both the manufacturer and the retailer have lost money on the product, which isn't likely. Check the merchandise. Is it out of date? Are parts for it available?
- **Comparable to $49.95 value.**A statement like this is just the opinion of the advertiser. The merchandise may be worth only the $29.95 you pay for it.
- **Special purchase.**Special purchase items are merchandise sold at a lower price than usual, especially for a sale. These may not be of the store's usual quality.

Points to Remember at Sales

Sales can offer excellent bargains for consumers who evaluate merchandise carefully.

- Is the product worthwhile? Examine the item carefully and check the label to see if it says "as is," "seconds," or "irregular." All of these phrases indicate that the product has a flaw, but if the flaw is minor, it may still be a worthwhile purchase. Labels that say "final sale" or "as is" mean the product is not returnable.
- Is the sale price really lower than the usual price? Some stores will advertise that a product that "regularly sells for $9.95 is now $5.95." In some cases, the store never sold the item at the higher price and never intended to. The lower price therefore is not a sale price but the store's regular price.
- Do you really need or want the product? Discount stores often put a large selection of products on sale, knowing that shoppers will be tempted to buy several items that they don't really need.
- Are coupons, rebates, or special offers really saving you money? In some cases, even with the coupon or saving, the product may cost more than the brand you usually use.

When buying items on sale, evaluate them for quality and price. If you are a careful shopper, you can get very good bargains at sales. When is a sale item not a good bargain?

CHAPTER
30 REVIEW

1. Name the three main consumer resources.
2. What is the difference between a specialty store, a department store, a discount store, and a factory outlet?
3. Name three ways you can shop without leaving home.
4. Why should you shop carefully when buying goods at a flea market or garage sale?
5. What are two reasons why stores use sales?
6. What is a clearance sale?
7. Why is the statement "comparable to a $40 value" misleading?
8. List four things you should remember when buying merchandise.

Sharing Your Ideas

1. If you were interested in buying a radio, would you buy it in a store, through direct mail, or at a flea market or garage sale? Explain your answer.
2. Identify the last sale item you bought. Was the sale associated with a particular holiday or event? Did you get a bargain? Why or why not?

Applying Your Skills

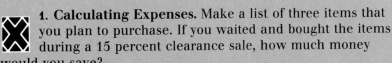

1. Calculating Expenses. Make a list of three items that you plan to purchase. If you waited and bought the items during a 15 percent clearance sale, how much money would you save?

2. Justifying a Choice. If you were buying a pair of running shoes, what type of store would you choose—a department store, a discount store, or a specialty store? Which kind of store would you expect to offer the greatest selection? the lowest prices? the highest quality shoes? Write a brief report in which you tell which kind of store you would patronize to purchase running shoes. Explain why.

3. Designing an Ad. Design a sales ad for a mountain bicycle that is regularly priced for $225.00 and is discounted 30 percent.

Price and Quality

OBJECTIVES

This chapter will help you to:

■ Judge the quality of a product or service.
■ Choose the most appropriate product to satisfy your wants and needs.
■ Explain the purpose of comparison shopping.
■ Give examples of hidden costs.

WORDS TO REMEMBER

comparison shopping
goods
service

Underwriter's Laboratory
unit price
warranty

Jason bought a portable tape player for a very low price at a going-out-of-business sale. He thought he had a real bargain, but the tape deck kept snagging and ripping his tapes.

Jason attempted to return the tape player and get his money back, but the store had gone out of business. In addition, the tape player did not come with a warranty from the manufacturer.

Jason was stuck with a bad buy because he had been overly influenced by the price of the tape player and he neglected to examine it for quality. Has this ever happened to you? You can learn how to be a better consumer by looking closely at both price and quality.

When you go to a store to shop, you can buy goods or services. **Goods** are material things, such as clothes and records, that you can use. A **service** is the work performed for one person by another. The person who cuts your hair provides a service, as do doctors, dentists, gardeners, travel agents, and plumbers.

Evaluating Purchases

Whenever you shop, you have to choose from a variety of goods and services. How then do you choose? What do you look for and what should you avoid?

You can compare the price and quality of goods by examining them, by reading about them, and by talking to people who have used the items. Were other people pleased with their purchases? Would they buy the same items again? It is a little harder to compare the price and quality of services. To compare the price of a service, you can ask several people who provide the same service to give you their price lists or estimates of their charges. To compare quality, you have to look at the work the people who are providing the service have already done for others.

If money were no object, you could always buy the highest-quality item available. For most people, however, money is limited. They often have to make trade-offs or compromises between what they can afford and what they really need or want. The best trade-offs result from planning before you shop. Planning requires thinking about quality and price.

Quality

What is quality anyway? How can you tell when a product is of poor or high quality? Quality depends on five factors:

- **Performance.** How well does the product work? Is the video game fun? Is the cereal nutritious as well as delicious?
- **Durability.** How strong, sturdy, or well made is the product? Will the sweater shrink after being washed? Will the schoolbag hold your books, or will it fall apart in a few weeks?
- **Convenience.** Is the product easy to open, close, use, and store? Do you have to fight those boots to get them on? Does the shampoo bottle tend to pour more than it should?
- **Maintenance.** How much care will a product require during its lifetime? Will the watch need expensive repairs if you get it wet? Does the portable television come with a warranty? Are there service centers nearby in case repairs are needed?

■ **Safety.** Are there any potential hazards involved in using the product? Is the handle of the typewriter case strong enough? Does that hair dryer come with the Underwriter's Laboratory (UL) seal of safety? The **Underwriter's Laboratory** is an agency that tests electrical products for safety.

Sometimes you can't answer all these questions before you buy a product. You can't try a hair dryer or play a compact disc in the store, for example, so it is always a good idea to make sure you can return the product if it proves to be defective. That is why it's important to keep sales receipts. You'll learn how to return damaged or defective goods in Chapter 32.

Safety is an important factor in judging the quality of a product. Electrical products should carry labels assuring they have met inspection standards.

Price

You need to consider several things when you decide how much you're willing to spend on a product. A higher price doesn't always mean better quality, and paying a low price at a discount store may not be a bargain if you have to travel far to get to the store.

Emergencies may cause you to pay more. If your glasses break and only an expensive repair shop is open, the price may be less important than getting your glasses fixed in a hurry. Your need for a product is as important a consideration as its price.

You'll usually get more for your money when you plan ahead. If those $6 pierced earrings are a perfect gift for your sister, buy them now if you can afford it. Six months from now, when her birthday arrives, you might pay $10 for a last-minute gift that you like less.

Suitability

Having some idea of what you need before you shop can make all the difference when you're in the store looking at rows and rows of products. This will help you select a suitable model—one that meets your needs and resources.

You won't always want or need the highest-priced, best-quality item. For example, if you shop for an electronic keyboard, you can choose from a small, inexpensive one with few features or one costing several hundred dollars. The high-priced keyboard includes many extra features and is intended for professional musicians who play in bands.

If you are a professional musician or if you are aspiring to be one, you might choose the expensive keyboard. If you just want a keyboard to play for fun, you should probably choose a much less expensive one with fewer features.

MANAGING RESOURCES

Clubs Are More Than You Bargain For

When Jeremy joined a record club, he thought he had found a real bargain. He not only got to select eight albums or tapes for one low price, but also was promised a monthly magazine on all the hottest new releases. A few months later, after Jeremy had a chance to discover some of the hidden costs, he felt disappointed.

Record and book clubs are very popular. When people join a club, they get to select a large number of records, tapes, or books from a list of current favorites. The club then sends all those selections for a very small charge. There's a catch, though: Members are usually required to purchase a certain number of full-priced items within a given time period. In addition, there are other hidden costs that consumers aren't usually aware of when they join.

- How do club prices compare with similar products bought in a store? If a club's prices are higher, it may be better to buy the items locally.
- Are costs for handling and postage added to the price? If so, those charges usually put the total cost of the item above the retail price.
- How does the quality of club products compare? For example, the quality of the paper used in a book can be much thinner than in a similar book bought at a bookstore.

- What do you have to do if you don't want the club to send you the items featured in its monthly catalog? You may have to return a postcard with the appropriate boxes crossed off. If you forget to send the postcard back, or if it gets lost in the mail, the club will send you all its featured selections of the month.
- What do you have to do if you don't want to keep the items? Usually, you are responsible for packaging the returns and mailing the items back.

- If the club has special sales or bonuses, do these items go towards fulfilling your membership requirements? If not, you may have to purchase full-price items instead.

Think It Through

1. Do you think Jeremy made a good choice in joining the record club? Why or why not?
2. Why do you think record and book clubs are so popular?

Comparison Shopping

If you're about to make an expensive purchase—a home video game system, for instance—you probably won't want to buy the first one you see. More than likely you'll want to look at several models and compare the features and prices of each before you buy. Such **comparison shopping** is a good habit even if the product is a relatively small item, like a box of cereal. It's even more important when buying a high-priced item.

In Chapter 29, you learned how to compare products by researching them in articles in consumer magazines and by reading the labels on similar products. Your comparisons should include price, performance, contents, durability, convenience, maintenance, and warranties.

Remember that the most expensive model is not always the one that best suits your needs or wants.

Price and Performance

You may think that a difference of a dime on a food purchase isn't that much, but what are the reasons for the 10-cent difference? Read the labels of two similar products carefully. Is the nutritional value the same? Is there as much in one package as in the other? Should you buy the larger or smaller size?

Using **unit prices**, or the prices of items per ounce or by count, will help you find the best value. Unit prices are usually found on the store shelf under the item.

Suppose that 15 ounces of your favorite shampoo costs $3.69, and 12 ounces of a new brand is $3.39. You wonder if the new brand is cheaper. Reading the unit prices of the two shampoos shows that your brand costs less. The other is priced at $4.52 per pint, but yours is only $3.94 per pint.

Prices are a good way to compare products, but at the same time you should consider performance. You may

Unit prices help you compare prices for the same quantities of similar items.

want to buy a more expensive model of a product such as a typewriter because it has more features or works better. To compare performance, start by looking up the product in the *Consumer Index*. Read all you can find about different brands and models. A more expensive brand may not be better. It might not have the features you want, or it may have features you don't need. It might have gotten a very low rating from a consumer magazine.

Next, go to the store and ask for a demonstration. You may prefer the sound of one keyboard over another.

Contents and Durability

Labels and packages will tell you about the contents of most products, but whenever you can, you should also get a "hands-on" feel for what you're buying. Try on clothes and shoes and examine them carefully to see how well they're made. Check tools and machines to see if they are sturdy and well constructed. You can't always depend on manufacturers' sizes or brands to determine the quality. Look at labels on food packages to see whether the item is as nutritious as you would like.

Convenience and Maintenance

Another factor to consider when choosing one brand of product over another is instructions for its assembly and care. If you're buying something that you'll need to assemble yourself, be sure that the instructions are included in the package. Ask at the store if someone will be available to answer questions should you have trouble with the item you have purchased.

Look for care instructions on clothing labels, and consider the cost of such care before you make your purchase. Most wool clothing, for instance, requires dry cleaning. Appliance packages should come with service manuals. These booklets describe how to use and care for the appliance properly.

Warranties

A **warranty** (or guarantee) is a written statement from the manufacturer or retailer, promising to repair or replace a defective product, or to refund your money. Because warranties vary from company to company and from state to state, you should examine them carefully. A warranty should include the following information:

- Name and address of the company.
- An exact statement of what is covered. Does the company agree to pay for parts and labor, or only parts?
- The length of time of the coverage.
- The procedure to be followed in case of a defect. For example, who will pay shipping costs to send the product back?
- Whom the owner must contact to get the warranty fulfilled.
- The length of time the company has to take action on a problem.

■ Any requirements that the purchaser must meet to validate the warranty.

Remember to keep your warranties and sales slips in a safe place in case you need them.

Avoiding Hidden Costs

Some costs are hidden because they are not part of the price of something, but they still must be paid. Some common hidden costs include:

■ **Travel.** When comparison shopping, don't forget to include the cost of transportation. Consider the time, energy, and money required to have your hair cut across town. It might cost less to go to a more expensive salon around the corner.

■ **Repairs.** Before buying a product, check the warranty for coverage. There may be a copy attached to the floor model. If not, ask to see one. Stores are required by law to show you warranties. Ask about the cost of repairs not covered by the warranty. If they seem high, compare them to repair costs for other models of the same products. If you buy an item that needs frequent or expensive repairs, in effect the item costs more.

■ **Additional parts.** "Battery not included" can mean another expense before the product you've bought is actually going to work. Some accessories, such as shoulder straps for schoolbags and stuff sacks for sleeping bags, are conveniences you might need as much as the item itself.

■ **Exchanges.** If something goes wrong with a product you purchased, take it back to the store with the receipt. Usually, stores have policies and time limits for refunds and exchanges. For your own protection, find out about these at the time of purchase. If you can't return a defective product, you've spent money for nothing. You'll learn more about refunds and exchanges in Chapter 32.

Accessories such as batteries are hidden costs that add to the price of some products.

CHAPTER

31 REVIEW

Reviewing the Facts

1. What is the difference between goods and services?
2. What are the five factors that define quality?
3. Why do people sometimes pay a higher price for a product during an emergency?
4. What does suitability mean?
5. How can comparison shopping save you money?
6. What is a unit price?
7. What is a warranty?
8. How can repairs be a hidden cost?

Sharing Your Ideas

1. Have you ever made a purchase that dissatisfied you? Why were you dissatisfied? What comparison shopping techniques could you use the next time to prevent this from happening?
2. Identify five recent purchases that you or your family have made. Determine whether there are hidden costs associated with any of the products. Discuss with the class.

Applying Your Skills

1. Evaluating Quality. Bring to class two new shirts or blouses. Read the labels and note the prices, fibers, and care instructions. See if the labels indicate where the garment was manufactured. Also look for details such as the tailoring of collars and cuffs, and examine the pockets, buttons, and stitching. Which do you think is the better quality garment? Why? What is the difference in prices? How do you account for the difference? Write a report describing your findings.

2. Comparing the Cost of Goods. Go to a supermarket or store that posts unit prices for products. Examine a group of products, such as aspirin, shampoo, or cookies, and write down the unit prices for each product in the group. Draw a graph showing each of the products from the least to most expensive according to their unit prices.

3. Evaluating Qualities. Identify a product you are interested in buying. Find an account of the item in a consumer magazine. Read about the quality, performance, durability, safety, and features of several brands. Which one would best fit your needs?

Voicing Your Opinion

OBJECTIVES

This chapter will help you to:

- List the rights of consumers.
- Explain how to make a complaint in person and by letter.
- Identify and describe sources of help for consumers.
- Explain why consumers should voice their opinions.

WORDS TO REMEMBER

Better Business Bureau (BBB)
redress
small claims court

eff had saved $35 to buy a video game disk for use on his home computer. When he and his friends tried to play the game, it wouldn't work. Just to make sure it was the disk and not the computer that was at fault, Jeff tried several other disks on the computer and each one worked fine.

Jeff took the disk, along with the sales receipt, back to the store where he bought it. When he explained the problem, the store manager gave him his money back.

Jeff was exercising his rights as a consumer. When you aren't happy with a purchase you've made, you do have certain rights. At such times, it's important to know how to voice your opinion so that you can obtain those rights.

Your Consumer Rights

When you purchase a product that is damaged, inferior, or unsafe, you have a right to make a complaint and to be heard. In the last 25 years, the U.S. Government has enacted many laws to protect the rights of consumers. These rights include:

- **The right to safety.** Consumers are protected from the selling of dangerous products.
- **The right to be informed.** Consumers are protected from misleading advertising. They can ask for all the facts needed to make good choices.
- **The right to choose.** Consumers are given the chance to make their own choices.
- **The right to be heard.** Consumers can speak out when they aren't satisfied. They have a voice in the making of consumer laws.

- **The right to consumer education.** Consumers have the right to learn about consumer issues.
- **The right to redress. Redress** means consumers have the right to get a wrong corrected.

When You Have a Complaint

Consumers expect manufacturers and sellers to be fair. They expect to be offered goods and services at fair prices, and they expect the things they buy to perform well. Consumers must also be fair by voicing their opinions only when their complaints are real ones.

For example, Donna bought a wool-blend sweater. The care label on the sweater said, "Hand wash, using a cold-water wash product." Donna followed the directions and washed the sweater by hand in cold water, but it shrank. Donna has a real complaint against the sweater manufacturer.

Generally, a complaint is fair if you purchased a product that was damaged, or if it was not sold at the advertised price. You would also have a right to complain if a service you paid for was not done correctly.

Complaining in Person

If you do have a fair complaint, act soon. A delay in making a complaint makes it harder for you to solve the problem. First, find your sales receipt and warranty. Always save these because they can help you state your case.

Then follow these five steps:

1. Check to see if the problem is covered by the warranty. If so, follow the directions listed on it. If not, take the next four steps.

2. Write down exactly what's wrong with the product. Use these notes to guide you as you explain the problem.

3. Go to the store where you made your purchase. Ask a salesperson to help you or to direct you to someone who can, such as the store manager or store owner. Bring your receipt and warranty. Some large stores have a customer service department for handling customer complaints.

4. Explain your problem clearly and briefly. Be polite, firm, and willing to compromise. Remember that the store employee will probably want to settle the problem. A satisfied customer means future sales.

5. Propose a solution to the store employee. You may want the product to be repaired, to receive a replacement, or to get your money back.

You are the head of a recording company. One day, you receive the following three complaint letters. How would you react to each one?

741 Planter Way
Dallas, Texas 75218
March 15, 19____

Ms. Joan Snelling
President
Top Quality Records
32 Platter Drive
Columbus, Ohio 43224

Dear Ms. Snelling:

Last week I bought the tape, Reaching for the Stars, made by your company. Unfortunately, my copy is broken.

I took the tape back to the store, Sound Effects, but the manager said that he had no more copies and suggested I write to you. I'm enclosing a copy of the sales slip.

I would like a new copy of the tape please. Also, please tell me what to do with the broken copy.

Thank you for your help.

Sincerely,

Wanda Ramirez

Writing a Letter of Complaint

The problem may not be solved by visiting the store. If it isn't, it's time to write a letter. Send your letter to the company that makes or sells the product or supplies the service. Whenever possible, address the letter to a particular person, such as the president, rather than "To Whom It May Concern." This makes it more likely that your letter will be read.

775 West 82 Street
New York, New York 10024
March 15, 19____

Company Head
Top Quality Records
32 Platter Drive
Columbus, Ohio 43224

Dear Company Head:

Your company made Reaching for the Stars, but my copy is broken.

I want my money back.

Yours truly,

Barbara Palatino

13 Weston Court
St. Louis, Missouri 63116
March 15, 19____

President
Top Quality Records
32 Platter Drive
Columbus, Ohio 43224

Dear President:

I bought the tape, Reaching for the Stars. It is broken and will not play properly.

Please send me a new copy of the tape or a refund. I would like your help in this.

Thank you very much for your time and attention.

Sincerely,

Alan Yamashita

If the company is local, check your phone book for name and address. For a national company, go to the library. You can find the company's address in a business reference book or in a consumer complaint guide.

A complaint letter should have the following information:

- Your name and address.
- The date you are writing the letter.
- The name, job title, and address of the person you're writing to.
- The product or service name, style, and model number.
- The name and address of the store where you made your purchase, and the date you bought it.
- What sales receipts, bills, or warranties you are including with your letter (always send copies of these papers, not the originals).
- A simple and brief explanation of why you are unhappy with the product or service.
- A statement telling how you would like the problem solved.

Taking Further Action

In most cases, visiting the store or writing a letter will settle the problem, but sometimes these actions are just not enough. In those cases, the consumer can get help from other sources.

If you cannot resolve a consumer complaint through the store or manufacturer, you can contact a consumer agency for assistance. The Better Business Bureau tries to resolve complaints between consumers and member businesses.

Consumer Agencies

Most large companies have public relations or customer relations departments that are staffed by people who are paid to help dissatisfied customers. Some companies have toll-free 800 numbers. You can use this number to call the company. Ask to speak to someone in the public relations department.

If the company fails to satisfy you, you can contact the **Better Business Bureau (BBB)**. This is an organization formed by businesses. Member businesses promise to abide by strict business standards, and the Better Business Bureau in turn tries to resolve consumer complaints against its members and other businesses in the community. There are 178 branches of the BBB helping consumers. Check for your nearest branch.

Consumer Advocates: They're on Your Side

Jane purchased a clock radio because of the special offer that went with it. After she bought the clock radio at the regular price, she was supposed to mail the receipt and a rebate form to the company and she would get a $5 refund. She followed these steps but never received the refund. She wrote a letter to the company but got no response. Is there anything else she can do? Should Jane just give up? She, like all consumers, should be aware that there are people and organizations called consumer advocates, who will help solve such consumer problems.

Consumers such as Jane can take their problems to local consumer organizations. Many communities have private, nonprofit consumer organizations that lobby for changes in consumer laws, organize protests, and help individual consumers.

Other consumer groups focus on particular issues. For example, the Aviation Consumer Action Project helps airline passengers obtain fair treatment from the airline industry. You could also try local newspapers or television stations, which often have consumer reporters or "Action Line" columnists who help with consumer problems.

In addition to solving individuals' complaints, consumer advocates have changed the attitudes of millions of Americans. Today cigarette smoking is far less socially acceptable in the United States than it was in the past, partly because of the activities of consumer groups. Various groups have helped in treating drunk driving as a serious crime.

You might consider joining or supporting a consumer organization to help protect all consumer rights. "There's strength in numbers" when it comes to being a consumer.

Think It Through

1. What are some of the general benefits to society of actions taken by leading consumer advocates?

2. Give an example of a community problem that could benefit from consumer advocate attention. How would this help?

Consumer Hotline

Consumer action panels (CAPs) are groups formed by industries—automakers, for instance—to handle consumer complaints. If a consumer is not satisfied after complaining directly to the manufacturer, the CAP will try to find a solution.

Your city, county, and state may each have a consumer protection agency that receives complaints from consumers and enforces local and state laws. If you believe that a business has not dealt fairly with you or that it has broken a law, you can file a complaint with the nearest consumer protection agency.

The federal government has several consumer agencies that are responsible for enforcing certain laws. The FDA, for example, regulates the quality of food, medicine, and cosmetics, whereas the Postal Service enforces laws to protect consumers from mail fraud.

Consumer agencies in the national government have three major jobs that they are responsible for:

1. Making safety rules to protect consumers.
2. Making sure that manufacturers do not offer unsafe products.
3. Keeping manufacturers and sellers from doing things that will mislead consumers.

The chart below lists nine federal agencies that help consumers in various ways. These agencies touch all aspects of our lives. If you wish to make a complaint to a federal agency, you can call or write to the nearest Federal Information Center for help on how to do so. These centers are located in several large cities around the country.

Joining with Other Consumers

Another way to get help is to join together with other consumers. All manufacturers and stores know that when customers are dissatisfied, they are likely to tell their family and friends.

Bad publicity and word-of-mouth complaints give a company or store a bad name and hurt sales. That is why you should only take action when you have a fair complaint and have been unable to resolve the problem in any other way.

Federal Consumer Agencies

Agency	Responsibilities
Consumer Product Safety Commission	Sets safety standards for household products
Department of Agriculture	Grades and inspects foods
Federal Communications Commission	Sets standards for radio and television advertising and broadcasting
Federal Trade Commission	Prevents misleading advertising and selling practices; regulates competition among businesses
Food and Drug Administration	Regulates food, drug, and cosmetic quality; inspects food and drug production plants
Interstate Commerce Commission	Regulates rates and sets standards for bus and train travel
Office of Consumer Affairs	Educates consumers
Postal Service	Regulates mail practices; protects consumers from being cheated through the mail
Securities and Exchange Commission	Regulates the sale of stocks and bonds

Legal Assistance

If a complaint is still not settled, you can get legal help to solve the problem. Hiring a lawyer to handle the complaint is one way, but it can be costly. Consumers usually choose this method only for serious problems. Legal aid and legal services provide free legal help to consumers who can't pay lawyers' fees.

Most consumers with less serious complaints use the **small claims court**. In this court, consumers and businesses present their complaints informally, and a judge decides the case. Because you can present your own case without a lawyer, there are no legal fees. The court's fee to file a small claim ranges from $5 to $30. This fee is often paid back if you win your case.

In a small claims court, you serve as your own lawyer when you present your case to the judge.

The Positive Power of Consumers

Suppose that you purchase a hair dryer. The first time you plug it in and turn on the switch, smoke pours out of the dryer's vent. That day, you write a letter to the maker of the hair dryer and describe what happened.

Your letter does something very important. It gives the manufacturer the chance to hear your complaint. The company may not even know the problem exists. A poorly made product could damage the company's name. This could mean that fewer dryers will be sold. The business would rather know about the problem and fix it, not only to make sales but also to prevent possible injuries to consumers.

Putting in a Good Word

Consumers are often quick to complain, but they rarely take the time to tell a business when it's doing something right. The next time you are happy with a purchase, think about writing a complimentary letter. Putting in a good word will encourage a business to continue providing high-quality goods and services. It will also encourage the business to care about consumer opinion.

Voicing your opinion takes time. It also takes extra effort, but it's worth it. By voicing your opinion, you can make a difference. With your complaints and your compliments, you help businesses learn about the needs and wants of consumers.

CHAPTER

32 REVIEW

Reviewing the Facts

1. What are the six consumer rights?
2. What two items should you take with you when making a complaint in person?
3. List the five steps to follow when making a complaint in person.
4. If a complaint is not resolved by visiting the store, what should you do?
5. What are three major functions of government consumer agencies?
6. What type of legal action is usually best for less serious consumer complaints?
7. Why should you write a complimentary letter to the company when you are pleased with a product?

Sharing Your Ideas

1. What are some situations in which you might not be able to resolve a complaint in a store? Why do you think it would be in a store's best interest to try to solve the problem?
2. Why do you think so many people avoid returning defective products?

Applying Your Skills

1. Giving Constructive Criticism. Write a letter of complaint to a manufacturer of a digital clock that didn't work. Exchange letters with a classmate and discuss what each of you could do to make your letters more effective.

2. Planning a Course of Action. Assume you have purchased a defective pair of shoes. You have a sales receipt, but the store refuses to take the shoes back or refund your money. List the agencies that could help you in the order in which you would approach them. Write a paragraph describing the information you would present to each agency.

3. Discovering Cause and Effect Relationships. Take a poll of your classmates. How many would keep a purchase if it didn't fulfill its purpose, how many would return it, and how many would exchange it? How many would write either a complimentary or negative letter to a company? What effect could these actions have on other customers and the businesses themselves?

Being a Responsible Consumer

This year Marlene did her Christmas shopping by mail order. She sent away for several gifts from a catalog. When she opened the box from the mail-order company, she discovered not only the gifts she had ordered but a very expensive watch. When Marlene looked at the shipping receipts enclosed in the box, she realized that a clerk at the mail-order firm had accidently packed another order in with hers.

Marlene knew that she could keep the watch and no one would ever know what had become of it. At the same time, she remembered how long it had taken her to save for the gifts she had bought, and how much they had cost her in time and energy as well as money. She realized that eventually someone—the company, the shipping clerk, or the other customer—would have to pay for the lost watch as well.

Marlene promptly returned the watch to the mail-order company with a written explanation of how she had received it by mistake. By taking this action, Marlene was acting as a responsible consumer.

Being Honest

Consumers expect merchants to be honest with them. If a can of food is spoiled, they expect it to be taken off the shelves. If they ask the difference between one guitar and another, they expect an honest answer. Consumers, in turn, should be honest with sellers.

Honest or Dishonest?

Honest consumers pay the price that is marked on an item. Some consumers put saving money ahead of honesty.

They may switch price tags, putting a lower price on the item they plan to buy. This practice is unfair to other consumers, who paid the correct price. In fact, this cheating makes prices higher because the store has to make up the money it loses this way by charging more for the product.

If a store cashier gives a customer too much change, an honest consumer returns it. It would be unfair for the store to charge too much for a purchase; keeping extra change is just as unfair. It could be costly for the cashier, too. Some stores make cashiers pay for missing money out of their own pockets.

No Shoplifting

Have you ever entered a store where you were asked to leave your shopping bag at the cashier's counter? The owners wanted to be sure that you wouldn't hide anything in your bag. They were trying to prevent **shoplifting**, or stealing goods from stores.

Some people believe that shoplifting is harmless, that it only hurts businesses and stores, not people. Nothing could be further from the truth; shoplifting hurts everyone. Such stealing costs $24 billion each year. That figure covers the cost of the goods stolen, the cost of security systems aimed at preventing shoplifting, and the cost of taking shoplifters to court. Store owners pay for some of these things, but consumers pay for most shoplifting costs by having to pay higher prices. In the end, everyone pays for the dishonesty of a few.

To try to stop shoplifting, stores are taking extra steps. They are putting special tags on clothes. These tags are removed by the cashier when the garment is purchased. If not, the tags sound an alarm if the clothing is taken out the door.

Taking a Bite Out of Crime

Imagine that you are in a large department store when you notice a nearby shopper taking wallets off a counter and stuffing them into a shopping bag. The person is shoplifting and you are the only one who notices. Would you know what to do? Here are the steps you should take:

- Do not speak to the shoplifter or indicate in any way that you have seen the theft.

- Make a mental note of what the person looks like and what he or she is wearing.

- Report the theft to the nearest salesperson or store employee. Do not point or stare at the shoplifter but describe him or her to the employee.

- Tell the salesperson what items were taken and where the shoplifter hid them. The salesperson will probably check to make certain that the items are missing.

- Remain in the area until you know you are no longer needed. The sales clerk may ask you to wait to talk to a store security guard, or you may be asked to be a witness in the event the shoplifter is arrested.

Reporting a stranger for shoplifting is one thing, but what would you do if you knew a close friend were shoplifting? Here are some suggestions:

- Avoid going to stores with your friend. If your friend is caught, you will be suspected of being an accomplice and you might be arrested as well.

- Talk to your friend. Find out if he or she is troubled about something. People who shoplift sometimes have emotional problems that require professional help.

- Ask your friend to think about what would happen if he or she were caught.

- If you are convinced that your friend is continuing to shoplift

tell your parents, guidance counselor, or other trusted adult. Your friend may resent you for telling, but if you remain silent, the chances are that sooner or later your friend will be caught and suffer much worse consequences.

Think It Through

1. Have you ever witnessed anyone shoplifting? If so, what did you do? What would you do if you saw someone shoplifting now? Why?

2. Which step would be the most difficult for you to follow if you saw a friend shoplifting? Why?

Shoplifting is a crime that is punishable by a fine and/or imprisonment.

Some stores hire security guards and use mirrors or cameras. Many stores are no longer letting shoplifters go with only a warning. When people are arrested for shoplifting, they are taken to a police station where they are questioned, fingerprinted, searched, photographed, and held until they can raise bail. If they are convicted, they can be imprisoned and fined. Children and teens also face stiff penalties for shoplifting. A judge may place shoplifters in a correctional facility or require them to perform a community service. Shoplifters may also acquire a criminal record that can cause them problems later in life.

Being Fair

Consumers expect stores to sell their goods at fair prices and to give them good service. They expect sellers to answer complaints fairly. Consumers should also be fair toward sellers.

Many stores have a **return policy**, a specific set of rules for returning or exchanging merchandise. A customer can return an item in exchange for another item, or perhaps for a cash refund. Whenever you buy an item in a store you are also agreeing to abide by the store's return policy. You should make a point of finding out what the policy is when you make your purchase, especially if you are buying an expensive item.

Fair consumers use the store's return policy when they need to—perhaps to return something that doesn't fit. Unfair consumers try to take advantage of this policy. They buy a sweater, wear it once or twice, and then return it. In the long run, this behavior hurts consumers. Handling too many returns and giving refunds force a store to raise its prices. Some stores adopt very strict policies—such as exchanges only, no refunds—to discourage returns.

Being Considerate

A considerate consumer remembers that the store and merchandise belong to someone else. Littering makes a store unpleasant for everyone. When trying on clothes, do so carefully so they don't become torn or stained.

Vandalism is an even more serious problem. This is when someone mars or destroys someone else's property, such as spraying paint on a store building or breaking products. Just like shoplifting, vandalism forces store owners to raise prices.

When shoppers open boxes, they sometimes lose, damage, or soil parts of a product.

Considerate consumers also think of others. Have you ever brought home something new, only to find that one piece was missing? The piece could have been lost when a thoughtless shopper opened the box in the store. If you need to see the product, ask the store clerk to show you a floor sample, rather than opening the box yourself. The person who buys the product wants it to be new, not dirty and incomplete.

Being Responsible

Consumer responsibility goes beyond how you act in stores. It also includes how you use the products you buy, and how you use both your own resources and the resources of the whole nation.

Using Products Safely

Consumers should follow manufacturers' instructions. Many products, such as lawn mowers and floor cleaners, can be very dangerous if they are used improperly. A responsible consumer is aware of the possible dangers and uses products carefully.

Consumers should stay informed about safety problems. News reports and articles tell the public about products that are found to be unsafe, such as dangerous toys and tainted foods. Many foods and medicines have special safety seals to prevent people from tampering with products on store shelves. Don't buy products with broken safety seals. If you notice a torn or opened box, point it out to the manager.

By staying alert and informed, consumers can protect themselves. They can also protect each other. If you hear of a product with a safety problem, tell your friends and neighbors. Then call the company that manufactures it, and report it. If the person you speak to is not interested in the problem, you can contact one of the agencies listed in Chapter 32.

Using Resources Responsibly

In this chapter and in Chapter 25 you learned that there are some steps you can take to become a responsible consumer. You have read about using human, material, and community resources carefully and honestly, but what about the natural resources that go into making these other resources?

Because natural resources—just like other resources—are limited, they must be used responsibly. How can you help conserve natural resources?

For example, right now you are reading your textbook. This book is made out of paper, which is made from trees, a natural resource. However people don't always use resources, such as paper, responsibly. They often throw paper wrappers on the street. They use vast quantities of newsprint that they usually don't recycle. If this continues, manufacturers will have to use more trees to produce more paper, and eventually trees will be rare and so will paper.

You don't have to worry yet; the forests are not out of trees. Still, people need to change their habits in order to use all of their natural resources responsibly. If everyone were to act as a responsible consumer, all of society would benefit. Being honest, fair, and considerate makes relations between consumers and sellers better. In addition, consuming natural resources responsibly makes the world a cleaner, healthier place to live.

Reviewing the Facts

1. What are three ways that shoplifting costs businesses and consumers money?
2. What can stores do to prevent shoplifting?
3. What is a return policy?
4. What is vandalism?
5. Name three ways that consumers can be considerate to store owners and other shoppers.
6. Why shouldn't you buy a food or medicine package that has been opened?

Sharing Your Ideas

1. What could be some possible reasons that a person would resort to shoplifting? What would be some more direct ways of dealing with those causes?
2. Robert bought his little brother, Mark, a remote-control car for his birthday. Mark had only played with the car a few minutes when it hit a bump in the street and lost a wheel. Would it be fair for Robert to return or exchange the car? Why or why not?

Applying Your Knowledge

 1. Writing an Article. Write an article for the school newspaper warning teens about the consequences of vandalism and shoplifting.

 2. Researching a Topic. Look through newspapers and magazines to find articles about product safety. Write a brief report summarizing what you have learned about product safety.

 3. Planning a Strategy. Make a list of things that you and your family could do to cut down on the amount of natural resources you waste each week. Compare this list with your classmates' lists.

CHAPTER

34

Management and Consumer Careers

OBJECTIVES

This chapter will help you to:

- Explain how interests and skills influence management and consumer career choice.
- Discuss different kinds of management careers.
- Describe several different kinds of consumer-related jobs.

WORDS TO REMEMBER

capital
entrepreneur
telecommunication

In the next few years, you will probably spend a lot of time thinking about the kind of work you want to do when you finish school. You will spend about a third of your life working, so one of the most important factors in choosing a career is finding one that you will really enjoy.

You may decide to choose a management or consumer career. Managers direct other employees and they organize the way in which work is done. People who work in consumer careers use their skills to assist others.

You can choose from thousands of different kinds of jobs in the management and consumer fields. These include being a store clerk, a lawyer, a financial adviser, a comparison shopper, an office manager, a bank teller, and many more. Some jobs require only a few days training, whereas others require several years of college or graduate-level education.

Characteristics for Consumer Careers

Studying home economics has helped you develop many skills that you will be able to use in a management or consumer career. You've learned to manage resources, make decisions, keep schedules, and set priorities. These are the same skills that people in management and consumer careers use every day, no matter what particular job they do. In addition, people in these careers usually possess several personal characteristics that help them work well with other people.

Interests and Skills

- **Can you communicate clearly?**For example, are you good at giving directions? If you have ever explained to a brother or sister how to play a game, you know how important it is to be able to give clear directions and be a good listener.

Good managers know how to be good leaders and how to communicate with their employees.

- **Are you good at math?** Management and consumer workers usually need good math skills. Bank tellers and store clerks count out money all day as part of their jobs, whereas financial advisers and accountants work with figures constantly. All of these kinds of workers must be able to make calculations without making mistakes.

- **Can you make decisions and solve problems?** Managers and consumer workers must be able to consider all of the pros and cons of an action and make the right decision. Sometimes, millions of dollars or thousands of jobs can depend on the decision a manager makes.

- **Can you set goals for yourself and then plan how to meet them?** Planning is an important skill for any responsible job. Organizing is, too. Can you order your schoolwork and your chores so that you get both done? You must have this important quality for a management or consumer-related job.

- **Are you good at making and keeping a schedule?** People in consumer jobs need to make the best use of their time and to see that the work they are doing is being carried out on time. This means being able to keep a schedule.

- **Are you a good leader?** Have you ever led a group of classmates in a school project or been the captain of a team? If so, you are learning a good management technique: how to guide and direct other people in order to accomplish a goal. Consumer workers must be able to judge the needs of others and know how to work efficiently with people.

- **Do you like working with other people?** Some people are task-oriented. They prefer a job where they are given a task and are left alone to com-

plete it. Managers and consumer workers, however, work with co-workers and with members of the public all the time. They must genuinely like people and must know how to treat them with courtesy and respect.

If you have these skills, interests, and abilities, you may want to think about some of these careers.

Management Careers

With the skills you have, you can work in many different types of management and consumer-related jobs. Because these jobs call for similar skills, you can even start in one area and change to another. You may start out working in a bank or department store. Years later you may use your skills to sell computers to businesses or plan how to use natural resources. You will still be using similar skills, though.

Entry-Level Jobs

Many businesses keep all their supplies or products in large rooms or warehouses. They hire stock clerks to work in these areas and to locate items when they are needed in the store, office, or factory. These workers may be part-time or full-time. The experience they gain in being part of a business will be very valuable in their future jobs, even if they do other work.

Managers are often helped by administrative assistants. These workers prepare reports, schedule meetings, and communicate with other workers. They must be well organized. Many use computers and word processors to do their work.

A wide variety of workers is involved in managing natural resources. Fish hatchery workers, park groundskeepers, and farm workers, for instance, are outdoors much of the time. Depending on where they live, these people may be seasonal workers—very active in some months, but less so in others.

Jobs That Require Training

If you enjoy working with numbers, you may want to become a bookkeeper. These workers keep financial records so that managers know how much money is being spent and in what way. Bookkeepers are trained in two-year college programs.

People who want to be their own bosses become **entrepreneurs** (AHN-truh-preh-nors). They open a new business to provide a product or service that they think people will want to buy. Being an entrepreneur is challenging and rewarding. You work for yourself instead of for other people, you set your own goals, and the money you make depends on how profitable your business becomes. Being an entrepreneur also presents many responsibilities and pressures, and it can also be risky. Entrepreneurs usually use their own savings to get the business going. If the new business does not do well, they can lose everything.

Many people start a business based on something they learned about in school, like hairstyling. Others learn by working for someone else first. Someone who works in a bookstore, for example, may eventually open his or her own store. Many business owners take courses in business management and financial planning to increase their knowledge so they can operate their businesses more successfully. Several government agencies and business groups also provide training and advice to new business owners.

Businesses around the globe can communicate almost instantly with each other thanks to the telecommunications revolution. **Telecommunications** workers install and repair electronic systems that transmit voices, images, and information from one place to another. This includes telephones, televisions, computers, and satellites. People who work in telecommunications jobs need specialized technical training to perform their jobs.

Entrepreneurs own their own businesses. They can achieve many rewards but must also assume the financial risks.

Jobs That Require an Advanced Degree

Many people and groups turn for money information to financial advisers. These experts in managing money help clients set financial goals. Then they write a savings or investment plan to meet those goals. Advisers have a college degree in business, finance, home economics, or economics. This career is expected to become very important in the future.

Most businesses have a personnel manager to help plan the company's employee needs. These managers make rules about hiring and firing and how workers should act on the job. They handle the health and life insurance policies provided by the company for the workers. They often have a college degree in business or a related area.

Environmental scientists plan how people use natural resources. They study an area to identify its resources and try to predict how long these resources will last. They may study how people and industry affect plant and animal life in an area. These scientists have at least four years of college and many have graduate degrees as well.

Consumer-Related Careers

Many people work with and for consumers. They provide goods and services, or they help consumers get the most for their money.

Entry-Level Jobs

A person interested in working in a bank often starts out as a bank teller. A teller handles deposits and withdrawals for bank customers. Tellers must be very careful in their work to avoid making mistakes.

Comparison shoppers work for large stores. They travel to competing stores to check the prices and quality of similar products. Then they report to their managers. The store uses these reports to plan its own pricing and advertising.

Market survey interviewers ask people what they like. They take surveys at public places such as shopping malls to find out how people will respond to a new advertising campaign or a new product. They should be friendly and willing to work with the public.

Market survey interviewers seek out people to test new products or new advertising campaigns.

Jobs That Require Training

Many magazines and newspapers print articles about new products or how to manage resources. The consumer writers who write these articles learn about these topics from research and from their own experience. They must be able to write clearly so that their readers understand what they say.

Credit managers work in banks or stores. They read the loan applications made by consumers and businesses. They must decide whether the person or business will be able to pay back the money borrowed. Some credit workers have attended college. Most of their experience, however, is received through on-the-job training.

Jobs That Require an Advanced Degree

Many lawyers work on behalf of consumers. They study laws and court decisions about product safety and consumer rights. They may practice alone or work as part of a consumer group. Some write books or articles giving consumers advice. These professionals go to college and then go to law school for three years to earn a law degree.

Home economists have college degrees. They perform a wide variety of jobs. Some teach in public schools, of course, and nearly every county in the United States employs a home economist through the Cooperative Extension Service to answer consumer questions and to develop family living programs. They also organize 4-H clubs.

Many businesses such as banks and electric and gas companies hire home economists to advise families about how to manage their resources. Home economists also write pamphlets, explaining how to use and care for appliances. Stores and manufacturers also hire home economists. They work with the public, explaining new products or new uses for old products.

Training in home economics, then, opens up many career possibilities. If you like managing and you like working with people, it may be for you.

Getting a Job

If you think you might decide to pursue a career in a management or consumer-related field, there are many things you can start planning to do. Most of the jobs described in this chapter require high school diplomas. Technical training or some college education is necessary for some of these positions. Advanced degrees will aid you in getting more experience and gaining more knowledge in order to obtain one of the more specialized positions that have greater responsibility.

MANAGING RESOURCES

Make It Your Business

Have you ever considered becoming an entrepreneur? Have you ever wondered what it takes to start your own business? No matter what type of business you're thinking of, a lawn service or dog walking service, you'll need three basic resources: money, knowledge, and time.

- **Money.** You will need some money to start your business and keep it going until you start making money. You will need to use this **capital,** the money you invest in your business, to buy supplies—such as a lawn mower and gasoline to power the mower in a grass-cutting business, for example. You may need to save this money, borrow it from someone, or go into business with a partner who can provide some money.

- **Knowledge.** Entrepreneurs need to know a great deal about the kind of business they are starting. For example, if you are starting a babysitting business, you need to know how to care for infants and children, how to entertain them, and how to deal with emergencies. Many entrepreneurs acquire the knowledge they need by taking courses, by doing the same job for others, or by turning their hobbies into paying businesses.

- **Time.** A new business needs time to become established. It takes time to make people aware that you are available to walk dogs or cut lawns. You may have to advertise to attract customers. Some teens hand out flyers or cards to announce their businesses. Once you have customers, you have to do your job well so that they will want to hire you again. You have to be willing to put as much time into your business as it takes to become successful.

Running your own business is hard work, but it is also very satisfying. You make all of your own decisions about the business and you earn money by using your own resources and abilities.

Think It Through

1. Why do you think many people prefer to start their own businesses while others don't?

2. Give an example of a business that you think would be a hit in your neighborhood. What would it take to start this business?

Reviewing the Facts

1. Name three skills needed by people in management and consumer-related jobs.
2. What do administrative assistants do?
3. What is an entrepreneur? List one possible risk that entrepreneurs take.
4. What do telecommunications workers do?
5. What do financial advisers do?
6. What are two characteristics that a market survey interviewer needs to have?
7. Name two consumer-related jobs that require college degrees.

Sharing Your Ideas

1. If you could have any job in this chapter, which would you want? Why? What skills or interests do you have that would prepare you for the job?
2. What's the relationship between management in business and everyday management?

Applying Your Skills

1. Researching Career Information. Check the classified ads in your local Sunday newspaper for job opportunities in management and consumer-related fields. Clip out five ads and circle the education or experience requirements. Be prepared to discuss the ads in class.

2. Organizing Consumer Careers. Make a list of the jobs discussed in this chapter. On another piece of paper, make a chart with three columns. Title each column with one of the following: Entry-level jobs, jobs requiring training, jobs requiring an advanced degree. List these and other consumer-related and management jobs in the appropriate categories.

3. Preparing Questions. Prepare a list of questions you as an interviewer would ask a person applying for a position in the management or consumer field.

TEEN TIPS

Using Sense to Make Dollars
Babysitting and lawn mowing are not the only ways to earn money.

Study Time—Dos and Don'ts
No tricks—just some helpful hints to help you maximize your study time.

Beyond Computer Games
How to use a computer to help manage your time and money.

Using Sense  to Make Dollars

Would you like to earn extra money and still be your own boss? Here are 55 ideas for increasing your income—and learning how to run your own business:

- **Help People**
  - Tutor younger children
  - Be a mother's helper after school for a working mom
  - Pack for people who are moving
  - Shop and run errands for people who can't leave home
  - Deliver balloons or specialty baskets
  - Walk kids to school and home again

- **Provide a Service**
  - Coordinate a baby-sitting service
  - Bake cookies, brownies, or nutritious muffins
  - Walk dogs
  - Take care of pets when people are out of town
  - Wash and groom pets
  - Water and take care of plants
  - Start a telephone wake-up service
  - Make clothing repairs and alterations
  - Address and stuff envelopes

Clean Things
Clean homes
Wash windows
Clean barbeque grills
Wash and wax cars and boats

Do Yard and Garden Work
Mow lawns
Weed gardens
Turn sprinklers on and off
Rake leaves
Shovel snow

Holiday Projects
Make and sell pinecone or candy wreaths
Wrap gift packages
Deliver valentines
Make Halloween costumes
Deliver gifts as the Easter Bunny or Santa Claus
Hold a holiday boutique to sell craft items

Recycle Things
Repair, redesign, and sell used clothing
Organize a garage sale
Sell used toys
Reclaim scrap lumber for craft projects
Collect and sell jars and bottles
Sell used books and magazines
Collect and sell sea shells and pinecones

Make Things to Sell
Start plants from cuttings
Make wooden or stuffed toys
Decorate T-shirts, sweatshirts, sneakers
Make wall hangings for children's rooms

Use Your Computer
Publish a newsletter
Write computer programs
Publish a list of babysitters
Word process reports and papers
Publish a cookbook
Maintain mailing lists for clubs and organizations
Design craft projects and write instructions

Party Services
Be a disc jockey
Take pictures at parties and family occasions
Be a clown for children's parties
Run a party clean-up service
Be a waiter or waitress
Organize and run children's birthday parties
Decorate cakes

Study Time 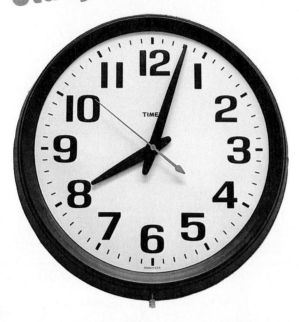 Dos and Don'ts

DON'T sleep, eat, or watch TV where you study.

DO sit in a comfortable chair at a desk or table where you have a good light.

DON'T get *too* comfortable. Easy chairs, sofas, and beds tell your body "It's time to relax."

DO study in a quiet place when you need to concentrate. If there's background noise that disturbs you, wear headphones and listen to quiet music.

DON'T listen to loud music while you study.

DO take the first 10 minutes to outline your priorities. What is due tomorrow? What is due in two days? What is due next week?

DO schedule your time. Estimate how long it should take you to accomplish each task.

DON'T let others misuse your time. If family members interrupt your study time, they may need a gentle reminder. Try hanging a "Do Not Disturb" sign on the door.

DO study when you're most productive. Some people are "morning people" and others are "night people."

DO use a regular study area. When you study in the same place every day, your body becomes trained to respond.

T E E N   T I P S

DON'T

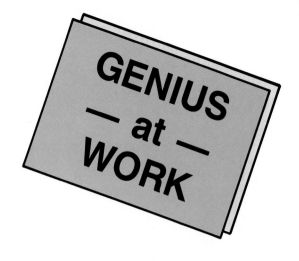

DO study your most difficult subjects first.

DO break up big projects, such as book reports and term papers, into small segments to do each day. Then you won't have to panic at the last minute to get the project done.

DON'T let the phone interrupt your study time. Tell the caller that you are studying and will return the call during your break.

DO allow for breaks. Use this time to do some exercises. Touch your toes. Do side bends. Roll your shoulders to get the kinks out.

DO set realistic goals. Say to yourself, "I'll study for an hour, then I'll watch TV for 30 minutes, then I'll study for 40 minutes and have a snack." It usually doesn't work to say, "I'll study for 4 hours straight."

DON'T waste time. If you find you aren't accomplishing anything, take a minute to evaluate what you're doing. Are you trying to avoid an unpleasant task? Face the task and get it over with.

DO spend the last 10 minutes to organize what you have done. Check your priority list again to be sure that you've completed everything you had planned.

Beyond Computer Games

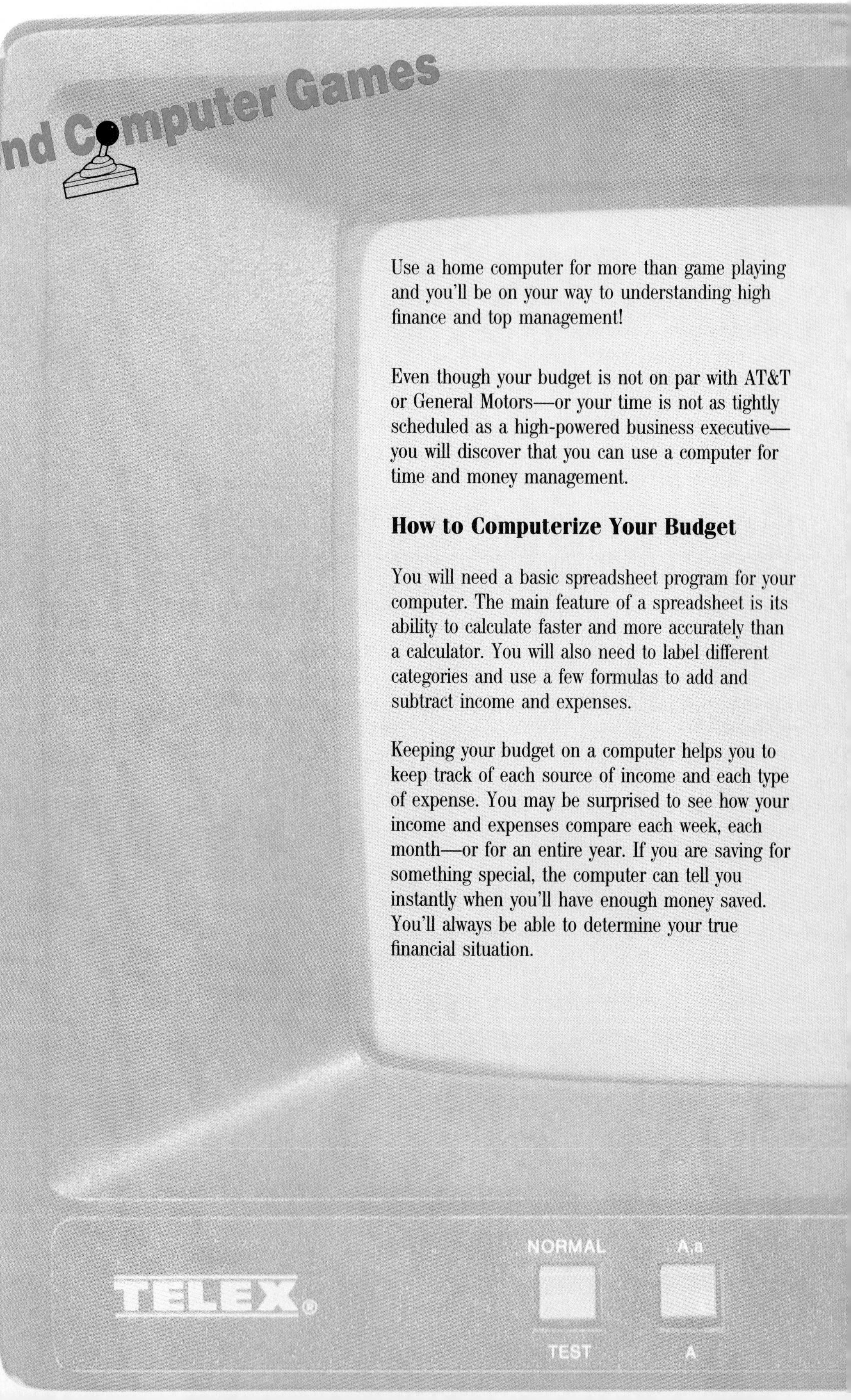

Use a home computer for more than game playing and you'll be on your way to understanding high finance and top management!

Even though your budget is not on par with AT&T or General Motors—or your time is not as tightly scheduled as a high-powered business executive— you will discover that you can use a computer for time and money management.

How to Computerize Your Budget

You will need a basic spreadsheet program for your computer. The main feature of a spreadsheet is its ability to calculate faster and more accurately than a calculator. You will also need to label different categories and use a few formulas to add and subtract income and expenses.

Keeping your budget on a computer helps you to keep track of each source of income and each type of expense. You may be surprised to see how your income and expenses compare each week, each month—or for an entire year. If you are saving for something special, the computer can tell you instantly when you'll have enough money saved. You'll always be able to determine your true financial situation.

NORMAL

A,a

TELEX.

TEST

A

How to Computerize Your Time Schedule

You can use spreadsheet and word processing programs to set up your weekly schedule. At the beginning of the semester, you can enter your schedule at school. Then, as homework, papers, and tests are assigned, you can add them to your weekly plan. Include after-school activities, sports, and household chores. If you have a part-time job, add that to your schedule. You can plan time for studying, relaxing—and even to watch your favorite TV program.

If you also have a database program, you can add special information about your activities. For example, make a list of families who ask you to babysit regularly. Include their phone numbers, addresses, and other helpful information. If you're on an athletic team, enter your coach's name and phone number, practice times, and the dates and locations of games or matches.

CONTRAST BRIGHTNESS

POWER

178
Display Terminal

FOODS AND NUTRITION

Health and Fitness

erschel wants to help his friend Ty. They are both on the school basketball team, but Herschel is a first-string player, while Ty spends a lot of time on the bench. Ty wants to improve his game. He has some great moves and shoots well from outside, but he tires too quickly.

"Coach said I would make the starting lineup if I could keep up with everybody else," Ty told Herschel. "He told me to cut down on junk snacks like candy and cookies. But I need the snacks, especially now with all this exercise—why else would I get so hungry? Food provides energy, right? Still, you don't snack like I do, Hersh, so how come you seem to have more energy?"

Herschel didn't know what to say. Not only does he play more during games than Ty, he also trains more on his own. Still, he actually eats less than Ty.

Herschel, too, had always thought that people ate food to meet their energy needs. Then shouldn't he need more food than Ty? Is their information about energy wrong?

What Food Does for You

Herschel and Ty are not wrong. Food *does* supply the energy that people need for their activities. However, it also contributes many other things to our lives. In addition to physical needs, food can meet emotional and social needs as well. It also plays a vital part in the growth and repair of body tissues.

Physical Needs

Your body is active all the time. Food provides you with all the energy you use—energy for walking, talking, writing, and more strenuous activities. Food also helps your heart to beat, your body to maintain its temperature, and the cut on your finger to heal.

If you go without eating, you will become tired, listless, unable to concentrate—and hungry. **Hunger** is the body's physical signal that it is short of energy and needs food. However, people often feel the urge to eat without being hungry. This is because we use food to satisfy emotional needs, too.

Studying and concentration take energy—which is best provided by nutritious food.

Emotional Needs

The urge to eat often comes from your emotions. You might have a second helping of meat loaf because it is your favorite food. You might go into the bakery on impulse because you smell the freshly baked bread and see the beautiful display of pastries in the window. These reactions are automatic, as is the urge to eat because it's lunchtime. This desire to eat is called **appetite**.

Your appetite is linked to your emotions in many ways. Food gives people a sense of security and well-being. When you are tense or upset you may eat excessively to comfort yourself—or you may lose your appetite entirely.

Social Needs

Eating also plays an important part in our social lives. Preparing and cooking food for others can be very satisfying. Most people enjoy the social pleasure of getting together to eat.

In fact, people spend a lot of time around the dining table enjoying each other's company. Do you sometimes sit and talk to a relative or friend at the table? Do you often stop with friends for pizza or ice cream after school?

In addition, of course, special social occasions often center around food—a birthday cake, a Thanksgiving dinner, a cookout on the Fourth of July. Food is a social experience. It is more than just a way to soothe your emotions or satisfy hunger.

Health Needs

Another major benefit you gain from food is health and well-being. When people don't get enough of the right kinds of food for a long time, they may get sick and even die.

Young people need certain foods to grow normally. Your body cannot combat diseases or heal properly unless it is well nourished. This is because food provides the raw materials that help build and maintain a healthy mind and body.

Families and friends enjoy getting together for a meal or to celebrate a special occasion.

U.S.A.: Land of Food Opportunity

Have you ever been surprised to see one of your friends enjoy a meal you never imagined she or he would eat? All people have favorite foods, and they aren't always what you would expect.

Your idea of what tastes good is based largely on what you eat in your own home, what you see on TV ads, and what your friends eat when you go out together.

However, taken together, American families probably eat a wider variety of foods than any other people in the world. There are several reasons for this:

- **Ethnic background.** Because the United States is a nation of immigrants, foods from many countries are eaten here—not only in ethnic restaurants but in people's homes. There are sausages from Germany, pasta from Italy, tortillas from Mexico, rice dishes from China and Japan—to name a few.

- **Religious customs.** The United States is also home to many religious groups, each with their own customs. Families often eat special foods on their religious holidays—egg dishes at Easter, matzoth during Passover. Some religions encourage the eating of fish; others have rules that forbid the eating of pork, shellfish, or any type of meat. Some religious groups fast—or do not eat—on certain holidays or at certain times of the year.

- **Regional traditions.** Many food specialties developed in different regions due to the foods that were plentiful there and the ethnic backgrounds of the settlers. Today, although most foods are available in all parts of the United States, certain dishes are still associated with a specific region: New England clam chowder, Southern fried chicken, Texas barbeque, Creole gumbo, or sourdough bread from San Francisco.

As a result, the United States offers a wide choice of healthful foods. True, *your* tastes have been shaped by your family, with its special ethnic, religious, and regional traditions. Our country, however, offers many opportunities to broaden your tastes. Take advantage of these opportunities; sampling the variety is not only fun, it's good for your health and fitness.

Think It Through

1. **What foods are considered typical of where you live? Why do you think that they became popular in your region?**

2. **Why do you think people are often unwilling to try new foods? Give some reasons for and against eating something you have never tried before.**

The Importance of Fitness

Fitness, which can be achieved through good nutrition and regular exercise, is important for everyone, not just for athletes like Ty and Herschel. When you are fit, you are strong and healthy enough to participate in a wide range of physical activities. Because your body is conditioned, you are less likely to suffer injuries.

Fitness improves other aspects of your life, too. You look better, and you feel calmer and more relaxed.

Good Nutrition

The way that your body uses food is called **nutrition**. When you eat the right combinations of foods, your body receives all the nourishment it needs; this means you are practicing good nutrition. Much research has been done to find out exactly which combinations of foods are most healthful. You will learn some of the results of this research in the next few chapters.

Without good nutrition, your body cannot manufacture the thousands of new cells that it needs every day. Good nutrition can help you to control your weight, avoid many illnesses, and reach your full height. Eating right and getting enough exercise is the key to strong muscles and healthy looking skin, hair, and nails. Understanding nutrition is an important part of managing your own life.

Regular Exercise

Exercise doesn't mean only sports and the activities you do in physical education class. When you walk to your friend's house instead of taking a bus, that is exercise, as are bicycling to the store and washing the kitchen floor at home. If activities such as these are not a part of your daily routine, however, set aside time for exercising regularly.

Regular exercise not only helps you become physically fit, it often gives you the opportunity to be with friends. In addition, as you read in Chapter 3, exercise can help you deal with stressful situations in your life. By helping with stress, exercise can lessen emotional dependence on food. People often feel fewer appetite urges when they exercise regularly.

Not only are you being good to your dog by going for a walk, you are doing yourself a favor by getting some exercise.

Types of Exercise

Regular exercise can contribute to your fitness in three important ways:

- **Strength.** Many types of exercise are designed to make you stronger. Weight training and similar activities usually benefit particular parts of your body. For example, push-ups strengthen your arms, full knee bends strengthen your legs, and sit-ups tighten your stomach muscles.

- **Endurance.** Endurance exercises increase your **stamina**, or staying power, by building up your blood circulatory system. They strengthen your heart and lungs, increasing the amount of oxygen that your body can use. Some activities that promote endurance are called **aerobic** (uh-ROH-bic) exercises because they improve your ability to use oxygen from the air. They include running, swimming, cycling, fast walking—in fact, any exercise that requires sustained regular movement for 30 minutes or more, with *no* rests. Endurance is probably more important than strength for general fitness, because it means that your whole body is working efficiently. It also helps your body make better use of the food you eat.

- **Flexibility.** Exercises that increase flexibility, such as stretching, are important to fitness. They help to make you more agile—whether you are dancing or playing football. If your body is flexible, you are less likely to pull a muscle during exercise.

Before you begin an exercise program, check with your doctor to be sure you do not have a condition that could be aggravated by strenuous exercise. Start each workout with warm-up activities such as stretching and bending. This helps to prevent muscle pulls and other injuries. When you are finished, a cool-down period of stretching or slow movement lets your body return to a relaxed state.

Each type of exercise provides different benefits for your body.

STRENGTH

ENDURANCE

FLEXIBILITY

Analyzing Your Own Eating Habits

By paying attention to your eating habits, you can learn if you are choosing foods that help promote health and fitness. A healthy **diet**, the food and drink you typically consume, will help you feel and look good.

The best way to become aware of your eating habits is to keep a record of everything you consume for a week or two. Exactly what did you eat, and how much? What time of day was it? What were you doing at the time? When you review this record, you will see how frequently you eat and what foods you choose. You might discover there are certain times that you always eat—such as when you watch television.

To help you analyze your eating patterns, here are some questions you can ask yourself:

- Do you usually eat three meals a day?
- Do you ever skip meals?
- What foods do you enjoy the most?
- What foods do you seldom eat?
- When do you snack?
- What do you order when you eat out?

Your answers to these kinds of questions can make you more aware of your eating habits. Some of these habits may be very good; for example, you might always eat a nutritious breakfast. Other habits, however, may be bad; you might find that you eat candy and fried foods for snacks instead of more healthful foods like fruits, yogurt, or popcorn.

As you read the rest of this unit, you will learn which foods are better for you and why. You will learn the importance of exercise and good eating habits, and how you can control your weight and improve your fitness. You will also find out how to prepare meals and snacks for yourself, your family, and your friends. You will thus be more able to take responsibility for the foods you eat and get the maximum benefits that food can provide.

When analyzing your eating habits, be sure to include snacks as well as regular meals.

CHAPTER
35 REVIEW

Reviewing the Facts

1. What four needs does food supply?
2. What is the difference between hunger and appetite?
3. How are your emotions linked to your appetite?
4. What does it mean to be fit?
5. List two benefits of being fit.
6. How do exercise and good nutrition contribute to a person's fitness level?
7. What types of exercise would you choose if you wanted to increase your strength? Your stamina? Your flexibility?

Sharing Your Ideas

1. What is your personal definition of fitness? Compare it to a classmate's. How is it similar? In what ways does it differ? Why do you think people may have different definitions?
2. Why do you think it is important to begin an exercise session with a warm-up and end it with a cool-down period? What could be some hazards if you did not warm up and cool down?

Applying Your Skills

1. Analyzing Your Diet. Keep a record of what you eat for a week: when, what, how much, and why. Do you see any patterns in your eating habits? Were you surprised at any aspects of your diet? Do you eat a variety of different foods, or do you eat the same ones over and over again?

2. Developing a Workout. Develop a personalized 30-minute workout including exercises that build strength, stamina, and flexibility. Include a warm-up and cool-down period. What percent of your program consists of strength exercises? What percent are endurance exercises? What percent promotes flexibility? Go over your program with a physical education teacher, then present it to the class.

3. Drawing Conclusions. Make a list of the exercise you get in an average week and a record of everything you eat in a week (see activity #1). What might be the relationship between your physical fitness and the amount of exercise and the foods you eat? What changes might you make in your lifestyle?

CHAPTER

36

Nutrients

OBJECTIVES

This chapter will help you to:

- Explain the importance of nutrients in food.
- List the six classes of nutrients and their functions.
- Identify foods that are good sources of carbohydrates, proteins, fats, water, vitamins, and minerals.

WORDS TO REMEMBER

amino acid	fiber
calorie	mineral
carbohydrate	nutrient
cholesterol	protein
	vitamin

Nutritionists are scientists who study food and its effects on the body. They have found that food contains many nourishing substances, or **nutrients**. These nutrients are all needed for your health; if your diet lacks any, you won't feel your best and may even become sick.

More than 40 key nutrients have been identified. They can be grouped into six classes: carbohydrates, proteins, fats, water, vitamins, and minerals. Knowing about nutrients and the foods that contain them will help you plan for a healthy life.

Carbohydrates

Starches and sugars are two main categories of **carbohydrates,** nutrients that provide your body with ready energy. However, your body cannot store them in large quantities. If you need energy but haven't eaten carbohydrates recently, your body has to make energy from other body tissues.

Therefore, foods containing carbohydrates should be a major ingredient in your diet—especially grains, vegetables, and fruits. These foods are complex carbohydrate foods; they contain other nutrients besides starch or sugar, making them particularly valuable.

How can you include carbohydrates in your diet?

- **Starches.** Rice, potatoes, and grain products such as bread and pasta are examples of foods high in starch. Starch is digested to form a simple sugar called glucose, which is a major source of energy for your body.

- **Sugars.** Glucose can also be formed from the sugar in fruits. To most people, however, sugar means refined sugar, which is found in foods such as cakes, candy, cookies, and many soft drinks. Refined sugar is a poor source of energy because it lacks other nutrients. Too much refined sugar can lead to weight gain and dental problems and it can cause complications in diseases such as diabetes.

Grains—breads, cereals, pasta, rice—are excellent sources of carbohydrates. The starch in these foods provides energy for your body.

An important benefit of eating certain carbohydrate foods is that they contain indigestible threadlike cells called **fiber**. Fiber is not strictly a nutrient, but it is important because it helps to move food through the digestive system. Whole-grain cereals and breads are excellent sources of fiber, as are fruits and vegetables, especially the peels and seeds.

Fiber can also promote a feeling of fullness, making you less hungry. This is helpful if you are trying to lose weight.

Proteins

Anyone who is growing needs a diet high in **proteins**, the nutrients necessary for building and repairing body tissues. Proteins are the basis of all the body's cells, and form the major part of hair, nails, and skin. The body includes more proteins than it does any other nutrient except water.

Though your body needs many different types of protein, all proteins are made from the same basic chemicals. These chemicals are called **amino acids**, and 22 different kinds have been identified.

While it is useful to have most of the amino acids present in your food, only 9 are absolutely necessary—the other 13 can be created by your body from other food substances. These nine are called the essential amino acids. The foods that contain them—animal proteins like meat, poultry, eggs, and milk—are said to have complete proteins.

Vegetables, fruits, and grains have incomplete proteins. They contain many amino acids, but not all of the essential ones. You can get the essential nine, however, by combining certain incomplete proteins, such as beans with rice, or nuts with whole grains. This is called protein complementing. People who do not eat meat or dairy products can use protein complementing to get the nutrients necessary for good health.

Complete proteins come from animal sources, such as meat, poultry, fish, eggs, and milk. Incomplete proteins come from plant sources, such as grains, vegetables, and fruits. Combining certain incomplete proteins, such as rice and beans, is called protein complementing.

Fats

Some fats are necessary for good health. The body uses them for reserve energy. Fats also allow your body to store and use other nutrients, such as vitamin A, and they help regulate body temperature. Without fats in the diet, skin and hair problems can develop.

However, too much fat in your diet is stored as fatty tissue and may make you overweight. It can lead to serious health problems.

Fats are present in most foods, especially meat, butter, salad dressings, nuts, milk, cheese, baked goods, and snack foods. Some fats are visible—such as butter or the layer of fat on meats. Other fats are hidden in foods such as egg yolks, french fries, hard cheeses, ice cream, and chocolate. Fats are also obtained from excess carbohydrates, which are converted to fat if not immediately needed for energy. Nutritionists recommend that fat intake be reduced for better health.

There are two types of fats: saturated and unsaturated. Saturated fats are found in the animal fats in meat, milk and butter, as well as in tropical oils such as coconut and palm oils. Saturated fats are particularly undesirable in the diet because they may lead to high levels of cholesterol in the blood. **Cholesterol** (kuh-LESS-tuh-rahl) is a white, waxlike substance that plays an important part in transporting and digesting fat. However, high cholesterol levels can lead to heart disease, high blood pressure, hardening of the arteries, and other health problems.

Unsaturated fats are better for you. They are found in vegetable oils which come from fruits and vegetables like corn or olives. Whenever possible, unsaturated fats should be substituted for saturated fats.

Water

Close to 75 percent of your body is water. Water is found in all cells and is the basic material of your blood. It transports nutrients throughout your body and carries away waste products. It also helps to move food through the digestive system and to regulate the temperature of your body.

Your body loses water continually, so it is important that you take in enough. Foods especially high in water are milk, soups, many fruits, and vegetables such as lettuce and celery. Health care professionals also recommend drinking between six and eight glasses of water daily. You need more water when it is hot and after you exercise or do physical work.

Your body needs six to eight glasses of water a day.

The Truth About Calories

What is a calorie? You hear a lot about calories, but you may not know what they are. A **calorie** is no more than an amount of energy; specifically, a measure of heat. A food's calorie count is the amount of energy the food provides. This energy may be used by the body or stored as fat.

In terms of calories, not all nutrients are created equal. There are four calories in every gram of protein and four in every gram of carbohydrate (starch or sugar). In every gram of fat, however, there are nine calories. Water, vitamins, and minerals, on the other hand, have no calories at all.

Let's look at an example. One 5-ounce (150g) baked potato has approximately 100 calories—it consists mostly of carbohydrates and has no fat. A 5-ounce steak, which is 80 percent fat, has 550 calories. Five ounces of butter has 1,000 calories!

Many people try to lose weight by counting calories, but it is important to understand that this is only half the story. Body weight is really a reflection of the energy balance in your body. If you eat more calories than your body uses up, the extra calories are stored as fat. If, on the other hand, you eat fewer calories than you use, your body burns stored fat to make energy. For most people

the problem is not so much the calories that go in, but rather those that do *not* go out. In other words, they may not overeat so much as under-exercise.

If you are trying to lose weight, don't just count calories. Instead, eat to get the most out of your calories. Choose foods that are nutrient-rich. At the same time, exercise to be sure you are burning calories as well as taking them in.

Exercise has benefits beyond the calories used during the activity. In a half-hour bicycle ride, you might use up 250 calories, but your exercise keeps on working for you. It helps your body burn calories faster all day long.

Think It Through

1. What do you suppose is the danger in fad diets that call for a person to eat only one or two kinds of food for a period of time?
2. How might teens who don't get regular exercise encourage themselves to exercise?

Vitamins

Vitamins are nutrients that help the body stay healthy, function properly, and make use of other nutrients. They are needed in very small amounts. Vitamins do not provide energy or form tissues, but if you don't get enough of each, you may become seriously ill. Vitamins can be water soluble or fat soluble.

Water-Soluble Vitamins

The B vitamins and vitamin C are water-soluble vitamins. That means that they are easily absorbed and can move through the body in water. However, since water is constantly being lost from the body, you need fresh supplies of these vitamins every day.

Citrus fruits are an excellent source of vitamin C.

There are eight B vitamins. They are especially important in helping nerve and brain tissue to develop and work well. They also aid in digestion. The most important of the group are thiamine (B_1), riboflavin (B_2), and niacin. B vitamins are found in milk products, meats, and breads and cereals.

Vitamin C, also called ascorbic acid, helps the body build cells. This makes it important in healing cuts and bruises. It also helps form strong teeth and bones and healthy gums. Vitamin C is found in many fruits and vegetables. Citrus fruits (such as oranges and grapefruits), strawberries and cantaloupes are excellent sources. Vegetables high in vitamin C include broccoli, raw cabbage, and turnip greens.

Fat-Soluble Vitamins

Vitamins A, D, E, and K are fat-soluble. This means that they travel through the bloodstream in droplets of fat. They can also be stored in fat cells for long periods of time.

Vitamin A is found in yellow and dark green vegetables, such as carrots, sweet potatoes, broccoli, and spinach. You need it for good vision, healthy teeth and gums, and strong bones. It also helps the body resist infections.

Vitamin D, another key substance in the formation of bones and teeth, helps you use minerals like calcium and phosphorus. Your body makes its own vitamin D if it gets enough sunlight. The dairy industry helps by adding vitamin D to many milk products.

Vitamin E helps keep red blood cells healthy. It is found in vegetable oils as well as foods such as grains, nuts, and green leafy vegetables. Vitamin K, which helps your blood to clot, can be obtained in vegetables such as broccoli and cauliflower.

Vitamins at a Glance

Vitamin	Source	Function
Vitamin A	Yellow and dark green vegetables: carrots, sweet potatoes, broccoli, and spinach	Builds good vision, healthy teeth and gums, and strong bones
Vitamin B thiamine (B_1) riboflavin (B_2) niacin	Milk products, meats, breads, and cereals	Helps nerve and brain tissue to work well; aids in digestion
Vitamin C (ascorbic acid)	Fruits: citrus fruits (such as oranges and grapefruits), strawberries, cantaloupe. Vegetables: broccoli, raw cabbage, and turnip greens	Helps body build cells—important in healing cuts and bruises; helps form strong teeth and gums
Vitamin D	Your body makes it and it is in many milk products	Helps you use minerals like calcium and phosphorus; forms bones and teeth
Vitamin E	Vegetable oils as well as foods such as grains, nuts, and green leafy vegetables	Helps keep red blood cells healthy
Vitamin K	Vegetables like broccoli and cauliflower	Helps blood to clot

Minerals

Minerals are simple substances that form parts of many tissues and are needed to keep body processes operating smoothly. Your body contains large amounts of some minerals and tiny quantities of others. All are vital to your health.

Calcium and Phosphorus

Calcium and phosphorus work together in the body as a team. They are essential for building and maintaining strong bones and teeth. Both help keep the nervous system working properly.

Calcium also helps normal growth to take place and keeps muscles healthy. It must always be present in the blood so that your heart beats regularly and blood clots normally.

Although calcium is found in many foods, it is not uncommon for teens to take in too little calcium. This is particularly true of girls, who need more calcium than boys.

A condition known as osteoporosis can develop later in life if you skimp on calcium foods when you are young. When osteoporosis occurs, bones lose their density and become brittle. Such bones are much more likely to fracture. Osteoporosis is a special problem for older people, especially women. However, by taking in enough calcium throughout your life and exercising regularly, you can help to prevent osteoporosis.

Milk and other dairy products provide calcium, which is needed for building strong bones and teeth.

Sodium

Sodium—found in table salt—plays an important part in controlling the movement of water in your body. Too much of it can disrupt the system, leading to high blood pressure and swelling of the hands and feet.

Unfortunately, sodium is widely used in processed food; not only chips and pretzels but even canned soups, catsup, and soft drinks. People often use extra salt to flavor their food, but today many individuals are cutting down on their sodium intake. See "Kicking the Salt Habit" on page 359.

Other Minerals

Other important minerals include potassium, magnesium, zinc, and iodine. Potassium regulates muscle contractions, transmission of nerve signals, and fluid in the cells. Your body may lose potassium when you perspire heavily, exercise strenuously, or become ill. Orange juice and bananas are good sources of potassium.

Magnesium helps the body use proteins and carbohydrates. It also helps regulate the nervous system. Good sources include whole-grain cereals and breads, dried beans, and green leafy vegetables.

Zinc is used to make insulin, which helps the body use glucose. People who eat no meat or eggs may get too little zinc. Iodine, available in iodized salt and seafood, helps the thyroid gland work properly. If the diet lacks iodine, a goiter, or enlarged thyroid gland, may develop.

Dairy products such as milk, cheese, and yogurt are the best sources of calcium. Dark green leafy vegetables and canned fish with soft bones (such as sardines and salmon) provide calcium also.

Phosphorus also helps the body use other nutrients. Good sources of phosphorus are milk, cheese, yogurt, meats, fish, poultry, and whole-grain breads and cereals.

Iron

Iron is vital for building red blood cells. When people do not get enough iron, they develop anemia—their blood cannot carry enough oxygen, causing a lack of energy and low resistance to infections. Liver, spinach, and raisins are good sources of iron.

Reviewing the Facts

1. List the six classes of nutrients. What is a major function of each?
2. What substance do the two major types of carbohydrates form when they are digested by the body?
3. How does fiber benefit you?
4. Describe protein complementing.
5. What are the two types of fats? Which one is better for you and why?
6. Explain the importance of vitamins.
7. Why is calcium important to your body, and what foods contain it?
8. What type of nutrient (carbohydrate, protein, vitamin, etc.) is each of the following: starch, sugar, vegetable oil, iron, riboflavin.

Sharing Your Ideas

1. Why is it important for you to know about nutrients in food? What could be done to encourage teens to become more concerned about nutrition?
2. What factors can you think of that contribute to the high amount of fat in the American diet? What alternatives are available that can help people lessen their fat intake?

Applying Your Skills

1. Preparing a Chart. Select two of the following vitamins: thiamine, niacin, vitamin C, vitamin D. Identify at least three foods which contain large amounts of the two nutrients you have chosen. Make a wall chart and illustrate it with pictures of these foods.

2. Recognizing Potential Problems. Describe your intake of fat—remember to include hidden fats. Keep in mind the warnings against having too much fat in your diet and the warnings about saturated fats. How healthy is your diet? Explain your answer.

3. Research a Topic. Select one of the following health problems: anemia, scurvy, osteoporosis, goiter, high blood pressure. Gather information about how specific nutrients can prevent or cause the problem. Report your findings to the class.

CHAPTER

37

Food Groups

OBJECTIVES

This chapter will help you to:

- Explain the purpose and principles of dividing food into four basic groups.
- Outline the general nutritional differences among the food groups and give examples of foods in each group.
- Specify typical serving sizes recommended by the Daily Food Guide.

WORDS TO REMEMBER

cereal
Daily Food Guide
enriched
fortified
legumes
nutrient density
processed
serving

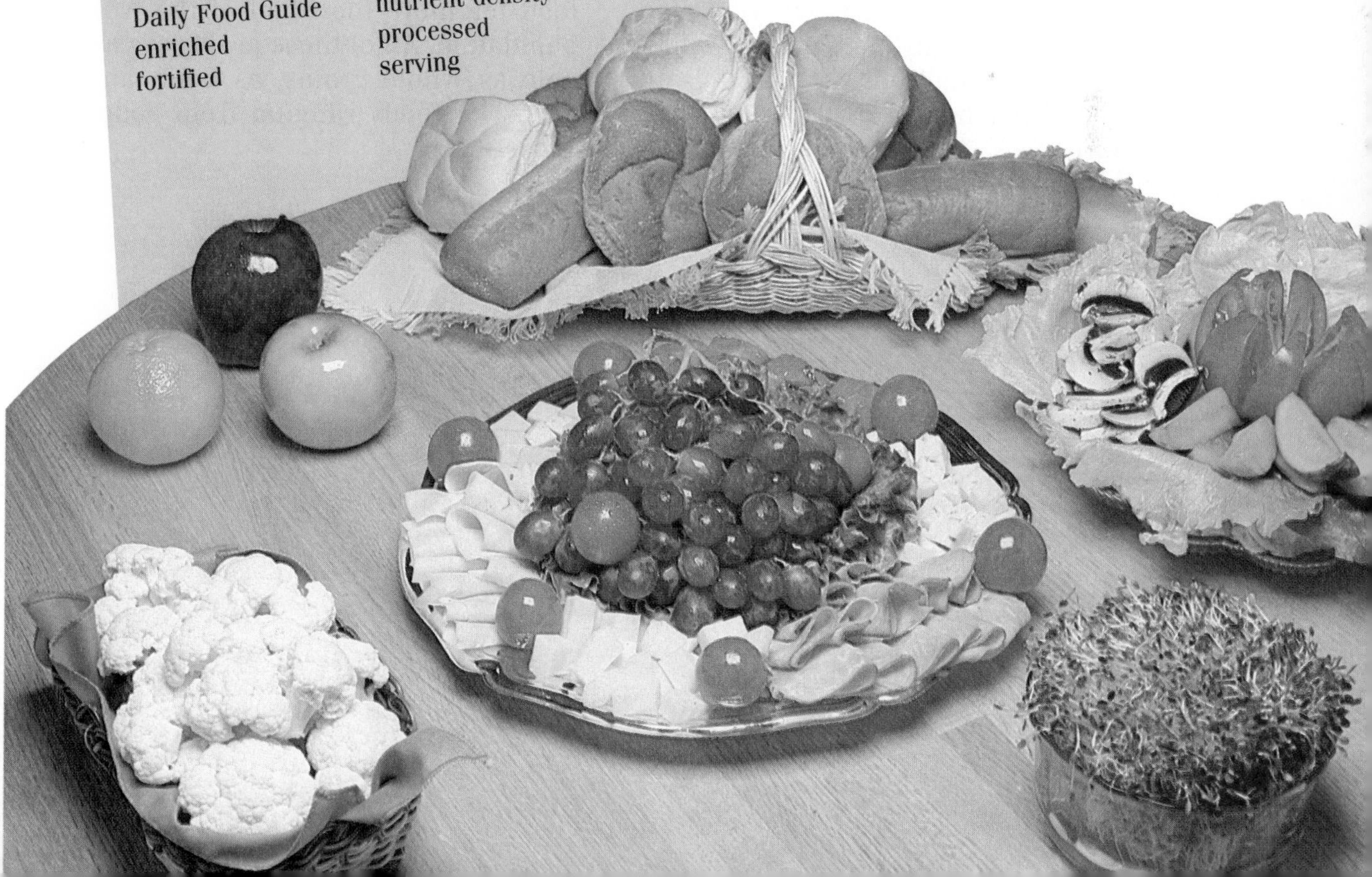

You have learned the importance of nutrition and good eating habits to your health, and you resolve to follow a nutritious diet—but where do you start? Will you have to consult long food tables with your pocket calculator handy? No, it's much easier than that. Nutritionists have divided foods into four basic food groups, according to the nutrients that different foods contain. These groups, which are discussed in more depth in chapters 49 through 52, are:

- Breads and cereals.
- Fruits and vegetables.
- Milk and milk products.
- Meats, poultry, fish, eggs, nuts, and beans.

Nutritionists have also developed the **Daily Food Guide,** which lists the number and size of servings needed every day from each food group. A **serving** is a portion of a food that a person needs to supply nutritional needs. If you plan your daily diet to include the right amounts of foods from each group, you will get all the nutrients your body requires.

The Breads-Cereals Group

Breads and cereals are the richest source of our most important energy nutrient, carbohydrates. The foods from this group also provide B vitamins, vitamin E, iron, fats, and several incomplete proteins. In addition, bread and cereal foods are good sources of fiber.

Most people think of cereal as the food they eat with milk and fruit for breakfast. **Cereal,** however, refers to any grain. Since breads, breakfast cereals, rice, and pasta are all made from grain, they are all cereal foods.

Types of Breads and Cereals

Important grains include wheat, rice, oats, corn, barley, and rye. Wheat is the main ingredient in most breads, pastries, breakfast cereals, crackers, spaghetti, and macaroni. Rice is a major food for more than half of the world's population. All of these grains are available as whole grains, as flour, and in prepared foods ranging from soups to desserts.

You need four servings per day from the breads-cereals group. One serving equals a slice of bread; a roll, biscuit, muffin, or bagel; or ½ to ¾ cup of cooked rice, cereal, or pasta.

Most grain products are **processed**, or changed from their raw form before being sold. During processing, some of the nutrients may be stripped away. For this reason, processed grain products are **enriched**—many of the lost nutrients are replaced. Sometimes the products are **fortified**, or given additional nutrients. Whole-grain products, like whole-wheat bread, are foods from which the natural nutrients were never removed.

Servings per Day

Nutritionists recommend that you eat *four* servings a day from the breads and cereals group. One serving would be a slice of bread; 1 cup (250 mL) of ready-to-eat cereal; 1/2 to 3/4 of a cup (125–175 mL) of cooked cereal, rice, or pasta; or 1 roll or muffin.

You need four servings daily from the fruits-vegetable group. A piece of fruit, a tossed salad, ½ cup of cooked vegetables, or one medium potato equals one serving.

The Fruits-Vegetables Group

Fruits and vegetables are valuable sources of carbohydrates and fiber. They provide many important vitamins and minerals, including vitamins A and C, potassium, iron, and calcium.

Types of Fruits and Vegetables

All fruits and vegetables are plant products. Different parts of plants are harvested:

- **Roots.** Several vegetables, such as carrots, beets, turnips, and potatoes grow underground.
- **Stems.** Some plants have edible stalks, such as asparagus, broccoli, and celery.
- **Leaves.** Leafy vegetables include lettuce, chicory, romaine, spinach, and cabbage.
- **Flowers.** Broccoli and cauliflower are both flowers of plants.
- **Seeds.** This group includes corn, beans, and peas.

■ **Fruits.** Apples, oranges, and melons are fruits. Did you know that squash, cucumbers, tomatoes, and peppers are also the fruit part of plants? Like other fruits, they have seeds inside the fleshy part.

Bananas, potatoes, beets, peas, beans, and turnips are especially good sources of carbohydrates. The carbohydrates in fruits are mainly sugars. Those found in vegetables are in the form of starches. Fruits and vegetables are generally high in fiber. The peel, skin, and stems contain the most fiber.

Yellow, orange, and dark green fruits and vegetables are good sources of vitamin A. These include apricots, peaches, sweet potatoes, carrots, spinach, and broccoli. Citrus fruits like oranges and grapefruits are especially high in vitamin C. Other good sources of vitamin C include potatoes, broccoli, tomatoes, cabbage, and peppers. Some, such as broccoli, are excellent sources of many important nutrients.

Fruits and vegetables are also good sources of minerals. For example, bananas and orange juice have lots of potassium. Green leafy vegetables, such as spinach, are high in calcium and iron.

Servings Per Day

To gain full benefit from the nutrients in the fruits and vegetables group, you should eat *four* servings every day. One serving is an apple or orange, 1/2 grapefruit or banana, 1/2 cup (125 mL) of fruit juice or fruit pieces, 1/2 cup (125 mL) of cooked vegetables, 1 carrot or celery stalk, 1 medium potato, or a bowl of tossed salad.

The Milk-Milk Products Group

Milk is a source of carbohydrates, fat, and protein. It is rich in riboflavin, one of the B vitamins, as well as vitamin A, and it is often fortified with vitamin D. Drinking milk is an excellent way to get the important minerals calcium and phosphorus.

Teenagers need four servings daily from the milk group. An 8-ounce glass of milk, two slices of cheese, or one cup of yogurt equals one serving.

Types of Milk and Milk Products

Milk is available in a variety of types, including whole milk, low-fat milk, and dried milk. You will learn more about milk and milk products in Chapter 51.

Many products, including cheese, yogurt, sour cream, and ice cream, are made from milk. These foods are nutritious, but the amount of nutrients and calories they contain varies, depending on how they were processed.

Nutritionists recommend the use of low-fat milk and milk products for adults. However, young children should drink whole milk to maintain growth.

Servings per Day

The milk group is the only one for which recommended servings change as you grow older. When you were a child, two or three daily servings were enough. As a teen, you need *four* servings to supply you with enough milk nutrients. Most adults require only two servings. A serving could be an 8-ounce (250 mL) glass of milk, 1 1/2 cups (375 mL) of cottage cheese, 1 cup (250 mL) of yogurt, or an ounce (30g) of cheddar cheese.

The Meats-Poultry-Fish-Eggs-Nuts-Beans Group

The foods in this group—which we will call the meats-to-beans group for short—are important sources of protein and B vitamins. They also provide vitamins A and E, iron, and other minerals. Many foods in this group contain saturated fats, though excess fat can often be removed.

There are two different kinds of protein in the meats–to–beans group—animal protein and vegetable protein.

Animal Protein

- Beef, which comes from cattle, is rich in iron.
- Lamb, from young sheep, has nutrients similar to those of beef.
- Pork, from pigs or hogs, is very high in thiamine.
- Liver, kidney, heart, and sweetbreads are packed with nutrients. For example, liver contains large amounts of vitamins A, B, and D, as well as iron.

You need two servings per day from the meats-to-beans group. One serving equals 2-3 ounces of meat, 1 chicken leg, ⅓ cup of tuna fish, 2 eggs, 4 tablespoons of peanut butter, or 1 cup of cooked beans.

- Poultry includes chicken, turkey, duck, and goose. Chicken and turkey have less fat than beef, lamb, and pork, but duck and goose have high amounts of fat.
- Fish is high in protein and low in fat, and is a good source of iodine.
- Eggs supply complete protein and some of almost every nutrient except vitamin C.

Vegetable Protein

Some vegetables—nuts, seeds, and beans—also provide high amounts of protein. *Beans* here means **legumes** (LEG-yooms), the dried seeds of the bean plant. Kidney beans, butter beans, lentils, and chick-peas are legumes. However, fresh beans—green beans, wax beans, and green peas—are classed as vegetables.

Vegetable protein foods are rich in carbohydrates, the B vitamins, and iron, but the protein they contain is incomplete. They should be eaten with complete proteins like meats, or with complementary protein foods like grains. Peanuts and other nuts are also good protein foods. They, too, must be eaten with grains (for example, peanut butter with whole-wheat bread) to make complete proteins.

Servings per Day

Your diet should include *two* servings in this food group each day. One serving is 2 to 3 ounces (60–90 g) of lean beef, lamb, pork, poultry, or fish. That would be 1 chicken leg, 2 slices of meat, or a hamburger patty. You can also consider 2 eggs, or 4 tablespoons (60 mL) of peanut butter, or 1 cup (250 mL) of cooked beans to be one serving.

Other Foods

You will notice that several fairly common foods have not been mentioned as part of the four basic food groups. These include *fats*, such as butter, margarine, oil, mayonnaise and salad dressings, and *sweets*, such as sugar, honey, syrup, jam, and candy. Pies, cakes, and soft drinks are also included in this category. These foods are often called "others" because they provide few nutrients.

Foods in the "others" group share one important trait: low nutrient density. **Nutrient density** is the proportion of nutrients to the calories a food contains. Soft drinks have a low nutrient density because they contain few nutrients, but their sugar provides many calories.

Nutritionists advise people to eat as little of these foods as possible. The few nutrients they provide can be obtained easily from the four basic food groups.

A Balanced Diet Plan

In addition to the four basic food groups, nutritionists have developed tables of Recommended Dietary Allowances (RDAs for short). These tables suggest how much of certain nutrients different people should eat each day to stay healthy. They have also prepared tables of food values which show how much of the nutrients are provided by portions of different foods.

However, the four basic food groups and their recommended daily servings are easy to use for everyday planning. These groups were established according to the nutrients they contain and are simple to remember. Using the Daily Food Guide to plan your meals and snacks can be a valuable lifelong habit.

MANAGING RESOURCES

Being Flexible with the Food Groups

Eating foods from the four basic food groups assures you of good nutrition, but what if you can't eat the foods from one group? Vegetarians, for example, do not eat meat for religious or personal reasons. Some people have food allergies, a physical reaction or illness caused by eating certain foods such as berries or nuts. Many people cannot digest milk.

When you don't eat the foods from one group, you have to get the nutrients provided by that group from other foods. You may have to consult a table of food values to find out which foods are high in the nutrients your diet lacks.

If you can't drink milk, for instance, you should get calcium and vitamin A from other sources. One serving of collard greens will give you almost as much calcium as a glass of milk, and many times as much vitamin A. Other leafy vegetables—like spinach or chard—and broccoli are also high in these nutrients.

You can also get calcium from certain seafoods: scallops, oysters, canned salmon, and sardines. Dates, rhubarb, and blueberries are high-calcium fruits, and almonds and Brazil nuts also contain this mineral. By choosing carefully, you can make sure your diet gives you the nutrients that you need.

Vegetarians must choose their foods carefully to get enough protein, because the proteins in plants are incomplete. Iron and B vitamins are also hard to get if you don't eat meat. If you are a vegetarian, be sure to use the protein complementing techniques described in Chapters 36 and 52.

Think It Through

1. What other food allergies do you know of? How do people with food allergies get the nutrients that those foods usually provide?
2. Imagine that bread and cereal products suddenly became unavailable. What substitutions could you use to ensure that you get the nutrients normally obtained from these foods?

Reviewing the Facts

1. What are the four basic food groups?
2. What word is used for food that has had nutrients added, often to replace natural substances lost during processing?
3. Which important nutrients do fruits and vegetables provide?
4. If you do not eat meat, how can you be sure to get the protein you need?
5. Describe serving sizes for two foods from each of the four food groups.
6. How many servings of food from each food group should you include in your diet each day?
7. What is nutrient density? Give an example of a food with low nutrient density.

Sharing Your Ideas

1. The four basic food groups make it easy for people to plan a nutritious diet. Yet many Americans eat too many of the wrong foods. Do you think this is due to lack of knowledge, or can you suggest other reasons? Explain your answer.
2. What measures can you think of to persuade Americans to cut down their intake of candy bars, doughnuts, and other foods in the "others" category?

Applying Your Skills

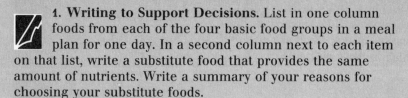

1. Writing to Support Decisions. List in one column foods from each of the four basic food groups in a meal plan for one day. In a second column next to each item on that list, write a substitute food that provides the same amount of nutrients. Write a summary of your reasons for choosing your substitute foods.

2. Calculating Nutritional Information. Check the nutrition labels on three foods from one of the four basic food groups. Calculate and compare the nutrient density of each of the foods. Write a brief analysis of your findings.

3. Researching a Topic. There was a time when people could not purchase a loaf of bread in a store. Use an encyclopedia to discover the history of bread making. Present your findings in an oral report.

CHAPTER

38

Healthy
Eating
Habits

OBJECTIVES

This chapter will help you to:

- Use the Daily Food Guide and Dietary Guidelines to develop good eating habits.
- Describe ways to carry out each Dietary Guideline.
- Explain the importance of regular meals.
- Give examples of different meal patterns.
- Describe healthy eating habits for snacking and eating out.

WORDS TO REMEMBER

Dietary Guidelines
entrée
moderation
malnourished

Carl doesn't feel hungry when he first gets up in the morning. He never wants to eat breakfast, but every morning his mother fixes him breakfast anyway. "Eat something!" she always tells him. "You can't do well in school on an empty stomach."

Carl's mother is right. It's very important to eat a good breakfast because breakfast restores your body's energy and nutrient levels after several hours of sleep. Other meals and snacks are important too. Food is the fuel your body uses for energy throughout the day.

To be healthy, you must eat enough foods to meet your body's daily energy needs. Not just any foods will do, however. Your body must get vitamins, minerals, and other essential nutrients. Making the right food choices is a major step toward enjoying a healthy, active life.

Choose healthy snack foods, such as a piece of fruit. Try to avoid snacks that are high in sugar, salt, or fats—usually these are high in calories too.

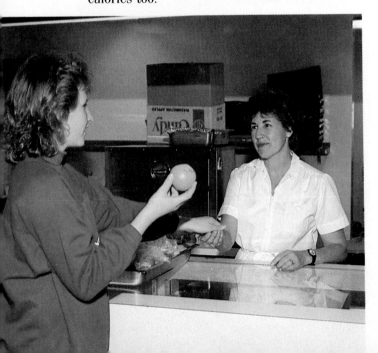

Guidelines for Selecting Foods

In this chapter, you will learn how to select nutritious meals and snacks. Two guidelines—the Daily Food Guide and the Dietary Guidelines—can help you make wise choices.

Using the Daily Food Guide

In Chapter 37, you learned that the Daily Food Guide lists the number and size of servings needed daily for each of the four food groups. Just remember the four food groups and the numbers 4-4-4-2.

- 4 servings of breads and cereals.
- 4 servings of fruits and vegetables.
- 4 servings of milk or milk products (2 servings for adults).
- 2 servings from the meats-to-beans group.

Using the Dietary Guidelines

As you have learned, the Daily Food Guide is a good way to keep track of the foods you need day by day. In addition, a set of **Dietary Guidelines** has been developed by the United States government. These recommendations for improving your eating habits offer a number of suggestions:

- **Eat a variety of foods.** Most foods contain several nutrients but no food provides all the nutrients in the amounts you need. When choosing foods within a food group, don't limit yourself to only a few foods. For example, if you eat only apples and green beans from the fruits-vegetables group, you will not get all the nutrients you need.

■ **Maintain desirable weight.** Eating nutritious foods and exercising can help you achieve and maintain your ideal weight. Being overweight or underweight can cause health problems (see Chapter 39). Try to always eat in **moderation**—neither too much nor too little.

■ **Avoid too much fat, saturated fats, and cholesterol.** These can contribute to high blood pressure and heart disease. Choose lean meats and poultry and trim off excess fat and skin. Switch to low-fat or skim milk, limit the number of eggs you consume to two a week, and broil or bake rather than fry foods.

■ **Eat foods with adequate starch and fiber.** Starchy foods, such as potatoes, pasta, and bread provide lots of carbohydrates for energy. Fibrous foods, such as fruits, vegetables, and whole-grain products, keep your digestive system in good order.

■ **Avoid too much sugar.** Sugar can lead to cavities in your teeth and weight gain. Eat less sugar, honey, syrup, and foods that contain sugar. Read food labels for ingredients such as sucrose, glucose, maltose, dextrose, lactose, fructose, and syrups.

■ **Avoid too much sodium.** Too much salt contributes to high blood pressure. Don't add extra salt to food, and limit the amount of salty foods and snacks that you eat.

■ **Avoid alcoholic beverages.** Drinking alcoholic beverages is illegal for young people. Alcoholic drinks are high in calories and provide few nutrients—they are part of the "others" group. More important, alcohol can cause serious health problems. Also, pregnant women who drink alcohol can harm their baby's health.

Meal Patterns

What you eat affects your health, and how you eat does, too. Do you often eat on the run, or skip breakfast, or eat lots of snack foods instead of regular meals? These and other eating habits are likely to affect your energy and fitness.

Mealtimes should be relaxed. They should give you a chance to unwind and enjoy time with your family and friends. You should be able to eat slowly, enjoy the taste of your food, and digest it comfortably. Slow eating allows time for your stomach to sense that it's full. If you eat too fast, you often eat more than you really need.

Families follow different meal patterns. Some eat breakfast followed by a light lunch and a large dinner. Others have their main meal at midday and eat a light supper in the evening. No matter what pattern your family follows, stick to a regular schedule of meals and snacks. Your body can then prepare itself to digest meals at specific times. If you miss one of these regular meals, it disturbs your system.

Any food is fine for breakfast as long as it's nutritious. Some people prefer traditional breakfast foods, such as milk and cereal, while others enjoy a sandwich.

Breakfast

The day's first meal is particularly important because you have not eaten for many hours. Carbohydrates and water-soluble vitamins are not stored in the body—they must be replaced every day. A good breakfast will restore these nutrients and energize you for the day ahead.

You don't have to limit your food choices only to breakfast foods. Instead of cereal and milk or bacon and eggs, you could have a cheese sandwich, soup, yogurt, a piece of chicken, or peanut butter on toast.

Lunch

By midday, your body has used up much of the energy it gained from breakfast. You need a healthy lunch to keep going through the rest of the school day. Whether you pack your own lunch or purchase lunch at the school cafeteria, make sure that it has servings from the four food groups.

A good lunch could include a sandwich made with meat, cheese, or peanut butter on whole-grain bread, a piece of fruit, and a container of milk. What do you usually eat for lunch?

Dinner

Dinner allows you to eat the remaining number of servings you need from the four food groups. You should not skip dinner. However, it is not necessary to make it the largest meal of the day, since most of your day's activities are behind you.

Snacks

As a growing teen, you may find you get hungry between meals. Snacks can provide quick energy and help satisfy your hunger until the next meal. Here are some guidelines:

- Snack midway between meals. If you snack too close to a meal—you'll spoil your appetite.
- Choose snacks from the four basic food groups; avoid foods in the "other" group like chips and candy.
- Remember that snacks are part of your total daily food intake—consider serving size and calories.

Be creative with snack ideas. Alternatives to junk food can give you more nutrients and less sugar, salt, and fats. If you have missed one of your food-group servings, you can make up for it with a snack. Try:

- A fresh apple, orange, or banana.
- Plain yogurt with fresh fruit.
- Celery sticks with peanut butter or cream cheese.
- Whole-grain cookies, breads, and muffins.
- Raw vegetables with a yogurt dip.
- Plain, unsalted popcorn.
- Dry-roasted, unsalted nuts.
- Ice milk.
- Pizza.

Eating Out

Most restaurant menus make it possible for you to select healthy foods while eating out. To avoid excess fat, choose an **entrée** (AHN-tray), or main dish, that is broiled or baked rather than fried. Order side dishes such as a baked potato and tossed salad instead of french fries. Choose fresh fruit for dessert.

A salad bar can be a low-calorie, low-fat alternative to many fast foods. Which salad bar items give the most nutrition for the fewest calories?

With care, you can eat nutritious foods at fast-food restaurants also. Pizza and tacos include foods from three and often all four food groups. Broiled hamburgers have less fat and calories than fried ones. If you order fried chicken, remove the skin and breading and eat only the meat.

Some fast-food restaurants offer a salad bar where you can make your own salad. Choose fresh salad greens and vegetables—macaroni and potato salads are much higher in calories. Go lightly on the salad dressing.

Choice of beverage in a restaurant is also important. Milk shakes and soft drinks are loaded with calories; fruit juice and milk have greater nutrient density.

Eating Habits and Your Future

If you regularly eat fewer than the required number of servings in each group, you run the risk of becoming malnourished. A **malnourished** person is not getting enough of the nutrients essential for growth and development. Get into the habit of thinking about what you eat each day. Are you getting the number of servings that you need from each food group?

Your food needs as a teen are greater than at any other point in your life. You are more active than many adults and, more important, you are still growing. Growth requires extra energy, as well as nutrients to build body tissue.

Infants obtain most of the energy and nutrients they need from milk. As they are introduced to solid foods, they must get nutritious meals and snacks. During the toddler, preschool, and elementary school years, children develop their eating habits. It is important for them to learn to eat a variety of foods, to eat regularly, and not to overeat.

Adults, whose growth has ended, usually need fewer calories than teens. If they continue to eat the same amount of food as they did while they were still growing, they will probably gain weight. The amount of food adults require depends on their age, body size, and how active they are. For example, a construction worker will need more food than an office worker of the same age and size.

Good eating habits are especially important when a woman is pregnant and if she is nursing her baby. Her need for nutrients increases as the baby grows and develops. She should get some extra protein and additional servings from the milk-milk products group. Poor nutrition during pregnancy, as well as the use of tobacco and alcohol, affect the health of both the mother and the child.

Older adults continue to need well-balanced diets. They should choose nutrient-rich foods and snacks to maintain their health and avoid weight gain. Good nutrition and exercise are essential for a long and healthy life.

A pregnant woman needs to increase her daily servings of some food groups—especially milk-milk products and meats-to-beans. She also needs an additional 300 calories per day.

HEALTH WATCH

Kicking the Salt Habit

Salt was very precious in ancient times because it was difficult to mine and transport. The ancient Chinese used it as money, and the word "salary" comes from "salarium," the salt allowance given to Roman soldiers as part of their pay.

Salt is no longer so rare or precious. In fact, it is by far the most common additive in our diet. Our bodies must have some salt, but most Americans consume two to four teaspoons (10 to 20 mL) every day—more than 20 times more than they actually need!

Common table salt is the chemical sodium chloride. The sodium it provides works with potassium from other foods to control movement of fluids and nutrients in your body. However, too much of a good thing can be dangerous. Overuse of salt leads to high blood pressure, which can contribute to heart disease, strokes, and kidney failure.

Start now, in your teen years, to prevent these often fatal diseases from striking you. Cut down on obviously salty foods like potato chips, pretzels, and crackers. Go easy on pickled foods, cured meat, and sausage, all of which contain a lot of salt. When you shop for groceries, study the nutritional information on the package or can. Avoid foods that show high levels of sodium (Na), sodium propionate, sodium bicarbonate, soda, or monosodium glutamate (MSG). These are all forms of salt that your body probably doesn't need.

In addition, you could look for alternative, safe flavor enhancers. You can use herbs and seasonings instead of salt to make favorite foods more appetizing.

Think It Through

1. **What are your favorite fast foods? Why? What can you do to reduce the amount of salt you take in from eating fast foods?**
2. **What are your favorite convenience foods? How can you find out how much salt they contain? What foods could you substitute for the salty convenience foods you like?**

Substitute Flavor Enhancers

Food	Seasoning
Baked potato	Basil, Thyme, Oregano, Paprika
French fries	Vinegar
Salad greens	Basil, Chives, Dill, Tarragon
Tomato	Basil, Celery seed, Oregano, Sage, Thyme
Meat roasts	Pepper, Paprika, Thyme, Garlic, Parsley
Fish, seafood	Vinegar, Lemon juice, Thyme, Oregano, Parsley

Reviewing the Facts

1. List the seven Dietary Guidelines.
2. Why should you eat a variety of foods?
3. What are three ways you can reduce saturated fats and cholesterol in your diet?
4. Why do you need to eat starchy and fibrous foods?
5. Why is it important to eat slowly?
6. How can eating breakfast help you meet your body's daily nutritional needs?
7. What benefits can snacks provide?

Sharing Your Ideas

1. Your parent has to leave very early tomorrow morning, and you will have to get your younger brother or sister off to school. Plan a breakfast that will energize you both for the day. Why did you choose these foods?
2. Describe your regular routine for eating meals. Is it a healthy routine, based on what you now know? How can you improve it?

Applying Your Skills

 1. Examining Your Eating Habits. Keep a diary in which you list all the foods you eat each day for a week. (If you did this in Chapter 35, use the record you made then.) Determine from the diary how many servings you chose each day from each of the four food groups. Did you choose the correct servings, or did you choose more from one food group and less from the others? Did you eat a lot of foods that contain saturated fats, salt, and sugar? Write a brief report explaining how you plan to correct any bad eating habits.

 2. Planning a Course of Action. Use the four basic food groups and the Dietary Guidelines to plan nutritious and varied meals for a week. Consult cookbooks and nutrition books to help you plan your meals.

 3. Graphing Information. Use a line graph to demonstrate the number and size of servings needed daily for each of the four food groups. On the same graph, chart your food intake for one day. Compare the positions of the lines. What does this tell you about your eating habits?

CHAPTER
39

Weight
Control

Have you ever gazed in a mirror, wishing you were as slim as the model on the cover of your favorite magazine? Do you sometimes flex your arm muscles in secret, imagining they are stronger and heftier?

Comparing your appearance with others is a normal part of adolescence. Often, however, those "others" are models, actors and actresses, or athletes who spend a lot of time and money maintaining their weight and appearance. Concern about looking perfect can cost you time and cause you dissatisfaction. Also, it distracts you from a more important issue—weight as it relates to fitness.

Weight and Fitness

In Chapter 35, you read about the importance of being fit. Fitness makes you feel good and look your best. It gives you strength, endurance, and flexibility, and it helps promote high self-esteem.

Your weight is affected by the same two things that influence your fitness— the foods you eat and the exercise you get. With the right mix of nutritious foods and exercise, people can achieve and maintain a healthy weight.

Individual Differences

Healthy weights differ for different people, however. Many athletes have less fat and more muscle than other people. This makes them relatively heavier because muscle is heavier than fat. However, other people may *look* heavier, because their bodies have a little more fat.

Your ideal weight is dependent on different factors, such as your age, height, bone structure, and muscular development.

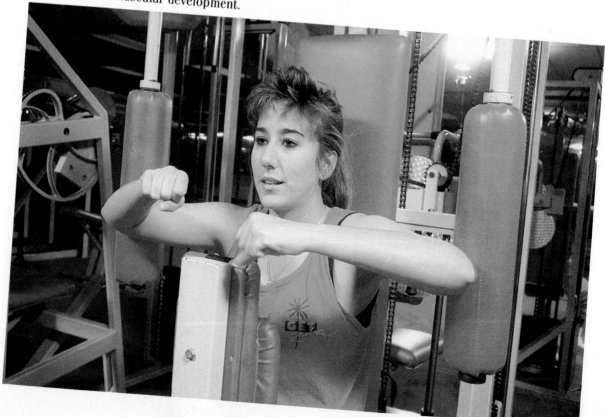

Physical activity isn't the only factor that affects a person's ideal weight. Several other things make a difference:

- Your age, sex, and height affect your weight. In general, adults weigh more than teens, and men weigh more than women of the same height. The taller a person, the more he or she can weigh.
- Bone structure also makes a difference. People with larger body frames should expect to be heavier. You can judge the size of your frame by looking at your wrist. If it is slimmer than most people your age, sex, and height, you have a small frame. If it is sturdier you have a large frame.
- Your heredity may affect your ideal weight. Scientists believe that a tendency toward being thin or being overweight may be inherited.

An Ideal Weight for You

If people are so different, how can you decide how much you should weigh? One clue is how you feel. If you feel mentally and physically good most of the time, you may be at your ideal weight. Other clues include how your family and friends evaluate your appearance.

You can consult charts and graphs showing ideal weights for males and females of different heights, ages, and body-frame types. However, the best way is to talk to your family doctor.

Exercise will help you firm up, look good, and have more energy.

What Affects Your Weight?

To maintain your ideal weight, the food you eat should supply exactly the right amount of energy to meet your needs. Several factors are involved in this balance: basal metabolism, exercise, food, and calories.

Basal Metabolism

Your **basal metabolism** (BAY-sul muh-TAB-uh-liz-uhm) means all the automatic functions of your body, including breathing, tissue repair, blood circulation, and growth. It consumes well over half the energy most people use up in a day—more than they use for exercise and other activities.

The energy used for basal metabolism differs for different people. Do you eat a lot of food and yet not gain any weight? This could mean that your basal metabolism uses energy at a high rate. Other people have smaller food needs, because their metabolisms are lower.

Your activity level also affects your metabolism. After vigorous exercise, your body continues to use up more energy, even when you are resting. The

more exercise you get, the higher is your metabolism. On the other hand, when people are starving their metabolism becomes lower. This "starvation reflex" occurs as the body adapts to having fewer calories to burn. It helps explain why some people have difficulty losing weight.

Exercise, Food, and Calorie Balance

Besides your basal metabolism, your weight is affected by the exercise you get and the food you eat. To maintain your weight, the calories your body burns up must equal the calories in the food you eat. If you increase your exercise, you will need to eat more to stay the same weight. If you get less exercise, you will need to eat less. Fortunately, most people instinctively adjust food intake to match their exercise, so their bodies maintain their weight.

Calories Burned in Various Activities

Activity	Calories burned per hour
Basketball	360–660
Bicycling (5 mph)	240
(10 mph)	420
Dancing, fast	240–360
Soccer	600
Housework, light	240–300
Karate and judo	700
Mowing lawn (hand mower)	450
Reading	125
Running (5 mph)	600
(8 mph)	1020
Swimming, most strokes	360–750
Table tennis	300–420
Walking, leisurely	300
Watching TV	125

Changing Your Weight

It may be, however, that you need to change your weight. An important part of adjusting—and then maintaining—your weight is developing new exercise and eating habits. Your present habits have resulted in your becoming overweight or underweight, so changing those habits is the way to reach your new goal. However, if you plan to lose or gain more than a few pounds, consult your doctor first.

The Importance of Exercise

Whether you plan to lose or gain weight, exercise should play an important part in any weight-change program. Exercise will make your body more fit. It will also help you to deal with stress, which causes overeating in some people and loss of appetite in others. Finally, exercise can provide the satisfaction of knowing that you are taking good care of yourself. All of these are pluses whether you are seeking weight loss or weight gain.

Dieting to Lose Weight

If you increase the exercise you are doing, you may find that changing your eating habits isn't necessary. Your body will use up more calories—perhaps enough to result in a weight loss. The chart on this page indicates how many calories are burned per hour in various activities.

Weight loss can also be helped by **dieting**, which means controlling your food intake for a specific purpose. An effective weight-loss diet cuts the amount of calories in the foods you eat to below the calories your body is using.

HEALTH WATCH

Fad Diets Aren't Worth Their Weight

"I lost 45 pounds in two months, and I kept the weight off." "With these pills, I wasn't hungry between meals." Do these lines sound familiar? They come from advertisements for popular fad diets. These diets are often seen in books and magazines.

People follow fad diets because they believe the diets will help them lose weight or make them healthier. In reality, most such diets fail to accomplish either goal. They sometimes even cause serious illness.

Crash diets are diets that promise quick and easy weight loss. They are almost always dangerous to your health, and usually fail. They encourage bad eating habits because they may exclude one or more food groups.

Some popular diets tell people to eat large amounts of protein, but almost no carbohydrates. People on these diets seem to lose weight—at first—but most of what is lost is water. As soon as the dieter goes back to normal eating, the water weight is regained. If people stay on these diets for a long time, the body even begins to break down muscle to get needed glucose.

Some weight-loss diets are based on the mistaken idea that certain foods, such as grapefruit, help the body burn fat. This is not true, and people on this kind of diet can suffer from weakness, dizziness, low blood pressure, and intestinal upsets.

People may also purchase diet pills or candy to lose weight. These substances are supposed to reduce the appetite, so the dieter eats less. Once dieters go off the pills or candy, they usually regain any weight they lost.

Some advertised diets, however, *are* healthy and effective. You can tell which ones are good by checking if they are based on principles of good nutrition and if the weight loss they promise is slow.

Think It Through

1. Do you know anyone who is on a popular weight-loss diet? What is the diet called? How successful has it been? What details do you know about the diet? Does it seem nutritionally sound to you?

2. There are many fad diets that advertise weight loss, but few that advertise weight gain. Why do you think this is? What is the most common type of weight-gain advertisement?

Here are three important points to consider when trying to lose weight:

- Some people can cut down their calorie intake by no longer eating high-calorie snacks like soft drinks and potato chips. Others find it helpful to refer to a calorie chart when they select foods for meals and snacks.

- Your body needs all the nutrients even though you are eating less food, so stick to the Daily Food Guide and choose foods that are high in nutrients and low in calories. For example, choose lean poultry or fish rather than red meat. Eat fresh fruit for dessert rather than fruit pie.

- Be content to lose weight slowly—one or two pounds per week. Crash diets (see page 365) are hard to stick to and can cause physical problems. Many people who lose weight this way find the pounds creeping back again because they haven't altered their habits. If you slowly adjust your eating and exercise habits as you diet, you will find it easier to maintain your new weight. You'll be able to enjoy some treats, too.

Dieting to Gain Weight

When people are underweight, it may be caused by a variety of reasons. Perhaps mealtimes make them tense. If so, an exercise program may help them to relax and enjoy mealtimes more. They should plan meals around foods they like, eat more frequently, and try to eat larger portions. They can snack on high calorie, nutritious foods such as milk shakes, cheese, and whole-grain sandwiches.

If you are underweight, think whether other parts of your life may be affecting your weight. Are you getting enough sleep? Do you try to do too much every day? If so, try to slow down, and leave yourself enough time for eating and sleeping.

Also, be patient. As with weight loss, rapid weight gain is undesirable and should not be expected. It takes time to build healthy muscle. Avoid any solutions—such as steroid drugs—that promise speedy results. These could be very dangerous to your overall health.

Even though you are dieting, be sure to eat a variety of foods from the four basic food groups. This boy enjoys low-fat cheese and fruit as an after-school snack.

Eating Disorders

Occasionally, some people become so obsessed with control over their bodies that they resort to drastic measures. The result may be anorexia nervosa or bulimia, two serious eating disorders that can cause severe health problems and even death. Most victims of eating disorders are females in their teens or early twenties, though some males are affected too.

- **Anorexia nervosa.** This disorder can result in starvation. Typically, people with **anorexia nervosa** (an-uh-REK-see-uh ner-VOH-suh) believe they are overweight even when they are painfully thin. They force themselves to diet still further, even though parents and friends try to get them to eat more.

- **Bulimia.** People who suffer from **bulimia** (buh-LEE-mee-uh) may be normal weight, but they maintain that weight in a very damaging way. They have sudden bouts of secret overeating, perhaps eating a gallon of ice cream at one time. Then, out of guilt and fear of gaining weight, they get rid of the food by using laxatives or forcing themselves to vomit. Both these methods of losing food are very damaging to the body.

If you recognize your own behavior in one of these descriptions, or if you think that a friend may be anorexic or bulimic, it's important to contact a counselor or doctor. Victims of these disorders can be helped by professional counseling.

The most successful method of losing weight is to increase exercise and decrease calorie consumption. Go for a walk, jog, jump rope, or do aerobic exercises.

Changing Your Habits

For less serious problems with weight control, you can often change your habits by yourself. Willpower is important, but if you focus on weight-control techniques that make you feel good, your goal will be easier to achieve. For example, if you are an individualist, your best form of exercise may be running. If you are sociable and like music, aerobic dancing classes may be more to your liking.

Look for small things about your new diet program that you enjoy. Maybe you've noticed that you like the taste of the food more when you eat slowly. Perhaps the taste of salad without dressing struck you as surprisingly good, particularly if you sharpen it with a little onion or radish. Focus on elements in your weight-control program that give you pleasure—it will make permanent results far more likely.

Reviewing the Facts

1. What is the relationship between fitness and a healthy, ideal weight?
2. What factors affect a person's ideal weight?
3. Identify some ways you can tell if you are at your ideal weight.
4. What does basal metabolism have to do with weight and weight control?
5. How does exercise contribute to weight control?
6. Describe three important concerns for a weight-loss diet.
7. What are some sound strategies for weight gain?
8. Name and describe two serious eating disorders.

Sharing Your Ideas

1. What aspects of American life can you think of that contribute to people's being overweight? Try to think of at least four.
2. If you had a friend who appeared to have an eating disorder, how might you try to help him or her?

Applying Your Skills

1. **Researching a Topic.** In the library, find three books or magazine articles that describe weight-loss diets. Read the diets carefully, and use your nutrition knowledge to decide how sound each one is. Then write a report on them, including your opinion on how easy it would be for a person such as you to succeed at each diet.

2. **Computing Calories.** Your friend is dieting with your help and advice. In the first week of summer vacation he did a lot of physical work: three hours cleaning house, five mowing lawns, two each day swimming, and riding 20 miles on his bicycle (five mph). With the chart on page 364, figure out how many calories he used. Then use a table of food values to calculate portions of nutritious meals and snacks that total the same number of calories. Write a note to your friend telling him what extra he could eat on his diet, and why.

3. **Promoting a Strategy.** Write a script in which you encourage a friend to lose weight. Suggest healthy ways of losing weight as well as the disadvantages of fad diets.

CHAPTER

40

Planning Meals

OBJECTIVES

This chapter will help you to:

- Explain the main considerations for planning a healthful and appetizing meal.
- Describe five ways in which to make meals appealing.
- Use newspapers, magazines, and cookbooks as planning tools.
- List the types of resources needed to carry out a recipe.
- Develop a shopping list for quick and efficient shopping.

WORDS TO REMEMBER

food preference
ingredient
portion
recipe
staple

In Nick's family, his father takes the main responsibility for meal planning. Each week he looks over the food supply, decides what the family will need for the week, and makes a shopping list. Sometimes Nick or his elder brother shop, but it is his father who determines what they will have each day. He follows a routine—a pot roast on Sunday, cold cuts on Monday, and so on.

At breakfast each morning, Melanie's family discusses what they will eat that night and who will buy the food. When they decide to have fish and vegetables, her father stops at the supermarket. Her mother buys meats at the butcher near where she works; and sometimes Melanie picks up pizza on her way home from school.

Meal planning is a very important step in food preparation. A good plan will ensure that you and your family eat a variety of nutritious meals that taste good and are within the family's budget.

Meal Planning Considerations

If you're like most teens, you are already responsible for preparing some family meals, and may even do so on a regular basis. It should come as no surprise that there are many things to consider such as:

- How many people will be eating?
- What type of meal will it be (breakfast, lunch, dinner)?
- What foods will be included (appetizer, main course, side dishes, desserts, beverages)?
- How much of the family budget can go toward the meal?
- What items must you shop for?
- What time will the meal be served?
- What can be done ahead of time?
- Will anyone be late and need food kept hot?
- Will there be any small children or other family members who need special foods served at certain times?

In addition, you could ask what people's **food preferences** are—what foods they like best. You should also find out if there are any foods that some people cannot or will not eat.

However, two of the most important considerations for planning a healthful and appetizing meal are nutrition and appeal.

When planning meals, you need to consider many different factors. Explain why this meal would be nutritious and appealing to a young child.

Nutrition

As you have read in earlier chapters, good nutrition is vital for everyone, so as you plan one or more meals, don't forget the four basic food groups. All four groups don't have to be included in each meal. However, during the day everyone should get the required number of servings from each group: four servings of breads and cereals, four of fruits and vegetables, two or more of milk and milk products, and two from the meats-to-beans group.

The heart of most meals is a combination of proteins and carbohydrates. Some examples are meat and potatoes, beans and rice, chicken and noodles, macaroni and cheese, or a tuna salad sandwich.

To round out these basic meals, add fruits and vegetables—as appetizers, salads, side dishes, or desserts. The dairy group could be included as a dessert (yogurt or ice cream), as a drink (plain milk or milkshake), or even as a topping on the main course (cheese on pizza or a casserole).

Meal Appeal

Have you ever had a meal that looked and tasted just delicious? How did the cook achieve this success? A well-planned meal successfully blends food flavors, colors, shapes, textures, and temperatures.

■ **Flavor.** The right combination of flavors makes a meal more enjoyable. Sweet flavors can often be paired with savory ones (applesauce and pork; cranberry sauce and turkey). Strong flavors go best with mild ones (tomato sauce on spaghetti; salsa on tacos; cheddar cheese on crackers). Two very strong flavors in the same meal are rarely successful.

■ **Color.** Think about what colors you'll include in your meal. A meal with only one color is far less appealing than one with a variety. If you plan to serve two vegetables, match carrots with string beans or tomatoes with spinach. A lemon wedge, a slice of orange, or a sprig of parsley can also provide an attractive color contrast.

Which meal has more appeal? Can you explain why?

- **Shape.** The size and shape of foods can be varied for an appetizing look. Serving meatballs and peas together is less interesting than replacing those peas with green beans or broccoli.
- **Texture.** The texture of foods can add interest to a meal also. How do foods feel in your mouth when you bite into them? Try for contrasting textures, such as meatloaf, a baked potato, a crisp salad, and an apple. Doesn't this sound more appealing than a meal of creamed chicken, mashed potatoes, applesauce, and other foods with the same texture?
- **Temperature.** Finally, consider varying the temperature of foods in your meal. Combine a cool salad with a hot soup, or serve warm scrambled eggs and cold orange juice.

Sources of Recipes

Once you have chosen the essential elements of your meal, you will need to decide how to prepare each of these foods, or which recipes you plan to follow. **Recipes** are detailed instructions for preparing foods. They come from many sources.

- **Cookbooks.** Your best meal-planning aid may well be your family's favorite cookbook. Some cookbooks include recipes for everything from appetizers and snacks to main dishes and desserts. These general cookbooks may offer suggestions for planning entire meals. They may have instructions on cooking methods and equipment. Other cookbooks are more specialized, with recipes only for desserts, or for vegetarian meals, or for Mexican food.
- **Newspapers and magazines.** Good recipe ideas are often featured in newspapers and magazines. You can clip ones that you like or copy them onto recipe or file cards. Newspapers and magazines also contain food ads, which can help you decide what to serve.
- **Other sources.** Recipes can often be found on food packages or cans. Many recipes are family favorites—passed on to relatives or friends.

Choosing a Recipe

When you are deciding what recipe to use to prepare a particular food, ask yourself these three questions:

- Will it taste good?
- Is it complete?
- Do you have the resources?

Will It Taste Good?

Sometimes, reading a recipe can cause your mouth to water. You just *know* how good it will taste. Other times, you see a food or a combination of foods that doesn't really appeal to you.

If a recipe sounds strange, it's probably not a good idea to try it when you're cooking a special meal for friends. You'll be safer if you test it first. This is also true when the cooking method is one you've never used before. In fact, you may want to give every new recipe a test run before you serve the dish to guests.

Is It Complete?

Be sure a recipe tells you everything you need to know to prepare the food successfully.

- **Ingredients and portions.** Obviously, the recipe must list all **ingredients,** the individual food items needed to make the recipe. In addition, it should tell you the number of **portions** it will yield, that is, the number of people it will serve. This number can often be adjusted, as you will read in Chapter 45.
- **Equipment.** The recipe should make clear what equipment is required. Different cooking methods—microwave cooking, for example—may require special cookware or utensils. It helps if the recipe offers practical tips, such as how to tell when the pan is hot enough for frying.
- **Full instructions.** Finally, the recipe should tell you exactly what to do with the ingredients step-by-step. You may need to peel or slice the foods, mix them together in the right order, or arrange them in a certain way. If a food is to be cooked, the recipe should tell you at what temperature or power setting to cook the food and for how long.

It should also tell you how to determine when the food is done. For instance, a cake recipe might tell you to bake it at 350°F (180°C) for 30 minutes or until a toothpick gently inserted into the middle comes out clean.

Do You Have the Resources?

Even if a recipe is complete and tells you everything needed to make the meal successful, you may not have the resources necessary to complete the project. Try to be realistic when planning meals. Consider these four factors:

- **Time.** If you try to make a long, complicated meal when you're short on time, you'll feel rushed. Washing, chopping, and mixing can each take several minutes. Keep in mind how much time is needed for the food to cook or cool. Some salads and desserts, for example, need to be refrigerated for several hours before serving.

This recipe includes a listing of all the ingredients needed, step-by-step directions for preparing the food, the size of dish to use, how long to cook the food, and how many people the recipe will serve.

- **Money.** Plan your meal within the family food budget.
- **Skill.** Don't take on a project that's more complex than you are ready for.
- **Supplies and equipment.** Check the refrigerator and kitchen cabinets for necessary ingredients. Be sure you have all the tools and appliances that you will need.

Making a Shopping List

Once you've chosen your recipe, check over the list of ingredients. Will you need to make a trip to the store for some of them? If so, make a shopping list—write down which items you will need to buy, along with the amounts needed.

You will find it more economical to plan several meals at a time. Check with other family members who prepare meals to see whether there are items that they will need. Also, look over supplies of **staple** foods—the basic food items that are used regularly, such as milk, bread, and eggs. Perhaps you need to add these to your shopping list.

Shopping will be easier if you organize your list logically. List the same types of food together, such as all meats at the top of the list and milk products next. You can also list foods in the order that they are arranged in the store.

Keeping Your Plan Flexible

While you are checking your supplies, try to stay flexible. Perhaps you have some perishable foods on hand that will not stay fresh much longer, such as vegetables or fruits. If you can adapt your meal plan to use these in place of what you originally planned, you will be using your food resources more effectively.

Flexibility will make you a better shopper, too. Perhaps you will decide to buy a little extra in case a family member brings a friend home, or you may want to take advantage of a bargain you see when you are shopping. You may choose to substitute chicken for turkey if it's on sale. Green beans might look fresher than the broccoli that you had planned to serve. For more about shopping for food, see the next chapter.

Check your supply of staples before making a shopping list. It is easier if they are grouped together in one storage area. Remember that some staples, such as milk and eggs, must be kept in the refrigerator.

The Computer and Meal Planning

Any task that requires you to keep track of many different things at the same time can benefit from the computer. As the market for home computers increases, you will be able to find more and more software to use for meal planning.

Take a trip into the future of meal planning. Your kitchen computer will hold many thousands of recipes in its database. It will also be able to search through them very quickly to find, for example, a recipe for lamb that goes well with green peppers. Then it will check the latest nutritive values issued by the government to find the nutritional content of each food you plan to serve. It will tell you how much your meal will contribute to your Recommended Daily Allowances—and if you are watching your weight, it will count calories for you.

Further, the computer could tell you whether you have the equipment and food supplies needed to prepare a particular recipe—based on information stored in its memory. The computer's database might also contain the food preferences of all family members, enabling the computer to suggest changes you could make to please your brother or sister.

Finally, your computer could automatically contact the store and place an order for the foods you will need to prepare the meal, plus any staples that you are running low on.

Think It Through

1. What aspects of meal planning that are not mentioned in this feature might home computers be helpful with in the future?
2. What do you think you might lose by having so much computing power in the kitchen?

Reviewing the Facts

1. What are two important considerations when you are planning meals?
2. Name five qualities of foods that you can vary to make an appealing meal.
3. What sources can you consult if you are looking for recipes?
4. What should you look for in a good recipe?
5. What four resources should you consider in planning a meal?
6. What is the next step to take after choosing a recipe?

Sharing Your Ideas

1. Which of the five qualities that affect meal appeal is it most important to vary for a successful meal? Which is the least important to vary? Why did you choose these answers?
2. You have volunteered to help an elderly neighbor who expects some visitors for lunch. How would you go about helping him or her to make a meal plan?

Applying Your Skills

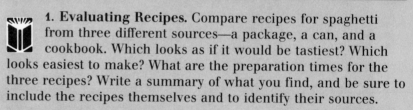 **1. Evaluating Recipes.** Compare recipes for spaghetti from three different sources—a package, a can, and a cookbook. Which looks as if it would be tastiest? Which looks easiest to make? What are the preparation times for the three recipes? Write a summary of what you find, and be sure to include the recipes themselves and to identify their sources.

2. Making a Plan. Prepare a shopping list for your family. Plan five meals and include the ingredients for each one on the list. Also include any staples, cleaning and household supplies, snacks, and other items your family customarily uses during an average week. Rearrange the list to follow the layout of the supermarket where your family shops, or according to groups of foods. Write a brief summary based on the list and share it with the class.

 3. Writing a Checklist. You are having a friend to dinner next week. Make a detailed checklist outlining all of the things you must accomplish to make the meal a success.

CHAPTER

41

Shopping for Food

OBJECTIVES

This chapter will help you to:

- Select the most appropriate store for your food shopping needs.
- Evaluate the quality and freshness of foods.
- Compare the nutritional value and price of foods.
- Describe how to get the best food buys.

WORDS TO REMEMBER

additive
brand
expiration date
generic product
preservative
pull date
universal product code

You've probably gone food shopping with a parent dozens of times, and may have gone by yourself for a few items needed to prepare a meal. You know that food shopping requires lots of decision making.

Some planning must be done beforehand—such as where to shop and what items are needed. Other decisions are made in the store. How fresh is the lettuce? What is the date on the yogurt container? Should I buy canned or frozen peas? How do prices compare? Efficient food shopping helps you select good quality foods and also saves you money.

Planning Where to Shop

Different kinds of food stores fill different customer needs, but prices, quality, and service can vary widely. Where you shop often depends on what you need and when you need it.

Supermarkets

Supermarkets are large stores that sell many brands of food and household products. They usually have counters where you can buy fresh cold cuts, salads, and pastries. The two main advantages of supermarkets are that they have lower prices and a wider selection than most other kinds of food stores.

Some communities have discount—or "no-frills"—supermarkets. While these stores have lower prices, they may stock fewer brands of basic items and may offer fewer services than regular supermarkets. At many discount supermarkets, customers select some items from cardboard boxes or barrels. They may also have to bag their own groceries or bring their own shopping bags to take their purchases home.

Gigantic supermarkets, also known as superstores, sell small appliances, books, automotive supplies, and many other goods, in addition to groceries. Superstores often feature fresh fish counters, gourmet foods, salad bars, and restaurants. They may also have small shops, such as a florist or a video rental outlet.

Specialty food stores, such as this fruit and vegetable store, sell one kind of food product. Their prices are usually higher than supermarket prices, but they offer a wide variety of high-quality food.

Convenience Stores

A convenience store is a small store with a limited selection of basic items that is open long hours. Some serve customers 24 hours a day and are open on holidays when other food stores are closed. Convenience stores are handy if you need to pick up a few food products quickly, but prices are usually higher and their selection is more limited compared to supermarkets.

Specialty Stores

Stores that sell only one type of product, such as meat, or fruits and vegetables, or baked goods, are called specialty stores. Their prices are usually higher compared to supermarkets, but they attract customers because they offer high-quality goods and a wide selection of their specialty.

Other Places to Shop

Some towns have a farmers' market, where shoppers can buy fruits and vegetables directly from the farm. The food is very fresh and prices may be quite low. Fresh fruits and vegetables are also sold from roadside stands right next to farms.

Some people belong to food co-ops (or cooperatives). A co-op is a group of shoppers who join together to purchase large amounts of basic food items at discount prices.

Judging Foods for Quality and Freshness

Wherever you decide to shop, you will find that successful shopping requires informed decision making in the store. The foods available may vary from day to day, and prices are continually adjusted also.

Judging Quality

The first thing you should do in selecting food items is to judge their quality. For example, you will want to choose the freshest fruits and vegetables, since they can lose nutrients while being stored and shipped to stores. Look for firmness, adequate color to indicate ripeness, and lack of bruises and breaks. Tips on buying fresh foods in the four food groups are included in Chapters 49 through 52.

Warning Signs

You can protect yourself from purchasing spoiled or tainted processed foods by looking for these warning signs:

- Bulging and dented cans may contain dangerous bacteria.
- Rusty cans may be old and have rust on the inside.
- Frozen-food packages that are soft or wet may be thawing.
- Frozen-food packages that are stained, covered with thin sheets of ice, or irregularly shaped may have thawed and been refrozen.

Product Dating

Dates stamped or printed on food packages can also help you to judge freshness. There are two major types of dates used on food products.

- The **pull date** is the last day a product may be sold. A label may say, "Do not sell after November 17."
- The **expiration date** is the last day a product can be used safely. This kind of label says, "Do not use after July 1994."

Other types of dates include the *pack date,* which states when the product was made or packaged, and the *freshness date,* which tells when the product will taste best or be most nutritious.

Reading Labels

Food labels tell you a lot about the contents and nutritional value of a product. This enables you to compare the features of different brands.

Basic Information

Almost every food label, by law, must contain the following information:

- Name of product.
- Weight of contents.
- Name and address of manufacturer, packer, or distributor.
- Ingredients.

Ingredients are listed in order by weight—the ingredient that weighs the most is listed first. A can of stew that lists beef first, for example, will have more meat than one listing potatoes first. Some standard foods such as catsup, mayonnaise, and peanut butter, however, do not have to list ingredients.

Nutrition Labels

By law, foods that have had nutrients added and products that are advertised as being nutritious must have nutrition labels. These labels include:

- Serving size and number of servings.
- Calories per serving.
- Grams of protein, carbohydrates, and fat per serving.

What information can you find on this food label?

Fiber Rich ® ——— PRODUCT

NUTRITION INFORMATION
SERVING SIZE: 1 OZ. (28.4 g, ABOUT ⅔ CUP) ——— SERVINGS
SERVINGS PER PACKAGE: 12

	CEREAL	WITH ½ CUP VITAMINS A & D SKIM MILK	
CALORIES	100	140*	——— CALORIES
PROTEIN	3 g	7 g	
CARBOHYDRATE	24 g	30 g	
FAT	0 g	0 g*	
CHOLESTEROL	0 mg	0 mg*	——— NUTRIENTS
SODIUM	170 mg	230 mg	
POTASSIUM	90 mg	290 mg	

PERCENTAGE OF U.S. RDA			
PROTEIN	4	15	——— % OF RDAs
VITAMIN A	25	30	
VITAMIN C	25	25	
THIAMIN	25	30	
RIBOFLAVIN	25	35	
NIACIN	25	25	
CALCIUM	**	15	
IRON	4	4	
VITAMIN D	10	25	
VITAMIN E	25	25	
VITAMIN B₆	25	25	
FOLIC ACID	25	25	
VITAMIN B₁₂	25	35	
PHOSPHORUS	10	20	
MAGNESIUM	8	10	
ZINC	25	30	
COPPER	6	8	

*WHOLE MILK SUPPLIES AN ADDITIONAL 30 CALORIES, 4 g FAT, AND 15 mg CHOLESTEROL.
**CONTAINS LESS THAN 2% OF THE U.S. RDA OF THIS NUTRIENT.

INGREDIENTS: WHOLE WHEAT KERNELS, MALT ——— INGREDIENTS
FLAVORING, SALT.
VITAMINS AND ZINC: VITAMIN C (SODIUM ASCOR-BATE AND ASCORBIC ACID), VITAMIN E (ACETATE), NIACINAMIDE, ZINC (OXIDE), VITAMIN A (PALMITATE), VITAMIN B₆ (PYRIDOXINE HYDROCHLORIDE), VITAMIN B₂ (RIBOFLAVIN), VITAMIN B₁ (THIAMIN HY-DROCHLORIDE), FOLIC ACID, VITAMIN B₁₂, AND VIT-AMIN D.

Made by CEREAL CO.
LAKE CREEK, MI 41265 U.S.A.
© 1984 by CEREAL CO. ——— MANUFACTURER
® CEREAL COMPANY

- Percentage of U.S. Recommended Daily Allowance (U.S. RDA) of protein, vitamins, and minerals per serving.

Labels also provide clues that indicate whether one product is less nutritious than another. For example, a drink labeled "orange juice drink," or one that says "contains 10 percent juice," usually has more water and sugar than actual juice.

Food Additives

A list of ingredients may indicate that a food contains **additives.** These are substances that are added to the food before it is sold. Additives can serve a variety of purposes. Food colors, sweeteners, and flavorings are all intended to make foods taste or look better. Additives help baked goods rise, keep ice cream smooth, and help soft foods like candy retain moisture.

Some additives are **preservatives,** which keep foods fresh and tastier longer. In the United States, all additives must be approved by the Food and Drug Administration (FDA), a federal agency. Because information about food additives is included on the labels of packaged goods, you can avoid some or all additives if you wish.

You can also look for foods that have been organically grown without chemicals. Such foods generally cost more than foods grown by standard procedures that use chemical fertilizers or pesticides.

Although the prices of different brands of food may differ, the quality is usually quite similar.

Brands

A **brand** is a particular name of a product; it is usually the first piece of information you notice on the package label. The brand name belongs to the company that makes that food product; no other company may use the same name or trademark. There are several brands of nearly every food product.

When you shop for food, you may encounter three different kinds of brands. National brands are sold across the country and are advertised on radio and television and in magazines. Store or house brands are products that have been produced by the supermarket chain that sells them. These usually cost less money than national brands. A third kind of brand, the **generic product,** is plainly packaged and is usually the cheapest of all brands.

You may find differences in quality among brands. These may be important to you for some products, such as canned vegetables or paper towels, but not for others, like relish.

TECHNOLOGY

High-Tech at the Supermarket

In the past ten years, more and more supermarkets have been using computerized checkout systems. You've probably seen these counters many times, but do you know how much work they save?

The checkout clerk guides each package over a window on the counter where an electronic scanner reads the **universal product code** (UPC). The UPC, also called the bar code, is an emblem of thick and thin black lines that is printed on virtually every item sold in the supermarket.

When the scanner reads the bar code, the computer consults its memory and prints the product name and price onto the sales receipt. This system reduces the time it takes a shopper to go through the checkout line, and it minimizes price errors. The system keeps track of the store's stock and can even forecast how many items will be sold on a given day, saving the store from bringing in too many perishable food products.

Here are some additional electronic systems that are already available for use in supermarkets:

- **Electronic coupon machines.** These are computers that can be programmed to give coupons for future purchases to shoppers at the checkout counter. If a shopper buys dog food, for example, the machine automatically provides coupons for pet-care products or doggy snacks.

- **Store directories.** A computer terminal shows customers a map of the store and pinpoints the location of any product the store sells. Some superstores already use these directories.

- **Cooking demonstration machines.** A videotape machine can provide cooking lessons and print out recipes requested by shoppers.

- **Self-checkout systems.** Some electronic scanning systems allow shoppers to check out their own groceries while store employees bag them. Shoppers pay a cashier on their way out of the store.

Think It Through

1. Which of the high-tech systems described above would you like to use the most? Which would you like the least? Why?

2. What is your opinion of computerized checkout counters? Do you see any problems or drawbacks to them? Do you think they are better than checkers using cash registers? Explain your answers.

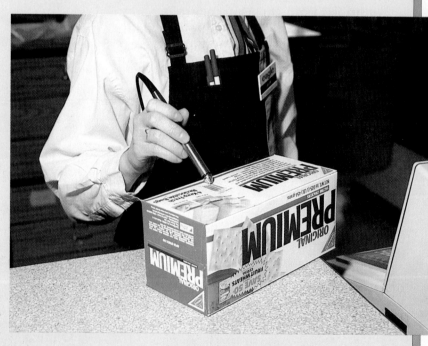

Locating the Best Buys

The choices you make in a food store are usually between different brands or different versions of the same food. Do you want fresh fish, frozen fish, canned fish, or a complete fish dinner? Will you buy a ready-made cake, a cake mix, or flour, eggs, sugar and baking powder to make a cake from scratch? Your decisions will be based on several factors such as the products' price, the amount of time you have, and your skills and preferences. Here are some general guidelines that may help you make shopping decisions:

- Decide if convenience is worth the extra money. Fresh foods which have been cut up generally cost more. Chicken parts are usually more expensive than a whole chicken. Shredded cheese usually costs more than a solid piece of cheese.
- Compare different forms of foods—fresh, canned, frozen, dried—to see which is the best buy. Consider taste, convenience, cost, preparation time, and storage.
- Take advantage of seasonal foods. Fresh fruits and vegetables in peak season will be high quality and often low in cost.

- Evaluate the extra expense of prepared foods. Frozen dinners, fresh salads, and packaged cookies are convenient but usually cost more than preparing the food from scratch.
- Learn to substitute one food for another. Buy cheaper cuts of meat or less expensive protein sources like poultry, eggs, and beans.
- Take advantage of sale items. If you need the item and have the storage space, you can save money by buying products on sale.
- Compare unit price labels, which are usually posted on the store shelves under each item. These help you to choose between different sized packages of similar items. For more on unit prices, refer to Chapter 31.
- Keep to your shopping list. Avoid impulse buying, especially at special displays and at the checkout counter.
- Use coupons for items that you usually buy. Coupons are found in newspapers, advertising fliers, and on some product packages and containers. Some supermarkets offer double or even triple value for coupons. That means that the store subtracts two or three times the coupon discount from a product's price.

Unit prices list the price per ounce, helping you to compare the cost of similar items. Coupons also help you save money—but only if they are for products that you will use.

G

WHOL KERNL GLDN CORN
03 27043 31 28 12OZ.

UNIT PRICE
5.67¢
PER OUNCE

68¢

Reviewing the Facts

1. Name three kinds of food stores. What is one advantage of each?
2. What warning signs should you look for to avoid buying tainted canned and frozen goods?
3. What is the difference between a pull date and an expiration date on a food package?
4. What four pieces of information are found on all food labels?
5. What are nutrition labels, and when are they required by law?
6. What is the difference between a national brand, a store brand, and a generic product?
7. List five guidelines to help you make wise shopping decisions.

Sharing Your Ideas

1. Rising food prices have a major effect on an average family's budget. What can people do to keep food costs down while ensuring that their families eat a nutritious diet?
2. What factors do you think affect the prices of national, store, and generic brands of foods? Do you usually buy national brands? If so, would you consider switching to a store or generic brand? Why or why not?

Applying Your Skills

1. **Making a Comparison.** Read and compare the nutritional labels on two brands of the same product. How large are the serving sizes? How many servings per package? Which product has more calories, protein, carbohydrates, and fats per serving? Which has more vitamins and minerals? Report your findings to the class.

2. **Computing Costs and Savings.** Clip coupons from your family's newspapers and magazines. Decide which ones you would probably use if you did your family's food shopping. How much money would you save if you used the coupons? What would be the savings if you received double the face value?

3. **Sharing Information.** Create a poster about helpful tips for buying food that would aid teenage shoppers. Use one or more ideas from this chapter or from other sources.

CHAPTER

42

Kitchen Know-How

OBJECTIVES

This chapter will help you to:

- Explain kitchen storage principles.
- Describe how to plan work areas for maximum efficiency.
- Discuss how to use and care for kitchen appliances.
- List ways to conserve energy in the kitchen.
- Describe how to use the kitchen efficiently and responsibly.

WORDS TO REMEMBER

appliance
perishable
rotation

utensil
work center
work triangle

itchens are workshops which surround you with equipment for working with food. You accomplish many tasks with **appliances,** kitchen equipment run by electricity or gas. For example, you store foods in a refrigerator, cook foods on a range or in an oven, and may wash dishes in a dishwasher. You may also use small appliances, such as a mixer, blender, or toaster, to prepare and cook foods. In addition, many **utensils,** such as knives, spoons, and other small tools, are needed to complete tasks in the kitchen.

In your kitchen at home you probably work alone or with another person. The foods laboratory that you use in school is more like a restaurant kitchen, with many people working on food preparation and cooking at the same time. In this chapter, you will learn how to organize equipment for work in the kitchen at home and at school.

Using the Kitchen for Food Storage

When you return from a shopping trip, your first task is to put the food away. Food should be stored where it will not spoil and you can find it easily. A large portion of most kitchens—the refrigerator, the freezer, and a lot of shelf space—is devoted to storing food. Storing foods properly can save you money and time.

Many fresh foods are **perishable** foods—they tend to spoil easily. Perishable foods should usually be stored in the refrigerator or freezer. Try setting up a system of **rotation,** so older supplies are used before newer ones. If you purchase a new carton of milk, for example, store it in back of any older ones. This helps ensure that you will use the older milk first.

Leftovers should be wrapped in airtight packages of aluminum foil, plastic wrap, sealed plastic bags, or covered bowls. You can purchase plastic storage containers with airtight lids which are specially designed to store refrigerated and frozen foods.

Not all foods should be kept in the refrigerator. Some perishables, such as potatoes and onions, do better in a dry, dark, and cool closet. Packaged and canned goods can be stored on shelves. Put soups together in one place, cereals in another; this will make everything easier to find.

Planning Work Areas

Food storage is only one task performed in the kitchen. Two other major kitchen tasks are food preparation and cooking. You can organize the kitchen for these tasks by thinking of it as divided into three areas.

Work Centers

Work centers are organized areas where the main kitchen tasks can be performed. A *food storage center* is most convenient if storage supplies like plastic bags and bowls are kept near the refrigerator. The main shelves for canned and packaged foods should be nearby. A surface for putting down grocery bags and wrapping foods is also important.

For a *food preparation center,* you need counter space to work. There should be nearby storage space for the equipment and utensils that are used to

A kitchen can be organized most efficiently by storing equipment, tools, and supplies near the area where they are used most frequently.

prepare food, such as bowls, knives, and measuring spoons. You could also use space for small appliances like blenders and mixers—and the sink should be close by for washing foods and keeping equipment clean.

Finally, the range and oven are important elements in the *cooking center*. Cabinets in the cooking center are convenient for storing pots, pans, lids, and hot pads. Utensils and supplies used during cooking can be placed here too. You may want to keep pepper, herbs, and spices nearby so you can add them to food as you cook.

The Work Triangle

As you have learned, the kitchen has three major work centers. The storage center is linked to the refrigerator. The food preparation center should be near the sink. The cooking center is around the range. The arrangement of these three centers in the kitchen is known as the work triangle. An ideal work triangle has equal sides, but is not too small or large.

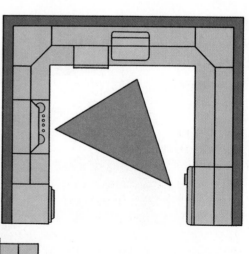

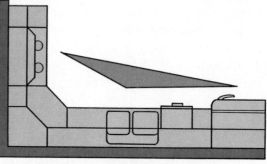

The U-shaped kitchen is usually considered the best work triangle, but the L-shaped kitchen is also easy to use. What other kitchen layouts have you seen? Why might an island be used in a large kitchen?

TECHNOLOGY

Smarter Appliances for Easier Living

Perhaps it seems like something out of a science fiction novel—appliances that turn themselves on and off and sense when your food is done—then tell you! But computer technology has brought this kind of magic into the kitchen. With the use of microprocessor chips, or micros, appliances are becoming "smarter" all the time.

Here are just a few of the innovations that are now available:

- **Self-checking appliances.** Some refrigerators have a light that signals a power failure, a door left open, or an overheating problem. Some dishwashers can tell you about a blocked drain.
- **Intelligent appliances.** Dishwashers, ovens, and coffee makers can be set to start whenever you want them to.

Even older appliances can be "educated" when you plug them into a central remote-control panel or a presetting device. Someday it may be possible to control appliances with your voice.

- **High-tech microwaves.** Some microwave ovens use a moisture sensor to tell when a food is ready. In other models, pre-programmed labels saying "baked potato" or "frozen dinner" make cooking as easy as pressing a button.
- **Computer cookbooks.** Are you stumped about what to make for dinner? Tell your computer software program what ingredients you have on hand. In seconds on your screen you'll have a list of recipes you can make using those ingredients. Tired of writing out your shopping list? Input a week of menus and the computer will produce a shopping list including everything you need to prepare those meals.

Maybe you don't feel like cooking tonight. Just say "pizza," and your preprogrammed, voice-activated telephone will start dialing your favorite restaurant—one that delivers!

Think It Through

1. How could some of the appliances named save you money as well as time?
2. Which of the appliances mentioned appeals the most to you? Why?

Kitchen Appliances

No matter how your kitchen is set up, your major appliances are basic necessities. This chapter discusses ways to use and care for these appliances to help you work efficiently. (Specific preparation and cooking techniques are covered in chapters 46 and 47.)

Types of Appliances

The most important appliances in every kitchen are the refrigerator, the range, and the oven.

- **The refrigerator.** Many fruits, vegetables, meats, and dairy products are stored in the refrigerator. Most refrigerators have special areas for vegetables, meats, and eggs. Refrigerators usually have a freezer section as well, where frozen foods are stored until they are used. Some kitchens include a separate freezer where large quantities of frozen foods can be kept for many months at a time.

  Caring for refrigerators and freezers means keeping them clean. If a freezer is not self-defrosting, it must be routinely defrosted to keep it operating efficiently.

- **The range.** The cooking surface with three or four gas or electric units is called the range. It may be on top of the oven or located nearby. A range top should be cleaned after each use. Safety while working with the range is especially important, since high temperatures can cause burns or even a fire.

- **The oven.** The oven is used for baking and roasting foods and may also be used to keep foods warm. It is usually located under or near the range. Like other appliances, it requires periodic cleaning to keep it working efficiently. Both ranges and ovens need to be kept clean for safety reasons as well; grease and food spills can cause fires.

Kitchens generally include the three appliances just listed. Other common appliances are dishwashers, microwave ovens, garbage disposals, and trash compactors.

Then there are the many small appliances available to make cooking easier—toasters, toaster ovens, blenders, food processors, electric skillets, and mixers. Many of these appliances have multiple uses. Toaster ovens, for example, can both toast and bake. Food processors do several different preparation tasks, and some mixers have grinding or dough-kneading attachments. These appliances should be wiped off or cleaned after every use.

Many portable appliances are very practical and useful. Some, such as the coffee maker, can also be used for serving.

Appliances and Energy

All appliances use energy in some form. The way you use and care for your appliances, however, can have an effect on how much energy they consume.

Major appliances come with an EnergyGuide label. This label allows the buyer to compare the energy consumption of various models.

There are other ways that you can make the kitchen more energy efficient. They include the following:

- Don't open the refrigerator or freezer door repeatedly. Take all that you will need and then close the door as soon as possible.
- Preheat the oven only if the recipe calls for it.

- Cook two or more items in the oven at the same time.
- Heat small things—such as frozen dinners—in a microwave or toaster oven rather than the oven itself.
- Run the dishwasher only when it is full.
- Use the shortest possible washing cycle of your dishwasher, and let the dishes air dry.

Using the Kitchen

Whether you are in the foods laboratory at school or in your own home, there are guidelines that help you work more efficiently and responsibly. Keep the following ideas in mind as you work in the kitchen:

- **Learn how to use various tools and appliances.** Later chapters will describe which tools are the right ones for which jobs. Before you use an appliance at home, read the instruction manual. The manual for a dishwasher, for example, will tell you the best ways to load it to get dishes clean.
- **Cooperate with others.** The kitchen belongs to everyone in your home and the foods laboratory belongs to all the students. At home, ask permission before using ingredients. Wherever you are, share responsibilities for preparation, cooking, and cleanup. When working with another person, try to plan so that you don't get in each other's way.
- **Keep the kitchen clean.** Clean the dishes, tools, and small appliances you use, and put away any foods or ingredients you have gotten out. Large appliances should be wiped down regularly. Try to leave the kitchen as clean as, if not cleaner than, you found it.

The EnergyGuide label gives information about the energy costs of appliances. Consumers can use this information to compare the energy efficiency of various models.

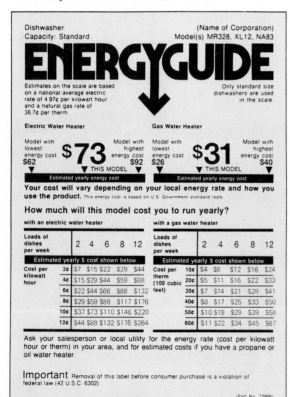

CHAPTER
42 REVIEW

Reviewing the Facts

1. What are the three main work centers in the kitchen?
2. What kitchen items would you store in drawers and cabinets by the food preparation center?
3. What is the work triangle?
4. Why should you keep the range and oven clean?
5. What are three things you can do to conserve energy in the kitchen?
6. What are three rules you should follow when you use the kitchen?

Sharing Your Ideas

1. Think about how your family stores food, dishes, and utensils in your kitchen. How could you rearrange these items to create work centers and to save time and energy when working in the kitchen?
2. What kinds of cooperative behavior, other than those mentioned in the text, can you think of that would contribute to smoother operations in the foods laboratory, or in your kitchen at home?

Applying Your Skills

1. **Evaluating Data.** Select a type of small kitchen appliance that your family is thinking of buying, or that you would like them to buy. Find a recent report about it in a consumer magazine, and compare the different brands for quality, features, cost, and, if possible, care and warranty information. Report to the class which one you think your family should buy, and why.

2. **Collecting Information.** Study the owner's manual or manufacturer's instructions for two major appliances (either from home, or in your home economics laboratory). Analyze the two documents, and write a report describing the kinds of information that they provide. Note whether they cover the same general topics, and indicate which document is likely to be more helpful, and why.

3. **Diagramming an Efficient Work Center.** Diagram the way you would set up your kitchen for maximum efficiency. Include the storage of tools and supplies, as well as the placement of major appliances.

Safety and Sanitation

OBJECTIVES

This chapter will help you to:

- Identify the sources of danger in an average kitchen.
- Demonstrate basic safety rules to avoid cuts, burns, and electrical shocks.
- Suggest ways to prevent food poisoning and contamination.
- Explain the use of heat and cold to destroy bacteria.

WORDS TO REMEMBER

contaminated
danger zone
food poisoning
sanitation

Safety and sanitation are vitally important whenever you work with food. Safety means following careful work habits to avoid accidents like burns, cuts, electrical shocks, and falls. **Sanitation** means storing, washing, and cooking food properly, as well as keeping the kitchen, appliances, tools, and yourself clean. In restaurant kitchens, workers are continually reminded of good safety and sanitation practices by signs at key points:

- Danger—open flame area.
- Keep floors clean.
- Put glasses in racks.
- Put knives in knife slots after use.
- Do not stand near dining room doors.
- Wash hands before returning to work.

Professional kitchen workers know that if they ignore these warning signs, they endanger not only themselves, but everyone around them. If they don't observe strict safety rules, their co-workers may be injured. If they ignore good sanitation practices, their customers could become very sick.

The same rules apply to you. Safety and sanitation practices are as important when you are cooking at home or in the home economics laboratory as they are in restaurants.

Safety in the Kitchen

One of the most important resources for working in a kitchen is knowledge. You need to know what dangers might occur and how to avoid them. You should pay close attention to your work, develop careful work habits, and follow safety rules consistently.

Sources of Danger

Some kitchen dangers are obvious. Knives and open cans are sharp, and an oven or range gets hot rapidly when it is turned on. There are other, less obvious dangers as well. Metal pots, pans, and tools can get very hot very quickly. Electric burners retain their heat for some time after being turned off. Hot grease can spatter, causing burns or fires. Even food can be so hot that it can scald you or others.

Many electrical appliances can cause shock if they have frayed cords, are used without following instructions, or are used near water. In addition, leaks from gas appliances such as ranges are very dangerous because they can cause explosions and fires.

Finally, cleaning products stored in the kitchen can cause serious injuries. Many common cleaning agents are poisonous if swallowed and can irritate or damage eyes if accidently sprayed in someone's face. These products can be very dangerous, especially in a house with young children.

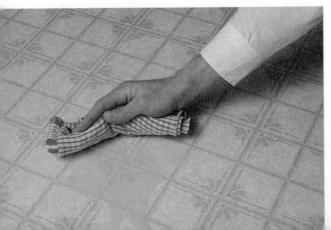

Wipe up spills immediately to prevent anyone from slipping and falling in the kitchen.

Precautions

The safety rules that follow will help you prevent cuts, burns, electrical shocks, and other serious injuries that can occur in the kitchen. The list is long, but it is important that you learn and follow these rules so you can prevent accidents to yourself, your family, friends, or classmates.

To prevent cuts:

- Always hold a knife by its handle and cut by moving the knife away from your fingers. Use a cutting board.
- Wash knives separately.
- Insert beaters into a mixer or cutting blades into a food processor before plugging it in.
- Watch out for sharp edges on the lids and rims of opened cans.

When using knives, always cut down or away from you to avoid cutting your fingers. Use a cutting board.

To prevent burns and scalding:

- Use a wooden spoon to stir hot foods—metal spoons get too hot.
- Always use pot holders to handle hot pots, pans, and utensils.
- Keep pot handles turned in over the center of the range—not over other burners—or over a counter so they won't get knocked over.
- Lift the far side of a pot's lid first so the steam won't burn you.

To prevent fires:

- Keep paper, dish towels, cleaning rags, and all other flammable materials away from the range.
- Don't wear loose, flowing garments while working in the kitchen. Keep sleeves and other parts of clothing away from flames and hot burners.
- Clean all grease from the surfaces of the oven and the range top. Check the vent above the burners, where grease collects.
- Smother a grease fire with baking soda or baking powder, or use a fire extinguisher. Never use water.

To prevent electrical shocks:

- Plug only one electrical appliance into an outlet at a time.
- Unplug appliances when they aren't in use, pulling on the plug, not on the cord.
- Don't use appliances with frayed cords, and don't drape cords over the countertop.
- Keep electrical appliances away from water, and don't touch them with wet hands.
- Don't stick metal objects (like knives or forks) inside a toaster or other electrical appliance.

To prevent other kinds of injuries:

- Wipe up spills immediately.
- Never leave anything on the floor where you might trip on it.

- When reaching to a high shelf, stand on a ladder or stool, not on a chair or box.
- Turn all the dials or controls of a range or appliance to "off" when you finish cooking.
- Never turn on a gas range if you smell gas. Report a gas leak to your gas company immediately, and follow the company's instructions precisely.
- Store dangerous chemicals well out of the reach of children. Keep cupboard doors closed and, if necessary, secure them with childproof locks.

Kitchen Sanitation

Some dangers in the kitchen are invisible. Microscopic bacteria and viruses can grow unseen in foods and cause serious, sometimes fatal, illnesses.

Prevent Food Poisoning

One way that germs can cause disease is by **food poisoning.** This happens when bacteria grow in food until the food actually becomes poisonous. Food containing large amounts of bacteria is said to be **contaminated.** A person who eats contaminated food may suffer nothing worse than stomach cramps, but very serious reactions are possible.

Salmonella is a bacteria that grows in raw foods like chicken and eggs. Salmonella poisoning is very hard to cure. Always use a plastic cutting board when cutting up raw chicken, because germs can lodge in the cracks of a wooden board. After the chicken is cut, wash the cutting board and knife thoroughly in hot, soapy water.

Another very serious type of food poisoning is called botulism. Botulism is caused by a bacteria which grows in food that has been canned improperly. That is why you should throw a can away if it bulges. The contents may be infected with botulism.

Use Good Sanitation Practices

A cook who has a cold or the flu can pass these illnesses to others by carelessly handling food or silverware. To prevent the spread of infection when you are preparing food, follow these six basic rules for personal hygiene:

1. Wash your hands well before working with food and after using the bathroom.
2. Keep your hair out of the food. If your hair is long, tie it back. Many food workers are required to wear a hat or hairnet to keep hair from falling into the food.

One of the most important sanitation practices is to wash your hands thoroughly before handling any food.

3. Use a separate spoon—not your fingers—for tasting food. If you've used the spoon for tasting once, wash it thoroughly before using it again.

4. Do not sneeze or cough on food. Use a tissue and turn your head away. (This is the reason for the plastic shields over many restaurant salad bars. These sneeze guards prevent the spread of germs.)

5. Rinse fresh fruits and vegetables thoroughly to remove dirt and insecticides. Wash the tops of cans before opening them.

6. Clean all kitchen equipment every time you use it. Wash all dishes and tools in hot, soapy water and rinse them in warm water.

Guard Against Pests

A pest is an insect or small animal that carries dirt and germs. Ants, cockroaches, mice, and rats contaminate foods and surfaces with their eggs or with diseases they carry.

Many insecticides and traps are sold to get rid of these creatures. Use a method that is safe and effective. Don't spray insecticides around food storage areas, or allow any pest killers to come in contact with food. If your pest problem persists, you may want to call a professional exterminator to deal with it.

Rinse fresh fruit and vegetables to remove dirt and insecticides.

Refrigeration Storage	
One to two days	**Two to three days**
ground meat	berries
variety meats	cherries
(liver, etc.)	asparagus
poultry	ham slices
fish	
sweet corn	**Three to five days**
sausage	
leftover cooked	broccoli
poultry	lima beans
	spinach
Three to four days	green onions
	green peas
leftover cooked	milk and cream
meats and meat	grapes
dishes	peaches
	apricots
Up to one week	fresh meats
	cold cuts
cottage cheese	
tomatoes	**Up to two weeks**
cauliflower	
celery	butter
eggs in shell	dried beef, sliced
bacon	lemons
whole ham	carrots (tops
lettuce	removed)
	cabbage
Up to one month	
apples	

The Danger Zone

Bacteria grow and produce poisons most rapidly at temperatures between 60° and 125°F (16° and 52°C). This range is called the **danger zone.** You should not keep perishable and cooked foods within this temperature range for more than two or three hours.

Heating Foods

High temperatures, such as those reached when boiling food, can kill bacteria. Different foods need to be heated to different temperatures for different lengths of time to accomplish this. For example, pork must be cooked until its internal temperature is 170°F (80°C). If not, tiny worms in some pork may survive, to cause a serious disease called trichinosis. To be safe, never eat pork that is still pink inside. All tools used to cut or grind raw pork should be washed thoroughly with hot water and soap.

Once food is cooked, keep it hot until it's eaten. Then cover and refrigerate leftovers as soon as possible. However, be sure to remove stuffing from inside a roasted chicken or turkey before storing. If left in place, the stuffing does not cool down quickly enough, and bacteria will begin to grow.

Cooling Foods

Low temperatures slow down the growth of bacteria in food. For this reason, food stays fresh in the refrigerator, but only for a limited time. The chart in this chapter lists the refrigerator storage times for some common foods. Take extra care with foods that spoil quickly, like milk, eggs, and meat. Pay particular attention to custards, and chicken and egg salads—these provide bacteria with a rich environment in which to grow. Always keep these foods cold, especially in hot weather.

Freezing food stops bacteria from growing altogether until the food is thawed out. However, during and after thawing you should take care to avoid the danger zone, because the bacteria may still be alive.

Chapters 49 through 52 give additional information on the best way to store many foods.

Germ Warfare

°F	°C	
250	121	Canning temperatures in pressure canner.
240	116	
212	100	Canning temperatures for fruits, tomatoes, and pickles in waterbath canner.
165	74	Cooking temperatures destroy most bacteria. Time required to kill bacteria decreases as temperature is increased.
140	60	Warming temperatures prevent growth but allow survival of some bacteria.
125	52	Some bacterial growth. Many bacteria survive.
60	16	**Danger Zone.** Temperatures in this zone allow rapid growth of bacteria and production of toxins by some bacteria. (Do not hold foods in this temperature zone for more than two or three hours.)
40	4	Some growth of food-poisoning bacteria may occur.
32	0	Slow growth of some bacteria that cause spoilage.
0	−18	Freezing temperatures stop growth of bacteria, but may allow bacteria to survive. (Do not store food above 10°F for more than a few weeks.

FOR FOOD SAFETY KEEP
HOT FOODS HOT
AND COLD FOODS COLD

Outdoor Dining

Whether you are barbecuing or backpacking, safety and sanitation are as important outdoors as they are in the kitchen. Here are some health and safety pointers for outdoors:

Water

- Don't drink from lakes or streams. The water may be contaminated.
- Make sure a safe supply of water will be available, or bring your own.
- Don't wash dishes or put soaps in any body of water.
- Avoid throwing garbage into or near a water supply.

Food

- Keep hot foods hot and cold foods cold. Wrap casseroles in layers of newspaper, and use insulated containers for hot soups or drinks. Keep cold fluids in ice chests, coolers, or insulated bags.
- Take special care with foods that spoil quickly, such as milk and egg dishes, and foods like chicken salad.
- Keep foods wrapped to protect them from bugs and animals.
- Don't eat wild berries or mushrooms—many are poisonous.
- Throw all garbage in the containers provided, or take it back home with you.

Fire

- Never use a charcoal grill indoors because the fumes are dangerous.
- Never leave a fire, grill, or gas stove unattended.
- Keep a container of water nearby in case a fire flares up.
- Use long matches to light a fire; never use gasoline or kerosene.
- Rearrange coals with long tongs.
- Use long-handled utensils and mitts to handle foods on the grill.
- Watch children around fires and grills. The coals and the equipment can remain hot for hours after you have finished using them.
- Be sure that the fire is completely out before you leave. Pour water on the coals and scatter them, then cover them with dirt.

Think It Through

1. What do you think are the most common hazards when cooking and eating outdoors? How would you prevent them?
2. What would you do if you were camping and saw other campers dumping their garbage into a lake or stream?

CHAPTER
43 REVIEW

Reviewing the Facts

1. What are four types of accidents that can occur in the kitchen?
2. List three ways to prevent burns.
3. Name two bacteria that cause food poisoning.
4. List three personal habits you should follow when handling food.
5. What is the purpose of washing fresh foods before cooking?
6. What is the danger zone for food?
7. What causes trichinosis? How can it be prevented?
8. How can you keep food cold when dining outdoors?

Sharing Your Ideas

1. You are served tuna salad in a restaurant. When you taste it, you think it tastes just the slightest bit odd, but you are really not sure whether there is anything wrong with it. What would you do? Why?
2. While working in the home economics laboratory, you notice a student who keeps using the same spoon to taste the food he is working on. You remind him of the rule about washing the spoon thoroughly, but he continues to ignore it. What should you do?

Applying Your Skills

1. Researching Topics. At your library, research salmonella poisoning, botulism, or trichinosis. Find out what are the most frequent causes and the most common symptoms. Also look for information about how to prevent the illness. Present an oral report to your class.

2. Evaluating Statistics. Look up the statistics for common home accidents in a recent almanac. Make a chart showing what percentage of the total number of accidents are burns, cuts, falls, poisoning, and electric shock. If possible, make another chart that shows which accident totals went up and which went down over a period of several years.

3. Promoting Public Safety. Choose a kitchen appliance and prepare a safety borchure about it. The brochure should include a description of the appliance, its uses, and safety precautions.

Getting Ready to Cook

OBJECTIVES

This chapter will help you to:

- Use recipes and package directions to help plan meals.
- Create a schedule for preparing and cooking a meal.
- Assemble equipment and ingredients to make a meal.

WORDS TO REMEMBER

abbreviation
dovetail
format
sequence

Fifteen minutes before her friends were expected, Karen started preparing lunch. However, the kitchen was such a mess that she first had to spend seven minutes cleaning it up.

Then, while she was preparing the soup, the grilled cheese sandwiches burned. As she started to make more sandwiches, the soup boiled over and spilled on the range. When she wanted to make the salad, she discovered she was out of lettuce.

"What a disaster!" Karen thought, "What am I going to do?" Just then the doorbell rang. Karen's meal didn't turn out right because she failed to plan ahead. As you will learn in this chapter, planning is as important for meal preparation as cooking the food. You must study the recipe or directions, then make a schedule, and finally assemble the equipment and ingredients.

Before beginning to cook, read through the recipe or package directions. Do you have the necessary ingredients? Do you have the proper pans or equipment? Do you understand the steps to follow?

Study the Recipe or Directions

Recipes and package directions are your instructions for preparing food. Though you may have looked at them as you made your shopping list or while you were in the store, you will need to reread them now.

What a Recipe Tells You

Recipes in cookbooks and magazines can be arranged in several different **formats,** or ways to present information. For example, ingredients may be listed first, or mentioned as you need them. However recipes are written, a good one includes:

- The name of the food.
- The name and exact amount of each ingredient to be used.
- Directions for assembling and cooking the food.
- The oven setting, if necessary.
- The number of servings yielded.

To save space, recipes often use **abbreviations,** shortened forms of words. Some common abbreviations are:

teaspoon—t. or tsp.
tablespoon—T. or Tbsp.
cup—c.
pint—pt.
quart—qt.
ounce—oz.
pound—lb.
milliliter—mL
liter—L
gram—g
kilogram—kg

Standard Format

Applesauce

8 apples
½ cup (125 mL) water
2 Tbsp. (30 mL) sugar
½ tsp. (2 mL) ground cinnamon
¼ tsp. (1 mL) ground cloves

1. Peel and core apples. Cut into chunks and put in saucepan.
2. Add water, sugar, cinnamon, and cloves.
3. Cover and cook slowly until tender, about 20 minutes. Mixture should be thick.
4. If desired, mash or puree to remove any chunks.

(Yield: about 2 cups)

Narrative Format

Applesauce

Peel, core, and cut 8 apples into chunks; put in saucepan. Add ½ cup (125 mL) water and 2 Tbsp. (30 mL) sugar. Stir in ½ tsp. (2 mL) ground cinnamon and ¼ tsp. (1 mL) ground cloves. Cover and cook slowly until tender, about 20 minutes. Mixture should be thick. If desired, mash or puree to remove any chunks.

(Yield: about 2 cups)

Action Format

Applesauce

Peel, core and cut into chunks: 8 apples
Put in saucepan: cut-up apples
       ½ cup (125 mL) water
       2 Tbsp. (30 mL) sugar
       ½ tsp. (2 mL) ground cinnamon
       ¼ tsp. (1 mL) ground cloves
Cook mixture slowly in covered pan until tender, about 20 minutes. Mixture should be thick.
Mash or puree mixture to remove any chunks, if desired.

(Yield: about 2 cups)

Four types of recipe formats include: standard, action, narrative, and descriptive. Which type do you think is easiest to follow?

Descriptive Format

Applesauce

Ingredients	Amount	Procedure
Apples	8	Peel, core, and cut into chunks; put in saucepan.
Water	½ cup	Add to pan.
Sugar	2 Tbsp.	Add to apples and water
Ground Cinnamon	½ tsp.	Add to mixture.
Ground Cloves	¼ tsp.	Add to mixture. Cover and cook slowly until tender, about 20 minutes. Mixture should be thick. If desired, mash or puree to remove any chunks.

(Yield: about 2 cups)

Reading Package Directions

The package directions on convenience foods such as cake mixes, soups, or pasta are usually simple to understand and follow. However, check whether you need to add anything. Some packaged mixes only require water. To others, you may need to add oil, eggs, milk, or some other ingredient.

Also, be sure you are reading the directions for your area and cooking method. Baking mixes may include special high-altitude directions. Microwave oven directions differ from conventional oven directions.

Understanding the Terms

When you read recipes or package directions, be sure you understand the terms. The terms tell you what techniques to use as you work with the food. Understanding terms is important because one mistake in the preparation, cooking, or measurement of ingredients can ruin an entire recipe. See listed below, preparation and cooking terms. You will learn more about these in the next four chapters.

Preparation and Cooking Terms

bake: cook by dry heat, usually in an oven

baste: to moisten food while it cooks, using its own juices as a sauce

beat: to mix smoothly, using rapid, regular strokes with a spoon, wisk, or electric mixer

blanch: to slightly precook foods such as vegetables

blend: to mix two or more ingredients together thoroughly

boil: to cook in a liquid that is bubbling

braise: to cook slowly in a small amount of liquid in a covered pan

broil: to cook by direct heat, especially in a broiler

brown: to make brown by cooking at high heat, usually in a pan

chop: to cut into small pieces

cube: to cut into small cubes or squares

deep-fat frying: cooking in hot fat deep enough for the food to float

dice: to cut into very small cubes

drain: to place food in a sieve or colander to allow it to lose excess moisture

dredge: to cover with a light coating of flour or crumbs

grate: to rub food against a grater to make small particles

melt: to heat a solid until it becomes a liquid

mince: to cut into tiny pieces

panfry: to cook in a pan with a small amount of hot fat

poach: to cook in a simmering liquid

puree: to blend into a smooth, thick paste

reduce: to decrease the amount of liquid by boiling

sauté: the same as panfry

scald: to heat almost to the boiling point

sear: to blacken the surface by cooking at a high heat

shred: to tear into fine pieces, or grate coarsely

simmer: to cook in a liquid just below the boiling point

slice: to cut into thin, flat pieces, using a sharp knife

steam: to cook over boiling water

stew: to cook in liquid at low heat for a long time

stir fry: to cook very quickly in very little fat

strain: to remove seeds or pits by pressing food through a wire mesh or colander

toast: to brown food with dry heat

whip: to add air and increase volume by beating food rapidly

Make a Schedule

Once you have read the recipe or directions, your next step is to work out a schedule so all the foods will be ready on time.

Note the Times

Estimate preparation time—the time it will take you to chop, mix, and assemble the ingredients before cooking begins. In addition, you may need to prepare equipment beforehand—to preheat the oven or grease a baking pan. These tasks also take time.

Some recipes may call for ingredients that have already been prepared, such as hard-cooked eggs, crisp bacon, or firm gelatin. Check how long it will take each item to cook or chill. If the recipe does not contain this information, consult other recipe books or talk with someone who has used a similar recipe.

Plan the Sequence

Next, you need to decide exactly what steps you will take and in what order, or **sequence**. Should you measure out all the ingredients beforehand, or as you need them? Is there anything you can do while waiting for the water to boil or the meat to brown? Deciding on a sequence helps you to work productively and make the most of your time.

When working with others, you need to divide the tasks efficiently. Everyone should have something to do. For example, you might prepare the pasta while someone else makes the sauce. In the foods laboratory, learning to assign tasks and work together is very important.

A Sample Schedule

Julie and Binh plan to prepare and serve the following meal to two of their friends:

Macaroni and Cheese
Garden Salad
Apples
Milk

They plan a simple salad of lettuce, carrots, and cucumbers, so they have only one detailed recipe to follow—"Creamy Macaroni and Cheese." (See page 405).

Before they started preparing the meal, Julie and Binh sat down to plan their schedule. They figured that the macaroni and cheese would take about an hour to prepare. They decided to make the salad while the macaroni and cheese was baking. Here is the schedule they planned:

11:00	
Binh:	Heat water for macaroni. Wash apples, put in bowl, place in refrigerator. Grease casserole.
Julie:	Measure ingredients for cheese sauce and grate cheese.
11:10	
Julie:	Preheat oven. Make cheese sauce.
Binh:	Place macaroni in boiling water. Melt butter and mix with bread crumbs for topping. Set table.
11:25	
Binh:	Drain macaroni and put in casserole.
Julie:	Pour sauce on macaroni and add topping.
11:30	
Julie:	Put casserole in oven. Wash and dry lettuce, break up leaves, put in salad bowl.
Binh:	Wash and shred carrots. Wash and slice cucumbers. Add to salad and refrigerate.
11:50	
Binh:	Add dressing to salad and place bowl on table.
Julie:	Set out apples.
NOON	
Julie:	Bring casserole to table.
Binh:	Pour milk.

CREAMY MACARONI AND CHEESE

Exact Amounts

8 oz.	(240 g)	elbow macaroni
¼ cup	(50 mL)	butter or margarine
¼ cup	(50 mL)	flour
½ tsp.	(2 mL)	salt
¼ tsp.	(1 mL)	pepper
2 cups	(500 mL)	milk
1 cup	(250 mL)	grated cheddar cheese

Topping:

| ½ cup | (125 mL) | dry bread crumbs |
| 1 Tbsp. | (15 mL) | butter or margarine, melted |

Ingredients listed in order of use

Pan Size

Time

Temperature

Cook macaroni according to package directions and drain. Place in greased 1½ qt. (1.5 L) casserole.

To prepare sauce, melt butter or margarine in 1 qt. (1 L) saucepan over low heat. Add flour, salt, and pepper and stir until mixture is smooth and bubbly. Remove pan from heat and add milk. Stir mixture over medium heat until boiling, then stir one minute longer. Reduce heat. Add cheese and stir until melted. Pour cheese sauce over macaroni and mix.

Combine bread crumbs and melted butter, and sprinkle mixture over macaroni and cheese. Bake uncovered at 375°F (190°C) for 30 minutes, or until top is brown and sauce bubbles. Makes 4 servings.

Step-by-Step Instructions

Servings

Making a schedule helps you manage the meal preparation so all the foods will be ready to eat at the same time.

Cooperating in the Foods Lab

Working in a foods laboratory is different from doing tasks by yourself in your own kitchen. You are working in a group, and that means cooperation; you have to take turns, share ingredients, and wait to use some appliances and tools. Here are a few guidelines that will help you:

- Plan your work ahead of time. Decide what has to be done when. Make a list of the ingredients, equipment, and utensils you will need.

- Share preparation with other students so you can get all your work done faster. For example, if your group is making beef stew, one student can trim and cube the beef while a second chops the onions. A third stu-dent can peel and slice the carrots, and a fourth can peel and cut up the potatoes.

- Follow all rules and procedures that your home economics teacher has established. These rules are important for safety and sanitation.

- Remember that laboratory time is limited. If you waste time, you and your classmates may not be able to finish preparing a recipe.

- Be courteous to other students. Show the same good manners you would in any social situation. Wait patiently for your turn at the range, or volunteer to help others when you have nothing to do. This will contribute to making the foods laboratory an enjoyable experience for everyone.

Think It Through

1. What would you do if you needed to use one of the home economics laboratory's food processors, but other students were using all of the available appliances and the class period was nearly over?

2. Your teacher has a rule that students must clean up each work center as soon as they finish using it. Why is this a good rule? What would you do if you saw a student leave a work center without cleaning it up?

Simplify Your Work

Once you've made a plan, look it over to see if you can make it simpler or more efficient. Some things to look for are:

- **Can you dovetail any tasks?** When you **dovetail** tasks, you combine them in such a way that one task overlaps another, saving time. Check the schedule on page 404—while the macaroni is cooking, the cheese sauce and crumb topping can be prepared.

- **Are you doing the job in the most efficient way?** When you are chopping onions, cut up peppers and celery, too. If you need to use flour, sugar, and baking powder, measure them all at the same time, and keep them in a bowl or on wax paper until needed.

- **What can you prepare ahead of time?** Sometimes you can prepare food earlier in the day or even the day before you plan to serve it. Perhaps you can bake a cake in the morning for dessert that evening. You can make potato salad one day to eat the next.

- **Is your plan flexible?** Even though you plan for all items to be completed at the same time, some foods may get done before others. However, most foods can be kept warm in the oven or on the range or kept cold in the refrigerator.

Assemble the Equipment and Ingredients

The final stage before preparation and cooking can begin is assembling the equipment and ingredients.

1. Clear the kitchen counters to give yourself room to work. For good sanitation, wipe off the counters and range to make sure they are clean.

2. Lay out the equipment and utensils you will need. Many recipes call for special pans, such as cake pans or cookie sheets, or they require bowls or casseroles of a certain size or capacity. For microwave cooking, you will need microwave-safe dishes or containers (see Chapter 48). In addition, some recipes require you to measure, cut, or mix ingredients. For each task, locate the right tools or appliances to do the job. You will learn how to do these tasks in the following chapters.

3. Lay out the ingredients you will need, including herbs and spices. However, keep refrigerated items in the refrigerator until you are ready to use them.

4. Plan to clean up as you work, so you won't have so much to do afterward. Fill a dishpan or one-half of a double sink with hot sudsy water. Rinse bowls, utensils, and pans immediately after using them, and place in the hot water to wash or to soak until you have time to wash.

Assembling all the necessary ingredients and equipment ahead of time will make the preparation and cooking steps much easier.

Reviewing the Facts

1. What five pieces of information should a recipe include?
2. What are abbreviations? What are the abbreviations for table-spoon, pound, and milliliter?
3. Name one important item to note when reading package directions.
4. Why is it important to understand all of the terms in a recipe?
5. What is the purpose of making a schedule for preparing a meal?
6. List three things you should consider when simplifying your work plan.
7. What are the four steps to follow during the final stage of getting ready to cook?

Sharing Your Ideas

1. Karen's lunch for her friends, described at the start of this chapter, was a disaster. If you planned to make the same meal for your friends, what would you do differently?
2. How can you ensure that you have enough preparation time for tasks such as chopping, mixing, and preparing equipment, so that you don't have to rush through the later steps of creating a meal?

Applying Your Skills

1. Making a Schedule. Assume that you intend to cook the following meal for three friends: hamburgers, corn on the cob, salad, and pudding. Consult cookbooks for the cooking times for each of these foods and make a schedule, similar to the one Binh and Julie planned in the chapter. Show each step you would take to complete this meal. Be prepared to present it to the class.

2. Evaluating Seasonings. Make a list of the herbs and spices you find in the home economics laboratory. Then go through some cookbooks and find recipes that use these spices or herbs. Make a chart showing the seasonings and the recipes they are used in.

3. Assessing Formats. Look at the recipe formats presented on page 402. Then look through cookbooks and identify which formats were used. Why do you think some formats are more popular than others? Which do you find easiest to follow, and why?

Measuring Basics

OBJECTIVES

This chapter will help you to:

- Identify customary and metric terms of measurement.
- Describe measurement utensils and their use in the kitchen.
- Demonstrate how to measure liquid and dry ingredients accurately.
- Adapt recipes for smaller or greater amounts.

WORDS TO REMEMBER

customary system   metric system
equivalent   volume

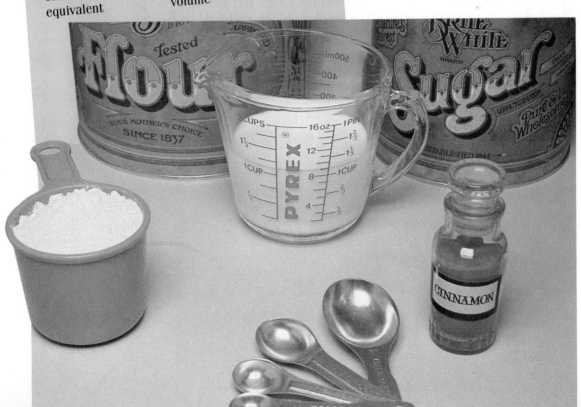

hen you watch experienced cooks, it often seems that they follow their instincts as they prepare food. A pinch of this combined with a dash of that results in something delicious. However, even an experienced cook relies on recipes for most food preparation. Following a recipe starts with careful measurement of the ingredients. If you don't measure precisely, the food won't turn out the way you expected.

Measuring Terms

Before beginning to cook, you need to understand the terms used for measuring food. This section explains the most common measurement terms and their abbreviations.

Two different systems of measurement may be used to give the ingredient amounts in a recipe. The standard one in the United States is the **customary system**, which measures in teaspoons, tablespoons, cups, pints, quarts, ounces, and pounds. Most of the world, however, uses the **metric system**, which measures in grams and liters. The metric system is also used by scientists, nutritionists, and other health professionals in this country. Remember that the two systems are just different ways of expressing amounts. It is helpful to know how to measure using both systems.

See "Measure for Measure: Equivalents" on page 414 for a comparison of customary and metric measurements. Both systems can be used for measuring volume, weight, temperature, and length.

Measurement by Volume

The most usual method of measurement for cooking in America is measurement by **volume**—the amount of space taken up by an ingredient.

Common terms for volume measurement include:

- Customary—teaspoon (tsp. or t.), tablespoon (Tbsp. or T.), fluid ounce (oz.), cup (c.), pint (pt.), quart (qt.), and gallon (gal.).
- Metric—milliliter (mL) and liter (L).

How many of these tools can you identify? See page 412 for a description of each.

Measurement by Weight

Solid ingredients in recipes are often described in terms of their weight. Most packaged foods, such as meat, poultry, pasta, and canned foods list the weight on the package. For other ingredients you can sometimes use **equivalents**, or comparison facts. These can help you convert weight measurements into volume.

The following are common terms for measuring weight:

- Customary—ounce (oz.) and pound (lb.).
- Metric—gram (g) and kilogram (kg).

Notice that ounce is used both as a volume measure (for liquids) and as a measure of weight. You may have to figure out which is called for when you read the recipe.

Other Types of Measurements

Volume and weight are not the only types of measurements needed in cooking. Temperature is measured in degrees—degrees Fahrenheit (°F) in the customary system and degrees Celsius (°C) in the metric system.

Length measurements may be used in recipes to indicate the size of a vegetable, the thickness of a cut of meat, or the size of a pan. In the customary system, length is given in inches (in.). For metric recipes, millimeters (mm) or centimeters (cm) are used.

Time is also important in cooking. To prepare a recipe successfully, the cooking or baking time should be followed carefully. Time is measured the same way in both systems—hours, minutes, and seconds.

Measuring Equipment

There are many tools used for measuring, and each plays a vital part in food preparation. Learning how to select and use the proper equipment will make measuring easier and more accurate for you.

On page 410 you will see pictures of various measuring utensils. Volume is measured with liquid measuring cups, dry measuring cups, and measuring spoons. A kitchen scale is used to determine weight. Oven thermometers show the temperature of the oven while food is cooking. Special meat and candy thermometers are available to check the temperature of those foods. You can keep track of cooking or baking time with a timer.

Measuring Accurately

Correct measurements depend on using the right equipment in the proper way. Cups and spoons used for drinking and eating can vary considerably in size. That is why special measuring cups and spoons should always be used for measuring ingredients.

When you measure most ingredients, you can either pour the ingredient into the measuring utensil or dip the utensil into the ingredient, whichever is more convenient. If you are dipping, wash and dry the cup or spoon before you measure a different ingredient. If you are pouring, never hold the utensil over the bowl in which you are mixing. You might pour too much, and the extra amount that falls in the bowl could affect the results.

Measuring techniques differ depending upon whether the ingredient is liquid or dry. Some techniques are even special for particular ingredients.

LIQUID MEASURING CUP
Used to measure liquids. Made of glass or clear plastic and graded on the sides to show cups, ounces, and often milliliters. Extra space at the top and a pouring spout help prevent spills. Common sizes are 1 cup and 2 cups.

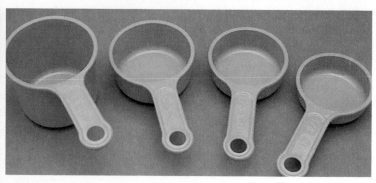

DRY MEASURING CUPS
Used to measure dry ingredients. Made of plastic or metal, and sold in sets that include several sizes, such as 1/4 cup, 1/3 cup, 1/2 cup, and 1 cup.

MEASURING SPOONS
Used to measure small amounts of liquid and dry ingredients. Come in sets, such as 1/4 teaspoon, 1/2 teaspoon, 1 teaspoon, and 1 tablespoon.

SIFTER
Removes lumps and adds air to flour and other dry ingredients.

TIMER
Usually has marks from 0 to 60 minutes and numbers at 5-minute intervals. A bell or buzzer signals when the set time is reached.

KITCHEN SCALE
Used to measure ingredients by weight. Usually marked in both customary and metric terms.

MEAT THERMOMETER
Measures the internal temperature of meat to determine when it has finished cooking. The stem is inserted into the center of the meat.

Liquid Ingredients

To measure liquid ingredients, place the measuring cup on a level surface, such as the countertop. Add the liquid until it reaches the correct mark. Check the measurement at eye level by crouching down to look through the side of the cup. Never lift the cup to check the amount, because you might tilt it and get an inaccurate reading. If necessary, pour some liquid out or add some more until it reaches the right mark.

Small amounts of liquid are measured in measuring spoons. Select the correct size spoon and fill it up to the brim.

Dry Ingredients

Dry ingredients such as flour, sugar, baking powder, and spices can be measured in dry measuring cups or measuring spoons. Select the correct size cup or spoon and fill it above the brim. Then level it off with a straight-edged knife or spatula.

Sometimes recipes call for an amount smaller than your smallest measuring spoon. Suppose your recipe calls for ⅛ teaspoon and you only have a ¼ teaspoon measure. Fill and level the ¼ teaspoon. Then, using a knife, divide the amount in half and push one half off the spoon.

When measuring liquids, place the cup on a level surface and bend over so you can read the measurement accurately.

To measure dry ingredients, spoon the required amount into a dry measuring cup or measuring spoon and level with a knife.

Measure for Measure: Equivalents

Here are some common equivalents that can help you when measuring.

The different measures used for volume and weight relate to each other. If your recipe calls for ¼ cup of flour but you can only find the measuring spoons, the chart of equivalents will help you figure out how many tablespoons would make ¼ cup. If the recipe uses metric measuring terms, but you only have customary measures, you can also consult the chart.

Sometimes equivalents are useful for particular foods. As the food equivalent chart shows, different foods weigh different amounts—a cup of flour weighs ¼ pound, while a cup of butter weighs ½ pound.

Judging the amount of different foods needed to fill certain measures is a matter of experience. How many eggs equal one cup? Some cookbooks may include such charts.

Food Equivalents

¼ pound butter (1 stick)	= ½	cup
¼ pound flour	= 1	cup
¼ pound macaroni (dry)	= 1	cup
1 pound apples	= 3	cups (chopped)
1 pound cocoa	= 4	cups
1 pound cheese	= 5	cups grated
1 pound cabbage	= 6	cups (minced)
1 cup rice (uncooked)	= 3-4	cups rice (cooked)
1 cup heavy cream	= 2	cups whipped cream
1 medium lemon	= 3-4	tablespoons juice
4 large eggs	= 1	cup of eggs
1 square of chocolate	= 1	ounce of chocolate

Customary Measure	Customary Equivalent		Approx. Metric Equivalent
¼ teaspoon			1 mL
½ teaspoon			3 mL
1 teaspoon			5 mL
1 tablespoon	3	teaspoons	15 mL
¼ cup	4	tablespoons	50 mL
⅓ cup	5⅓	tablespoons	75 mL
½ cup	8	tablespoons	125 mL
¾ cup	12	tablespoons	175 mL
1 cup	16	tablespoons or	250 ml
	8	fluid onces	
1 pint	2	cups	500 mL
1 quart	4	cups or 2 pints	1000 ml or 1L
1 gallon	4	quarts	4 L
1 pound	16	ounces	500 grams
2 pounds	32	ounces	1000 grams (1 kg)

Think It Through

1. What do you see as the advantages and disadvantages of the American customary system compared to the metric system?
2. If a recipe called for the following, what shortcuts could you find to assemble the ingredients, based on the figures in this feature: 1 pound of flour; 2 tablespoons of butter; 1 kilogram of grated cheese.

Special Measuring Techniques

Some ingredients require special techniques when measuring.

- **Flour.** Always spoon the required amount gently into a dry measuring cup. Don't dip the cup into the flour or shake it once you have filled it. The flour will pack down and you will get too much. If your recipe calls for sifted flour, sift the flour onto wax paper and then measure it.

- **Brown sugar.** Spoon into a dry measuring cup, pressing down firmly. Level off the top. If the sugar is lumpy, place it in a plastic bag and roll a rolling pin over the bag before measuring. Or place the sugar in a microwave oven for a few seconds.

- **Shortening.** Spoon the shortening into the dry measuring cup, packing it firmly. Level off the top, and scrape it out, with a rubber scraper.

- **Thick liquids.** Pour honey, syrups, and other thick liquids into a measuring cup. Dipping a measuring spoon or cup into these liquids will coat the utensil and give you too much.

When measuring brown sugar, pack each spoonful down firmly before leveling off the top.

Adjusting Measurements

Sometimes you need to prepare a recipe for more or fewer people than the recipe serves. In these cases, you may be able to adapt the recipe by adjusting its measurements.

Adjusting measurements works well for mixtures of foods like stews, salads, desserts, or casseroles. Recipes for baked products like breads, cakes, and cookies are harder to adapt—both the cooking time and the exact size of the cooking pan may be important. You may be able to make a larger cake by adjusting measurements, but a smaller cake may not be a success.

The following pointers will help you adjust recipe measurements to fit your needs:

- Use your math skills to find out how much you will need to increase or decrease the ingredients in the recipe. If your recipe has 4 servings and you need 8, you should multiply all ingredients by 2. If, however, the recipe yields 12 servings and you need only 4, divide each ingredient by 3.

- Write down the adjusted measurements of all ingredients. Then you won't forget the new amounts as you follow the recipe.

- Select appropriate-sized containers for the adapted recipe. Some recipes require cooking pans of a specific size. For example, to make twice the amount of bread in a recipe, you may need to use two loaf pans rather than one larger one. For other recipes, you can use a different sized pan, though you may need to change the cooking time.

If a recipe is difficult to adapt, you could always make it in two separate batches, rather than adapting the measurements for a single, larger batch.

Reviewing the Facts

1. What are the two major systems of measurement?
2. Name four measuring utensils found in the kitchen, and describe their use.
3. Describe the technique for measuring liquids, and explain why it is important.
4. How should you level off a measuring spoon with a dry ingredient? Is the technique the same with dry measuring cups?
5. How should you measure brown sugar?

Sharing Your Ideas

1. What types of measuring utensils do you consider vital in the kitchen? Which are less important, and why? Can you think of a different type of measuring utensil that you would like to see produced by a manufacturer?
2. Decreasing recipes is often harder than increasing them. Why do you think this is? What else might you do if the recipe yields too much food?

Applying Your Skills

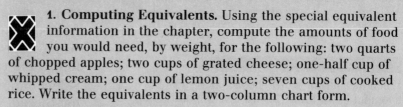 **1. Computing Equivalents.** Using the special equivalent information in the chapter, compute the amounts of food you would need, by weight, for the following: two quarts of chopped apples; two cups of grated cheese; one-half cup of whipped cream; one cup of lemon juice; seven cups of cooked rice. Write the equivalents in a two-column chart form.

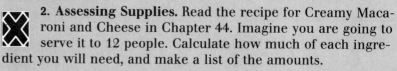 **2. Assessing Supplies.** Read the recipe for Creamy Macaroni and Cheese in Chapter 44. Imagine you are going to serve it to 12 people. Calculate how much of each ingredient you will need, and make a list of the amounts.

3. Checking Your Sources. Demonstrate that the equivalents described on page 414 are correct. Select four equivalents for which you have ingredients and measuring equipment, and perform four experiments. For example, measure 2 tablespoons of water into a liquid measuring cup. Boil a cup of dry rice and see how many cups it becomes. Record your results.

Preparation Skills

OBJECTIVES

This chapter will help you to:

- Identify different food preparation utensils.
- Describe cutting techniques and safety precautions.
- Explain different mixing techniques.
- Identify three special techniques used during food preparation.

WORDS TO REMEMBER

beat   garnish
blend   peel
chop   puree
            shred

Have you ever seen a professional chef prepare food? In some Japanese restaurants, you can watch as the food is prepared and cooked at your table. The skillful way in which the chef cuts vegetables becomes an impressive display of showmanship. A chef who can do this knows a great deal about techniques as well as equipment.

How does your knowledge compare? Do you know the difference between dicing and mincing? Can you distinguish between blending and folding? Each term names a technique for using certain equipment in specific ways to get the right results.

Preparing Food

Preparing food means getting cold foods ready for the table and hot foods ready for cooking. The steps you must follow often involve cutting or mixing ingredients. Your recipe will guide you through the preparation techniques required. However, you need to know what equipment to use, what the terms mean, and how to perform certain tasks.

Cutting Techniques

For the preparation jobs that involve cutting food into slices or smaller pieces, many specialized tools and appliances have been developed. Learning about each will help you choose the right equipment for each job. You will also need to know the terms that describe different cutting tasks. Since cutting involves using sharp tools, safety rules must always be followed.

Cutting Tools and Equipment

A well-stocked kitchen has several types of knives, each of which can be used for many tasks. Other tools—from shears to peelers to cutting boards—are needed for special cutting jobs. In addition, cutting appliances like the blender and the food processor can handle many tasks. See these tools on page 419.

Cutting Terms and Tasks

Cutting tools are helpful only if you know how to use them for different tasks.

- **Peel.** Use a knife or peeler to **peel** or remove the skin of fruits and vegetables. For soft fruits and vegetables, such as peaches and tomatoes, use a paring knife. Cut lightly into the food and lift the skin away. Dipping the fruit or vegetable in boiling water for 30 seconds will make peeling easier. A paring knife can also be used to cut away the skin of firm fruits, such as apples and oranges.

  Use a peeler for firm vegetables, such as carrots, cucumbers, and potatoes. This cuts a much thinner peel, leaving more of the vitamins that are concentrated just under the skin. A peeler can also be used to cut vegetables into thin, decorative strips. These can be used in a salad, or as a **garnish** to add color to other foods.

PEEL

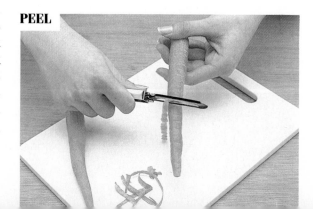

Peeler. Swivel blade is used to remove the skin from fruits and vegetables.

Kitchen Shears. Sturdy scissors used to cut foods such as meat, poultry, vegetables, pastry, and dried fruits.

Paring Knife. Use to peel fruits and vegetables.

Utility Knife. Use to cut and slice cheese and vegetables.

Slicing Knife. Use to slice meats and poultry.

Bread Knife. Has serrated edge for cutting bread and cake.

Chef's Knife. Use to slice, chop, mince, and dice fruits and vegetables.

Butcher Knife. Use to divide large cuts of meat or vegetables.

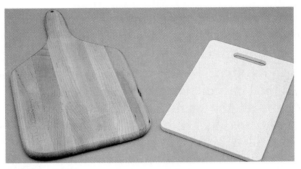

Cutting Board. Wooden or plastic board used to protect countertop when cutting or chopping foods. (Plastic should be used with meat or poultry.)

Grater. Sharp-edged holes are used to shred and grate vegetables and cheeses.

Blender. Appliance used to chop, blend, and liquify foods.

Food Mill. Used to puree foods.

Food Processor. Appliance used to slice, chop, mince, shred, and grate foods; knead dough; and mix ingredients.

- **Slice.** To slice food—carrots or meat, for example—cut it into thin, flat pieces using a sharp knife and a cutting board. Steady the food with your other hand or with a fork.

- **Chop and mince.** To **chop** is to cut food into small pieces. Tools used for chopping can range from a chef's knife to a food processor. Some foods, such as parsley, can even be chopped with kitchen shears. Food can be chopped coarse, medium, or fine. To mince, keep chopping until the food bits are as small as you can make them. Foods such as onions, garlic, and ginger give the most flavor when chopped or minced.

- **Cube and dice.** Use these techniques to cut food into small cubes or squares that are all the same size. You can cube cheeses, cooked meats, and vegetables. Slice the food in one direction, then grasp the slices all together and cut them in the other direction. Finally, grasp the resulting strips together, lay them on their sides, and cut again to make cubes. To dice, make the cubes very small.

- **Shred.** To **shred** is to grate or cut food into fine pieces using a grater. Foods such as carrots, cabbage, and cheese are often shredded or grated. Food processors are also excellent for shredding.

- **Puree.** To **puree** (pyu-RAY) is to cut or mash food so fine that no solid pieces remain. Foods such as vegetables are usually cooked first before being pureed. Small amounts of some foods can be pureed in a blender.

CUBE

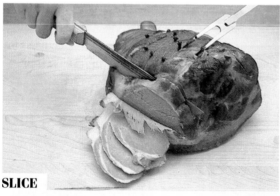

SLICE

CHOP

SHRED

PUREE

Cutting Safety

Cutting usually requires the use of knives or other hazardous equipment, so it's important to follow safety precautions to avoid accidents.

- Keep knives sharp. Dull knives slip easily and can cut your fingers.
- Always cut with the blade of the knife slanting away from you.
- Use a cutting board each time you use a knife.
- If you drop a knife, let it fall. Never try to catch it on the way down.
- Wash knives one at a time. Never place them in soapy water where they cannot be seen.
- When working with a food processor or blender, don't put your hand or a tool inside while the blades are moving or the motor is turned on.

Safety is very important when using appliances with motor-driven blades.

Mixing Techniques

Food preparation often requires combining one ingredient with another—or mixing. Ingredients must be combined in the correct way for the recipe to turn out well.

Mixing Tools and Equipment

Mixing is usually done with a variety of mixing bowls and spoons. Some mixing tasks, however, require specialized equipment, such as an electric mixer. How many of the items shown on page 422 would you use to make a cake?

Mixing Terms and Tasks

Mixing tasks differ according to the speed at which the mixing is done, and whether any air is introduced into the mixture.

- **Stir and combine.** These are slow mixing techniques usually done with a spoon. To stir, you use a circular motion to mix the ingredients.

Stirring can be done with a wooden or metal spoon.

Mixing Bowls. Available in different sizes, usually as a set, and used for mixing food. Made of glass, metal, plastic, or pottery.

Mixing Spoons. Made of wood, plastic, or metal; used for combining ingredients.

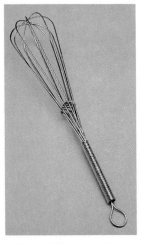

Wire Whisk. Used for blending, stirring, and beating.

Rubber Scraper. Used to fold ingredients and to scrape food from bowls and pans.

Rotary Beater. Used for beating ingredients, especially eggs and thin batters.

Electric Mixer. Appliance used to mix, beat, and whip ingredients. Comes in hand-held or stand models.

Pastry Blender. Used to cut shortening into flour for biscuits and pie crusts.

Rolling Pin. Used to roll out dough for biscuits, pies, pastries, and cookies.

- **Cream.** Sometimes a fatty ingredient like shortening must be mixed with another ingredient like sugar until the mixture is very creamy and smooth. Creaming is done with a spoon, rotary beater, or electric mixer.
- **Blend.** To **blend** means to mix two or more ingredients thoroughly with a spoon or wire whisk so that they lose their original appearance.
- **Beat.** To **beat** is to mix ingredients thoroughly so that air is introduced. Beating involves a strong, circular motion. When you do it by hand with a spoon or wire whisk, you use a quick over-and-under motion that lifts the mixture on each rotation, adding air. You can also use a rotary beater or electric mixer.
- **Whip.** Whipping is a very rapid beating that incorporates so much air that it increases the volume. For example, whipped cream is twice the volume of the original heavy cream. To whip, use a wire whisk, rotary beater, or electric mixer.
- **Fold.** You use a spoon or rubber scraper to fold—or slowly combine—air-filled ingredients. For example, whipped egg whites can be folded into a cake mixture to make it lighter. If you stir them together, some of the air will be lost.

Use a whisk to blend, beat, or whip.

Use a rotary beater to cream, beat, or whip.

An electric mixer has multiple speeds for various mixing tasks.

Fold gently with a spoon or rubber scraper.

Salad tongs can be used to toss and serve salads.

- **Toss.** To make a tossed salad, you tumble the ingredients lightly together using a spoon and fork.
- **Cut-in.** When pastry is made, the shortening is cut-in, or mixed with the dry ingredients using a pastry blender or two knives (see "Making Do" on page 425).

Mixing Tips

Here are some tips to help you when mixing.

- Choose the right size bowl for the job. Base your decision on the amount of ingredients and the method of mixing. Beating or whipping will require a larger bowl than stirring.
- Choose the best tool or appliance for the job. You might use a food processor to chop a large amount of cabbage for coleslaw, but a chef's knife to chop one onion.
- Place a wet cloth under the mixing bowl to keep it from sliding.
- When adding dry ingredients to a wet mixture, add only a small amount at a time, mixing until the dry ingredients disappear.
- Use a rubber scraper to remove food from a mixing bowl.

Special Techniques

Some other techniques used in food preparation deserve special mention. Here are some guidelines to help you master these techniques.

- **Separating eggs.** To separate an egg, or divide the white from the yolk, tap the egg lightly on the edge of a bowl, just enough to crack one side of the shell. Gently separate the halves of the shell so some of the white slips into the bowl. Transfer the yolk carefully from one half of the shell to the other, allowing more white to drop into the bowl until only the yolk remains.

- **Breading.** Foods such as fish or chicken are sometimes breaded, or covered with a light layer of flour, crumbs or cornmeal before cooking. Roll the food in seasoned crumbs, or place crumbs in a paper or plastic bag, add the food, close the bag tightly, and shake.

MANAGING RESOURCES

Making Do

In a perfect world, all kitchens would be stocked with every useful tool. However, in your kitchen at home, and even in your school foods laboratory, some equipment may not be available. Even if a particular tool is around, someone else might be using it.

When this happens, you can usually substitute another tool for the one you preferred. For example:

- **Peeler.** If a peeler is unavailable when you need it, a sharp paring knife can be used to remove the skins of firm vegetables. Work slowly and carefully, however, so you peel away only the necessary amount of skin. Going slowly will also help you avoid cutting yourself.

- **Wire whisk.** If a whisk is unavailable, a fork or rotary beater can be used for beating foods such as eggs. To blend a smooth sauce or to beat a cake mix, you might use a long-handled spoon.

- **Sifter.** If you can't find a sifter, use a fine mesh strainer to sift flour and other dry ingredients. Gently tap the strainer or stir the ingredients until they pass through the mesh.

- **Pastry blender.** A pastry blender is used for cutting shortening into flour, but you can also do the same job with two table knives. Hold one knife in each hand with the blades down. You will have better control if you extend your forefinger along the back of the blade. Cross the knives in an X and cut through the mixture repeatedly, pulling the knives apart as you cut. Between cuts, use the sides of the knives to push the ingredients together again.

These are just a few of the ways that you can substitute one tool for another. You may be able to think of more. The more familiar you become with the kitchen and with cooking, the better you will get at making emergency substitutions.

Think It Through

1. You have just looked at some substitutions for common tools. What are the advantages of using the right tool if you can get it?
2. Name two hand tools that could do some of the work done by a food processor.

Reviewing the Facts

1. Name and describe the uses of four cutting and chopping utensils.
2. When would a paring knife be used instead of a peeler?
3. List four safety rules for cutting foods.
4. What do the mixing methods whipping and beating have in common?
5. What is the difference between beating and creaming?
6. What does it mean to separate an egg?
7. Describe an easy way to bread food.

Sharing Your Ideas

1. If you were making a stew with meat and vegetables, which preparation tasks would you do and in what order?
2. What is the most impressive food preparation technique that you have seen a chef use?

Applying Your Skills

1. Identifying Words. Prepare an 18-word matching exercise, using the food preparation terms you have learned in this chapter. Instead of the definitions given in the chapter, use a brief description of a food or the name of a particular food as the clue to the term. For example, whipped cream (whip). Exchange papers with a classmate, and see how many preparation terms you both know and how often you came up with the same foods for the same terms.

2. Making Comparisons. Prepare two identical bowls with ingredients for scrambled eggs. Pour one into a blender and mix it for 15 seconds. Whisk the other one by hand for 15 seconds. Do you think there will be any difference when the two mixes are cooked? Make a prediction, and then test it by cooking the two mixes. Was your prediction correct? Write a report, and present it to your class.

3. Writing a Recommendation. Your friend asks your advice on what three cutting tools to purchase for a kitchen. Consider how often you and your family use different cutting tools at home. Write your recommendations, giving specific reasons for each of your selections.

CHAPTER

47

Cooking Techniques

OBJECTIVES

This chapter will help you to:

- Identify equipment used for cooking and baking.
- Describe different kinds of cooking using moist heat, dry heat, and fat.
- Determine when foods are done.

WORDS TO REMEMBER

braise
broil
casserole
poach

sauté
simmer
steamer
stir-fry

Have you ever had a boiled steak or an egg roasted in its shell? What about broiled spaghetti? You can probably tell just by imagining it that these foods would taste wrong, and look wrong, too. The steak would be watery and not browned. The egg would probably explode. The spaghetti would be crisp and inedible. Why?

There are many different ways to apply heat to foods. Some methods suit some foods, and some suit others. This chapter explains the different equipment used to heat foods, and describes the different techniques for cooking. In chapters 49 to 52 you will learn more about which techniques to use for which foods.

Wooden spoon. Use to stir hot foods.
Long-handled fork. Use to lift or turn hot foods.
Slotted spoon. Use to lift food out of a liquid.
Steamer. Use inside a covered saucepan to steam vegetables.
Ladle. Use to dip out soup or stew.
Tongs. Use to lift and turn hot foods without piercing.
Turner. Use to flip foods such as pancakes and hamburgers.
Strainer. Use to drain liquid from fruits or vegetables.
Colander. Use to drain liquid from cooked pasta.
Cooling rack. Use to cool cakes, cookies, and breads.

Cooking Equipment

Will you heat food in cookware or bakeware? It depends on what you are preparing and the cooking method you have chosen.

Cookware and Bakeware

Cookware—pots and pans used on top of the range—comes in many sizes. Most have lids to retain steam and nutrients during cooking. Cookware also has handles for safe and easy handling when hot. A pot with small handles on each side is lifted with both hands. A saucepan that has a long handle can be lifted with one hand. Even though handles may not get hot, you might touch a hot lid or pan accidentally. Use a hot pad or mitt to prevent accidents and burns.

Bakeware consists of containers that are used in the oven. Like cookware, these come in many sizes. Some dishes, or **casseroles**, can be used for both cooking and serving. Casseroles usually have lids and small handles. Other pieces of bakeware may have a ridge around the edge to allow for easy gripping. Hot pads or mitts are essential when removing bakeware from the oven.

Know Your Materials

Cookware and bakeware can be made from different materials. Each type of material has its own characteristics. These affect how food cooks, how long the cookware or bakeware will last, and how it should be cleaned.

Many pieces are made of aluminum or stainless steel. Aluminum is lightweight, heats rapidly and evenly, but may stain. Stainless steel is durable, heats slowly and unevenly, but is easy to clean. Some metal pans have nonstick surfaces to make them easier to clean.

Enamel pots and pans are attractive but chip easily and cannot be scoured. Cast-iron pots and skillets are durable and heat well, but they are heavy and may rust.

Some pieces, especially bakeware, are made of glass or glass-ceramic. Many can go from freezer to oven to table, but they may not heat evenly. Glass is inexpensive but can break. Glass-ceramic is attractive, durable, and easy to clean.

COOKWARE

Saucepan. Comes in several sizes; has one long handle and lid. Used for cooking foods in liquids.
Pots. Large pans with two handles and lid. Used for cooking pasta, soups, corn-on-the-cob.
Dutch oven. Large heavy pot and lid used for slow cooking of meats and poultry.
Double boiler. Two saucepans, one inside the other, used for heating foods that burn easily.
Frying pan or skillet. Low-sided pan, usually with lid; comes in several sizes. Used for frying.
Griddle. Flat surface used for cooking eggs and pancakes.

BAKEWARE

Roasting pan. Large shallow pan with rack. Used for roasting meat and poultry.
Broiler pan. Shallow pan with slotted tray for fat to drip through when broiling meats.
Casserole. Dish used for baking and serving.
Cake pan. Round, square, or rectangular. Used for cakes, brownies, and bar cookies.
Muffin pan. Has individual cups for muffins or cupcakes.
Pie Pan. Round pan with sloping sides for pie.
Loaf pan. Deep, rectangular pan for bread, cake, or meat loaf.
Baking sheets. Large, flat, metal pan (sometimes with narrow sides) for cookies.

Cooking With Moist Heat

Moist-heat cooking methods use liquid or steam to cook the food. Boiling, simmering, poaching, braising, and stewing all use liquid. Steaming and pressure cooking use steam.

Boiling, Simmering, and Poaching

In boiling, simmering, or poaching, the food is partially or completely covered with water or gravy as it cooks. To boil foods such as spaghetti and noodles, first bring the water to a boil—212°F (100°C). Bubbles should rise continuously to the surface of the water and break. Add the pasta and cook until softened. Boiling is not used for most foods, however, because this heating method robs food of nutrients, and it often results in overcooking.

To **simmer** means to cook food in liquid at temperatures just below the boiling point. A few bubbles should rise slowly but not break the surface of the liquid. Foods lose fewer nutrients when simmered rather than boiled, so vegetables are frequently simmered.

To **poach** means to simmer in a small amount of liquid so the food keeps its original shape. Tender foods such as fish, eggs, and fruit are sometimes poached.

When a liquid simmers, the bubbles do not break the surface.

Because boiling can toughen many foods and destroy nutrients, use this method only for foods such as pasta or corn. Be careful not to overcook.

Use a wooden spoon—not metal—when stirring hot foods.

Braising and Stewing

You can braise or stew foods that require long, slow cooking for tenderness or taste. Sometimes the food is browned, or cooked in a little oil first, for added color and flavor.

To **braise** food—a pot roast, for example—place it in a small amount of liquid in a pan that has a tight-fitting lid. Cook it slowly in the oven or on top of the range until tender. Check occasionally to be sure the liquid is not drying up.

Stewing is similar, but the food is cut into small pieces and covered with water before cooking. Braising and stewing are used for less tender cuts of meat and for poultry, vegetables, and some fruits.

Steaming and Pressure Cooking

Steaming helps preserve the nutrients in food. The most common method is to boil a small amount of water in a pan, then put the food in a **steamer**, a metal basket that holds the food above the water. After the pan is covered with a tight-fitting lid, the water continues to boil and the steam cooks the food in the basket. Steaming is recommended for cooking vegetables.

Pressure cooking requires an airtight pan in which the food cooks quickly by means of hot steam that is under pressure. The manufacturer's directions should be followed carefully. This method is used for less-tender meats, poultry, and vegetables such as potatoes and carrots.

Braising is a good method for cooking less tender cuts of meat.

Stews may be cooked for several hours to achieve maximum tenderness and to blend the flavors.

Steaming is recommended for cooking vegetables. The food is held above the water and retains nutrients such as water-soluble vitamins.

Cooking with Dry Heat

Cooking with dry heat means cooking without liquid. The heat may come from hot air in the oven or from a direct heat source such as a broiler or grill. Dry-heat cooking includes roasting, baking, and broiling.

Roasting and Baking

Roasting and baking are methods of cooking food uncovered in the oven. The term *roasting* is usually used to describe cooking meat or poultry by this method. *Baking* refers to cooking foods such as potatoes, fruit, fish, breads, cakes, cookies, and pies.

When food is roasted or baked, the outside cooks first and often becomes brown or crisp. The inside is usually softer.

Broiling

To **broil** means to cook food directly with a glowing heat source. You can broil food under a broiler or on an outdoor grill. As the food broils, any fat released drips away. The outside of the food browns quickly. Broiling is often used for tender meats such as steaks and hamburgers, chicken, and some fruits and vegetables.

Roasting two or more foods together in the oven saves energy.

Baking is used for many foods, such as pies, cookies, cakes, muffins, and breads.

Tender meats, such as hamburgers, can be broiled indoors or out.

Working in a Restaurant Kitchen

Have you ever been in the kitchen of a busy restaurant? You might be surprised at the feeling of pressure. Everyone is working to meet the customers' needs. Certain principles and procedures help the staff work efficiently and safely. Kitchen organization and teamwork are two of these principles. Here are some others:

■ **Cooperation.** Workers need to help one another and follow general rules. If someone spills some oil while making a cake, another worker could offer to help clean it up. To avoid accidents, everyone needs to observe traffic rules within the kitchen—keeping to the right in any passageway, and correctly using doors marked "entrance" and "exit."

■ **Communication.** Kitchen workers need to warn each other about dangers and problems, such as spills, obstacles, and broken equipment. Also, they need to let others around them know their intentions. For example, people carrying hot food should announce when they are passing behind other workers by saying, "Behind you."

■ **Keeping cool.** The kitchen is a hot place. Workers should keep paper and clothing away from flames and use hot pads whenever necessary. They need to know what to do if a fire starts, and learn where fire extinguishers are and how to use them. They must also know where to get help if someone is hurt.

Keeping cool has another meaning as well. In a restaurant kitchen, many things are happening at once, and tempers may flare. To be effective, kitchen workers need to practice remaining calm no matter what is said to them. They'll work more safely and efficiently if they have themselves under control.

Think It Through

1. What problems could be caused by workers not putting tools and utensils back where they belong?
2. Describe a potentially dangerous kitchen problem and how it could be prevented through good communication.

Cooking with Fat

Sautéing, panfrying, stir-frying, and deep-fat frying are methods of cooking with fat. The food cooks fast and gets a crisp, brown crust. However, some of the fat gets sealed into the food, adding calories.

- **Sautéing or panfrying.** To **sauté** (saw-TAY) means to cook food, such as onions, mushrooms, and peppers, slowly in a little fat until tender but not brown. Panfrying is used to cook tender meats such as chops, chicken, eggs, and vegetables until brown. Extra fat from foods like bacon should be poured off during cooking.

- **Stir-frying.** To **stir-fry** is to cook food very quickly in very little fat until the food is just tender. This method is used for vegetables and thin slices of meat, poultry, and fish. Many oriental dishes are stir-fried.

- **Deep-fat frying.** This method is used to cook foods, such as french fries and doughnuts, in a deep kettle of hot oil or shortening.

When Food Is Done

How do you judge when food is cooked properly? Here are some suggestions:

- **Check the appearance.** Many foods can be judged by the way they look. Toast is brown when it is done. Sautéed onions become transparent.

- **Pierce the food with a fork.** Do this for vegetables, such as potatoes, carrots, beans, and asparagus. The fork should insert and pull out easily.

- **Use a thermometer.** Insert a meat thermometer in the center of a roast before cooking. When the recipe temperature is reached, the meat is done.

- **Use a wooden or metal tester.** When cakes are done, a toothpick or skewer inserted into the center will come out clean. Use a knife for custards.

- **Test a sample.** Remove a piece of vegetable or pasta, let it cool slightly, and taste. Vegetables should be crisp; pasta should be slightly chewy.

- **Use the time listed in the recipe.** Many recipes give estimated cooking times, though actual time may vary.

SAUTÉ

STIR-FRY

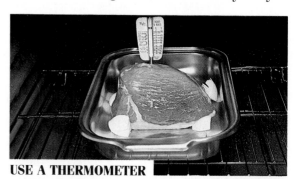

USE A THERMOMETER

PIERCE WITH A FORK

CHAPTER
47 REVIEW

Reviewing the Facts

1. What is the difference between cookware and bakeware?
2. Name three materials used for making cookware and bakeware. What are the characteristics of each?
3. Why is simmering a good cooking method?
4. What is the difference between braising and baking?
5. What is the difference between stewing and broiling?
6. What is one point to remember about cooking with fat?
7. What are three ways to tell when food is cooked?

Sharing Your Ideas

1. Assume that you are helping a friend shop for cookware and bakeware to furnish his or her kitchen in a college apartment. Which cooking equipment and utensils would you consider essential, and which would you advise could wait to be purchased at a later date? Why?
2. Foods such as potatoes, fish, and eggs can be cooked in several different ways with equal success. Assuming that you like the taste of each method equally, which cooking technique would you favor and why?

Applying Your Skills

1. **Writing Descriptions.** Using a catalog from a mail-order company that sells kitchen supplies, find at least four items that you would like to have in your "dream" kitchen. Note the prices, and write a short paragraph on each item describing its usefulness to you.

2. **Using Reference Materials.** Go to the library and look up the history of dry-heat cooking, from prehistoric to the present time, across cultures. Be sure to find information on peoples of desert, tropical, and temperate lands, and find out how they bake, roast, or broil. Make illustrations of their "ovens" or cooking utensils. Label these items and write a brief description of how each is used.

3. **Forming Hypotheses.** Cookware is used on top of the range, while bakeware is used in the oven. Why do you suppose that pots and pans are not used in the oven? Why are baking pans and cookie sheets not used on the range top? What would happen if they were?

Microwave Cooking

OBJECTIVES

This chapter will help you to:

- Describe the uses of the microwave oven.
- Explain how microwaves cook food.
- Describe various techniques for cooking with microwaves.
- Name the variables in microwave cooking and tell how they affect the cooking time.

WORDS TO REMEMBER

arcing
microwave
rotate

shield
standing time
variable

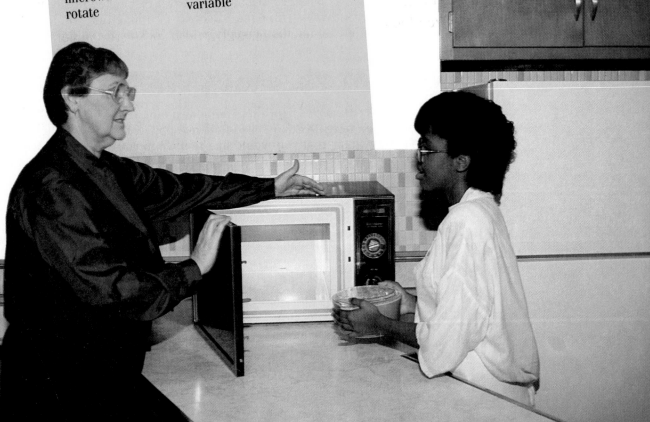

In recent years, microwave cooking has become popular in the home kitchen because the microwave oven performs many cooking tasks faster and more easily than a conventional oven does. Using a microwave oven, you can cook a meal in a matter of minutes or prepare a snack in seconds. Microwave ovens are cleaner and more economical than conventional ovens. They also have an added advantage in hot weather—they do not heat the kitchen.

To make the best use of microwave cooking, you need to know when to use a microwave oven and when to use other cooking methods. Most microwave ovens are best suited for cooking relatively small amounts of food; large amounts usually call for a conventional oven or range top. Microwave ovens are particularly useful for preparing quick snacks such as hot cereal, soup, melted cheese sandwiches, nachos, or popcorn. They are also ideal for reheating cooked foods and defrosting frozen foods.

Some microwave ovens have different power settings. Although higher power cooks foods faster, some foods cook better at a lower power.

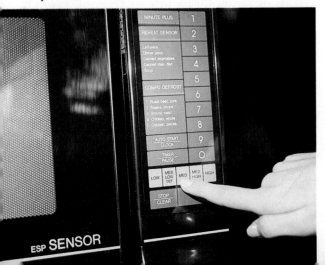

ESP SENSOR

How a Microwave Oven Works

Microwave ovens vary in size, features, and power, but they all work in a similar way. They differ from conventional ovens in that they themselves do not get hot. With microwave cooking, only the food gets hot.

When you turn on a microwave oven, you activate a magnetron tube that produces microwaves. A **microwave** is a type of energy wave that operates at a very high frequency. A stirrer, or fan, at the top of the oven spreads the microwaves around the oven.

Microwaves can penetrate most materials except metal. The walls of the microwave oven are lined with metal. The microwaves bounce off the oven walls and penetrate the food, causing its molecules to vibrate and rub against each other. This causes friction, producing the heat that cooks the food.

Microwaves cook foods without greatly changing their appearance and texture. Usually this is an advantage—broccoli and carrots, for example, retain their bright colors. For foods which are traditionally baked, however, microwave cooking may be perceived as a drawback because foods do not brown in this type of oven.

Settings

Microwave power is measured in watts. The maximum power of most microwave ovens is 500 to 700 watts, but some recipes may call for lower power settings. You can usually control the amount of power you use for different tasks and recipes—the more power used, the faster most foods will cook.

The power control on the microwave may be a single dial or a control panel.

This control is usually numbered from one to ten; each number represents the fraction of power used. Thus, number one gives you one tenth or 10 percent of the available power, and number ten gives you 100 percent. Some models have low, medium, and high settings, with the percent of power provided by each setting varying among brands.

In addition to selecting a power setting, you also need to decide how long to cook the food. Another control on the microwave oven enables you to key in the exact cooking time required.

Cookware

Not all cookware is suitable for microwave cooking. Ceramic, glass, plastic, and paper containers are usually appropriate, but you should look for a label indicating that they are microwave-safe.

Microwave-safe ceramic, glass, and plastic are unaffected by microwaves. Their molecules are not disturbed enough by the microwaves to cause friction, and therefore they do not get hot. They are also heat resistant, so they do not crack or melt when the food becomes hot. Ceramic dishes that are not microwave-safe may shatter in a microwave oven.

Metal pans and bowls should never be used. Because microwaves cannot pass through metal, some parts of the food will not be heated. More serious, metal containers may cause **arcing** (ARK-ing), sparks that can damage the oven and start a fire.

Some dishes have metallic trim or a metallic glaze, and they too should not be used. Even recycled paper sometimes contains metal. Metal *can* be put in many microwave ovens, but only with great care, as you will read later.

Microwave Techniques

For most microwave cooking, you need to use certain techniques when preparing and cooking the food. Because food heats up so fast in a microwave, moisture can escape very quickly and foods can burst. Also, evenness of cooking is a concern.

Stirring and Rotating

Microwaves penetrate food to a depth of about an inch from all of its surfaces. The heat generated by the microwaves is then conducted toward the center of the food. That is why the center of a large piece of food, or of a container of soup or stew, takes longer to cook than the outer edges.

Special microwave cookware is available, but you can use many dishes and containers that you already have. Check for labels that state "microwave-safe."

You can help soups, stews, and other foods containing liquids to heat up evenly by stirring them occasionally. For best results, stir from the outer edge toward the center. When food can't be stirred, you may need to **rotate** it. Turn the dish a quarter- or half-turn in the oven. This allows the microwaves to penetrate the food evenly on all sides.

In some cases you may need to rearrange food pieces or turn them over. For example, you would rotate a tuna casserole, rearrange baking potatoes, and turn over a ham.

Covering

Most foods should be covered in a microwave oven to hold in moisture and to prevent spattering. Choose the cover according to the type of food:

- White paper towels or napkins work well for covering bacon, sandwiches, and appetizers.
- Waxed paper is often used on meats or vegetables to hold in some of the moisture while letting steam escape.
- Microwave-safe dishes with lids are ideal for vegetables and casseroles.
- Vegetables can also be covered with plastic wrap. However, because plastic wrap forms a tight cover, it must be pierced or turned back at one corner to keep it from bursting.

Puncturing

Foods that are encased in a skin or seal should be pierced before they are placed in a microwave oven. Otherwise, steam will build up inside the food and cause it to burst. A quick jab or two with a fork or a small slit with a knife will prevent the pressure buildup. Puncture whole potatoes, egg yolks, hot dogs, and vegetables in plastic pouches.

Shielding

As a rule, you should not place metal in a microwave oven. However, you can use small pieces of aluminum foil to **shield** parts of food that might overcook. For example, you might shield the small end of chicken drumsticks, or the corners of a rectangular casserole. Be careful that the foil does not touch the sides of the oven and cause arcing. Check the instruction manual for any cautions.

Standing Time

A mistake that many people make when cooking in a microwave oven is to ignore the standing time called for in a recipe. **Standing time** is the time you should allow for the food to continue to cook after the microwave oven is turned off. You may think that the food is just sitting there, but the food molecules are still moving inside. Standing time is almost as important as cooking time for the food to turn out just right.

Recipes usually call for a cooking time slightly less than what is needed for doneness. Then, during standing time, the center of the food can cook some more, yet the outer edges do not dry out.

Whole potatoes must be pierced before being cooked. After they are removed from the oven, potatoes can be wrapped in tinfoil to retain moisture as they continue cooking during standing time.

A New Wave in Microwave Cooking

Hungry for a hot after-school snack? There's a new wave of convenience foods coming to the supermarket shelves—snack foods made specially for microwave cooking.

When microwave ovens were first sold to consumers, convenience foods manufacturers weren't ready for the new cooking technology. TV dinners were still packaged in trays made of metal foil, which could cause arcing. To cook them in a microwave oven, you had to empty each section from the tray and cook the dinner on a plate. Now, TV dinners have plastic trays which are safe in the microwave oven.

Food technologists, the people who devise new methods of preparing food, are beginning to go a step further. They are finding clever ways to package foods that have been hard to cook in a microwave. For example:

- Pizza is a favorite snack, but the crust gets soggy when heated in a microwave. Now you can buy pizza in portions that are microwave-ready. It comes with a paper tray lined with a metallic substance that heats up enough to crisp the pizza crust.

- TV dinners can now follow the meal-planning principle of variety in temperature. You can get a dinner in which the dessert stays cold while the meat and side dishes are heated.

- A milk shake in less than a minute? Many stores now sell packs of paper cups filled with frozen milk shakes. After 45 seconds in the microwave, and a quick stir, the milk shake is ready to enjoy.

- Even hot fudge sundaes can now be prepared in a microwave. The sauce heats up—but the ice cream stays cold and doesn't melt.

Think It Through

1. What types of foods are manufacturers choosing to market in microwaveable packages? Why do you think this is? What foods would you like to see made microwaveable?

2. Why do you think it has taken so long for food companies to develop foods specifically for the microwave oven?

Variables in Microwave Cooking

Variables are conditions that determine how long a food needs to be microwaved and at what power level.

- **Type of food.** Foods vary in moisture content, fat and sugar content, and density. Foods high in moisture cook more slowly than dry foods.

  Because microwaves are attracted to fat and sugar, these portions of foods cook faster. That is why the sugary top of a microwaved cinnamon roll may burn your tongue even though the center may not be warm.

  Foods that are porous, such as breads, cook faster than dense foods, such as meats. In general, the more compact and solid a piece of food is, the longer it will take to cook.

- **Volume.** Volume refers to the amount of food, or number of servings. The smaller the volume, the faster the food cooks in a microwave oven. Cooking time generally doubles if you double the amount of food. Often there is no saving of time when cooking large amounts of food in a microwave oven.

When cooking foods of different shapes, place the thicker pieces toward the outside.

- **Shape.** Shape also determines how evenly and how fast foods cook. Round pieces cook more evenly than square pieces, because they do not have corners that overcook.

  Thin pieces of food cook more rapidly than thick ones. Therefore, when cooking foods that are uneven in thickness, place the thin pieces toward the center of the pan or dish and the thick pieces toward the outside.

- **Starting temperature.** Foods that are at room temperature cook faster than foods that are colder. Most recipes assume the foods are at room temperature, so you may have to add to suggested cooking time if the food has been refrigerated.

Safety Considerations

Microwave cooking is easy but, as with conventional cooking, you need to follow certain safety precautions:

- Remove the cover from microwaved food very carefully, because the escaping steam could burn you. The tighter and less porous the cover, the greater the buildup of steam.

- Do not use dishes that are not microwave-safe because they might shatter.

- Do not use an extension cord with a microwave oven. The oven should be grounded with a three-prong plug and should not be on the same electrical circuit as other appliances.

- Keep your microwave oven in good working order. The waves that bounce off the metal-lined walls must be kept inside the cavity of the oven. An oven should be serviced if the door does not seal tightly or if the oven makes any unusual sound when it is turned on.

Reviewing the Facts

1. What cookware can be used for microwave cooking? What material should you not use for microwave cooking?
2. Why is it sometimes necessary to stir food at intervals during microwave cooking?
3. When foods cannot be stirred, what can you do to help them cook faster and more evenly?
4. Why should you puncture food or plastic wrap before placing it in the microwave oven?
5. What are four variables in microwave cooking, and how do they affect cooking time?
6. Give four safety precautions to follow when cooking with a microwave oven.

Sharing Your Ideas

1. If you had to choose between either a microwave oven or a conventional oven, which would you choose, and why?
2. If you were in charge of the household cooking and had a microwave oven in the kitchen, for what purposes and foods would you use it?

Applying Your Skills

1. Supporting Decisions. Bring to class several cookbooks or magazines containing microwave recipes. Make a list of some of your favorite foods, and from that list choose at least five that could be cooked in the microwave oven. From the cookbooks or magazines, find two microwave recipes for each food. Decide which recipe of each pair is most suitable for your family. Explain what your choices are and why you selected them.

2. Explaining Techniques. From the cookbooks or magazines that you have brought to class, find examples of rotating, stirring, covering, puncturing, shielding, and leaving to stand. For each of the five recipes you selected in Activity 1, check to see which of these techniques are used. Using your recipes as examples, write a paragraph or two explaining how two of these techniques are used in microwave cooking.

3. Comparing Results. Cook broccoli, carrots, and baked apples in a microwave oven and by conventional methods. Compare the appearance and taste of each item. Which method of preparation do you prefer, and why?

CHAPTER

49

Breads and Cereals

OBJECTIVES

This chapter will help you to:

- Identify and select foods in the breads-cereals group.
- Explain how to store breads and other cereal foods.
- Describe the best methods of cooking breads and other cereal foods.

WORDS TO REMEMBER

knead
quick bread
yeast bread

mong the four food groups, the breads-cereals group holds a special place. Cereal grains like wheat and rice are the main source of nutrients for well over half the world's population. In addition to providing carbohydrates for energy, they supply protein and important vitamins and minerals. They are a valuable source of fiber, too.

Many food products come from grains—breads, breakfast cereals, pasta, biscuits, muffins, tortillas, pancakes, waffles, and even pizza crusts. Grains and grain products should be a part of everyone's diet because of the nutrients they provide.

Some breakfast cereals are ready-to-eat, while others need either cooking or mixing with hot water.

Selecting Breads and Cereals

You will find a wide variety of breads and cereals to choose from in most markets. Your decisions may be based on personal taste, convenience—and also nutrition. An important question to ask is, how was the grain processed to make the product you are choosing?

Many products sold in America are made of white flour. This type of flour has been refined, meaning that the bran and the germ are removed during milling to give the flour a finer texture and to make it last longer. See "Whole and Hearty" on page 446 for an explanation of the parts of a grain.

Together with the bran and the germ, refining removes important nutrients, such as iron and the B vitamins. The flour is then enriched—federal law requires nutrients lost in processing to be replaced—and may also be fortified with additional nutrients.

Whole-grain products are made from the entire grain, including the bran and germ. They do not have to be enriched. Whole-grain products often have a distinctive, nutlike taste, and are higher in fiber than refined flour products.

Breads

There are many types of breads— white, whole wheat, rye, pumpernickel, and oat bran are just a few examples. Bread products include rolls, muffins, and biscuits, as well as loaves.

In addition to bread that has been commercially baked, you can buy bread mixes or ingredients to make the bread yourself. For extra convenience, you can also buy frozen bread products such as waffles or rolls. These merely need thawing or heating to be ready to eat.

Breakfast Cereals

Breakfast cereals are made from grains such as wheat, oats, corn, rice, and barley. Some are ready to eat—wheat flakes or corn puffs, for example—and can be served with milk and fruit. Others are cooked in water or milk and served hot. Some hot cereals are instant—you only have to add boiling water.

Read the labels carefully for nutrition and ingredient information. Many breakfast cereals contain large amounts of sugar and salt, and are high in calories. However, many cereals are fortified with added nutrients, and whole-grain cereals are also available.

Rice

White rice has had its outer coverings, the hull and bran, removed by polishing. Because most of the vitamin B and fiber is in the bran layer, enriched rice, like enriched bread, has had the vitamins put back in. You can also buy brown rice, which has been hulled but is unpolished. Much of the nutritious, fiber-rich bran is retained in brown rice, which has a nutlike flavor similar to whole wheat.

Other rice products include rice that is packaged with a sauce or seasoning packet, and instant rice which can be cooked quickly. These rices usually cost more than regular rice.

Pasta

Macaroni, spaghetti, and noodles are also in the breads and cereals group. These products are called pasta, which comes from the Italian word for dough. Most pasta keeps its shape and stays firm even after it has been cooked be-cause it is made from a special flour called semolina.

Pasta comes in all sizes and shapes—from thin strands of spaghetti to little shells and pieces that look like wagon wheels. Some pasta products have spinach or tomatoes added to the dough for color. They all usually taste the same, but the difference in texture or appearance may be important in your recipe.

Flour

You can purchase several kinds of flour for making bread products. All-purpose flour is used for general baking and cooking. Self-rising flour is an all-purpose flour with baking powder and salt added for baking.

Other types of flour include whole-wheat flour, rye flour, oat flour, and buckwheat flour. Cornmeal is used for baking corn bread, tortillas, and hush puppies. Other grain products are discussed in the feature on page 446.

Pasta comes in assorted shapes and is a good source of carbohydrates.

Whole and Hearty

A grain of wheat measures no more than one quarter of an inch, yet wheat has been a staple food throughout the world for thousands of years. How can you get the most out of this important source of energy, nutrients, and fiber?

A grain of wheat has four parts and is crammed with nutrients. The germ, which is at its core, contains vitamins and minerals that your body needs to stay healthy. Surrounding the germ is the endosperm, with nutrients to nourish the seed if it were allowed to sprout. These include starchy carbohydrates for energy, and most of the grain's protein. Outside the endosperm are layers of bran, covered by an outer protective case called the hull. The germ, bran, and hull all contain cellulose, or fiber.

The germ, the endosperm, and the bran are all retained in whole-wheat flour, which can be used in bread, graham crackers, pasta, and even pizza crust. Here are some other healthful grain products:

■ Wheat berries, or whole-wheat kernels, can be cooked much like rice and served in similar ways.
■ Bulgur, or cracked wheat, is the pasta of the Middle East and can be used in place of pasta or rice.

■ Wheat germ can be sprinkled on cereal, yogurt, or ice cream.
■ Barley, which usually has the bran removed, can be used in soups or served as a side dish.
■ Grits, or ground white corn, are used as cereal or instead of rice or mashed potatoes.
■ Kasha, or ground buckwheat with the bran removed, is used in Eastern European cooking instead of rice.

These grains can provide lots of nutrients. They are delicious and fun to eat as well!

Think It Through

1. What arguments would you use to convince someone who eats only white bread to try whole-grain varieties? Which argument would be most likely to convince you?
2. What breakfast foods can you think of that are made with whole grains?

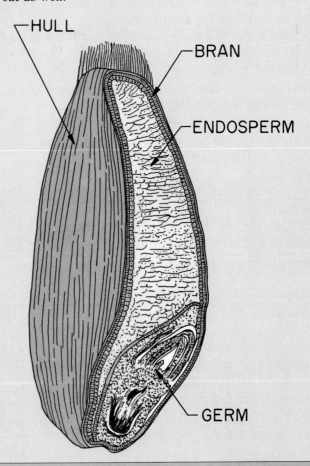

HULL — BRAN — ENDOSPERM — GERM

Storing Breads and Cereals

One of the advantages of products in the breads and cereals food group is that they can easily be stored. Many items keep well for long periods of time without refrigeration.

Breads

Bread tastes best when it's fresh, but it can also keep for some time. Always wrap breads tightly and store them in a cool, dark place, such as a breadbox or cabinet. In hot weather, keep bread in the refrigerator to slow down the growth of mold. Refrigeration will cause breads to get stale quickly, so do not store them this way unless it is necessary. Refrigerator rolls should remain refrigerated after you bring them home from the store.

Bread freezes well if it is tightly wrapped. It can be kept in the freezer for several months. Bread products that come frozen should be kept in the freezer until they are used.

Cereals, Rice, Pasta, and Flours

Dry cereals keep well in tightly closed packages or airtight containers. Rice, pasta, and flours also stay fresh for a long time if kept air-tight. Refrigeration is not needed for most cereal products except in hot, humid weather or if insects are a problem. However, whole-grain flours should be refrigerated.

Cook pasta in a large pot so it can move around freely and not stick together. First bring the water to a boil and then slowly add the pasta so the boiling does not stop.

Cooking Breads and Cereals

Breads and cereals may be cooked in liquids, baked, or heated in the microwave oven. Learn how to prepare them correctly, so the finished food will have good taste, texture, and appearance.

Cooking in Liquids

Many cereal products, including rice, pastas, and hot breakfast cereals, are cooked in water, and sometimes other liquids. They expand to two or three times their original size when fully cooked, so it is important to use a large enough pot.

Nutrients, especially the B vitamins, escape into the liquid during cooking. The key to preparing cereal products, therefore, is to use just the right amount of liquid. The package will tell you how much water or broth to use and how long to cook the product.

Rice and breakfast cereals absorb all the liquid used to cook them, so no nutrients are lost. Do not rinse rice before or after cooking, because the water may wash away nutrients.

Pasta should be cooked until just tender, or "al dente" (meaning "to the tooth" in Italian). Drain pasta in a colander but do not rinse after cooking.

In contrast, pasta is cooked in a large amount of water and then drained. Use 2 quarts (2 L) of water for every 8 ounces (250 mL) of pasta. Add the pasta slowly.

Pasta is done when it has expanded and softened. Overcooking destroys the texture and nutritive value. The pasta must be drained, using a colander. Do not rinse it or additional nutrients will be lost.

Baking

When you bake muffins, biscuits, or a loaf of bread, chemical and physical changes take place. The dough rises or puffs up because ingredients in the dough release gases. There are two basic types of breads—quick breads and yeast breads. Each type uses different ingredients to make the dough rise.

Quick breads use baking soda or baking powder to rise. These ingredients work fast, so that the bread is ready for baking right away. Examples are muffins, biscuits, pancakes, waffles, and banana bread. Most quick breads are made by combining the dry ingredients in one bowl and the liquid ingredients in another. The liquid is poured all at once into the dry ingredients, and the mixture is stirred only until the dry ingredients are moistened. Overmixing will cause the baked product to be tough.

Muffins, biscuits, and pancakes are quick breads.

Some biscuits are made by cutting the shortening into the flour mixture with a pastry blender or two knives. Then the liquid is added. After the ingredients are mixed together the dough is **kneaded**. To knead dough, press and fold it by hand several times. Then the dough is rolled, or flattened with a rolling pin, and the biscuits are cut out and baked.

Quick breads should be baked or cooked until lightly brown. When they are done, they spring back when touched lightly.

Yeast breads rise through the action of yeast, a tiny plant. They take longer to make than quick breads because the dough must be left to rise, often for half an hour or more, before it is put in the oven. Common yeast breads include white bread, whole-grain bread, raisin bread, rolls, and pizza crusts.

To make a yeast bread, combine the ingredients according to the recipe. When the yeast is mixed with warm water, it becomes active and slowly releases the gas that makes the dough rise.

After the flour and other ingredients are combined, most yeast breads are kneaded for at least eight to ten minutes.

Then the dough is allowed to rise, punched down, shaped, and allowed to rise a second time. This process may be repeated more times for heavier breads. Finally, the dough is put into the oven.

You can test yeast breads for doneness by rapping the crust with your knuckles. A hollow sound means the bread is done.

Microwave Cooking

A microwave oven can be used to defrost or warm prepared rolls, pancakes, waffles, bagels, and other breads. Baking in a microwave is also possible, though microwave baked breads are pale in color, not brown. Chopped nuts, cinnamon and sugar, or frosting can be added as a topping.

Hot breakfast cereals can easily be cooked in a microwave oven. Make sure, though, that your dish is microwave-safe—and large enough to allow for expansion of the cereal.

Rice and pasta take as long to cook in a microwave oven as they do on the range. Time is needed for them to absorb the liquid and soften. However, precooked rice and pasta can be quickly reheated in a microwave.

Most yeast doughs are kneaded for about 8 to 10 minutes. This develops the gluten which forms the structure of the bread. Then as the yeast releases carbon dioxide gas, the dough rises.

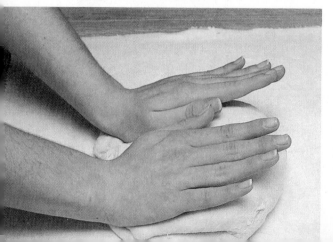

Reviewing the Facts

1. What is the difference between bread and cereal products that have been enriched and those that have been fortified?
2. When buying cereals, what can you find out by looking at the label?
3. When should breads be stored in the refrigerator?
4. What can you do to conserve nutrients in pasta and rice when cooking them?
5. What is the difference between quick breads and yeast breads?
6. How do you test quick breads and yeast breads for doneness?
7. What is the best use of a microwave oven for bread and cereal products?

Sharing Your Ideas

1. You make a pasta salad for lunch, but when you are eating it you find that the pasta is mushy and it breaks when you try to pick it up on your fork. What might you have done to cause this? Did it affect the nutrient value? What should you do next time?
2. What reasons do you think that people have for baking their own bread at home when so many varieties can be bought in the store?

Applying Your Skills

1. Researching Processes. Another type of rice is *converted* rice. Using the resources of your classroom and the library, find out what converted rice is. Why is the conversion process used? Does it relate to the way that rice is normally cooked? Explain the process to the class.

2. Giving Instructions. Prepare a chart that gives simple instructions on making bread. Divide all the steps into three parts: preparing the dough; kneading; rising. Write the steps for each part in a list on one half of a sheet of paper. Create simple illustrations of each step on the other half.

3. Identifying Objects and Phenomena. Several types of bread rise through the action of yeast. Use an encyclopedia to learn what yeast is and how it works. In one small bowl, mix yeast with warm water. In another bowl, mix yeast, warm water, and sugar. Then explain what happens.

CHAPTER

50

Fruits and Vegetables

OBJECTIVES

This chapter will help you to:
- Identify and select foods in the fruits-vegetables group.
- Explain how to store fruits and vegetables.
- Describe the best methods of cooking fruits and vegetables.

WORDS TO REMEMBER

concentrate
produce
seasonal
spoilage

Plants have provided people with important foods for thousands of years. Early people wandered over great distances to find roots, stems, leaves, berries, and fruits to eat. Today, however, refrigerated transportation brings a wide array of fruits and vegetables right to your neighborhood stores.

Fruits and vegetables are valuable sources of vitamins and minerals. Oranges, tomatoes, and green peppers, for example, are rich in vitamin C. Carrots, cantaloupes, and apricots contain a lot of vitamin A. Collard and turnip greens are valuable sources of vitamins A and C, calcium, and iron.

In addition, fruits and vegetables provide carbohydrates—starches and sugars. They also are excellent sources of fiber.

The way fruits and vegetables are handled, processed, and cooked can affect these nutrients. Thus, learning how to select, store, and prepare fruits and vegetables will do more than improve the taste of your meals and snacks—it will add to their nutritional benefits, too.

Selecting Fruits and Vegetables

There are probably more varieties of fruits and vegetables than of any other food. Most people can easily name ten fruits and vegetables that can be found in the produce section of their local supermarket. **Produce** (PRAH-doos or PRO-doos) is a term used to describe fresh fruits and vegetables. In fact, new transportation techniques are increasing the variety of produce in supermarkets, as described in "Strawberries in December" on page 454.

You can buy fruits and vegetables in several different forms—fresh, frozen, canned, and sometimes dried. Many types of juices are available too.

Fresh

Fresh fruits and vegetables—crisp, tart apples, steaming baked potatoes—have tastes and textures that many people find irresistible. In general, fresh also means more nutritious, because fruits and vegetables may lose some of their nutrients during processing. However, some of the vitamins in fresh produce deteriorate after harvest. So you should select fruits and vegetables that look fresh and crisp, and have not wilted.

Fruits and vegetables should also have a healthy color, with no bruises, spots, or sticky areas. Fruit that is soft to the touch may be overripe. For maximum juiciness, fruit should feel firm but not hard.

Examine fresh vegetables and fruits for color, ripeness, and texture. Don't buy any that are wilted, bruised, spotted, or damaged—they have lost nutrients and will not keep well.

Some produce is **seasonal**, meaning that it is more plentiful at certain times of the year, when it is usually less expensive. For instance, fresh corn is available in the summer but rarely in the winter. Buying produce in season can save money, and it also assures you that the food is fresh. Out-of-season produce may have been artificially ripened, or have traveled a long distance; either way, it will probably be more expensive, less nutritious, or both.

Processed

Perhaps you want a particular kind of produce, but its fresh form is either unavailable, in poor condition, or expensive and out of season. Maybe you want to stock up on fruits and vegetables so you don't have to go to the store so often. You may just prefer the convenience of processed foods—frozen, canned, or dried.

- **Frozen.** Frozen fruits and vegetables retain almost as many nutrients as fresh produce, and they keep their flavor and color better than canned products. However, frozen fruits usually have a softer texture than fresh fruits. Frozen vegetables are available whole, cut in pieces, and in special sauces.

- **Canned.** Fruits and vegetables in cans also come in many forms, such as whole, halved, sliced, or in pieces. Which form you choose depends on how you will use the item. Whole fruits and vegetables usually cost more than those in pieces. Most canned fruits are sold in a sugar syrup. For fewer calories, look for fruits packed in their own juice.

- **Dried.** Many fruits and vegetables are available dried, from raisins and apricots to mushrooms and onions. They can all be used in cooking, and dried fruits can be eaten as snacks.

- **Juices.** Apples, oranges, prunes, and tomatoes are just some of the many fruits and vegetables that are made into juices. Juices may be sold fresh, canned, or as frozen **concentrates**— juice products from which most of the water has been removed. Concentrates may be less costly than other forms of juice.

Many fruits and vegetables are available in several different forms. Your choice depends on how and when you plan to use the food, as well as availability and price.

Strawberries in December

Strawberries in December? Blueberries in February? Yes, these summer pleasures can brighten up a dreary winter weekend, thanks to modern technology.

Alongside the familiar fruits and vegetables, you may also find new and strange-looking varieties. The kiwi fruit from New Zealand and Australia; the carabola, or star fruit, from South America; winged beans from the Philippines; and the chayote, or vegetable pear, from Mexico are among the new "residents" of the produce sections in today's supermarkets.

How is it possible to have this rich variety of fresh produce from thousands of miles away? Improvements in the following areas help to bring produce from all over the world to your local markets, from January to December:

■ **Storage.** Warehouses and storage facilities can accommodate varied produce for longer periods because of refrigeration equipment that adjusts automatically to maintain the proper temperature.

■ **Transportation.** Airplanes, boats, and trucks, have specially insulated refrigerator compartments for shipping produce long distances. The temperature is controlled automatically while fruits and vegetables are in transit.

■ **Packaging.** Perishable produce is protected from jolting and bruising in transit. Individual fruits are wrapped and separated from each other with molded plastic wrapping, and containers are insulated with foam.

■ **Computerization.** A microprocessor chip can record and time the number of jolts, collisions, or any serious disturbances of a shipment of produce in transit. The little computer is enclosed in a piece of hard beeswax that has been molded in the shape of a fruit or vegetable; it is then packaged with the produce. It provides information that can lead to improved packaging, or a change in the transportation method.

Think It Through

1. What are some advantages of more fruits and vegetables being available in supermarkets year round?
2. Now that techniques have been developed to transport produce great distances, are there any advantages in buying fruits and vegetables that have been grown locally?

Storing Fruits and Vegetables

Storing fruits and vegetables properly helps prevent **spoilage**, damage that happens when food is too old to eat or contains bacteria or mold.

- **Fresh.** In general, fresh fruits and vegetables need refrigeration. Lettuce and other leafy vegetables, should be refrigerated in airtight containers to retain their moisture. Bananas and a few other products do much better stored at room temperature.

  You can wash and dry fresh fruits and vegetables before storing. However some, like berries, are best kept as dry as possible until they are served.

  Most fresh produce should be used within a few days of buying it. Apples, though, can stay fresh for three or four weeks, while oranges and other citrus fruits can keep for five weeks in a plastic bag in the refrigerator. Potatoes and onions can be kept a long time—two or three months—in a cool, dry, dark place. If you have a question about a specific product, ask the produce manager at your supermarket.

- **Frozen.** Frozen products keep well for several months if the temperature in the freezer or freezing compartment is no higher than 0°F (-18°C). If the freezer or freezing compartment is not this cold, frozen foods should be stored for only a few days.

- **Canned.** Canned fruits and vegetables keep for a year or more if they are stored in a cool, dry place—70°F (21°C) is recommended.

- **Dried.** Dried and freeze-dried products do well on the cupboard shelf, tightly wrapped. In humid weather, dried fruit should be refrigerated.

- **Juices.** Juices should be stored according to the package directions.

Preparing Fruits and Vegetables

Nutrition and flavor are the words to remember when preparing fruits and vegetables.

Serving Fresh Produce

Fresh fruits and vegetables may be eaten as snacks, in salads, as appetizers, as side dishes, or for dessert. Produce such as apples, grapes, celery, and tomatoes can simply be washed and served. Other produce, such as oranges, bananas, and carrots, are peeled before being eaten.

Some peeled fruits and vegetables darken in color if not eaten or cooked immediately. This is especially true of apples, bananas, peaches, and avocadoes. To prevent this, sprinkle the cut surfaces with lemon juice and wrap the produce in plastic or another airtight covering. You can also put them in a bowl of water with lemon juice added.

Salad greens should be washed, drained thoroughly, and torn into bite-size pieces before tossing. To prevent wilting, add dressing to greens just before the salad is served.

Before using fresh fruits and vegetables, wash them carefully under cold running water to remove dirt, bacteria, and pesticides.

Cooking with Moist Heat

Vitamin A, vitamin C, and the B vitamins are easily destroyed or dissolved by water, heat, and air, so follow the cooking suggestions given in Chapter 47. Use a heavy-bottomed pan so fruits and vegetables can cook at a low, even temperature. Add a minimum amount of water and cover the pan with a lid. This prevents the steam from escaping with valuable nutrients.

The general rule is, the less water used, the better the result will be. Steaming is ideal for most vegetables. Any water leftover from cooking vegetables contains valuable nutrients and is good to save for use in soups and stews.

Canned vegetables are already cooked and only need to be heated. The water from canned vegetables can also be saved if you wish.

Baking

Baking is an excellent way to cook many fruits and vegetables; it preserves the nutrients well. You can bake pears, apples, potatoes, and all forms of squash. Sometimes a very small amount of liquid is added to the pan to prevent the skins from becoming too dry. Potatoes, however, are baked entirely dry after their skin has been pierced to release steam.

Stir-Frying

Stir-frying—cooking quickly in very little fat—is another good method of preparing vegetables. Stir-fried vegetables should remain a little crisp and not be overcooked. You can test for doneness by poking them with the point of a knife or a sharp fork.

Microwave Cooking

Fruits and vegetables can be cooked to perfection in a microwave oven. Very little water, if any, is needed so nutrients are not lost. Because microwaves cook fruits and vegetables from within, there is no change in the color, flavor, or texture.

Cut pieces into equal size and pierce unpeeled apples, potatoes, and other foods with skins to prevent bursting. Usually the foods should be stirred or re-arranged once or twice for even cooking. Fruits and vegetables should be taken out of the microwave while they are still slightly crisp and allowed to stand a few minutes. Be careful not to overcook them. (See Chapter 48 for the general rules of microwave cooking.)

Microwave cooking is an ideal way to cook vegetables. For fresh vegetables, you can add a very small amount of water—no more than two tablespoons. Don't add water to frozen vegetables. Cover with plastic wrap and pierce, or pierce a plastic pouch. Check the manual for cooking times.

CHAPTER
50 REVIEW

Reviewing the Facts

1. Name five forms in which you can buy fruits and vegetables.
2. What important fact related to nutrition should you consider when buying fresh produce?
3. Describe features to look for when you are buying fresh produce.
4. What does the term *seasonal* mean?
5. Name advantages of buying fresh fruits and vegetables, of buying frozen, and of buying canned.
6. How long can you store most fresh produce?
7. Why is steaming vegetables preferable to boiling them?
8. Why is microwave cooking a good method of cooking fruits and vegetables?

Sharing Your Ideas

1. What steps would you suggest to encourage young people to eat a wider variety of fruits and vegetables?
2. Deep-fat frying is a common way of cooking some vegetables. Why do you think this might not be the ideal method?

Applying Your Skills

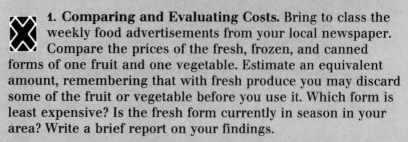

1. Comparing and Evaluating Costs. Bring to class the weekly food advertisements from your local newspaper. Compare the prices of the fresh, frozen, and canned forms of one fruit and one vegetable. Estimate an equivalent amount, remembering that with fresh produce you may discard some of the fruit or vegetable before you use it. Which form is least expensive? Is the fresh form currently in season in your area? Write a brief report on your findings.

2. Using Reference Materials. Select your favorite fruit or vegetable, and find a recipe that uses it as an appetizer, a side dish, and a main dish or dessert. Make a poster showing the versatility of the fruit or vegetable and listing the various recipes.

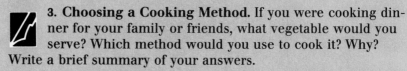

3. Choosing a Cooking Method. If you were cooking dinner for your family or friends, what vegetable would you serve? Which method would you use to cook it? Why? Write a brief summary of your answers.

Milk and Milk Products

OBJECTIVES

This chapter will help you to:

■ Identify and select foods in the milk-milk products group.
■ Explain how to store milk and milk products.
■ Describe the best methods of cooking milk and milk products.

WORDS TO REMEMBER

coagulate   homogenized
dehydrated   pasteurized

The milk group is unique among the food groups in that it includes products made from just one substance: milk. In the United States, *milk* usually means cow's milk. In some other countries, people drink milk that comes from goats.

Milk is an excellent source of many nutrients. It provides complete proteins, carbohydrates, and fats—the last in varying amounts depending on how the milk is processed. Milk is also an excellent source of calcium and phosphorus. Together, these two minerals make bones and teeth strong.

Milk is a good source of riboflavin, a B vitamin, as well as vitamin A. (Since vitamin A is fat soluble, milk from which the fat has been removed must be fortified with vitamin A.) Most milk is also fortified with vitamin D, a nutrient that must be present for calcium to be used by the body. Because vitamin D occurs naturally in very few foods, adding it to milk makes it possible for people to get enough.

Selecting Milk Products

Milk products come in many varieties. You can buy whole milk or milk with less fat. You can choose from yogurt and hundreds of cheeses. In addition, there are many delightful flavors of ice cream available.

Milk

You can buy milk in liquid form or **dehydrated**, meaning that some or all of the liquid has been removed. Milk sold as a liquid is usually **pasteurized** (PASS-chuh-ryzed), or heated and cooled to kill harmful germs. It is also **homogenized** (huh-MAHJ-uh-nyzed), to blend the creamy fats into the liquid. Some or all of the fats may be removed, making lowfat milk or skim milk.

- **Whole milk.** Whole milk has all the original nutrients of milk, and at least 3.5 percent fat.
- **Lowfat milk.** Lowfat milk has less fat than whole milk, but more than skim

Milk is available in several different forms. What are the characteristics of each? Which ones have you used?

milk. Lowfat milk comes in different varieties—2 percent and 1 percent fat content are common. Although lowfat milk is a little higher in calories than skim milk, many people prefer its flavor and texture.

- **Skim milk.** Skim milk is whole milk from which almost all the fat has been removed. It has most of the nutrients supplied by whole milk, except for fat, and it is fortified with Vitamin A.

- **Cream.** Cream is the fat in milk. It rises to the top of the container if milk is not homogenized. An ounce of cream contains 110 calories. An ounce of whole milk, in contrast, has only about 20 calories.

- **Half-and-half.** Half-and-half is a mixture of cream and milk. It offers some of the rich taste and texture of cream with less fat and fewer calories.

- **Evaporated milk.** Canned evaporated milk is whole milk that has been heated to remove more than half the water content. If you add the right amount of water, you have a product like fresh whole milk.

- **Sweetened condensed milk.** Canned sweetened condensed milk has half the water removed and sugar added. It is a rich concentrated milk that can be used in baked desserts and candy.

- **Nonfat dry milk.** This is milk from which all the moisture and most of the fat has been removed before packaging. Nonfat dry milk is an inexpensive powder that contains all the nutrients found in skim milk with about half the calories of whole milk. It can be used for cooking and, with water added, for drinking.

Cheese can be used for appetizers, dips, salads, sandwiches, sauces, in cooked foods, and with fruit for dessert.

Cheese

Cheese is made from the milk of cows or goats. The type of cheese depends on what milk it is made from and how it is made. There are more than 400 types of cheeses, with over 2,000 different names. Some cheeses are fresh, such as cottage cheese, and must be used within a short time. Other cheeses, such as Swiss and Parmesan, are aged or ripened for as long as two years. Each type of cheese requires a specific length of time to develop.

Cheese is a milk product and is a good source of complete proteins, carbohydrates, and calcium. For example, the calcium content of 1 cup (250 mL) of milk can be provided by 1 1/2 cups (375 mL) of cottage cheese or by two 1-inch (2.5 cm) cubes of cheddar cheese. However, cheeses are higher in calories than milk is, although lowfat varieties are now available. Almost all cheeses can be put into one of four groups:

- **Soft.** These range in flavor from mild types such as cottage cheese, cream cheese, and ricotta to the tangy French Brie and Camembert.
- **Semisoft.** Mild cheeses such as Muenster, Gouda, and Mozzarella are semisoft. So are many strong-flavored blue cheeses.
- **Hard.** Hard cheeses range from mild to sharp flavors, such as Cheddar, Swiss, and Parmesan.
- **Processed.** These are mixtures of different cheeses, sometimes combined with flavorings such as pepper, olives, or pineapple.

Milk and milk products are excellent sources of calcium, which is needed for strong bones and healthy teeth.

Other Milk Products

Some milk products are formed by adding new ingredients to milk, while others are developed through a freezing process.

- **Cultured milk products.** The taste and texture of milk and cream can be changed by the addition of certain harmless bacteria. These bacteria, grown in colonies called cultures, turn milk and cream into products that have a tangy taste and a thick texture. That is why yogurt, sour cream, and buttermilk are called cultured milk products. Yogurt can be made from either whole or skim milk, sour cream is made from cream, and buttermilk is made from skim milk.
- **Frozen milk products.** Ice cream, ice milk, and frozen yogurt are all popular desserts made from milk. Ice milk and frozen yogurt contain less fat and fewer calories than ice cream. However, all three are sweetened with sugar and contain more calories than liquid milk or regular yogurt.

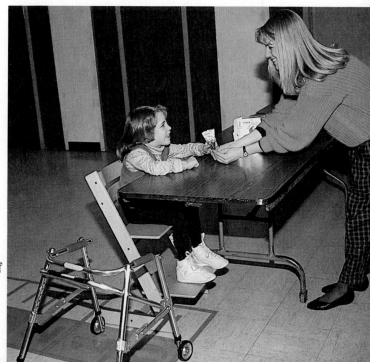

HEALTH WATCH

The Truth About Yogurt

Over the years, many claims have been made about yogurt—if you believe one company's commercials, yogurt is the key to long life. Even though this claim may be exaggerated, no one questions that yogurt is a nutritious and highly beneficial food.

Nutritionally, yogurt almost exactly matches the milk from which it is made; and milk is one of the most nutrient-rich of all foods. Like milk, yogurt has calcium, phosphorus, B vitamins, and high-quality protein.

The cultures in yogurt release lactase, a chemical that allows milk to be digested. People who cannot digest milk can usually eat yogurt.

For those who like to eat yogurt straight from the cup, there are hundreds of varieties—whole milk, lowfat, and nonfat yogurt; yogurt flavored with fruits or other flavorings; liquefied, custardized, and frozen yogurt.

Many people consider yogurt a low-calorie food. Plain yogurt contains only a fraction of the fat and cholesterol of ice cream. However, many flavored yogurts have sweetened fruit sauces added. Though low in fat, these yogurts are relatively high in calories. A healthier alternative is to add fresh fruit to plain yogurt.

Plain yogurt can also be used in place of sour cream on baked potatoes, and in salad dressings, dips, and dessert toppings. It can also be substituted for some of the mayonnaise in potato salad. Yogurt is a nutritious snack food and a healthful addition to any meal.

Think It Through

1. Why might a person choose to eat eight ounces of yogurt rather than drink an eight ounce glass of milk?
2. Why do you think yogurt has become so popular in the last two decades?

Storing Milk Products

Once you get milk products home, keeping them fresh is important. Most dairy products are perishable. Storing them properly helps you use them safely, enjoy their flavor, and avoid wasting money.

Milk

All fresh milk should be kept in the coldest part of the refrigerator to retain nutrients and freshness for as long as possible. Putting the milk container away as soon as you have used what you need is important, since warmth and light both harm fresh milk. Warmth allows the growth of harmful bacteria, while light destroys the riboflavin, a B vitamin in milk. Cream and half-and-half should also be refrigerated.

Evaporated and sweetened condensed milk are canned and can be stored for long periods of time on the shelf. Once you have opened the cans, however, refrigerate any unused portions and use them within a day or two.

Nonfat dry milk keeps well on the shelf as long as it is kept away from moisture. When you add water to dry milk and restore it to a liquid, refrigerate it immediately after use, just as you would fresh milk.

Cheese and Other Milk Products

All cheese should be kept in the refrigerator. Soft cheeses, like cottage cheese, keep for a few days if tightly covered. Hard cheeses, like Cheddar and Swiss, remain fresh for weeks or even months if they are tightly wrapped.

Cultured milk products also need refrigeration. They keep longer unopened than fresh milk, but once opened, they spoil quickly. Use them by the dates stamped on their packages.

The freezer, of course, is the place for ice cream, ice milk, and frozen yogurt. If the freezer temperature is above 0°F (-18°C), the product should be used within a few days.

Cooking Milk Products

Proteins **coagulate** when they are heated. This means that they change from a fluid state to a thickened mass. In order to prevent proteins from becoming tough and stringy at high temperatures, low heat is the rule for cooking milk and milk products. Often, the difference between success and failure is a matter of a few degrees; all the stirring in the world won't save a cream sauce that's been cooked at too high a temperature.

Low-temperature cooking and frequent stirring keep the proteins in milk from coagulating.

Cooking Milk

Because milk can burn easily, cook milk products in heavy pans that allow slow, even heating. This keeps the milk from burning on the bottom of the pan and prevents it from boiling over.

Low temperatures also prevent proteins from forming a skin over the top of the milk. If a skin does develop, beat it back into the milk so the valuable proteins will not be lost. Covering the pan will also discourage a skin from forming. At the same time, this will help retain the milk nutrients, since light quickly destroys riboflavin.

To cook milk and milk mixtures in a microwave oven, follow the same general rules but watch the mixture very closely. Because milk boils over easily, the glass or bowl you use should be no more than two-thirds full. Puddings will scorch if they are in the microwave too long.

Cooking Cheese

Cheese can be served uncooked, melted in a sandwich, or added to a creamy sauce. It can also be sprinkled on top of casseroles or vegetables near the end of the cooking period. Baking or broiling quickly melts the cheese.

Cheese, like milk, toughens when overcooked. To prevent this, chop, grate, or slice the cheese before adding it to a recipe. Low heat and constant stirring also help.

The same principles apply if you cook cheese in a microwave. Cheese dishes and toppings need to be watched for signs of overcooking or toughening.

A double boiler can be used to heat milk. The heat from boiling water in the lower pan cooks the food in the upper pan without scorching or curdling it.

Cheese can be grated and sprinkled on top of casseroles to provide color, taste, and added nutrition.

CHAPTER

51 REVIEW

Reviewing the Facts

1. Name four forms of liquid milk. What are the differences among them?
2. What are the four basic types of cheese?
3. What produces a cultured milk product? What is its effect on the taste of milk?
4. Name three popular frozen desserts made from milk. Which one contains the most butterfat?
5. How should you store fresh milk?
6. What is the rule of heating that applies to cooking milk and milk products? Give the reason for this rule.

Sharing Your Ideas

1. What might be some of the advantages and disadvantages of adding cheese to vegetables and sauces?
2. Why might it be a good idea to keep a supply of evaporated and dried milk on hand?

Applying Your Skills

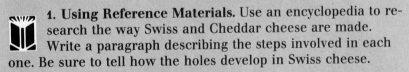 **1. Using Reference Materials.** Use an encyclopedia to research the way Swiss and Cheddar cheese are made. Write a paragraph describing the steps involved in each one. Be sure to tell how the holes develop in Swiss cheese.

2. Comparing Costs. Check newspaper advertisements or food stores for the prices of whole milk, nonfat dry milk, and evaporated milk. How much evaporated and how much dry milk is needed to prepare one gallon of milk? Compute the costs of a gallon of milk made from these two sources. Then compare the costs per gallon for both to the price of a gallon of whole milk. Which one of the three is the most expensive? Can you think of any reasons for the price differences?

3. Performing an Experiment. There are many types of milk, all with different qualities. Obtain small amounts of as many types as possible, and pour each one into a separate cup that has been labeled on the bottom. Rearrange the cups, then taste. Try to correctly identify the types of milk. Document your procedures and results.

Meats, Poultry, Fish, Eggs, Nuts, and Beans

OBJECTIVES

This chapter will help you to:

- Identify and select foods in the meats, poultry, fish, eggs, nuts, and beans group.
- Explain how to store foods in the meats-to-beans group.
- Describe the best method of cooking foods in the meats-to-beans group.

WORDS TO REMEMBER

cut
marbling
processed meat
variety meat

The milk group depends on one substance—milk—for all its products. In contrast, the meats-to-beans group includes foods as varied as pork, Cornish game hens, flounder, eggs, and navy beans.

The meats-to-beans group is a major source of protein in your diet. Even after you have finished growing, your body will continue to need protein every day. Proteins are the nutrients that maintain healthy muscles, tissues, and cells in your body. Most foods in this group also contain iron and important vitamins, such as the B vitamins or vitamin A.

Selecting Meats, Poultry, Fish, Eggs, Nuts, and Beans

You have a great range of choice when you are shopping for foods from the meats-to-beans group. Do you want a steak, a chop, a roast, or ground meat? Do you prefer beef, lamb, or pork? Would you rather have poultry or fish? What about **variety meats**, which are organ meats such as liver, heart, and kidney? If none of these appeal to you, what about eggs for an omelet or beans for a casserole?

When comparing the costs of different cuts of meat, compare the price per serving rather than the price per pound. Although boneless cuts usually cost more per pound than similar cuts with bones, they provide more meat per pound and may be the better buys.

Meats

Beef, veal, lamb, and pork are the most common types of meats. Beef and veal come from cattle, lamb from sheep, and pork from hogs. Meat is a good source of complete protein, B vitamins, and iron. However, it also has saturated fat, so choose lean cuts and trim away excess fat.

Each type of meat is sold in many different **cuts**, sections or parts, such as loin chops, spare ribs, flank steaks, and ground chuck. The name of each cut indicates what part of the animal the meat is from (for example, the flank or the chuck), and how it has been prepared (as a steak or as ground meat). **Processed meats** have been seasoned, smoked, or prepared in some other way before they are brought to the store. They include hot dogs, bacon, sausages, ham, and luncheon meats.

Both the type and cut of meat determine its flavor and tenderness. Expensive cuts of meat are usually more tender, because they are taken from parts of the animal that have less connective tissue and get less exercise—the

ribs and the loins, for instance. High-quality pieces will have **marbling**, fine streaks and flecks of fat within the lean area of the meat. However, less expensive cuts are just as nutritious, and they can be delicious when appropriately cooked.

Both processed and unprocessed meats may be available fresh, frozen, or canned. They may also be available fully cooked—canned meats are nearly always ready to eat. Check fresh meat for its color, and for how much bone and fat are included in the package. Meat that looks brown and dry is probably not fresh. Read the label to learn the weight of the package and to check the pull date, the last day the meat should be sold.

Poultry

Poultry includes chicken, turkey, duck, and other birds. They are good sources of complete protein, B vitamins, and iron, just like meats. However, chicken and turkey are relatively low in fat.

Poultry can be bought whole, cut up, or in packages of separate pieces such as legs, breasts, or wings. Processed forms of poultry include chicken hot dogs and turkey cold cuts.

The names given to types of chicken are a clue to age and tenderness. Broiler-fryers are young and tender, roasters are older, and stewing chickens are the oldest. The names also tell you the best cooking methods to use for each type. Stores sell fresh, frozen, and canned poultry products. Whole poultry generally costs less per pound than cut-up poultry. Boneless pieces usually cost the most per pound.

Fish

Saltwater fish, like tuna and flounder, come from the ocean. Freshwater fish, such as trout and catfish, come from lakes, rivers, and streams. There are also many types of shellfish, such as clams, scallops, shrimp, and lobster. Fish is a good source of complete protein, the B vitamins, and important minerals, such as phosphorous.

You can buy fresh, frozen, or canned fish. Fresh fish is sold in three ways:

- Whole, with only the scales and insides removed.
- Dressed, with head, tail, fins, scales, and insides removed.
- Cut into steaks or into boneless strips (fillets).

Fresh fish should not have a strong smell, and the flesh should be firm when pressed. Some frozen fish and shellfish are sold completely cooked; frozen fish and shrimp can be bought plain or batter-dipped. Canned fish, like tuna or salmon, comes packed in water or in oil.

You can buy a whole chicken and cut it up yourself, or you can buy just the parts that you like. Cut-up and boneless chicken parts cost more, but have less waste than whole chickens.

Eggs, Nuts, and Beans

Eggs are a source of complete protein, vitamin A, B vitamins, and iron. However, egg yolks contain fat and cholesterol. Eggs are usually bought fresh in cartons of a dozen. Brown eggs and white eggs have exactly the same quality and taste. Eggs can be small, medium, large, or extra-large in size. Many stores also sell dried eggs, which keep for a long time, and egg substitutes, which contain less fat and cholesterol.

Nuts and other seeds contain incomplete protein, but they are high in fat and calories. Nuts and seeds are sold in packages or loose from bins. Shelled nuts are usually more expensive and can be whole, halved, slivered, or chopped.

Finally, there are many varieties of beans, or legumes, including soy, navy, pinto, lima, and kidney beans. These are excellent sources of incomplete protein, B vitamins, and iron. They come dried and canned. Before being cooked, most dried beans must be soaked in water, which allows them to expand greatly in size.

Storing Meats, Poultry, Fish, Eggs, Nuts, and Beans

Proper storage is the first step in using meat and meat-group products wisely. You can leave fresh meat, poultry, and fish in its original store wrapper, but you need to place it in the coldest part of the refrigerator. If it has been wrapped only in butcher paper, however, rewrap it in foil or plastic wrap before storing.

Meat, poultry, and fish can also be frozen. Wrap it tightly in freezer paper or some other moisture-proof wrap, and write the date of storage on the package. When you thaw the product, do so in the refrigerator or microwave oven—not at room temperature.

Refrigerated meat, poultry, and fish should be used within one or two days of purchase. Ground meat should be cooked within 24 hours. Variety meats keep only for one to two days. Processed and cooked meats can be kept longer.

Eggs, too, need refrigeration to retain nutrients and flavor. They should be stored in their original covered carton to keep them from absorbing food odors.

Nuts, seeds, and dried beans will stay fresh in the cupboard if they are kept in a tightly sealed container. Canned meat, poultry, fish, and beans keep well on cool, dry shelves until they are opened. However, some canned hams need to be refrigerated.

Five methods for cooking eggs (clockwise from top): baked, poached, cooked in shell, scrambled, and fried.

Cooking Meats, Poultry, Fish, Eggs, Nuts, and Beans

The general principles for cooking foods in the meats-to-beans group are based on how proteins react to heat. The more heat, the less tender the foods become.

The cooking method you choose is also important. Moist heat, dry heat, and fat are all used to cook the foods in this group.

Moist Heat

Moist-heat cooking methods use liquid or steam to cook the food. Braising, stewing, poaching, simmering, boiling and steaming are all moist-heat methods. Tougher cuts of meat and poultry become more tender when cooked slowly with moist heat.

Pot roasts and short ribs are braised using a small amount of liquid. Chunks of meat can be stewed with vegetables in water or other liquid. Brown the meats first in a hot pan—this helps seal in their juices and produces a more fla-

Less tender cuts of meat should be cooked slowly in a liquid to make them tender and flavorful.

vorsome dish. Processed meats too are often braised or stewed with a vegetable; common combinations are sausage and sauerkraut, and corned beef and cabbage.

Tender cuts can also be cooked using moist heat. For instance, veal is often braised for additional flavor. However, more expensive cuts of meat are usually roasted or broiled, which are dry-heat methods.

Moist heat is frequently used for cooking other protein foods. Fish can be poached or used to make fish stew. Eggs can be boiled in their shells, poached, or beaten and added to soup. When beaten eggs are added to a hot sauce or pudding, first stir a little of the hot liquid into the egg mixture. Then slowly stir the egg mixture into the rest of the sauce. If the eggs are added all at once, the egg will cook too fast and look curdled.

Dried beans are always boiled in large amounts of water or meat-flavored liquid. Despite their name, baked beans are not baked, but are simmered in a liquid.

Dry Heat

Many meats, poultry, and fish can be cooked with dry heat. Baking or roasting in the oven, broiling in a broiler pan or on a barbecue, and grilling in a skillet are all dry-heat methods.

- **Meats.** Tender meats such as legs of lamb and certain cuts of beef, pork, and veal can be roasted in the oven. Place on a rack so that the fat drips down into the pan. Beef, lamb, and veal can be cooked to different degrees of doneness—rare, medium, and well-done. Pork should always be well cooked, however, and should not be served if it is still pink inside.

Broiling is often used for steaks, chops, and hamburgers. Broiling sears meat on the outside and seals in juices and nutrients.

- **Poultry.** Chicken, turkey, and other birds can be filled with a stuffing of bread, rice, vegetables, or fruits and roasted. Chicken parts can also be baked or broiled.
- **Fish.** Like poultry, fish can be baked or broiled. Fish cooks quickly—you can tell it's done when the flesh flakes or separates easily when touched by a fork. Do not overcook fish or it will dry out and toughen.
- **Eggs.** Overcooking toughens eggs, too. Baked eggs need to be timed according to a recipe.
- **Nuts and beans.** Nuts can be roasted, but beans are almost never cooked with dry heat. You can toast chickpeas in the oven.

Cooking with Fat

Meat, poultry, and fish can also be cooked in butter or oil. Some methods are sautéing, stir-frying, or deep-fat frying. The fat should be very hot so that the foods will cook quickly without absorbing the fat. Sometimes chicken and fish are breaded before being fried.

Eggs can be fried in a small amount of fat or beaten first to make scrambled eggs. It is important to watch fried eggs and scrambled eggs closely as they cook. If they are undercooked, they will be soft and runny; if overcooked, eggs will get tough and rubbery.

Fish is done when it is firm and flakes easily with a fork.

Microwave Cooking

Microwave cooking preserves the natural juices of foods because the foods cook from within.

- Meats remain more moist and shrink less in a microwave than they do in conventional cooking. Fat on the outside must be removed, however, because it spatters and could cause a fire. Moist meat dishes such as stews, pot roasts, and Salisbury steaks should be covered with plastic that has been pierced to prevent bursting.
- Poultry can be microwaved whole, or cut up into pieces. If in pieces, place the thicker, meatier parts toward the outer edge of the dish. Remember the importance of rotating the dish every few minutes for even cooking.
- Fish must be watched carefully and removed before it is fully cooked because it continues to cook during standing time.
- If you cook eggs in a microwave oven, break them into a bowl and pierce the yolk with a skewer; otherwise, they may burst. Eggs can be scrambled in a microwave oven, but they should never be cooked in the shell.
- Beans cooked in a microwave do not need to be presoaked. Preparation time is therefore much faster.

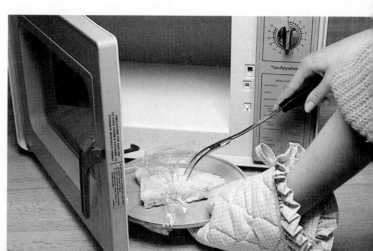

Protein Complementing

Meats, poultry, and fish are expensive, so you plan to have baked beans for lunch and several spoonfuls of peanut butter as a snack. Will you be satisfying your meats-to-beans group requirement?

Not necessarily. Remember the difference between complete and incomplete proteins from Chapter 36? A complete protein contains all nine essential amino acids, the ones that the body *must* have from foods you eat. Incomplete proteins are missing one or more of these amino acids. Animal proteins are complete; vegetable proteins are incomplete.

To benefit fully from the vegetable members of the meats-to-beans group, you must eat foods that contain the missing amino acids in the same meal. This isn't as hard as you might think. A glass of milk with your baked beans will do the trick, as will a slice of bread with the peanut butter. This is called protein complementing.

Many traditional dishes supply economical complete proteins in this way:

- **Pea soup with ham.** Dried peas, like beans, are legumes. Simmer them with some ham for a tasty, nutritious soup.
- **Black-eyed peas and rice.** The missing amino acids aren't only present in meats. Grains such as rice can also complement legumes.

- **Hummus and pita bread.** Hummus—ground chick peas with sesame seed oil and other ingredients—is often eaten in a tasty sandwich of pita bread.
- **Succotash.** Lima beans with corn is a traditional American dish that uses the principle of protein complementing.
- **Chili.** Chili beans are served *con carne*, with meat, and often topped with grated cheese.

As you see, legume foods should be paired with milk products, grain products, or other meats-to-beans group foods to provide the complete proteins needed.

Think It Through

1. What other common or not-so-common dishes can you think of that supply complete proteins using little or no meat? Do they all include foods from the meats-to-beans group?

2. Think of other combinations of legumes and grain or milk foods that might taste good. How would you cook them?

CHAPTER
52 REVIEW

Reviewing the Facts

1. What nutrients do you get from the meats-to-beans group?
2. What is a cut of meat?
3. What are processed meats?
4. What is the significance for the consumer of the different names given to chicken in the store?
5. List three ways fresh fish are sold.
6. What is the benefit of egg substitutes?
7. How should you store fresh meats and fish if you plan to use them very soon?
8. What is the benefit of cooking foods in the meats-to-beans group in a microwave oven?

Sharing Your Ideas

1. If you were purchasing fresh fish, in what form would you buy it? Why?
2. If you were buying a cut of meat, what factors would you take into account when making your choice? What would be the best way to cook the meat you choose?

Applying Your Skills

1. Preparing a Menu. Plan your lunches for the next week including different foods from the meats-to-beans group. Write a summary as to why you picked these items.

2. Researching a Topic. Look through a cookbook and find two recipes for chicken and two for beef. Name the cuts necessary and the methods of cooking used.

3. Comparing Fat Content. Prepare hamburger patties of equal weight from different types of ground beef, such as extra lean, lean, and chuck. Broil each patty separately for the same length of time. Compare the weight of each patty after cooking, and the amounts of fat in the broiler pan.

CHAPTER

53

Serving Meals at Home and Eating Out

OBJECTIVES

This chapter will help you to:

- Explain several ways to serve a meal at home.
- Describe some important points of table manners and etiquette.
- Demonstrate appropriate behavior in restaurants.

WORDS TO REMEMBER

buffet
etiquette
family style
flatware
menu
place setting
table service
tipping

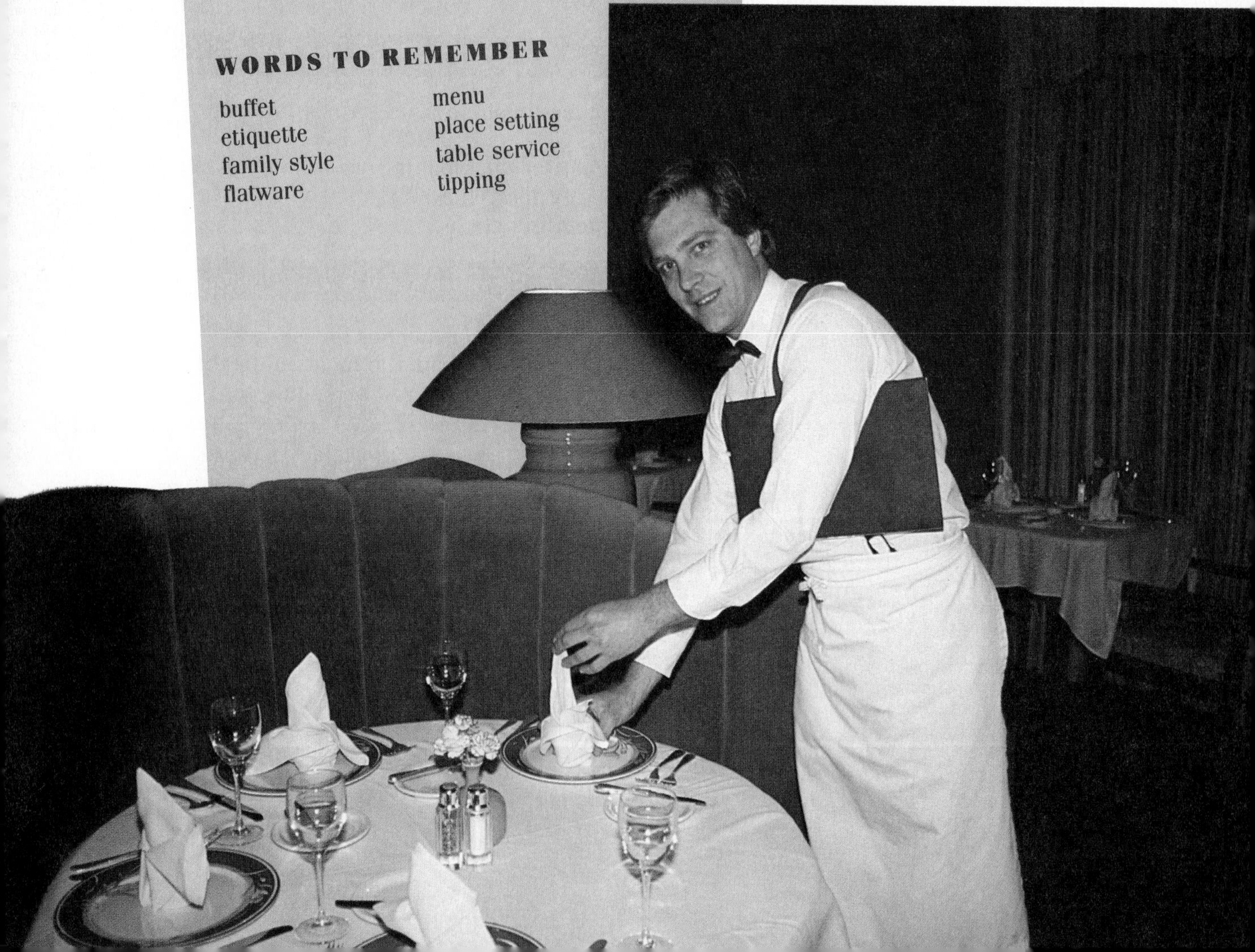

Mealtime customs differ from meal to meal, and from household to household. Some meals may be eaten almost like snacks—people help themselves to what they want. For others, the family sits down together at the table and the food is passed around in serving bowls. More formal meals, particularly when guests come over, may be served with the best dishes and table linen.

Restaurant service, too, ranges from the informal to the formal. Some restaurants serve fast foods, while others offer expensive meals in a fancy environment. This chapter will help you feel more confident in different types of eating situations.

Eating at Home

In today's busy families, meal times are often informal occasions. Each family has its own customs regarding how such meals are served and who sits where. If you are in someone else's home, you can ask what to do or watch the others and follow along.

However, even informal meals are usually served in certain customary ways. The mealtime patterns that families follow help make group meals pleasant, orderly occasions.

A Style for Each Occasion

In America, one of the most common styles of serving a sit-down meal is family style. Other styles include plate service and buffet.

- **Family style.** In **family style**, food is brought to the table in bowls and serving platters, which are passed from

person to person. Sometimes, however, the main dish—a roast or a casserole, perhaps—is served from the head of the table. Then, only the vegetables and extras like gravy are passed around the table.

- **Plate service.** Plate service means the food is put onto each person's plate in the kitchen and then brought to the table.

Buffet style is a convenient way to serve food to any size of group. The serving table can be set up indoors or outdoors.

■ **Buffet style.** When all the food is arranged on a serving table for people to select from and make up their own plates, it is called a **buffet** (buh-FAY). After choosing their food, people sit somewhere else to eat. This style of service is good for large parties—indoors or outdoors.

Buffets can be quite informal, with paper plates, or very formal; the choice depends on the occasion. For a casual buffet, the food should be easy to eat with fingers or a fork. Casseroles are often served at an informal buffet. At a formal buffet, people are usually seated at tables, so all types of food can be served.

Setting the Table

If you are helping to arrange a group meal, you may need to set the table.

■ **Place setting.** For sit-down meals, you will make individual place settings. A **place setting** is the arrangement of the tableware each diner will need for the meal. There should be a plate, a glass, a napkin, and **flatware**—knives, forks, and spoons. A more formal place setting might include additional flatware, a bread-and-butter plate, a salad plate, and perhaps a coffee cup.

In addition to the place settings, salt, pepper, and serving spoons will be needed. If the meal is to be served

A place setting includes the dishes, glasses, and flatware needed for a meal. For more formal place settings, the flatware is placed in the order in which it is used, starting at the outside and working toward the plate.

from the head of the table or in the kitchen, stack the main plates there rather than placing them at each place setting.

- **Buffet table.** A buffet table should be arranged so that people can easily serve themselves. Put plates at the beginning so guests can take food from bowls and platters as they walk along the table. Put serving forks and spoons, gravies, and sauces near the appropriate serving dishes. Flatware, napkins, and beverages should be placed at the end or on a separate table.

- **Special touches.** When you want a meal to be something special, you can add a few decorations. A tablecloth—cleaned, pressed, and hanging evenly around the table—adds elegance. Its color should go well with the dishes and the napkins.

    You could use placemats instead of a tablecloth. You may also want to add a centerpiece, such as a flower arrangement, candles, or a decorative bowl of fruit.

Good Manners: Rules of Thoughtfulness

The food, the style of service, and the appearance of the table all help to make a meal a success and so does the behavior of the people who are there. Good manners are emphasized at mealtime because people want to have a comfortable and enjoyable experience.

The main basis of manners is thoughtfulness toward others. The way you look at mealtimes, the way you eat at the table, and how you talk to others can indicate your respect for both family and friends.

Appearance and Hygiene

Good hygiene is important not only for your own health, but for the health of others. No one wants to be passed a piece of bread by someone with filthy hands. Be sure you wash your hands before you eat. Also, use a comb or makeup *before* you sit down—not at the table.

Good manners make mealtime more enjoyable both at home and when eating out.

Etiquette at the Table

Etiquette (ET-ih-ket) means accepted customs of behavior. While good manners are generally aimed at setting people at their ease, some rules of etiquette have no logical reason—just as there is no logical reason why America chose to drive on the right-hand side of the road. However, when people follow the same customs, life can seem much calmer and easier.

Here are some points of table etiquette that could help you if you are invited to a luxury restaurant or a dinner party.

- **Dealing with flatware.** Formal place settings are laid with flatware for the first course placed on the outside, flatware for the second course inside that, and so on. For each course, always use the outermost knife, fork, or spoon.

- **Using a soup spoon.** Dip the far side of the spoon into the soup first. Then raise the spoon to your lips and quietly sip the soup from the near side of the spoon. For the last spoonfuls, tip the bowl away from you.

- **Eating bread.** Use your hands to break off a bite-sized piece of bread or roll when you want to eat it, instead of biting into the entire piece or cutting with a knife.

- **Cutting up foods.** Cut one or two bites as you need them, rather than cutting up all your food before you start eating.

Then place your knife on the edge of the plate as you eat the food with a fork.

- **Eating finger foods.** At home and in informal restaurants it may be acceptable to eat chicken, chops, and french fries with your fingers. At more elegant parties and restaurants, however, only a very few foods are "finger foods"—celery and carrot sticks, olives, bread and rolls, cookies, and some small appetizers.

- **Signaling that you have finished.** The accepted custom is to place your knife and fork together across the center of your plate. This tells your hosts, waiter, or waitress that you are done.

Think It Through

1. Some people dislike many of the rules of etiquette, finding them senseless and inconvenient. Others enjoy learning to follow the accepted customs. Can you come up with two arguments to support one side, and two to support the other?

2. What unusual foods have you seen eaten, or what common foods have you observed people eat in unusual ways? Describe the methods used, and try to think why these methods might have been developed.

Eating the Meal

When the serving bowls are passed around, use the serving forks and spoons, not your own flatware, to serve yourself. This is especially important when you are taking a second helping. Also, if you can't reach a serving dish, ask someone to pass it to you instead of reaching across the table.

At most meals you should not start eating until everyone is served. An exception, however, is when a parent or host urges you to start while the food is hot.

Try not to take large bites of food, and don't speak with your mouth full or blow on your food. Doing so might offend—or even spatter—others at the table. Don't eat with your elbows resting on the table, and keep your napkin on your lap except when you need to use it. If you must remove something from your mouth, don't spit it out; calmly use your hand or a spoon and place the food on the edge of your plate. "Etiquette at the Table" on page 478 gives other tips on good manners while eating.

Conversation

Mealtime conversation is an important part of dining, and it should be pleasant and enjoyable. For many families, mealtime provides an opportunity to talk about the day's events, share ideas, and enjoy each other's company. Meals are a time for warmth and friendship, not for arguments or disputes between family or friends.

When you're a guest at a friend's home, don't leave without thanking your friend's parents. A special word of thanks for the food and hospitality is always appreciated.

Eating Out

Good manners are as important for eating out as they are for eating at home. When you eat out, however, there are other considerations, too—the type of restaurant you choose, what you select to eat, and how to interact with the restaurant staff.

Types of Restaurants

There are four main types of restaurants:

- **Fast-food restaurants.** You're probably very familiar with the fast-food restaurants in your town, since they're often popular spots for young people. Many fast-food restaurants specialize in hamburgers, tacos, fish, or chicken. They may also offer items such as salads, baked potatoes with toppings, and breakfast foods. They're usually clean, bright, and inexpensive. You order food at a central area, then take it to a table—and you may be responsible for cleaning up afterward. You can also take your food home to eat.

- **Family-style restaurants.** These places include coffee shops, diners, and specialty restaurants like those that cook only steak or fish. The term can be applied to any restaurant with a casual atmosphere and good, simple food—meat and potatoes, egg dishes, salads, and hot and cold sandwiches. Usually, these restaurants offer **table service**, in which waiters and waitresses take your order at the table, bring the food, and clean up after the meal.

- **Ethnic restaurants.** These places specialize in food from other countries, such as Italian or Japanese, or from special regions, such as Cajun or Southern. The number of ethnic res-

Different types of restaurants offer different types of service. Sometimes the check is paid at the table; other times you pay a cashier as you leave. The standard tip for service is 15 percent of the bill.

Feel free to ask waiters and waitresses any questions you have about the food, such as how it's prepared. You might even ask for their advice about what to order. Don't forget to consider what other foods you've already eaten that day or plan to eat later. For example, if you didn't eat a vegetable or fruit at lunch, be sure to choose at least one for your dinner. Good nutritional choices are as important when you eat out as when you eat at home.

taurants in the United States has grown recently because of Americans' increasing interest in different food traditions. Ethnic restaurants allow people to sample unusual foods. They can be casual, family style, or elegant, and often offer take-out foods.

■ **Luxury restaurants.** Such restaurants offer specially prepared food in elegant surroundings. Luxury restaurants provide their customers with excellent personal service. They're often chosen by business people who want to entertain clients, or by families who are celebrating a special occasion, such as a birthday or anniversary.

Looking at the Menu

The kind of food you order depends on your likes and dislikes. Start by checking the **menu**, the list of foods that the restaurant offers. As extra help, some restaurants put pictures of their food on the menu, on table displays, or on the walls.

Restaurant Service

When you enter a restaurant for the first time, look around. Is this an informal restaurant where you seat yourself? Sometimes a sign asks you to wait to be seated. If you see such a sign, wait until a host or hostess comes to take you to your seat.

If you wish to get the attention of a serving person to make a request, never shout. Speak in an ordinary voice as he or she passes your table. If the waiter or waitress is across the room, raise your hand and try to catch his or her eye.

After you have received the bill, quickly add it up to be sure that the total is correct. If there has been a mistake, as occasionally happens, bring the error politely to the server's attention. It will be taken care of quickly.

Tipping—giving extra money to waiters and waitresses for good service—is customary in all table-service restaurants. Usually, 15 percent of the cost of the food (before taxes) is an acceptable tip. Many customers tip 20 percent of the food's cost in luxury-class restaurants.

CHAPTER

53 REVIEW

Reviewing the Facts

1. What is the difference between a family-style dinner and a buffet?
2. Draw or describe a simple place setting.
3. What should you say to the host or hostess when leaving a home after a meal?
4. What are the four types of restaurants?
5. What should you consider when looking at a menu?
6. How should you get a food server's attention?

Sharing Your Ideas

1. If you were inviting a large number of people over for dinner, what serving style would you use? Why?
2. What are some advantages and disadvantages of the various types of restaurants? Which type of restaurant do you eat in most often?

Applying Your Skills

 1. Planning a Meal. Plan a buffet-style meal for a group of 30 people. Would it be formal or informal? Where would you hold it and what would you serve? What would you do differently if you were serving a group of ten people? Write a detailed account.

 2. Creating a Poster. Create a poster illustrating one or more rules of etiquette. You could use cartoon or stick figures and a humorous approach, if desired.

 3. Ranking Preferences. Which of the four types of restaurants do you like best? Rank them by assigning a number from 1 to 5 (5 = strongly agree) depending on how well the statement reflects your feelings.
1. I like the choice of food.
2. I like the atmosphere.
3. I like the service.
4. I can afford the prices.
Add up the numbers for each type of restaurant. Is the type with the highest total the one where you eat most often? If not, why?

Careers in Food and Nutrition

OBJECTIVES

This chapter will help you to:

- Identify the interests and skills required for a career in food and nutrition.
- Give examples of jobs in food processing.
- Give examples of jobs in food service.

WORDS TO REMEMBER

apprentice
inventory
promoted

o you like to measure and combine ingredients to create a tasty bread? Do you enjoy making people feel comfortable and at ease so that they can enjoy their meal? Do you like to plan menus to meet a variety of people's needs? If your answer to any of these questions is yes, a career in foods and nutrition may be for you.

Careers in foods and nutrition are plentiful. Such jobs are among the top ten career slots in the country. These career positions range from farm workers and supermarket checkers to meat cutters and food technologists. Waiters, restaurant hostesses, chefs, and food writers for newspapers and magazines are all part of the foods and nutrition industry.

Characteristics for Careers in Foods and Nutrition

There are a variety of careers in this area, from dishwasher to chef, from food server to menu planner. While the careers vary, they all call for similar interests and skills.

Interests and Skills

- **Can you pay close attention to details?** Bakers must measure carefully, food servers must take orders accurately, and supermarket checkers must ring up the correct prices using advanced machines.
- **Are you calm under pressure?** Creating a calm atmosphere can be hard at times. The hurried pace of a restaurant kitchen or the late hours of a supermarket can put pressure on the workers.

- **Are you creative?** Chefs often need to devise new menus to satisfy tastes and attract customers. Dietitians need to create healthy recipes that are appealing to people on special diets.
- **Can you work well and get along with others?** Few people in foods and nutrition careers work alone. A restaurant staff is a team composed of waiters and waitresses, hosts and hostesses, food preparers, and dishwashers. The ability to cooperate with others is essential.
- **Do you have a pleasant and friendly personality?** Many people in this field spend much of their time working closely with the public. Helping customers feel at ease and happy promotes business and encourages them to return.

When you are an employee, remember that customers appreciate efficient and courteous service.

■ **Are you interested in knowing about food and food preparation?** The short-order cook must know the correct cooking time for hamburgers. The dishwasher must know how to make plates and utensils sanitary.

If you have these characteristics, a career in foods and nutrition may be for you. In the next few pages, you can learn about some of these careers. There are many more, of course, but this chapter will give you a sampling of what's available in this field.

Jobs in Food Processing

Many food careers involve producing and selling food products. Some people in these careers grow the food we eat, while others make sure that the food is of good quality. Still others deal directly with the consumer, selling food in supermarkets or other stores.

Entry-Level Jobs

Canners are the people who process foods in cans, bottles, and cardboard cartons. Their work includes washing, peeling, pitting, and cooking the food. Some food is processed entirely by machinery, but delicate foods must be prepared by hand. Food processing jobs may be seasonal.

Stock clerks make sure that the shelves and refrigerated units in supermarkets are stocked with foods. They also unpack shipments of food, put prices on items, and help keep the store clean by wiping up spills and broken glass. Many stock clerks work only part-time.

Jobs That Require Training

The person who runs the supermarket is called the manager. Managers must keep track of the store's **inventory**, or the amount of each product in stock. They also oversee the store's workers and budget. Supermarket managers often have taken college courses. Many are promoted from checker to department head to store manager.

Meat cutters cut and package meat. They too may keep track of inventory and help with buying new supplies. They must be extremely careful because the equipment they use is dangerous. Most cutters learn their job by becoming **apprentices**, helpers who are trained on the job by senior workers. Others are taught in vocational or trade schools.

A quality-control inspector checks the food that is produced in the processing plant. He or she makes sure that the taste, texture, and appearance of the food is up to the company's standards. Some inspectors work for the federal government, checking the safety and cleanliness of different plants. Food inspectors are trained on the job.

Jobs That Require an Advanced Degree

Agricultural researchers study ways to make crops yield more produce, and try to develop new types of crops that resist disease. Researchers can work for the government, for universities, or for agricultural companies. They usually have advanced training beyond a college degree.

Food technologists try to improve existing methods of processing food. They work on new ways of canning, freezing, packaging, and storing foods that will cause fewer nutrients to be lost or make

A food technologist examines foods to find ways to improve nutritional content, flavor, appearance, and preparation techniques.

products easier to prepare. At the same time they are concerned with preserving a food's flavor, texture, and appearance. These scientists study chemistry and biology in college.

Jobs in Food Service

The other major group of careers in the foods and nutrition field relates to food service. People in these careers work mostly in restaurants and cafeterias, making sure that customers get the foods that they want and enjoy their meals.

Entry-Level Jobs

Waiters and waitresses are a familiar sight in many restaurants. They take customers' orders and bring them their food. The job goes beyond that, however. Many food-service workers are asked by customers to recommend dishes. Enjoyment of a meal often begins with how comfortable the waiter or waitress makes customers feel. Many of these workers work part-time. Salaries are fairly low, but tips add to income.

Dishwashers work in the kitchen removing all food and germs from plates and utensils. In smaller restaurants, they might also work at cleaning the kitchen or clearing the dining room. Dishwashing is often a part-time job.

Jobs That Require Training

A restaurant host or hostess usually learns on the job, although some take courses in food service. These workers supervise the waiters and waitresses, take reservations, greet customers, and show them to their tables. They may also operate the cash register. Many hosts and hostesses begin their careers as waiters and waitresses.

The star of a restaurant, of course, is the chef who prepares the food. A small restaurant may have only one or two chefs, but a larger one will employ many chefs. Each chef prepares a certain kind of food, such as pastries, roasts, or soups.

The head chef acts as manager of all kitchen activities. He or she also has experience with cooking, and may plan the menu and even create new dishes. Chefs spend many years learning their profession. Some attend a culinary institute, take vocational courses, or learn from other chefs.

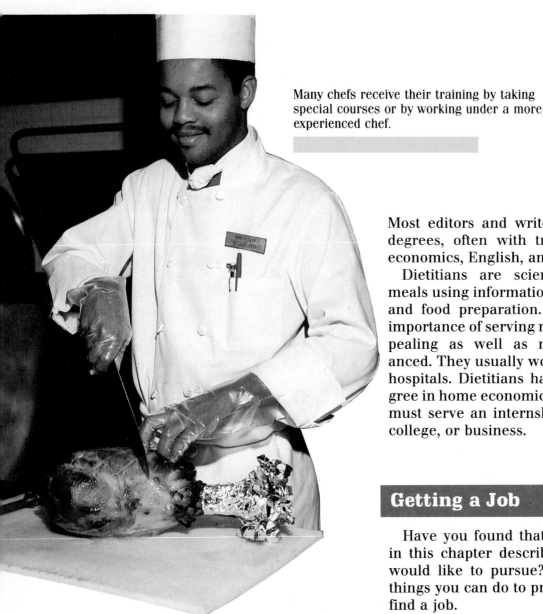

Many chefs receive their training by taking special courses or by working under a more experienced chef.

Jobs That Require an Advanced Degree

Editors and writers help the public learn about foods and nutrition. They write newspaper and magazine articles explaining new ways of using food or describing the latest discoveries in nutrition. They also write books, and they prepare reports for food manufacturers.

Most editors and writers have college degrees, often with training in home economics, English, and journalism.

Dietitians are scientists who plan meals using information about nutrition and food preparation. They know the importance of serving meals that are appealing as well as nutritionally balanced. They usually work for schools or hospitals. Dietitians have a college degree in home economics or dietetics and must serve an internship in a hospital, college, or business.

Getting a Job

Have you found that the information in this chapter describes a career you would like to pursue? If so, there are things you can do to prepare yourself to find a job.

Many of these careers require a high school diploma. While you are still in school, however, you can often get a part-time job as a waiter, waitress, or stock clerk. This will give you a feel for the work and hands-on experience.

Some of the more involved careers, like dietitian or food technologist, require a college education or specialized training. The more education you have, the more responsibility you'll be prepared to handle. This will make you very valuable to your future employers.

Special Order: Your Career in Food Service

"Two cheeseburgers, a small order of french fries, and a *job*, please!" said Josie when she went to the fast-food restaurant for dinner. She had seen a "Help Wanted" sign as she walked in. It was an opportunity to learn more about the food-service field.

You too could take advantage of such an opportunity. Employee schedules in fast-food restaurants are usually flexible because managers realize that students can only work part-time. Many of their teenage employees work after school and on weekends, and then full-time during the summer.

Usually you will be hired as an entry-level, general fast-food worker, to be assigned to different work stations. One day you may be responsible for cooking the hamburgers, while the next day you may be in charge of the french fries.

Doing a good job and conveying your interest to your supervisors can help you get **promoted**, or advanced, to a position of higher rank and greater responsibility, such as assistant manager. Assistant managers supervise general workers, keep track of inventory, count money in the cash registers, and deal with any customer complaints. When the restaurant gets busy, they often pitch in to help the general workers.

Later you could be appointed store manager, overseeing all of the restaurant employees. Store managers look after everything from maintaining the health and cleanliness standards of the store, to hiring and firing employees. A successful store manager might one day become an executive who manages a whole region or takes care of services like advertising and transportation.

As an employee in a fast-food restaurant, you will gain valuable experience, work with people your own age, and make money. So go ahead, put in your order for a food-service career!

Think It Through

1. In what ways do you think being a fast-food worker could prepare you for a food-service career? Would you consider taking such a job? Why or why not?

2. What points would you bring up if you were trying to convince your superior that you deserve a promotion?

Reviewing the Facts

1. List four interests and skills useful for a career in foods and nutrition.
2. What are the two general fields foods and nutrition can be divided into?
3. What is a store's inventory?
4. What does a food technologist do?
5. List some functions of a chef.
6. Describe the work of a dietitian.
7. How can you prepare for a job in food processing or food service?

Sharing Your Ideas

1. Would you prefer working at a food-processing plant that uses a lot of machinery, or one that requires people to work by hand? What do you see as the advantages of each method for the worker, the plant owner, and the public?
2. What are some traits a waiter or waitress should have? How could these be important to the server, the customer, and the restaurant?

Applying Your Skills

 1. Researching a Topic. Choose any career in this chapter and read about it in a book selected from your school library. Write a short summary including a job description, education and training requirements, and salary information.

2. Making a Plan. Pretend you are opening a new restaurant. Describe how you would go about hiring workers and what skills they would need. Research how you would go about getting supplies. Write a paper describing your findings.

3. Analyzing a Situation. Choose any career in this chapter, and pretend you were hired for such a position. Describe a situation that you might encounter on your first day on the job. How should you handle the situation? What skills would you need?

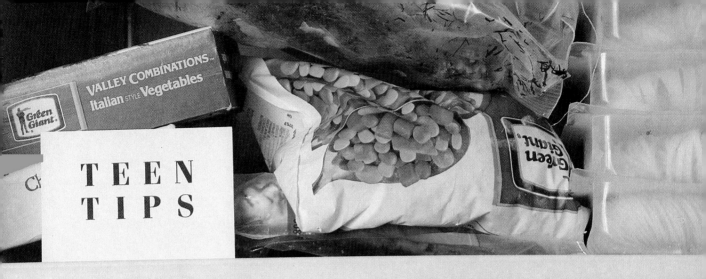

TEEN TIPS

50 Snacks Under 75 Calories

Would you rather snack on fresh fruit or chips? Here's how their calories compare.

Breakfast On-the-Run

If you'd rather sleep than eat, here are some quick breakfasts to get you going in the morning.

Fast Foods: Cutting the Calories

How to eat better and healthier in a fast food restaurant, without becoming a slave to the salad bar.

50 Snacks under 75 Calories

Do you need a quick snack after school or to get you through the evening? All of these snacks are under 75 calories—but you have to watch some amounts carefully, or the calories will add up fast!

FROM THE GARDEN

Artichoke, 1 medium	53
Carrot, raw, 1 cup	45
Cauliflower, florets, 1 cup	28
Celery, 7 large ribs	49
Mushrooms, 10	50
Potato, baked, 1/2 medium	73
Snow Peas, cooked, 4 ounces	49

FRESH FRUIT

Apple	75
Apricots, 4	72
Banana, 1/2	50
Blueberries, 3/4 cup	68
Grapefruit, 1/2 medium	40
Grapes, 1 cup	70
Kiwi	60
Orange	60
Peach	40
Strawberries, 1 cup	55
Watermelon, diced, 1 cup	42

SAY CHEESE

Cottage Cheese, low-fat, 1/3 cup	67
Parmesan, grated, 2 tablespoons	55
Provolone Cheese, 1/2 ounce	50

TEEN TIPS

ODDS 'N' ENDS

Almonds, 8 whole	48
Dill Pickle, medium	8
Green Olives, 15 large	68
Pecan Halves, 9	72
Yogurt, low-fat, lemon, vanilla, coffee, 4 ounces	75

SWEET TALK

Animal Crackers, 7	74
Graham Crackers, 4	60
Chocolate Kisses, 3	72
Oatmeal Cookie, 2 1/2" diameter	60
Mini Marshmallows, 24	40

MUNCHIES

Date-Nut Bread, 1 ounce slice	40
Goldfish Crackers, 25	75
Popcorn, unbuttered, 3 cups	69
Potato Chips, 6	66
Pretzel Logs, 3" unsalted, 3	59
Raisins, 1 ounce	75
Rice Cakes, 2	70
Rye Toast Crackers, 4	64
Taco Chips, 1/2 ounce	64

SIPPERS

Milk, low fat, 8 ounces	75
Apple Juice, 6 ounces	60
Beef Bouillon, 1 cup	30
Orange Juice, reconstituted, 6 ounces	68
Tomato Juice, 1 cup	45

POWER FROM PROTEIN

Chicken Roll, 2 ounces	75
Ham, extra-lean, 2 ounces	74
Hard-Cooked Egg, medium	72
Peanut Butter, 2 teaspoons	60
Shrimp, 10 medium	37

Breakfast On-the-Run

No other meal is skipped as often as breakfast. Often the reason is "I don't have time." Yet breakfast gives you the energy you need to start the day. Here are 15 breakfast ideas that take only a minute or two to prepare:

1 Toss your favorite fruit juice in a blender and add milk or yogurt, a banana, and some ice. If desired, add a dash of cinnamon or nutmeg.

2 Sprinkle grated cheddar or mozzarella cheese on an English muffin or pita bread. Pop in a microwave or toaster oven until the cheese melts.

3 Top a bowl of yogurt with granola, wheat germ, coconut, or raisins—or all four!

4 Spread peanut butter on rice cakes or whole-wheat bread and sprinkle with sunflower seeds.

5 Warm up a leftover slice of pizza. You'll get three or four of the basic food groups in one quick breakfast.

6 On a cold morning, nothing beats a bowl of hot cereal. Try the instant varieties that cook in a microwave oven. Top with a banana or fresh strawberries.

T E E N   T I P S

7 Raid the refrigerator and eat a leftover chicken leg.

8 Make an open-faced sandwich with leftover meat or a sliced hard-cooked egg. Top with a slice of cheese and melt quickly in a microwave or toaster oven.

9 Add sliced peaches or berries to cold cereal.

10 Make a homemade trail mix ahead of time. Combine 3 cups Chex cereal, 1 cup sunflower seeds, 1 cup nuts, and 1 cup raisins. Spread on a baking sheet and bake 8-10 minutes at 375°F. Store mix in individual plastic bags and enjoy for breakfast with a frozen yogurt bar.

11 Stuff celery with peanut butter or cottage cheese mixed with raisins.

12 Grab a whole-grain muffin and a slice of individually wrapped cheese to eat on the way out the door.

13 Keep low-fat yogurt and yogurt drinks in convenient serving-size containers in the refrigerator. Eat the yogurt with a banana, orange, apple, pear, or grapes.

14 Try cream cheese and a tomato slice on a bagel.

15 Keep a supply of emergency rations such as peanut butter, whole-grain crackers, and raisins in your locker for when you need a morning pick-me-up. That way you can avoid the candy machines.

Fast Foods ✂ Cutting the Calories

Did you know that a fried chicken dinner—or a burger, fries, and a shake—can have more than half the calories you need for an entire day! Many fast foods are high in fat, salt, and sugar, but must you always limit yourself to the salad bar? Here's some help in making good choices when you're choosing from a fast-food menu:

T E E N   T I P S

- Order what you want on your burger. Fast-food beef is usually lean, but the special sauces and mayonnaise boost up the calories and fat content. Instead, top your burger with lettuce and tomato.

- Skip the french fries and order a baked potato or mashed potatoes instead. Remember, however, that adding lots of butter, sour cream, or gravy quickly increases the calorie count.

- Watching the sodium? Hold the pickles and don't add extra salt to your food.

- Order skim milk instead of a milkshake.

- Save 85 calories on the fast-food chicken by not ordering the extra crispy. Cut even more calories and fat by removing the breading and skin from the chicken.

■ Looking for all four basic food groups in one item?
Order pizza or tacos.

■ Try some chili—it has less calories than a burger.

■ Skip the snack-type fruit pies and other sugary
desserts. Eat a piece of fresh fruit instead.

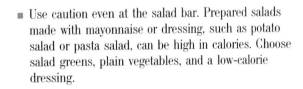

■ Use caution even at the salad bar. Prepared salads
made with mayonnaise or dressing, such as potato
salad or pasta salad, can be high in calories. Choose
salad greens, plain vegetables, and a low-calorie
dressing.

CLOTHING AND TEXTILES

Clothing and You

The first decision you have to make nearly every day of your life is what to wear. One day you want to feel comfortable, and you don't really care what others think of your clothes. On another day you dress so you can fit in with your friends. Some days you have to dress up for a special occasion. There are also days when nothing in your closet seems to suit you.

Experimenting with clothing is part of finding out about yourself. As you try different styles and fashions, you learn what kinds of clothes make you feel comfortable—with yourself and with others.

The choices you make about clothes depend on many things:

- Your self-concept.
- Your personality.
- Your coloring and body type.
- The climate you live in.
- Your activities and interests.
- The groups you belong to.

Clothing Choices

Some clothing choices depend on your activities. You need certain clothing for school, other outfits for special occasions, and some comfortable clothes for exercise or relaxation. You may also select clothes based on the weather. Heat, cold, sun, rain, and snow all affect your choice of clothing.

Some choices are not so clear-cut. You may need to make a decision between what you want and what you need, considering the amount of money that you have to spend.

In making these choices you have to decide what is important to you. Do you want to dress like your friends or in your own way? Do you want clothes that are easy to care for, or are you willing to iron some items? Do you like to sew, or would you rather buy your clothes ready-made?

Your clothing choices can tell others something about your personality, your interests, and your values.

The other members of your family may have different factors to consider when selecting their clothing:

- **Occupation.** Where a family member works influences the kinds of clothing chosen. A person who works outdoors has different needs from an office worker, and someone who wears a uniform to work does not need as large a wardrobe as someone who works in an office or retail store.
- **Type of community.** The type of community your family lives in can affect clothing choices. For example, small towns usually have a more casual style of dress than large cities.
- **Family structure.** People have different needs at different times in their lives. Young children, who quickly outgrow their clothes, are often dressed in inexpensive, practical outfits. Many older children are involved in activities such as sports and dancing, which require special clothing. A family member who has retired might prefer casual clothing to business attire. A family member who is disabled might have special clothing needs.
- **Values.** Family values also influence clothing choices. Some families value easy care in clothes. Others like handmade items, such as hand-knitted sweaters. Still others might favor designer labels.

Clothes and Your Appearance

Clothes are like the wrapping on a package. When you meet people for the first time, you often make a judgment about them based on the way they are dressed, just as you might guess what is in a package according to the way it is wrapped.

Your clothing tells others about your lifestyle, your interests, and how you feel about yourself. Your willingness to select your clothes carefully and keep them in good condition indicates that you feel good about yourself and take pride in your appearance.

Expressing Your Personality

Your clothes also express your personality. If you wear unusual clothes that set you apart from the crowd, you may like to show your **individuality,** the ways in which you are different from others. You think for yourself and enjoy being original.

When you wear the same type of clothing that your friends wear you dress to **conform**—to be like the people around you. Being part of the group makes you feel comfortable. Can you conform and still be an individual? Even if everyone in your group wears jeans and T-shirts to an event, the design, style, and color of your T-shirt is your special choice.

The colors you choose often reflect your inner feelings and preferences. When you wear cool, quiet colors such as soft blue or green, you may be showing a calm mood. Bold, bright colors and splashy prints show the fun-loving, outgoing side of your personality.

Making You Look Better

You can use your clothing to change your appearance. Some designs make your shoulders look broader or your body seem slimmer. Color and accessories can call attention to your best features. For example, you might use a wide belt to highlight your slim waist or a shirt with a contrasting collar to accent your face.

Which styles and colors are best for you? You can learn how to select clothing that will accent your best features.

Colors play an important part in the way you look. The same style can have different effects in different shades, depending upon your skin tone and hair color.

Learning how color and design can change your appearance will help you make clothing decisions. You'll be able to choose clothes that express your personality and help you look your best. Chapter 56 has more information about using color and design to enhance your appearance.

Clothes and Comfort

Comfort has a lot to do with clothing choices. It's hard to be good-tempered if you're shivering with cold, or if the sandals you're wearing on city streets are made for use on the beach.

Dressing for Climate and Weather

If you are like most people, you will switch on a weather report or glance outside before deciding how to dress for the day. On a cold day, you might wear a parka, a hat, gloves, and boots for comfort. Underneath your parka you might wear a sweater and a shirt. Wearing several layers of clothing helps the body to retain heat.

If the weather is warm, you will probably wear light-colored, loose-fitting clothing. You will wear less clothing than in cold weather, so that body heat can escape. In hot climates people often cover their heads to protect themselves from the sun. Raincoats and umbrellas offer protection from the rain.

Dressing for Activity

You also select clothing based on what you do. In a given day, you probably participate in a variety of activities. You may go to school, practice with a sports team, work at a job, play in the marching band, go out on a date. The clothing that is appropriate for one activity may not be suitable for another. Casual clothes are fine for school, but you may need to dress less casually at work. Some jobs and sports require a uniform.

Certain activities call for clothing that serves a specific purpose. A helmet protects a bicyclist's head, and shoulder pads cushion the shocks endured by a football player. Like athletes, some laborers need protective clothing, such as hard hats, fireproof suits, or plastic aprons.

Clothes and Groups

The people around you also influence your clothing choices. You are a member of many groups—your friends, your family, a club or athletic team, or a religious organization. Clothes have always been useful in identifying certain people in a community. Police and fire fighters, for example, are known by their uniforms. The business executive's suit, the cheerleader's outfit, and the bride's white gown all identify these people and what they are doing.

Belonging to a Group

Being comfortable in a group is important to nearly everyone. When you're dressed like the others in your group, you feel confident that you are a part of that group.

Sometimes people in a group dress identically, as when members of a school athletic team or band wear uniforms. Clubs may have matching jackets or sweaters. When you wear these special clothes you are identified and recognized by others as belonging to a particular group. Wearing a uniform also carries a special responsibility. You represent the entire group—the band, team, or school. Your actions tend to influence what other people think of the group as a whole.

Sometimes clothing shows favored position, or **status**, within a group. The leader of a marching band may wear a tall fur hat. Scouts wear badges on their uniforms to show that they have mastered certain skills. Some people believe that designer labels indicate status.

Respecting Others' Feelings

You usually choose what you wear based on how you feel. However, there are times when you choose clothes to show your respect for others.

If your family has a large celebration—such as a party for your grandparents' anniversary held in a restaurant—your parents want to feel especially proud of you. Dressing less casually than you usually do is an easy way to show that you care about your parents' and grandparents' feelings.

On special occasions, you are expected to wear a certain kind of clothing. Dressing in an **appropriate** manner, that is, in clothes suitable for the occasion, is important. For many of these occasions, dressing appropriately means dressing up.

- **Parties.** The person who invites you may tell you whether it is a dressy or casual party. Otherwise, ask the person who is giving the party or check on what your friends are wearing.

Uniforms identify members of a particular group and help to create a special image for the group.

- **Weddings.** Members of the wedding party often wear **formal clothes**—tuxedos for the men and long dresses for the women. The guests, however, are not required to dress formally. Females can wear knee- or calf-length dresses. For a male guest, a jacket, shirt, and tie is generally accepted.
- **Funerals.** At one time, black was considered the only proper color for funerals. This is no longer the rule everywhere; simple, dark- or neutral-colored designs are now considered appropriate.
- **Religious services.** Some groups have strict rules about dress. If you're not sure what to wear to a service or inside a particular house of worship, ask a member of the congregation.
- **Trips to stores and restaurants.** You may not be permitted to enter certain places if you are dressed inappropri-

ately. Stores in many areas are forbidden by law to admit customers who are barefoot or without shirts. Restaurants require shirts and shoes. Some insist on ties and jackets for men.

Clothing Decisions

In the following chapters of this unit, you'll learn how to make important decisions about your clothing. You'll find out how to choose fashions and designs that are right for you and how to plan your wardrobe. You'll discover what to look for when buying clothes and which stores to shop in. You'll learn how you can make your own clothes and choose the patterns and fabrics that are best for you. In addition, you'll find out how to care for your clothes so they'll look better and last longer.

INTERPERSONAL SKILLS

Peer Pressure and Clothes

How much time do you and your friends spend talking about clothes, shopping together, or reading the fashion magazines to see what other people your age are wearing? Keeping up with the current clothing styles may be an important interest that you share with your peers.

Clothing expresses the behavior, tastes, and interests of a group. If a style is popular with a group you belong to, you will probably want to wear it to show that you are part of that crowd. You may even change your style of clothing in order to gain acceptance in a group.

A group of peers can have a positive influence on your clothing choices. Your peers can, for example, help you journey toward independence. Perhaps your parents no longer choose your clothing or tell you what to wear. Shopping with your friends can help you adjust to this new responsibility.

Your peers can also help you develop your self-concept. When you dress to identify with a group, you are making a choice about who you want to be. You are showing that you care about yourself and how you look.

Peers can also help you learn appropriate behavior. By dressing like the group you learn the acceptable standards for your age, lifestyle, and society. From your friends you learn how to deal with new situations.

Although a group of friends can provide positive support, a group may also have a negative influence. The group may pressure you to adopt a style that causes conflict with your parents or another group to which you belong.

Some groups may put pressure on you to wear only designer labels. If you don't wear a certain brand, you will not be considered part of the group. What if you simply cannot afford expensive designer jeans?

In addition, peer pressure to conform can suppress your individuality. In all the choices you make, be sure to pay attention to your own feelings and values. If they are different from what the group demands, you may need to say no—or find another group that better reflects what is important to you.

Think It Through

1. What positive influences has your peer group had on your appearance?
2. Describe an occasion when you had a conflict with someone because you expressed your individuality through your clothing. How did you feel about it?

CHAPTER
55 REVIEW

Reviewing the Facts

1. List five factors that affect clothing choices.
2. What does your clothing tell other people about you?
3. How is your personality expressed through your clothing?
4. What type of clothing do you need for a hot climate? What type of clothing do you need for a cold climate?
5. Why does wearing a uniform carry a special responsibility?
6. Give an example of clothing that shows status.
7. What is meant by dressing appropriately?
8. List four occasions for which it is usually necessary for people to dress a certain way.

Sharing Your Ideas

1. Give three examples other than those discussed in the chapter in which appropriate dress is important. Discuss why.
2. How have your clothing tastes changed in recent years? Can you identify the reasons why they have changed?

Applying Your Skills

1. Writing a Description. Write a humorous short story in which a character finds himself or herself in a social situation wearing inappropriate clothing.

2. Using Reference Materials. Select a country that interests you. In the library, research the traditional clothing for males and females of that country. Find out how the clothing reflects the climate, lifestyle, and culture of the country. Are traditional clothes still worn today? Prepare a report for the class. Include drawings or photos.

3. Presenting Two Sides of an Issue. List two activities or jobs that require a uniform, and explain the advantages or disadvantages of the uniform in each example.

Design and Your Appearance

Rita was trying to decide what to wear to school. She wanted to look especially nice, and she was looking forward to wearing the blouse she had just bought. As she tried on the blouse with a few different skirts, she realized that it just didn't look as good on her as it did in the store window. For some reason, her old plaid blouse seemed to give her face more color and sparkle. Maybe that's why she got compliments every time she wore it.

Have you ever wondered why you look better in some clothes than others? Why doesn't everyone look great in the same outfit? You will discover the answers to these questions as you study the elements of design as applied to clothing.

Elements of Design

Deciding what to buy and which article of clothing to combine into an outfit are some of the most common clothing decisions you will make. To choose wisely, you need to be aware of the basic elements of design and how they can be used to create pleasing effects in clothing.

If you look carefully at any garment, you can pick out the five elements of design:

- Line.
- Shape.
- Space.
- Texture.
- Color.

All five design elements affect the way clothing makes you appear to yourself and others.

Line

The stripes on a shirt, the creases in a pleated skirt, and the seams on a pair of jeans are examples of line. Line defines the form of a garment. Line can also be used to create an **illusion**—an image that fools the eye.

Vertical lines can make you look taller and thinner. Because these lines lead the eye up and down, the distance from side to side seems less significant.

Horizontal lines have the opposite effect. They lead the eye from side to side, making the wearer seem shorter and broader. Wide waistbands and belts and wide horizontal stripes are lines that make you look heavier.

Diagonal lines can give the illusion of either height or width, depending on their length and angle. Curved lines, such as the curved front of a vest, create a softer effect than either vertical or horizontal lines.

Shape

The outline of a garment is its shape. A leotard closely follows the shape of the body. A dress that is loose and full creates a triangular shape. A shirt that hangs straight from the shoulders creates a boxy shape. The shape of a garment can cover up or draw attention to certain parts of your body. As you choose clothing, you need to consider the way the garment's shape accents your best features or hides those that are not your best.

Space

Space is the area between or inside lines. One way to think of space is as the entire area within a garment. Garment lines break up this total space. Pockets,

LINE
vertical vs horizontal

PROPORTION
short vs long

TEXTURE
smooth vs bulky

PRINTS
small vs large

COLOR
solid color vs
contrasting colors

seams, buttons, and trim divide a garment into different shapes. For example, a belt at the waist of a dress breaks the dress up into two spaces.

Proportion is the relationship between spaces within a garment. Proportion in a man's suit would be the length of the jacket in relation to the length of the pants.

By changing the proportions of your clothes, you can change the way you look. For example, a short, waist-length jacket can make your legs look longer. A long, hip-length jacket can make your legs seem shorter and your upper body look longer.

Patterns within an outfit have proportion, too. These should be appropriate in size to the person wearing the clothing. Large plaids and prints look better on a tall person. A short person should choose smaller plaids and prints.

Texture

Texture is the way a fabric looks and feels. Leather is smooth and slippery. Denim is rough and rugged. Corduroy is ribbed and bulky. Texture can also create illusions. Bulky fabrics usually make you look heavier. Smoother fabrics tend to make you look slimmer.

Not all textures are equally appropriate in all situations. Some textures, such as bulky, ribbed sweaters, are traditionally casual. Fabrics that reflect light and have a shimmery texture—such as velvet, satin, and taffeta—are dressy and suitable for formal occasions.

Color

You will learn about color and its many effects in the following section.

Understanding Color

If you ever told a friend that your new shirt was light, bright, fire-engine red, you were describing the shirt's color. Color is an element of design which is described in terms of hue, value, and intensity.

Hue is a specific color name such as green, red, or blue-violet. A color wheel is an arrangement of basic hues. It shows how the colors are related to each other. Although there are hundreds of hues, they are all blends of the three primary colors: red, yellow, and blue.

A secondary color results when two primary colors are mixed in equal amounts. Orange, green, and violet are the secondary colors. Orange is a mixture of red and yellow, and appears on the color wheel halfway between these hues. Green is a mixture of blue and yellow, and violet is a mixture of red and blue.

Other hues can be made by mixing the primary colors in different amounts. For example, both pine trees and olives are green, but they are two different hues. The green of a pine tree has more blue than yellow in it. The green of an olive has more yellow than blue in the blend.

White, black, and gray are considered neutrals. They are not included on the color wheel, but they are used to create different values of a hue. **Value** is the lightness or darkness of a color. Darker values result when black is added to a hue. These darker values are shades of the hue. Burgundy is a shade of red. When white is added to a basic hue it creates a tint of that color. Pink is a tint of red.

Intensity is the brightness or dullness of a color. Hot pink and lemon yellow are bright. They are high in intensity. Subdued colors like navy blue and rust are low in intensity.

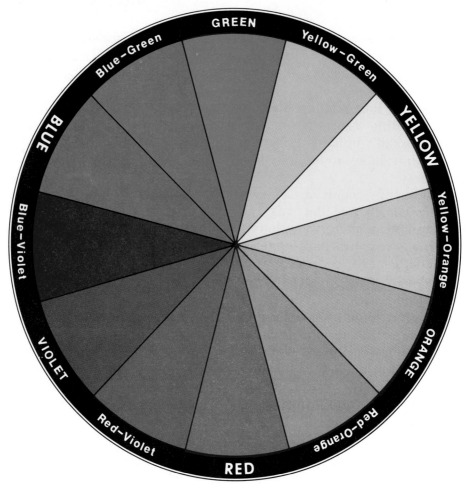

THE COLOR WHEEL
All the colors on the color wheel are blends of the three primary colors—red, yellow, and blue.

Color Schemes

How do you put colors together for a pleasing effect? The color wheel is useful for making up combinations or color schemes. There are three common color schemes.

A **monochromatic color scheme** uses variations of the same color. If you wore a light blue sweater and dark blue pants, your outfit would be monochromatic.

An **analogous color scheme** uses colors that are closely related, such as yellow, yellow-orange, and orange. If you topped your blue pants with a blue-green sweater, your color scheme would be analogous.

A **complementary color scheme** uses colors that are direct opposites on the color wheel, such as red and green. Different values and intensities can also create an interesting effect. Suppose you decide to use the complementary colors blue and orange in an outfit. With pants that are navy blue (a shade of blue), you may choose a peach (a tint of orange) sweater for a pleasant complementary color combination.

Visual Effects of Color

Like the other four elements of design, color can be used to create illusions. Colors that are light and bright tend to make a person look larger. Warm colors, such as red, yellow, and orange, also give the appearance of added weight. Darker shades and less intense colors tend to minimize size, as do the cool colors, blue, green, and violet.

If you wear a solid color outfit, you will probably seem taller. Contrasting colors, such as a yellow shirt and dark blue pants, break up the outfit and can make you appear shorter.

Contrasting colors can also create emphasis, or a center of attention. For example, a bright contrasting scarf or tie at your neckline draws attention to your face. Contrast can emphasize your best features and draw attention away from other areas.

When choosing colors to wear, consider your personal coloring. Your eyes, hair, and skin have their own combinations of tones. Your wardrobe can include a variety of colors, but you should

learn which values and intensities of a color look best on you: a clear green, forest green, mint green, blue-green, or olive green. Some people look best in bright, bold colors. Others find that softer, paler colors are most attractive. Ask a friend to help you analyze what looks best on you.

The Whole Effect

Your appearance is created by the lines, shapes, and spaces found in your clothing, combined with texture and color. When you know how these elements work together, you can choose clothes that are right for you.

Take a look at some of your favorite outfits. What features make them look especially good on you? Could using the same design elements in the same way work for other outfits?

Don't be afraid to try a style or color that you've never worn before. You may discover a look that suits you perfectly.

Study your skin, eyes, and hair coloring to determine which colors look best on you. What colors do you recommend that each of these teens wear?

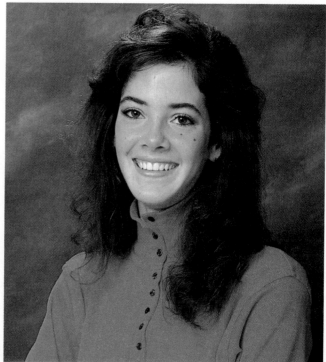

Paying Compliments

When people comment on something that is attractive about you, it makes you feel good and builds your self-esteem. When a person has self-confidence and a positive self-image, that person can acknowledge good things in someone else with a compliment.

A compliment is an expression of esteem or admiration, given freely and honestly. A true compliment is not given to get something in return. If you compliment Mark on his haircut only because you want him to help you with your math homework, you have not been fair to him or yourself.

Avoid the "backhanded compliment," one that masks a criticism. If you said "Hey,

Mark, your haircut looks nice. It was much too long before," you would actually be criticizing Mark, not complimenting him.

Be careful not to go too far in the other direction. Be generous, but don't say something that isn't true. Most people can spot insincere flattery immediately.

One way to give compliments is to ask people about themselves. Most people like to talk about their hobbies and other concerns. Maybe you noticed a piece of jewelry that a friend received as a gift. Asking about it shows your interest and approval.

For many people, however, responding to a compliment is much harder than giving one. The best answer is a simple "Thank you" or "Thanks." Avoid

belittling yourself or the compliment by saying something such as, "Oh, I never like the way my hair looks." That makes the person who gave the compliment feel silly for saying it. And don't feel you have to give a compliment in return. Just accept and enjoy the fact that someone appreciates something good about you.

Think It Through

1. Think of a compliment that you gave to someone. How did you feel after you gave this person a compliment? How do you think he or she felt?
2. Why do you think some people become embarrassed when others compliment them?

CHAPTER

56 REVIEW

Reviewing the Facts

1. What are the five elements of clothing design?
2. How do vertical and horizontal lines in clothing affect a person's appearance?
3. How can proportion affect the way you look?
4. Define texture. How does texture in clothing affect a person's appearance?
5. Name the primary and secondary colors.
6. What is the difference between value and intensity? Give examples of each.
7. Give an example of each of the three common color schemes.
8. What aspects of your own appearance should you consider when choosing colors to wear?

Sharing Your Ideas

1. In terms of shape, space, and proportion, how would you describe the "look" of today's clothing? Find drawings or photographs in current fashion magazines to illustrate the elements of design in today's fashions.
2. Suppose your friend Cliff has asked you to go shopping with him and help him pick out some clothes. He is somewhat uncomfortable about his height because he is taller than most people in his class. What kinds of styles and colors would you suggest that he choose? What should he avoid?

Applying Your Skills

 1. Writing a Description. Find a picture of an outfit in a newspaper or magazine. Write a description of the clothing in terms of the five elements of clothing design.

 2. Comparing and Contrasting Colors. Colors are affected by different types of light. Examine several colored fabrics under incandescent light, fluorescent light, and natural sunlight. Describe any difference in value and intensity of each color. What similarities do you observe?

 3. Expressing Your Feelings. List the colors on the color wheel. Beside each color write the feelings that you associate with it. Compare your color associations with those of your classmates.

Clothes and Fashion

OBJECTIVES

This chapter will help you to:

■ Explain why fashions change from year to year.

■ Identify several ways in which fashions get started.

■ Distinguish between a classic fashion and a fad.

■ Describe how to display good judgment in building a wardrobe.

WORDS TO REMEMBER

classic
designer
fad
fashion
garment industry

A fashion is a style of clothing that is accepted in a society at a given time. During any one period, certain lengths, shapes, colors, proportions, and fits are favored above others. The fashion of the day sets broad guidelines that help people decide which clothes they will purchase and wear.

Today, hundreds of millions of dollars are spent on advertising to promote a certain fashion. Nevertheless, you must be careful not to build your wardrobe based on commercials and other types of persuasion. Rather, your clothing purchases should reflect:

- Your tastes.
- Your need to express yourself.
- Your lifestyle.
- Your need for comfort.

What Makes Fashion Change?

Fashion changes quickly. A certain style suddenly becomes popular and everyone seems to be wearing it. Skirt lengths go up or down; pant legs get wider or narrower; jackets are longer or shorter. Today, a new look may not replace a previous fashion, but merely add another alternative from which to choose.

Social Changes

One reason that fashions change is that people change. They have different clothing needs from those of their parents and grandparents.

When your parents, grandparents, and great-grandparents were teens, life was much more formal than it is today. Now the emphasis is on comfort and leisure, and fashion has changed to reflect this fact. Today's clothes have been adapted to the active lives people lead.

What similarities and differences are there between these two outfits? What social changes do they reflect?

Technical Changes

Some new fashions result from changes in technology. The new fibers and fabrics that can now be produced are easier to care for and more comfortable to wear than the fabrics available to previous generations. For example, knit and stretch fabrics can be used for all types of clothing. Special finishes make fabrics wind-resistant and water-resistant.

Besides creating new fabrics, technologists have changed the way fashions are produced. The development of high-speed communications and computers has enabled clothing manufacturers to see and copy fashions from anywhere in the world. A new fashion can be put into production and shipped to hundreds of stores much more quickly than before.

How Do Fashions Start?

Fashion ideas come from many different sources. Much of current fashion, however, is a reflection of our society and of the things that our society considers important.

The Garment Industry

Clothing fashions are created by the **garment industry**—the many companies involved in manufacturing clothing. A **designer** is a person who creates new styles. Designers get their ideas from many sources—history and current events; books, movies, and television; and styles of other countries. Designers also create new styles of their own based on what they feel will be acceptable to the public.

At one time high fashion—the expensive clothing created by world-famous designers—was made entirely by hand in France, which was then the center of the fashion world. The influence of the Paris fashion market is not as strong today as it used to be. Many other fashion centers, including London, Milan, Tokyo, New York, Los Angeles, and Dallas, produce original clothes.

Designer labels have become popular in recent years, mostly because they are considered to be status symbols. Many people believe that wearing such labels shows that they are in fashion. Famous labels and symbols may mean that clothes are particularly well made or well designed, but this is not always true. They are, however, usually more expensive.

Some designer labels are so popular, in fact, that counterfeit, or imitation, clothing bearing a fake label may be produced. These fashions are often made from cheaper fabrics or with poorer construction methods than are the designer fashions.

Personalities and the Media

Fashion is influenced by famous people. Millions of people notice what movie and television stars, rock singers, politicians, and athletes wear. Some fashions become popular because they're seen on a hit television show or movie.

People and events in the news also affect fashion. Clothing associated with a particular ethnic group may become fashionable if members of the group are featured in the news long enough for their fashions to capture the imagination of the public. Concerts, videos, and television bring fashions to the public instantly. Before you know it, they're available in many stores.

Blue jeans originally were considered work clothes. What other current fashions started as clothing worn for work or sports?

Groups of People

Blue jeans, overalls, and cowboy boots started out as practical work clothes. Then people began to wear these familiar garments in a new way—and they became fashionable.

Fashions like these start when a few people try out a new idea. Soon it seems that everyone is wearing the same thing. Often, no one knows who first created the fashion.

Consumer Demand

When there is a need for a different type of clothing, manufacturers start producing it. The popularity of certain sports activities and the current interest in physical fitness, for example, have created a demand for clothing that is both comfortable and functional.

Some sports, such as bicycling and running, involve speed and require a wide range of body motion. Clothing for these sports has been designed to cut down on wind resistance and increase speed. The clothes are made of stretch fabrics to provide ease of movement and comfort. Bicycle shorts and leotards are examples of fashions that allow the wearer to move freely.

Sweatsuits, T-shirts, jogging outfits, and rugby shirts were designed for active sports, but now have become fashion items. One of the reasons for their popularity with people of all ages is their comfort.

Fashions and Fads

Some fashions are popular for short periods and then suddenly lose their appeal. Other fashions are enduring favorites for several decades, even generations.

Extremes in Fashion

If the Surgeon General had been around throughout history, there might have been labels on certain clothing that said: "SURGEON GENERAL'S WARNING: The wearing of this fashion may be hazardous to your health."

You can blame the button for the development of some extreme fashions. The introduction of buttons in the thirteenth century made it possible to cut garments to fit the shape of the body. By the fourteenth century, men and women were tightly lacing and binding their bodies with stiff undergarments called corsets so that they could fit into the fashionable clothes of the time.

The dangers of the corset were many. It caused deformities of the spine, respiratory and digestive problems, and pregnancy complications. In the late 1800s doctors encouraged abolishing the corset.

In the 1920s the ideal fashion figure was a thin, boyish body. Women tightly bandaged their chests to get a stylish straight-up-and-down look. Even though most women no longer wore corsets, starvation diets became a fad. Later, very high "spike" heels for women increased the potential for ankle injuries. In addition, wearing such heels required posture adjustments that often led to back strain.

Although today's fashion trend is toward a natural look, ultra-slim fashion models and body-conscious fashions still promote fashion-related health hazards, such as fad diets.

When you choose fashions, try to think about your health as well as what is in style. Fashions will come and go, but a healthy body is an asset for your whole life.

Think It Through

1. Why might it be easier for people today to recognize dangerous fashion trends than it was for people in previous centuries?
2. Do you think their own health is a consideration for most people when they choose clothes? Explain.

Classics vs. Fads

Some styles are **classics**—they stay popular for a long time. Classics were probably worn by your parents or grandparents. They may be part of your wardrobe, too. Examples of styles that have been around for years are blazers, pullover sweaters, pleated skirts, and polo shirts.

Other fashions may gain popularity quickly, but then lose their appeal. Fashions that are very popular for a short-time are called **fads.** Hi-top sneakers with colorful laces and oversized sweaters are clothing fads that have been popular with teens in the recent past.

Other styles seem to go through fashion cycles—periods when they are in and out of fashion. Short skirts, for example, were popular in the 1920s, then again in the 1960s. They came back in style in the 1980s.

Building Judgment

It takes experience to be able to tell which styles will stay popular for a while and which will disappear quickly. One way to learn about fashion trends is to talk to one of your parents, an older friend, or even an experienced clothing salesperson. Writers in fashion magazines also give their opinions about trends. Usually styles that are simpler and less innovative are likely to last longer: a basic skirt, a solid-color blazer, or a classic shirt with a conservative collar and cuffs.

Consumer Strategy

Most wardrobes contain both fashions and fads. Fad items carefully chosen can add sparkle to your wardrobe. Although some fad items are not expensive, others cost a lot of money. In that case, a fad may be a very poor buy.

You can compromise by selecting classic styles when you make an expensive clothing purchase, and by looking for bargains when you buy fad items. T-shirts are examples of inexpensive fad clothes that can keep your wardrobe up-to-date at little cost. You can also follow fads when buying accessories, the smaller items that are not part of your basic outfits. Belts, scarves, and jewelry can perk up your clothes for a reasonable amount of money. You can look fashionable without spending more than you can afford.

Some clothing styles are classics that never go totally out of fashion. Others are fads that may be popular for only a short time.

Reviewing the Facts

1. Define the term *fashion*. List two reasons why fashions change.
2. Name one way that advances in technology affect fashion.
3. Where do designers' fashion ideas come from?
4. How do famous people influence fashion?
5. What are three examples of clothing classics?
6. What is the difference between a classic and a fad?
7. How can you mix fashion and fad items effectively in your wardrobe?

Sharing Your Ideas

1. Name a popular television star, movie star, or rock star who started a fashion trend. What is the fashion? When people wear this fashion what are they saying about the person who started the fashion? What are they saying about themselves?
2. Particular fashions tend to project special images. Choose a fashion popular with teens in recent years. Why do you think it was popular? What image does the fashion project?

Applying Your Skills

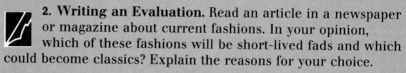

1. Judging Historical Information. Look through a book on the history of fashion and choose two illustrations. Describe each fashion to the class and tell about the time in which each fashion was popular. Could these designs be popular today? How could they be modified for today's lifestyles.

2. Writing an Evaluation. Read an article in a newspaper or magazine about current fashions. In your opinion, which of these fashions will be short-lived fads and which could become classics? Explain the reasons for your choice.

3. Comparing Prices. Look through newspapers, magazines, or catalogues for clothing with designer labels. Record the prices of three items. Then find three similarly styled garments or accessories that do not have designer labels. What is the difference in prices? How much would you save by buying the lower-priced item?

Fibers and Fabrics

OBJECTIVES

This chapter will help you to:

- Summarize the characteristics of various natural and manufactured fibers.
- Identify woven, knitted, and nonwoven fabrics.
- Describe how color applications and finishes affect clothing care.

WORDS TO REMEMBER

blend
dyeing
fabric
fiber
finish
manufactured fiber
natural fiber
yarn

Steve bought a warm-up suit that looked great in the store, but he got very little use out of it because it was not comfortable to wear. Kim spent a week sewing a pair of shorts in just the color she wanted, only to give them to her younger sister a few weeks later because they shrank when she washed them. What could have prevented these mistakes?

There are more things to know about clothing than how it looks on a hanger or even how it looks on you. One of the most important considerations is the fabric. Knowing about fabrics can help you:

- Be a smarter shopper.
- Look and feel better in your clothing.
- Get more satisfaction from the things you make.
- Care for garments correctly so they look better and last longer.

The natural fibers come from plants and animals.

COTTON
LINEN

Fibers

Fibers are the basic components of all fabrics. They are the tiny strands that, when twisted together, make up yarns. Fibers are made into yarns, yarns into fabrics, and fabrics into clothing. There are two kinds of fibers: natural and manufactured.

Natural Fibers

Natural fibers come from plants or animals.

- Cotton is the most common plant fiber. It comes from the seed pod of the cotton plant.
- Linen is another common plant fiber that comes from the stalk of the flax plant.
- Wool is from the fleece of sheep. Camels, alpacas, goats, and rabbits also provide hair that is used for speciality wool.
- Silk is made by an insect—the silkworm. The fibers come from a cocoon that the silk worm spins around itself.
- Ramie comes from the stems of china grass.

WOOL
SILK

Each natural fiber has its own special characteristics, but they all absorb moisture and allow air to reach your skin. They are comfortable to wear, keeping you warm in winter and cool in summer. Natural fibers usually require more care than manufactured fibers.

Manufactured Fibers

Until the end of the last century, all fabrics were made of natural fibers, but today many fabrics are made of **manufactured fibers.** These are fibers formed all or in part by chemicals.

Many manufactured fibers were made to replace or copy natural fibers. For instance, nylon was made to look like silk and acrylic is a substitute for wool in sweaters and blankets. One advantage of manufactured fibers is that they are easy to care for.

Characteristics of Natural Fibers

Fiber	Characteristics
Cotton	soft, comfortable, absorbent strong even when wet takes finishes well wrinkles & shrinks unless treated easily laundered
Wool	warm, retains body heat resists wrinkles naturally water repellent can shrink with heat and moisture can be damaged by moths usually drycleaned; sometimes washable
Silk	natural luster soft, flexible, but strong can be damaged by perspiration usually drycleaned; sometimes washable
Linen	comfortable, absorbent strong, but stiff wrinkles & shrinks unless treated easily laundered
Ramie	very strong, stiff natural luster absorbs moisture often combined with other fibers washable

Characteristics of Manufactured Fibers

Fiber*	Characteristics
Acetate Celanese Chromspun	attractive silk-like look soft, drapeable may wrinkle and fade, heat sensitive, usually drycleaned
Acrylic Acrilan Creslan	soft, lightweight yet warm blends with other fibers for added bulk resists wrinkles does not cause allergy heat sensitive drycleaned or laundered
Nylon Antron Cantrece	very strong, holds shape well doesn't absorb moisture heat sensitive washable, dries quickly
Polyester Dacron Fortrel Kodel Trevira	resists wrinkles blends with other fibers for wrinkle resistance holds oily stains washable, dries quickly needs little or no ironing
Rayon Avril Fibro	absorbs moisture soft and comfortable may wrinkle or shrink unless treated usually drycleaned, sometimes washable
Spandex Lycra	excellent stretch and recovery combines with other fibers for stretchability washable, avoid chlorine bleach

*Listings under each fiber type are trademark names.

Yarns

Fibers are twisted together to form **yarn.** Long, straight fibers usually create smooth, silky yarns. Short, curly fibers tend to make softer, fluffier yarns. The thickness of the yarn also depends on how tightly the fibers are spun. The qualities of the fiber and yarn affect wear and care of the fabric.

A **blend** is a yarn made from two or more different fibers. The blend can be made of natural fibers (cotton and linen), manufactured fibers (rayon and acetate), or natural and manufactured fibers (cotton and polyester). Blends combine the best characteristics of both fibers.

The percentage of each fiber in a blend determines which characteristics will dominate. A common blend for shirt fabrics is 60 percent polyester/40 percent cotton. The result is a shirt that has the good looks and comfort of cotton and the easy care features of polyester. This combination does not require ironing but may not be as comfortable as a 100 percent cotton shirt.

yarns, called the filling, is passed over and under the warp yarns in a crosswise direction.

There are three basic types of weaves:

- **Plain.** Each filling yarn passes over and under a warp yarn.
- **Twill.** Each filling yarn passes over at least two, but not more than four, warp yarns. This produces a diagonal line in the fabric.
- **Satin.** Each filling yarn passes over four or more warp yarns.

Fabrics are woven on industrial looms that produce many different variations of the basic weaves. Each weave produces a different fabric. For example, pile fabrics such as corduroy and velvet are made from three sets of yarns. The extra set of yarns forms the pile, or cut surface, on the plain, twill, or satin weave base.

The type of weave, along with the type of fiber and yarn, determines whether the fabric will be soft or crisp, smooth or textured. Woven fabrics generally hold their shape better and are stronger than knits.

Fabric Construction

Yarns are made into **fabric,** also called material or cloth. Most fabrics are made by one of three basic methods: weaving, knitting, and bonding the yarns or fibers together.

Woven Fabrics

You may have seen people weave yarn by hand on a loom. Weaving is the interlacing of yarns to form woven fabric. The warp yarns are lined up in lengthwise rows on a loom. Another set of

PLAIN WEAVE   **TWILL WEAVE**

SATIN WEAVE   **KNIT**

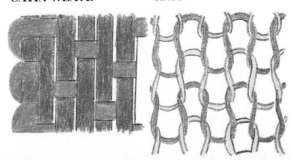

Knit Fabrics

Knitting is another way of creating fabric from yarns. Knitted fabrics are made by looping yarns together, row after row, on special knitting machines. Unlike weaving, knitting can be done with a single strand of yarn, just as people do by hand with knitting needles. Many kinds of clothing, from sport shirts and dresses to T-shirts and underwear, are made of knitted fabrics.

Knitted fabrics are comfortable because they can stretch with movement and return to their original shape. They don't wrinkle easily. Although knits do not fray or ravel, some may run if snagged.

Nonwoven Fabrics

Nonwoven refers to fabrics made from fibers that are matted or bonded together. They all share one special quality—their edges do not fray or ravel when cut. That means they need no special finishing.

Felt, a nonwoven fabric, has long been used for hats and craft projects. Other nonwoven fabrics are used on the inside of garments, to shape collars or add firmness to belts.

Certain nonwovens—called fusible webs—will melt when heat is applied. These fabrics can fuse other materials together and are used for hems or to attach trimmings.

Color and Finishes

Color is applied to fabrics by dyeing or printing. **Dyeing** is using a substance to change the natural color of a fiber, yarn, or fabric. Dyeing can be done at any stage of fabric making. Manufactured fibers and yarns can be dyed, or an entire finished fabric can be soaked in a dye bath. Designs can also be printed on the surface of fabrics using a variety of methods.

A **finish** is a substance added to a fabric to change the appearance, the feel, or the performance of the fabric. Some finishes are used to make the fabric look or feel more appealing. In napping, the fabric is brushed to raise the fiber ends. The result is a smooth, soft look. Other finishes make a fabric shinier or crisper.

Some finishes affect the performance of a fabric. How will the fabric be used? How will it wear? What care will it require? Cotton is usually preshrunk, for instance, so that it will not shrink when washed. Fabrics used for raincoats or all-weather bags usually have water-repellent finishes. Other finishes are applied to provide wrinkle resistance, stain resistance, and flame resistance.

A finish may be permanent or temporary. Special care may be needed to make the finish last longer. Some finishes, such as water-repellency, can be renewed at home or by a professional drycleaner.

Care Labels

To keep a fabric looking its best, you must care for it properly. Laws require fabric and clothing manufacturers to provide permanent labels that tell what fiber the fabric is made of and how to care for it. These labels should be on all the clothes and fabrics you buy.

Fiber content greatly determines the care your clothing requires, but you also need to consider fabric construction, fabric finishes, and the way the garment is stitched together. In Chapter 66 you will learn more about how to care for your clothing.

TECHNOLOGY

Battling the Elements

If you camp or ski, you are probably familiar with some new fabrics and what they do. Whether you need protection from rain, cold, heat, or wind, there's a fabric on the market to meet your needs. Some of these fabrics are also becoming more popular in everyday clothing.

- **Coated nylon ripstop.** This strong, lightweight fabric does not tear and is used in fabrics for ski clothing and outerwear. The strength of nylon, plus the coating, provides excellent protection from the weather.

- **Polypropylene.** This lightweight, manufactured fiber doesn't absorb moisture. It keeps your skin dry by transferring moisture outward to your next layer of clothing. Polypropylene is used in turtlenecks, underwear, hats, and gloves.

- **Teflon®.** This flame-resistant material can be adapted to fabrics so they do not melt at high temperatures.

- **Gore-Tex®.** This very thin fabric is laminated between layers of sturdier fabrics to provide water-repellency with breathability and wind resistance. It is most often used in rainwear and skiwear, such as jackets, parkas, and pants.

- **Aramid.** This fabric is similar to nylon but with flame resistance and more strength. It is currently used in astronaut's space suits but may be adapted to other uses in the future.

There have been other fabric developments. A line of liquid-cooled sportswear for joggers and other athletes has been developed by engineers who design clothes for outer space. This sportswear prevents athletes from overheating during strenuous activity. Other applications of modern technology include special-purpose clothing, such as gowns for lowering the risk of infection in surgery, and survival gear, such as bulletproof vests.

Think It Through

1. If you were a firefighter, what fibers would you want your uniform to be made of? Why?
2. Imagine a clothing fabric that would never wear out. What would be some advantages and disadvantages of such a fabric for the wearer?

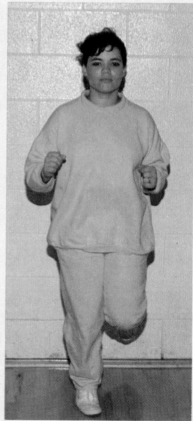

CHAPTER
58 REVIEW

Reviewing the Facts

1. How will knowing about fabrics help you make clothing decisions?
2. What are fibers? What is the difference between natural fibers and manufactured fibers?
3. Name four natural fibers. What are two advantages of natural fibers?
4. What is the advantage of a blend?
5. What is the difference between a woven fabric, a knit fabric and a nonwoven fabric? What is one advantage of each?
6. How are fabrics given color or design?
7. In what ways do finishes affect fabrics?
8. What do care labels tell us? Why are they important?

Sharing Your Ideas

1. Do you prefer garments made of natural fibers or manufactured fibers? Explain your choice.
2. What fabric characteristics would you look for in a warm-up suit intended for jogging? Which fiber, or combination of fibers, would you choose?

Applying Your Skills

1. Evaluating Consumer Information. Bring in one item of clothing from home. Examine the garment for the following information: Was the care label easy to find? Was it easy to read? Were the care instructions easy to understand? Do you have suggestions for garment manufacturers to improve their labeling? Read the notes to your class.

2. Examining Characteristics. Examine a variety of fibers and yarns under a microscope. Describe the physical characteristics of each. Using a reference book on textiles, try to identify the fibers.

3. Comparing Fabric Preformance. Select a woven fabric and a knitted fabric made of 100% cotton, and a woven fabric and a knitted fabric made of a manufactured fiber. Test each fabric for wrinkle resistance, stretchability, absorbency, and stain resistance. Wash the samples and compare appearance and shrinkage with unwashed samples. What conclusions can you make about fabric characteristics and perfomance?

Planning Your Wardrobe

OBJECTIVES

This chapter will help you to:

- Determine how well your inventory of clothes matches your clothing needs.
- Use the principle of mixing and matching.
- Evaluate different ways of adding to your wardrobe.
- Develop a wardrobe plan.

WORDS TO REMEMBER

coordinated pieces
inventory
versatile
wardrobe

ave you ever stood in front of your closet wondering what to wear? Even though there were clothes in the closet, nothing seemed quite right. You are not alone if you felt like that. Almost everyone has said "I have nothing to wear" at one time or another. What can you do to turn your closet's mistakes into a set of clothing that works?

One way to get the most out of your clothes is to plan your **wardrobe**—the clothes that you own. As you have learned, a plan helps to solve a problem or reach a goal.

A good wardrobe plan requires many decisions as you think about various aspects of your life. You need clothes that allow for physical growth and changing moods. You need different clothes for different activities.

Finally, you must consider your resources. One resource is the amount of money you have to spend. The ability to sew some of the items in your wardrobe is a resource you may be able to apply. Time for shopping or sewing is another resource you should include in your plan. By looking closely at the clothes that you have and carefully determining what you need, you can use your resources wisely.

A Wardrobe Inventory

One way to decide what clothes you need is to take an inventory of the clothes you already have. An **inventory** is a detailed list of everything on hand. Don't forget to include items that are in the wash or at the drycleaners. Your inventory can help you analyze your wardrobe and learn which clothes are best for you and your lifestyle.

What Do You Have Now?

Go through your closet and drawers and divide your clothes into three groups:

- Clothes in good condition that you like to wear.
- Clothes that you like, but that need to be repaired.
- Clothes that you don't wear because you have outgrown them, they are worn out, or you don't like them.

Make a list of the clothes in each group, noting type of clothing and color.

Start by looking at the clothes that you listed in the first group. What are the characteristics of the clothes you like? Is it the color? The texture? The style? Do you like how **versatile** they are—how many different ways you can use them? If you discover why you like some clothes, you will have set a standard for judging your entire wardrobe.

Now take a close look at the garments in the second group. By removing a stain or mending a tear, can you make these clothes wearable again? Is a favorite shirt at the back of your closet because it needs a button? Spend a few minutes fixing it and bring it back into your active wardrobe. You will learn more about clothing care and repair in Chapters 66 and 67.

By looking at the third group of clothes, you will learn the most about your clothes-buying habits. Why have you decided to put these items in the third group? If you have outgrown or worn out a shirt, do you need to replace it? Will you choose the same kind of shirt, or something different? If a pair of pants is in the group because you never wear them, can you figure out why? Are they an unflattering style or do they feel uncomfortable? Did you find that you had nothing to wear them with after you bought them?

By taking an inventory of your clothes, you can discover why you enjoy wearing some clothes more than others.

Look back at your list of clothes that you like—the first group. Can any of these items serve more than one purpose? A football jersey is a specialty item that can be combined with a pair of jeans for a casual outfit. The same is true for a leotard, which you can wear for exercise class or combine with a skirt and blouse for a layered look.

Your goal is to have a versatile wardrobe. The more uses you get from your clothes, the further your money will stretch. A shirt that can be worn in three different combinations is more practical than one that can be worn with only one other item.

Creative Combining

One way to stretch your wardrobe without buying new clothes is to combine pieces to make new outfits. Look again at your closet. You'll probably see a few things you always wear together. These may be the outfits you wear most often. If you take a new look at your clothes, you will find that you have even more possibilities if you mix and match your clothes.

Sometimes different combinations of clothes won't occur to you because you are used to wearing certain pieces together as an outfit and with nothing else. Perhaps the tan sweater will go with blue pants as well as with the brown ones. If you have a two-piece outfit, try wearing the top with different bottoms and the bottom with different tops. You will be surprised at how many different outfits you can create this way.

Types of Clothes

Your wardrobe probably consists of five basic types of clothes. They can be grouped according to their use:

- School clothes.
- Casual clothes.
- Dressy clothes for special occasions.
- Work clothes for a job or for working around the house.
- Specialty clothes, such as uniforms or swimsuits.

Create new outfits by mixing and matching your clothes. This shirt can be worn in several different ways.

Think of the variety of ways that clothes can be combined. A shirt can be worn by itself, under a sweater, or as a jacket over something else. That's one shirt and three entirely different looks. Combine a dressy item, like a silky shirt, with a more casual one, like tweed pants. By doing this, you'll get more use out of dressy garments and create an interesting new look as well.

Experiment with your accessories, too. Adding scarves, belts, ties, and vests can change the look of an outfit. Browse through fashion magazines for more ideas on how to make your wardrobe more versatile.

Adding to Your Wardrobe

Now you have looked at your wardrobe to see what you own and how to put outfits together. How do you decide what you need to add?

What Do You Need?

As you looked at your clothes, you probably realized that you should add a few items. Maybe you need a new shirt to go with a suit. Perhaps your old blue sweater should be replaced. You might have realized that a bright red belt would add color to two or three outfits.

You may need to replace some clothes for your regular activities. Think about your hobbies and other interests and write down how you dress for them. For example, you may need a swimsuit and biking shorts for the sports you participate in.

You also need to identify some clothes for activities such as parties, proms, and vacations. These special events may require additions to your wardrobe.

Changes in season may require new clothes, too. Have you outgrown last year's ski jacket? Do you need new shoes?

Deciding on Additions

When you are ready to buy new clothing, do some thinking before you begin to shop. To determine whether a specific item is important to your wardrobe, answer these questions:

- What do you really need?
- Will you be able to wear the new item for different occasions?
- Will you be able to wear the new item with other clothes in your current wardrobe?
- Can you make your wardrobe more versatile by adding accessories?

If you are going to be matching a new piece of clothing to an old one to make an outfit, you should decide which colors and fabrics will go with the item you already have.

Although you can combine colors any way you like, be aware that some combinations look better than others. For example, you probably would not want to wear a black top with navy. That combination isn't interesting because it lacks contrast. Why not add excitement by choosing a bright color instead, such as red or yellow?

Fabric and texture combinations need to be planned, too. Some textures do not work together as well as others. You may want to try to match a fabric you already have or find one that is compatible with it. Two good combinations are corduroy with tweeds and velvet with satin.

When you shop for the new addition, try to take along the article of clothing that you plan to wear with it to make sure that your new clothes will go well with what you already have. Also, think again what you like about your current wardrobe. When you are sure of the colors, textures, and styles that you prefer, you will choose additions that will please you.

A wardrobe plan can help you make decisions about what new clothes and accessories to add to your wardrobe.

Trading clothes with a relative or friend is one way to add new items to your wardrobe.

Making the Additions

You can add to your wardrobe in four ways: buying, sewing, redesigning, and trading.

- **Buying additions.** You can buy ready-to-wear clothes from stores and catalogs. By buying ready-to-wear clothes you are able to build your wardrobe with little work. Chapter 60 has information on how to shop for clothing.

- **Sewing additions.** You can choose to make your clothes. Being able to sew gives you a chance to make a garment that's exactly what you want. When you gain experience, you might even design your own clothes.

  Sewing has another benefit, too. It allows you to make minor changes in ready-to-wear clothing. You can also take advantage of bargains by fixing used or discounted clothes. Chapters 64 and 65 introduce you to basic sewing skills.

- **Redesigning.** You can put the clothes that you no longer wear to use. Go back to your wardrobe list and look at those items you have outgrown or don't like. Could you lengthen or shorten something to make it wearable again? Would a change of style make a sweater more appealing? Chapter 67 has more ideas on how to turn old clothes into new.

- **Trading.** You may have something that you don't wear because you don't like the color, or it doesn't go with anything else in your wardrobe, or it just isn't comfortable. Could you trade it for something that you need with a friend or a family member?

Buying Coordinated Pieces

Building a wardrobe is easier when you plan it around **coordinated pieces**—garments that can be worn together in several different ways. You will have a maximum number of outfits for a minimum amount of money.

Classic items are basic to a coordinated wardrobe. To think that classics are boring is a mistake. Classics can be selected in fabrics and colors that are suited to your personal style. Buy the best quality in fabric and workmanship that you can afford. Then, buy or sew some trendy pieces or accessories that add spice to the classics.

Here are some points to remember when you go shopping:

- Can the jacket be worn with two pairs of pants? You get more wear out of a jacket when you have two or more bottoms to wear with it.
- Shirts and blouses with a finished bottom edge can be worn out and belted or worn as lightweight jackets.
- Cotton knit T-shirts are classics; mix with jeans, pants, and skirts. Sweaters can be worn in different seasons and change the mood of an outfit.
- Patterns can be mixed together. However, the decision to mix should be evaluated by current fashion. To coordinate prints, plaids, and stripes, use different patterns that contain the same or related colors or use the same patterns in different colors. Small patterns are easiest to mix.

How many combinations can you get from these items?

Think It Through

1. If you could add two items to your wardrobe, what would they be? With what would they coordinate?
2. Do you think you have a good wardrobe? Why or why not? If not, what could you do to improve it?

CHAPTER
59 REVIEW

Reviewing the Facts

1. What is a wardrobe inventory?
2. Why should you look carefully at the clothes in your wardrobe that need to be repaired?
3. What is the advantage of mixing and matching different clothing items?
4. Before adding an item to your wardrobe, what four questions should you ask yourself?
5. Name two ways to add to your wardrobe without buying new clothes.
6. Give two advantages of sewing your clothes.

Sharing Your Ideas

1. What do you think is the most versatile item in a typical teen's wardrobe? Why?
2. How could you make the clothes you are wearing right now more versatile?

Applying Your Skills

1. Judging Versatility. You have been invited to your cousin's wedding and plan to purchase an outfit for this special occasion. Study catalogs or store circulars and choose an appropriate outfit. From the illustration and description, how versatile would it be for other occasions? How could accessories be used to increase its versatility?

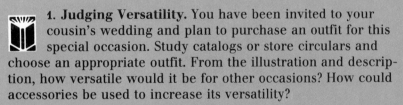

2. Writing Descriptions. Choose your favorite season of the year. Using what you have learned in Chapters 55–59, plan a wardrobe that you could wear during this season. Describe each garment in terms of type and color (for example, red shirt) rather than specific brands or styles.

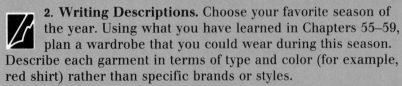

3. Making a Budget. Using a wardrobe plan, determine which items of clothing you will need to purchase during the next six months. List an approximate price for each item. What is the total of the estimated costs? How could you distribute these costs evenly over the six-month period? If necessary, how could you reduce some of these costs?

Shopping for Clothes

OBJECTIVES

This chapter will help you to:

- Explain how to prepare to shop for clothes.
- Identify the places where you can buy clothing.
- Discuss how to determine your size.
- Describe how to evaluate clothes for fit and quality.

WORDS TO REMEMBER

cost per wearing
end-of-season sale
facing
hem

inseam measurement
seam
size range
trimmings

Have you ever bought a skirt that you felt you "couldn't live without," only to have it pushed to the back of your closet in a short time? Have you ever bought a sweater at one store—only to see it three days later at another store for less money? Have you ever bought a pair of slacks in "your size" that just didn't fit? What about the brand new shirt that came apart at the seam and frayed when it was washed?

We can all answer "yes" to at least some of these questions. Buying wearable clothes takes skill. You should know:

- What you want.
- Where to buy.
- How to find your size.
- How clothes are made.

The more you know about clothes, the more success you'll have in shopping and finding the right garment for you.

Getting Ready to Shop

The first step is to write down exactly what you have decided to buy. Next to each item, write what you plan to wear it with and possible colors and fabrics. This information is part of a wardrobe plan. You might wear or bring along the clothes you're trying to match when you go shopping. If you want to match a color or fabric and cannot bring the whole garment along, take samples such as the belt or a tiny piece of fabric cut from the inside. If you plan to wear a specific pair of shoes with your new purchase, bring them along when you try on the new clothing.

There are still two decisions to be made before you begin shopping: you must decide where to shop, and you must decide how much you can afford to spend. Then you will know how much money to take with you.

Where to Shop

Where you buy your clothes will determine the selection you'll find, the prices you'll pay, and the quality you can expect. Convenience and atmosphere are also factors to consider when deciding where to shop.

- **Department stores.** These stores are divided into sections that offer many clothing styles and sizes for men, women, and children. They also sell accessories. Most offer extra services, such as credit cards, gift wrapping, and free delivery. Department stores may have slightly higher prices than some other stores, but they almost always have certain items on sale.

Stores differ in type of merchandise, prices, and services offered. This specialty store carries one particular brand of clothing.

- **Specialty stores.** These stores sell only one type of clothing, such as sportswear, shoes, children's apparel, or a particular brand of clothing. A specialty store may carry labels that most department stores do not stock. Prices may be higher than at a department store, but many specialty stores offer extra personal services and handle special orders.

- **Discount stores.** These stores sell clothing and other items at lower prices than department stores. Discount stores do not always carry the same merchandise as department stores. Don't expect to find the *same* item for less, but you can probably find a *similar* item. Discount stores offer fewer services than department stores.

- **Factory outlets.** These stores are run by a manufacturer or factory. Prices are low because few customer services are offered. Some factory outlets may look like warehouses and may not accept returns or exchanges. You'll find a mix of merchandise in these stores, from high-quality clothes to clothing that is labeled *seconds* or *irregulars.* These have flaws or are otherwise not perfect. If the flaws aren't noticeable, the item may be worth buying. You may also have the sewing skills to repair some of the imperfections.

- **Mail-order catalogs.** These books and pamphlets are sent out by many stores and companies. They are convenient to use, but you'll have to wait from a few days to several weeks for your order to be delivered. A decision about which size to order should be made carefully. Catalogs usually explain how to measure for your correct size. Catalog prices vary and you will usually have to pay mailing or shipping charges. It's a good idea to compare prices with those in local stores.

- **Resale shops.** These shops sell secondhand garments that often look new. Some may specialize in antique clothing or designer clothing. A resale shop may be sponsored by a charitable organization, or it may be a consignment shop where the person bringing the clothing to be sold will get a percentage of the selling price. The clothing cannot be returned.

- **Garage sales, yard sales, and rummage sales.** These are other sources of used clothing. Clothing items at these sales can often be purchased for a few dollars or less. You have to check very carefully to be sure that items are not stained or worn beyond repair since they cannot be returned.

- **Flea markets.** These can offer everything from first-quality merchandise to seconds and irregulars. Some items labeled as "designer" may be poor-quality copies. Prices are usually below retail store prices, but many flea markets do not allow customers to try on or return items.

- **Art and craft fairs.** These can be sources of original, one-of-a-kind designs. You may find hand-painted, quilted, patchwork, hand-woven, and hand-knitted garments, as well as handcrafted jewelry and accessories. Although you will pay a premium price for these unique designs, a special item may be worth the extra cost.

When to Shop

Stores generally market clothes for different seasons, so the time of year will affect prices and selection. At the beginning of each season, prices tend to be at their highest, but more clothing is available. During the season, the selection decreases and prices usually go down.

Most stores hold some type of clearance sale at the end of each season to make room for new merchandise.

In addition, stores usually hold sales at regular times throughout the year. If you are aware of the sale schedule, you can plan ahead for larger purchases such as a winter coat. Sales are important to anyone buying clothes, but remember that stores hope you'll also buy their regularly priced items when you shop during a sale. Keep in mind, too, that no item is worth buying if you have no use for it, no matter how much of a bargain it is.

Here are traditional types of sales:

- An **end-of-season sale** is held to clear out merchandise to make room for the next season's styles. Winter coats, sweaters, and ski clothes go on sale in February; bathing suits and summer sportswear go on sale in July.

- Annual holiday sales, such as those on Columbus Day or Washington's Birthday, aim to bring in business on a day when more customers can shop.

- Markdowns, or reduced-price items, are almost always available. These are clothes that, for some reason, didn't sell as fast as planned. The longer an item remains in the store, the more it is marked down.

- Special purchases are items that the store has bought for a lower than usual price. The store then passes on the savings to their customers.

Know Your Size

Knowing what size you wear involves knowing which **size range** or category you fit into. If you shop in the right size range, you'll get a better fit. For teens there are several possible size ranges.

Size Ranges

There are so many terms used in sizing clothes today. Here are some guidelines to use when trying to decide which size range will fit you best.

- **Female sizes.** Most females wear either a misses or a junior size. Misses sizes are even-numbered (4, 6, 8, 10, 12, 14, 16) and designed for a well-proportioned figure. Junior sizes are odd-numbered (3, 5, 7, 9, 11, 13, 15) and cut for a trimmer, shorter-waisted figure. Teen sections in some department stores carry clothes made for developing teen figures.

- **Male sizes.** Male clothing comes in men's and boys' sizes. Some stores have special teen departments with clothing sized for this age group. Boys' and mens' pants are sold by waist and **inseam measurement**—the length of the pants leg from the bottom to where the two legs meet.

■ **Special sizes.** Some manufacturers make special sizes such as *petite*, *women's*, *slim*, *husky*, *tall*, and *short*, to better fit different body shapes.

Finding Your Size

Sizes in ready-to-wear clothing are based on the measurements of typical bodies, but no one is typical, so finding the right size can be difficult. Unless you're familiar with a particular label or brand name, never buy clothing without trying it on.

Some clothing is marked *extra-small*, *small*, *medium*, *large*, or *extra-large*. These categories will fit two or three standard sizes. For example, a small will fit sizes 6 and 8; medium fits sizes 10 and 12. It's best to try these on because there can be a great variation in manufacturers' sizing.

If you are having trouble choosing between two sizes, it's smart to buy the larger size. Because you're probably still growing, you will be able to wear the item longer.

You can also allow for growth by looking for skirts and pants with wide hems. You'll be able to let them down later to lengthen the garment if you grow taller. Elasticized waists that leave room for expansion are good ideas, too.

Evaluating Your Choice

How can you tell whether you are getting good value in a garment you are considering buying? What do you look for? Fit, comfort, fabric quality, construction details, and cost all determine the value of a garment.

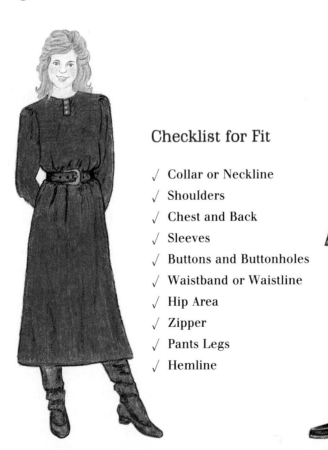

Checklist for Fit

√ Collar or Neckline

√ Shoulders

√ Chest and Back

√ Sleeves

√ Buttons and Buttonholes

√ Waistband or Waistline

√ Hip Area

√ Zipper

√ Pants Legs

√ Hemline

Checking the Fit

To find out if a garment fits properly, you'll have to try it on. When you are in the dressing room, don't just stand still. Move around, sit down, reach up, bend over. If you cannot do any of these things easily, or if the garment sags, gaps, or pulls anywhere, it's probably too large or too small. If it doesn't fit right, don't be discouraged. Remember what you learned earlier in the chapter—clothing is manufactured according to typical body measurements as well as the manufacturer's own specifications. Try another size.

Never compromise on fit. An uncomfortable garment will end up at the back of your closet and never be worn. Avoid buying too small a garment in the expectation that you will lose weight. Poor fit also leads to broken zippers, split seams, and worn fabric.

Checking the Fabric

You really like the jacket you found. It fits nicely and goes well with your pants. What questions about its quality should you consider before making it your final choice? First take a look at the fabric:

- **Wrinkling.** Grab a handful of fabric, crush it in your hand, and release it. Do the wrinkles stay or fall out quickly? If the wrinkles don't fall out, the garment will look rumpled when you wear it.
- **Pattern.** If the fabric is a plaid or a print, check that the pattern is straight and even all around. The pattern should run in the same direction in all pieces. Plaids should match at the seams.
- **Wearing qualities.** Hold the garment up to the light. If patches of light come through the fabric unevenly, it will

probably wear unevenly. The tighter the knit or weave, the better the garment will hold its shape.
- **Care information.** Look at the labels for the fiber content and care information. You want clothes that you wear often to be made of easy-to-care-for fabrics.

Checking the Construction

Next look at how the jacket is made. Check its construction in these areas:

- **Seams.** First, check each **seam**, the line of stitching that joins the pieces of the garment together. Make sure they're straight and smooth with no puckering. Stitches should be secure so the seams won't come apart. Check the inside of the garment, too. The seams should be finished, with no raw edges to ravel.

Examine the way a garment is constructed inside, as well as outside. Look for straight, smooth seams that won't pull out, and for pucker-free facings and hems.

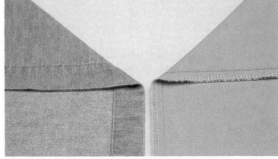

■ **Edges and corners.** Collar points and lapels should be flat and smooth without bulk or puckers. Some edges, such as necklines and armholes, have **facings**—extra pieces of fabric sewn on the outside and turned to the inside to finish an edge. Facings should lie flat and be anchored so they won't show when the garment is worn.

■ **Hems.** The **hem** is the bottom edge of fabric turned up and sewn to the wrong side of the garment. Hemmed edges should be smooth. Stitches should be invisible from the right side, with no wrinkles or puckers.

■ **Fastenings.** Make sure zippers are sewn in securely, and that they slide evenly and smoothly. Buttonholes should be even and without loose threads. Check that buttons, hooks, eyes, and snaps are firmly attached.

■ **Trimmings.** Look at any **trimmings**. These are the decorations sewn on a garment. They should be attached with even, secure stitches. Topstitching thread should match the fabric, unless done for contrast. It should be even, without any puckers.

Cost

The overall cost of a garment is very important. Some questions to ask when purchasing an item are:

■ Is the price within your budget?

■ How long might you wear it or how long might it last?

■ Can you buy something similar for less?

■ Can you get it cheaper somewhere else?

■ Could you save money by waiting for it to be put on sale?

■ Could you make the item?

The more times you wear a garment, the more value you will get from the money you spent on it. One way of finding that value is to compute the **cost per wearing.** This is the total of the purchase price and the cost of cleaning divided by the number of times you wear a garment. See the chart below.

Although cost is important, you also need to evaluate your purchases as to your needs and wants, color and design, fit and quality. If all these factors are met, you can be sure of making good choices.

Estimating Cost Per Wearing

Suppose you buy a dressy sweater and a pair of pants. The sweater had been marked down to $24.99. The pants cost $25.00.

Through the year you wear the pants 39 times, but you wear the sweater only 5 times. The next year you wear the pants another 25 times until they are too short and too tight. The sweater still fits and you wear it 5 more times.

You have the sweater drycleaned three times in two years, for a total of $8.25. The pants are washable, so their cleaning cost is only a fraction of the family laundry—about 50 cents a year.

To figure the cost per wearing for each garment over two years, add the purchase price and the cleaning cost then divide by the number of wearings.

Sweater: $24.99 + $8.25 =
$33.24 ÷ 10 = $3.32
Pants: $25.00 + 1.00 =
$26.00 ÷ 64 = $0.41

The cost per wearing of the sweater is eight times that of the pants. The pants are a better value than the sweater, even though they were not marked down. When you consider buying a garment, weigh its price against the cleaning cost and the number of times you expect to wear it.

Choosing Accessories

Accessories include items such as scarves, shoes, boots, gloves, hats, belts, socks, jewelry, sunglasses, ties, handbags, backpacks, and tote bags. They are a way to brighten your wardrobe. They also help you express your unique personality and creativity. Use accessories to:

- Update a classic or favorite outfit with the latest fashion colors.
- Make a quick change from a school outfit to a party outfit.
- Add color and life to neutral colors.
- Focus attention wherever you want it.

Check fashion magazines, catalogs, and pattern books to see the new trends in colors and accessories. In one season you may see that wide belts are being shown in bright, fluorescent colors. In another season, the emphasis may be on natural accessories, such as wood jewelry or rope belts. These are small items that can inexpensively update and accent your wardrobe.

Some other accessories are not so inexpensive. It's possible to spend more for a pair of leather boots than for a coat, and a silk scarf can cost more than a blouse. When you are deciding how much money to spend on accessories, it is best to spend more money on items that will last for several seasons and limit fad purchases to low-priced items.

- Select accessories that are appropriate for a person of your size. If you are short, a large tote bag may make you look even smaller.

- Use accessories to set the tone of your look. A whimsical piece can put a little humor into your appearance.
- Classic leather belts are 3/4″ to 1 1/4″ wide. Collect them in a variety of colors.
- Carry a list of the garments you have and their colors when you shop. Fabric samples from your clothing will help you match accessories.
- Think of new ways to wear accessories you already own. Try wearing a tie or a scarf as a belt. Or twist two scarves together and knot.

Think It Through

1. **What are some additional ways of using accessories you already own, such as belts, scarves, hats, or ties?**
2. **What is your favorite accessory and why?**

Reviewing the Facts

1. What are two things you should do to get ready for a shopping trip?
2. List six places where you can buy clothing. What is one advantage and one disadvantage of each?
3. Name three traditional types of clothing sales.
4. What are two female and two male clothing size ranges?
5. Even if you know your size, why should you always try on clothing before buying?
6. When checking the fit of a garment, what should you do?
7. What are four factors to check when evaluating fabric quality?
8. How does the cost per wearing help you determine the value of a garment?

Sharing Your Ideas

1. When planning a wardrobe, why does it help to read advertisements in a newspaper or special store circular?
2. Which of the following are most important to you when you are shopping for clothes: *price, style, fit, color, fiber content and care, appearance, quality.* Which characteristics, if any, are least important to you?

Applying Your Skills

 1. Analyzing Quality. Examine a garment that you recently purchased. Check the quality of the fabric and construction, and write a brief quality analysis of the garment. Did you make a good purchase?

 2. Judging Advertising Techniques. Collect five clothing ads from newspapers or catalogs. Compare the information they give. How does each persuade customers to buy?

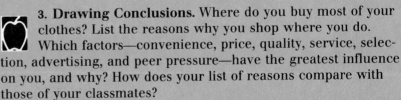 **3. Drawing Conclusions.** Where do you buy most of your clothes? List the reasons why you shop where you do. Which factors—convenience, price, quality, service, selection, advertising, and peer pressure—have the greatest influence on you, and why? How does your list of reasons compare with those of your classmates?

CHAPTER

61

Selecting Patterns, Fabrics, and Notions

OBJECTIVES

This chapter will help you to:

- Determine the correct pattern size to buy.
- Explain how to select a pattern.
- Use the information on the pattern envelope.
- Suggest factors that affect your choice of fabric and notions.

WORDS TO REMEMBER

bolt-end label   pattern
figure type   pattern catalog
notions   view

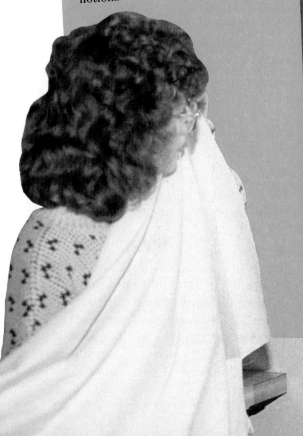

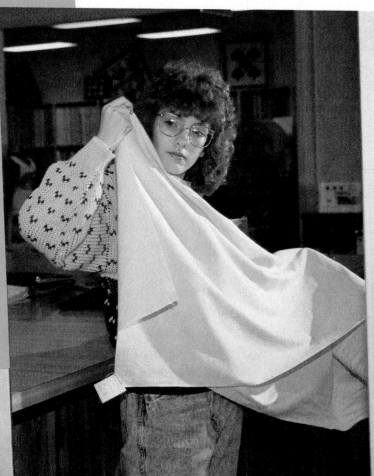

When you sew you can choose from the hundreds of patterns, fabrics, and colors available to make the item you want. You can make it in the exact size that you need, and in the color that does the most for you and your wardrobe. You can also sew accessories, gifts, and practical items like backpacks, duffel bags, and pillows. You can get satisfaction and pride from sewing something to wear or use. You may even be able to earn extra money with your sewing skills.

Body Measurements

The first step in making clothing is selecting a pattern. A **pattern** is a set of written directions and printed paper pieces that show you how to put a sewing project together. The pattern also tells you how much fabric you need and shows you how to lay out and cut the pieces. To know what size pattern is right for you, you must first know your body measurements.

Taking Measurements

Here are a few things that you can do to make measuring easy and accurate:

- Ask a friend or relative to help you take your measurements and write them down for you.
- Wear smooth-fitting clothes, a leotard, or underwear when measuring. Do not measure over a bulky sweater or jacket.
- Wear shoes. That will make your posture close to what it will be when you wear the clothing.
- Tie a string or piece of narrow elastic around your waist. You'll use it to lo-

cate your waist and for measuring the length of your back, hips, and legs.
- Stand straight and tall.
- For measurements around the body be sure that the tape measure is parallel to the floor.
- For accurate measurements, pull the tape measure snugly, but not too tight, around your body.
- Before writing down any measurement, double-check it. See page 547 for the measurements to take.

Figure Types and Pattern Sizes

To help you choose the correct pattern size, compare your measurements with the pattern size charts. These charts are found in the back of a **pattern catalog,** a book that shows all the patterns available from one company.

Pattern sizes are divided by **figure types,** size categories determined by height and body proportions. The major pattern companies use common figure types. Which description most closely describes your figure type?

- **Misses** patterns are designed for the well-developed figure about 5'5" to 5'6" in height.
- **Girls** patterns are for the petite figure, 5'1" or shorter.
- **Mens** patterns are for the average adult build, about 5'10" tall.
- **Teen-Boys** patterns are for boys who are still growing.

Because each body is built differently, it is not always possible to match your measurements exactly to a pattern size. Choose the size within your figure type that comes closest to your measurements. A few patterns are not identified by size but by measurements, such as by waist size for pants. Others may be sized small, medium, large, and extra-large.

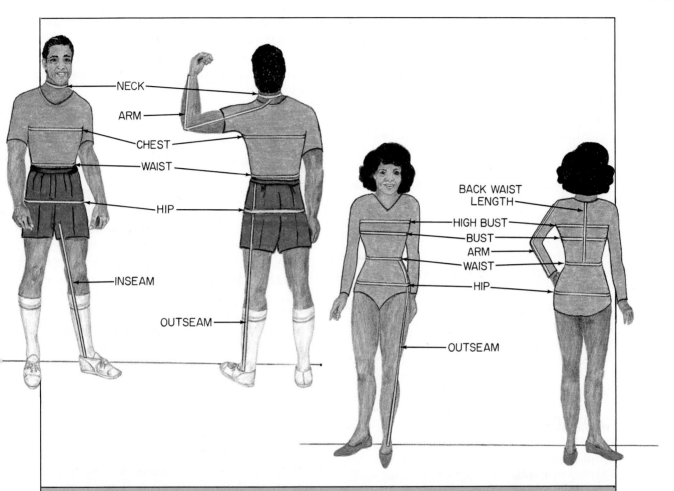

Measuring Up

Height Stand tall against the wall, barefoot. Have another person make a mark level with the top of your head. Measure from this point to the floor. For pants and skirt measurements, it is best to wear shoes.

High Bust For females, measure around body, under the arms. This measurement is not found on pattern size charts. It is used for comparison with bust measurement to help select pattern size.

Bust For females, measure at fullest part of bustline. If bust measure is 2 in. (5 cm) or more larger than high bust, use the high bust measurement to select pattern size.

Chest For males, measure the fullest part of the chest.

Waist For females, measure where string or elastic falls. For males, measure around the natural waist where a belt or waistband feels most comfortable.

Back Waist Length Measure from the base of the neck to the waistline.

Hips Measure around the fullest part of the hips. For females, this is 7–9 in. (18–23 cm) below the waist. For males, this is usually about 8 in. (20 cm) below the waist.

Outseam Measure along the outside of the leg from waist to desired length of pants.

Inseam For males, measure along inside of leg from crotch to desired length of pants. Or measure a pair of pants that fit well, measuring from bottom of one leg to where the two legs meet.

Neckband For males, measure around the fullest part of the neck, adding ½ in. (1.5 cm) for wearing ease.

Sleeve Bend arm up. Measure from base of neck across center back to elbows, across elbow crook, and up to wrist bone.

Selecting a Pattern

Pattern catalogs provide lots of information about patterns. First, look for the type of garment or item you want to sew. Clothes patterns usually are grouped according to the type of garment (such as sportswear or dresses) or by figure type (such as men and boys, or children). Other categories are based on sewing skill, such as easy-to-sew patterns. Catalogs also have sections for gifts, home decorating, toys, accessories, and crafts.

Each catalog page has illustrations or photographs showing how the project will look when sewn. This often includes a number of views. A **view** is a different version of the pattern. For example, a sweatshirt pattern might include views for long and short sleeves.

When you look through a pattern catalog, study the illustrations to get an idea of what the finished item will look like. Read the descriptions for information about sewing difficulty.

Don't overlook patterns that may be shown on special display racks in the store. These may be best-selling patterns, seasonal selections, or easy-to-sew patterns.

Choosing for Style

When you buy a pair of pants or a shirt in a store, you can see the style, color, and fabric together. You can also try the item on to see how it looks and feels. With patterns, you have to rely on the way the pants or shirt look in the pattern catalog. Study the photograph and illustrations carefully. Check the design lines, the shape, the length, and the fit. What details are there? Read the description under the pattern. This will tell you how it fits. Is it snug-fitting or loose? Pattern catalogs also feature a drawing of the back of the garment.

You may still wonder if the garment will look good on you. One clue might be whether the item is similar to something you have worn in the past. If not, look for a similar garment in a store and try it on. Be sure to select a pattern that you really like. Half the fun of sewing is showing off what you've made.

Choosing for Your Sewing Skills

When picking a pattern, consider your sewing skills. If you are a beginner, look for patterns marked "easy to sew" or "very easy." The number of pattern pieces is a clue to the difficulty of the pattern. The fewer the pieces, the easier the pattern. Details such as shirt cuffs, collars, fly-front zippers, extra darts, tucks, and topstitching make a pattern more difficult to complete. Easy-to-sew patterns include few of these details.

The back of the pattern envelope includes information about design details, measurements, fabrics, and notions.

8959
17 PIECES

MISSES', MEN'S OR TEEN BOYS' KNIT PANTS, SHORTS AND TOP: Long sleeved crewneck top has side sections and ribbed knit bands. V. 1 top has pockets and contrast sleeves and side sections. V. 3 top has contrast side sections. Pants and shorts have side sections and elastic waistline casing. Pants have ribbed knits bands. V. 1 pants and V. 3 shorts have contrast side sections.

1,2 & 3

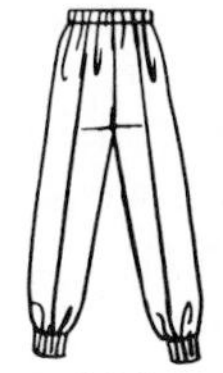

1 & 2

3

Fabrics—Knits only such as: sweatshirt knits, velour, stretch terry, cotton interlock. Bands in stretchable ribbed knit fabric. (SEE PICK-A-KNIT® RULE FOR BANDS ONLY.) Not suitable for obvious diagonals. Extra fabric needed to match plaids, stripes or one-way design fabrics. For pile, shaded or one-way design fabrics, use with nap yardages/layouts.

Notions: Thread, straight seam tape. Look for Simplicity notions.

BODY MEASUREMENTS						
Chest/Bust	30-32	34-36	38-40	42-44	46-48	Ins.
Waist	26-27	28-30	32-34	36-39	42-44	"
Sizes U.S.A. ONLY	X-Small	Small Small	Medium Medium	Large Large	X-Large X-Large	
View 1 Top and Pants						
60"**	1½	1⅝	1⅝	1¾	1¾	Yds.
Contrast side sections and sleeves (top and pants)						
60"**	1½	2	2	2	2	Yds.
Bands—Stretchable ribbed knit fabric—18" to 20" tubular **OR** 36" to 40"						
flat**	⅝	⅝	⅝	¾	¾	Yd.
View 2 Top and Pants						
60"**	2⅝	3¼	3¼	3¼	3⅜	Yds.
Bands—Stretchable ribbed knit fabric—18" to 20" tubular **OR** 36" to 40"						
flat**	⅝	⅝	⅝	⅝	¾	Yd.
View 3 Top and Shorts						
60"**	1½	1½	1½	1⅝	1¾	Yds.
Contrast side sections (top and shorts)						
60"**	⅞	1⅛	1⅛	1⅜	1⅜	Yds.
Bands—Stretchable ribbed knit fabric—18" to 20" tubular **OR** 36" to 40"						
flat**	½	½	½	⅝	⅝	Yd.
View 1, 2 or 3 Elastic—1¼ yds. of 1" wide						
Pants side length V. 1 or 2	43	43½	44	44½	45	Ins.
Shorts side length V. 3	15	15½	16	16½	17	"

*without nap **with nap ***with or without nap

Using the Pattern Envelope

The pattern department in most stores is self-service. That means you find the pattern you want in the large file drawers that hold the patterns by number. After you find the right number, be sure to select the correct size. Most stores will not allow you to exchange or return a pattern.

Once you have chosen your pattern, take a good look at the pattern envelope. The outside of the envelope contains important information.

- **Front of the envelope.** The front of the envelope shows the same drawings and photographs of the pattern views that were in the catalog. You will also find the figure type and size the pattern is made for, along with the pattern number and the price.
- **Back of the envelope.** On the back of the envelope, the garment description lists the design details that may not be obvious in the illustration. A sketch is given of the back of each pattern view, along with a size chart of the body measurements for each pattern size.
- **Other information.** The back of the pattern envelope is your shopping list. The yardage chart shows how much fabric you'll need for each pattern size. It will tell you whether you need extra material for napped fabric, such as corduroy, velvet, and velveteen. Under the heading "Suggested Fabrics," it will list the types of fabric that are appropriate for the pattern. It will also say whether a fabric such as a plaid or diagonal is not suitable. Finally, you'll find information on the notions that you will need to buy. **Notions** are the supplies needed to complete a project. They include thread, zippers, buttons or other fasteners, elastic, seam binding, hem tape, and trimmings.

MANAGING RESOURCES

Deciding Whether to Make or Buy

Do you enjoy shopping and have good luck finding what you need at the right price? Maybe you feel you can have more clothes for less money when you sew.

Ask yourself these questions when you are deciding whether to make or buy. Then, consider the following:

- **Time.** Does it take more time to shop or to sew? How much time do you have?
- **Money.** Can you save money by sewing the item or can you find it on sale for the same price or less?
- **Skill.** Do you have the sewing skills necessary to complete the project?
- **Sewing equipment.** Will you have to invest in new tools and sewing supplies?

One way to determine what to sew and what to buy is by degree of difficulty. Plan to sew garments that can be simply constructed. Sometimes you can make something in less time than it takes to shop for it.

It makes sense to sew when you cannot find what you want in ready-to-wear. It also makes sense to sew when you can copy an expensive item. For example, you can make a simple belt from a braid trim or an interesting ribbon for about one-fifth the cost of a similar, ready-made belt.

You may decide to sew something that you can wear often. You will get the most wear out of seasonless fashions that can be worn year round. You may decide to sew something that is expensive to buy but that you will wear only once or twice, such as a prom or bridesmaid's dress.

It makes more sense to buy than to sew when you don't have the time to make what you need, and the pattern details or fabric is beyond your sewing skills. Other times you may find a garment that seems just right—the color, fit, design lines, and price tag are perfect for you.

You may find something great in a perfect fabric at an ideal price, but it requires some minor adjustments of detail or fit. Then you can use your sewing skills to improve something that you buy.

Think It Through

1. Do you think your family would rather receive ready-made gifts or a gift you sewed? Why?
2. Why is purchasing a ready-to-wear item sometimes a better use of your resources than sewing one?

Selecting a Fabric

The array of different fabrics in a store can appear overwhelming. There are so many fabrics to choose from that you may not know where to start.

What the Pattern Tells You

Luckily, the pattern envelope tells you what type of fabric will be most suitable for a particular pattern. A lot depends on the shape and style of the garment. A soft fabric, such as challis, will be suggested for a soft, gathered shape. For casual clothes, the envelope will suggest a more durable, sturdy fabric. Dressier fabrics will be recommended for a special-occasion item, such as a formal for a prom.

Using Your Knowledge

Ask yourself some questions about which fabric is right for your project. Here are a few guidelines that will help you decide.

- **Your own experience.** Your feelings about yourself and the clothes you wear will help you make a decision about fabric. What feels comfortable and seems to express your personality? What will the item be used for and where will it be used? For instance, backpacks need durable, sturdy fabric, and placemats require medium-weight washable fabric.
- **Seasonal wear.** What time of year do you plan to wear the item? You wouldn't want a heavy wool for summer or a lightweight cotton fabric for winter. If you plan to wear the garment often, you want to buy a fabric that wears well.
- **Fabric care.** If you don't want to spend a lot of time hand-washing and ironing, pick an easy-care fabric. If your budget is limited, avoid a fabric that needs drycleaning. You will find the fiber content, recommended care, the fabric width, and price per yard on the **bolt-end label.** When you pay for the fabric ask the salesperson for a sew-in care label for your garment.
- **Sewing difficulty.** Some fabrics are easier to work with than others. Fabrics with a one-way design or a nap are more time-consuming to lay out because all pattern pieces must be placed in the same direction. Then, when the pieces are sewn together the nap will retain the same look throughout the garment.

Plaids need to be matched at the seams and are more difficult to lay out and cut. Fabrics that ravel easily can be frustrating to work with. Lightweight silky fabrics are slippery to lay out and cut. They may need special sewing techniques. Firmly woven or knitted fabrics are easier to handle.

Looking for Quality

Find a mirror and drape some of the fabric over your shoulder to see how it looks on you. Consider not only the color and design, but also the softness or firmness. Does it drape nicely for a garment with soft gathers? Is it crisp enough for the details in the pattern that you have selected.

When you've found a fabric that you like, examine it for flaws. These may be torn threads, snags, holes, or grease stains. Crumple it in your hand to see if the wrinkles disappear when you release it. If it's a knit, stretch it across the cut edge and see if it goes back into shape after you let go.

Buy the best quality fabric that you can afford. You waste time and money by working with poor quality fabric. You want to enjoy your sewing and end up with something that lasts and is a pleasure to wear.

Deciding How Much Fabric to Buy

Check the chart on the back of the pattern envelope to find out the amount of fabric to buy. Look at the correct size of the pattern, the view you'll be using, and the width of the fabric. The envelope will also tell you if extra fabric is needed for napped or plaid fabrics.

Estimate the total cost of the project by multiplying the cost per yard of the fabric by the number of yards you need. Add the cost of the pattern, buttons, zipper, and thread. If that total cost is more than you planned to spend, look for a less expensive fabric or shop at another store.

Before buying a fabric, check for characteristics—such as drapability, wrinkle resistance, or stretchability—that could affect your sewing project.

Selecting Notions

When you're buying a pattern and fabric, also buy your notions. The pattern envelope lists the notions that you'll need.

Choosing Colors

Notions should coordinate with your fabric. When buying thread, zippers, seam binding, or bias tape, pick a color that matches or is slightly darker than the fabric. Buttons can match the color of the fabric or contrast with it for accent. If you're unsure about what style or color notions to buy, look at some ready-to-wear clothing for ideas.

Choosing Thread

The thread you use depends on the fabric you are working with. All-purpose thread, such as cotton-wrapped polyester and 100 percent polyester can be used for almost all fabrics. These threads are strong, stretch slightly, and don't shrink. They're especially good for knit and stretch fabrics, as well as fabrics made from manufactured fibers.

If you will be using a serger or overlock machine, buy special serger thread on cones. Because three or four spools of thread are used at once, serger thread is finer and more lightweight than all-purpose thread.

Specialty threads are available for machine embroidery, quilting, topstitching, and sewing on buttons. In addition, there are cotton, silk, rayon, and nylon threads for other specialty sewing.

Reviewing the Facts

1. Why is it helpful to know how to sew?
2. Before picking out a pattern, what do you need to know about yourself?
3. What are two female figure types and two male figure types?
4. Name two non-clothing projects included in pattern catalogs.
5. Why does a page in a pattern catalog often have several different drawings or photos?
6. What are two clues that would help you determine that a pattern might be easy to sew?
7. Where do you find suggestions for the kind of fabric that is suitable for a pattern?
8. List three things to consider when selecting a fabric.

Sharing Your Ideas

1. How can sewing help you use all five design elements to create an illusion that highlights your good features?
2. Why is it a good idea to estimate the cost of a project before making a final decision on the type of fabric you will use?

Applying Your Skills

1. Taking Body Measurements. Have a friend or classmate take your measurements, following the guidelines on pages 546–547. Using the pattern size charts found in a pattern catalog, determine the best figure type and pattern size for you to use.

2. Computing and Comparing Costs. Go to a fabric store and select a pattern for a sewing project. Also, choose the fabric and the notions. Record the prices and calculate the total cost of the project. Don't forget the cost of the pattern. Could you have purchased a garment of similar style and quality for less money in a department store? At a discount store? On sale?

3. Predicting Results. Look through several crafts or women's magazines (for example, *McCall's, Woman's Day, Family Circle*). Choose a project that you would like to make. Are the instructions clearly written? Are the terms similar to those in pattern instructions? Do you have the necessary skills to complete the project?

Sewing Equipment

OBJECTIVES

This chapter will help you to:

- Describe the parts of the sewing machine and the serger.
- Use a sewing machine.
- Identify and describe the purposes of many pieces of sewing equipment.

WORDS TO REMEMBER

bobbin
feed
lockstitch
looper
serger

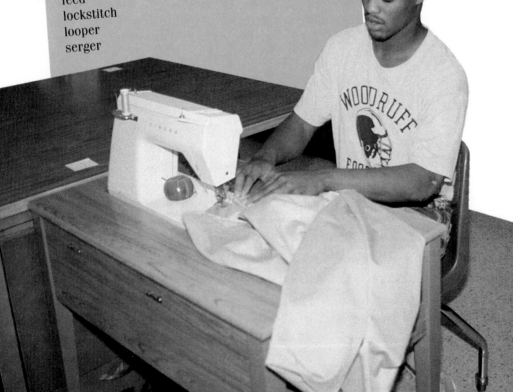

Many centuries ago, people sewed clothes using long thorns and strips of leather to attach pieces of animal skin together. The results were crude, but sufficient for the way most primitive people lived. Until the 1800s all sewing was done by hand. Then, in 1845, a Massachusetts machinist named Elias Howe invented a workable sewing machine. His invention revolutionized the making of clothing.

We've come a long way since then. We now have electronic, computerized sewing machines that allow you to complete sewing projects with speed and efficiency. **Sergers**, high-speed overlock machines developed for industrial sewing, are now available for home use, helping even more do-it-yourself sewers to achieve professional results.

The Sewing Machine

A sewing machine is the most important piece of sewing equipment. Although sewing machines vary in capabilities and accessories, each machine has the same basic parts and controls. Refer to the chart on page 556 as you read the information in this chapter.

How It Works

Sewing machines join pieces of fabric together with a **lockstitch.** This stitch requires a thread above the fabric to meet another thread coming from below the fabric. The top and bottom threads should link or lock in the middle of the fabric layers. A special tension control on the sewing machine helps form a balanced stitch.

The fabric is moved along by a part of the machine called the **feed.** The feed positions the fabric for the next stitch. The process is repeated over and over again to create a row of stitching.

The machine is operated by a foot or knee control. You can also turn a hand wheel to raise and lower the needle as you begin and end stitching.

Threading the Machine

Each sewing machine model is threaded a bit differently. The basic steps, however, are the same for all machines. The thread goes from the spool to the upper tension control to the take-up lever and down to the needle. Thread guides keep the thread from tangling along the way. You can find diagrams in your machine's manual that will explain how to thread that particular machine.

You must also wind and insert the **bobbin,** a small spool that holds the bottom thread. Wind the bobbin on the machine and insert it in the bobbin case according to the directions in your machine's manual.

Adjustments

You must adjust the type and length of your stitches to suit each sewing job. There are four main types of stitches:

- Regular stitch is a medium-length stitch used for most purposes.
- Basting stitch is a long stitch used for holding layers of fabric together temporarily. It is also used for gathering.
- Reinforcement stitch is a short stitch used to strengthen the stitching area at a corner or point.
- Zigzag stitch is a sideways stitch used to finish seam allowances, make buttonholes, and sew special seams.

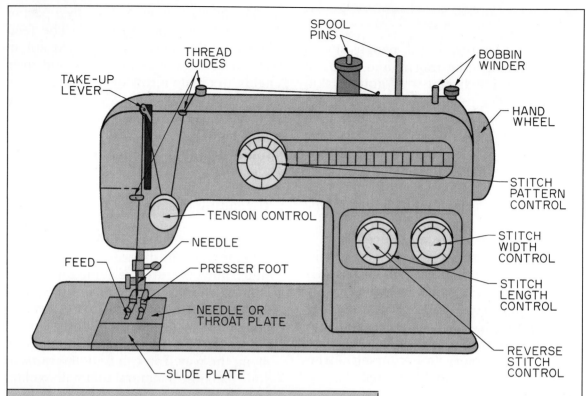

Basic Parts of the Sewing Machine

Bobbin Holds the bottom thread which forms the under half of the stitch.

Bobbin case Holds the bobbin and the tension adjustment for the lower thread.

Feed Rises through the throat plate and moves fabric forward with each stitch.

Presser foot Helps hold fabric in place to keep stitches in a straight line.

Stitch length control Used to adjust stitch length.

Reverse stitch control Allows machine to stitch backward.

Stitch width control Used to adjust stitch width.

Stitch pattern control Used to make different stitching patterns.

Thread guides Hold thread in place.

Needle or throat plate Plate directly under the needle; it has guideline markings to help you keep your stitching straight.

Slide plate A metal plate that covers the bobbin and opens to let you remove the bobbin.

Hand wheel Turns to raise and lower the take-up lever and needle.

Bobbin winder Used to wind the bobbin.

Spool pins Hold spools of thread.

Tension control Regulates how tightly the thread is pulled as a stitch is formed.

Take-up lever Keeps thread feeding evenly through the needle.

Needle Feeds the upper thread, which forms the upper half of the stitch.

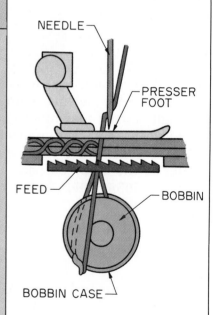

Adjust the stitch length control for basting stitches (6 per inch), standard stitches (10-12 per inch), and reinforcement stitches (20 per inch). Adjust the stitch width control for zigzag stitches, which can also vary in length.

TYPES OF STITCHES

BASTING — — — — — — — —

STANDARD – – – – – – – – – –

REINFORCEMENT - - - - - - - - - - -

ZIGZAG /\/\/\/\/\/\/\/\/\/\/\

Specialty stitches are built into some machines and used for hemming, stitching on stretch fabrics, and decorative stitching.

All machines have a dial or lever, called the stitch length control, for adjusting the stitch length. The higher the number on the control, the closer together the stitches. Some machines also have a lever for setting the width of zigzag and other specialty stitches.

You can also change the tightness of the stitches with the tension control. This adjusts the tension on the upper thread so that the stitches interlock in a different place. The tension needs adjusting if one thread lays flat against one side of the fabric while the other thread forms loops on the other side.

Needles

Needles come in different sizes and types for different fabrics. There are two basic types:

- General purpose or universal needles have a sharp point for use with most fabrics, wovens or knits.
- Ball-points have a rounded point and are used for knits.

A bent or damaged needle can cause stitching problems. If a needle seems to be dull, replace it right away.

Accessories

Modern machines have features for many kinds of sewing. A special presser foot or a separate attachment may be needed for some of these operations. To sew zippers, you need a zipper foot that allows you to stitch close to the zipper teeth. Other attachments are used for hemming, gathering, and attaching binding.

Caring for the Sewing Machine

A sewing machine is a finely engineered piece of equipment that needs regular maintenance and careful handling. After each use, unplug the machine and put it away in its cabinet or case, or cover it.

Clean the machine regularly with a soft sewing machine brush to keep the moving parts free of dust and lint. Be especially sure to keep lint away from the feed area and the bobbin case. Directions for cleaning the machine are in the manual.

The machine needs to be oiled occasionally with sewing machine oil. Refer to the manual to see where to place the drops and how often to oil the machine. Carefully wipe away any excess oil to avoid spotting your fabric.

Electronics in Sewing Equipment

In just a little more than a century, we've gone from foot-pedaled treadle machines to sewing gear with "brains"—computerized machines with memories. The computer enables sewing equipment to feed thread evenly, adjust for different weight fabrics, and, at the touch of a finger, form any number of decorative stitches.

Electronic Machines

An electronic sewing machine is any sewing machine with a form of electronic circuitry. The most common electronic element is speed control. This allows you to sew various thicknesses and layers of fabrics without losing speed or power. For example, you could sew over 10 layers of heavy denim and go right to the finest silk, at any speed and without any pressure or tension adjustments.

You can also stitch slowly without limiting the piercing power of the needle. Other mechanical functions, such as moving the needle up or down, may also be controlled electronically.

Computerized Machines

Computerized machines are electronic machines with a microcomputer, central processor, and memory bank. They memorize, store, and retrieve data just like any other computer. Computerized sewing machines offer the following features:

- **Automatic stitch selection.** The most appropriate stitch length, width, and tension are selected according to the fabric and the type of sewing.
- **Stitch patterns.** Computers string a series of stitch patterns together, reverse images, produce mirror images, or double the stitch pattern length.

- **Touch control panel.** Stitches are clearly illustrated on the machine. By touching the stitch picture you select the pattern.
- **Digital readout panel.** This panel shows the program that has been set.
- **Memory cassettes.** With some machines, you can add hundreds of designs or patterns to the basic machine.

Think It Through

1. Do you think you would enjoy working on a computerized sewing machine? Why or why not?
2. Can you think of some advantages of a basic sewing machine that doesn't have electronic or computerized features?

The Serger

The serger, or overlock machine, trims, sews, and overcasts in one step. It creates the special stitches that you see on seams of ready-to-wear garments. Sergers sew at extremely high speed and can form up to 1,500 stitches per minute.

Sergers are known as 2-thread, 3-thread, 4-thread, or 5-thread, depending on the number of threads used to make the stitch. Each thread goes through a separate tension disc. Sergers do not have bobbins. Instead they have **loopers** that perform like bobbins do in conventional sewing machines. The looper threads loop around each other and are interlocked with the needle thread, or threads. Depending on the model, sergers may have one or two needles. A well-adjusted serger stitch interlocks exactly on the cut edge of the seam.

Another difference between sergers and sewing machines is the cutting knife. There are small knife blades on the serger that work like scissors to trim the fabric to the width of the stitch.

In addition to stitching seams, sergers can do narrow rolled hems, similar to the hems on napkins or silk scarves. With other adjustments they can produce a blind hemming stitch and a flatlock stitch. The flatlock stitch is a flat seam that can be used to decorate lingerie, T-shirts, and sweatshirts.

The serger can stitch, trim, and overcast a seam in one step. What are the similarities and differences between a serger and a conventional sewing machine?

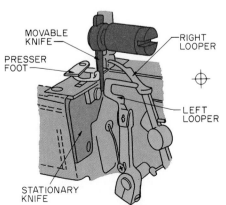

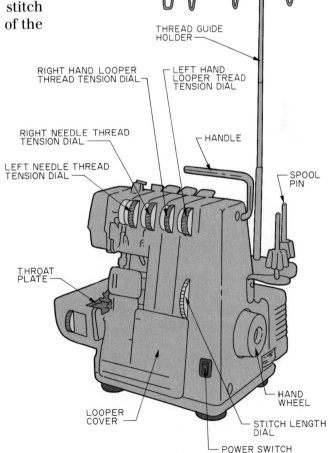

Other Sewing Tools and Equipment

You will need additional supplies to do sewing projects. These special tools are used for measuring, cutting, marking, pinning, hand stitching, and pressing.

Measuring Tools

- **Tape measure.** You need this to take body measurements. It should be flexible and 60 in. (1.5 m) long.
- **Yardstick/meter stick.** This is used to measure fabric, check grain lines, mark hems, and draw long lines. The sticks are 36 in. or one meter (39.5 in.) long and are made of wood.
- **Ruler.** A 12 in. (30.5 cm) ruler with 1/8 in. (3 mm) markings can be used to measure and mark lines. A see-through plastic ruler is practical.
- **Sewing gauge.** This is a 6 in. (15 cm) ruler with an adjustable sliding marker that is used to measure small areas, such as seams or hems.

Cutting Tools

Scissors and shears should cut along the whole blade. Buy good cutting tools, which will last a long time. Oil and sharpen your cutting tools regularly to keep them in good working order.

- **Shears.** These have long blades, and the two handles are shaped differently. They are used to cut fabric.

Which of these sewing tools and equipment can you name?

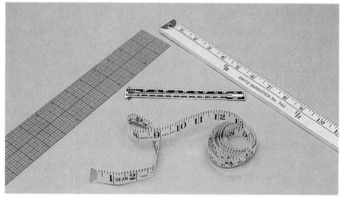

MEASURING

CUTTING AND SEWING

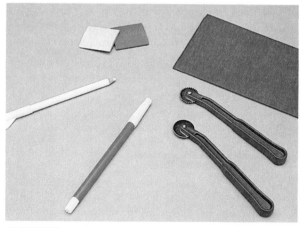

MARKING

PRESSING

Bent-handled shears are easiest to use because the fabric can stay flat on a surface as you cut.

- **Scissors.** These are smaller than shears and are used for trimming and clipping. Both handles are the same shape.
- **Pinking shears.** These shears have zigzag-shaped blades. They can be used to finish the edge of firmly woven fabrics and help prevent raveling.
- **Seam ripper.** This penlike object has a sharp, pointed end and small blade for removing stitches.

Marking Aids

Here are some of the marking tools that are used to transfer pattern symbols to fabric.

- **Tracing paper.** This comes in several colors. Choose a color that will show up on the fabric without being too dark. Double-faced tracing paper allows you to mark two layers of fabric at one time.
- **Tracing wheel.** This device is used with tracing paper to transfer pattern markings. Wheels with sawtooth edges can be used for most fabrics. Smooth-edged wheels are best for delicate fabrics.
- **Chalk.** Chalk can be used to mark most fabrics. The markings can be brushed off or will disappear when pressed with an iron. Chalk is available as colored squares, pencils, or powder.
- **Liquid marking pencils.** These make quick work of marking tucks, darts, pleats, and pocket locations. Use the type that washes off with water. Pressing may set the marks permanently, so remove the marking before pressing the area.

Small Equipment

Some additional items are essential for pinning and hand sewing.

- **Pins.** These are used to fasten the pattern to the fabric and to hold fabric layers together for stitching. Pins with colored heads are easy to see and use.
- **Needles.** Needles for hand sewing come in a variety of sizes and lengths. The smaller the number, the larger the needle. Sizes 7 and 8 are good for most purposes.
- **Pincushion.** This is better than a box for holding pins because the pins can't spill onto the table or floor. Magnetic pin holders are convenient to use and are handy for picking up spilled pins.
- **Thimble.** A thimble made of metal or plastic is used to push the needle through the fabric when hand sewing. Wear it on your middle finger.

Pressing Equipment

Pressing as you sew will make your sewing easier and more accurate.

- **Steam iron.** An iron that steams and sprays at any setting, not just the high settings, gives best results.
- **Ironing board.** Your ironing board should have a well-padded, clean cover. It also should be adjustable for your height.
- **Press cloth.** For some fabrics, a press cloth is needed to prevent shiny marks caused by the iron's heat. It can be dampened to provide additional steam for hard-to-press fabrics.
- **Tailor's ham.** This firm cushion, shaped like a ham, is used for pressing curved seams and darts.

Reviewing the Facts

1. When and by whom was the sewing machine invented?
2. How does the sewing machine join pieces of fabric together?
3. What part of the sewing machine moves the fabric along?
4. How should a sewing machine be cared for between uses?
5. What are the three things that a serger does in one step?
6. List three measuring tools used in sewing.
7. What is the difference between shears and scissors?
8. Name three useful marking tools.

Sharing Your Ideas

1. When purchasing a sewing machine or a serger, what factors do you think you should consider?
2. How can knowing how to use a sewing machine be valuable?

Applying Your Skills

1. Writing Instructions. Make up a game to identify and explain the important terms in this chapter. Be sure to develop a key for reference later. Terms should include parts of the sewing machine and serger, and sewing tools and equipment.

2. Compare Costs. List any sewing tools and equipment that you already have. What additional tools would you need to begin a sewing project? Estimate the cost of these tools, and add the total to the cost of the item you would like to make. Would it be more or less expensive to buy a ready-made item? What other options might you have?

3. Comparing Techniques. Demonstrate the use of various sewing tools and equipment on different types, weights, and colors of fabrics. For example, cutting with shears, scissors, and pinking shears; marking with tracing paper, chalk, and pencils; and pressing with and without a press cloth. How do the results differ? What recommendations can you make for different fabrics?

CHAPTER
63

Lay Out, Cut, and Mark

OBJECTIVES

This chapter will help you to:

■ Adjust a pattern to fit your body shape.
■ Prepare the fabric and lay out the pattern pieces.
■ Cut out and mark the fabric pieces.

WORDS TO REMEMBER

directional cutting
ease
grain
layout
seam allowance
selvage

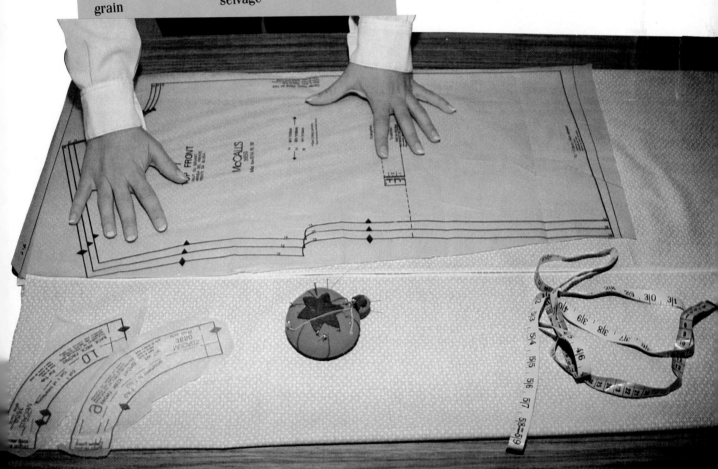

You are now probably anxious to start sewing. You have your pattern, fabric, notions, and sewing equipment; you're ready to start the sewing process.

In this chapter, you will learn the four steps to go through before you can actually begin sewing on the machine.

The four steps are:

1. Preparing your pattern.
2. Preparing your fabric.
3. Laying out the pattern pieces and cutting the fabric.
4. Marking the fabric.

The result of careful preparation will be a garment that looks good and fits well.

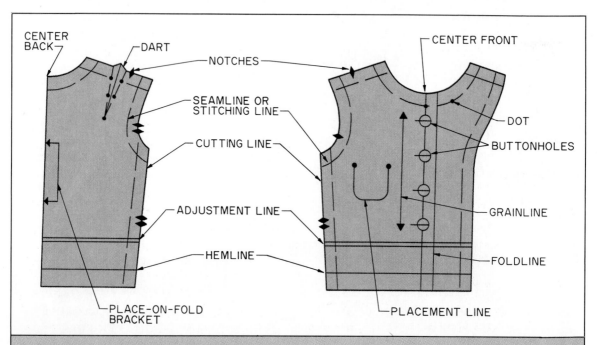

Patterns and Pattern Terms

Adjustment line A double line, where the pattern may be lengthened or shortened.

Buttonholes Marked by lines that show the exact location and length.

Center front and center back Solid lines that show the center of the garment.

Cutting line The heavier outer line, along which you cut.

Dart Consists of two broken lines and corresponding dots.

Dots Used for matching seams and construction details.

Foldline A solid line showing where the fabric is to be folded.

Grainline The heavy solid line with arrows at each end that shows the direction of the grain.

Hemline A solid line indicating the finished edge of the garment.

Notches Diamond-shaped symbols along the cutting line that are used for matching seams.

Placement line Line showing the exact location of pocket, zipper, or trim.

Place-on-fold bracket The symbol which shows that the pattern piece is to be placed along a fold of fabric.

Seamline or stitching line A broken line ⅝" inside the cutting line (unless otherwise noted).

Preparing Your Pattern

First, take out your pattern guide sheet. This sheet gives you step-by-step information for cutting, marking, and sewing the garment or accessory. The front of the guide sheet contains general instructions, information about pattern symbols, and diagrams for laying out the pattern pieces. Circle the layout for your pattern size, view, and width of fabric.

Now, take out the pattern pieces that you'll need. Press them with a warm, not hot, dry iron to make them smooth and flat. Write your name on all your pattern pieces, the pattern envelope, and the guide sheet.

Next, find the measurements that you took before you bought the pattern. Compare them with those listed on the pattern envelope to see if you'll need to adjust the pattern to make it fit better.

Checking Pattern Measurements

If your body measurements do not exactly match those listed on the back of the pattern envelope, you may have to make adjustments. You must change the pattern so that the finished garment will fit you properly.

If there's a difference of an inch (2.5 cm) or more between your measurements and the size measurements on the envelope, you'll probably have to make adjustments. You can check with your instructor to be sure, because if a pattern style is loose or full, adjustments may not be necessary.

You can also compare your measurements to those of the pattern by actually measuring the pattern pieces. Measure only from seam to seam. Don't include the **seam allowance**. This is the fabric between the line for cutting and the line for stitching. The seam allowance is 5/8 in. (1.5 cm) from the cutting line. If your pattern has three sizes printed on it, the seam allowance line is not marked. You will have to measure it yourself.

Remember that the pattern includes **ease**. This is extra room that a pattern allows for clothing to fit comfortably. Because of the ease, pattern pieces measure larger than size measurements. The difference might be 3 to 4 in. (7.5 to 9.5 cm) at the bust, 3/4 to 1 in. (2 to 2.5 cm) at the waist, and 2 in. (5 cm) at the hips. Thus, a pattern for 34 in. (87 cm) hips would actually measure 36 in. (92 cm). Patterns for bathing suits and leotards will have little or no ease because they fit close to the body.

Simple Adjustments

Lengthening or shortening a pattern is the easiest adjustment to make. An adjustment line is printed on some pattern pieces to show where they can be lengthened or shortened; others can be adjusted at the lower edge.

Shorten a pattern piece by taking a tuck at the adjustment line or at the bottom. If a pattern must be made longer, cut it apart at the adjustment line. Insert and tape a strip of tissue paper between the two pieces, or add it to the bottom of the pattern. Don't forget to adjust the front and the back.

Adjusting for width is a little more complicated. An increase or decrease of 1 in. (2.5 cm) or less can be done at the side seams. Just draw new seamlines parallel to the old, adding tissue paper if necessary. If you have to add or subtract more than 1 in. (2.5 cm), get assistance from your instructor. Multi-sized patterns have three separate cutting lines. You may be able to make a width adjustment by using two sizes. Blend gradually from one size to the next in areas where you need to adjust the width.

HEALTH WATCH

Safe Use of Sewing Tools

You will prevent accidents and injuries in the sewing room by following a few general safety tips.

- Keep pins in a pincushion or magnetic pin holder, never in your mouth or stuck in your clothes.
- Keep scissors, shears, and seam rippers closed when you are not using them.
- When passing scissors or shears to another person, pass them with the handle out.
- Keep your tools and supplies in your sewing box when they are not being used.
- Use a magnetic pin holder to pick up loose pins around your sewing machine. Be careful not to drop pins.

Using a sewing machine:

- Keep the sewing machine cord out of the way so that no one trips over it.
- If you are learning how to use a sewing machine or serger, use a slow speed until you are comfortable enough to sew faster.
- Keep your fingers away from the needle of the sewing machine and the cutting knives of the serger.
- Do not lean your face too close to the machine when stitching in case the needle breaks.
- Remove pins as you come to them. Do not stitch over them as they might break or dull the sewing machine needle.

- When you are not using the sewing machine, unplug the cord from the outlet and then disconnect the cord from the machine.
- Close the sewing machine carefully or cover it when you are finished sewing.

Using an iron:

- Don't touch a hot iron anywhere but on the handle.
- Keep your fingers and face away from the steam.
- Place the iron cord so that the iron cannot be accidentally pulled off the ironing board.

- Rest the iron on its heel when not in use.
- Unplug the iron when finished. Empty any water from it. Be sure the iron has cooled completely before putting it away.

Think It Through

1. If you were a sewing instructor, what steps would you take to ensure that your students were following safe sewing practices?
2. How many more sewing safety tips can you list?

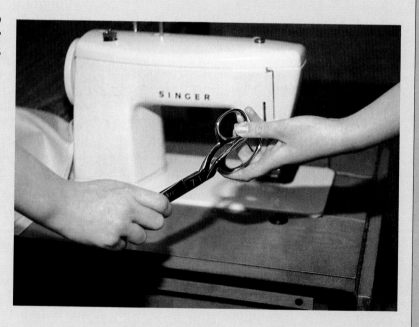

Preparing Your Fabric

The next step is to decide if your fabric needs to be preshrunk or straightened. Read the label on the bolt of the fabric to check if the material has been preshrunk. If the label says it will shrink more than 1 percent, or if no information is given, you should preshrink the fabric before cutting out the pieces. To preshrink washable fabrics, wash and dry the fabric according to the care instructions. Fabrics that cannot be machine or hand washed must be taken to a drycleaner for preshrinking.

Straightening grain is another step in preparing your fabric. Fabric **grain** is the direction in which the yarns run. Lengthwise and crosswise grains should meet at right angles. If the fabric is not straightened before the pieces are cut out, the hemline may hang unevenly or the garment may twist to one side. To check grain, first straighten the fabric ends. For a woven fabric, pull a thread across the width of the fabric and cut along this crosswise thread or cut along a woven stripe or other woven line. For a knit, cut along a row of loops.

Next, fold the fabric in half, matching lengthwise and crosswise edges. If the fabric isn't smooth, and the corners do not match exactly, it is off-grain. You may be able to straighten it by steam pressing. Pin the fabric along the **selvages**, the finished edges of the fabric, and along both ends. Press from the selvage to the fold. Fabrics that have a permanent finish can't be straightened.

Layout and Cutting

The laying out and cutting of pattern pieces and fabric should be done in a comfortable place. It is best to work on a large, flat surface such as a table topped with a cutting board.

Laying Out the Pattern

The pattern **layout** is a diagram that shows how to place the pattern pieces on your fabric. Its purpose is to help you use fabric as economically as possible, with little waste. Special layouts may be given for fabrics with a nap or directional print.

Follow the layout that you circled on the pattern guide sheet. Fold your fabric as shown on the layout, with the right sides together. Smooth the fabric flat on a surface that is large enough to hold the fabric width. Then follow the layout as you arrange your pattern pieces on the fabric. To avoid mistakes, lay out all the pieces before starting to pin and cut.

First, pin any pattern pieces placed along the fold line. These pieces have a bracket arrow on a straight edge. Next, pin the pattern pieces that have grainline arrows in the center of the pattern piece.

Smooth out each pattern piece and pin it diagonally at the corners. Then place pins about 6 in. (15 cm) apart at right angles to the edges. Make sure that the pins don't extend into the cutting lines.

To be sure the pattern piece is exactly on grain, measure from each end of the arrow to the selvage. If the distances are not equal, move the pattern and remeasure.

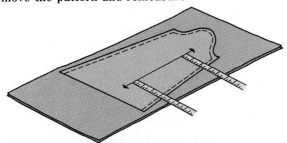

Cutting

Before cutting your fabric, double-check the layout. Are all your pieces laid out? Are grain lines accurate?

Use sharp shears to cut accurately and evenly. With your free hand, hold the fabric flat on the table. Cut with long, even strokes, following the cutting line exactly. If the pattern is printed with more than one size, be sure to cut on the line that is your size. Use **directional cutting**, which is cutting with the grain of the fabric. The direction may be shown on the pattern by arrows on the stitching line or by illustrations of tiny scissors positioned on the cutting line.

Use the points of your shears to cut corners, curves, and notches. Always cut notches *outward* from the cutting line. Cut two or three notches together as one long notch.

Double-check to be sure that you have cut each pattern piece as many times as necessary. Do not remove the pattern from fabric pieces after cutting. Now the pieces must be marked.

Marking the Fabric

Each pattern piece is printed with markings that must be transferred to the wrong side of your fabric. You will use these markings as you stitch the pieces together. Choose the marking method most suitable for your fabric, testing it first on a fabric scrap.

- **Tracing paper and wheel.** Slide the tracing paper under the pattern so that the color is against the wrong side of the fabric. If you have two layers of fabric to mark, use two pieces of tracing paper, or fold one in half. Roll the tracing wheel once along the line that you want to mark. Use a ruler to keep the lines straight. Mark dots with an X.

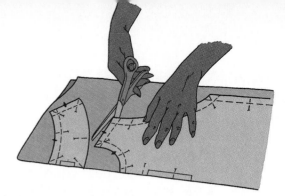

Use sharp shears and cut with long, even strokes on the pattern's cutting line.

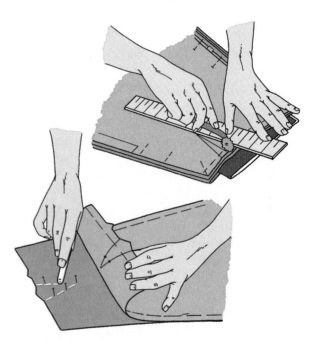

Use a tracing wheel with tracing paper, pins and chalk, or a liquid marking pen to transfer pattern markings to fabric.

- **Pins and chalk.** Push a pin through pattern and fabric at the symbol to be marked. Then make a chalk mark on the wrong side of both fabric layers at the pin marking.
- **Fabric markers.** Special liquid marking pens allow temporary markings to be made on fabric. Some markings can be removed with a bit of water; others fade within a few hours. Test such markers on a scrap of your fabric to be sure the markings come out.

CHAPTER
63 REVIEW

Reviewing the Facts

1. What are the four steps to take before sewing a garment?
2. Why do pattern pieces measure slightly larger than the size measurements?
3. Describe two simple adjustments you can make to a pattern.
4. Why should you straighten fabric that is off-grain?
5. What does the pattern layout show you? Where is it found?
6. Which pattern pieces should be placed on the fabric first?
7. Describe how to cut around notches on the cutting line.
8. Why is it important to transfer markings to your fabric?

Sharing Your Ideas

1. What do you think would happen if you began to sew without properly adjusting the pattern? Without following the pattern layout? Without marking the fabric pieces?
2. Which of the methods of marking fabric do you prefer? Why?

Applying Your Skills

1. Identifying Details. Using two or three pieces from any pattern, identify, list, and define all the markings and pattern terms printed on the pattern pieces.

2. Creating a Safety Poster. Create a poster that emphasizes one or more safety tips to follow when using sewing tools and equipment. Use stick figures, cartoons, or pictures to illustrate the safety tips.

3. Solving Measurement Problems. Marsha is making a skirt. Her measurements are 1 in. (2.5 cm) larger at the waist and hips than those shown for the pattern size. She also needs to make the skirt 1½ in. (3.8 cm) longer. The skirt pattern has three pieces—a skirt front, a skirt back, and a waistband. How must it be adjusted so the skirt will fit Marsha?

Basic Construction

ow that you have marked all your fabric pieces, spread them out and look at them. Can you see how to put the pieces together and where to stitch? Are there areas that are marked for pleats, gathers, tucks, or darts? Markings make your job easier and your work more accurate.

You are now ready to assemble—or construct—your project. Soon you'll see it begin to take shape using a basic technique called unit construction. In **unit construction,** you prepare the separate pieces first, then assemble them in a specific order. For example, a shirt has a back, two fronts, two sleeves, and maybe a collar. Each part is a unit and each unit is constructed separately. Then you simply put them together.

Staystitching

Before you start assembling your project, you have to prepare the pieces to prevent them from pulling out of shape while you're working with them.

Look for all edges that are curved or cut on the **bias.** Bias is any curve or angle that is not cut on the lengthwise or crosswise grain of the fabric. Bias-cut edges stretch as you work with them, so you'll need to put a row of stitching on these curved edges to keep them from losing their shape.

This row of stitching is called staystitching. **Staystitching** is a line of machine stitches sewn through one layer of fabric. The stitches are placed in the seam allowance, 1/2 in. (1.3 cm) from the edge of the fabric. You should stitch in the same direction as the grain, usually from the wide section of the piece to the narrow part.

Shaping to Fit the Body

Darts, tucks, pleats, and gathers are used to shape a flat piece of fabric to fit the shape of your body. Each creates a different effect.

- **Darts.** A **dart** is a triangular fold of fabric stitched to a point. Darts help shape the fabric to body curves. They're usually located at the waistline, the bustline, the back of the shoulder, and the elbow. Darts can also be used to shape curved areas in hats and tote bags.

On the outside of your garment, darts will look like short seams. They should not have bubbles or puckers at the points. Darts in the right and left sides of a garment should be the same

Fold the dart in half, matching markings, and pin. Stitch from the wide end to the point. Tie a small knot at the point.

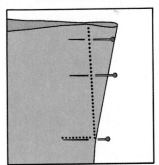

PIN

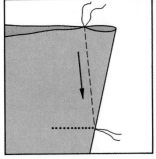

STITCH

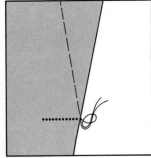

TIE

length, and they should be the same distance from the center. Vertical darts should be pressed toward the center of the garment. Horizontal and diagonal darts are usually pressed downward.

- **Tucks.** Like a dart, a **tuck** is a small, stitched fold used to give shape. However, a tuck doesn't taper at the end; it makes a small, unpressed pleat in the fabric. Tucks may be stitched on the inside for shaping, and on the outside for decorative detail as well as shaping.

- **Gathers.** Soft folds of fabric stitched into a seam are called **gathers.** They are created by sliding the fabric along a line of basting stitches in order to fit a larger piece of fabric to a smaller one. Gathers can be used at a waistline, cuff, shoulder, or sleeve. Ruffles on clothing, pillows, and placemats are also gathered.

Stitch two rows of machine basting next to the seam line in the seam allowance. Pull up both bobbin threads at one end and gently slide fabric along threads. Repeat at other end until fabric is proper length. Distribute gathers evenly.

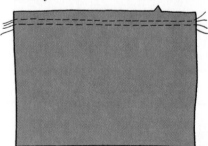

STITCHING

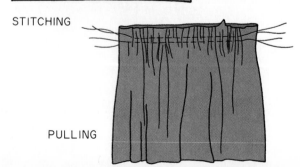

PULLING

- **Pleats.** Stitched pleats, such as on a classic pleated skirt, give the same close fit as darts. Unpressed pleats, such as on shorts and trousers, give the ease of gathers. Both styles of pleats result in a straight, vertical line. Accurate marking and stitching are important to be sure that the width of each pleat is even.

Assembling the Pieces

After you have staystiched the pieces and built in the shape, you are ready to start assembling your garment. You begin with the seams.

Stitching Seams

Pin the two layers of fabric together with the right sides facing each other, matching the notches. Use a regular stitch length and **directional stitching,** that is, stitching with the grain of the fabric. This will keep your seams from stretching as you work on them. Backstitch at the beginning and end of each seam to secure the stitching. Most seams are 5/8 in. (1.5 cm) wide, unless the pattern has different instructions.

Press the seam before going on to the next one. First, press the seam flat, just as it was stitched. Then, press the seam allowance open.

Finishing the Seams

Seams need to be finished to prevent fabric edges from fraying or raveling and to create a neat appearance. There are four ways that seam allowances can be finished.

- **Pinked or stitched-and-pinked.** Trim the edges with pinking shears. For fabrics that ravel easily, stitch 1/4 in. (6 mm) from the edge and then pink.
- **Zigzagged.** Zigzag by machine near each raw edge, using a narrower stitch for lightweight, closely woven fabrics and a wider stitch for heavy, bulky, or loosely woven fabrics.
- **Hemmed.** This method, also called clean finishing, can be used on light- and medium-weight fabrics. Turn the edge of the seam allowance 1/8 in. (3 mm) under and press. Then stitch along the edge of the fold.
- **Bound.** This method is good for medium- and heavy-weight fabrics. Put double-fold bias tape or sheer bias tricot strips over each raw edge. Place the slightly narrower folded edge of tape on top, and stitch through all the layers.

- **Serged or overlocked.** Stitch a regular width seam with the sewing machine. Overedge each side of the seam allowance using the serger. You can also stitch and overedge seam at the same time on the serger. These seams will only be about 1/4 in. (6 mm) wide, so mark seams accordingly.

Stitching Facings

Facings are cut in the same shape as the edges and used to finish a raw edge such as a neckline, armhole, or waistline. A facing is stitched to the right side and turned to the inside of the garment. Separate pieces for facings are included in the pattern.

The type of fabric and the amount of raveling determines what seam finish to use.

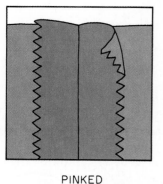

PINKED

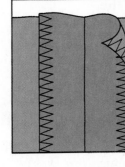

ZIG ZAG

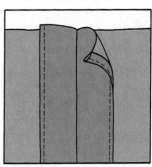

HEMMED

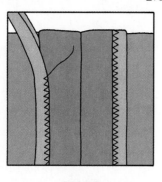

BOUND

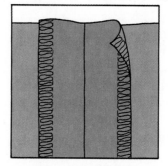

SERGED

Trimming, grading, clipping, and notching are done to help facings lie flat and smooth by reducing fabric bulk. These steps are often necessary when stitching collars, necklines, armholes, and waistbands.

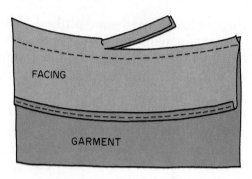

TRIMMING

A facing may also be cut as an extension or a part of the garment. Fold the extended facing to the inside along the foldline. Extended facings are used on straight edges, such as the front openings of shirts and jackets.

To sew a facing, stitch the facing pieces together. Then press the seams open. Finish the outer edge with one of the seam finishes on page 573. Stitch the facing to the garment, with right sides together, matching notches and seams.

For a facing to lie flat and smooth when turned to the wrong side, trim, grade, clip, or notch it as follows.

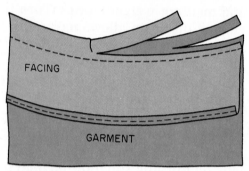

GRADING

■ Trim the seam allowance to half its width.

■ Grade or layer seam allowances if the fabric is thick or if the seams have three or more layers. Trim each layer of a seam allowance slightly narrower than the previous one. Leave at least 1/8–1/4 in. (3–6 mm) of seam allowance to prevent raveling.

■ Clip seams that curve inward to let the fabric lie flat. Clip the seam allowance by making small, evenly spaced cuts up to, but not through, the staystitching line.

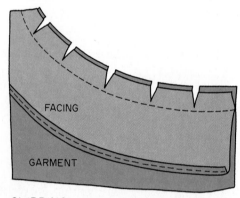

CLIPPING

■ Notch the seams that curve outward. To notch, cut V-shaped wedges from the seam allowance. When you press the notched seam allowance open, it will be smooth and the notched edges will meet.

Press the facing seam flat. Then, turn the facing to the inside of the garment and press again.

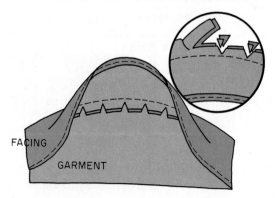

NOTCHING

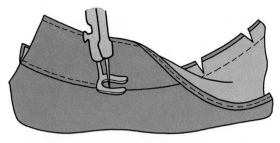

Understitching helps to hold the facing flat and prevent it from showing along the seamline.

To hold the facing flat, use one of three methods:

- Understitch the facing and seam allowance together. Open out the facing and machine stitch through the facing and seam allowance. Do not stitch through the outer layer of fabric.
- Topstitch from the right side of the fabric through all the layers.
- Tack or stitch the facing to the seam allowances on the inside.

Adding Interfacing

Faced edges are sometimes interfaced to prevent stretching and to give them extra body and shape. Interfacing fabrics are available in a variety of types and weights.

Fusible interfacings are applied to the fabric with an iron. Most fusibles come in plastic wrappers that include specific directions for applying the product.

Sew-in interfacings must be pinned or machine-basted in place and then stitched into the seam. Both types of interfacing are available in woven and nonwoven fabrics.

Pressing

Pressing isn't something you do only when you have finished your garment, although you do that, too. Pressing is an important part of unit construction and guarantees that your seams will lie flat, darts and pleats will be shaped accurately, and facings will lie smooth.

When **pressing** a seam or garment, lift the iron and set it down on the fabric. Do not slide the iron back and forth, which would be ironing the fabric. Ironing can stretch the fabric.

If you're not using a steam iron, use a damp press cloth to create steam. After you've steamed one section, lift the iron just above the fabric and move your press cloth to the next section to press. Then lower the iron again.

To avoid shine, press on the inside of the fabric whenever possible. Do not use heavy pressure. Let the steam do the work.

If you are pressing curved seams and darts, use a tailor's ham so that the curved shape will not be flattened. Press as you finish each unit and before going on to the next.

Press carefully after each step of construction to achieve the best results.

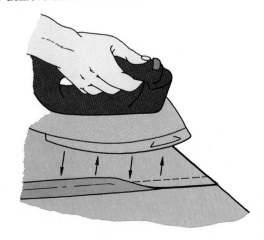

Using Videos to Learn to Sew

Videos have changed the way people learn to do many things, including how to sew. You may be using sewing videos in school, or you can rent or buy them at fabric and video stores or through the mail.

If you are going to buy a sewing video, you will want to preview it to see if it helps you realize your sewing and wardrobe goals. Here's what to look for:

- **Good close-ups.** If the steps are at the sewing machine, is the camera focused on the stitching? Does it show exactly how to stitch? Does it show how the garment should look when finished? When the video is exhibiting how to cut, trim, or use any equipment, the sewer's hands should not block the demonstration.
- **Lively action.** Look for a video that moves quickly and features many exciting ideas that you can apply to your sewing projects.
- **Small tasks.** Look for videos that break up the sewing tasks into several brief segments. For example, if you are using a video to learn how to sew pants, you may want to view only the section on how to insert a zipper during one sewing session.

- **Rewards.** Does the finished garment inspire you? Your goal is to learn to sew, but your reward is a garment that you will enjoy wearing. The video should enable you to approach that goal by helping you select clothes that are right for you.

First, watch the video for the general information. Then you can watch the segments that interest you.

After viewing the video, check to see that you have everything on hand that you need. If you are putting in a zipper, do you have the right length zipper, a zipper foot, and the machine set up as directed on the video? You may want to watch the video again.

An advantage of videos is that you can rerun them as many times as you like. You can also stop a video at any point to check your progress against the action on the video.

Think It Through

1. If you are learning to put in a zipper, which do you think is the most helpful aid—a sewing book, a video, a filmstrip, a movie, or a demonstration by your instructor? What are the advantages and disadvantages of each?
2. Do you think that you could learn to make a pair of shorts by watching a video? Why or why not?

CHAPTER 64 REVIEW

1. What is unit construction?
2. Why is it important to staystitch around curved or bias-cut edges? How is staystitching done?
3. What purpose do darts, tucks, pleats, and gathers serve? How are darts and tucks different?
4. Name four ways to finish seam allowances.
5. What is the purpose of a facing?
6. Explain the difference between grading and notching. When would you use each?
7. What is the purpose of understitching? How is it done?
8. What is the difference between pressing and ironing?

Sharing Your Ideas

1. What factors influence your choice of interfacing? How would you decide which interfacing to use for a particular fabric?
2. On garments that you are wearing, or with pictures from magazines and catalogs, point out ways in which the garments have been shaped to fit the body.

Applying Your Skills

1. Writing a Script Imagine that you are making a video to help others learn basic sewing techniques. Write a video for one of the following activities: use of gathers in different fashions; use of different seam finishes on various fabrics; decorative stitching. Demonstrate your project to the class, using the script you prepared.

2. Comparing Techniques Cut an inward curve (similar to that of a garment facing) through two layers of fabric. Stitch a ⅝ in. (1.6 cm) seam along the curved edge. Press the seam open and note the result. Then, trim and clip the seam. Press the seam again and compare the results.

3. Creating a Progress Chart Using the unit construction method, prepare a step-by-step chart for the project you are sewing. Start with preparing the pattern and fabric, laying out the pattern, and cutting and marking the fabric. Use the pattern guide sheet to list each construction step including pressing. As you complete each step, check it off on the chart.

Adding
the Details

OBJECTIVES

This chapter will help you to:

- Describe the details that give a quality look to sewing.
- Demonstrate techniques used for sewing fashion details.
- Identify common closures and describe how to attach them.
- Select trimmings and trimming techniques to personalize your sewing projects.

WORDS TO REMEMBER

appliqué
sew-through button
shank button

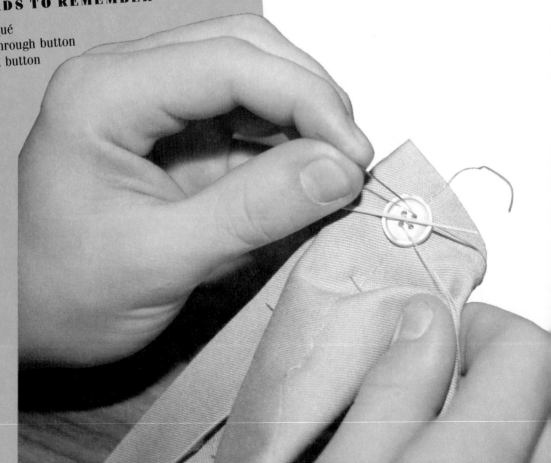

ashion details come and go as styles change, but the fundamentals of good sewing can be applied to any design. To achieve a look of quality, you will need to decide on the best techniques for sewing the details you choose. Many of your options depend on your pattern and fabric selection. You may also need to make a choice between finishing something by hand or machine, so your sewing skills will also influence your decisions.

You will be better able to pick out fashion details if you can visualize and evaluate what the finished detail will look like. In this chapter, you will learn some of the sewing techniques needed for:

- Special details such as collars, cuffs, sleeves, pockets, waistbands, casings, ribbings, hems, and trims.
- Closures such as buttons, snaps, hooks and eyes, zippers, and hook and loop tapes.

Special Techniques

If you're just learning to sew, you may want to practice your skills on an easy project before choosing a pattern with several special details. Once you master these techniques, you will have a wider choice of patterns that you will be able to handle.

Collars and Cuffs

You'll find specific instructions on your pattern guide sheet for your garment's collar or cuffs. However, there are some general guidelines for all collars and cuffs.

On a collar, the curved edges should be smooth and the collar points should be even. The undercollar or underside should never show. Interfacing is necessary for some collars and cuffs. Use short reinforcement stitches for the sharp points so fabric threads will not pull out. Trim and grade the seam allowances. Understitch so that they will lie smooth and flat. Press carefully.

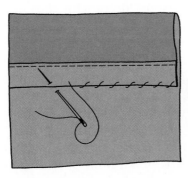

HEMMING STITCH

Most projects require some hand sewing—finishing a hem, attaching fasteners or trims, repairing a seam, or basting fabrics together. These illustrations show how to do four hand stitches. When might you use each stitch?

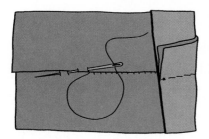

SLIPSTITCH

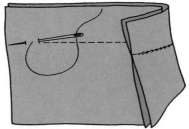

BACKSTITCH

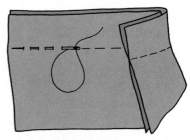

RUNNING STITCH

RAGLAN

KIMONO

SET-IN

There are three basic types of sleeves: kimono, raglan, and set-in. All styles are variations of these basic types.

Sleeves

There are three basic styles of sleeves:

- Kimono sleeves are cut in one piece with the top of the garment. They are usually short and loose-fitting.
- Raglan sleeves have two diagonal seams that run from the neckline to the underarm. They are easy to sew and comfortable to wear.
- Set-in sleeves are attached by one seam that goes in a circle over the shoulder and under the arm. The sleeve can be stitched into the armhole before the side seam and underarm seam are completed, as in a shirt. The sleeve can also be attached to the armhole after the two seams are done. The ideal set-in sleeve should have no gathers or puckers in the seam.

Pockets

Two different types of pockets that are particularly easy to sew are in-seam and patch pockets. In-seam pockets are usually cut along with skirt or pants sections and stitched at the same time as the side seams. A patch pocket is sewn to the outside of a garment. Patch pockets are also popular on tote bags, duffels, and other projects. Topstitch the pocket in place, using the edge of the presser foot as a guide for straight stitching. The top corners of the pocket should be reinforced with triangular stitching or a bar-tack.

Waistbands

Waistbands need to be strong and sturdy to support a skirt, shorts, or pants. Interfacing is essential to keep the waistband from rolling and stretching.

Most waistbands call for a turned-under edge as a finish on the inside. A faster method requires laying out the pattern so that one long edge of the waistband is cut on the selvage. Because the selvage does not ravel it will not need to be turned under. This eliminates extra bulk. Another way to eliminate extra bulk and smooth the edges of your sewing project is to trim, grade, and clip the seam edges.

Some directions call for topstitching the waistband from the right side, while others instruct you to stitch by hand on the inside.

Hems

Hems are used at the bottom edge of pants legs, skirts, shirts, and jackets. They are the last step in constructing a project. To determine the right length, try on the garment wearing the shoes you expect to wear with it.

Stand up straight and have someone mark the hemline with pins or chalk. Fold the hem up and pin it. Check the length and evenness in a mirror.

Next, trim the width of the hem to the desired depth. Pants, sleeves, and shorts usually have hems of 1 to 2 in. (2.5 to 5 cm). On dresses and skirts, the hem could be up to 3 in. (7.5 cm) deep. Straight hems can be wider than curved hems. If you are still growing, you may want a wider hem that can be let down in the future.

The hem edge on woven fabric should be finished to prevent raveling. Use one of the seam finishing techniques or apply seam tape, bias tape, or lace.

Stitch the hem in place with small, invisible hand stitches, or topstitch using straight, zigzag, or decorative stitches. Hems can also be secured with a fusible web. Fusing is good on garments that will not need to be lengthened.

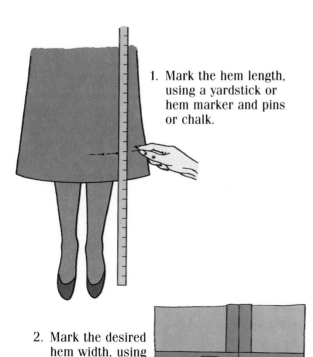

1. Mark the hem length, using a yardstick or hem marker and pins or chalk.

2. Mark the desired hem width, using a sewing gauge and chalk.

The hem can be attached to the garment by hand stitching, machine stitching, or fusing.

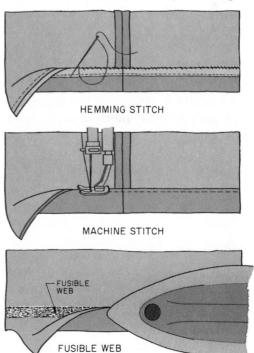

HEMMING STITCH

MACHINE STITCH

FUSIBLE WEB

FUSIBLE WEB

Casings

Casings are used for drawstrings or elastic at the waistline of pants, shorts, and skirts, or on one-piece outfits such as dresses and jumpsuits. They are also used at necklines and at hemlines of sleeves and pants.

You can create a self-casing by folding back an extension of the fabric at the edge of the garment and stitching it in place. Some casings—for example those at the waistline of one-piece garments—are made by stitching a strip of bias tape to the inside of the garment.

Leave an opening at the seam to insert the elastic or drawstring. Attach a safety pin to the end of the elastic or drawstring to pull it through the casing.

Ribbings

Ribbing is a knit with lengthwise ridges and crosswise stretch and recovery. Recovery is the ability of a stretch fabric to go back to its original shape. Ribbing may be used instead of a hem to finish necklines, wrists, ankles, armholes, and waistlines. The ribbing provides a snug but comfortable fit for pullover and pull-on garments, such as sweatshirts, sweatpants, and T-shirts.

To maintain stretchability, apply ribbings with a flexible stitch, such as narrow zigzag, overlock stitch, or overedge stretch stitch. Stretch the ribbing to fit the garment edge as you sew.

For sew-through buttons, you have to make a thread shank. The shank provides room for the fabric to stay smooth beneath the button when the garment is fastened.

Closures

Closures include buttons and buttonholes, snaps, hooks and eyes, zippers, and hook-and-loop tapes. Buy your closures when you buy your pattern and fabric. The quantity and size you'll need are listed on the pattern envelope.

Buttons

There are two kinds of buttons: sew-through and shank. A **sew-through button** has two or four holes through it and no shank or loop on the back. You'll need to make a thread shank when you sew the button on. The shank leaves room for the thickness of the buttonhole when the button is closed.

To make a thread shank, lay a toothpick or pin on top of the button between the holes. Use double thread and secure the thread with one or two stitches. Sew several stitches over the toothpick or pin and through the fabric. End stitches with the needle and thread under the button. Remove the toothpick or pin and wind the thread several times around the thread shank under the button. Fasten the thread on the underside of the fabric.

A **shank button** has a built-in shank, or loop, on the back. It does not have any holes through it. Sew it in place with several small stitches through the shank and into the fabric.

SEW-THROUGH BUTTON

SHANK BUTTON

Patterns have markings showing the location and length of each buttonhole on the pattern. Buttonholes can be made with a zigzag machine or with a special buttonhole attachment. Well-made buttonholes should all be the same length and the same distance from the edge of the garment. Carefully cut the buttonhole open with the points of a scissors.

Snaps

Sew-on snaps are suitable for areas where there is little strain, such as at the neckline to hold a facing edge flat. Snaps consist of two parts: a ball and a socket. The section of the snap that has the ball should be sewn on the wrong side of the overlap. Then sew the socket on the right side of the underlap so they are perfectly aligned. Make several small stitches through each hole. Secure your thread when you begin and finish your work.

Heavy-duty snaps can be used instead of buttons and buttonholes on jackets and shirts of sturdy, heavyweight fabrics. Each side of a heavy-duty snap is in two sections, applied with a special tool. Follow instruction on the package. Because of their weight, these snaps must be used with at least two thicknesses of fabric reinforced with interfacing.

When sewing on snaps, sew three or four stitches through each hole—carrying the thread under the snap from one hole to the next. Be careful not to have any stitches show on the outside of the garment.

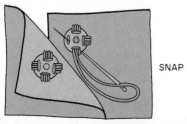

SNAP

Hooks and Eyes

Hooks and eyes are used on waistbands or above zippers where they are not visible. If the finished edges just meet, use a hook with a round eye. If the edges overlap, use a hook with a straight eye. Attach hooks and eyes with small stitches around each loop. Finish with three or four stitches across the end of the hook to make sure it lies flat. Heavy-duty hooks and eyes, also called skirt or pants hooks, are used on waistbands as a sturdier closure for skirts and pants. The hooks are strong and flat so they will not slide out of the eye.

A straight eye is used for edges that overlap; a round eye for edges that meet. Heavy-duty hooks and eyes are used for waistbands.

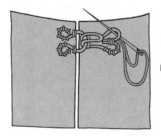

ROUND EYE

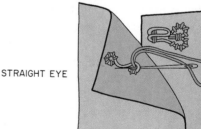

STRAIGHT EYE

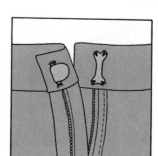

HEAVY-DUTY

Zippers

Detailed instructions for inserting zippers are given on the zipper package. Zippers can be inserted in a seam in two ways—centered, with a row of stitching on each side of the zipper, or lapped, with just one row of stitching showing on the outside. A special zipper foot on the sewing machine makes it easy to stitch close to the zipper teeth.

In fly-front zipper applications the overlap side of the zipper is stitched to a facing, not to the garment. Topstitching holds the facing and zipper in place. On the right front of men's pants, an extension may be a separate piece or cut in one piece with the garment and folded back.

Separating zippers are used in jackets and sweatshirts. They may be inserted to allow the zipper teeth to remain covered or exposed. The method you use for inserting a zipper depends on the garment and the location of the zipper in the garment.

Colorful appliqúes can be attached by machine stitching. Use a close zigzag stitch, covering the edge of the appliqúe completely.

Hook-and-Loop Tapes

Hook-and-loop fasteners consist of two pieces of nylon tape that stick to each other when pressed together. Velcro is the trademark name for hook-and-loop tapes. Though they're too bulky for lightweight fabrics, these closures are common on parkas, jackets, camping equipment, pillows, and totes. They are particularly useful on clothing for people who find it difficult to handle regular closures. Hook-and-loop tape fasteners are available as rectangular strips or circles. Attach the rectangular strips to fabric by machine stitching around all four sides. Attach the circles with a triangle of stitching.

Trims

Trims such as braid, ruffles, lace, and appliqués are wonderful for decorating and emphasizing the lines of garments, accessories, and household items. Almost all can be bought ready-made and can be easily attached with machine stitching or fusible webs.

An **appliqué** (ap-li-KAY) is a cutout fabric decoration sewn onto another fabric background. You can buy appliqués or make them yourself. Use a firmly woven fabric that does not ravel easily. Appliqués can be cut in any shape you choose. Sew on by machine or by hand or use a fusible web.

Embroidery can be used to personalize almost anything that you make or buy. You can add your initials or name to a pocket, pillow, or totebag. You can also use embroidery to create a unique design on a T-shirt or place mat.

INTERPERSONAL SKILLS

Closures to Help People with Disabilities

People with disabilities can gain added independence through clothing adaptations. Being able to manipulate closures is important in maintaining or acquiring self-sufficiency.

Whether a disability is temporary or permanent, a simple task such as opening and closing a zipper can be frustrating. Some disabled people have difficulty grasping the small tab slider, so a zipper pull such as a large metal ring, a tassel, a chain, or a large bead provides something that is easier to grasp. A simple leather thong, large enough to accommodate the thumb, may be looped through the zipper. For separating zippers, knot leather thongs through holes punched in the bottom of the zipper tape. This provides something to hold with one hand while pulling up the zipper with the other.

Zippers may be inserted in leg seams to enable clothing to go over braces or casts. A zipper in a raglan sleeve seam makes clothing easier to pull over the head.

Some people with disabilities find it difficult to handle small buttons. Use large buttonholes and large buttons with raised rims. Toggles may be easier to manage than buttons. Buttons or toggles can be sewn on with elastic thread or with a loop of narrow flat elastic. Horizontal buttonholes are easier to handle than vertical ones.

One of the most adaptable closures is hook-and-loop tape. Because it is easy to open and close with one hand it can replace zippers, buttons, or snaps.

To adapt a garment for hook-and-loop tape, cut the tape in pieces the size of a postage stamp. For the front opening of a shirt, jacket, or dress, sew the buttonholes shut and remove the buttons. Stitch the loop side of the tape behind each buttonhole. Then sew the hook side to where each button was stitched. This method helps prevent the scratchy hooks from irritating the skin. Finish by sewing the buttons on top of the buttonholes.

Think It Through

1. Do you know anyone who could benefit from some of these suggestions for closures? How can these adaptations be helpful?

2. Jason broke his arm playing football and has to keep it in a cast for several weeks. How could his clothing be adapted so that he would be able to dress himself?

Reviewing the Facts

1. What will influence your decision when choosing a technique to use on special details and closures?
2. What are three basic styles of sleeves?
3. What are two types of easy-to-sew pockets?
4. Where might casings be used?
5. When would you use a ribbing instead of a hem?
6. Describe the difference between attaching a sew-through button and a shank button.
7. What kinds of closures can be used on pants?
8. Name two kinds of decorations that can be added to a sewing project.

Sharing Your Ideas

1. How will well-sewn details on the garments or projects that you sew increase your self-esteem?
2. If you had to decide between finishing something by hand or machine, which would you choose? What are the advantages and disadvantages of each method?

Applying Your Skills

1. Using Reference Materials. Visit the library and read about the history and use of embroidery or appliqué. How can embroidery or appliqué be used to personalize everyday items? Suggest five projects anyone could make using these techniques.

2. Evaluating Alternatives. Using mail-order or pattern catalogues, select ten garments that use some type of fastener. List alternative types of fasteners that could be used for each design. What would be the advantages and disadvantages of each? How could each garment be adapted for easier use by a person with a physical disability?

3. Rating Workmanship. Compare an expensive garment and an inexpensive garment for quality of workmanship. Evaluate details, such as collars, sleeves, cuffs, pockets, waistbands, casings, hems, fasteners, and trims. How does the workmanship differ? Is the best workmanship always on the more expensive garment? Write a report of your findings.

CHAPTER

66

Clothes Care

OBJECTIVES

This chapter will help you to:

■ Explain how to care for your clothes.
■ Describe different ways to clean clothes.
■ Identify some simple clothing repairs.

WORDS TO REMEMBER

detergent
dryclean
mildew
snag
stain
texturizing

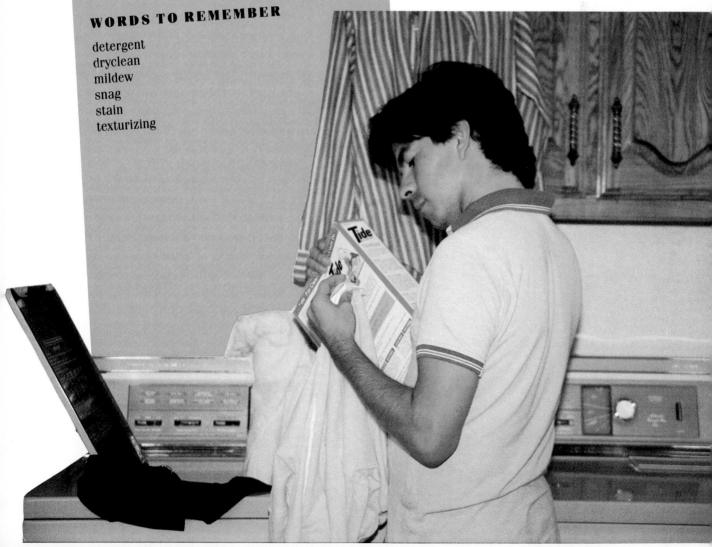

Who takes care of household chores in your home? In increasing numbers of families, jobs such as doing the laundry and repairing clothing are shared among several family members. As you accept responsibility for selecting and purchasing your own clothing, you must also accept responsibility for its care.

Caring for clothing rarely takes longer than a few minutes each day, but the results are well worth the effort. Proper care means that you:

- Put on and take off clothes carefully.
- Open zippers and buttons fully to prevent breaking them or ripping seams.
- Bathe daily and use deodorant or antiperspirant.

- Protect clothes by using a napkin while eating and by wearing old clothes when doing messy chores.
- Take care of stains immediately. The longer a stain remains, the harder it is to remove.

General Care

There are three basic types of clothing care. Keeping clothes in good condition depends on performing some tasks every day, others only occasionally, and still others seasonally.

Daily Care

Take these steps each day to keep your clothes in good condition:

- Before putting clothes away, air them out. Spread them flat on your bed or drape them over a chair.
- Brush off lint and dust. Check each garment to see if it needs repair or has a spot that needs cleaning. A small rip or a loose button takes only a few minutes to fix. If you ignore it, however, the repair may become a major job.
- Set aside any clothes that need to be washed or drycleaned.
- Once your clothes have aired, hang them up or fold them and put them away. Use curved or wooden hangers for jackets and padded hangers for delicate fabrics. Close zippers and one or two buttons on each garment.

Take time to check your clothes before putting them away—brush off lint and remove stains promptly. Set aside clothes that need to be cleaned or repaired.

Occasional Care

Set aside some time each week for making sewing repairs. This is also the time to hand wash clothing that can't be put in the machine. If clothes need ironing or pressing, do it all at one time to save effort and energy.

You might also collect all your clothes that need to be fixed and put them in one place, such as a clothes basket or a dresser drawer. Then, when you have a few minutes to spare, make the necessary repairs. You could even repair your clothing while watching television.

Follow the directions on the care labels when deciding how to clean your clothes.

Seasonal Care

When the seasons change, people often change their wardrobes and put clothes in storage. A winter coat, for example, may not be worn for several months. When clothes aren't worn for a long time, they can become damaged if not stored properly. To protect stored clothes:

- Make sure that the clothes are clean, dry, and free of stains. If the garments are not cleaned before they are stored, any leftover perspiration and skin oils may weaken the fabric. Insects such as silverfish can attack food stains and damage the fibers, also.

- Treat woolens with moth repellent to prevent moth larvae from eating the fibers. If possible, seal woolens in an airtight bag.

- To prevent **mildew**—a fungus that grows on damp fabric, causing stains—make sure that clothes are completely dry before you put them away. Also, store them where they will remain dry.

- You can also put stored clothes in garment bags or boxes to protect them.

Cleaning Clothes

All clothes need to be cleaned, but different garments need different types of cleaning. Jeans with a grass stain will require a more thorough washing than will a shirt that is only slightly soiled. Some fabrics require drycleaning, and delicate items need to be washed by hand.

To choose the correct cleaning method, check the care label. It will tell you what procedure to follow, such as machine wash, hand wash, or dryclean. A label will also tell you whether to machine dry or line dry a garment and any cautions about ironing temperatures. The label also tells you what not to do, such as "Do not bleach."

Removing Stains

Sometimes dirt is concentrated in one spot in a garment. Such a spot is a **stain.** You may need to give a stain special treatment before adding the garment to a load of laundry. The chart on page 590 lists removal procedures for some common stains. Some stains can be removed by spraying them with a prewash spray, letting the spray set, and then washing the clothing normally.

Always try to treat stains either when they occur or soon afterward. A quick rinse with cold water helps remove many stains from washable fabrics. For nonwashable fabrics, sponge with water or club soda, wetting the fabric as little as possible.

Sorting Clothes

Before washing clothes, you must decide which items can be washed together. First, separate the clothing according to care labels. Put together all clothes that can be machine washed at the same temperature and all those that must be hand washed. Hand washing is best for delicates, woolens, and silks, as well as for single items that should be washed separately.

Next, sort out fabrics that might leave lint, such as terry cloth bath towels and corduroy. Separate bulky items like sheets that might tangle with and tear delicate clothes.

Finally, sort by color. The dye from bright colors may stain whites, so whites should be washed separately. Even if your red cotton T-shirt has the same care instructions as your white cotton underwear, do not wash them together. You may not want pink underwear!

Stain Removal Chart

Stain	Cleaning Method
Blood	Soak in cold water and detergent or presoak. Wash using bleach if safe for fabric.
Candle wax, chewing gum	Harden by rubbing with ice cube, then scrape off with a dull knife or your fingernail.
Chocolate	Soak in cool water. Rub in detergent and wash. If brown stain remains, use bleach if safe for fabric.
Cosmetics	Rub detergent into stain and wash.
Grass, flowers, foliage	Rub detergent into stain and wash. If stain remains, sponge with alcohol. For stains on acetate, dilute alcohol with two parts water.
Grease	Apply prewash soil-and-stain remover, then wash. If stain remains, sponge with cleaning fluid and rinse.
Ink	Sponge with rubbing alcohol or spray with hair spray. Rinse. Rub any remaining stain with detergent and wash.
Nail polish	Do not use polish remover. Sponge with amyl acetate and wash. If necessary, sponge with alcohol mixed with a few drops of ammonia.
Paint, varnish	Rub detergent into stain and wash. If stain is only partially removed, sponge with turpentine or mineral spirits. Rinse.
Perspiration	If garment color has been affected, sponge fresh stains with ammonia, old stains with white vinegar. Rinse and launder.
Soft drinks	Sponge with cold water, or soak in cold water. Wash using bleach if safe for fabric.

Washing will be easier if you sort your laundry into piles of items that can be washed together. You might have quite a few piles: sheets, towels, dark colors, light colors, whites, and delicate fabrics such as laces and sheers.

Washing Clothes

Washing cleans clothes by pushing water between the yarns and fibers. The water either dissolves the soil or lifts the particles of dirt away from the fabric. Cleaning agents are usually used to help remove soil. Two products, soap and detergent, perform the same function but are chemically different. Soap is made from animal or vegetable fat; **detergent** is made from chemicals or petroleum. Sometimes one is preferred over the other. Detergent, for example, is usually recommended for garments treated with a flameproof solution.

The following laundry products may be used for special purposes:

- Presoak helps remove protein stains like egg, meat juices, and blood.
- Prewash spray helps dissolve or lift out many stains before washing.
- Water softener softens hard water, which has lots of mineral deposits preventing thorough cleaning.
- Disinfectant destroys bacteria. It may be used if the water is not hot, or if there is an illness in the family.
- Bleach removes stains and soil. It acts as a disinfectant, and it brightens white items.
- Fabric softener decreases static electricity and makes fabric feel softer.

You can wash your clothes in two ways—by hand or in a washing machine. The chart on page 592 shows different washing machine settings. Whether the machine is in your home or in a laundromat, you should follow these steps:

1. Check garment pockets to make sure they are empty. Close all fasteners.
2. Select water temperature as directed on the garments' care labels. To save energy, wash with warm or cold water instead of hot water.
3. Add the clothing and the soap or detergent to the machine. (Read the instructions on the machine or in the machine's operating guide first. Some require that you add the soap or detergent before putting the clothing into the machine.) Add bleach if appropriate. If you're using fabric softener, follow package directions.

It's important to sort your clothes into groups of fabrics and colors that can be washed together.

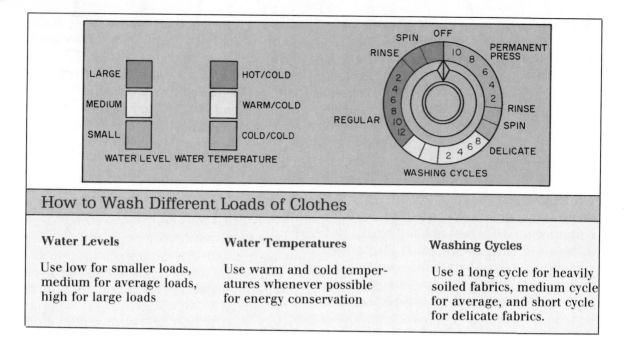

How to Wash Different Loads of Clothes

Water Levels	**Water Temperatures**	**Washing Cycles**
Use low for smaller loads, medium for average loads, high for large loads	Use warm and cold temperatures whenever possible for energy conservation	Use a long cycle for heavily soiled fabrics, medium cycle for average, and short cycle for delicate fabrics.

4. Adjust the water level. If you are not washing a full load of clothing, reduce the setting to conserve water.
5. Turn on the wash cycle.
6. When the cycle is over, remove the garments from the washer and clean the filter.

Drying and Ironing

For best results check the care labels again and set the correct temperature on the clothes dryer. Fabrics made of manufactured fibers are usually dried at a lower temperature than cotton fabrics. Be sure to remove your clothes as soon as they're dry. Fold them or hang them up immediately to prevent wrinkling.

Some clothes should not be put in a dryer. The care label will tell you whether you should hang the garment on a clothesline or lay it flat on a towel to dry. Line drying can help give your wash a pleasant, fresh smell. If you only have a few items to dry, hanging them saves energy and avoids shrinkage.

Some fabrics require pressing or ironing to get a smooth finish. Knits and woolens should be pressed, not ironed, to avoid stretching. To iron a woven fabric, be sure to iron with the grainline.

Drycleaning

You will have to **dryclean** some fabrics, that is, they must be cleaned with chemicals rather than soap or detergent and water. After they are cleaned, the clothes are put on forms that are in the shape of a body and steam is blown through them to remove wrinkles. Special touches, such as creases in trousers, are added by a steam-pressing machine or by hand with a steam iron.

Some fabrics and trimmings are harmed by drycleaning. Vinyl, for example, cannot be drycleaned. Leather and suede need special handling. If the care label says not to dryclean, follow the advice. The manager of the drycleaning store will tell you if any trim must be removed before cleaning.

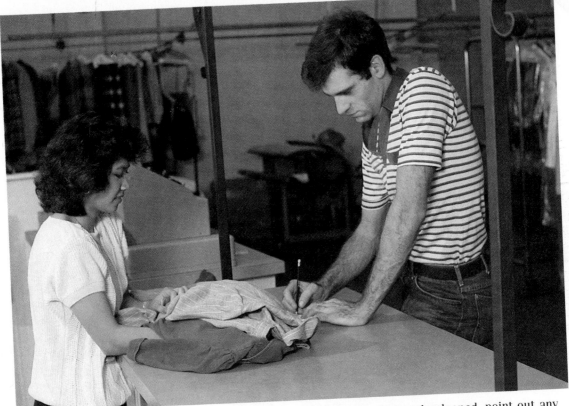

When having clothes drycleaned, point out any stains so they can be specially treated.

Cleaners may miss spots and stains unless you point them out. If you know what caused the stain, tell the drycleaner. Otherwise, it may not be identified correctly. The more information you provide, the better the results.

Some laundromats offer coin-operated drycleaning machines. These cost less than professional drycleaning and remove most soil quite well. They don't, however, provide special treatment for spots and stains.

Simple Repairs

No matter how careful you are you will need to repair your clothing at some point. Here are some ways to make simple repairs.

- **Repairing snags.** Knits often **snag** which means that loops of yarn are pulled out of the knit. To repair these, use a crochet hook or a snag fixer, which can be bought wherever notions are sold. Grasp the snag with the hook and pull it back through to the underside of the fabric. Gently stretch the fabric to smooth out any puckers that the snag caused.

- **Mending seams.** Seams that are coming apart can be stitched by machine or by hand, using a strong backstitch.

- **Patching a hole.** For jeans and casual clothes, use iron-on patches that you can buy in fabric stores. For dressier clothes, matching is important. Cut a piece of fabric from the hem or seam allowance, and place it under the hole. Turn in the torn edges and stitch around the opening with tiny, hardly visible stitches.

- **Replacing fasteners.** You may have to mend the fabric underneath before replacing a fastener.

Easy-Care Fabrics

When you want to save time on clothing care, look for garments that don't need ironing. Manufacturers create easy-care garments by using special fibers, special finishes, and special fabric treatments.

- **Fiber content.** The fiber content is generally a very good clue to how much ironing will be needed to maintain a garment's new look. Most manufactured fibers tend to wrinkle less than natural fibers and require relatively little ironing if care instructions are followed. Acrylic, polyester, and nylon are popular manufactured fibers used in garments that need no ironing. These fibers are often blended with natural fibers.

- **Finish.** Crinkles, wrinkles, and puckers are seen in both casual and dressy wear. Ironing would damage these textures. Some fabrics have a permanent heat-set texture. Others may be woven or knit with texturized yarns. **Texturizing** is a process that adds crimp or curl to a normally straight yarn. Knit or woven fabrics may be treated with finishes to create crinkles or a puckered surface, as in seersucker.

- **Fabric manufacture.** Certain fabrics have been prewashed to give them a worn look when you buy them. These fabrics may be called "washed cotton," "laundered sheeting," "prewashed" or "stone-washed" denim. Such fabrics have an uneven surface texture that is desirable in casual sportswear and comfortable activewear. Knits are also manufactured for easy care. Knitted clothes need little ironing, even those that are made of cotton. If you remove them from the dryer immediately they can be hand-smoothed to be wrinkle-free.

Think It Through

1. Can you think of two specific ways that an easy-care garment affects a person's lifestyle?
2. Why do you think there is such a demand today for easy-care garments?

CHAPTER
66 REVIEW

Reviewing the Facts

1. Describe four steps you should take every day to care for your clothes.
2. Why are care labels so important in helping you keep your clothes looking attractive?
3. Explain how clothes should be sorted before you wash them.
4. What do the following laundry products do: presoak, bleach, fabric softener?
5. List three common stains and explain how to treat each.
6. When using an automatic washer, what four steps should you follow before starting the machine?
7. What are two methods of drying clothes?
8. How are clothes drycleaned?

Sharing Your Ideas

1. What sort of impression is given by a person who wears stained or unmended clothing?
2. How does taking care of your clothing show a sense of responsibility?

Applying Your Skills

 1. Classifying Information. Make a care chart for your clothes. Using the care labels as your guide, classify the different types of care into different columns for your chart. List each item under the appropriate heading.

2. Computing and Comparing Costs. Visit a supermarket and write down the prices and sizes of five brands of detergent. Check the package directions and note how much detergent is recommended per wash load. Calculate which brand and size is the least expensive per washload.

3. Performing Experiments. Stain separate swatches of fabric with items such as chocolate, lipstick, grass, grease, ink, and soft drinks. Cut each swatch in half. Using the Stain Removal Chart on page 590, try cleaning each stain from one of the fabric halves. Then wash all fabric swatches—both the treated and the untreated—and compare the results.

Redesigning and Recycling

OBJECTIVES

This chapter will help you to:

- Describe ways to get more use out of your favorite garments.
- Determine how to make old or ill-fitting clothes wearable again.
- Suggest uses for clothes that you can no longer wear.

WORDS TO REMEMBER

patchwork
recycle
redesign

Think back to the first step of planning your wardrobe, in Chapter 59. You made three piles of clothes:

- Clothes in good condition that you like to wear.
- Clothes that you like, but which need fixing.
- Clothes that you do not wear because you've outgrown them or you don't like them.

In the third pile, you put clothes that no longer appeal to you or that you cannot wear. Did you find some pants that were too short or a dress that was no longer "you"? You don't have to throw those clothes away. You might be able to **redesign** the garment—change it so that it's more in fashion or has an exciting new look. Perhaps you can **recycle** the garment—find a new use for it.

Redesigning and recycling offer many personal rewards. You can use your creativity to alter a poor-fitting pair of pants, redesign a shirt bought at a garage sale, or change a garment in your closet to better suit your tastes. It's a good way to save money by extending the life of your clothes.

Redesigning a Garment

One of the easiest ways to make a garment wearable again is to change the way it fits. You may be able to do this by simply adjusting the hems or seams.

Adjusting Hems

Have you suddenly grown two inches and your clothes are too short or are the newest fashions showing longer or shorter hemlines? If so, you can lengthen or shorten your clothes.

If there is too little fabric for lengthening the garment, stitch a strip of wide hem facing to the bottom edge. Turn the facing to the inside along the new hemline and sew in place. You could also add a fabric band or ruffle.

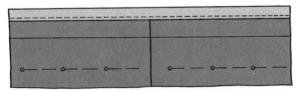

1. To lengthen or shorten a hem, remove stitching and press out old crease. Try on garment and have someone mark the new hem length with pins or chalk.

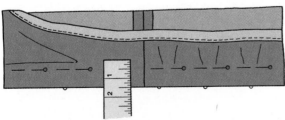

2. Turn up hem along marked line and pin in place. If hem is too wide, cut off extra fabric and finish raw edge with seam tape or stitching. If hem is too narrow, sew on wide hem facing.

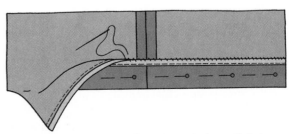

3. Sew hem in place, keeping stitches slightly loose to avoid puckering. Be sure stitches do not show on outside of garment.

Altering Seams

It is easier to take in seams than to let them out. To take in a seam, put on the garment and pin a new seamline. Baste the new seam, and check the fit by trying on the garment to be sure it feels comfortable. Rip out the old seam as far as necessary. Stitch the new seam, overlapping the old stitching with the new stitching for 1 inch (2.5 cm).

If you want to let out a seam, check the seam allowance to be sure that there is enough fabric to make the change. Many ready-made garments have serged seams that are usually less than 1/4 in. (6 mm) wide. Rip out the old seam as far as necessary. Pin and baste the new seamline, and check the fit. Then stitch the new seam, overlapping the stitching lines.

Changing the Style

You can also change the style of clothes to get more use out of them. Consider making changes in one of the following ways:

- **Use.** You can turn a garment from one type into another. By removing sleeves from a sweater, you make a vest. Shorten pants legs to make cropped pants or shorts; turn sweatshirts into cut-off tops; alter coats to make jackets.

- **Shape.** Reshape a garment. Turn flared pants into straight legs or bring a full garment closer to the body by taking in the side seams. Shortening also changes the shape.

- **Details.** Give a shirt or blouse a new look by shortening the sleeves, removing a collar, or adding patch pockets. Collars or cuffs can be replaced with knitted ribbing.

- **Trimmings.** Add an appliqué, ribbon, buttons, or other trimmings. Replace original buttons or trim to update the design of a garment or accessory.

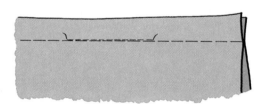

1. When repairing or altering seams, overlap the old stitching lines about 1 in. (2.5 cm) as you start and finish the new stitching.

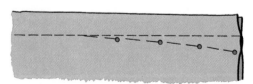

2. To take in a seam, pin new seamline and machine baste. Remove old stitching, and try on garment to check fit. Stitch new seam, overlapping stitches, and press.

3. To let out a seam, check seam allowances for extra fabric. Baste new seam and remove old stitching. Check fit, stitch seam, and press.

Creative Measures

You can make old or damaged clothes bright and lively by adding decorations. Patches, appliqués, trims, and embroidery can cover holes, hide stains, or liven up your clothing. Even if your sweatshirt doesn't have a hole, decorate it with an appliqué, costume jewelry, a painted design, or a sports-team emblem. Use these decorations to make garments that show your individuality.

Dyeing

Perhaps the only thing wrong with a garment is its color. If you don't like the color or it doesn't go with the rest of your clothes, you can consider dyeing, or changing the color of the fabric.

You can dye your clothes at home, or you can have them dyed professionally. For successful home dyeing, follow the directions on the dye package.

Home dyeing works best when a light-colored fabric is darkened. Mix the dye with hot water, and then soak the fabric in a sink, a washing machine, or another container. You must simmer the fabric in the dye if you want it to come out very dark. Natural fibers absorb dye better than manufactured fibers.

In tie-dyeing, parts of the fabric are tightly wrapped or tied, so that the dye penetrates unevenly, producing many different shades of the color. One or several colors may be used in this process.

Dyes may stain containers and other materials, so you should always get permission to use the equipment with which you plan to dye your clothes. Never dye clothes in a laundromat.

Fabric Painting

An old shirt may be given a new look with fabric paint. Acrylic paints, cold-water fabric dyes, tube paints, waterproof markers, and fabric marking pens can be used to cover a stain or reclaim a comfortable old T-shirt, sweatshirt, or skirt.

Wash and dry the garment before painting to soften the fabric and remove any finish that might repel the dye. Then follow instructions for the type of paint or dye that you are using. When the dye dries, cover the painted area with a clean cloth. Use an iron at the proper setting for the fabric and iron over the entire painted area to set the dye.

Give old clothes a new look by dyeing, painting, or adding colorful trims.

MANAGING RESOURCES

Putting a Little into Your Wardrobe

When clothing is so ragged that it cannot be worn, is there anything you can do with it besides throwing it away? You can save money by using old fabrics to make an accessory for yourself, or the material can be used in any number of crafts projects. Keep in mind, too, that children love to play "dress up" with older people's discarded clothing.

Brainstorm all the possible uses for your worn-out clothing. Start by considering these options:

- Fabric from an adult's garment may be ideal for making children's jumpers, pants, or other clothing. Children like garments made from well-worn fabrics because they are soft and comfortable.

- Old clothing can also be used by children for all types of creative play. They love to wear old clothes for costume parties, Halloween, and class plays at school.

- In some cases, you may be able to cut the worn area away and save the rest of the garment. A comfortable sweater that is worn out at the elbows may make a fine vest.

- Make accessories from old clothes or household fabrics. Convert the legs of a pair of jeans into a backpack or a book bag. Make place mats from a tablecloth that is badly stained.

- Save buttons, zippers, and usable trimmings to use on future projects.

- Use fabric scraps for **patchwork,** a method of sewing small fabric shapes together to create a decorative piece of fabric. Such pieced fabric can be made into one-of-a-kind vests, shirts, place mats, totes, handbags, pillows, or quilts.

- Recycle fabrics for craft projects such as braided rugs or hand crafted rag baskets. Many of these traditional American crafts were created by frugal early settlers who had learned the fine art of recycling. No scraps were ever wasted and clothing was never thrown away because new fabrics were hard to obtain.

Think It Through

1. Jenny has a red raincoat that she never wears because the sleeves are worn out at the elbows, the lining has faded, and it has a bad stain on the front. How could she recycle it?

2. What are some things that you have in your home that are recycled from old clothing or household fabrics?

Recycling a Garment

When a garment has reached the end of the road for you, the fabric or its fibers may still be useful for someone else if you recycle it. Here are three ways to recycle clothes.

Passing it On

During your teen years, you're likely to be growing fast. This means you may outgrow garments long before they are worn out. It's wasteful to throw them away because there may be several years' wear left for someone else.

One of the oldest forms of recycling clothing is the hand-me-down. Clothing that you no longer wear or that no longer suits you can be passed on to a younger brother, sister, cousin, niece, or nephew. You might give it to a friend. A shirt or sweater that is no longer right for you may be perfect for someone else. You and your friends could hold a swap meet and trade garments.

If you don't know anyone who can use the clothes you no longer want, look further. You might earn some money by selling these garments through a consignment shop that buys and sells used clothing. You could also give the clothing to a religious organization or a charity such as the Salvation Army. They may repair and fix used clothing and give it to shelters for the homeless or other people in need. Clothes that you give away may help a family that has lost everything in a fire or a flood. Check in your area for organizations that accept used clothing.

A common method of recycling is to pass garments on to younger family members.

Using the Fabric Another Way

Even if only small pieces of the fabric are in good condition, you can save them for patchwork or crafts projects. If you don't use the fabric scraps yourself, there may be a nursery school, retirement home, or community group that can use fabric for projects.

Worn-out garments of soft cotton make good cleaning rags. It's a good idea to remove all fasteners from the rags to protect furniture from being scratched by sharp hooks or button edges. Save trim, decorations, and fasteners for future projects.

Reusing the Fiber

Even if the fabric cannot be redesigned or given away, the fibers may be recycled—to be used as padding, for instance. Fibers are also used as an ingredient in paper. Some cities have organizations that collect old clothes for such recycling.

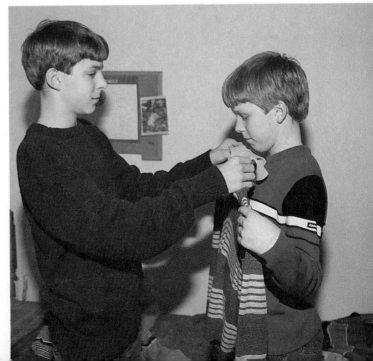

Reviewing the Facts

1. Why is it useful to know how to redesign and recycle garments?
2. How do you lengthen a hem? What could be used if the hem does not have enough fabric to lengthen?
3. What are the steps for taking in a seam?
4. List two specific ways to change the style of a garment.
5. What are three functions that trimmings, dye, or fabric paint on garments can achieve?
6. What are three ways to recycle clothes?
7. How can you pass on clothing that you no longer wear?

Sharing Your Ideas

1. Have you ever worn used garments, handed down by older brothers or sisters, other relatives, or neighbors? If so, how did you feel about wearing these clothes?
2. Have you ever bought used clothing at a garage sale or rummage sale? What are advantages and disadvantages of buying resale clothing?

Applying Your Skills

1. Writing Instructions. Assume you are preparing an article for a crafts magazine. Make up a recycling project that uses everyday objects, such as fabric scraps or old clothing. Include specific cutting and sewing instructions and a sketch of how the finished product should look.

2. Evaluating Historical Information. Research the history of patchwork quilts. Find examples of old scrap quilts that were made in America. Report to the class how fabrics were recycled in these traditional quilts.

3. Performing an Experiment. Obtain two different fabrics—one made of natural fibers and the other made of manufactured fibers. Dye both fabrics, using fabric dye and following the package directions. What are the results? What might account for any differences?

CHAPTER

68

Careers in Clothing and Textiles

OBJECTIVES

This chapter will help you to:

- Identify the interests and skills required for a career in clothing and textiles.
- Give examples of jobs available in design and marketing.
- Give examples of jobs available in clothing construction and care.

WORDS TO REMEMBER

buyer
fashion coordinator
interview
pattern maker

Did you ever wonder who designs the spacewear that keeps space shuttle crews safe and comfortable? Who is responsible for the strong and flexible action-wear garments worn by members of Olympic teams from around the world? Experts in fibers, fabrics, and clothing construction work together to outfit astronauts, Olympic athletes, and other people with special clothing requirements. These experts are some of the hundreds of thousands of workers who also put their talents toward meeting the everyday clothing needs of individuals and families.

The clothing and textiles industry is one of the largest industries in the country. Every year new styles and new developments in fibers and technology are introduced. People are needed to manufacture fabrics and sew garments. Others become entrepreneurs—they start new businesses to provide products or services that consumers want.

Careers in clothing and textiles cover a broad range of endeavors, from designing clothing to working in a textile mill or managing a retail store. Jobs are available in all parts of the country. In this chapter, you'll learn about a few of the fascinating careers in clothing and textiles.

Characteristics for Careers in Clothing and Textiles

Although many types of jobs exist in this field, several of them attract people with similar characteristics. If you have these traits, a clothing career may be for you.

To be successful in a clothing career, as in any career, you need a strong interest and desire to work in your chosen field. Many of the jobs are demanding and put people under a great deal of pressure. Deadlines must be met, and workers frequently put in long hours. Positions in sales, design, and buying require the ability to predict future trends in styles, colors, and fabrics.

For a career in clothing and textiles, you should have an interest in fashion, color, and fabrics.

Interests and Skills

■ **Do you have a sense of color and design?** Do you also enjoy working with shapes? For almost all clothing careers, a sense of color, design, and shape is essential. Clothing workers combine these elements in their work to create attractive, usable products.

■ **Are you well organized?** Clothing jobs often involve following many steps and combining many pieces. To get the job done, you must plan your tasks carefully.

■ **Do you pay careful attention to detail?** This trait is very important for a clothing worker, whatever the job. Careful attention to detail results in a quality product—one that people will buy and recommend to friends. Consumers want to be satisfied with how they spend their clothing dollars.

■ **Are you interested in the technical side of fibers and fabrics?** Because fibers are the basic building blocks of fabrics, an understanding and knowledge of fiber characteristics are valuable. This information is needed in every area of the garment industry, from the design and manufacture of clothing through clothing care.

If you have the abilities outlined here, you might want to pursue one of these careers.

Jobs in Design and Marketing

Many clothing and textile careers have to do with the design, marketing, and selling of clothes. In any one of these jobs, you could combine an interest in fashion with a career in the world of business.

Entry-Level Jobs

Salespeople in retail stores assist customers in making important decisions about their wardrobes. If salespeople know about fabric and wardrobe planning and have the ability to judge quality in clothing, they can answer questions about the fabrics or garments they sell. This helps build the store's credibility and prestige. The ability to meet and work with the public, a pleasant personality, and a well-groomed appearance are qualities that employers look for in their sales personnel.

Being a salesperson is often the first step in a retail clothing career. Some stores require that a full-time salesperson have a high school diploma, but there are many part-time employment opportunities available for students. A part-time sales job can start you on your career path.

Another entry-level position at a department store is that of a stock clerk. Stock clerks check incoming orders, put price tags on garments, and keep track of how the stock is moving. A stock clerk doesn't need special training, but a good background in math and spelling is helpful. It's also useful to enjoy detailed work and to have good organizational skills.

Jobs That Require Training

Buyers are some of the most important people in the fashion industry. **Buyers** connect designers and garment makers with the stores and shops where clothing is sold. They must be able to spot fashion trends many months in advance as well as have a sense of the colors and styles their customers like. A buyer may work for a large department store, a chain of stores, a mail-order house, or a local specialty store. Large stores have a number of buyers who travel to fashion centers to select merchandise for their departments. Fashion centers are buildings that house the sales offices of garment manufacturers. In a small specialty store, the owner of the store is often the buyer.

Large clothing stores have promotion and publicity departments where copywriters and artists prepare ads and displays. College writing or journalism courses will help prepare you for a copywriter's job. Artists and display workers should be talented in art. In addition to what they have learned in school, these workers acquire many skills while on the job.

Some department stores offer their customers the services of personal shoppers. A personal shopper selects fashion merchandise that answers a particular customer's needs, saving time and energy for a busy consumer. A personal shopper must have good taste, be able to work within a predetermined budget, and have the ability to choose clothing that is suitable and pleasing to the customer.

Jobs That Require an Advanced Degree

Large stores have **fashion coordinators** who develop advertising themes and plan fashion events that will bring people into the store. The fashion coordinators often involve community groups, such as school clubs, in their projects. You may have attended or modeled at a fashion show put on by a store.

Working closely with the buyers, the fashion coordinators also make sure that different departments of the store sell clothing and accessories that go well together. They keep the buyers informed about the newest colors and styles. They want to make sure, for example, that a customer who selects a suit in a new color can find matching accessories in other departments.

Fashion coordinators are usually college graduates who majored in home economics or art. In addition, they may attend special fashion and merchandising schools where they get work/study experience. They need experience in various positions within a clothing store.

Stores employ stock clerks and salespersons, sometimes on a part-time basis. What skills are needed for these entry-level jobs?

The designer is another important person in the fashion industry. Every piece of clothing that a buyer selects, and every piece that you wear, first takes shape in the mind of a designer. Designers choose the fabrics and plan the lines of new garments. They make sketches, and sometimes samples, from which a pattern can be made.

Designers usually get their training in college programs for fashion design and by working with experienced designers. To be successful, designers must follow fashion trends closely.

In addition to fashion design, job opportunities exist in fabric design, weaving, and knitting. Today, many fabric designers are creating a variety of textures by using computers to weave different kinds of yarn into different patterns. They can quickly color the designs in a variety of combinations and print a copy of each design on paper—all by computer.

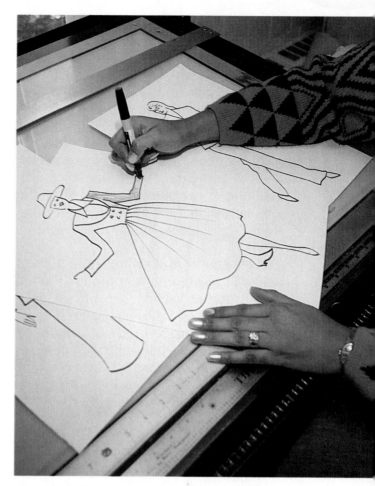

Clothing designers must have a knowledge of art, as well as clothing construction.

Jobs in Clothing Construction and Care

The clothing industry also employs thousands of people who work behind the scenes. These workers are involved in the manufacture of fabrics or garments. They may develop new fibers, dye fabrics, or sew clothes. They also are involved in caring for clothes.

Entry-Level Jobs

The largest number of workers in the garment industry are sewing machine operators. These are the people who do the stitching. Most machine operators are trained on the job to sew on special machines, but they may receive training at a technical or vocational school. Beginners start out stitching the easiest seams. Their wages begin with the legal minimum pay, but they can earn more as they gain skill and responsibility. Operators who show an ability to work with people can become supervisors.

Skilled sewers can work in other businesses. Drycleaning companies employ menders to repair and alter customers' clothing. Resale clothing stores also hire workers with sewing skills for repair work. Many large clothing stores hire alteration workers to alter garments, such as suits, to fit customers.

Jobs That Require Training

Drycleaners must know how to choose the right chemicals to remove stubborn spots and stains without damaging a garment. They learn the techniques to use for each type of fabric and stain. Because the job involves making complex decisions, it takes six to twelve months to learn. This training can be obtained in a vocational school or on the job. Drycleaners who own their own shops need some business training as well.

The **pattern maker** holds the highest paid and most important production job in a garment factory. He or she is a skilled worker who makes a pattern from the designer's original sample. All the patterns of a garment are copies of this first one, so accuracy is very important. Many years of on-the-job experience are needed for this career.

Jobs That Require an Advanced Degree

Not all textiles are suitable for making clothing. To find the right types, research is necessary.

Textile chemists develop new fibers and finishes. Manufactured fibers such as nylon and polyester, as well as durable press and water-repellent finishes, are the result of textile research. Textile engineers develop new techniques for making yarns and fabrics. They seek to improve quality yet keep production costs down. These workers must have college degrees and be skilled in math and chemistry.

Garment manufacturers need pattern makers, cutters, sewing machine operators, pressers, and inspectors to produce the clothes that people wear.

Dyers are also highly skilled workers. They work in textile mills and choose the formulas used for dyeing the fibers or fabrics. They must know chemistry and understand how the dyes and fibers will react together. They should be familiar with computers, which play a major role in controlling color and dyeing fabrics.

Getting a Job

If you have an interest in a career in the textiles and clothing industry, there are many avenues of experience and study that you can follow. High school diplomas are required for most of the jobs described here. Technical or vocational schools, apprenticeship programs, or some other form of post-high school training may be required for some positions. College or fashion merchandising degrees will help you gain the knowledge and skills necessary for specialized positions offering greater responsibility.

What to Wear for an Interview

According to one major university's research, the most common reason that employers give for not hiring an applicant is poor personal appearance. Here are some general grooming tips to help you make a good impression during an **interview**—a meeting between an employer and a job applicant.

- Take a bath or shower before dressing for the interview. Men should shave, if necessary, for a neat appearance.
- Hair should be clean and well-trimmed.
- Fingernails should be clean and trimmed.
- Avoid extremes. Don't dress too casually or too formally.
- Perfume or cologne, if used, should be applied sparingly. A woman should use only a small amount of makeup.

Men can use the following guidelines in dressing:

- Wear a solid-color shirt and a tie. A sports jacket or suit gives a more professional look for offices or stores.
- Choose well-pressed casual or dress pants, not jeans.
- Wear tie shoes or loafers that are polished and neat.

For women, the following guidelines are appropriate:

- Wear a classic dress, a skirt with a sweater, or a skirt-blouse-jacket combination. Pants are not appropriate for an interview.
- Choose sheer or plain-colored pantyhose, coordinated to your outfit.
- Wear classic pumps or flat shoes. Boots are appropriate if they coordinate with your outfit.
- Be conservative in your choice of jewelry.

It is important to make a good impression at a job interview. You're more likely to make that impression if you prepare yourself in advance to look your best.

Think It Through

1. Why would a neat, well-groomed appearance be especially important for a person employed in the clothing and textile industry?
2. Describe in detail an outfit that you now own that would be appropriate for a job interview. What makes the outfit appropriate?

Reviewing the Facts

1. Identify three characteristics useful for careers in clothing and textiles.
2. What are three qualities that an employer looks for when hiring sales personnel in a retail store?
3. Describe the work done by a stock clerk.
4. What is the function of the buyer?
5. What kind of advanced training is usually necessary for a fashion coordinator? A designer?
6. Name three jobs in clothing construction and care, one at each level.
7. In which position in the garment industry are the largest number of workers employed?

Sharing Your Ideas

1. What are some of the ways that you might use your knowledge and skills in clothing and textiles to become an entrepreneur while you are in high school?
2. How can entry-level jobs help prepare you for other jobs within the clothing and textile field?

Applying Your Skills

1. Forming Questions. Make up some basic questions you might want to ask on any job interview, as well as a list of questions you think employers will ask you. Compare your lists with those of your classmates. How do they differ?

2. Comparing Professions. Select two careers in clothing and textiles that you're interested in finding out more about. Ask your librarian to help you find career books, career encyclopedias, or magazine articles about them. Compare the details of each and explain which you would prefer.

3. Planning a Product. Working with two or more classmates, select a textile product that could be made and sold by students. Plan the production steps and estimate the costs of materials and other expenses. Determine a selling price for the product in order to make a profit for the group.

TEEN TIPS

Create Your Color Palette
To look your best and feel your best, wear the colors that do the most for you.

T-Shirt—Make It Unique
Some great ideas for adding a unique design to a T-shirt or sweatshirt.

Designer Jeans—Worth the $$$?
Are designer jeans worth the price? Here are some facts.

Create Your Color Palette

Have you ever heard people ask each other if they are a "summer" or a "winter?" No, this is not a new horoscope. It's a way of analyzing your skin tone and using this analysis to find the colors that look best on you. Both males and females find that this analysis helps them choose the colors that make them look and feel better.

The basis of the seasonal color system is that skin has blue or yellow undertones. Blue undertones are associated with the cool color seasons—winter and summer. People whose skin has blue undertones look best in cool, blue-based colors. Yellow undertones are associated with the warm color seasons—autumn and spring. People whose skin has yellow undertones look best in warm, yellow-based colors.

Use these steps to choose your best colors:

1. Think about your wardrobe. Which colors do you wear over and over again? Which colors bring compliments from others? Which colors make you look dull or washed-out when you wear them?

2. Look at your skin. Hold a piece of white paper next to the inside of your arm and examine your skin tone. Natural light will give you the truest picture, so stand by a window or go outdoors to do this. If you have a hard time seeing yellow or blue undertones, compare your skin with others to see the differences more clearly.

3. Drape colored fabric beneath your face, or use colored paper—try colors from all four seasons. Your best colors will make your skin look bright and healthy. The wrong colors will make your skin look dull, and any shadows or lines will be more obvious.

Look at the four illustrations of teens as you read the descriptions of the color seasons. Decide in which color you feel each teen looks best. Does each have a color season? Then, put yourself into one of the four color seasons.

WINTER

SUMMER

AUTUMN

SPRING

- **Winter.** This is the most common season type. People in this group have beige, taupe, olive, or brown skin and dark hair. They look best in clear, vivid colors such as royal blue, true red, hot pink, emerald green, purple, and lemon yellow. Primary colors look better on them than pastel or muted colors.

- **Summer.** People in this group also have blue undertones, but they're more delicate in coloring than the winter group. Their skin may be very fair or pink. Soft, cool pastels—especially blue—look great on them, as do pink, lavender, and mauve. Blue-green and light yellow are good, but steer clear of royal blue and yellow-green.

- **Autumn.** People in this group have skin with rich golden tones. Most redheads with freckles and medium-to-deep brunettes with peach, ivory, or golden beige skin belong in this group. These people look best in brown, gold, mustard, rust, and moss green. Ivory and beige look good on them, too.

- **Spring.** People in this group have skin with golden undertones but it is more fair and delicate than people in the autumn group. Clear, delicate colors look better on them than dark, muted, or muddy colors. They look best in ivory, warm beige, peach, apricot, salmon, light aqua, turquoise, and yellow-green.

Remember—most colors can be worn by anyone. You just need to pick the right value and intensity. You can use colors that are not in your season as accents, trims, or accessories.

T-Shirt—Make It Unique

You can use T-shirts, sweatshirts, sleepshirts, jeans—even athletic shoes—as a canvas for self-expression. This "art" that you wear can be individualized with designs that vary from the witty to the beautiful. Dare to be different with bright colors and bold designs, or show your more gentle side with soft pastel colors.

1 Stencil or paint a design with liquid dyes.

2 Trim a shirt with ribbons and fabric hearts. Tack on ribbon bows with small hand stitches. Cut out hearts and apply with fusible web.

3 Tie-dye a plain white shirt. Tightly tie or wrap parts of the fabric so the dye will penetrate unevenly, producing many different shades of the color.

4 Use acrylic paints to create a design or write a message.

5 Add a colorful, gathered border to the bottom edge of a shirt. Stitch a seam in 1/2 yard of fabric to make a tube. Hem one edge and gather the other edge. Stitch gathered edge to bottom of shirt.

6 Make appliqués using fabric scraps. Fuse cut-outs to shirt, then outline with closely spaced zigzag stitches on the sewing machine.

7 Collect buttons in different sizes, shapes, and colors. Sew them on a shirt in a sunburst pattern.

8 Use puff paints, sequins, and jewels to add glitter and glamour to ordinary designs.

I ♥ School

Designer Jeans — Worth the $$?

American consumers buy about 385 million pairs of jeans a year. You might pay anywhere from $20.00 to $50.00 or more for a pair of jeans, depending upon the brand, the style, and the store where you buy it. Yet an average pair of jeans is worth about $7.00 in materials. Where does the rest of the money go?

Let's take a look at the manufacturer's costs for a pair of jeans:

- $6.00 for denim fabric (about 1¾ yards)
- $1.00 for buttons, rivets, and thread
      (standard jeans use 5 buttons, 6
      rivets, and 2⅓ yards of thread)
- $1.40 in salaries and benefits for designers
      and sewing machine operators (14
      minutes and 40 separate steps for
      each pair of jeans)
- $2.50 for packaging, shipping, and other
      overhead costs
- $1.10 for advertising, public relations, and
      other marketing costs
- $1.30 in salaries and benefits for salespeople
      and executives
- $1.70 in profits

$15.00 wholesale price to the store

Styles with certain extras usually cost more to manufacture. For example, stone-washed, acid-washed, or whitewashed jeans must go through an extra manufacturing step, which increases the wholesale cost.

Stores usually sell clothing for twice the wholesale cost, so a pair of jeans that a store buys for $15.00 would sell for $30.00 retail. Stores—just like manufacturers—have many costs, including salaries and benefits for employees, advertising, displays, lighting and heating, markdowns, shoplifting, and security. Some stores have much higher overhead costs than others, depending on their location and services offered. Thus you may pay a higher price at one store than at another for the same brand of jeans.

Why are designer jeans usually more expensive? If a famous designer or celebrity endorses a brand of jeans, he or she receives a fee for each pair of jeans sold. Usually designer labels are widely advertised and promoted—in magazine, newspaper, radio, and television ads—resulting in expensive marketing costs. All of these fees and costs are added to the wholesale and retail prices of designer jeans.

Are you getting a better product with designer jeans? They may be better designed or may fit you better—but not necessarily. It's up to you to decide if they are worth the price.

HOUSING AND LIVING SPACE

Living Space and You

OBJECTIVES

This chapter will help you to:

- Describe how living space meets psychological needs.
- List the physical needs that housing meets.
- Explain how location, lifestyle, and budget affect housing decisions.

WORDS TO REMEMBER

condominium
facility
location

mortgage
personal space

Have you ever claimed some space on a beach by putting down your towel, sunglasses, and radio? When you did this, you said to all the world, "This is my place. Please do not disturb it." Then you filled up your space with the things that were important to you. For a few hours, you created a home base at the beach—a place where you belonged.

Your home is the place where you always feel that you belong. It is the place where you can meet your needs for warmth, companionship, privacy, safety, and self-expression. It is also the place where you keep your possessions and do the things you want to do. Most importantly, your home is where your family is—where you live with the people you love and the people who love you.

Meeting Psychological Needs

Most of us think of home as a warm, comforting place where we can relax and please ourselves. Our homes fill several emotional needs in us that aren't fulfilled by school or work or other places.

A Sense of Belonging

Your home should provide you with a sense of belonging. You should feel that your home is a place where you can unwind, where you can do things with your family and friends or just be by yourself. A sense of belonging makes you feel that you are a member of the household. You may have to follow certain rules as a member of the family, but you also feel comfortable raiding the refrigerator or participating in family decisions. This is what is meant by a sense of belonging.

Privacy

The need for a place of one's own—**personal space**—is basic to all people. Even if you share your personal space, it's still a place that you feel is your own. You have the privilege of asking people in when you want to and of keeping them out, when that is what you want.

People need private, personal space where they can read, listen to music, study, talk with friends, or just be alone to think and dream.

This privilege allows you to have privacy—the ability to be alone. Everyone needs to get away from others at times, even if it's only for a couple of hours. People use that time away from other people in any way they want to, whether it's to think, to dream, or to make decisions.

Individuality

Just as the way you dress expresses your personality, the way you arrange and use your living space enhances your self-concept. You can put up posters of your favorite rock stars or classical musicians. You can display your collections or work on your hobbies. You can keep your favorite books, tapes, and other possessions around you. All of these things say, "This is who I am."

Later, when you set up your own home, some of these personal possessions will help you feel comfortable in a new place. An empty room quickly becomes yours when you put up your favorite pictures or arrange a few of your mementos.

Values and Goals

How you live also reflects your values. If you value neatness, you will have a well-organized space. If you appreciate family heirlooms, you may have antique furniture that belonged to another generation of your family.

How you live also reflects your goals. If getting a good education is an important goal of yours, you will probably have a comfortable place to study and lots of book shelves. If being popular is important to you, you may want space in your home to have parties and entertain friends.

Your home also reflects the goals of other members of your family. For example, your mother may need room to write or sew, and your brother may need some space to keep his hamster cage.

Meeting Physical Needs

In addition to meeting your psychological needs, a home also meets the following physical needs for you and your family.

- **Shelter.** One important job of a home is to provide shelter from the weather outside, whether it is wind, rain, snow, or extreme heat.
- **Safety.** A home also protects your family and your possessions from dangers such as accidents, injuries, and crimes.
- **Space for possessions.** A home provides you with space for your possessions, such as your books, clothes, and furniture.
- **Space for activities.** A home provides a place for activities, such as cooking, bathing, entertaining, working on hobbies, exercising, and talking. Many of these activity areas can be used by more than one person.

Housing Choices

When your parents chose the home where you now live, they had to ask several important questions about how the home would fulfill their needs and wants:

- How many people are in your household? A large family needs more bedrooms and baths than a small family.

A home provides space for possessions and activities, such as listening to music.

■ How old is each member of your family? If there are small children in your family, your parents may have wanted a house with a fenced-in yard. If one or more grandparents live with you, they might want rooms on the first floor to avoid the need to climb stairs.

■ What are the special needs of family members? For example, does anyone with disabilities need wheelchair ramps or extra wide doors? Are there other children in the neighborhood? Is the school system a good one? Can you walk to shopping areas?

When making housing choices, people also have to consider four important factors: where the housing is located, what type of housing to choose, whether to rent or buy, and how much to spend on housing.

Where?

The first decision to make when choosing a home is to decide where it will be located. **Location** refers to the region of the country where you will live. The availability of work may be a major factor in determining in what part of the country you will live. For example, if you go to work for an airplane manufacturer in the Pacific Northwest or an oil company in Louisiana, you would have to live where the company is located.

Location also refers to the kind of community you choose to live in—urban, suburban, rural, or small town. People are attracted to a place that offers the lifestyle and the **facilities,** or goods and services available in a community, that they desire. For instance, if they like museums, shopping, and lots of activities, they will choose to live in a city or large suburban area. If they like quiet and the outdoors, they will choose a rural setting for their home.

The facilities and services offered by communities include schools, fire and police protection, parks, libraries, and trash pickup. You might choose a home because it is in a nice neighborhood and has a good school system. Someone else may choose a home that is close to public transportation systems or recreational areas. Others may want to be able to walk to a church or to stores.

A family that enjoys outdoor activities will want housing that has convenient access to recreational facilities and parks.

What Type?

A home can be any size, shape, and style. Here are a few examples:

- **Single-family house.** This home provides living space for one family. It is not attached to any other building. It stands on its own, usually on a separate lot with a lawn and outdoor living space.
- **Townhouse.** This is one of many single-family units attached to other units on its sides. In the city, these may be called row houses. Each family lives in a different unit.
- **Duplex or triplex.** This is a building divided into living spaces for two or three families. The spaces can be side by side or one on top of the other.
- **Apartment building.** This building contains a number of separate living units. The living spaces may range in size from one-room studio apartments to three-bedroom units. If the people who live in each unit have a patio or bit of lawn, the units are called garden apartments. If the building is very tall, it is called a high-rise.
- **Mobile home.** This is a factory-built house that is moved to the home site by truck. It is then usually permanently parked in a mobile home park or on the individual owner's property. Many mobile homes come with furniture and built-in appliances. These homes are very compact, but some owners build porches or decks to add more space.

Rent or Buy?

You can either rent or buy your home. When you rent a house or apartment, you pay a monthly fee—the rent—to the owner in exchange for the right to use that space. When you buy a home, you usually have to take out a long-term

There are many different types of housing from which to choose. What are the advantages and disadvantages of each of these types?

loan called a **mortgage**. Then you have 15 to 30 years to pay back the loan.

A **condominium** is one of a group of apartments or townhouses that you buy rather than rent. When you purchase a condominium, you also agree to pay a monthly service fee to pay for things that all of the owners use in common, such as lawns, swimming pools, tennis courts, and hallways.

Owning a home has some advantages and some drawbacks. One advantage is that owning your own home gives you a sense of permanence or belonging. Also, your home may increase in value, and as you pay off your mortgage, you own more and more of your home. Another advantage of home ownership is that you can decorate or remodel it any way you like.

Some of the disadvantages of owning a home include being responsible for all of the maintenance and upkeep and having to sell the home if you move.

Renting also has advantages and disadvantages. If something breaks in a rented apartment or house, such as the plumbing or heating system, the building's owner is responsible for making the repairs. Renters can also move more easily than homeowners. Often, they need to give only a month's notice so the owner can find new occupants.

There are, however, some disadvantages to renting. You probably won't be able to decorate or remodel, and the money you pay every month isn't a part of a larger investment. Also, the building owner can raise the rent.

How Much to Spend?

Another decision you need to make about housing is determined by how much you can afford to pay. Housing prices vary in different areas, such as in a city or a suburban or rural setting, as well as in different parts of the country. When you have a limited amount of money to spend on housing, location is a very important factor in deciding what kind of home you will be able to afford.

Housing costs are also determined by the size of the house or apartment. Usually the larger the space, the higher are the costs.

When choosing housing, many people face trade-offs. They are willing to spend a little more money for a better location, or walk a few blocks more to the bus stop to save on rent. How you make these decisions will depend on what is most important to you.

Decisions About Housing

Even now you make many decisions about your living space, even if you share a room with a brother or sister. Where will you put your tapes or disks? How can you store your clothes? If you want to redecorate, can you use materials you have on hand, or do you need to buy new supplies?

As you read the following chapters, you'll find information that will help you make these decisions and many others.

- You'll find out how to plan and organize your space for your activities and your belongings.
- You'll learn how to use some basic principles and elements of design to give your space the look you want.
- You'll discover ways to care for your space to make it more comfortable.
- You'll learn how to use your knowledge to help keep your home safe and control the energy you use.

The more you learn about housing choices now, the better prepared you'll be to make decisions in the future.

Adapting Space for Independent Living

If a family member is disabled, living space can be modified so that the person can live independently. Here are some adaptations that can make a home accessible for everyone who lives there:

- **Special equipment.** People with physical disabilities often require some special equipment to allow them to move about safely at home, especially in the bathroom. They may need grab bars around the tub and toilet, nonskid mats in the tub or shower, and perhaps a tub seat or hand-held shower head. They may also require special faucets if they are unable to turn regular ones.

  If they use crutches or a walker, loose scatter rugs should be removed and objects, such as shoes, books, and toys should be kept off the floor and out of the way. If necessary, have railings installed along hallways or wherever the person has difficulty walking.

  Stairs are a special hazard for people who must use walkers or who have certain heart conditions. Special lifts can be installed that allow them to go up and down the stairs sitting down.

- **Wheelchairs.** People who are confined to wheelchairs need wide, clear paths to allow them to maneuver around the house. It may be necessary to widen doorways and lower light switches and countertops to prepare a home for a wheelchair-bound family member. Also, shelves and clothes poles can be lowered so the disabled person can reach them.

  A family member in a wheelchair will require ramps to go up or down any steps, both indoors and out. In addition, it is difficult to move a wheelchair across deep pile carpets or rugs. Replace thick carpeting with tile, hardwood floors, or flat, tightly woven carpeting.

- **Visual aids.** People who are blind or visually impaired quickly learn where things are located in their homes. Tell them if you move anything so they don't become disoriented, bump into objects, or fall. Special equipment such as braille knobs and control panels can be installed on appliances, as well as braille labels on packaged goods.

Think It Through

1. How would you prepare a bedroom for a family member who has recently become wheelchair-bound?

2. Suggest some ways that you could prepare a kitchen for a person who is blind.

Reviewing the Facts

1. What psychological needs does a living space meet?
2. What are the four physical needs that a home can fulfill?
3. List the four basic factors to consider when choosing a place to live.
4. What are two important influences when choosing the location of a home?
5. List five different styles of housing.
6. List two advantages and two disadvantages of owning a home and of renting a home.
7. How do an apartment and a condominium differ?
8. Name two factors that help determine the cost of housing.

Sharing Your Ideas

1. How is your home a reflection of your individuality?
2. Discuss the facilities and services that your community offers. Which of these are the most important to you and your family?

Applying Your Skills

1. Computing Costs. Check the real estate ads in your local newspaper. Cut out at least five listings for any one of the following: single-family homes, duplexes, townhouses, or mobile homes. What is the average price? Then cut out five listings for rental housing offering similar space and features. What is the average price of a rental in your area?

2. Presenting Two Sides of an Issue. Using your own experience and opinions, list the advantages and disadvantages of renting vs. buying a home. Write a report on the advantages and disadvantages of each, which you would prefer, and why.

3. Writing a Description. Find a picture of a home or room in a magazine that clearly shows the interests of the people who live there. Cut out the picture from the magazine. On a separate piece of paper, write a brief description of the people who might live in the room or home.

70

How to

Organize

Your Space

OBJECTIVES

This chapter will help you to:

- Use floor plans to improve the use of space in rooms.
- Organize specific areas in a room.
- Follow examples of ways to organize and store possessions.

WORDS TO REMEMBER

floor plan
layout
multiple use

scale drawing
traffic pattern

Y ou probably do more than sleep in your room. You may study, dress, read, listen to music, and perhaps even eat there. You might use your room to have private talks with a friend or for a chance to get away from family noise. Your room is also the place where you keep your clothes, schoolbooks, cassette tapes, and other personal possessions. Your living space, then, provides you with a place to relax and enjoy yourself, perform many activities, and store your things.

Other people use their living spaces in many different ways to meet their own special needs and particular goals. Some people like uncluttered, functional rooms, with a minimum amount of furniture. Other people prefer rooms with lots of furniture and places to display their keepsakes. In this chapter, you will learn how to get the best use out of the space you have, and how to arrange it according to your own tastes and needs.

Organizing Your Furniture

When you open your closet door, does it bang into your desk? Is there a dresser drawer that you can't open because your bed is in the way? Rearranging the furniture in your room could eliminate problems like these and enable you to make better use of the space that you have available.

Making a Floor Plan

A good way to organize your space is to start with a **floor plan,** an illustration of the arrangement of elements in a room or home. With a floor plan, you can change your furniture around on paper without having to actually move the furniture.

A floor plan is a sketch of a room and the furniture drawn to scale. You can try different arrangements to find the best use of the available space.

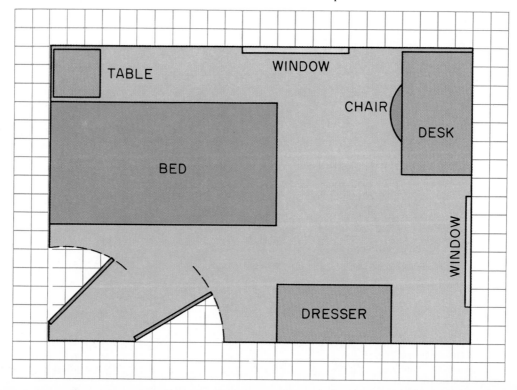

TABLE

WINDOW

CHAIR

DESK

BED

WINDOW

DRESSER

To make a floor plan, start by measuring your room and all the furniture in it. Then make a scale drawing of your room on graph paper. A **scale drawing** is one in which the relative sizes of objects are the same as the relative sizes of those objects in that actual space.

Follow these steps:

- Allow a certain number of graph paper squares to equal each foot of space that you measured. For example, if the scale you choose allows two squares per foot, a room measuring 8 ft. x 12 ft. would be drawn as a rectangle 16 squares by 24 squares.
- Indicate features such as doors and windows on the plan. With a dotted line, show which direction the doors open.
- Add your furniture, allowing the correct number of squares per foot for each piece.

By using a floor plan, you can see how furnishings will look in a particular **layout**, or arrangement of furniture. If you want to try another arrangement, draw separate scale drawings of the furniture on graph paper and cut them out. Try several different layouts until you find one you like. This saves you the trouble of having to rearrange your furnishings several times to find the best arrangement. If you are buying furniture, a floor plan can help you make sure that your choice is the right size and shape.

Considering Traffic Patterns

Think about **traffic patterns**, or how people move through the space. Can you move freely from one area of your space to another without tripping over things? If you have to squeeze past a dresser every time you walk into the room, the dresser is interfering with an easy flow of traffic through the room.

You should also think about how an arrangement will look. Depending on how furnishings are placed, a room can look cramped and cluttered or spacious and neat.

Creating Different Areas

One key to organizing space is to group together furnishings and other items that you use together. You can make a special area for each of your activities:

- A study area might include a desk, chair, bookcase, and desk lamp. In your desk drawer would be paper, pens, and pencils.
- A music center would contain all your records or tapes, your cassette tape player or stereo, and a cozy chair.
- A computer area would include your computer, monitor, printer, and storage for disks or computer games, joysticks, and computer projects.
- A science area might include a microscope, magnifying glass, collections of rocks or butterflies, and reference books.
- A game area might include your playing cards, games, puzzles, and a table and chairs.
- A fitness area could include an exercise mat, jump rope, weights, clothes for working out, and a radio or tape player.

Activity Areas

People use living spaces for the activities they enjoy. Whether you sew, build models, read, or program a computer, you want space in your room to pursue your hobby.

Not all of your activities are going to be done in your bedroom. Woodworking or staining furniture is best done in a workshop or garage. Some families use spare rooms in their homes for offices, workrooms, exercise rooms, or sewing rooms, and everyone in the family can use the equipment that is kept there.

In most homes, many areas are used for more than one activity. This **multiple use** of space is more efficient than using each area for only one activity. A desk can be used for doing homework, working with a computer, or building models. Your bed can double as a place for playing cards, reading, or listening to music. If you push the bed to the wall and add big, comfortable pillows, you've made a couch that can be used for many activities during the day while still serving as a bed at night.

Storage Areas

Everyone needs to have space for storing possessions and protecting them from damage. This storage space should be convenient and accessible, and with a little work it can also be attractive.

Solving Storage Problems

Whether you are organizing your closet, your room, the kitchen, or the garage, there are four principles of organization that you should consider:

- **Group similar items together.** Hang or store similar items in the same area so they are easy to find.
- **Keep items within easy reach.** Avoid high shelves or low drawers for items that you use often.
- **Keep items clearly visible.** Use clear plastic storage containers, wire mesh baskets, and open shelves so that you can easily see what you're looking for.
- **Compartmentalize space.** Divide space in the closet or drawers into smaller categories, designating a place for each type of item. For example, hang shirts in one section, and pants in another.

Decide what your storage problem is. You might want a place to store your athletic equipment. Your sister may need a place for her books. Someone else may need a place to put out-of-season clothes.

Some hobbies or activities, such as refinishing furniture, require a space where you can work on the project. Do you have any hobbies that need a special work area or equipment?

Closet Space: The Final Frontier

Is your closet uncharted territory? Do you feel that even an astronaut wouldn't be able to discover the space that lies within your closet?

Here are some storage aids that can expand your closet space:

- Double rods expand the space for hanging clothes in a closet. Raise one pole to 80 in. (200 cm) and install a second pole 40 in. (100 cm) from the floor.
- Plastic-coated wire shelves are lightweight and easy to install for storing sweaters, shorts, T-shirts, and accessories.
- Tubular plastic hangers hold clothes in shape better than wire hangers. Use sturdy wooden hangers for coats and heavy suit jackets. Use padded hangers for lightweight silky blouses and for other garments made of fine fabrics. Use multiple skirt and pants hangers to keep garments accessible and wrinkle-free.
- Plastic hooks can be used to hang hats, belts, bags, robes, and pajamas.
- Kitchen towel racks can be hung on the wall or back of a door to hold scarves and ties.
- Mug racks, used to hold cups, are an easy-to-install way to hold scarves, ties, belts, and bags.
- Clear plastic boxes keep items dust-free and easy to see.

- Shoe racks provide storage for several pairs of shoes and can be used on the wall or on the back of the door.
- Wire basket drawers can eliminate cramped dresser drawers. You can see underwear, socks, and sweaters at a glance. The wire permits air to circulate keeping clothes fresh.
- Open plastic bins can be stacked to hold shoes, accessories, equipment, or games.
- Corkboard is handy for posters, photos, notes, and mementos.
- Modular storage units are versatile for use as shelves and drawers. They can be arranged in interesting ways.

- Fishing tackle boxes and small metal tool chests with see-through plastic drawers can be used to store small items used for a hobby or a collection.

Think It Through

1. One business that is gaining in popularity is closet planning and organizing. Why do you think this field has become popular?
2. If you could redo your closet, how would you change it? If you wouldn't, then what makes it work?

Before deciding how to store things, ask yourself four questions:

■ **How often is the item used?** Something used frequently should be easier to get out than something you rarely need.

■ **Do other family members use it?** If so, you'll need to take their use into account when choosing a storage space. You might even want to store the item in a different room.

■ **Does it look good on display?** Many objects can be stored and used as decoration at the same time. Chapter 71 offers some ideas.

■ **Does it require other tools or supplies?** You don't want to have to go to two or three places to collect the things you need for one activity.

You can store possessions in many different ways. Your closet, dresser, and desk are the obvious places to store your clothes and school supplies.

Here are some suggestions for other storage areas in your room.

■ The space under your bed can be used as a storage area. Cut off the upper sections of cardboard boxes so they'll fit under the bed. Use these boxes to store sweaters, games, or out-of-season clothes.

■ Bookcases can hold more than just books. If your bookcase holds books that you seldom use, pack them up and use the shelf space for frequently used items instead.

■ Wall shelves are good for storing all sorts of items besides books. Shelf storage space can be attractive as well as useful. Mount shelves on the wall with brackets. You might want to paint, stain, or cover the shelves with adhesive-backed paper.

■ Walls can be used for storage in other ways. Put up hooks or pegs and use them to hang jewelry, tote bags, jackets, belts, hats, and sporting goods.

Baskets of all types can be hung from the wall and ceiling and used for light-weight items.

■ Another area that often goes unused is the back of the closet door. Attach shoe racks, belt racks, hooks, and baskets to extend the use of this space for storage.

In choosing between one storage method and another consider your resources, such as money, skill, and time. If your money is limited, shop for bargains at garage sales or flea markets. Perhaps you could build a room organizer out of wood, or make storage shelves out of boards and cement blocks. Paint or refinish an old bookcase, or get cardboard boxes free from stores. Use your imagination to think of other ways to solve your storage problems.

Use boxes for under-the-bed storage to keep items neat and easy to find.

CHAPTER 70 REVIEW

Reviewing the Facts

1. Why are floor plans a good way to decide how to organize your space?
2. How do you make a floor plan?
3. Why should you think about traffic patterns when organizing your space?
4. List five kinds of activities for which teens might create specific areas in their bedrooms.
5. What is multiple use of space?
6. When solving storage problems, what four questions should you ask?
7. List five kinds of storage items that can help you organize your closet or room.
8. What must you consider when deciding which storage method to use?

Sharing Your Ideas

1. If you wanted to improve your room's organization or appearance, what would you do?
2. What area would you set up in your room if you had the resources? What items would you need for this center?

Applying Your Skills

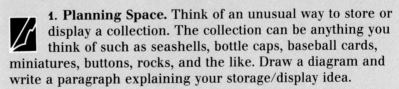

1. Planning Space. Think of an unusual way to store or display a collection. The collection can be anything you think of such as seashells, bottle caps, baseball cards, miniatures, buttons, rocks, and the like. Draw a diagram and write a paragraph explaining your storage/display idea.

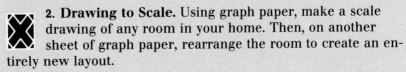

2. Drawing to Scale. Using graph paper, make a scale drawing of any room in your home. Then, on another sheet of graph paper, rearrange the room to create an entirely new layout.

3. Researching Ideas. In the interests of energy and space efficiency, many people are combining spaces in their homes for a single multiuse area. Read several home decorating or home remodeling magazines and report to the class on this or other housing trends.

Designing Your Space

OBJECTIVES

This chapter will help you to:

■ Describe the elements of design and how to work with them.

■ List the principles of design and use examples of each.

■ Explain how accessories can be used to add interest to a room.

WORDS TO REMEMBER

accessory
balance
contrast
emphasis
proportion
rhythm
unity

hireen was embarrassed to invite friends to her room. She thought the pink ruffled curtains and pink dresser seemed childish. Although her toy box held sewing supplies, it still looked like a toy box. Her one new possession, a desk, didn't fit in with anything else in the room.

You may feel this way about your own room. What can you do? Shireen and her mother started by buying plaid fabric to make new curtains. Shireen repainted her toy box and dresser. She also made some big pillows to match the curtains and put these pillows on top of the toy box. Next, she rearranged her furniture to make her new desk the center of interest.

Shireen found it didn't take much money to give her room a new look. She applied a knowledge of the elements and principles of design and made creative use of accessories.

The Elements of Design

You can make your personal space more attractive by working with the basic elements, or tools, of design. Those five elements are color, texture, space, shape, and line.

Color

Interior designers give a lot of thought to the colors they use in a room. Color has a powerful, immediate effect on a person's mood. Warm colors, such as red, yellow, and orange, are bold, cheerful, and exciting. Cool colors, such as blue, green, and purple, are quiet, calm, and soothing. If your favorite color is red, but you feel that a whole room in red would be too much, you could use that color for a bedspread or draperies.

When choosing colors for a room, first choose a dominant color. It could be your favorite color, the color of a particular item in the room, or a color that would set the mood you want to create.

You may need to work around colors that are already in your room. Perhaps you can paint the walls, but you can't change the floor color. Choose a light background color for the walls and accent it with colorful accessories. Light colors, such as white, tan, and soft tones of yellow, blue, or green are easily combined with other colors. Many colors work well together, so you'll have quite a few to choose from. Look at the color wheel in Chapter 56 to see how colors can be combined.

Texture

Another important element of design is texture, or how the surface of an object feels. Is it silky or fuzzy? Rough or polished?

For a more formal look, designers use the smooth surfaces of chrome, glass, and polished wood. A formal look is also created with fabrics that have a sheen such as silks and taffetas. A more informal look is achieved with deeply grained woods, such as pine and oak, and with nubby fabrics, woven baskets, and deep pile rugs.

You can also combine textures. A smooth laminated desk contrasts nicely with a woven rag rug, and a knitted afghan accents a smooth comforter.

Space

You can't change the size of your room or the room you share, but you can make it appear larger or smaller with the right use of space. Arranging your furniture along the wall will give the room the feeling of more space. Using one color throughout the room will unify the space. Bright, light colors also make a room appear to be larger.

Space looks larger and less cluttered if you have few items on the floor. Use hanging shelves and sturdy hooks to hold everything from your bookbag to your bicycle.

You can make a room look larger or smaller by your choice of colors and how you arrange the furniture.

If your room is large, you can move the furniture toward the center of the room to fill in space and make the room seem cozier. Darker, rich colors make the space look smaller. You could also divide larger spaces into two living areas, one for sleeping and one for activities. A folding screen divider can make one room seem like two smaller ones.

Shape

The shapes of objects in a room can have a strong effect on a room's atmosphere. A matching set of furniture usually repeats certain forms. The arms of a chair, the shape of a headboard, or the frame of a mirror may be curved or straight. Repetition can set a tone for the room.

When you use many curved shapes in a room, the result is a soft effect. If most of the furniture is square or rectangular, the effect will be harder. When many different forms are mixed together, the effect will be informal, or even confusing. It's a good idea to think carefully about how different shapes look together in a room.

Line

Every room has many lines. There is a line at the top of the door, for example, and a line around the base of a lamp. The atmosphere of a room is most affected by the bold lines that stand out and are the most obvious, such as those around windows and moldings.

In a room with tall windows, you could use floor-to-ceiling draperies for the windows and paper the walls with vertically striped wallpaper. If you added a tall bookcase and some full-length posters, the vertical lines would be the boldest element in the room.

Some people feel comfortable in such a vertical room. Others prefer more horizontal lines, because they give the room a more restful effect. These lines could be created with a low bed, a long dresser, and shelves. Still other people like the feeling of motion and excitement that is created by diagonal lines on walls and furniture.

The Principles of Design

Now that you've learned about the elements of design—color, texture, space, shape, and line—it is time to learn about the principles of design. The principles of design are a set of guidelines or rules about how to make color, texture, and the other elements of design work together to create a pleasing appearance. The principles of design are unity, contrast, balance, emphasis, proportion, and rhythm.

Unity and Contrast

Imagine a room with square chairs, curved chairs, tall chairs, and short chairs of many styles and colors. It might be hard to relax in such a room. Designers usually advise clients to choose one color scheme and perhaps one general style of furniture in a room. This helps create a feeling of **unity**, a feeling that all objects in a room look like they belong together.

Unity doesn't mean that a room must have only one color or only one style. You can accent a major color such as beige walls with red and yellow draperies and pillows.

In fact, a room can be more interesting if there is some contrast. **Contrast** is the difference in color and shape among objects. For example, brightly patterned upholstery can make an interesting contrast with a solid-colored carpet. Similarly, you can contrast shapes by hanging an oval mirror over a rectangular dresser or mixing angular and rounded tables in a room.

Balance and Emphasis

Another effect designers work to achieve is **balance**. Balance means that objects are arranged in even, pleasing ways. Balance can either be formal or informal. When you place identical end tables at each end of a sofa or arrange four photographs in a square on the wall, you are using formal balance. If you were to display several antique bottles of different sizes and shapes in an eye-pleasing arrangement on a table, you would be using informal balance.

An object that stands out in a room receives **emphasis**, or more attention than the other objects. When you emphasize an object, it becomes the focal point, or center of interest, and it draws the eye to itself. For example, a large dramatic painting hung on the wall or a brightly colored rug on a hardwood floor can be used for emphasis in a room.

Proportion and Rhythm

A pleasing size relationship among objects is called **proportion**. A big oak desk that came from your mother's office is out of proportion to the wire ice cream parlor chair you use to sit at the desk. To achieve better proportion, find a larger and more comfortable chair to use at the desk.

The regular repetition of line or shape is called **rhythm**. Rhythm in design is similar to rhythm in music. Striped fabric or pictures hung at regular intervals create a rhythm that can be pleasing in a room. Gathered curtains with a soft gathered valance and a bed with a gathered dust ruffle have a rhythm.

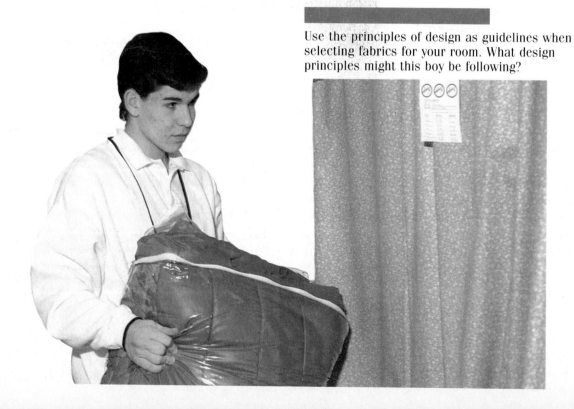

Use the principles of design as guidelines when selecting fabrics for your room. What design principles might this boy be following?

TECHNOLOGY

Computers Can Design, Too

Will a computer completely eliminate the pencils and drawing aids used by designers and architects? It seems entirely possible.

Computer graphics use the computer to design or draw an object on a computer screen. It is being used by designers to lay out and plan the interiors of homes and offices.

■ **What is it?** The process is computer-aided design (CAD). A CAD system for an interior designer has been compared to what a bulldozer is to a shovel. In a fraction of the time that it would take to hand-draw a floor plan, the computer presents the plan on the screen.

■ **What does it do?** After the scale drawing of the room is completed, the computer user goes to a data base, or catalog, of furniture to lay out and plan the space in the room. When the designer gives the computer further instructions, it can show the room three-dimensionally so you are able to "walk" through the space as if it were actually there.

The computer can also display the room in hundreds of color schemes that can be instantly changed. The colors can be shown in a variety of textures, in light and shadow, and from any angle.

The major benefit of computer-aided design is the ability to look at all possible solutions to a problem with amazing speed. Not only is computer-aided design faster, but it is also cheaper and more accurate than hand drawings.

■ **Who will use it?** These computer systems are already being used by many high-tech engineering and architecture firms for interior and exterior design. As prices for these systems go down, more designers will be able to own and use these programs. Schools and universities are installing these systems for use by engineering, interior design, and architecture students.

Think It Through

1. What effect do you think CAD could have on people's jobs?
2. Do you think computers take the creativity out of design? Why or why not?

Accessories: The Personal Touch

When planning rooms, designers often speak of two things: the major furnishings and the accessories. In a bedroom, the major furnishings may be a bed, a dresser, and a desk. They are expensive items that are not often replaced.

Accessories are the small objects that add visual appeal to a room. They do a great deal to improve the look of a room, are fairly inexpensive, and are easily changed. Posters, for example, don't cost much money and can reflect your interest in music, art, or sports. When your interests change, you can easily get a new poster.

Using Accessories

Accessories add interest to a room, such as a splash of color. They can accent or highlight an area, especially if you keep the room's color scheme in mind when you choose them.

Some accessories are strictly for decoration. A painting, for example, adds beauty to a room. Other accessories have a double purpose. In addition to improving the appearance of a room, accessories can also be useful, such as a calendar that features art prints or colorful baskets that hold craft supplies.

Accessories and You

Your accessories say a lot about you. By looking at them, a stranger might be able to get an idea of the kind of person you are. A ceramic cat, for example, might show your interest in pets and animals. Posters of dirt bikes suggest that you like that sport. By displaying your drawings or sports trophies, you are saying something special about yourself.

Accessories also please your senses. They help satisfy your sense of beauty. Your plants may give you the pleasant feeling of being in a garden. Even on the darkest day, a bright quilt or a cozy afghan may make you feel cheerful.

An accessory can bring back memories of places you've been and people you've known. By looking at a collection of seashells, you can remember the beach where you gathered them. Choose accessories that reflect your own life and have special meaning for you.

Give your room a personal touch by selecting accessories that reflect your interests. What do these items say about the person who lives here?

Reviewing the Facts

1. What are the five elements of design?
2. Give two examples of how colors affect mood.
3. What kind of texture creates a formal look? An informal look?
4. Describe three ways to make a small space look larger.
5. What are the six principles of design?
6. Define unity as a principle of design.
7. What is the most effective way to use emphasis in decorating a room?
8. How can your choice of accessories reflect who you are?

Sharing Your Ideas

1. What other suggestions would you give to Shireen to make her room more "grown-up"?
2. If you could change one element of design in your room, what would it be? How would you change it?

Applying Your Skills

1. Describing a Design. Using your own artwork or photos from magazines, put together a picture of your "dream" room. On one page, describe the elements and principles of design you used to get the look you want.

2. Searching for Ideas. Look through several issues of craft or decorating magazines. Cut out five simple projects that could be made easily and inexpensively to accessorize a teen's room. Report to the class on one project.

3. Budgeting a Project. Describe how you would like to redecorate your room. Establish a cost that the project should not exceed. Then estimate the cost of each specific item or supply that you would have to buy. What is the total estimated cost? If this total exceeds your budget, what changes could you make in your plan? Give specific examples.

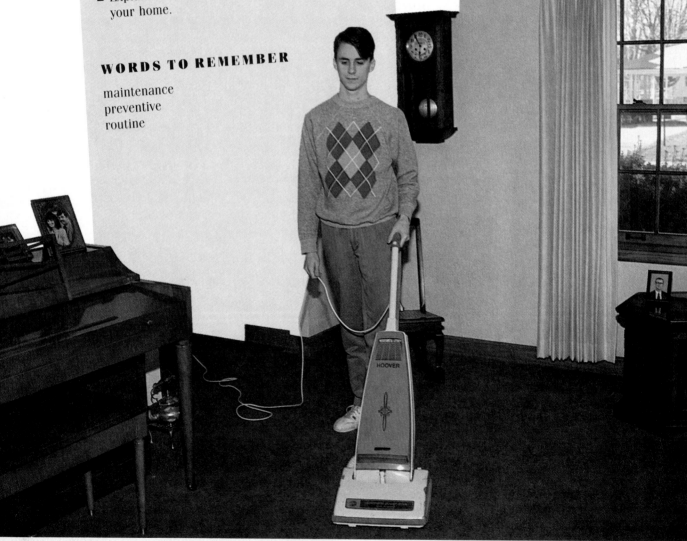

CHAPTER

72

Caring for Living Space

OBJECTIVES

This chapter will help you to:

- List three reasons why caring for living space is important.
- Describe a routine for keeping your personal and shared space clean.
- Explain how to clean some of the areas in your home.

WORDS TO REMEMBER

maintenance
preventive
routine

Kirsten always got home from school first. She dumped her schoolbag and her shoes on the floor in front of the TV. Then she made a snack in the kitchen and left the milk, peanut butter, and crackers on the counter.

After she finished her snack, Kirsten called a friend to go skating. When Kirsten couldn't find her skates in the hall closet, she emptied the closet, throwing articles on the floor until she found them. She left 30 minutes later without putting anything back.

When her brother Chad got home later, he put his books in his room. Then he made himself a snack in the kitchen. When he finished he cleaned up the kitchen including the mess left by Kirsten.

In the same amount of time it took Kirsten to create a mess, Chad took responsibility for the comfort and convenience of everyone in the family. He cared for his own space and the space he shares with other family members.

Why Care for Space?

With more family members working outside the home, traditional family roles are changing. Each person in the family now needs to care for the family's living space, not just the adults.

Caring for space means keeping it neat and clean. Possessions should be stored where they belong, and floors, walls, and furniture should be kept clean. There are three good reasons for caring for your living space. Each reason has to do with things you value—your money, your time, and your feelings about yourself.

- **To avoid waste.** If you care for your things, they will last longer and stay in better condition. It is expensive to replace things that have been abused or carelessly treated. If you leave audio cassette tapes on the floor, they can get stepped on and broken.

- **To make life easier.** It is easier to live in a tidy space than in a cluttered one. Whether you want to find a pen, a book, or a baseball mitt, it's easier and less frustrating to find the item if it's where it's supposed to be. With outside work and activities, all family members place more value on their free time. They would rather spend their time doing something they enjoy, instead of searching for a misplaced item.

Get into the habit of putting away your possessions after using them. They will stay in better condition—and you will be able to find them when you need them.

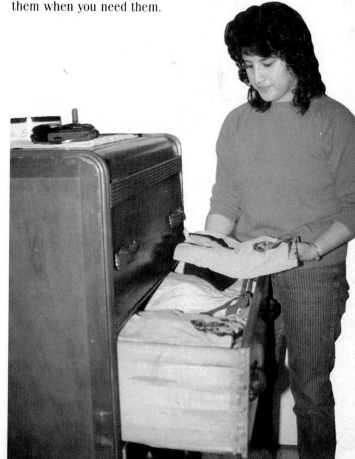

■ **To make you feel better.** A cluttered room can reflect the way you feel about yourself. People who are surrounded by disorder may feel nervous, depressed, or anxious. A neat room, on the other hand, usually makes you feel organized and in control of things.

Even people who say they don't mind clutter would prefer a neat room. There's a feeling of satisfaction and pride that comes when you see that your room is clean and everything has been put away. The reward for your efforts is that you can relax and enjoy your space.

Keeping your room neat and clean is easier if you spend a few minutes each day straightening it up.

Caring for Your Own Space

Even though you probably feel that your room is your personal space, it's still a part of your family's home. How you keep your room is not just a matter of what makes you feel comfortable. It has an effect on the overall condition of your home.

Home furnishings and home repair are expensive. If you don't bother to clean up spilled nail polish, glue, or fruit juice, what will it cost to repair the damage? If you make big holes in the wall when putting up a poster, who will pay to repair the damaged wall? What you do in your own space clearly affects other members of your family.

By caring for your own space and keeping it neat, you are helping the whole family. Money spent on fixing damage caused by carelessness is money that could have been spent on something that could have benefited you and others in your family.

Getting Started

The first step in keeping your living space neat is to find storage space for your possessions. A good system of storage and organization will make it much easier to keep things looking neat. Follow the old adage "A place for everything, and everything in its place."

Establishing a Routine

Once you have found places for the different items in your room, you must see that they all end up there. Putting things away as soon as you finish using them is a big help. It will be easier for you to keep things neat if you get into a **routine**, or set sequence, for cleaning and straightening up your room.

Some tasks, such as making the bed, should be done daily, while others need to be done only weekly or occasionally.

■ **Daily chores.** You need to do some cleaning chores every day and other chores less often. You might divide up the daily chores like this:

Make your bed in the morning.

Put school things away when you get home from school or when you're finished studying.

Put your clothes and shoes away. Put dirty clothes in the laundry after school or at night.

Put your athletic, hobby, or music equipment where it belongs when you're done with it.

■ **Weekly chores.** Other tasks need to be done only once a week. You may do one of these tasks each day, or set aside a time to do all of them at once. If you do just one thing a day, however, it probably won't take you longer than 10 minutes at a time.

Straighten your desk and study area.

File papers, stack books, and organize magazines.

Empty the wastbasket.

Straighten drawers and closets.

Change the sheets on your bed.

Dust the furniture and other objects in your room.

Vacuum or sweep the floor.

Clean or wipe off walls, light fixtures, and windowsills.

Caring for Shared Space

Maintenance of a home, the things that have to be done to keep living space and joint belongings in good working order, is a job for everyone. Each family

may have a way of dividing the responsibilities for maintaining the family's living space according to the interests, skills, and time that each family member has to contribute. It's a good idea for the family to get together and talk about the chores that need to be done, who will do them, and when they will be done.

Making a schedule for maintenance of the home may be done differently in each family. Sometimes each family member is made responsible for a particular task. For instance, one person vacuums, and another dusts. The chores can also be divided on a room-by-room basis. You may clean the bathroom and kitchen, while your brother or sister cleans and straightens up the family room or living room.

Sometimes a cleaning job is passed around from one family member to another. You might be responsible for cleaning the bathroom one week, and the next week your brother or sister would have the job. This kind of system is called rotating chores.

In the spirit of cooperation, if you see that your mother or older brother is very busy on a particular day, you could volunteer to clean up the living room, even if that's not your job. Likewise, if you see your father and sister working hard to clean out the garage or shovel snow off the walk, you can offer to give them a hand.

Prevention

One of the important areas of maintenance in a home is the **preventive** one. This means making sure that accidents and damage do not occur. You can do your part in preventive maintenance by keeping all the shared spaces in the home neat and safe for anyone who wants to use them.

You can keep the range clean so that grease won't build up and start a fire. You can put snack items such as crackers and chips away after you use them so they won't attract insects. You can wax wooden furniture so that spills won't spoil the finish. These are all examples of preventive maintenance.

What to Do

Cleaning isn't difficult; you probably know many of the procedures already. There are certain steps for cleaning

each area of a home. If you use commercial cleaning products, follow the directions on the product containers. Misuse of a product can ruin what you're cleaning; it can also be dangerous. Chemicals in cleaning solutions may be very strong, and combinations may be deadly. For example, you should never use ammonia with liquid bleach.

■ **Walls.** Check the walls for dirt and fingerprint marks. Use a sponge dampened with a cleaning solution to wipe fingerprints off doors, moldings, switches, drawers, and cabinets. Some paint and wallpaper can be washed, but others cannot, so if you're not sure, test in an inconspicuous spot.

For the most satisfactory cleaning results, follow the instructions on the product containers.

MANAGING RESOURCES

Who Does the Chores in Your Home?

A popular sign hangs in some offices where a microwave oven and refrigerator are available for use by the employees. It says, "Clean up your mess. Your mother doesn't live here." Most of these people might be surprised to find that even if their mother did live there, she would not clean up the mess.

In many of today's families, because of busy lifestyles, everyone needs to help with the housework. One way for everyone to share these tasks is to use problem-solving techniques to make a family cleaning plan:

■ **Define goals.** An order of importance has to be established for each family. Some families have the goal of straightening up the living room before everyone goes to bed. Another goal may be to put the house in order on the weekend.

■ **Make decisions.** Decide when and how each person will do his or her part of the cleaning. Will he or she have a specific job to do each week or will the chores be rotated?

■ **Adjust your attitude.** If you do the cleaning as willingly and as cheerfully as possible, it will be less of a chore and more of a pleasure. Play music or listen to the radio to get you into a good rhythm for your duties. Think of how good you will feel after you have cleaned a room and everything is neat.

■ **Analyze the steps.** The most efficient method for cleaning uses the fewest steps and the least amount of effort. Compare the amount of time that it takes to make a bed with a top sheet, two blankets, and a bedspread, or with only a sheet and a comforter.

■ **Use resources.** Look at each job and collect the necessary equipment and cleaning aids. Gather paper towels, dust mop, dust cloth, furniture polish, and anything else that you need, before you begin to work. Try new products that may make your work easier.

Think It Through

1. What other resource management skills can be applied to doing chores?
2. What decisions does your family make together about cleaning in your home? Why do such decisions need to be made?

■ **Windows.** To clean windows, you can use a cloth or paper towel with a window cleaner. For a cheaper cleaning product, mix four cups of warm water, four teaspoons of baking soda, and one-fourth teaspoon of liquid bleach. Dry the window immediately, using a very dry, lint-free cloth or paper towel, otherwise it will streak.

■ **Furniture and other objects.** Wooden furniture needs an occassional dusting. A dust cloth or duster will do the job. Some people use dusting sprays. You may wish to use furniture polish or wax occasionally.

Upholstered furniture should be vacuumed to remove dust, lint, and pet hair. Use a special vacuum cleaner attachment to pick up dirt and hairs that collect in cracks. Turn cushions over occasionally to let the fabric wear evenly on both sides.

When you clean the furniture in a room, you should also dust or clean the other objects in the room, such as the pictures, books, knickknacks, and lamps.

■ **Floors.** How you clean a floor depends on the type of floor that it is. Carpeted floors can be vacuumed. If you spill something on carpeting, clean it up immediately with a sponge or brush and cold water. Clean smooth floors with a broom or dust mop. Vinyl and tile floors can be washed with a mop and water or with cleaning products designed for these kinds of floors. Hardwood floors may also need to be waxed occasionally with a good floor wax, and vinyl floors can be coated with an acrylic floor finish to shine and protect them.

■ **Bathroom.** Use a sponge or cloth and scouring powder or liquid to clean the sink basin and bathtub. Then rinse them carefully. You'll need a toilet brush and toilet cleaner to clean and sanitize inside and outside the toilet. For this kind of cleaning, you may want to wear rubber gloves.

When to Do It

Some cleaning jobs need to be done more frequently than others. Cleaning your room and wiping out the sink and bathtub or shower after using them are routine chores. The kitchen counter needs to be cleaned after every meal.

Other day-to-day considerations will make cleaning easier for everyone. Clean up and put away food that you take out for an afterschool snack. If you take a snack to your room or have it in front of the TV, return your dirty dishes to the kitchen. Rinse them off or put them in the dishwasher.

Clean the floors and dust furniture on a regular basis. Waxing floors and washing windows can be done monthly or even less frequently. No matter how the cleaning chores are divided, it's important that they be done and that each family member does his or her part.

Some tasks, such as washing windows, can be rotated among different family members.

CHAPTER

72 REVIEW

Reviewing the Facts

1. Give three reasons for caring for your personal space.
2. How can caring for your own space be beneficial to your whole family?
3. What is the first step in keeping your living space neat?
4. After creating storage space, how can you make sure your room will be neat and clean?
5. What is home maintenance?
6. What are some ways to divide up chores in a home?
7. How can you help in the preventive maintenance of your home?
8. What two things can happen if you misuse a cleaning product?

Sharing Your Ideas

1. Do you think it is OK for one family member to do most of the housework? Why or why not?
2. What do you like and dislike most about cleaning? Can you think of any way to make what you dislike more pleasant?

Applying Your Skills

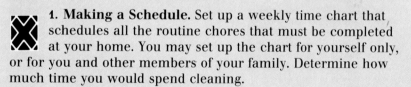

1. Making a Schedule. Set up a weekly time chart that schedules all the routine chores that must be completed at your home. You may set up the chart for yourself only, or for you and other members of your family. Determine how much time you would spend cleaning.

2. Figuring Costs. Make a list of cleaning products and supplies you would need to thoroughly clean your home. Then realistically estimate how much you would have to spend. Assume you have *no* supplies at home, such as mops, pails, cleaners, and the like. How long do you think your newly purchased supplies will last?

3. Looking for Ideas. Skim a book on household hints for ten helpful ideas on caring for your living space. Write a short paper describing the ideas and explaining why they would be helpful. Be prepared to share the ideas with your class.

Safety in the Home

OBJECTIVES

This chapter will help you to:
- Describe the most common dangers in the home.
- Prevent accidents such as falls, cuts, poisoning, electrical problems, and fire.

WORDS TO REMEMBER

accident
fireproof
pilot light
smoke detector

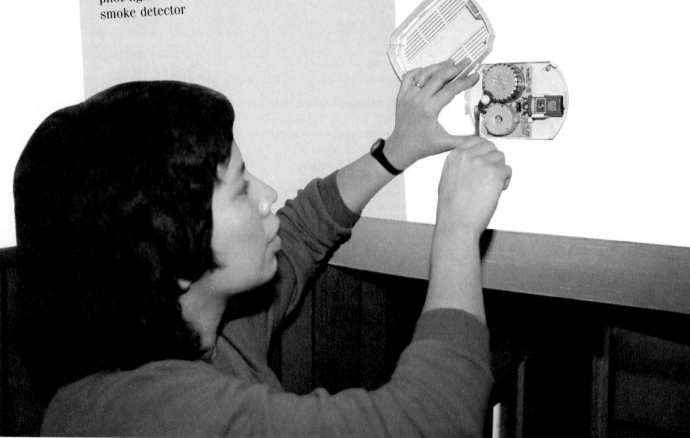

A baseball player dashes from third base to home, trying to score a run. Because she has to take some risks to get home safely, she took some precautions before she left third base. She watched the other players and she got some signals from her coach. Her goal is to get home and hear the umpire yell "Safe!"

We like to think of our homes this way, but the truth is different. Each year in the United States, unexpected falls, fires, drownings, and poisonings injure about 4 million people and claim more than 25,000 lives in the place we like to consider the safest, our homes.

An **accident** is an unplanned, sudden event, and unfortunately, people often have accidents in the most familiar part of their homes. Many accidents don't have to happen if you take steps to make your home safe.

Assessing the Dangers

To prevent accidents from happening in your home, you must make responsible decisions, be aware of the dangers, stay on guard, and plan for prevention.

Before you take steps to avoid accidents, you need to know what the dangers are. Here are the most common causes of home accidents:

- **Falls and bumps.** One-third of all injuries and deaths in the home are the results of falls. Older people and children fall most often, but anyone can fall down a flight of stairs or slip on a wet floor.
- **Cuts.** Knife or scissor cuts may not be as serious as some other injuries, but they are avoidable if sharp objects are stored and used properly. Power tools and equipment such as saws and lawn mowers can cause serious injuries.

Preventing accidents in the home is the responsibility of all family members. What could you do to help make your home safer?

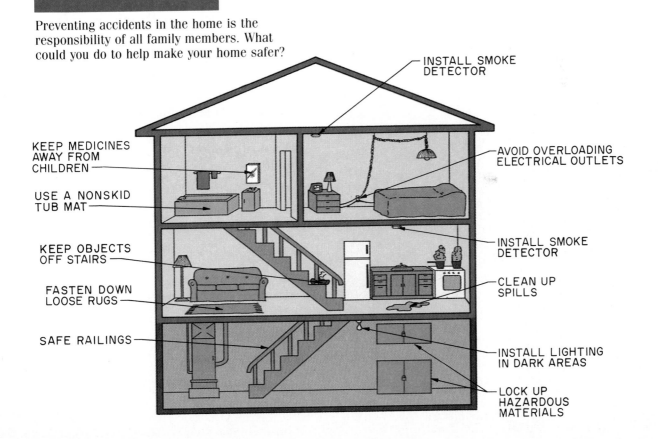

INSTALL SMOKE DETECTOR

KEEP MEDICINES AWAY FROM CHILDREN

USE A NONSKID TUB MAT

AVOID OVERLOADING ELECTRICAL OUTLETS

INSTALL SMOKE DETECTOR

KEEP OBJECTS OFF STAIRS

FASTEN DOWN LOOSE RUGS

CLEAN UP SPILLS

SAFE RAILINGS

INSTALL LIGHTING IN DARK AREAS

LOCK UP HAZARDOUS MATERIALS

- **Poisonings.** Little children, who can't read labels, are the most likely victims of poisoning. Children are very curious and not likely to know about poisonous substances.

- **Fires and electrical problems.** Fire is the second biggest killer in the home. A carelessly tossed, lighted match can set a sofa on fire. Grease can start an oven fire. Electrical shock accounts for accidental home deaths.

Preventing Accidents

Human factors should be considered when analyzing the causes and prevention of accidents. If you are alert to these conditions and know how to avoid them, you could save a life.

- **Carelessness.** Many accidents happen when people are under stress or when they are upset. People who are in a hurry or are tired are also more likely to have an accident.

- **Physical needs.** Young children have not developed the physical coordination and awareness to avoid many accidents, whereas elderly people may not be able to react quickly in the face of an emergency. Special cautions may be necessary to keep such family members safe from accidents, especially falls.

Preventing Falls

Falls can happen anywhere, but they're most likely to happen on cluttered or slippery floors. Keep toys, books, and newspapers off the floor, especially where people may be walking, such as from a bedroom to the bathroom. People can slip on freshly scrubbed or waxed floors. Simply putting up a sign—CAUTION: WET FLOORS—will tell others that you've cleaned the floors and warn them to walk carefully.

Six other steps will help you make floors safe:

- Wipe up spills immediately, so people won't slip.
- Keep rooms and hallways well lit, so people can see objects.
- Anchor throw rugs with carpet tape or hook-and-loop tape, so they won't skid.
- Arrange furniture so it will not be in people's way.
- Shorten long electrical cords or speaker wires, or secure them with electrical tape to keep them out of walkways.
- Use stepladders to reach high shelves.

To help prevent falls, secure small rugs with carpet tape.

Lighting is very important on stairways. Stairways should also be kept clear of clutter; an open stairway is not for storage. Don't put a throw rug at the top of the stairs where someone could slip and fall down the stairs. Stairs should have sturdy handrails, and small children should never be left around open stairs without gates at the top and bottom. Be careful, also, to lock basement doors when there are small children in the home.

Many falls happen in the bathtub and shower because of slippery conditions. Nonskid mats or strips that stick to the bottom can help prevent these falls. Install handrails on the wall near the tub or toilet, and a tub seat for elderly family members who have trouble sitting or standing steadily.

Preventing Cuts

The kitchen, workrooms, and the outdoors are the danger areas where cuts and injuries from tools and equipment most often occur. Proper storage and proper use of knives and other sharp cooking utensils can prevent cuts from occurring in the kitchen. Store knives with their handles toward the person opening the drawer. Keep all knives and scissors out of the reach of children.

Power tools and saws, stored in workrooms and garages, are dangerous objects. These tools should be stored out of children's reach, and their blades should be safely covered.

Care must be taken when operating outdoor tools and machinery. Do not wear jewelry or loose-fitting clothing that could get caught when using these machines. Always wear shoes with closed toes when running a lawn mower. Leather shoes are safer than canvas. Turn off the power before adjusting or fixing any tool.

Preventing Poisoning

Most poisonings occur in the kitchen, bathroom, and bedroom. Many poisonings involve young children, whose curiosity leads them to explore things that they don't know are dangerous.

Closets, medicine chests, cabinets, laundry areas, and other storage areas hold many poisonous substances. Ammonia, bleach, cleansing powders, cosmetics and perfumes, detergents, furniture polish, fertilizers, gasoline, kerosene, paint thinner, and weed killers are all poisonous.

Medicines such as aspirin and prescription drugs are poisonous if they are taken in excess. Children are the most likely to swallow medications that they see adults regularly take. You should never refer to medicine as "candy."

Keep medicines and other dangerous substances high and out of the reach of children. Buy medicines that come in child-proof containers.

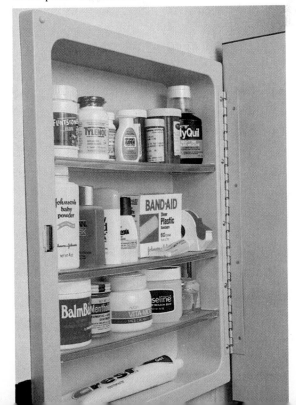

Preventing poisoning involves these steps:

- Lock all cabinets, closets, or other storage areas that contain poisons.
- Keep dangerous substances high and out of children's reach.
- Warn children not to swallow these products.
- Purchase medicines that come in childproof containers.
- Never place medicine in a container that lacks a warning label.

Preventing Electrical Problems

Most electrical accidents are caused by problems with plugs, outlets, and extension cords and by the improper use of electrical appliances. Here are steps you can take to prevent electrical problems:

- **Plugs and outlets.** Pull furniture away from the wall and inspect electrical cords. Pay special attention to plugs. Unplug and plug them in again while you watch for sparks. If you see any sparks, pull the plug out slowly and don't use it again until it's fixed. When there are small children in the home, cover all unused outlets with plastic safety covers to prevent children from sticking their fingers or other objects into the outlets.

- **Extension cords.** Avoid plugging too many electrical appliances into the same outlet. Otherwise you could overload the circuits and start a fire. Use extension cords to distribute the appliances among several outlets. Keep extension cords out of traffic areas so that no one trips over them, but do not run the cords under rugs or carpeting.

- **Appliances.** Check all appliances for safe wiring. Cords should be well covered with insulation and there should be no fraying. Unplug small appliances and put them away when they're not in use, and clear all dust away from the appliances' motors after you unplug them. Never use electrical appliances when you're wet or have wet hands as you could suffer a serious electrical shock. Also, never use appliances around sinks or bathtubs—they might fall into the water and cause you to be electrocuted.

Learn how to detect electrical hazards. Check electrical cords for broken plugs or exposed wires. Be sure that outlets are not overloaded with too many plugs.

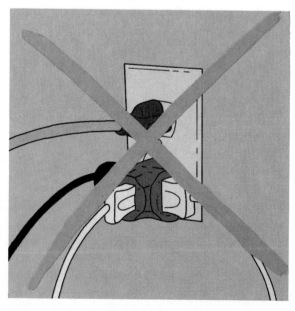

Preventing Fire

No home can be made **fireproof**, completely protected from the danger of fire, but steps can be taken to reduce the chances of a fire's occurring. Check electrical outlets and appliances as the first step. Don't store anything near the heater or the furnace. Don't pile papers, wood, or oily rags in a corner, especially near a range, a fireplace, or an electrical source.

Keep the kitchen clean to prevent grease fires. Avoid clutter around the range and check the pilot light on a gas range to be sure that it is working properly. A **pilot light** is a thin stream of gas burned constantly and used to light a gas burner on a range. Because many fires start in the kitchen, keep a fire extinguisher there.

Use matches and candles safely. Always be sure that a burned match is cold and wet before throwing it in the trash. Cigarettes should be completely put out and smokers should never smoke in bed. Finally, use fireplaces and wood stoves carefully.

Sometimes, despite all precautions, a fire occurs. Your family is more likely to survive a fire if it has **smoke detectors**. When they sense smoke, these devices, usually battery-operated, sound an alarm to warn occupants of the home. There should be a smoke detector on each level of your home, and one near the sleeping area. Check the battery regularly to see that the device is working.

A major part of fire safety is knowing how to leave the home if a fire occurs. Be sure that everyone in the home knows an escape route. Home fire drills should be a part of this procedure.

Smoke detectors can save lives by alerting family members to smoke or fire. Is your home protected by smoke detectors?

Home Fire Drills

Schools have them. Businesses have them. Have you ever had a fire drill in your home? Does everyone in your family know the best exits from the house or apartment in case of fire? Proper planning for a fire emergency can—and does—save lives.

Here are seven steps to follow:

- **Have a planning meeting that everyone in the family must attend.** Discuss safety measures.

- **Establish escape routes.** Everyone should know the best way to get from each room in the home to the outdoors. Determine alternative exits, if the first escape route is blocked. Where should a chain ladder be kept? Does everyone know how to attach it?

- **Set up a buddy system.** If there are small children in the home, determine who could get to them fastest. You may decide that each family member should be responsible for one other family member.

- **Plan a meeting place.** Establish a meeting place outdoors where everyone should come immediately after leaving the home. This way you will know that everyone is safe. Call the fire department from a neighbor's home. Never go back into a burning home to save pets or possessions.

- **Try out each escape route.** Time the route and make changes, if necessary. Draw all the routes on a floor plan and review the plan with the whole family.

- **Hold a fire drill with all family members.** Have it at a time when everyone is home, and preferably when people are in different areas of the house. Set off the smoke detector alarm and check that it can be heard all through the house. Can it be heard in the bathroom when the water is running?

- **Follow up with a meeting to discuss and analyze the results.** If there are changes, have another drill a week or so later.

Think It Through

1. Why do you think that people do not bother to have home fire drills? Are these valid reasons?
2. Do you have any family members who would have difficulty in getting out of the building in case of a fire? What special plans are made for their safety?

CHAPTER

73 REVIEW

Reviewing the Facts

1. Approximately how many home injuries occur yearly in the United States?
2. What are four main types of accidents that occur in the home?
3. List three ways to prevent falls.
4. What can you do to prevent cuts from occurring?
5. Name five common household substances that are poisonous.
6. List two ways to prevent electrical problems.
7. Where should smoke alarms be placed?
8. What is a major part of fire safety?

Sharing Your Ideas

1. What family members live in or visit your home who need to pay special attention to safety features? What have you done to make your home safer for them?
2. Have you ever had an accident because you were in a hurry or upset? What precautions should you have taken so it wouldn't have happened? Why?

Applying Your Skills

1. Making a Diagram. Draw a diagram of your home marking the best escape route out of the building from your bedroom in case of fire.

2. Evaluating Your Home. Make a safety survey of your own home. List preventive measures that have already been taken in one column, and those that need attention in another column. Compare lists with your classmates.

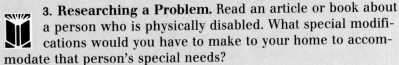
3. Researching a Problem. Read an article or book about a person who is physically disabled. What special modifications would you have to make to your home to accommodate that person's special needs?

Managing Energy Costs in the Home

OBJECTIVES

This chapter will help you to:

- Explain the importance of using energy wisely.
- Improve the comfort level of your home.
- Decrease energy use and become a responsible energy consumer.

WORDS TO REMEMBER

energy
home automation
hydroelectric power
insulation
weather stripping

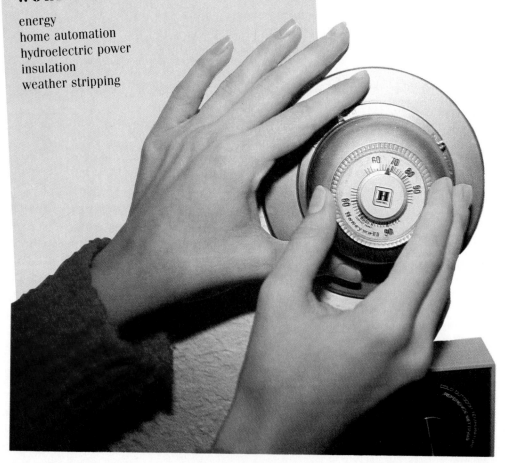

Do you turn the lights off when you leave the room? Do you take quick showers? When you're chilly, do you put on a sweater instead of turning up the heat? Has your family put insulation into the walls of your home?

You've probably heard your parents and others talk about the costs of electricity, gas, and oil. Energy-saving steps such as these actions help keep energy bills manageable.

Some Uses of Electricity in the Home

Heating & Cooling	• Electric furnace • Electric heater • Water heater • Air conditioner • Fan
Food Preparation	• Refrigerator • Electric range • Microwave oven • Toaster • Food processor • Blender • Mixer
Cleaning	• Washer • Dryer • Vacuum cleaner • Dishwasher • Food waste disposal • Trash compactor
Entertainment	• Television • VCR • Computer • Radio • Cassette player • Stereo • CD player
Lighting	• Ceiling fixtures • Lamps • Outdoor lights
Personal Care	• Iron • Electric razor • Hair dryer • Curling iron • Electric curlers

What Is Energy?

Energy is the capacity for doing work. We use energy for two important purposes—to make electricity and to produce heat.

Types of Energy

Electricity is power provided to homes and businesses by local utility companies. Most utilities produce electricity by burning fuels such as oil, coal, or natural gas. Some use **hydroelectric power**, which is generated by the force of falling water. Others use nuclear reactors to make electricity.

Home-heating energy sources vary. Your home might be heated by electricity, oil, or natural gas, the three main sources of heat. Some alternative sources of heat in homes are wood-burning stoves and coal-burning furnaces. Solar panels, using the heat from the sun, are used in some homes, primarily as a supplemental energy source to heat water.

Uses of Energy

If you've ever had a power blackout during a storm or peak usage period, you know how helpless you feel without electricity. Almost everything we do requires electrical energy of some kind. The chart on this page lists many uses of electricity in your house. How many more can you think of?

Steps to Save Energy

What can you do to manage energy wisely? First, think about how you use energy. Of the average home's energy bill, approximately 40 percent of the cost is for heating and 15 percent is for heating water. Cooling totals 7 percent. The other 38 percent goes for all the appliances, machines, and lights that are run by electricity. Your family's actual energy use may be different, because climate, the size and age of your home, and the size of your family all affect energy use.

Heating and Cooling

Cold winter winds and summer heat waves affect the comfort levels in your home. You want to make your home warmer in the winter and cooler in the summer to be comfortable. Although you can't control the weather, you can control the amount of heated or cooled air used in your home. Because heating and cooling amount to almost half of the average family's energy bill, they are two good areas for managing your use of energy.

- Utility companies recommend that in the winter you set your thermostat to 68 degrees when family members are home during the day. Set the thermostat at 58 degrees while you're asleep or away from home for four or more hours. If you reduce your home temperature by 5 degrees for four or more hours each day you can save 5 to 10 percent on your fuel bill.

- If possible, put thermostats in more than one room. Then you can control the temperature better. Don't heat rooms that aren't used.

- If you use an air conditioner in the summer, the recommended setting for your thermostat is 15 degrees below the outside temperature, or a minimum of 78 degrees.

- Use fans instead of air conditioners. They are less costly to run.

- Use drapes to help you control the temperature. On cold days, open draperies on the sunny side of the house. Close draperies on cloudy days or as soon as the sun sets. During the summer, you can keep the house cooler by closing drapes and shades on the sunny side of the house.

- Close the fireplace damper when the fireplace is not in use to prevent warm air from escaping up the chimney.

To help save on energy costs, put on a warm sweater instead of turning up the thermostat. Several layers of clothing are warmer than a single sweater or shirt.

One way to keep your home more comfortable in extreme temperatures is to use insulating materials. **Insulation** goes inside walls or ceilings to keep cold out and heat in. In some houses, good insulation can lower heating bills by 30 to 35 percent.

Insulation is measured by its R-value. This stands for its resistance to heat loss. The higher the R-value, the better the insulation. Building materials such as glass and wood have low R-values; insulating materials such as polyester fill and fiberglass have high R-values. Because heat rises, ceiling insulation should have a higher R-value than that of wall insulation. Homes in colder climates need insulation with higher R-values than do homes in warmer climates.

A lot of heat is lost because warm air escapes through cracks in the walls or around windows and doors. You can prevent this problem from happening by using double-glass or triple-glass windows, and by adding caulking or weather stripping around doors and windows. **Weather stripping** is the material used to fill gaps between the door and the door frame and around windows so that less air leaks in and out. These strips are made of fiber, vinyl, or metal.

Lighting and Appliances

You can manage electricity costs in two ways—by using it carefully and by buying efficient appliances. Here are some ways to save electricity.

- Keep the refrigerator defrosted so it works more efficiently. Don't leave the refrigerator door open.
- If you have a dishwasher, wash only full loads. Open the door once the dishes are clean and let them dry in the air. Use a dishpan to wash dishes if you are doing them by hand. Don't leave the hot water running.
- Wash clothes on warm or cold water settings. Many laundry detergents can be used in cold water instead of hot, and you can always use cold water for rinsing.
- Do not overdry clothes in a dryer.
- Dry clothes by hanging them up, rather than in a dryer.

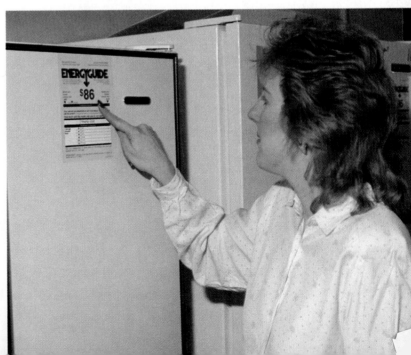

When buying major appliances, read the EnergyGuide labels for information about operating costs. Then you can compare the energy efficiency of different models.

- Turn off electric lights and appliances such as the radio and TV when no one is in the room.
- Replace high-wattage bulbs with low-wattage ones if light isn't needed for reading or close work.
- Use fluorescent bulbs in the kitchen, bathroom, and workroom. They use less energy than incandescent bulbs.

When buying large appliances that use a great deal of energy every day, look for the EnergyGuide labels on many of these appliances. These labels estimate the cost of running the appliance for one year. You can use these labels to find the model that uses energy most efficiently.

You can also check appliances for energy-saving features. Dishwashers should have controls to allow the user to skip the drying cycle. Instant-on TV sets use more energy then those that take time to warm up.

Gas

Four important pieces of home equipment can run on natural or propane gas—the heating system, the water heater, the clothes dryer, and the range. Follow the tips for managing electric energy mentioned earlier.

Another way to save gas is to buy equipment with an electronic ignition. On standard gas equipment, the pilot light burns constantly even when the equipment isn't in use. By lighting the flame electronically, newer models no longer need the pilot light.

Turn faucets off completely after use. Fix dripping faucets as soon as possible.

Water

Water is an important and increasingly scarce resource. In some parts of the country, water is scarce because of the terrain, and in others, people sometimes have to ration water because of droughts. You can easily save water by following these suggestions:

- Wash clothes and dishes only when the washing machine and dishwasher are full.
- Take showers instead of baths and keep your daily showers short. A typical tub bath uses 10 to 15 gallons of water, whereas a five-minute shower uses 8 to 12 gallons.
- Don't let water run continuously while shaving, brushing your teeth, or working at the sink. Turn faucets off and on as needed, and turn them off completely after you use them.
- If you wash dishes by hand, use a dishpan or put a stopper in the sink. Washing dishes under continually running water wastes about 30 gallons of water per meal.
- Always fix dripping faucets and other water leaks promptly. A faucet that leaks one drop of water per second wastes 192 gallons of clean water per month.

TECHNOLOGY

The Smart Home

How smart is your home? Can it turn off the lights? Can it lock doors and windows? Can it turn on the water in the bathtub so that your bath is ready when you get home?

The home of the not-so-distant future will be able to do all of these things, and more, through the technology of **home automation.** This technology can automatically control systems in a home using electricity, electronics, and appliances equipped with microchips. The appliances "talk" to each other and to the house. The "smart house" is convenient and energy efficient.

The level of automation can range from a basic on-off system for lights to a fully automated home where the climate, security, entertainment, and all other systems are controlled through a central panel.

The simplest approach to home automation is a product that plugs into any home. Any electric appliance with an on-off switch can be plugged into a module that is controlled by a hand-held cordless device similar to a TV remote control. The system can be programmed to turn heat up or down automatically or to turn TV, stereos, and lights on or off.

The next level of automation is aimed at home security. Window and door sensors respond if they are opened, closed, or tampered with.

The fully automated home requires complete rewiring, or installation at the time the home is built. Any appliance can be plugged into it and activated from any location. It can be controlled from a phone or TV.

Engineers estimate that energy costs can be cut by 20 to 50 percent through the use of this system. It will be able to turn lights out when no one is in the room, automatically control the water temperature and usage in a dishwasher, control the temperature and humidity in the home, as well as choose music and cook meals.

The engineers and architects who are designing these homes are making every effort to make these systems easy for anyone to understand. They believe that today's teens, who are growing up with computers, will have no problem adapting to fully automated homes.

Think It Through

1. What features of the automated homes appeal to you the most? Why?
2. Suggest some ways that your home is automated or could be automated now.

Reviewing the Facts

1. What three sources of power can a utility company use to produce electricity?
2. What are three main sources of home-heating energy? What are two alternate sources of heat?
3. List three factors that affect your family's energy use.
4. Suggest four steps a family can take to cut down on its home-heating costs.
5. How can you compare different types of insulation?
6. What is weather stripping?
7. In what two ways can you manage electricity costs better?
8. List three ways that you can save water.

Sharing Your Ideas

1. If you had your own home, what would you do to manage energy efficiently? Explain your answer.
2. What, in your opinion, is the best source of energy for housing? Why?

Applying Your Skills

 1. Writing Directions. Think of a project you could sew or build yourself that could save energy in your home. Write out instructions and include a diagram.

 2. Evaluating Energy Use. If you were in charge of maintenance at your school, what actions would you take to conserve energy in the school? Write a detailed description to be shared with the class.

3. Recognizing Solutions to a Problem. Create a brochure suggesting ways to cut down on energy costs. This brochure should be aimed at elementary school children, so they may start learning how to conserve energy. Include suggestions listed in this chapter, as well as additional ideas.

CHAPTER

75

Careers in Housing

OBJECTIVES

This chapter will help you to:
- Develop the interests and skills needed for careers in housing.
- Identify various jobs available in housing.

WORDS TO REMEMBER

architect
blueprint
construction
visualize

Shelter is one of the basic human needs. Comfortable, affordable housing must be planned, built, furnished, decorated, maintained, and sold. Because of this, the housing industry provides jobs and careers for hundreds of thousands of people.

The largest segment of careers in housing is in **construction**, the building of homes. Over one and a half million homes are built every year. These homes may be single-family dwellings or multiple family units.

In the building industry, people are needed to become carpenters, masons, plumbers, plasterers, electricians, painters, and paperhangers. Carpenters are by far the largest group in the building industry.

Many people who start in the home building industry move into commercial construction of stores, office buildings, warehouses, restaurants, apartment buildings, and factories.

Characteristics for Careers in Housing

People who work in the housing industry do not work simply with houses. First and foremost, they work with people. Whether they are designing, constructing, selling, or maintaining a house, people in this business must have a feeling for people and their lifestyles.

Interests and Skills

- **Can you see a finished product by looking at a plan?** Housing workers must be able to **visualize**, or see in their minds, how a completed project might look. Carpenters must be able to read a **blueprint**, the architect's plan or mechanical drawing, to visualize a room so they can know how to build it. Interior designers look at a floor plan and then picture how the furniture can be arranged.

- **Do you communicate with people easily and work well with them?** Designers, builders, and salespeople work closely with their clients, learning what the client wants and making him or her feel comfortable. It makes the work satisfying and leads the clients to recommend the expert or worker to their friends.

- **Do you like fixing up your room by selecting new colors or rearranging your furniture?** Do you have fun picking out new posters for your room? Your interest in colors and shapes may mean that you can use your skills in a housing career.

- **Are you interested in learning how buildings are created and how to use the materials that go into construction?** If you're interested in learning how to work with plastics, pipes, concrete, wood, and bricks, there are many jobs that use these abilities. In addition, the knowledge of plumbing, heating, and air conditioning leads to well-paying jobs. This knowledge is often learned on the job or in a technical school that prepares people for a career.

- **Do you pay attention to detail?** Housing workers must be thorough and complete. A cabinetmaker must make the tops of cabinet doors line up perfectly. A building inspector must check carefully for safety hazards. If you are patient and thorough in your work, you have this characteristic.

Jobs in Design, Construction, and Sales

You might want to consider being part of the housing business that plans, builds, and sells homes. These jobs are open to men and women who have the interest and have learned the skills that are in demand.

Entry-Level Jobs

Landscape gardeners must like to work with plants, bushes, trees, and flowers. Generally they work outdoors and many jobs in this field are seasonal. However, there is a growing demand for gardeners to work year-round at offices and shopping malls taking care of indoor plants. Some landscape gardeners have their own businesses, working at many different locations during the week. Others work at apartment and office buildings, or on college or government campuses, caring for larger areas.

Construction workers include carpenters, electricians, masons, painters, plumbers, and roofers. These workers are usually good at working with their hands and have learned special skills for their trade. Many begin their work as apprentices, helpers who are trained on the job by the senior workers. Construction workers can work for building contractors or be self-employed.

Jobs That Require Training

Retail wallpaper, fabric, and furniture stores often have decorating consultants to help customers select appropriate colors, fabrics, and furniture for new homes or redecorating projects.

Some people hire an interior designer to help them improve the appearance of their homes. This is a professional who is trained to work with colors, line, form, texture, unity, and composition to design or redesign one room or a whole house. Depending on the client's budget and wishes, an interior designer might decorate new walls or suggest new arrangements of furniture to make the home more functional.

Decorating consultants and interior designers help people plan living space that is comfortable, attractive, and appropriate to their lifestyle.

Real estate agents help people who want to buy, sell, or rent homes and office space.

Consultants and designers usually take special courses in interior design at a professional school. Most designers are members of the American Society of Interior Designers (ASID). They may work for furniture stores or architects or have their own businesses.

A real estate salesperson helps people buy and sell homes. Buyers consult with a realtor and explain what size home they want, what location they want, and how much they can pay. The real estate salesperson tries to find a house or condominium that matches their needs.

A real estate career requires special training in housing financing and sales. The field is highly competitive, but other sales jobs provide good experience for real estate sales.

Jobs That Require a Degree

Architects actually design buildings and homes. They may design houses for individual families or huge apartment buildings for hundreds. They may create a new house or redesign an older one.

Architects must know about the materials used for building and about people's living patterns. They must also be able to visualize a completed project while it's still on the drawing board. Computer skills and the ability to work with computer-aided design are especially important to architects. A college degree and a license in architecture are required.

City planners work for local governments to guide the growth of an area. First they predict the future population of the area. Then they predict the people's needs for the facilities and services that make the area livable, such as housing, schools, shopping, recreation, and transportation. City planners suggest ways to meet future needs so that the city can grow in pace with the population. A college degree and computer skills are definite assets.

INTERPERSONAL SKILLS

Success on the Job

What do you think is the key to success on the job? Did you ever take a class that taught that subject? Most people don't realize that they are developing the keys to on-the-job success while they are attending school.

The most important factor is a good attitude toward your work. If you have a positive attitude, you will find satisfaction in your work and in pleasing your employer. Optimistic employees have a positive affect on the attitudes of coworkers and are often looked to for leadership.

Here are some additional skills that contribute to a worker's success:

■ **Be reliable.** When given a task, do it willingly and on schedule. Follow directions, and ask questions if you are not entirely sure of what you are to do. Always do quality work.

■ **Get along with others.** Whether working as part of a team or independently, be helpful and pleasant to coworkers.

■ **Be punctual.** This means coming to work on time everyday, taking breaks and lunches during the time allowed, and trying not to be absent.

■ **Work hard.** Don't loaf on the job. Your employer expects you to manage your time and equipment efficiently.

■ **Try to do your best.** If you try to do your job better every day, you will feel satisfied that you are doing your best.

■ **Be willing to learn.** This includes learning new tasks and improving the math, writing, and communication skills you already have.

■ **Follow rules and procedures.** Every organization has safety rules and business procedures. Be sure you know what your employer expects from you so you can act professionally.

■ **Learn to deal with stress.** Problems at home affect your work. Work problems can also affect your personal and family life. You can minimize such problems by learning how to deal with stress both at home and at work.

■ **Be cooperative.** If you are polite, considerate, and fair towards others, everyone will benefit.

■ **Give reasonable notice.** When you leave a job, two weeks notice is usually appropriate.

■ **Leave with a good impression.** You may want to return to the company later, or you may ask your employer for a reference in the future.

Think It Through

1. Which of these skills do you think you're strong in? Which can you learn? How would you go about learning them?
2. Why are these skills needed to succeed on the job?

Jobs in Home Maintenance and Use

The home maintenance industry is among the largest in the country. People are needed to repair everything in the home, including broken appliances, leaking roofs, damp basements, and faulty heating systems.

Entry-Level Jobs

As more people work outside the home, time for home maintenance is limited. Many people prefer to hire the services of others to clean and maintain their homes. Positions for private household workers are plentiful. This is a service-oriented business that requires efficiency and organization.

The rising number of office buildings, apartment houses, and hospitals, as well as day-care centers, nursing homes, and senior citizens' homes, increases the demand for maintenance services. These positions also offer good opportunities for part-time and evening hours. Hotels and motels also provide a growing demand for cleaning and maintenance workers.

Many people like to maintain or improve their homes themselves. They need knowledgeable sales clerks to advise them on what materials to buy and how to use tools and materials correctly and safely. These sales clerks work in hardware or in home improvement stores.

Jobs That Require Training

Large apartment buildings have superintendents who keep all the housing units in good repair. They must know how to fix leaks, check furnaces, repair broken windows, and do other similar jobs. Often, these workers live in one of the units in the building. They may need to be available for emergencies at all hours.

The home maintenance industry is among the largest in the country. People are needed to repair everything from water pipes to air conditioners.

People who work for home service and home repair businesses also require special training. They may learn how to repair major appliances, such as air conditioners and refrigerators, or to fix heating, electrical, or plumbing systems. Some businesses provide services such as exterminating insects and rodents or cleaning carpets and upholstery. In most cases, the company or employer provides training courses, on-the-job training, or pays for workers to take special courses.

Jobs That Require a Degree

Home economists with a college degree can work in the field of housing, just as they can in the areas of food or clothing. Some work in the extension service, an educational program run by the U.S. Department of Agriculture and county governments.

Some utility companies have home service advisers who work with the public, helping to manage resources. These workers do many of the same things for businesses that extension home economists do for government agencies.

In both of these jobs, home economists offer suggestions and ideas on how to get the most out of housing. They may run educational workshops, write articles, or give speeches. Whatever the methods, their goal is to provide information to the consumer.

Getting a Job

Did the information in this chapter make you think you would like a career in housing? If so, you might consider a job in this field. There are steps you can take to prepare for such a career.

On-the-job experience is a great help. You can get this by getting a part-time job in a related field while you are going to school or by finding an entry-level job as an apprentice upon graduation. A technical school will help you get the necessary skills. There are many opportunities for college graduates and graduates of specialized schools, such as professional interior design schools. Special training in sales, financing, or computers is very helpful.

Many teens have part-time or summer jobs that give them on-the-job experience in the construction or home maintenance fields. What jobs might be available in your community?

Reviewing the Facts

1. In what area of housing are the largest number of people employed?
2. List three interests or skills that are important for careers in housing.
3. Identify one career at each job level in home design, construction, and sales.
4. What is an apprentice?
5. Name two special abilities architects must have.
6. Describe the work of city planners.
7. List an entry-level job and a job that requires training in the home maintance industry.
8. Name two areas where home economists and home service advisers can work in the field of housing.

Sharing Your Ideas

1. What effect do you think changes in the way people live will have on careers in housing?
2. If you could have any job described in this chapter, which would you choose? Why?

Applying Your Skills

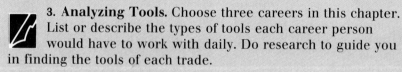 **1. Researching a Career.** Choose one career in the field of housing. Do library research or conduct an interview with someone in that career. Write a one-page report describing specific characteristics and qualifications necessary for that career.

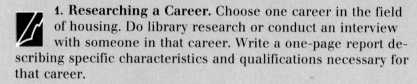 **2. Researching History.** Use your library and find books about the Middle Ages. Read about the lives of apprentices, or the history of craft unions and guilds. Report to your class.

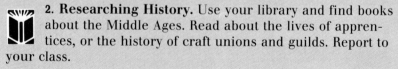 **3. Analyzing Tools.** Choose three careers in this chapter. List or describe the types of tools each career person would have to work with daily. Do research to guide you in finding the tools of each trade.

TEEN TIPS

Four Looks—One Room
Four ways to put your personal stamp on your room.

Living on Your Own
Dreaming of your own place some day? Here's what it takes to swing it.

Terrific Teenage Tool Kit
Here are some basic tools that you should know how to use for routine home maintenance.

Four Looks  One Room

Using different colors and accessories can change the look of any room. Start by choosing the main color for your room. Then select one or more colors as an accent. Your creativity, plus some time and effort, will help you achieve the unique look that you want.

Here are four possible ways to spruce up a room:

1 To create a country look, use a floral print, lots of ruffles and lace, and soft window treatments. Stencil a design on the walls, woodwork, furniture, or floor. You can buy ready-made stencils or make your own designs.

2 For a tailored look, choose plaid fabric for a bedcover and matching window shades. Select accessories that combine function and form, such as a swing-arm lamp that can light two areas. Highlight only a few carefully chosen items.

3 For a natural, outdoor look, add lots of texture to the room. Hang straw mats on the walls, and use baskets in various sizes for storage. Plants—both large and small—help create a feeling of the outdoors.

4 To create a dramatic look, use bold colors and patterns. Group pictures or photos together on the walls to create a gallery. Use mirrors to make the room look larger—look for inexpensive ones at flea markets and garage sales.

Living on Your Own

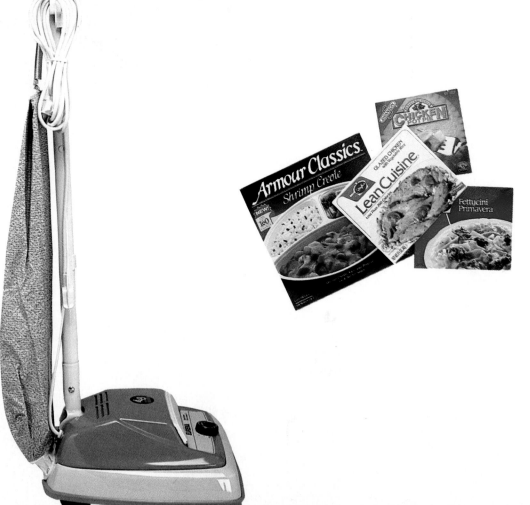

Growing up takes time. Accepting responsibility, learning from mistakes, and making your own decisions are important steps in the transition from being a child to becoming an adult.

You can prepare for your role as an adult while you are a teen. One way is to be a responsible person while you are living at home. This means caring for your own clothing, possessions, and room. You can practice making decisions based on your goals and values—and being flexible, too.

To help you better understand the responsibilities of living on your own, you may want to open your own checking and savings accounts and to take charge of your own appointments. You could earn money to pay for your own expenses—such as clothing, entertainment, car insurance, or telephone bill.

T E E N   T I P S

Most young people plan to leave home someday and live independently—either by themselves or with friends. When considering leaving home, ask yourself the following questions. If you can answer all of them positively, you might be ready to live on your own.

- Am I earning (or have the ability to earn) a steady living?

- Am I capable of managing my own finances?

- Am I able to provide my own food, clothing, and shelter?

- Can I handle housekeeping?

- Do I enjoy spending time alone, or can I get along with roommates?

- Do I avoid extreme reactions to difficult situations?

- Am I willing to accept the consequences of my actions?

Terrific Teenage Tool Kit

Are you handy with tools, or must you ask someone to help you when anything needs to be fixed? Could you hang up a picture? Put up a curtain rod? Take a door off its hinges? You could if you knew how to use these basic tools for some simple tasks:

> Hammer with claw end
> Nails, assorted sizes
> Picture hanging hooks
> Straight screwdriver
> Phillips screwdriver
> Pliers
> Adjustable wrench

How to put in a nail

Place masking tape over the spot on the wall where the nail will go. To start, hold the nail in place with one hand, and tap gently with the hammer. Be sure to hold the hammer near the end of its handle. Then hit the nail squarely and firmly until it is inserted the desired amount.

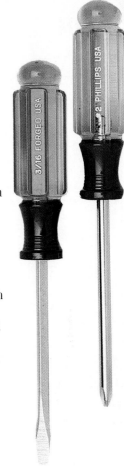

How to remove a nail

Use the claw end of the hammer to lift out the nail. When the nail is partly removed, place a piece of cloth or wood beneath the head of the hammer to prevent damaging the wall.

How to fill an unwanted hole

If you move a picture or make a mistake pounding in a nail, fill the hole with a bit of spackle or patching compound. Smooth with a putty knife. After it dries, sand with fine sandpaper and touch up the paint.

How to put up a curtain rod

First, measure the window accurately. Then insert the topmost screw part way at each end to hold the rod in place. You can start the screw holes by hammering a nail into the wall about 1/8"; remove nail. Use a straight screwdriver (for screws with a single slot) or a Phillips screwdriver (for screws with an X slot). Fit the screwdriver into the screw slot and push against the head of the screw as you turn it. Next, insert the other screws part way. Finally, tighten all screws.

How to take a door off its hinges

Sometimes a door has to be taken off its hinges in order to move a piece of furniture into a room. To do this, use a straight screwdriver and a hammer. Hold the screwdriver with the edge just underneath the ball top of the hinge bolt. Tap the end of the screwdriver with the hammer to loosen the bolt. Undo the bottom bolt first, then the top one. To replace the door, put it back on the hinges, insert the bolts, and hammer them down.

How to take off a bicycle wheel

Use an adjustable wrench or pliers to remove the nuts and bolts that hold the wheel in place. Put tape or a piece of cloth around each nut to prevent scratches. Then adjust the wrench or the pliers to fit snugly around the nut. Turn counterclockwise to loosen nut. If the bolt is a screw, you can use a screwdriver to hold it as you turn the nut. If the nut is hard to loosen, apply a few drops of oil and let soak for a few hours.

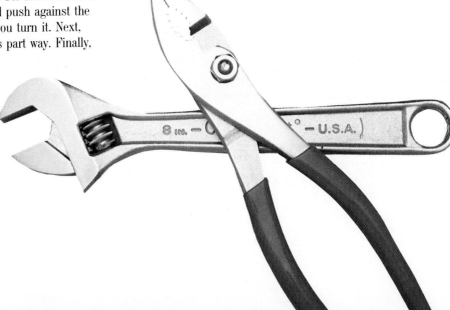

Appendix

Table of Food Values

Milk Group

	Amount	Calories	Carbohydrates (g)	Fat (g)	Protein (g)	Calcium (mg)	Iron (mg)	Vitamin A (IU)	Thiamin (mg)	Riboflavin (mg)	Niacin (mg)	Vitamin C (mg)
Cheese, American, process	1 oz/28 g	105	Tr	9	6	174	.1	340	.01	.10	Tr	0
Cheese, Cheddar	1 oz/28 g	115	Tr	9	7	204	.2	300	.01	.11	Tr	0
Cheese, cottage, creamed	½ c/120 ml	117	.1	5	14	67.5	.15	185	.025	.185	.135	Tr
Cheese, cottage, dry	½ c/120 ml	62.5	.5	Tr	12.5	23	.15	20	.02	.10	.1	0
Cheese, cream	1 oz/28 g	100	.2	10	2	23	.3	400	Tr	.06	Tr	0
Chocolate milk	1 c/240 ml	210	26	8	8	280	.6	300	.09	.41	.3	2
Cream, heavy	1 T/15 ml	80	.1	6	Tr	10	Tr	220	Tr	.02	Tr	Tr
Cream, light	1 T/15 ml	30	1	3	Tr	14	Tr	110	Tr	.02	Tr	Tr
Cream, sour	1 T/15 ml	25	1	3	Tr	14	Tr	90	Tr	.02	Tr	Tr
Ice cream 16% fat	½ c/120 ml	175	16	12	2	75.5	.05	445	.02	.14	.5	5
Milk	1 c/240 ml	150	11	8	8	291	.1	310	.09	.4	.2	2
Milk, low fat 2%	1 c/240 ml	121	12	5	8	297	.1	500	.1	.4	.2	2
Milk, skim	1 c/240 ml	85	12	Tr	8	302	.1	500	.09	.34	.2	2
Yogurt, fruit	1 c/240 ml	230	42	3	10	343	.2	120	.08	.4	.2	21
Yogurt, plain, skim milk	1 c/240 ml	125	17	Tr	13	452	.2	20	.11	.53	.3	2
Yogurt, plain, whole milk	1 c/240 ml	140	11	7	8	274	.1	280	.07	.32	.2	1

Meat, Poultry, Eggs, Fish, and Legumes Group

	Amount	Calories	Carbohydrates (g)	Fat (g)	Protein (g)	Calcium (mg)	Iron (mg)	Vitamin A (IU)	Thiamin (mg)	Riboflavin (mg)	Niacin (mg)	Vitamin C (mg)
Beef, lean (roasted)	3 oz/85 g	165	0	7	25	11	3.2	10	.06	.19	4.5	—
Beef, hamburger, 21% fat	3 oz/85 g	235	0	17	20	9	2.6	30	.07	.17	4.4	—
Chicken (broiled)	3 oz/85 g	240	0	7	42	16	3.0	160	.09	.34	15.5	—
Chicken (fried)	3 oz/85 g	160	1	5	26	9	1.3	70	.04	.17	11.6	—
Eggs (hard cooked)	1	80	1	6	6	28	1	260	.04	.13	Tr	0
Fish, bluefish (baked)	3½ oz/100 g	135	0	4	22	25	0.6	40	.09	.08	31.6	—
Ham, boiled	1 oz/28 g	65	0	5	5	3	.8	0	.12	.04	.7	—
Kidney beans (red beans)	1 c/240 ml	230	42	1	15	74	4.6	10	.13	.10	1.5	—
Lamb shoulder (roasted)	3 oz/85 g	285	0	18	23	9	1.0	—	.11	.2	4.0	—
Lentils	1 c/240 ml	210	39	Tr	16	50	4.2	40	.14	.12	.12	0
Peanut butter	2 T/30 ml	190	6	16	8	20	.6	0	.04	.04	4.8	0

	Amount											
Peas, dried, split	1 c/240 ml	230	42	1	16	22	3.4	80	.5	.18	1.8	—
Pork (roast)	3 oz/85 g	310	0	20	26	9	2.6	0	.46	.21	4.1	—
Sardines	3 oz/85 g	175	0	9	20	372	2.5	190	.02	.17	4.6	—
Tuna, canned in oil	3 oz/85 g	170	0	7	24	7	1.6	70	.04	.1	10.1	—
Turkey, dark meat (roasted)	3 oz/85 g	175	0	7	26	—	2.0	—	.03	.2	5.6	—
Veal cutlet	3 oz/85 g	185	0	9	23	9	2.7	—	.06	.21	4.6	—

Fruits and Vegetables Group

	Amount											
Apple	1 (2¾"/63 mm)	80	20	Tr	1	10	.4	120	.04	.03	.1	6
Apricots	3 med	55	14	Tr	1	18	.5	2,890	.03	.04	.6	11
Banana	1 med	100	26	Tr	2	10	.8	230	.06	.07	.8	12
Beans, green	1 c/240 ml	30	7	Tr	2	63	.8	680	.07	.11	.6	15
Bean sprouts	1 c/240 ml	35	7	Tr	4	20	1.4	20	.14	.14	.8	20
Blueberries	1 c/240 ml	90	22	1	1	22	1.5	150	.04	.09	.7	20
Broccoli	1 c/240 ml	40	7	Tr	5	136	1.2	3,880	.14	.31	1.2	140
Cabbage, shredded	1 c/240 ml	15	4	Tr	1	34	.03	90	.04	.04	.2	33
Cabbage, red, shredded, raw	1 c/240 ml	20	5	Tr	1	29	.6	30	.06	.04	.3	45
Cantaloupe	½ melon	80	20	Tr	2	38	1.1	9,240	.11	.08	1.6	90
Carrots	1	30	7	Tr	1	27	.5	7,930	.04	.04	.4	6
Celery, raw	3 stalks	15	6	Tr	Tr	48	.3	330	.03	.03	.3	12
Corn, sweet kernels	1 c/240 ml	130	31	1	5	5	.3	580	.15	.10	2.5	8
Cranberry sauce	½ c/120 ml	202.5	52	Tr	.5	8.5	.3	30	.015	.015	.5	3
Dates	10	220	58	Tr	2	47	2.4	40	.07	.08	1.8	0
Grapefruit juice[a]	¼ c/60 ml	25	6	Tr	.25	6	.05	5	.01	.01	.1	24
Grapes, seedless	10	81	9	Tr	Tr	6	.2	50	.03	.02	.2	2
Lettuce, iceberg	¼ head	17.5	2.6	Tr	.8	18	.45	297	.05	.05	.3	5
Mustard greens	1 c/240 ml	30	6	1	3	193	2.5	8,120	.11	.20	.8	67
Onions, boiled	½ c/120 ml	50	7	Tr	1.5	25	.4	Tr	.03	.03	.2	7.5
Orange	1 (3"/76 mm)	65	16	Tr	1	54	.5	260	.13	.05	.5	66

Note: Although ice cream is a good source of calcium, it also contains many calories, and may lead to weight problems.
Key: Tr—Nutrient present in trace amounts. [a] Made from concentrate.

Table of Food Values (cont.)

Fruit and Vegetables Group	Amount	Calories	Carbohydrates (g)	Fat (g)	Protein (g)	Calcium (mg)	Iron (mg)	Vitamin A (IU)	Thiamin (mg)	Riboflavin (mg)	Niacin (mg)	Vitamin C (mg)
Orange juice[a]	¼ c/60 ml	30	7.25	Tr	.5	6.25	.1	135	.05	.001	.22	30
Peaches, peeled	1 (2½"/65 mm)	40	10	Tr	1	9	.5	1,330	.02	.05	1.0	7
Pear, Bartlett	1 (2½"/65 mm)	100	25	1	1	13	.5	30	.03	.07	.2	7
Peas, green, frozen	1 c/240 ml	110	19	Tr	.8	30	2.3	960	.43	.14	2.7	21
Pepper, green sweet, raw	1 med	15	4	Tr	1	7	.5	310	.06	.06	.4	94
Pineapple, cubed	1 c/240 ml	80	21	Tr	1	26	.5	110	.14	.05	.3	26
Potato, baked	1 med	145	33	Tr	4	14	1.1	Tr	.15	.07	2.7	31
Potatos, French fried	10 pieces	155	18	7	2	9	.7	Tr	.07	.04	1.8	12
Prunes, dried	4 med	110	29	Tr	1	22	1.7	690	.04	.07	.7	1
Raisins (snack package)	½ oz/14 g	40	11	Tr	Tr	9	.5	Tr	.02	.01	.1	Tr
Spinach	1 c/240 ml	40	6	1	5	167	4	14,580	.13	.25	.9	50
Tomatoes, canned	1 c/240 ml	50	10	Tr	2	14	1.2	2,170	.12	.07	1.7	41
Tomato, raw	1 med	25	6	Tr	1	16	.6	1,110	.07	.05	.9	28
Tomato juice	6 oz/170 g	35	8	Tr	2	13	1.6	1,460	.09	.05	1.5	29
Bread and Cereals Group												
Bread, white enriched	1 slice	70	13	1	2	21	.6	Tr	.08	.06	.8	Tr
Bread, whole wheat	1 slice	65	14	1	3	24	.8	0	.07	.03	.8	Tr
Bread, pumpernickel (⅔% rye)	1 slice	80	17	Tr	3	27	.8	0	.09	.07	.6	0
Corn flakes, fortified (25% RDA)	1 c/240 ml	95	21	Tr	2	V	V	V	V	V	V	15
Crackers, saltines	4	50	8	1	1	2	.5	0	.05	.05	.4	0
Egg noodles, enriched	1 c/240 ml	200	37	2	7	16	1.4	110	.22	.13	1.9	0
Pasta, enriched (macaroni cooked, etc.)	1 c/240 ml	190	39	1	7	14	1.4	0	.23	.13	1.8	0
Rice, instant, enriched	1 c/240 ml	180	40	Tr	4	5	1.3	0	.21	V	1.7	0
Rice, enriched	1 c/240 ml	185	41	Tr	4	33	1.4	0	.19	.02	2.1	0
Rice, puffed, whole grain	1 c/240 ml	60	13	Tr	1	3	.3	0	.07	.01	.7	0
Wheat, farina, quick	1 c/240 ml	105	22	Tr	3	147	V	0	.12	.07	1	0

Food	Amount											
Wheat flakes, fortified, 25% U.S. RDA	¾ c/180 ml	105	24	Tr	3	12	4.8	1,320	.40	.45	5.3	16
Wheat, puffed, whole grain	1 c/240 ml	55	12	Tr	2	4	.6	0	.08	.03	1.2	0
Wheat, shredded, whole grain	1 large biscuit	90	20	1	2	11	.9	0	.06	.03	1.1	0
Wheat, whole grain cereal	1 c/240 ml	110	23	1	4	17	1.2	0	.15	.05	1.5	0
Other												
Bacon, fried crisp	2 slices	85	Tr	8	4	2	.5	0	.08	.05	.8	—
Butter	1 T/14 g	100	Tr	12	Tr	5	Tr	430	Tr	Tr	Tr	0
Doughnuts, glazed	1	205	22	11	3	16	.6	25	.1	.1	.8	0
Honey	1 T/21 g	65	17	0	Tr	1	.1	0	Tr	.01	.1	Tr
Margarine, regular	1 T/15 g	100	Tr	12	Tr	5	Tr	470	Tr	Tr	Tr	0
Mayonnaise	1 T/15 ml	100	Tr	11	Tr	3	.1	40	Tr	.01	Tr	—
Nuts, peanuts, salted	1 c/240 ml	840	27	72	37	107	5	—	.46	.19	24.8	0
Nuts, walnuts	1 c/240 ml	785	19	74	26	Tr	7.5	380	.28	.14	.9	—
Oil, corn	1 T/15 ml	120	0	14	0	0	0	—	0	0	0	0
Pizza, cheese	1 slice	145	22	4	6	86	1.1	230	.16	.18	1.6	4
Popcorn, plain	1 c/240 ml	25	5	Tr	1	1	.2	—	—	.01	.1	0
Salad dressing, Italian	1 T/15 ml	85	1	9	Tr	2	Tr	Tr	Tr	Tr	Tr	—
Salad dressing, Italian low calorie	1 T/15 ml	10	Tr	1	Tr	Tr	Tr	Tr	Tr	Tr	Tr	—
Seeds, sunflower	½ c/120 g	405	14.5	34.5	17.5	87	5.15	35	1.42	.17	3.9	—
Sugar	1 T/12 g	45	12	0	0	0	Tr	0	0	0	0	0

Note: All fruits and vegetables fresh unless noted. Vegetables fresh cooked unless noted.
Key: [a] Made from concentrate. Tr—Nutrient present in trace amounts. V—Varies by brand; consult label.

United States Recommended Daily Allowances (U.S. RDA)

The U.S. Recommended Daily Allowances (U.S. RDAs) for vitamins, minerals, and protein were developed from the Recommended Dietary Allowances of the Food and Nutrition Board, National Academy of Sciences—National Research Council (NAS-NRC) by the Food and Drug Administration for use in its nutrition labeling, nutritional guidelines, and dietary supplement regulations.

U.S. RDA		
Unit		**Adults and children 4 or more yrs.**
Vitamins		
Vitamin A	IU	5000
Vitamin D	IU	400
Vitamin E	IU	30
Vitamin C	mg	60
Folacin	mg	0.4
Thiamin (B_1)	mg	1.5
Riboflavin (B_2)	mg	1.7
Niacin	mg	20
Vitamin B_6	mg	2
Vitamin B_{12}	mcg	6
Biotin	mg	0.3
Pantothenic acid	mg	10
Minerals		
Calcium	g	1
Iron	mg	18
Phosphorus	g	1
Iodine	mcg	150
Magnesium	mg	400
Zinc	mg	15
Copper	mg	2

Protein
High quality g — 45
Lower quality g — 65

    IU = International Unit
     g = gram
    mg = milligram
   mcg = microgram

1000 mcg (micrograms) = 1 mg
1000 mg (milligrams) = 1 g

Percentages of U.S. RDA

This chart shows what percentage of the U.S. RDA you need for your age and sex.

Most people do not need 100 percent of the U.S. RDA for every nutrient. Use of 100 percent of the U.S. RDA as a nutritional goal is in no way dangerous. However, it may lead to needless changes in your diet and to spending more money on food than is necessary. It may also cause you unwarranted concern about nutrient shortages in your day's food choices. On the other hand, at certain stages of the life cycle, some people need more than 100 percent of certain nutrients.

For your daily nutrition goal, select the appropriate amounts of nutrients shown in this table. For example, the recommended amount of calcium for a 16-year-old male or female is 120 percent of the U.S. RDA. Therefore daily food choices by 16-year-olds should provide 120 percent or more of the U.S. RDA for calcium, rather than 100 percent.

Age	Food Energy[1]	Protein[2]	Vitamin A	Vitamin C	Thiamin	Ribo-flavin	Niacin[3]	Calcium	Iron
Years	*Calories*	*Percent of U.S. Recommended Daily Allowance*							
Child:									
1–3	1300	35	40	70	50	50	30	80	85
4–6	1800	50	50	70	60	65	35	80	60
7–10	2400	55	70	70	80	75	50	80	60
Male:									
11–14	2800	70	100	75	95	90	55	120	100
15–18	3000	85	100	75	100	110	55	120	100
19–22	3000	85	100	75	100	110	60	80	60
23–50	2700	90	100	75	95	95	45	80	60
51+	2400	90	100	75	80	90	35	80	60
Female:									
11–14	2400	70	80	75	80	80	45	120	100
15–18	2100	75	80	75	75	85	30	120	100
19–22	2100	75	80	75	75	85	35	80	100
23–50	2000	75	80	75	70	75	30	80	100
51+	1800	75	80	75	70	65	25	80	60
Pregnant	+300[4]	+50[4]	100	100	+20[4]	+20[4]	35	120	100+
Nursing	+500[4]	+35[4]	120	135	+20[4]	+30[4]	35	120	100

[1]Calorie needs differ depending on body composition and size, age, and activity of the person.

[2]U.S. RDA of 65 grams is used for this table. In labeling, a U.S. RDA of 45 grams is used for foods providing high-quality protein, such as milk, meat, and eggs.

[3]The percentage of the U.S. RDA shown for niacin will provide the RDA for niacin if the RDA for protein is met. Some niacin is derived in the body from tryptophan, an amino acid present in protein.

[4]To be added to the percentage for the girl or woman of the appropriate age.

Source: *Nutrition labeling, Tools for Its Use,* Agriculture Information Bulletin No. 382, U.S. Department of Agriculture, 1975.

Glossary

Note: Numbers in parentheses indicate the chapter in which the term appears.

abbreviation A shortened form of a word. (44)

abstract thinking A thought process that includes concepts that are difficult to understand. (2)

accessory A small object that adds visual appeal to a room. (71)

accident An unplanned, sudden event. (73)

acquaintance Someone you know, but not as well as you know a good friend. (7)

addictive A substance that is difficult, and sometimes impossible, to stop using. (3)

additive A substance added to food before it is sold. (41)

adolescence The period of life when you grow from being a child to being an adult. (2)

adopted A child who has been legally made a permanent member of a new family (10)

aerobic Any exercise that improves your ability to use oxygen by requiring sustained regular movement for 30 minutes or more, with no rests. (35)

aide Worker who assists higher-level workers with their jobs. (17)

alternative A choice (5)

amino acid Any of the twenty-two chemicals that make up all proteins. (36)

analogous color scheme A color scheme that uses colors that are closely related. (56)

annual percentage rate (APR) The percentage cost of credit on a yearly basis. (28)

anorexia nervosa An eating disorder in which people believe they are overweight even when they are too thin, causing them to diet even more. (39)

appetite The desire to eat. (35)

appliance A piece of kitchen equipment run by electricity or gas. (42)

appliqué A cutout fabric decoration sewn onto another fabric background. (65)

apprentice A helper who is trained on the job by senior workers. (54)

appropriate Suitable for an occasion. (55)

architect A person who designs buildings and homes. (75)

arcing Sparks that can damage a microwave oven and start a fire. (48)

attitude Thoughts and judgments you have about the world around you. (1)

back-up plan An alternative way of doing something if the original plan does not work out. (6)

bait and switch When a store advertises a product at a low price, but then tries to get you to buy a more expensive product. (29)

balance When objects are arranged in an even, pleasing way. (71)

barter The direct exchange of one resource for another. (25)

basal metabolism All the automatic functions of your body, including breathing, tissue repair, blood circulation, and growth. (39)

beat To mix ingredients thoroughly so that air is introduced. (46)

Better Business Bureau An organization formed by businesses that promise to obey business standards; in return, the Bureau tries to resolve consumer complaints against its members. (32)

bias Any curve or angle that is not cut on the lengthwise or crosswise grain of the fabric. (64)

blend To mix two or more ingredients together thoroughly; *also,* a yarn made from two or more different fibers. (46, 58)

blended family A family that joins two separate families through marriage. (10)

blueprint An architect's plan or mechanical drawing. (75)

bobbin A small spool that holds the bottom thread in a sewing machine. (62)

body language Your posture and the way you move, walk, or sit. (8)

bolt-end label A label on a fabric bolt that lists the fiber content, recommended care, fabric width, and price per yard. (61)

brainstorming A free-for-all approach to problem solving that lists as many ideas as people can think of in order to get ideas flowing and promote discussion. (11)

braise To cook food in a small amount of liquid in a pan that has a tight-fitting lid. (47)

brand The particular name of a product. (41)

broil To cook food directly with a glowing heat source. (47)

budget A plan for using your money. (27)

buffet A style of meal service in which all the food is arranged on a serving table for people to select from and make up their own plates. (53)

bulimia An eating disorder in which a person overeats, and then gets rid of the food by using laxatives or vomiting.

buyer A person who connects designers and garment makers with the stores and shops where clothing is sold. (68)

calendar A weekly, monthly, or yearly record of appointments, important events, holidays, birthdays, and other important dates. (26)

calorie An amount of energy; specifically, a measure of heat. (36)

capital The money you invest in a business. (34)

carbohydrate Any of the nutrients that provide your body with ready energy. (36)

caregiver A person who takes care of children or who cares for people who are sick or elderly. (18)

caring The emotional bond that one person feels for another. (13)

casserole A dish which can be used for both cooking and serving. (47)

cereal Any grain. (37)

characteristic A special feature or trait that distinguishes one individual from another. (1)

checking account An account on which you can write checks directing the bank to pay money as directed. (28)

child abuse The physical or emotional mistreatment of children. (21)

child care center A place where children are cared for while their parents work. (22)

childproof Safe for children. (21)

cholesterol A white, waxlike substance that plays a part in transporting and digesting fat. (36)

chop To cut into small pieces. (46)

citizen A member of a group such as a school, a community, or a nation. (16)

classic A style that stays popular for a long time. (57)

clearance sale A sale held by stores to get rid of old stock to make room for new items. (30)

clergy Religious workers such as priests, ministers, rabbis, and mullahs. (17)

client A person who is given help and information by a professional. (17)

clique A small, exclusive group of people within a peer group. (13)

coagulate To change from a fluid state to a thickened mass. (51)

communicating Sending messages from one person to another. (8)

community resource Any person or facility in your community that helps you enjoy your life, improve your skills, or achieve your goals. (25)

comparison shopping Comparing features and prices of different brands and models of the same item before you buy. (31)

complementary color scheme A scheme that uses colors that are direct opposites on the color wheel. (56)

compromise A way of solving a problem in which each person gives up something in order to come to an agreement. (7)

concentrate A juice product from which most of the water has been removed. (50)

condominium One of a group of apartments or townhouses that you buy rather than rent. (69)

confidentiality The complete privacy of a person's business. (11)

conflict A problem that arises in a relationship. (9)

conform To be like the people around you. (55)

conscience Your inner voice that tells you whether what you are doing is right or wrong, according to your values. (15)

conserve To save or use carefully so as not to deplete a resource. (25)

construction The building of homes. (75)

consumer A person who buys and uses things. (30)

contaminated Food containing large amounts of bacteria. (43)

contrast The difference in color and shape among objects. (71)

coordinated piece A piece of clothing that can be worn with another in several different ways. (59)

cost per wearing The total of the purchase price of a garment and the cost of cleaning it, divided by the number of wearings. (60)

counseling Advice and guidance from experts, religious leaders, or support groups. (11)

creativity The ability to use your imagination to do things in new ways. (24)

credit An arrangement for receiving money, merchandise, or a service now and paying for it later. (28)

custody The right of caring for children, granted by a court in case of divorce. (12)

customary system The measurement system that is standard in the U.S. which measures in teaspoons, tablespoons, cups, pints, quarts, ounces, and pounds. (45)

cut A section or part of a meat carcass. (52)

Daily Food Guide A guide, developed by nutritionists, which lists the number and size of servings needed daily from each food group. (37)

danger zone The range of temperatures in which bacteria grow and produce poisons most rapidly—between 60°and 125° F (16° and 52° C). (43)

dart A triangular fold of fabric stitched to a point to shape the fabric to body curves. (64)

day-care center A place where infants and pre-school children are cared for during the day while their parents work. (22)

deadline Date by which a task must be completed. (26)

decision The choice you make between different possibilities. (5)

dehydrated Any milk product from which some or all of the water has been removed. (51)

department store A store offering a wide variety of items, often in different price ranges, under one roof. (30)

depression A prolonged feeling of sadness or a serious emotional disorder characterized by hopelessness and an inability to enjoy life. (3)

designer A person who creates new styles. (57)

detergent A cleaning agent made from chemicals or petroleum. (66)

developmental task Any of the skills and abilities that children acquire as they grow. (19)

diet The food and drink you typically consume. (35)

Dietary Guidelines Recommendations for improving eating habits, developed by the U. S. government. (38)

dieting Controlling your food intake for a specific purpose. (39)

dietitian A person who has studied food and nutrition and their relationship to health and fitness. (24)

directional cutting Cutting with the grain of the fabric. (63)

directional stitching Stitching with the grain of the fabric. (64)

direct mail ad Advertisement that is delivered by the postal service. (29)

discount store A store that sells nationally advertised brands at reduced prices. (30)

distract To lead children away from something they should not do by interesting them in another activity. (21)

divorce The legal termination of a marriage. (12)

dovetail To combine tasks in such a way that one overlaps another, saving time. (44)

dryclean To clean fabrics with chemicals rather than detergent or soap and water. (66)

dyeing Changing the natural color of a fiber, yarn, or fabric using a substance. (58)

ease The extra room a pattern allows for clothing to fit comfortably. (63)

electronic funds transfer (EFT) The method of banking and paying bills automatically with the use of computers. (27)

emotional maturity Being secure enough with your own self-image to be able to meet the emotional demands and responsibilities you face. (23)

empathy The ability to understand what someone else is experiencing. (13)

emphasis When one object receives more attention than other objects in the room. (71)

end-of-season sale A sale held to clear out merchandise to make room for the next season's styles. (60)

energy The capacity for doing work. (74)

enriched Processed grain products which have had nutrients replaced. (37)

entrée Main dish. (38)

entrepreneur A person who starts a new business to provide a product or service that they think consumers want. (34)

entry-level job A job for which little or no experience is needed. (17)

environment Everything that surrounds you including your family, friends, teachers, and the neighborhood and society in which you live. (1)

equivalent Any of the comparison facts that help convert one measurement into another. (45)

etiquette Accepted customs of behavior. (53)

evaluate To judge an action or decision by studying it carefully. (5)

expectation What each person wants in a relationship. (9)

expense Any of the things that you spend your money on. (27)

expiration date The last day a product can be used safely. (41)

extended family A family that includes parents, children, and other relatives, such as grandparents, uncles, aunts, and cousins. (10)

eye contact Direct visual contact with another person's eyes. (8)

fabric Material, or cloth, made from yarn. (58)

facility Any of the goods and services available in a community. (69)

facing An extra piece of fabric sewn on the outside and turned to the inside to finish an edge. (60)

factory outlet A store in which a manufacturer sells goods directly to the consumer. (30)

fad A fashion that is very popular for a short time. (57)

family day care A child-care arrangement in which a small number of children are cared for in a person's home. Also called family child care. (22)

family life cycle The stages of life that the average family goes through. (12)

family style A style of meal service in which the food is brought to the table in bowls which are passed from person to person or served from the head of the table. (53)

fashion A style of clothing that is accepted in a society at a given time. (57)

fashion coordinator A person who develops advertising themes and plans fashion events to bring people into a store. (68)

feed Part of the sewing machine that positions the fabric for the next stitch. (62)

fetus An unborn child. (23)

fiber An indigestible threadlike cell that helps to move food through the digestive system; *also,* the basic ingredient of all fabrics, it is the tiny strand that makes up yarn. (36, 58)

figure type Size category determined by height and body proportion. (61)

finance charge The money you pay to the lender for allowing you credit. (28)

financial stability The ability to meet all your everyday living costs. (23)

fine-motor skills Ability to control the small muscles of the body, such as in the hands. (19)

finish A substance added to a fabric to change its appearance, feel, or performance. (58)

fireproof Protected from the danger of fire. (73)

first aid Emergency care or treatment given to an ill or injured person. (21)

first impression The image people have of someone they have just met. (8)

fixed goal A goal that can be met at a certain time. (4)

flatware Knives, forks, and spoons. (53)

flexible Having the ability to adapt to different plans if the original plans don't work out. (6)

flexible goal A goal that has no definite time limit in which it needs to be accomplished. (4)

floor plan An illustration of the arrangement of elements in a room or home. (70)

food poisoning A disease caused by bacteria growing in food until food becomes poisonous. (43)

food preference The food a person likes best. (40)

formal clothes Particularly dressy clothes, such as a tuxedo or long dress. (55)

format The way information is presented. (44)

fortified Given additional nutrients. (37)

foster child A child who is taken into a new family on a temporary basis. (10)

garment industry The many companies involved in manufacturing clothing. (57)

garnish A thin, decorative strip of vegetable used to add color to food. (46)

gathers Soft folds of fabric stitched into a seam. (64)

generic product Product that is plainly packaged and usually the cheapest of all brands. (41)

goal A target you set for yourself to accomplish. (4)

goods Material things, such as clothes or records, that you can use. (31)

grain The direction in which the yarns run in a fabric. (63)

gross-motor skills Ability to control the large muscles of the body, such as the arms and legs. (19)

guidance Advice or assistance that helps children learn what behavior is acceptable and what is not. (18)

hand-eye coordination Ability to get eyes and muscles to work together to make complex movements. (19)

Heimlich maneuver A procedure in which one uses pressure to force an object that is interfering with breathing from the throat. (21)

hem The bottom edge of fabric turned up and sewn to the wrong side of the garment. (60)

heredity The characteristics that you inherit from your parents and ancestors. (1)

home automation Technology that automatically controls systems in a home. (74)

homogenized Milk that has had its creamy fats blended into the liquid. (51)

hormones Substances in your body that trigger physical changes. (2)

hue A specific color name. (56)

human resource A personal resource such as knowledge, skills, imagination, energy, time, family, and friends. (25)

hunger The body's physical signal that it is short of energy and needs food. (35)

hydroelectric power Power generated by the force of falling water. (74)

illusion An image that fools the eye. (56)

image ad Advertisement that attempts to associate a product with a popular image so people will want to try it. (29)

implement To put a project into action and monitor it. (6)

improvise To come up with new ideas when some of your plans don't work out. (6)

impulse buying Buying things that you had not intended to buy. (30)

income The money you take in and have available to spend. (27)

individuality The ways in which you are different from others. (55)

infatuation An intense but usually short-term feeling of love for someone who may not even know the yearnings exist. (14)

information ad Advertisement that provides information about a specific product or service. (29)

ingredient Any one of the individual food items needed to make a recipe. (40)

inseam measurement The length of the pant leg from the bottom to where the two legs meet. (60)

insulation Material put inside walls or ceilings to keep cold out and heat in. (74)

intensity Brightness or dullness of a color. (56)

interest A fee paid for the use of money. (28)

interview A meeting between an employer and a job applicant. (68)

inventory The amount of each product in stock; *also,* a detailed list of everything on hand. (54, 59)

jealous Feeling hurt or resentful when a boyfriend or girlfriend spends time with or pays attention to someone else. (15)

knead To press and fold dough. (49)

layout A diagram included in sewing instructions that shows how to place the pattern pieces on fabric; *also,* the arrangement of furniture. (63, 70)

legume The dried seed of the bean plant. (37)

licensed A business that is given permission by the state government to operate. (22)

location The region of the country where you will live. (69)

lockstitch A sewing machine stitch in which a thread above the fabric meets another thread coming from below the fabric, and the two threads lock in the middle of the fabric layers. (62)

long-term goal Something you plan to accomplish sometime in the future. (4)

looper Part of the serger that performs like a bobbin in a conventional sewing machine. (62)

loyalty Being faithful to others, especially when they need it. (13)

mail order An order for products by mail. (30)

maintenance The things that have to be done to keep living space and joint belongings in good working order. (73)

malnourished A result of not getting enough of the nutrients essential for growth and development. (38)

management Making decisions about the things you want to do, and then accomplishing the goals you have set for yourself. (2)

manners The way you behave toward other people. (8)

manufactured fiber Fiber formed all or in part by chemicals. (58)

marbling Fine streaks and flecks of fat within the lean area of meat. (52)

material resource An object that you can use to provide or make other things. (25)

media The means by which ads are broadcast or displayed (television, radio, magazines, newspapers, direct mail). (29)

menu The list of foods that a restaurant offers. (53)

metric system The measurement system which measures in grams and liters. (45)

microwave A type of energy wave that operates at a very high frequency. (48)

mildew A fungus that may grow on damp fabric, causing stains. (66)

mineral Any of the nutrients that are simple substances form part of many tissues, and are needed to keep body processes operating smoothly. (36)

moderation Neither too much nor too little. (38)

money order A piece of paper that is sold in banks and post offices and can be used like a check. (28)

monochromatic color scheme A scheme that uses variations of the same color. (56)

mortgage A long-term loan that people take out when they buy a home. (69)

multiple use Using the same area for more than one activity. (70)

natural fiber Fiber that comes from plants or the hair of animals. (58)

natural resource Anything found in nature that people can use, such as air, water, and soil. (25)

nonverbal Without words. (8)

notion Any of the sewing supplies—including thread, zippers, buttons, and trimmings needed to complete a project. (61)

nuclear family Two parents and one or more children sharing a household. (10)

nurture To help children learn and develop by providing love, support, attention, and encouragement. (10, 18)

nutrient Any of the nourishing substances food contains. (36)

nutrient density The proportion of nutrients to the calories a food contains. (37)

nutrition The way that your body uses food. (35)

objective The ability to listen without becoming emotionally involved. (17)

parallel play Playing alongside each other, rather than together. (19)

parenting Taking care of children by meeting their physical, emotional, mental, and social needs. (18)

parliamentary procedure A democratic method which involves people voicing their opinions in order to reach a majority decision. (16)

passive activity An activity that a person watches or listens to, but does not join in. (20)

pasteurized Liquid milk that has been heated and cooled to kill harmful germs. (51)

patchwork A method of sewing small fabric shapes together to create a decorative piece of fabric. (67)

pattern A set of written directions and printed paper pieces showing how to put a sewing project together. (61)

pattern catalog A book that shows all the patterns available from one company. (61)

pattern maker A skilled worker who makes a pattern from the designer's original sample. (68)

pediatrician A doctor who cares for children. (24)

peel To remove the skin of fruits and vegetables. (46)

peer group People your own age. (2)

perishable Tending to spoil easily. (42)

personal inventory A review of your interests and skills. (17)

personality The combination of characteristics and actions that makes you different from every other person. (1)

personal space A place of one's own. (69)

pilot light A thin stream of gas burned constantly and used to light a gas burner on a range. (73)

place setting The arrangement of the tableware each diner will need for the meal. (53)

platonic A relationship based on friendship, rather than romance. (14)

poach To simmer in a small amount of liquid so food keeps its original shape. (47)

pollution Waste that has not been disposed of properly. (25)

portion One of the servings that a recipe yields. (40)

prejudice A fixed mental picture about a whole group of people on the basis of an opinion or feeling, not fact. (9)

premature birth A birth that occurs before development is complete. (23)

prenatal Before birth. (23)

preservative A substance added to food to keep it fresh and tasty longer. (41)

press To lift the iron and set it down on fabric, not sliding it back and forth. (64)

preventive Making sure ahead of time that accidents and damage do not occur. (72)

principal The amount of money you have in your account. (28)

prioritize To rank in order of importance. (4)

processed Food that has been changed from its raw form before being sold. (37)

processed meat Meat that has been seasoned, smoked, or prepared in some way before it is brought to the store. (52)

procrastinate To put off doing something. (26)

produce A term used to describe fresh fruits and vegetables. (50)

promoted Advanced to a position of higher rank and greater responsibility. (54)

proportion The relationship between spaces within a garment; *also,* a pleasing size relationship among objects. (56, 71)

protein Any of the nutrients necessary for building and repairing body tissues; it is the basis of all the body's cells and forms the major part of hair, nails, and skin. (36)

pull date The last day a product may be sold. (41)

puree To cut or mash food so fine that no solid pieces remain. (46)

quick bread Bread that uses baking soda or baking powder to rise. (49)

recipe Detailed instructions for preparing food. (40)

recycle To find a new use for a garment. (67)

redesign To change a garment so that it is more in fashion or has an exciting new look. (67)

redress To correct a wrong. (32)

reference A person who is willing to tell an employer more about you. (22)

reflex An automatic, involuntary response. (19)

relationship Any of your connections with other people. (7)

reliability Being a person others can count on. (13)

resource Something that you need to accomplish a goal. (4)

respect Being polite and considerate to a person because you find them worthy. (7)

return policy A store's rules for allowing a customer to return an item in exchange for another item or for cash. (33)

rhythm The regular repetition of line or shape. (71)

role A part you play when you interact with others. (9)

role model A person you admire and whose behavior you use as an example. (16)

role playing Pretending to be someone else. (20)

rotate To turn a dish a quarter or half-turn in a microwave oven. (48)

rotation A system in which newly purchased foods are put behind older foods so the older supplies are used before newer ones. (42)

routine A set sequence of events. (72)

sanitation Storing, washing, and cooking food properly, as well as keeping the kitchen, appliances, tools, and yourself clean. (43)

sauté To cook food slowly in a little fat until it is tender, but not brown. (47)

savings account An account that holds the savings you deposit. (28)

scale drawing A drawing in which the relative sizes of objects are the same as the relative sizes of those objects in the actual space. (70)

schedule A daily or weekly plan showing the time and length of each of your activities. (26)

seam The line of stitching that joins the pieces of a garment together. (60)

seam allowance The fabric between the line for cutting and the line for stitching. (63)

seasonal More plentiful at certain times of the year. (50)

self-concept The particular view that you have of yourself. (1)

self-confident Having confidence in or being sure of yourself. (13)

self-control An inner control over your own behavior. (15)

self-esteem The way you feel about yourself. (2)

selvage The finished edge of fabric. (63)

sensory toys An object that appeals to the senses—it can be touched, listened to, looked at, or put in the mouth. (20)

sequence The order in which steps are to be done. (44)

serger A high-speed overlock machine that trims, sews, and overcasts in one step. (62)

service Work performed for one person by another, such as a haircut. (31)

serving A portion of a food that a person needs to supply daily nutritional needs. (37)

sew-through button Button that has two or four holes through it and no shank. (65)

shank button Button that has a built-in shank, or loop, on the back but no holes through it. (65)

shield To cover parts of food with aluminum foil to protect them from overcooking in the microwave oven. (48)

shoplifting Stealing goods from stores. (33)

short-term goal Something you can accomplish soon. (4)

shred To grate or cut food into fine pieces using a grater. (46)

sibling Another word for brother or sister. (10)

simmer To cook food in liquid at temperatures just below the boiling point. (47)

single-parent family One parent and one or more children living in the same household. (10)

size range A size category. (60)

small claims court A court in which consumers and businesses present their complaints informally, and a judge decides the case. (32)

smoke detector Battery operated device that sounds an alarm when it senses smoke. (73)

snag A loop of yarn pulled out of a knit. (66)

specialty store A store that sells only a certain type of merchandise. (30)

spoilage Damage that happens when food is too old to eat or contains bacteria or mold. (50)

stages Periods during which a child can perform certain tasks. (19)

stain Dirt that is concentrated in one spot in a garment. (66)

stamina Staying power or endurance. (35)

standing time The time you should allow for food to continue to cook after the microwave oven is turned off. (40)

staple Any of the basic food items that are used regularly. (40)

status Favored position within a group. (55)

staystitching A line of machine stitches through just one layer of fabric that keeps the curved edge from stretching and losing its shape as the fabric is handled. (64)

steamer A metal basket which allows steam to pass through it as it holds food above boiling water. (47)

stepparent A person who marries a child's mother or father. (10)

stereotype An unfair label that is automatically given to strangers, based on the belief that all members of a certain group are alike. (9)

stir-fry To cook food very quickly in very little fat until the food is just tender. (47)

stress The physical and emotional tension that is caused by important happenings or changes in your life. (3)

table service Restaurant service in which waiters and waitresses take your order at the table, bring the food, and clean up after the meal. (53)

telecommunication Any electronic system that transmits voices, images, and information from one place to another. (34)

texture The way a fabric looks and feels. (56)

texturizing A process that adds crimp or curl to a normally straight yarn. (66)

tipping Giving extra money to waiters and waitresses for good service. (53)

tolerance The ability to accept people as they are. (9)

traffic pattern How people usually move through a space. (70)

traumatic An experience causing severe emotional shock that may take time to heal. (12)

trimming Any of the decoration sewn on a garment. (60)

tuck A small, stitched fold—which doesn't taper at the end—used to give a garment shape. (64)

Underwriter's Laboratory An agency that tests electrical products for safety. (31)

unit construction Preparation of separate pieces of fabric before assembling them in a specific order. (64)

unit price The price of an item per ounce or by count. (31)

unity A feeling that all objects in a room look like they belong together. (71)

universal product code An emblem of thick and thin black lines that is printed on items so price and product name can be read on an electric scanner. (41)

unrequited love Love that is not returned. (14)

utensil A small kitchen tool, like a knife. (42)

value Lightness or darkness of a color. (56)

values Guidelines you have for living with yourself and others. (4)

vandalism The marring and destroying of someone else's property. (33)

variable Any condition that determines how long a food needs to be cooked in a microwave oven and at what power level. (48)

variety meat Organ meat such as liver, heart, or kidney. (52)

verbal Using words. (8)

versatile Having many different uses. (59)

view A different version of a sewing pattern. (61)

visualize To see in your mind how a completed project might look. (75)

vitamin Any of the nutrients that help the body stay healthy, function properly, and make use of other nutrients. (36)

volume The amount of space taken up by an ingredient. (45)

wardrobe The clothes that you own. (59)

warranty A written statement from a manufacturer or retailer promising to repair or replace a defective product or to refund your money. (31)

weatherstripping Material used to fill gaps around door frames and windows so that less air leaks in and out. (74)

wellness A state of good health that you achieve by making a conscious effort to look after yourself. (3)

work center An organized area where the main kitchen tasks can be performed. (42)

work triangle The arrangement of the three major centers in the kitchen. (42)

yarn Fiber that has been twisted together in order to make fabric. (58)

yeast bread Bread that rises through the action of a tiny plant called yeast. (49)

Credits

Contents:

Index